A Clinician's Gui[de to] Functional Neurological Disorder

This manual for clinicians presents a ground-breaking, accessible and unifying new model for understanding functional neurological disorder (FND) that bridges the gap between theoretical FND-specific models and the more practical, but non–FND-specific Cognitive Behavioural Therapy (CBT) models. Grounded in psychology, the Pressure Cooker Model provides a clear metaphor for FND, focusing on intra-individual and inter-individual cognitive, emotional and behavioural processes. Developed based on years of clinical experience in the field, it is applicable to the assessment and treatment of every type of FND.

Viewed as a systemic condition with unique psychosocial features, the book will describe the rationale for radically transforming FND recovery by providing a treatment model that aims to resolve emotion dysregulation processes and repair relationships between the person and the system. It uses a unifying framework to guide the steps of intervention and can be adapted for work in a multidisciplinary team context to facilitate communication between disciplines. Enriched with case studies and research data, the book also highlights a plethora of clinical tools and strategies based on the Pressure Cooker Model, as well as contextualising its position alongside CBT models.

This manual is instrumental in educating and treating people with FND. It offers essential guidance for neuropsychologists, neuropsychiatrists and other health professionals, as well as students in these fields.

Dr Egberdina-Józefa van der Hulst, Phd, DClinPsy, is an inpatient psychologist with more than ten years of experience in clinical practice and research on functional neurological disorder (FND) and neuropsychology. As a firm believer in a systemic and interpersonal approach to FND, she is passionate about highlighting the power of neuropsychology for FND.

A Clinician's Guide to Functional Neurological Disorder

A Practical Neuropsychological Approach

Egberdina-Józefa van der Hulst

Routledge
Taylor & Francis Group

LONDON AND NEW YORK

Designed cover image: © Josué Borges Expósito

First published 2023
by Routledge
4 Park Square, Milton Park, Abingdon, Oxon OX14 4RN

and by Routledge
605 Third Avenue, New York, NY 10158

Routledge is an imprint of the Taylor & Francis Group, an informa business

© 2023 Egberdina-Józefa van der Hulst

British Library Cataloguing-in-Publication Data
A catalogue record for this book is available from the British Library

Library of Congress Cataloging-in-Publication Data
Names: Hulst, Egberdina-Józefa van der, author.
Title: A clinician's guide to functional neurological disorder : a practical neuropsychological approach / Egberdina-Józefa van der Hulst.
Description: New York, NY : Routledge, 2023. | Includes bibliographical references and index.
Identifiers: LCCN 2022047309 (print) | LCCN 2022047310 (ebook) | ISBN 9781032312842 (hardback) | ISBN 9781032312859 (paperback) | ISBN 9781003308980 (ebook)
Subjects: LCSH: Conversion disorder. | Conversion disorder—Diagnosis. | Conversion disorder—Treatment.
Classification: LCC RC552.S66 H85 2023 (print) | LCC RC552.S66 (ebook) | DDC 616.85/24—dc23/eng/20221202
LC record available at https://lccn.loc.gov/2022047309
LC ebook record available at https://lccn.loc.gov/2022047310

ISBN: 9781032312842 (hbk)
ISBN: 9781032312859 (pbk)
ISBN: 9781003308980 (ebk)

DOI: 10.4324/9781003308980

Typeset in Bembo
by codeMantra

This book is dedicated to my parents Gerrit and Halina van der Hulst-Wasieczko

Contents

1 The rationale for developing the Pressure Cooker Model to understand FND

Introduction

People with functional neurological disorder (FND) experience a range of neurological-like symptoms. Although organic causes for FND symptoms may not appear on regular brain imaging investigations, these symptoms are nevertheless real and genuine and can be very disabling. Treatment of FND is multidisciplinary in nature and consists of psychological therapy, pharmacotherapy, physiotherapy, occupational therapy, and speech and language therapy, as well as input from social services (e.g. Goldstein et al., 2010; Nielsen et al., 2015; Gardiner et al., 2018). In terms of epidemiology, approximately 5–10% of new neurology patients will have a diagnosis of FND and the condition affects people throughout the entire age range (Bennett et al., 2021). Females are more likely to be afflicted with FND than males, with a reported ratio of 3:1 (Bennett et al., 2021). Prevalence rates suggest that 16% of new referrals to neurology outpatient clinics were diagnosed with FND (Stone et al., 2010a, 2010b) and an estimated 12–18% of new-onset seizures are dissociative seizures (Baxter et al., 2012). In addition, the prevalence of psychogenic non-epileptic seizures has been estimated as 2–33 per 100.000 (Benbadis & Hauser, 2000). The "minimum annual incidence" rate for functional weakness was estimated as 3.9/100.000 (Stone et al., 2010a, 2010b).

Diagnostic criteria for FND

The diagnostic criteria for FND (Criteria for Conversion Disorder, Diagnostic and Statistical Manual of Mental Disorders, 5th edition; DSM-V, American Psychiatric Association, 2013) specify the presence of at least one symptom that affects the voluntary motor or sensory system. FND symptoms can affect the entire neurological system, and FND is an umbrella term that covers four main subtypes. FND can produce sensory symptoms (e.g. numbness, tingles and vision loss), motor-type features (e.g. tremors, limb weakness, dystonia and gait difficulties) and fluctuations in awareness and responsiveness (e.g. dissociative seizures or non-epileptic episodes), as well as cause cognitive dysfunction (e.g. functional cognitive disorder, "brain fog"

DOI: 10.4324/9781003308980-1

or amnesia). Often, people with FND experience symptoms from all these categories. In comparison to organic neurological symptoms, the criteria describe that FND symptoms are incompatible with an underlying, recognised medical or neurological disease process such as stroke, traumatic brain injury or dementia. The DSM-V criteria further specify that other medical or psychological difficulties do not explain the symptoms better than FND, for example substance misuse. Furthermore, the symptoms should generate significant distress or impaired social and occupational functioning in other life areas.

DSM-V criteria: diagnostic challenges

From a neuropsychological perspective, the DSM-V criteria for FND pose several challenges. For example, the criteria specify that FND symptoms should be incompatible with recognised neurological conditions; however, recent findings from neuropsychological and neuroimaging studies that have revealed subtle structural and functional abnormalities in people with FND oppose this notion to some extent. In addition, psychological difficulties tend to explain the symptoms, *as well as* the FND explains the symptoms (not necessarily better, worse or not at all). Emotions and FND are intricately linked, which means that psychological difficulties will explain the FND symptoms because they *are* the FND. For example, a patient who experiences brief periods of dissociation and a tremor in social situations may likely be displaying a psychological safety behaviour and the physical manifestations of social anxiety. According to the DSM-V criteria, this patient would not fully meet the criteria for FND since the criteria for social anxiety disorder are equally or more fitting "on paper". A parsimonious approach would be to slightly alter the criteria to state that the patient fits the criteria for FND and that psychological difficulties explain the FND.

The specification of distress, as well as the presence or absence of psychological stressors, is another problematic issue with the diagnostic criteria. A person with FND may initially not appear to experience or actively reject and deny the existence of any distress. This does not automatically indicate the absence of stressors in FND. On the contrary, plausible hypotheses exist for this phenomenon including a reluctance to express emotions due to underlying negative beliefs and embarrassment; a reduced ability to identify, describe, experience or remember emotions due to alexithymia (Demartini et al., 2014); or longstanding and high levels of dissociation. It is therefore unhelpful to attempt at specifying stressors, at first contact, during the diagnostic process with professionals who are not necessarily mental health–trained, as often a psychological therapy process may be needed to uncover stressors that the patient is not aware of due to dissociative tendencies.

The final criterion that specifies that the symptoms impair social and occupational functioning reflects reality since many patients with FND are socially isolated and unemployed. However, the criterion does not cover a subset of patients who are fully adapted with equipment and do not feel distressed due to the FND helping to reach psychological and interpersonal safety, two concepts that will be discussed in more detail in Chapter 3.

Explanatory models of FND

FND and its mechanisms are not well understood, are shrouded in mystery and frequently cause high levels of distress and confusion in individuals with FND and their environment including family members, friends and health-care professionals. In more recent times, awareness of FND has substantially increased. The number of research studies investigating the biological, psychological and social determinants of FND has almost exponentially risen. Peer-reviewed journals and conferences have embraced articles and communications on FND. Furthermore, clinical services have identified a pressing need for the development of new FND-specialist services or opened up existing services to incorporate the care for FND patients in existing community teams. In addition, FND is more known amongst the lay public, as the condition has had more media coverage than ever before and is frequently featured and discussed on social media.

The increased attentional spotlight on FND may create the false impression that FND is a newly discovered condition. However, this clinical entity has existed for many years under many different names including conversion disorder, "hysteria", "pseudoseizures", non-epileptic attack disorder ("NEAD") and dissociative seizures. FND has fascinated researchers and clinicians across centuries. Over the years, this has resulted in the development of a multitude of models that have greatly advanced our current conceptualisation of FND as a biopsychosocial condition. Research on FND considers psychological, biological and social factors in the emergence and maintenance of FND symptoms and has identified key maintaining processes including heightened self-focused attention (Edwards et al., 2012); anxiety and avoidance (Goldstein & Mellers, 2006); hormonal dysregulation (Keynejad et al., 2019); and social factors (Edwards et al., 2012; Brown & Reuber, 2016).

In the following section, we will highlight some of the most important and influential theories, which can be subdivided into historical and contemporary models.

Early theories of FND: a historic time-line

Historically, research on mechanisms in FND heavily emphasised psychological hypotheses. In the 19th and 20th centuries, FND was described as "hysteria" by prominent scholars (Janet, 1920) who implicated attentional mechanisms as important factors in FND. Janet was also one of the first clinicians to describe dissociation in the context of psychological trauma (van der Hart & Horst, 1989). Early psychodynamic theories (e.g. Freud & Breuer, 1895) viewed FND as an expression of unconscious conflicts where psychological distress is "converted" into physical symptoms via psychodynamic processes.

In contrast to these more psychologically minded theories and ideas on FND, Charcot (1889) conceptualised "hysteria" as a hereditary process and the result of a "weak" neurological system. Charcot maintained that hysteria could be triggered by trauma but was subsequently progressive and irreversible. He suggested that "dynamic or functional" brain abnormalities in the motor areas could play a role in hysterical paralysis. Interestingly, the notion of brain abnormalities in the motor areas of people with FND was confirmed by later neuroimaging studies. For example, Vuilleumier et al. (2001) conducted a SPECT study with n=7 patients experiencing unilateral sensorimotor loss as part of FND. The results showed reduced regional cerebral blood flow in the thalamus and caudate nucleus, but increased blood flow in the lenticular nucleus. N=4 recovered patients showed normal regional cerebral blood flow in the thalamus and the basal ganglia. In another study by Voon et al. (2010), an fMRI study showed increased amygdala-supplementary motor area functional connectivity.

Contemporary models of FND

Attentional and cognitive theories

Historically, explanations and theories of FND have often focused on intra-individual psychological mechanisms. More contemporary models of FND have invoked the role of socio-environmental factors in FND.

INTEGRATIVE COGNITIVE MODEL (ICM; BROWN, 2006)

The ICM is a model intended to explain Medically Unexplained Symptoms (MUS), an umbrella term that covers somatoform symptoms affecting a wide range of bodily systems. FND could be viewed as a subtype of MUS in that the term describes a specific family of unexplained symptoms in the neurological domain.

According to the ICM, MUS are caused by activated memory representations that bias an attentional system to select faulty information, resulting in "rogue representations". In MUS, rogue representations emerge because of a misinterpretation of sensory input which the person experiences as "real symptoms". Rogue representations originate from a variety of sources including personal past experience of an illness, exposure to a physical illness in another person, verbal suggestion and sociocultural ideas about illness. Furthermore, increased self-focused attention on the symptoms will activate a rogue representation more strongly and is viewed as a maintaining factor of MUS. Several factors heighten attention and maintain the MUS, including the misattribution of MUS to physical illness, distress, personality, illness worry and behaviours. One of the advantages of the ICM is its ability to explain the involuntary nature and "real" experience of somatoform symptoms in the absence of pathology.

Brown and Reuber (2016) applied the ICM to a subtype of FND: dissociative seizures. According to this adapted version of the ICM, dissociative seizures emerge due to a complex interplay of stress, elevated arousal and cognitive processes. The perception of threat cues in conjunction with the anticipation of a dissociative seizure activates a "seizure scaffold" leading to a dissociative seizure. A seizure scaffold is described as a mental representation of a dissociative seizure and is shaped by prior physical illness or injury, traumatic experiences, "seizure models", the media and importantly previous dissociative seizures that have effectively reduced the arousal and directly feed back this information into the seizure scaffold.

BAYESIAN MODEL (EDWARDS ET AL., 2012)

This neurobiological framework uses a Bayesian formulation of brain function. The Bayesian model shares some similarities with the ICM as it postulates an important mediating role for attention in FND, particularly in the context of heightened self-focused attention on symptoms. According to the model, FND symptoms are produced by abnormal prior beliefs about illness. Various factors predispose an individual to develop abnormal beliefs including personal experience or exposure to physical illness in family and media settings. These abnormal beliefs about illness are subjected to heightened self-focused attention and lead to misattribution of agency; that is, voluntary experiences are perceived as involuntary by patients.

Biological theories

In recent years, the historic notion of FND as a psychological entity shifted in favour of the examination of the neuroscientific and biological underpinnings of FND. Structural and functional neuroimaging studies revealed neural changes in the amygdala, motor and prefrontal cortical areas (Aybek et al., 2014; Voon et al., 2016), consistent with the clinical features of anxiety, trauma and emotion dysregulation often observed in people with FND. Other research highlighted a role for stress hormones including cortisol and hypothalamic-pituitary-adrenal axis dysregulation (Bakvis et al., 2010; Keynejad et al., 2019).

Keynejad et al. (2019) proposed a stress–diathesis model for FND describing a complex interplay between biological vulnerabilities, early-life adversity and later traumatic stress events. Specific configurations of these variables are required in order to trigger FND, in particular (1) high biological risk/

minimal early and later stress and (2) low biological risk/significant early and later stress. Keynejad et al. (2019) further highlighted the potential relevance of neurobiological processes triggered by stress in FND including hypothalamic-pituitary-adrenal axis dysfunction; allostatic load; changes to volume, activity and connectivity in brain regions; and genetic changes. Although FND patients do not always report stress experiences, the model is able to explain the individual differences in stress experiences in patients with FND and suggests the possibility of tailored treatment for FND.

Biological viewpoints continue to locate the problem within the individual. Moreover, ascribing a larger biological contribution to FND risks the condition being viewed as a more fixed and even unchangeable condition. Importantly, the strong emphasis on physical terminology provides a circumlocution around psychosocial explanations for FND. It is possible that systemic anxiety around the diagnosis and management of people with FND is perpetuated using biological explanations for FND, resulting in active avoidance of psychosocial explanations and a further shift away from psychology for FND.

Cognitive-behavioural theories

MULTIFACTORIAL MODEL FOR PSYCHOGENIC NON-EPILEPTIC
SEIZURES (REUBER, 2009)

This psychologically driven model resembles the longitudinal formulation of depression (Beck Judith, 1995) and incorporates four out of the five Ps, with the exception of a clear outline of protective factors. In the Multifactorial Model, dissociative, dissociative seizures ('the problem'), emerge as a result of predisposing, precipitating and perpetuating factors. Predisposing factors (e.g. genetic vulnerabilities, early traumatic and later interpersonal experiences) cultivate the conditions for the development of a "vulnerable state". Precipitating factors (e.g. stressful experiences, physical or mental health symptoms and models) subsequently lead to the rise of dissociative seizures. Once emerged, the dissociative seizures are maintained by a wide range of perpetuating factors including negative emotions, avoidance behaviours and cognitive processes such as misattributions. The maintaining factors of the model further incorporate social and interpersonal factors (e.g. mistreatment, sick role and isolation). More recently, Reuber et al. (2021) applied the Multifactorial Model to the social emotion of shame in people with dissociative seizures.

CONDITION-SPECIFIC CBT MODELS (VARIOUS)

Cognitive-behavioural therapy (CBT) models combine cognitive restructuring techniques and behavioural modification principles to alter cognitive distortions, irrational thinking patterns and maladaptive learned responses in order to change behaviours and relieve distress (Beck, 1976). CBT models are firmly grounded in principles from cognitive and behavioural therapy and supported by a large body of theoretical and practice-based evidence (Skinner, 1963; Beck Judith, 1995) including for a wide range of psychological conditions commonly encountered in FND (Salkovskis, 1985; Clark, 1986; Salkovskis & Warwick, 1986; Clark & Wells, 1995; Wells, 1995; Ehlers & Clark, 2000).

Over the years, numerous CBT models have been developed that focus on a specific psychological difficulty ("condition-specific CBT models"), for example social anxiety, panic disorder or depression, amongst many other psychological conditions. As a large subset of people with FND experience psychological difficulties (e.g. Binzer et al., 1997; Carson et al., 2000; Stone, 2009; Urbanek et al., 2014), it is not surprising that psychological intervention models have gained popularity in FND. Table 1.1 shows a range of condition-specific CBT models that are commonly used in clinical practice with people with FND. It should be noted that a lot of traditional CBT models have transdiagnostic features in common with existing FND-specific but non-CBT models (e.g. Edwards et al., 2012; Brown & Reuber, 2016). Both types of model share and highlight a subset of the maintaining factors of FND symptoms, for example the presence of unhelpful beliefs, the physical effects of anxiety and the existence of avoidance responses. Interestingly, theoretical FND models tend to have more in common with CBT-focused anxiety models than with depression models.

To date, the ICM adapted for dissociative seizures (Brown & Reuber, 2016) probably comes closest to a condition-specific CBT model for FND, in the same way as has been developed for psychological conditions such as obsessive-compulsive disorder, health anxiety or panic disorder. However, due to the heterogeneity of FND symptoms, this model has limited applicability beyond dissociative seizures. It should also be noted that for a subset of patients, invoking a condition-specific FND model to treat the symptoms would not be recommended. Traditional CBT models can be very helpful in a subset of cases with FND where the link between the FND symptom and psychological difficulty is obvious, for example in situations where the dissociative features can easily and automatically be subsumed into existing CBT models without changing its core elements or processes. Chapter 8 will explore this type of therapy work in more detail using illustrative case studies. For a significant subset of people with FND, traditional CBT models will not be sufficient.

Theoretical vs CBT models of FND

Over the past decades, theoretical models of FND have provided important theoretical insights into the emergence and maintenance of FND symptoms. Furthermore, more non–FND-specific but practical CBT models have

Table 1.1 Transdiagnostic features overlapping between CBT and theoretical FND models

Condition	Key belief	Transdiagnostic feature in CBT model	Equivalent feature in FND model
Health anxiety (Salkovskis et al., 2003)	Worries and preoccupation about health or illness	• Reassurance seeking (e.g. increased healthcare visits) • Illness beliefs • Preoccupation with/high attentional focus on health • Misinterpretation of bodily symptoms • Checking behaviour (as part of increased attentional focus) • Avoidance behaviours	• Heightened self-focused attention • (Brown, 2006; Edwards et al., 2012) • Brown's (2006) rogue representations (Brown, 2006)
Social anxiety (Clark & Wells, 1995)	Worries about negative judgements from other people	• Heightened self-focused attention • Safety behaviours that reduce anxiety and arousal • Perceived social danger	• Heightened self-focused attention (Brown, 2006; Edwards et al., 2012) • Perception of threat cues/reduction in arousal (=result of the safety behaviour of DS; Brown & Reuber, 2016)
Generalised anxiety (Hirsch et al., 2019)	Chronic worries	• "Habit to attend to threat" • "Try to suppress worry" • Reassurance seeking • Checking behaviours	• Heightened self-focused attention • (Brown, 2006; Edwards et al., 2012)
Post-traumatic stress (Ehlers & Clark, 2000)	Re-experiencing of trauma memories	• Dissociation (numbness, cut-off, out-of-body) • Negative appraisals of trauma or its sequelae and the notion of a "current threat" and "arousal" symptoms	• "Loss of consciousness", "traumatic experiences" and "trauma reminders" (Brown & Reuber, 2016). • Perception of threat cues and arousal (Brown & Reuber, 2016)

Condition	Key belief	Transdiagnostic feature in CBT model	Equivalent feature in FND model
Panic disorder (Clark, 1986)	Catastrophic misinterpretations of physical symptoms	• Misinterpretation of bodily symptoms	Brown's (2006) rogue representations (Brown 2006)
Obsessive-compulsive disorder (Salkovskis, 1985)	Obsessions and compulsions	• Checking behaviour • Attentional biases	Heightened self-focused attention (Brown, 2006; Edwards et al., 2012)
Depression (Beck Judith, 1995)	Beliefs around rejection and loss	• Predisposing, precipitating and perpetuating factors giving rise to the problem (psychogenic non-epileptic seizures) • The presence of a critical incident ("stressful experiences, conflicts, dilemmas")	Reuber's (2009) 4Ps

greatly improved our understanding of the treatment of FND. These models can be subdivided into "theoretical" models and "clinical" CBT models, each with their own advantages and drawbacks. Theoretical models can at times rely heavily on the physical aspects of FND, whereas CBT models focus almost exclusively on psychological features, which interestingly almost mirror the disjointed nature between the body and the mind that is so characteristic of FND. In the following section, the theoretical and CBT models will be directly compared with one another, on several indicators, in the context of their usefulness in FND treatment. Table 1.2 shows the characteristics of these models that tend to be mirror images of each other.

At present, the treatment of FND symptoms with existing theoretical models or CBT models will likely fall short if the abovementioned limitations are not addressed. The next section will introduce a new way of thinking and working in the psychological therapy of FND.

Bridging the gap: introducing the Pressure Cooker Model

Research from the last decade has greatly advanced our theoretical and clinical understanding of the emergence and maintenance of FND, as well as progressed knowledge on the diagnosis, management and treatment of FND. To further elaborate on these important findings and improve outcomes in FND,

Table 1.2 Comparison between theoretical vs CBT models in FND

Feature	Theoretical models of FND	CBT models
Description of the emergence and maintenance of FND	• Theoretical models help to explain in great detail the mechanisms involved in the emergence and maintenance of FND symptoms. • In contrast, CBT models do not directly incorporate FND symptoms or their nuances (e.g. heightened self-focused attention).	• CBT models describe the maintaining factors of psychological conditions that are commonly associated with FND (e.g. panic cycle, social anxiety, health anxiety, generalised anxiety and post-traumatic stress disorder). • Do not describe a clear pathway of how these emotional difficulties eventually may lead to FND symptoms in the same way that theoretical models do. CBT models do not incorporate FND symptoms. • A condition-specific CBT model for FND has not yet been described, in the same vein as CBT models for panic disorder, social anxiety, post-traumatic stress disorder and generalised anxiety disorder. • Some CBT concepts overlap with FND-specific processes ("transdiagnostic": e.g. self-focused attention, catastrophic misinterpretation). • However, these processes are not usually linked to FND symptoms within the specific CBT models. • The pathway of "conversion" of emotion to FND is somewhat unclear for most patients who are treated with a CBT framework. However, a highly obvious emotion–FND link in a CBT model will apply to a small subset of people with FND (see Chapter 8 for case studies). • CBT models also do not describe other important factors maintaining FND and that are commonly noted in the literature, including the characteristic two-stage process.
Incorporating FND-specific concepts, phenomena and processes	• Theoretical models are specifically tailored to FND and incorporate FND-specific concepts, phenomena and intricacies of the FND presentation, for example: • Heightened self-focused attention (Edwards et al., 2012) • The impact of the existence of prior "seizure models" from self, others or the media, as well as prior physical illness and injury on developing FND (Brown & Reuber, 2016). Delineate a characteristic two-stage process that has been described in the research literature: • Stage 1: (internal) elevated arousal that unfolds over time and reduces following the non-epileptic seizure (Brown & Reuber, 2016) • Stage 2: (external) "secondary" gains as a result of the FND including care from the environment, avoidance of responsibilities.	

Patient–friendliness and applicability in clinical practice	• Although theoretical models have greatly enhanced our understanding of FND, these models have limited practical and clinical utility. Some models could imply treatment strategies for FND (e.g. distraction for self-focused attention); however, this often pertains to one concept and not the whole model, in contrast to CBT models. • Theoretical models tend to map poorly onto individual patient experiences and are not easily translated into a practical formulation and treatment model for use either in individual therapy or within a group therapy setting. • Do not possess theory–practice links that plan and guide an intervention to reduce FND symptoms. • For example, Brown and Reuber's (2016) model describes the process of the unfolding of a dissociative seizure. However, the model does not clearly indicate the steps that can be undertaken at each stage of the seizure to intervene and prevent it. For example, how does one know when the seizure scaffold has been activated and how does the link between the activation of the seizure scaffold and the dissociative seizure be broken? What are the processes by which seizure models feed into the seizure scaffold?	• A major appeal of CBT models is the strong theory–practice links. They guide the assessment and formulation of psychological problems. Once an individualised formulation of a person's psychological difficulties is created, CBT models automatically provide a clear roadmap for intervention and highlight useful techniques. • For example, in the social anxiety model, the crux of the therapy is often focused on using a series of behavioural experiments to help break the link between the social fears and safety behaviours. • CBT tends to be time-limited and cost-effective.
Level of inclusion of psychological elements into models	• Approximately 70–80% of patients with "medically unexplained neurological symptoms" experience co-morbid psychological difficulties including anxiety and depressive symptoms (e.g. Carson et al., 2000); it is therefore crucial to incorporate psychology and emotions into any model of FND. • Theoretical models of FND often use a mixture of psychological elements and principles either re-interpreted or borrowed from the psychological literature.	• Psychology and psychological concepts are central to CBT models, with physical aspects secondary to the psychological problem (e.g. social fears are core to social anxiety. Treating social anxiety successfully will hinge on whether social fears have sufficiently been challenged and embraced by the patient, as opposed to whether the physical symptoms of social anxiety have reduced sufficiently with relaxation exercises).

(Continued)

Table 1.2 (Continued)

Feature	Theoretical models of FND	CBT models
	• **Re-interpretation of classic psychological processes.** Some concepts used in theoretical models could be re-interpreted as an already well-researched classic psychological process; for example, seizure models are part of the modelling process described in Bandura's social learning theory; the characteristic reduction in arousal following a dissociative seizure is akin to Skinner's negative reinforcement processes; some concepts in theoretical models refer to behaviourist concepts, for example "hard-wired behavioural tendencies" and "conditioned reflexes". • **Mixed use of CBT maintenance cycles.** Other concepts in theoretical models appear to be similar to processes and maintenance cycles that are pulled from various CBT models, for example panic disorder and the idea of "catastrophic misinterpretations of bodily symptoms"; post-traumatic stress disorder and "threat perception" or "trauma reminders"; and increased self-focused attention from the social and health anxiety models. • Theoretical models often lack a more in-depth view of core psychological phenomena in FND (i.e. adverse early experiences and their relationships with coping strategies that emanate from childhood).	• Heightened attention as a maintenance factor (Brown et al., 2006; Edwards et al., 2012) parallels the self/symptom-focused attentional biases found in obsessive-compulsive disorder, health and social anxiety, and the build-up of worries in generalised anxiety disorder.
Uniformity vs diversity of psychological difficulties	• Theoretical models tend to refer to psychological phenomena in FND in general and uniform terms, and do not address psychological conditions in specific detail. The uniform approach to psychological difficulties in theoretical models does not capture the diversity of mental health symptoms observed in FND.	• CBT models do capture the diversity of mental health difficulties. A wide range of models, particularly for a multitude of different anxiety disorders, have been developed over the years. These condition-specific models delineate the psychological processes that maintain these conditions more clearly.

(Continued)

	• For example, the ICM focuses on anxiety and anxiety-related symptoms (e.g. elevated arousal, threat); however, anxiety is not a uniform concept. It consists of various types (e.g. social anxiety, obsessive fears, worries and panic attacks), each with different nuances and requiring specific treatment. • Furthermore, many patients with FND will not have anxiety as their main problem, even if this may appear that way initially. It is often relationship and interpersonal issues that drive or significantly contribute to FND. None of the theoretical models clearly detail the processes by which relationship factors impact on FND. It assumes that anxiety, often in the context of trauma, wholly drives the clinical picture.
Evidence base including for clinical applicability in FND	• Theoretical models of FND tend to be generally rooted in a large body of research; however, studies have not firmly tested these theoretical models in clinical practice and generated any evidence-based or practice-based evidence from the clinic. Therefore, the effectiveness of theoretical models in treating FND remains unclear. • It may be better to view theoretical models of FND as explanatory as opposed to clinical treatment models.	• CBT is firmly grounded in the principles from cognitive and behavioural psychology, supported by a large body of theoretical and practice-based evidence (Skinner, 1963; Salkovskis, 1985; Clark, 1986; Beck Judith, 1995; Clark & Wells, 1995; Wells, 1995; Veale, 2007). • A growing body of evidence has demonstrated the effectiveness of both CBT-based individual and group approaches in the treatment of FND including improved psychological well-being, FND symptoms, healthcare utilisation, mobility, activities of daily living and the degree of disability and dependence (e.g. Goldstein et al., 2004, 2010; Kuyk et al., 2008; LaFrance & Friedman, 2009; Sharpe et al., 2011; LaFrance et al., 2014; McCormack et al., 2014; Baslet et al., 2015; Bullock et al., 2015; Cope et al., 2017; Petrochilos et al., 2020).

Table 1.2 (Continued)

Feature	Theoretical models of FND	CBT models
		• However, it should be noted that most studies on the effectiveness of CBT models were conducted with people who experience one subtype of FND, that is, non-epileptic episodes. Research on the effectiveness of CBT in the motor subtype of FND has largely been neglected.
Social context	• Theoretical models incorporate the relationship between socio-environmental processes and FND symptoms, for example by mentioning secondary gains and describing the impact of media health scares and symptom models on the emergence of FND. • Although the social context appears to be more emphasised in theoretical over CBT models of FND, interpersonal processes and relationships, and their association with FND symptoms, are not well outlined in any type of model.	• CBT models generally tend to focus strongly on formulating and changing the internal psychological processes and responses of the individual and have a relatively limited view of the role of the wider environmental context that may contribute to a person's FND symptoms, as well as mapping out the appropriate intervention for the environment surrounding the individual.
Emergence vs maintenance of FND	• Theoretical models describe both the emergence and the maintenance of FND symptoms. • Theoretical models take into account the past, for example, by highlighting that an accident set off the FND or having cared for an ill family member may have contributed to FND, although these models do not highlight the pathway between these experiences and FND.	• Although longitudinal CBT models of depression incorporate past experiences and thinking patterns to help understand a person's current psychological difficulties, most CBT-specific models for anxiety disorders (e.g. panic, social anxiety, generalised anxiety) tend to focus on the "here-and-now", with less emphasis placed on how past events might have shaped or set off the anxiety, as well as the FND.
Complexity of language	• Unlike CBT models, contemporary theoretical accounts of FND tend to use complex terminology, language and concepts. The models do not clearly elucidate how complex theoretical concepts can be easily translated into day-to-day clinical practice. The models often require an abstract level of "almost scientific" thinking. • This will limit a patient's ability to understand the formulation of their FND.	• CBT models use simple language and concepts, are intuitive and relatively easy to understand by patients. • Models tend to be straightforward and simplistic.

Dissociation and alexithymia	• Dissociative features, a central concept in FND, have been incorporated in theoretical models of FND (e.g. "loss of consciousness"; Brown & Reuber, 2016).
	• Prior to entering therapy, CBT requires patients to have a certain level of psychological awareness, "psychological mindedness" or introspection in relation to processing their emotions, in order to understand the psychological formulation. However, people with FND can present with a variety of psychological features that CBT models will struggle to accommodate.
	• For example, patients do not always identify with stress and, in some cases, deny any form of distress completely. Dissociation ("cutting off from emotions") is often a core feature. Some people fail to consistently identify or provide verbal descriptions of emotions ("alexithymia", e.g. Demartini et al., 2014) and report vague cognitions and emotions that are often poorly defined and do not fit well into traditional condition-specific models of CBT. In addition, people may struggle with labelling emotions and refer to emotions as "feeling tired" or "in pain".
	• CBT models therefore cannot accommodate every patient with FND.
Rigidity vs flexibility	• Theoretical models are rigid and "niche" in that they are entirely focused on FND or one subtype of FND.
	CBT models have flexible features: CBT models can be adapted, and used in a generic format (five areas model) or as a condition-specific model.

a need has arisen for the development of a new biopsychosocial and practical treatment model of FND, the Pressure Cooker Model (PCM), that attempts to bridge the gap between theoretical and practical models by combining the "FND-specific" maintaining factors identified by theoretical models with the strong theory-practice links of "non–FND-specific" CBT models.

The principles of the PCM will be discussed in more detail in Chapter 3. In a nutshell, the PCM aims to delineate and raise insight into the equal individual and systemic contributions to FND by exploring, identifying and addressing the impact of beliefs, emotions and actions between the person with FND and every individual in their direct environment that has a relationship with the person (e.g. family members, healthcare workers). The main goals of the PCM are to assess, formulate and treat the individual and systemic factors that contribute to FND, in particular:

- To identify the characteristic two-step process of FND: the first intra-individual step ("internal regulation") and the second inter-individual step ("external regulation") cognitive, emotional and behavioural processes of people with FND and their environment that are hypothesised to maintain FND. The model aims to enhance the view and position of psychology as a leader in the field of FND and puts psychology at the core of FND treatment.

- To conceptualise FND and its psychological features in a radical new way: FND is the product of an inter-individual emotion regulation problem shared between the person and the system that results in harmful person-system cycles that maintain FND and distress, resulting in detrimental effects on care and recovery.

- To resolve the "systemic emotional co–dysregulation" between the individual and the system to achieve the most optimal outcomes in treatment. It will make a case for the environment to start recognising their own significant contribution to FND, shift the responsibility for recovery away from the individual towards the individual and the environment, and make changes in every individual's way of thinking, feeling and behaving to minimise their impact on FND.

- To highlight the power of a neuropsychological approach in capturing a coherent, cohesive and joined-up narrative of FND in straightforward language that ties together all the disciplines involved in the multidisciplinary treatment of FND and is accessible to every individual involved in FND.

- To assume a unique social role in raising awareness of the environment's own detrimental contribution to FND and actively promote a radical shift from an individual towards a more systemic framework of new ways of thinking and working with FND to help improve recovery in FND, and reduce stigma and confusion and anxiety in the environment. The PCM will touch on the novel concepts of "reciprocal reinforcement" and "systemic re-traumatisation" providing a systemic explanation for the often reported "attention seeking" and "manipulative" behaviours reported in people with FND by their environment. It hopes to increase societal and media awareness in the general population of FND as a condition with strong psychosocial determinants using a simple and relatable model.

• To ultimately change care practices in FND by re-building a validating and compassionate environment that repairs relationships and sets healthy boundaries, with the aim to reduce FND symptoms and distress in both the individual and the system.

The next section will explore the advantages of the PCM over existing theoretical and clinical models of FND.

The PCM: a biopsychosocial model with a big P+S

The PCM is a biopsychosocial model of FND that incorporates biological, psychological and social factors to explain the emergence and maintenance of FND symptoms. However, in comparison to other models, the PCM places a larger emphasis on the active formulation and treatment of social and environmental processes in FND and, additionally, incorporates biological and medical factors. These biological factors are not neglected; however, these variables play a more facilitating or subsidiary role, as the PCM strongly conceptualises FND as a psychosocial condition with additional biological features. It should be noted that although physical symptoms are described in models of FND (e.g. Brown & Reuber, 2016) and form part of the "hot cross bun" in CBT models, the models struggle with accounting for co-existing pain, fatigue and other symptoms on the somatoform spectrum. In the PCM, these features are classified as "FND after-effects" and viewed as part of a wider psychological process. For example, a person with a non-epileptic episode can fall to the ground and hurt themselves or tense up their muscles for a prolonged period during an episode, both resulting in pain. Fatigue is another common FND after-effect. A non-epileptic episode can result in severe and prolonged fatigue. This state is psychologically highly reinforcing since people who are fatigued are far less likely to feel negative emotions or some other unpleasant state or arousal that they felt before the episode. Each of the PCM elements is heavily embedded within a psychosocial context and relates to psychosocial concepts and processes, for example interpersonal triggers of FND (Fuel), social emotions, beliefs and fears about other people's thoughts including the fear of recovery (Flames), the concept of enjoyable activities linked to a sense of social belonging (Valve), the importance of emotional expression in a safe and trusting relationship (Cover), and relationships and interpersonal functioning between people with FND and the individuals in their immediate environment (Kitchen). The PCM is different from other existing models that incorporate social features because it not only highlights the socio-environmental context, but it also hones in on the association between specific interpersonal mechanisms and relationships with FND symptoms.

The PCM: a practical model in the clinic

Confusion is prominent and has been widely reported in people with FND, their family and friends, and in healthcare professionals (Carton et al., 2003; Green et al., 2004; O'Sullivan et al., 2006; Shneker & Elliott, 2008; Ahern et al., 2009; Espay et al., 2009; Thompson et al., 2009; Kanaan et al., 2011; Monzoni et al., 2011; Edwards et al., 2012; De Schipper et al., 2014; McMillan et al., 2014; Fobian & Elliott, 2019; Lehn et al., 2019; O'Connell et al., 2020; Klinke et al., 2021; Barnett et al., 2022). This confusional state of affairs has not been helped by existing metaphors of FND that are commonly used in clinical practice to provide a definition of FND to newly diagnosed people. Examples include the software-hardware analogy and the idea that in FND, the "messages" from the brain are not passed on appropriately to the rest of the body, together with the perception of FND as a mind-body disconnect, with therapies attempting to "reconnect" the mind with the body. Although the intentions behind these tangible and relatable metaphors were good and have certainly supported clinicians in explaining the diagnosis to a person with FND, the metaphors provide a vague description of FND and do not elucidate the mechanisms, maintaining factors or steps towards remediation of FND. In addition, these metaphors have the potential to further increase confusion as they may imply neurological injury.

In contrast to previous metaphors, the PCM is capable of assessment and formulation of FND and intuitively provides a roadmap for intervention. The PCM uses patient-friendly language to explain jargonistic concepts (e.g. self-focused attention, boom-bust cycles) and may help foster engagement with FND as connected to psychological features, facilitating the "socialisation process to the model". The relatable visual pressure cooker metaphor easily lends itself to incorporating all the elements that are important in FND. This concrete model is easy to understand, visualise and memorise. It provides a containing structure to explain a confusing condition and helps to elucidate the mechanisms underpinning the emergence and maintenance of FND. A pressure cooker (or "stress bucket") is a practical and easily understandable metaphor that, across decades, has been used to explain psychological concepts including stress (Schreiber & Seitzinger, 1985), psychosis ("stress and vulnerability bucket"; Brabban & Turkington, 2002) and anger (French, 2001).

The proliferation of models in the field of FND has caused confusion and overwhelming feelings for practitioners who often have limited time in day-to-day clinical practice to decide on a therapy model. In a busy, oversubscribed clinic with long waiting lists, the PCM can be quickly accessed to help the practitioner share an initial "rough" formulation to a person with FND and their family. A PCM formulation provides a concrete explanation for the emotion–FND link. It should, however, be noted that the PCM is not intended as a "quick fix" model that can miraculously simplify the complexity of FND within a single therapy session or a review appointment. The model does not endeavour to minimise the complexity of FND but is meant as a starting point for people with FND and their environment to help reduce confusion and obtain an initial psychologically driven formulation of FND that can be used reiteratively for further elaboration. It aims to facilitate understanding and communication between various stakeholders involved in FND and provide a "lingua franca" to patients, families and healthcare professionals.

The PCM: a hybrid model

CBT models or theoretical models of FND apply directly to the person with FND, "the person with the problem". None of the models can be applied to individuals without FND symptoms who interact with people with FND and form part of their direct environment. Since relationships with the environment are often a core issue in FND, a model of FND aimed at recovery should be capable of treating not only the person with FND but also the individuals in their environment. The PCM radically assumes that FND is the product of emotion dysregulation between the person and the environment that equally contribute to maintaining FND (see Chapter 3 for more details). Therefore, the PCM can and should be used as a hybrid model that applies to patients, family and practitioners who are all assumed to contribute to the development and maintenance of FND. In PCM terms, all participant groups carry an official diagnosis of FND. The Overpressure Plug in the "patient" version of the PCM represents the FND symptoms and psychological safety behaviours, whereas in the "hybrid" versions, this element is reflected by environmental psychological safety behaviours that are not FND.

The PCM: an early intervention model

A common problem in FND is the entrenchment of symptoms and behaviours over time, particularly in people with longstanding FND. Entrenchment may present in different ways including overreliance on equipment that has increased in number over the years; permanent and sometimes irreversible home adaptations; the extent to which the environment has adapted around the person's symptoms and disabilities; the consolidation of patterns of caring and dependency that have been repeated and reinforced over many years and could be difficult to unlearn; and the provision of comprehensive care packages provided by external carers. Entrenchment can have far-reaching consequences, even resulting in permanent bodily changes ('fixed' dystonia).

There are many reasons for entrenchment in FND. Lack of knowledge and confidence in diagnosing FND can delay the diagnosis and treatment. Furthermore, the scarcity of FND-specialist services in the UK often means long waiting lists, due to a lack of resources and staffing but high demand. It is not unusual for people with newly diagnosed FND who are referred to a specialist service to wait for years before they can finally commence treatment. People who are left untreated during this long waiting time risk their symptoms becoming entrenched, making it harder to undo the symptoms in future. In addition, anxiety and confusion about FND may lead health and social care professionals to provide patients with an unusual amount of equipment, home adaptations and comprehensive care packages, which maintain the FND and can serve as psychological safety behaviours of the patients and the practitioners. Another reason for entrenchment is the fact that the maintaining factors of FND are often found in the family and healthcare systems around a person with FND. However, both systems are often "systematically" neglected during the treatment of FND. Systemic re-traumatisation (a key psychological process in FND that will be discussed in Chapter 3) can also prolong FND symptoms and therefore entrenchment.

Therefore, early intervention in FND, before the symptoms and behaviours become entrenched, is an area of great importance that not only can improve outcomes in FND, but also reduce healthcare utilisation and environmental dependency. The PCM can play an important role in this early intervention process on multiple levels. FND education based on the PCM can promote a greater understanding of the maintaining factors and mechanisms of FND to patients and families who are on the waiting list for treatment, as part of a low-intensity stepped-care model. The inclusion of the environment in the treatment programme from the very start can halt entrenchment.

The PCM can also be recommended as essential reading for first-year students of all disciplines that are commonly involved in the treatment of FND including psychology, medicine, nursing, occupational therapy, physiotherapy, speech and language therapy, social work, dietetics, paramedics and pharmacy. The earlier the education on FND starts in the healthcare system, the more systematic re-traumatisation can be suppressed and its impact on the maintenance of FND reduced.

The PCM: a versatile model

Table 1.3 demonstrates the endless flexibility and versatility of the PCM.

The PCM: embedded in evidence-based psychological principles

Although the PCM has not been investigated using gold-standard randomised controlled trials, it is a psychologically driven model that is rooted in practice-based evidence (see Chapter 2 for more details). The PCM uses widely researched transdiagnostic and evidence-based CBT principles including the concepts of reinforcement learning, increased self-focused attention and safety behaviours. Each element of the PCM represents a well-researched and/or clinically observed maintaining factor in FND; for example, the Warning light represents heightened self-focused attention (Edwards et al.,

Table 1.3 Versatility characteristics of the Pressure Cooker Model

Versatility feature	Details
FND subtypes	• FND is characterised by variability on many different levels including type, severity and frequency of symptoms, as well as psychological and medical co-morbidities. A model of FND should be able to accommodate for this variability. • The PCM can address the heterogeneity of FND subtypes including dissociative episodes, motor-type FND, sensory conversion symptoms, functional cognitive disorder or a mixture of these symptoms. In addition to FND symptoms, the model also addresses pain and fatigue symptoms commonly associated with FND, as well as psychological safety behaviours (e.g. caring behaviours from the environment).
Different populations with FND	• FND affects a wide range of different people and comes with co-morbidities. Chapter 6 will show that, with adaptations and simplifications (e.g. removing elements), the PCM can be applied to different populations with FND including children and young people, people with learning difficulties, autism, functional overlay (e.g. epileptic and non-epileptic seizures) and complex trauma.
Different formats	• The PCM can be adapted for use in different intervention formats including individual one-to-one, manualised group therapy and online therapy, as well as used as a model for team reflection (see Chapters 6 and 7) and training/FND education.
Anxiety, depression and complex trauma	• The PCM can easily accommodate two separate psychological presentations that often go hand in hand in FND: a more anxiety-dominated picture vs depression with or without complex trauma features. In addition, the PCM can formulate other safety behaviours in FND, including deliberate self-harm and aggression, in the context of complex trauma presentations. • The PCM can manage psychological features that resemble but may not invariably follow the expected pattern (e.g. classic panic cycle in FND is often self-terminating due to a dissociative episode). • It can formulate and address a mixture of dysregulated emotions that are experienced simultaneously, which a CBT model would struggle to accommodate.
Strong dissociation and "denial" of distress	• Some people with FND may not identify with emotions, reject the idea that FND is associated with any psychological features or adopt a highly defensive position towards stress and psychology. For these people, the PCM can be used to explain the general mechanisms of stress-coping without applying it to the individual's situation. Furthermore, in contrast to CBT models, the PCM does not require a person to identify with emotions. The model is capable of continuing the work even if the person identifies their emotions as an unpleasant state.

(Continued)

Table 1.3 (Continued)

Versatility feature	Details
Type of healthcare setting	• The model can be used in single therapist work and within a multidisciplinary context since every element of the PCM represents a discipline involved in the treatment of FND.
Preparatory model	• The model can be used as part of the standalone treatment in FND but is also easy to embed or use alongside other models including CBT models (e.g. stabilisation phase before reliving phase in PTSD treatment, or learning about emotions, their functions and physical features, as well as basic emotion coping skills to make the person ready for a condition-specific CBT model; see Chapter 8).
CBT × PCM hybrid models	• CBT models can be incorporated into PCM formulations, which augment the CBT model and can explain additional FND-specific features that CBT models struggle with (social aspects of FND, reduced verbal emotional expression), for example for social anxiety or panic disorder (see Chapter 8 for examples).
Biopsychosocial guide	• The model can also be used as a "biopsychosocial guide" for asking structured questions about various topics important in FND care including emotions, sleep and assertiveness (see Chapter 4 of this book, as well as Chapters 7 and 8 of the patient workbook for examples).
People with past FND that may return in future	• By the time that a person with FND is at the top of a waiting list for specialist support, the FND symptoms may not always be present. This could mean that the symptoms have naturally resolved over time and the person may have found their own coping strategies. However, without an understanding and explanation of the mechanics of FND, the person may experience a setback in future. The PCM lends itself well for generating formulations of past FND symptoms vs current absence of FND to provide an explanation of FND, steps to take if a future relapse occurs and creating a "stay-well" plan.

2012). It combines CBT principles with FND-specific factors and processes, for example the idea of a two-stage process of internal and external regulation of emotions. Although theoretical models of FND incorporate many FND-specific concepts and processes, these models miss other maintaining factors that have been consistently identified in the clinical practice and in the research literature including reduced verbal emotional expression (Griffith et al., 1998; Wood et al., 1998; Bowman & Markand, 1999; Krawetz et al., 2001), dissociation (Janet, 1920), abnormal activity levels and boom-bust behaviours (Lempert & Schmidt, 1990; Gardiner et al., 2018), and emotion dysregulation (Uliaszek et al., 2012; Brown et al., 2013). Furthermore, psychological factors relevant to FND that have been identified in the research literature are not commonly described in the models, particularly adverse childhood experiences, and upbringing and early coping mechanisms. The PCM includes all these key FND-associated variables that have not earlier been incorporated in other models including reciprocal reinforcement patterns between the person and the environment that maintain FND.

The PCM: a model that helps to reduce stigma

It may seem paradoxical to think that a psychologically driven model would possess the ability to reduce stigma in FND. After all, psychology has always been strongly associated with stigma and negative connotations. However, the PCM truly makes an attempt to reduce stigma on different levels. For example, the PCM conceptualises FND as a two-step process governed by intra-individual and inter-individual processes, holding true to the evidence base in FND. However, in contrast to previous models that consistently describe the second step as "secondary gains" and assumed a one-directional process with the person "manipulating" the environment, the PCM views the second step as part of a "social function" and assumes a bi-directional and interpersonal dynamic between the person and the environment. The PCM insists that both the person and the environment are "ill" and play an equal role in their contribution to FND and in need of treatment. This makes both parties "liable" to adopt a joint and equal responsibility towards recovery from FND, removing the responsibility and therefore the stigma from the individual. The model has the potential to reduce stigma and re-traumatisation in FND by highlighting and bringing to awareness the processes that contribute to these phenomena. Eventually, the reduction in stigma and re-traumatisation will lead to better outcomes in FND.

The PCM and relationships: transcending beyond the socio-environmental context

Traditionally, CBT models have strongly focused on treating the individual whilst de-emphasising the environment. Although theoretical models of FND describe the impact of the socio-environmental context on the emergence and maintenance of FND symptoms to a larger extent than CBT models do (e.g. symptom models), both types of model neglect to focus on relationships and interpersonal processes. Moreover, current models do not provide a practical solution to address these systemic issues and reduce their contribution to FND. This is surprising since a large body of evidence has demonstrated interpersonal triggers of FND and a wide range of abnormal features in the past and current relationships of people with FND with individuals in their environment. Moreover, a vast number of people with FND report upsetting and challenging interactions with healthcare professionals resulting in profoundly negative beliefs and emotions. Healthcare professionals often report beliefs and emotions about people with FND that exactly mirror the beliefs and emotions that people with FND experience in response to interactions with healthcare professionals (see Chapter 3). The PCM is a relational model and focuses on this core aspect of FND by not only focusing on "contents" but also equally highlighting the "process" and introduces two new interpersonal processes: reciprocal reinforcement and systemic re-traumatisation.

The PCM: a multidisciplinary model

The relatively recently published UK government white paper (2021) has detailed a range of healthcare priorities, in particular the need for more joined-up care in the NHS and social care. The joined-up care for FND remains a challenge in clinical practice for a variety of reasons. Although FND is a condition that requires a multidisciplinary approach, teams caring for people with FND are often incomplete, due to the complexity of FND and its psychological impact on staff, higher staff turnover or unavailability of specialist staff. At times, teams may lack psychological input despite psychological treatment representing a core feature in the treatment of FND. In this situation, a psychologically driven model such as the PCM may prove to be helpful in creating a formulation of FND that provides guidance to treatment planning in the absence of a psychologist. Another roadblock towards joined-up care in FND is the lack of a cohesive narrative in FND, in part due to the proliferation of numerous FND models over the years. A final issue pertains to the lack of interdisciplinary working in teams. Oftentimes, disciplines involved in the treatment of FND work alongside each other ("multidisciplinary") instead of closely collaborating together ("interdisciplinary"). This may lead to adverse effects including repetition of work, over-assessment, over-treatment and a lack of synergistic effects between the treatments delivered by the different disciplines. The PCM can help remediate these challenges in various ways.

Focusing solely on psychology may help a person with FND gain insight into the psychological mechanisms of FND and move the person along in their journey of recovery from FND. However, in moderate to severe cases, psychological treatment is likely not going to be sufficient. For example, a person with longstanding functional leg weakness and deconditioned muscles may have struggled to access the community, dropped hobbies and other meaningful activities, and collected a long list of interacting medications prescribed by different practitioners that need ratification, as well as a review of their dependency on equipment and regular care calls organised by social services. None of the models specifically highlight the contributions of physiotherapy, occupational therapy, psychiatry and social work to FND. None of the models can easily be adapted for work in a multidisciplinary team context or possess a "lingua franca" of FND to facilitate communication between disciplines. In their paper, Klinke et al. (2021) highlight the importance of working with "specialised FND vocabulary" and using similar terminology and metaphors to enhance care for people with FND.

Although the PCM is suitable for single therapist work, the model can be flexibly adapted in such a way that each element represents a discipline or multiple disciplines that are part of the treatment team responsible for the care of a person with FND (see Chapter 4 for more details). In a multidisciplinary context, the PCM framework can help develop a unifying, psychologically driven formulation that ties together different pieces of information from multiple disciplines into one coherent narrative. Once the multidisciplinary formulation is in place, with psychology permeating through every element, the PCM allows treatment to be planned in an interdisciplinary rather than a multidisciplinary manner and provides "discipline-specific" and "pan-discipline" guidance applicable to all disciplines (e.g. the identification of reciprocal reinforcement processes that all team members need to address). The model may help keep a multidisciplinary team on track throughout the assessment, formulation and treatment of FND. Importantly, by facilitating joined-up working, the PCM reduces team splitting and the persistent unhelpful use of mind-body distinctions.

The PCM: a positive model instilling hope

The PCM strongly assumes that FND is maintained by a collection of psychological safety behaviours and unhelpful relationship habits. Behaviours and habits have the potential to be learned or unlearned and can be subjected to remediation with new individual and relationship skills, giving hope for recovery. Instead of focusing on medically unexplained neurological symptoms, the PCM focuses on psychologically explained neurological symptoms. Importantly, unlike other models of FND that often focus on "pathology" and "what's wrong with the patient", the PCM actively incorporates protective and positive prognostic factors in FND (represented by the "Safety features" element).

The PCM: a model promoting a more positive role for psychology in FND

In recent years, the treatment options for FND have grown beyond historical disciplines (e.g. psychology and psychiatry) and have focused on a range of relatively new disciplines (e.g. physiotherapy, occupational therapy, and speech and language therapy). As the treatment of FND has become multidisciplinary, the perceived role of psychology as a vital discipline contributing to effective outcomes in FND has gradually decreased. Despite its core role in the treatment and resolution of symptoms in FND, people with FND can be highly rejecting of psychological therapy. Moreover, psychology as a profession has generally been associated with negative connotations in FND. Some of the reasons that may have contributed to the negative status of psychology in FND include prior negative experiences and suboptimal outcomes with psychological therapy carried out by "generic" rather than "FND-specialist" therapists; a psychologist uncovering the core of the problem with the patient unable to tolerate the distress, which leads to the mistaken belief that psychology will make you feel worse than better; healthcare professionals pushing the patient to try psychology but the person being too dissociated from emotions and perceiving the pushing as frustrating with psychology becoming synonymous to not feeling believed; the stigma of psychology as a therapy for "weak" people; the advance of biological approaches to FND that may feel less threatening than psychology; and the confusion about the difference between psychology and psychiatry with patients often believing that these professions are more or less similar with little awareness of the power of psychological formulation for FND.

In addition to the ambivalence around psychology in FND, a trend has been observed where non-psychology disciplines have started to use techniques that have traditionally been used by psychologists. Examples include reality grounding techniques, relaxation strategies, assertiveness and social skill training, and any other cognitive-behavioural therapy techniques, which may look simple on the surface. However, due to the less threatening nature of these disciplines, people with FND may become more inclined to engage with and even favour these professions over psychology. This can be dangerous as techniques such as reality grounding and relaxation may become ineffective or even counter-productive in FND, and, for example, actively used as safety behaviours by the patients, which subsequently maintain psychological difficulties and FND. In addition, non-psychology professions do not use psychological formulation and these techniques are often shared with patients "on a whim" without being driven by a strong psychological rationale.

Therefore, a need has arisen to improve and reclaim the status of psychology as a core part of the multidisciplinary treatment in FND. The PCM can be a powerful model in this process since it has the ability to generate a multidisciplinary formulation and may help promote a more positive view of psychology in the field of FND.

FND as a psychosocial condition: an unspoken and uncomfortable truth

The book does not deny the existence of the brain or biological processes operating in FND. Although the recent approach to FND has been slanted towards exploring a biological basis for FND, the book highlights that a biological approach provides only one piece of the puzzle of our understanding of FND. More importantly, the book recommends the reader to actively consider the overwhelmingly strong but consistently neglected evidence in favour of adopting a much stronger psychosocially informed approach towards FND than has previously been used. The book encourages clinicians and researchers to think more deeply along the lines of psychosocial perspective on FND and challenges clinicians working in the field in their thinking: By neglecting a psychosocial perspective in FND, have we missed a crucial and powerful forum for therapeutic change? The book challenges an unspoken and uncomfortable truth: that all along FND should have been regarded as a systemic condition rather than a condition solely caused by the individual, and that as a system, we are not only in control but also have an obligation to change these aberrant systemic processes that have been contributing to FND.

The book does not purport to force the reader to make a choice between a biological vs psychosocial approach to FND. This dichotomy is exactly what created the core problem in the world of FND: the persisting disconnection between the mind and the body, that is so symbolic of FND and that is in part caused by the confusion that this condition has generated in clinicians from many different psychological and physical disciplines. During times of confusion and discomfort, it is understandable that one holds on strongly to what is familiar, resulting in an incoherent constellation of snippets of psychosocial and physical formulations. The Pressure Cooker Model aims to move closer towards the resolution of this dichotomy and facilitate a more coherent, "joined-up" biopsychosocial understanding of FND.

Our understanding of FND is an "and-and" situation rather than "either-or". The book does not encourage the reader to challenge existing notions of FND but rather retain those notions that have been so crucial in furthering our knowledge on the emergence and maintenance of FND yet simultaneously invite a more psychosocial approach towards an explanation and treatment of FND. Not only will this reduce the confusion that still festers amongst patients and healthcare professionals, but it will also provide new and ground-breaking treatment avenues for FND to truly help people, families and healthcare professionals.

2 Evidence-based data for the Pressure Cooker Model

Introduction

The PCM is a newly developed model of FND that has not been subjected to scientific scrutiny. Although randomised controlled trials (RCTs) provide the most robust evidence to demonstrate the effectiveness of a treatment model, these research designs can be costly and time-consuming, and absorb clinical resources, particularly in busy clinical services with limited staffing and resources. One of the criticisms of the RCT approach concerns the mismatch between the often highly controlled "one-size-fits-all" style of intervention protocols on the one hand, and their relevance, feasibility and ease of implementation in routine clinical practice on the other hand (e.g. Cully et al., 2012), a particular important consideration for a heterogeneous patient group such as FND. The generalisability of the conclusions from RCTs beyond the studied sample that will have been subjected to strict inclusion and exclusion criteria is unclear ("external validity", e.g. Ammerman et al., 2014).

Assessing the effectiveness of a model or intervention as satisfactory, for example in reducing symptoms and improving well-being, does not provide a guarantee for its successful implementation into clinical practice and can even lead to a subsequent failure of adopting the intervention.

Fortunately, novel treatment models can also be assessed using alternative and less than "gold-standard" designs that, for example, use descriptive methods, practice-based evidence or more qualitative methods that investigate the feasibility of an intervention in day-to-day clinical practice and the acceptability of the model by the people who are going to use it including patients, families and healthcare professionals. The effectiveness of an intervention can be viewed as one of the many parameters at which an intervention can be assessed or will make an impact (e.g. see Ammerman et al., 2014). Furthermore, reality is chaotic, disorganised, cluttered, complex and not controlled (e.g. Swisher, 2010) – unlike the experimentally controlled, tightly organised and simplistic, reductionist conditions that tend to be set out as part of an RCT intervention. A descriptive research method that highly resonates with a "cluttered world" that is reflected by the heterogeneity in symptoms in a

DOI: 10.4324/9781003308980-2

condition like FND may be a better fit for an investigation of the features of the PCM.

Rationale of the study

Although the book recommends the use of a rigorous scientific methodology to test out treatment models as part of "evidence-based practice", the utility of a more descriptive approach that is deeply rooted in clinical practice for the investigation of a new, previously untested model such as the PCM will be highlighted here.

A starting point

A descriptive approach can be a helpful starting point for the collection of preliminary data on a novel model. Due to its nature, a practical model such as the PCM lends itself well to this type of research method. The results from this more qualitative approach may help determine whether there is future scope and rationale towards the development of a more rigorous research design using more time-intensive and effortful methods of measurement and study procedures. Therefore, descriptive data directly obtained from clinical practice may pave the way for a more evidence-based research study that in turn will feed back its findings to inform clinical practice.

Effectiveness, acceptability and feasibility

Even if the PCM as a treatment model was found to be effective using a more rigorous and time-intensive scientific methodology, an exclusive focus on the effectiveness of an intervention may not provide a full evaluation of the model and lose sight of other important factors in FND, for example the acceptability of a psychology-driven model to patients, families and clinicians who are using it and who may favour a more physical approach, as well as the feasibility of using the model in day-to-day clinical practice, multidisciplinary teams and its utility in a variety of inpatient and outpatient clinical settings.

Capturing the richness of FND

A descriptive approach can provide a far richer understanding of a condition than standard RCTs may likely achieve, which often require tightly controlled experimental conditions (e.g. experimental vs treatment-as-usual) with strict inclusion and exclusion criteria (e.g. only people with FND who experience the "pure dissociative seizures" subtype) and rely on quantitative measurements and whole-group analyses to obtain average scores across a group of patients with heterogeneous clinical presentations (e.g. dissociative seizures, motor-type FND) and that cuts across a diverse range of categories (e.g. age, presence of complex trauma, learning difficulties). The PCM aims to capture the intricacies of the multi-layered nature of the complex condition of FND by invoking relational concepts that are notoriously difficult to conceptualise and measure (e.g. reciprocal reinforcement). Measuring the validity or utility of the PCM using a more descriptive approach by providing a characterisation of clinical phenomena may do the FND patient group and the intricacies of the model more justice as it preserves the richness and nuances of FND.

A different but equally important question

Gold-standard RCTs investigating the effectiveness of psychological therapy in a patient group often ask the question whether an experimental treatment causes a significant reduction in symptoms or an increase in well-being, in comparison to treatment-as-usual. It often focuses on content rather than process, for example by examining whether the contents of a specific group therapy have therapeutic effects and ensuring that the same group therapy is delivered to every patient. However, we know that FND is a complex and heterogeneous condition where treatment may not always be as straightforward in its implementation. (Relationship) process rather than content is often the core issue, and any research design that does not incorporate this to a major extent will likely miss an important treatment target.

Aims of the study

The service evaluation consisted of two different studies. Study 1 focused on quantitative data that was collected as part of "real-world" routine clinical care in a neurorehabilitation setting. Study 2 served as a pilot study that used data from the same setting but that aimed to provide the reader with preliminary evidence for the usefulness of the PCM in clinical practice, using a descriptive and "rich formulation" method that captures the unique individual differences and heterogeneity of FND than a quantitative method on its own would be able to do. It aimed to show that these more qualitative findings provide a basis for further investigation of the PCM using a more rigorous scientific methodology.

Structure of Chapter 2

Chapter 2 will be divided into three parts. Before describing the PCM study, this chapter will start with presenting the results of a service evaluation on outcomes in psychological therapy based on principles of the PCM, either as part of psycho-education on FND; an addition to another treatment model (e.g. social anxiety model) to help fully capture the processes of FND; or as a broad-based core model of treatment (Table 2.1).

Table 2.1 Chapter sections presenting clinical and literature research evidence for the Pressure Cooker Model

Section #	Goals	Details
Section 1	Description of quantitative results from a service evaluation study.	Outcomes collected as part of routine clinical care in a service evaluation. The results from this evaluation provide an overview on important demographic and clinical characteristics of the sample.
Section 2	Descriptive evidence to assess whether clinical findings could lend support for the model.	This descriptive evidence was obtained from a clinical setting that used the PCM for formulation and treatment purposes, as part of psycho-education on FND and/or psychological therapy.
Section 3	Acceptability and feasibility of the model by patients and healthcare professionals.	Qualitative feedback on the model that was obtained from: • A small group of patients with FND who participated in a group therapy programme. • Healthcare professionals who attended a presentation on the PCM.
Chapter 3	Literature review of peer-reviewed findings from the scientific literature in support of the PCM.	Chapter 3 will focus on the discussion of evidence-based research that lends support to the inclusion of each element in the PCM.

Section 2.1: A service evaluation of clinical outcomes of psychological therapy in FND (Study 1)

Background and service context

In general, very few research studies have been published on inpatient outcomes in FND. These published findings will be later reviewed in Chapter 3 in more detail. The present service evaluation is based on clinical outcome data that was collected as part of routine clinical care in an inpatient rehabilitation setting. The service aimed to treat people with "category A rehabilitation needs" characterised by complex and unstable psychiatric needs, which required the involvement of at least five therapy disciplines including psychology, neuropsychiatry, physiotherapy, occupational therapy and speech therapy. Psychology was therefore part of a wider multidisciplinary treatment team that also consisted of other highly skilled professionals (e.g. support workers). Although outcome data will only be presented for people with FND, it should be noted that the neuropsychiatric team was embedded into a service that consisted of other teams that treated people with traumatic brain injury, stroke and spinal conditions without brain injury.

Ethical considerations

In agreement with local and national legislation, as well as in accordance with the institutional requirements, this service evaluation did not require ethical review, approval or written patient consent for the study of human participants. However, study authorisation for this service evaluation, with an explanation and a description of the procedures and methods, was sought and provided by the local trust.

Patient sample

The studied sample consisted of n = 49 adult patients with a diagnosis of FND who were consecutively admitted between 2018 and 2021 to participate in an intensive inpatient treatment programme for FND. No inclusion or exclusion criteria were applied; every patient's data was included for analysis.

Methods and procedure

On admission and at discharge, patients with FND completed a series of questionnaires that measured a variety of psychological difficulties and concepts, whereas clinicians rated the patients on a set of neurorehabilitation measures.

Psychology questionnaires

MOOD AND ANXIETY

The 9-item Patient Health Questionnaire (PHQ-9; Kroenke et al., 2001) consists of nine items that measure a range of self-reported psychological, behavioural and biological features of depression including anhedonia, sleep and appetite. Scores range from 0 to 27. Cronbach's alphas of .86 and .89 indicated good internal consistency. The 7-item Generalised Anxiety Scale (GAD-7; Spitzer et al., 2006) assessed the symptoms of anxiety. Scores range from 0 to 21. Cronbach's alpha of .92 has been reported, with a test-retest reliability of .83 and good validity of the scale (Spitzer et al., 2006). A score of ≥5 is deemed clinically significant on both measures ("mild", whilst scores of 10, 15 and 20 reflect "moderate", "moderately severe" and "severe" levels, respectively; Kroenke et al., 2001).

EMOTION DYSREGULATION

Emotion dysregulation has been reported in a subset of people with FND (Uliaszek et al., 2012; Brown et al., 2013; Williams et al., 2018). Using the original 36-item Difficulties in Emotion Regulation Scale (DERS; Gratz & Roemer, 2004), Uliaszek et al. (2012) found two clusters of high vs low emotion dysregulation in a sample of patients with non-epileptic episodes. Therefore, to reduce burden on the patients, the Difficulties in Emotion Regulation Scale – Short Form (DERS-SF; Kaufman et al., 2016) was included in the study. The DERS-SF consists of 18 statements that are each self-rated on a 5-point scale running from "almost never" to "almost always" (total score: 18–90). Six scales make up the questionnaire including Strategies, Non-acceptance, Impulse, Goals, Awareness and Clarity. These scales measure a range of features pertinent to the concept of emotion regulation including a person's tendency towards denial of distress, ability to control behaviour or concentrate when feeling distressed, as well as the level of emotional awareness. Psychometric properties of the DERS-SF were good with Cronbach's alphas ranging between .78 and .91 (Kaufman et al., 2016).

SELF-ESTEEM

The Rosenberg Self-Esteem Scale (Rosenberg, 1965; Gray-Little et al., 1997) consists of ten items that measure level of self-worth and self-acceptance. Patients are asked to rate each statement on a 4-point Likert scale running from "strongly agree" to "strongly disagree", with a maximum score of 30 and ≤14 suggesting low self-esteem. Test-retest reliability was found to be .82–.88, whilst Cronbach's alpha ranged between .77 and .88 (Rosenberg, 1986; Blascovich & Tomaka, 1993). Low self-esteem is a commonly observed clinical feature in FND, and this scale has previously detected low self-esteem in over 50% of a research sample of people with FND. Furthermore, the median score on admission fell just below the normal range, suggesting that as a group, patients were low in self-esteem (Petrochilos et al., 2020).

HEIGHTENED SELF-FOCUSED ATTENTION

Heightened self-focused attention on physical symptoms has been identified as a key maintaining factor in FND (Brown, 2006; Van Poppelen et al., 2011; Edwards et al., 2012; Nielsen et al., 2015). At the time of the study, no patient-rated measures were available that gauged a person's views on their level of self-focused attention to symptoms and that, following a course of psychological therapy, could be used to track the level of self-perceived attentional symptom focus over time. Therefore, to measure self-perceived pre-to-post therapy change in self-focused attention, a new Attention-to-Symptoms Questionnaire (ATSQ) was developed on the basis of two previously published questionnaires, using a similar coding system (i.e. Scale of Body Awareness: Hansell et al., 1991; Body Vigilance Scale: Schmidt et al., 1997). The psychometric properties of this short questionnaire were not examined; it was used in the context of clinical practice to provide some estimate of change in self-focused attention. The ATSQ is a 7-item questionnaire with response options running from 1 ("very little") to 5 ("very much"). Total scores range from 7 to 35.

Neurorehabilitation measures

Participants were "observer-rated" by their treating clinicians on all neurore-habilitation measures.

UK FIM+FAM

The UK Functional Independence Measure (FIM) and Functional Assessment Measure (UK FIM+FAM; Turner-Stokes et al., 1999) consists of 30 items and assessed a patient's level of disability and functional independence in activities of daily living. Staff members scored each item between 1 (complete dependence) and 7 (fully independent) on a range of motor and cognitive functions including self-care, bladder and bowel management, locomotion, communication, psychosocial functioning and thinking skills. The UK FIM+FAM generates a Total score (min-max: 30–210), Motor score (16–112) and a Cognitive score (14–98). Higher total scores suggest more independence.

MODIFIED BARTHEL INDEX

The modified Barthel Index (Wade & Collin et al., 1988; Nyein et al., 1999) was derived from the FIM and assessed a person's functional independence in activities of daily living and mobility. The index consists of 10 items including bowel and bladder management, grooming, toilet use, feeding, transfer, mobility, dressing, stairs and bathing. Scores range from 0 (totally dependent) to 20 (completely independent). Higher total scores suggest more independence.

NEUROLOGICAL IMPAIRMENT SCALE

The Neurological Impairment Scale (NIS; Turner-Stokes et al., 2014) measures the severity and extent to which different physical, psychological and cognitive impairments impact on functioning in the rehabilitation process. Using a functional impairment rating scale running from 0 (no impairment – normal function) to 3 (severe impairment – little or no useful function, effectively limiting rehabilitation), the NIS assesses a range of variables on their functional impact including motor and sensory function, communication, pain, fatigue, cognitive, mood and behavioural functioning. The maximum score is 50, and higher scores suggest more severe impairment.

REHABILITATION COMPLEXITY SCALE – EXTENDED

The Rehabilitation Complexity Scale – Extended (RCS-E version 13; Turner-Stokes et al., 2012) assesses the level of complexity of care needs. The total score (maximum = 22) consists of staff ratings of basic care needs, special nursing needs, medical needs, therapy needs and equipment for each patient. Higher scores mean more care needs.

ANALYSES

The distributions of all continuous variables were examined for normality via three different methods from the Statistical Package for the Social Sciences (SPSS; Nie et al., 1975): (1) statistics to test for the skewness of distributions (Kolmogorov-Smirnov's and Shapiro-Wilk's tests); (2) visual inspection of the histograms of each distribution to check for the shape of the curve (e.g. grossly normal, right- or left-skewed, bimodal); and (3) inspection of the position and deviation of the data-points from the reference line in the "normal Q-Q plot" of each variable. Based on the results of these three normality measures, which were interpreted in conjunction to determine normality, a decision was made whether to perform a parametric or non-parametric analysis on the variable. Since the data of only one sample of people with FND was examined without reference to a second, control group, statistical analyses consisted of within-subjects pre-to-post measure comparisons: parametric paired-samples t-tests for normally distributed variables and non-parametric Wilcoxon's signed rank tests for non-normally distributed variables. Categorical variables (e.g. gender, age strata, clinical classification categories for mood and anxiety symptoms) were examined with frequency counts (%). Exploratory non-parametric correlational analyses were undertaken using Spearman's rho.

Results

Sample characteristics

The patients were divided into six age strata. Figure 2.1.1 shows the distribution of the patients across age strata. A bimodal distribution was apparent, with one peak falling in the 21–30 age group (n = 15) and the second peak falling in the 51–60 age group (n = 10) (Table 2.1.1).

Approximately 30% of all patients (n = 14) experienced FND symptoms for less than six months by the time they had arrived on the unit. Slightly under half of the sample (22/49, 45%) had more recently developed FND, within two years, whereas about 55% (27/49) of the sample had been experiencing

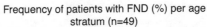

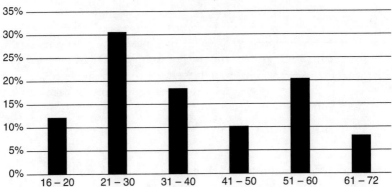

Figure 2.1.1 Frequency of patients with FND (%) per age stratum (n = 49).

Table 2.1.1 Demographic and clinical characteristics of the sample of people with FND (n = 49)

Demographic variable	Mean ± SD	Range
Age	38 ± 15.6	16–72
Gender (M/F)	n = 17 (35%)/n = 32 (65%)	–
Admission length (in days)	100.7 ± 56.9	41–329 days
Admission length (in months)	3.4 ± 1.9	1.4–11 months
Disease duration (in years)	4 ± 5.8	0–27 years

FND for at least two years. Approximately ~30% reported FND for at least two to five years. About 15% of the sample experienced long-term FND for at least ten years (Figure 2.1.2).

NEUROREHABILITATION MEASURES

All pairwise, within–subjects, repeated-measures comparisons between mean admission and discharge scores were highly significant, suggesting significant reductions in the impact of (functional) neurological symptoms, disability and dependency, as well as in relation to care needs (Table 2.1.2).

MOOD AND ANXIETY QUESTIONNAIRES: PHQ-9 AND GAD-7

In comparison to admission, people with FND appeared to obtain lower scores for depressive and anxiety symptoms on discharge. However, the difference between pre-to-post scores was non-significant for the PHQ-9 and trending towards significance for the GAD-7. On admission, as a group,

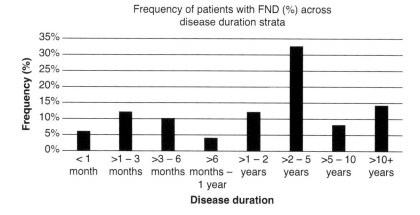

Figure 2.1.2 Frequency of patients with FND (%) across disease duration strata.

Table 2.1.2 Scores on neurorehabilitation measures of the FND sample

Measure	Admission (mean ± SD)	Discharge (mean ± SD)	Statistics (t or Z)
NIS	21.3 ± 5.3	11.3 ± 6.5	t = 11.6, df = 38, p < .001
UK FIM + FAM (Motor)	64 ± 21.3 (range: 22–100)	95.4 ± 17.2 (range: 34–112)	Wilcoxon's signed rank test Z = -5.3, p < .001
UK FIM + FAM (Cognitive)	66.5 ± 14.7 (range: 35–94)	85.3 ± 9.5 (range: 58–98)	Z = -5.2, p < .001
UK FIM + FAM (Total)	130.5 ± 31.6 (range: 68–183)	180.7 ± 25 (range: 92–210)	Z = -5.3, p < .001
Modified Barthel Index	11.1 ± 3.9 (range: 4–19)	17.1 ± 3.4 (range: 7–20)	Z = -5.38, p < .001
RCS-E	12.5 ± 1.7 (range: 9–17)	10.1 ± 3.4 (range: 3–18)	Z = -3.8, p < .001

Sample sizes for admission-discharge score pairs, all n = 37 except for NIS, Barthel and RCS, which are all n = 39; NIS = Neurological Impairment Scale; UK Functional Independence Measure (FIM) and Functional Assessment Measure (UK FIM + FAM); RCS = Rehabilitation Complexity Scale – Extended.

people with FND were found to be moderately depressed and anxious. On discharge, the mean group scores reduced but remained in the "moderate" range (Table 2.1.3).

On admission, 31 out of 40 patients (78%) reported clinically significant depressive symptoms. At discharge, this number reduced to 19 of 37 patients reporting depressive features (51.4%). After removing the n = 4 people who only completed a discharge questionnaire, an analysis was undertaken to explore movement between non-clinical vs clinical categories for n = 33 patients who had completed both questionnaires. Across the two time-points, n = 6 (18.2%) people remained non-clinical, whereas n = 13 (39.4%) people kept a clinical score. Although n = 3 (9.1%) people worsened from non-clinical to clinical, n = 11 (33.3%) people improved from a clinical to a non-clinical score (chi-square = 1.1, df = 1, p = .29/Fisher's exact test, p = .44) (Table 2.1.4).

On admission, 60% of patients reported anxiety symptoms that fell in the clinical range. At discharge, this percentage had slightly reduced to 48.6%. An analysis of movement between categories revealed that n = 11 people (33.3%) remained non-clinical with respect to anxiety symptoms and n = 12 (36.4%) people stayed in the clinically significant category. Improvement was observed for n = 7 (21.2%) people whose scores changed from clinical to non-clinical, as well as for n = 3 (9.1%) people who deteriorated from the non-clinical to a clinical category (chi-square = 5.7, df = 1, p = .02/Fisher's exact test, p = .03) (Table 2.1.5).

Table 2.1.3 Scores on psychological questionnaires of the FND sample (n = 33)

Measure	Sample size	Admission	Discharge	Statistics
PHQ-9 (total score)	n = 33	9.2 ± 5.9 (range: 0–25)	7.5 ± 5.8 (range: 0–22)	Wilcoxon's: Z = -1.4, p = .15
GAD-7 (total score)	n = 33	8.1 ± 6.2 (range: 0–21)	6.2 ± 5.7 (range: 0–20)	Wilcoxon's: Z = -1.8, p = .075

Table 2.1.4 Frequency of patients per level of severity on the PHQ-9

Categories	Admission (n = 40)	Discharge (n = 37)
Mild (0–5)	N = 9 (22.5%)	N = 18 (48.6%)
Moderate (6–10)	N = 19 (47.5%)	N = 7 (18.9%)
Moderately severe (11–15)	N = 7 (17.5%)	N = 5 (13.5%)
Severe depression (≥16)	N = 5 (12.5%)	N = 7 (18.9%)

* n = 4 people did not have an admission score but did complete a discharge questionnaire to gauge their level of low mood following rehabilitation.

Table 2.1.5 Frequency of patients per level of severity on the GAD-7

Categories	Admission (n = 40)	Discharge (n = 37)
Mild (0–5)	N = 16 (40%)	N = 19 (51.4%)
Moderate (6–10)	N = 10 (25%)	N = 7 (18.9%)
Moderately severe (11–15)	N = 8 (20%)	N = 5 (13.5%)
Severe anxiety (≥16)	N = 6 (15%)	N = 6 (16.2%)

EMOTION DYSREGULATION: DIFFICULTIES IN EMOTION REGULATION
SCALE – SHORT FORM

None of the DERS-SF comparisons were statistically significant. A case analysis revealed that approximately 23% (n = 7) of people scored at least 1.5 SD above the mean on the admission and discharge DERS-SF, in comparison to the means and SDs reported for a college student sample in Kaufman et al. (2016), suggesting that one-fifth of people with FND self-reported symptoms of emotion dysregulation. None of the patients exhibited an unusually low score (≥-1.5 SD below the mean) (Table 2.1.6).

ROSENBERG'S SELF-ESTEEM SCALE

Pairwise comparisons revealed no significant difference between admission and discharge scores in self-esteem (19.6 ± 6.3, range: 4–30 vs 20.1 ± 6.4, range: 10–30; Wilcoxon's Z = -.75, p = .46).

A subsequent case analysis revealed that, on admission, only seven out of 30 people with FND (23%) reported low self-esteem, whereas twice as many people (13/30, 43%) rated themselves as experiencing high to very high self-esteem. Interestingly, at discharge, a slightly higher number of people exhibited scores that indicated low self-esteem (9/28; 32.1%). The number of people indicating "very high" self-esteem rose with n = 3 more people on discharge, although generally, the absolute number of people who fell in the high self-esteem category (high + very high collapsed) remained the same (Table 2.1.7).

HEIGHTENED SELF-FOCUSED ATTENTION

There was no significant difference between self-perceived levels of self-focused attention to symptoms between admission (20.6 ± 8.4) and discharge (18.8 ± 7.0; t = 1.2, df = 31, p = .25), nor were any of the 7-item scores found to be significantly different between admission and discharge.

Exploratory correlational analyses with the ATSQ revealed highly significant correlations between the admission scores of the ATSQ with several

Table 2.1.6 Mean pre- and post-treatment scores on the DERS-SF in n = 31 people with FND

Variable	Admission	Discharge	Statistics
Total score	42 ± 12.1	40.6 ± 16.2	Wilcoxon's Z = -.65, p = .52
Strategies	6.4 ± 3.3	6 ± 3.8	Z = -.28, p = .78
Non-acceptance	7.7 ± 4.1	7.5 ± 4.3	Z = -.39, p = .70
Impulse	4.9 ± 2.5	5.1 ± 3.2	Z = -.33, p = .74
Goals	8.3 ± 3.8	7.6 ± 3.9	Z = -.89, p = .37
Awareness	8.2 ± 2.8	8.4 ± 2.5	Z = -.23, p = .82
Clarity	6.5 ± 3.1	6.1 ± 2.7	Z = -.55, p = .58

Table 2.1.7 Frequencies of patients per self-esteem score classification

Label	Score	Admission (n = 30)	Discharge (n = 28)
Very low	0–10	n = 2 (6.7%)	N = 1 (3.6%)
Low	11–15	n = 5 (16.7%)	N = 8 (28.6%)
Moderate	16–20	n = 10 (33.3%)	N = 6 (21.4%)
High	21–25	n = 7 (23.3%)	N = 4 (14.3%)
Very high	26–30	n = 6 (20%)	N = 9 (32.1%)

admission measures of psychological health including the DERS-SF (Spearman's rho = .54, $p < .001$, n = 36), PHQ-9 (rho = .66, $p < .001$, n = 38), GAD-7 scores (rho = .85, $p < .001$, n = 38) and Rosenberg's self-esteem scores (rho = -.41, $p = .03$, n = 30) (Table 2.1.8).

Interim conclusions (Study 1)

The present study explored outcomes in routine clinical care of a large sample of FND patients who had participated in a specialist intensive multidisciplinary rehabilitation programme. Several interesting results came to light. Participant age at the time of admission followed a bimodal distribution with two peaks in young adulthood (nearly a third of the sample) and middle age (one-fifth of the sample). Disease duration data revealed that the sample was more or less split in the middle, around the two-year mark. Almost one-third of the sample was "early intervention" on admission, with a short symptom duration of less than six months, whilst a chronic subgroup of n = 7 patients experienced long-term FND for at least ten years.

The results from the service evaluation revealed that, at discharge, people with FND showed highly significant gains on all neurorehabilitation measures including with respect to the severity of the functional impact of their symptoms; level of disability and dependency; and a reduction in care needs.

In contrast, whole-group analyses of psychological variables failed to show any significant pre-to-post changes over time, with only the level of anxiety trending towards significance. As a group, people with FND did not show significant improvements in psychological functioning, a phenomenon that has been reported elsewhere (e.g. Nielsen et al., 2017). However, case analyses yielded more informative results showing a significant clinical-to-non-clinical improvement in scores in a substantial subset of patients: 33% for depressive symptoms and 21.2% for anxiety.

Furthermore, 23% of patients self-reported significant emotion dysregulation. The two high vs low emotion dysregulation clusters reported earlier in people with non-epileptic episodes (Uliaszek et al., 2012) were not replicated in the current sample. Various reasons may exist including the use of a short form version of the DERS-SF, which may have been less sensitive in detecting emotion dysregulation; the large heterogeneity in FND symptoms of the

Table 2.1.8 Mean admission and discharge scores for each ATSQ item

ATSQ item #	Admission (mean ± SD) (n = 38)	Discharge (mean ± SD) (n = 33)
How much did you think about your symptoms?	3.3 ± 1.4	3.2 ± 1.3
How much attention did you pay to your symptoms, their internal sensations or warning signs?	3 ± 1.4	2.9 ± 1.4
How sensitive were you at noticing changes in your body/mind that your symptoms were about to come up or become worse?	2.95 ± 1.5	2.8 ± 1.3
How much time did you spend "scanning" or "being on the lookout" for sensations that may warn you for your symptoms?	2.3 ± 1.6	2.1 ± 1.2
How much did you try to figure out what was happening in your body and mind – whilst experiencing symptoms?	2.9 ± 1.7	2.5 ± 1.5
How much did you wonder about why you have these symptoms?	2.89 ± 1.6	2.88 ± 1.6
In general, how much did you pay attention to your body or notice changes in how your body feels?	3.1 ± 1.4	2.9 ± 1.2

inpatient sample, which also consisted of people with motor-type FND; and the quality of the norms used.

In contrast to the findings from Petrochilos et al. (2020), there were no significant differences in self-esteem found over time. It should be noted that this particular study reported only small improvements in self-esteem, with the admission score at the top end of the low range and the discharge score just within the moderate range. Although in the current sample only 23% reported low self-esteem on admission, twice as many people reported high levels of self-esteem. On discharge, slightly more people self-reported low self-esteem, probably owing to increasing levels of insight into psychological functioning; reduced levels of dissociation; or worries about their ability and self-belief in managing FND right before discharge.

The self-perceived self-focused attention on symptoms measure (ATSQ) did not show any significant change on discharge. There were several limitations to this new measure including the lack of a control group and information on what constitutes normal levels of symptom focus, as well as the relatively abstract and complex language of the items. Furthermore, the measure focused on only one aspect of self-focused attention that could be summarised as tapping into hypervigilance towards internal bodily sensations and physical symptoms. However, in clinical practice, increased self-focused attention transcends beyond perceptual and interoceptive processes and can manifest itself in many other domains, for example language and communication (e.g. expressing a strong preference for physical explanations over psychological formulations for FND), cognition (e.g. rigidity of thinking or mental inflexibility: difficulty disengaging from physical symptoms), behaviour (e.g. spending time searching, reading or speaking about FND; reassurance seeking behaviours), environmental (e.g. systemic hypervigilance that also contributes to self-focused attention; environmental "markers" of self-focused attention such as equipment) and person/identity-related (e.g. the level of entanglement of FND in a person's identity) processes. Therefore, a measure of self-focused attention should be multifaceted to fully capture the richness of the concept. The question also arose whether people with FND can accurately self-evaluate their level of symptom focus, as "being in the middle of it" may affect their insight into this process. A self-rated vs observer-rated assessment that considers discrepancies may prove to be a better measure. Self-focused attention is a maintaining factor in many psychological conditions. Interestingly, this measure found associations between self-perceived, self-focused attention and several psychological variables: the higher a person's self-perceived, self-focused attention on physical symptoms, the higher their levels of emotion dysregulation, and depressive and anxiety symptoms, as well as the lower their self-esteem.

Reflections and limitations

Questionnaire scores

A case analysis revealed that rather than decreasing, absolute scores on questionnaires increased before discharge for n = 10 (out of 33, 30.3%) people on the PHQ-9 and n = 11 (out of 33; 33.3%) people on the GAD-7. Across questionnaires, n = 4 people plateaued and exhibited similar pre- and post-treatment scores. This could have contributed to the lack of a significant pre-to-post difference for the whole-group analyses. Although scores increasing rather than decreasing appear paradoxical, from a clinical perspective this is unsurprising. People with FND may have obtained more insight into their emotions and reconnected with emotions due to therapy. As patients developed therapeutic relationships with staff and personal relationships with peers, their attitudes towards emotional expression may have changed with people becoming less opposed to the expression of their true feelings (opened Cover) than they were at pre-therapy. In addition, peers may have positively modelled these helpful coping strategies. The anxiety-provoking nature of transitioning back into the community has very likely resulted in expressing more distress for a subset of patients, which converged with clinical observations and verbal reports of not wanting to be discharged. However, since psychological difficulties are assumed to be strongly associated with physical symptoms in FND, verbal reports without the concomitant increase in physical symptoms may signify an actual improvement as people adopted the expression of emotions rather than a physical expression. In addition, the existence of a substantial number of missing values on psychological questionnaires should also be noted. Approximately one-third of the sample did not have PHQ-9, GAD-7 and DERS-SF scores. Reasons included the later introduction of these questionnaires into the programme, as well as staff failing to administer questionnaires due to time pressures in the service. As a result, level of depression, anxiety and emotion dysregulation is unclear in a significant subset of the patient sample. These missing scores could have influenced the statistical analyses and the final conclusions.

Measuring instruments

The discrepancy found between psychological vs physical/overall rehabilitation gains could also be explained by a qualitative difference in measurement methodology. Psychological measures were based on patient self-reports, whereas the more physical rehabilitation measures (e.g. UK FIM + FAM, NIS and RCS) all relied on staff reports. In addition, a range of different staff members ("observers") were involved in the collection of the physical measures, which introduced another confound. Plausible scenarios may include patients underreporting psychological problems and staff's perception of a patient's change in functioning at post-treatment coloured by a wish to see change, particularly in the context of reduced confidence that is often reported in staff treating people with FND (see Chapter 7 for more details).

COURSE OF PROGRESSION

In inpatient settings, with a full multidisciplinary team, motor gains are often seen to surface faster than psychological gains. It is conceivable that the natural recovery pathways of psychological vs physical symptoms may be qualitatively different. Maladaptive psychological coping strategies could take longer to undo or change than abnormal motor features because they may be lifelong or longstanding, whereas FND symptoms may have emerged more recently in comparison with less opportunity to become ingrained. The psychological difficulties, particularly in the studied sample, tended to be severe, and a relatively short inpatient admission may not have been sufficient to bring about a full recovery in psychological functioning that was noticeable on mood questionnaires. The admission often served the purpose of psychological formulation rather than intervention – which in itself was often part of the treatment.

It should also be noted that psychological coping strategies may have had a protective value to help a person survive (e.g. keeping self to self, dissociation) and a person may have been understandably reluctant to part ways from these strategies, even if unhelpful, whereas being able to walk, independently wash and dress, or accessing the community for shopping may have been more attractive goals to achieve. Furthermore, psychological strategies tend to rely on declarative, explicit memory and may take longer to become automatic than physical strategies that rely on non-declarative and implicit learning processes, for example relearning a new movement pattern (although it is acknowledged that some functional motor changes may become irreversible after a long period in a select few cases, e.g. severe dystonia).

SENSITIVITY: AN ISSUE OF CONTENT VS PROCESS

Although the psychometric properties of the selected questionnaires were satisfactory, the question arises whether the selected questionnaires were sufficiently sensitive to detect characteristic psychological difficulties in people with FND, in particular to beliefs and emotional phenomena that are commonly encountered in clinical practice in people with FND (see Chapters 3 and 4 for an in-depth discussion).

Common "FND-specific" beliefs and emotions include fears of recovery, relapse, falling, and more interpersonal fears of not feeling cared for, being abandoned, not being believed by other people and attachment anxiety. Other beliefs are associated with feeling trapped in the context of an unspeakable dilemma or around illness. Furthermore, people with FND commonly report anxiety and depression, but standard questionnaires used in clinical practice are unable to distinguish whether this distress is secondary to the development of FND (e.g. having to rely on equipment, not being able to access the community) or related to triggers preceding the FND (e.g. divorce, difficult family dynamics), a "chicken or egg" problem. Dissociation and alexithymia have likely further impacted on the detection and potential underrecognition of psychological distress on questionnaires.

What all these features have in common is "relationships" and "process". The FND-specific thoughts and feelings are all in some way associated with the process of relating to other people. Standardised questionnaires are more focused on content, quantification and scores: "How much depression does this person have?" "How many standard deviations is this person above or below a mean in terms of anxiety?" Alternative questions, specifically pertinent to clinical practice, include "How did the person come to experience psychological difficulties in the first place? What environmental and relationship conditions made the person vulnerable?" "Can we say anything about the way this person has always coped with emotions, shaped by past relationships and circumstances, that contributes to their current psychological difficulties?" "What characteristic beliefs, associated with other individuals, make this person feel depressed or anxious/are associated with this person's depression or anxiety?" "Does the person identify with negative emotions and is this discrepant with the way this person presents?" "Is there anything that we can say about the variability of the person's intensity of emotions in response to their environment?" "Are physical factors mediating or contributing to the person's psychological difficulties?" "How do other individuals in the person's life contribute to the psychological difficulties?" All these questions are not easily answered with quantitative methodology.

In the light of the reduced sensitivity of conventional quantitative methods in capturing the richness of FND-specific beliefs, and emotional and psychosocial features, the next section will focus on outlining the results of a descriptive study with qualitative aspects that focused on a detailed process analysis of (bio)psychosocial functioning in FND.

Section 2.2: The pressures of an inpatient environment: empirical evidence for the Pressure Cooker Model (Study 2)

Aims

Study 2 aimed to determine whether:

- A process approach as outlined in the PCM can more fully capture the complexity of psychological functioning in FND.
- There is evidence for the existence of the hypothesised elements and processes of the PCM in a sample of people with FND.
- The PCM is found to be an acceptable model by patients and healthcare professionals in clinical practice.

Description of the inpatient service context: richly connected social systems

Table 2.2.1 shows that the FND participants in this study were all part of a multi-layered social environment surrounded by a wide range of "social subgroups" on the inpatient ward.

Given this social context, the permutations of interactions between the person with FND and other individuals were endless and had the power to create significant interpersonal group dynamics. The inpatient unit enabled careful observations of the impact of introducing a new patient with FND on an existing richly connected social system ("ward life") that comprised continuously moving parts (e.g. admissions, discharges, staff turnover) and the impact of interpersonal triggers on a person's FND symptoms and behaviours.

The following questions guided and informed this investigation:

- When and where did the FND re-appear or worsen? In what situations were FND symptoms more likely to emerge? (e.g. in the gym, public spaces, unwitnessed at bedside, before or after a goal-setting meeting).
- What triggered an FND flare-up or relapse? Was this associated with interpersonal communication within the hospital ward or family environment?
- What intra-individual and inter-individual factors mediated the frequency of FND symptoms? What worsened and ameliorated the FND in response to the environment? Over time, could anything be concluded

Table 2.2.1 Multi-systemic inpatient ward environment

Group	Examples
Other patients	• From the same or different treating team • In the same bay or therapy groups • Mixed functional and organic patients – and considerable heterogeneity of symptoms within the FND subgroup • Females and males • Various cultural backgrounds • Different age ranges • Levels of cognitive/motor functioning and impairments
Multidisciplinary treating team dedicated to FND and neuropsychiatry care	Consisting of the following disciplines: psychology, physiotherapy, occupational therapy, neuropsychiatry, nursing, social work, speech therapy, therapy technicians and dietetics
Multidisciplinary teams dedicated to other non-FND patient groups	Staff with similar disciplines
Ward team	Consisting of charge nurses, specialist nurses and healthcare assistants, as well as ward doctors, junior medical fellows and pharmacists for medication management
Support staff	Activity coordinators, ward receptionists, pastoral, domestic, catering and security staff interacting with patients
Management team	Service management, secretarial staff
Personal relationships	Family members, friends, partners of the patient, as well as from other patients
"Outsiders"	Students, out-house social workers, healthcare professionals visiting the ward for in-reach consultations

about what moderated the FND symptoms, "the peaks and troughs" during the admission?

• What did the patients themselves report or conclude about the moderating factors of FND. What was the level of insight into the link between the triggers and FND?

• Were there multiple triggers of varying nature (e.g. physical, interpersonal) that drove the FND symptoms in patients with FND? Could patients have been re-triggered by current interactions that reminded them of past experiences?

Methods

Data was analysed from people with FND who were admitted to an inpatient ward for a period of intensive rehabilitation. Patients from studies 1 and 2 were identical. This study was highly descriptive in nature and did not make use of quantitative statistics, apart from relying on the use of frequency counts for analysis, in a similar vein to the methodology used in the study by Bowman and Markand (1999) who investigated life events in people with non-epileptic seizures.

Results

Focus of psychological therapy

Due to the high level of psychological complexity of inpatients with FND, it was common to "trial" and use a multitude of models in treatment. A common scenario in FND therapy involved multiple re-iterations of psychological hypotheses and re-formulations until arriving at a solid formulation of the FND, occasionally at the end of the admission, with the admission serving the purpose of psychological formulation rather than intervention (or the arrival at a shared formulation constituting the actual treatment). Across all psychological therapy work, the PCM formulation functioned as a "leitmotif", either as the main treatment model or as an adjunct model, for example when a CBT model was far more applicable to the person's psychological difficulties and the FND symptoms could easily be incorporated (e.g. social anxiety) (Table 2.2.2).

Engagement and acceptance in psychological therapy

Psychology was part of a wider multidisciplinary team. It was not uncommon for some patients with FND to prefer the more "physical" disciplines over psychology. This impacted on their level of engagement with psychology. Table 2.2.3 shows four categories of psychology engagement, which was defined by the following variables: (1) acceptance of a psychological model for FND, (2) attendance of psychological therapy sessions and (3) application of psychological strategies in between sessions (e.g. carry out behavioural experiments, engaging with an enjoyable activity, expressing emotions, distraction

Table 2.2.2 Frequencies of PCM configurations in the sample (n = 49)

Psychological models used	Frequency
PCM only	N = 18 (36.7%)
PCM+: panic model	N = 1 (2%)
PCM+: longitudinal depression	N = 20 (40.8%)
PCM+: social anxiety	N = 4 (8.2%)
PCM+: generalised anxiety disorder	N = 1 (2%)
PCM++: depression + another condition	N = 5 (10.2%)
Panic	N = 2
Social anxiety	N = 3

Panic model (Clark, 1986); longitudinal depression model (Beck Judith, 1995); social anxiety (Clark & Wells, 1995); generalised anxiety disorder (Wells, 1995).

Table 2.2.3 Acceptance, attendance and strategy application in n = 49 people with FND

Category	Accepting of psychology?	Attendance of psychology sessions? (regular)	Application of strategies?	Frequency (%)
1 – Active non-engagement	No	No – strongly preferred not to attend, either actively declining sessions or finding ways to avoid psychology	No – lack of evidence of strategy application, even with non-psychology staff	N = 4 (8.2%)
2 – Passive non-engagement	No	Yes	No	N = 12 (24.5%)
3 – Partial engagement	Yes	Yes	No	N = 15 (30.6%)
4 – Full engagement	Yes	Yes	Yes	N = 18 (36.7%)

techniques during a seizure). Acceptance of psychology was described as the person accepting a psychological cause or psychological factors contributing to the FND, even if partially.

Approximately two-thirds of the sample (67.3%) was accepting of psychological factors as significantly contributing to FND. Slightly over half of this accepting group (54.5%) fully engaged in psychological therapy. One could argue that these engagement categories reflected the level of participation in the actual intervention of "building a therapeutic relationship", which is core to FND. Interpreting the data from this perspective suggests that the ~25% of people with "passive non-engagement" were still engaging to some degree, based on their presence in the therapy room.

Layer 1: Ignition

Tables 2.2.4 and 2.2.5 display predisposing events in remote history that have likely contributed to a vulnerability towards the development of FND. The type of predisposing factors can be subdivided into two broad categories: factors affecting family and relationships, and factors affecting historical physical and psychological health. It should be noted that these life events are based on patient self-reports and may be underreported or the reporting process impacted in different ways due to the subjective nature of self-report. Factors including dissociation, nature of trauma memories and the highly sensitive nature of some memories that may not be disclosed (e.g. sexual trauma) could lead to a distorted view.

Historical emotional neglect and emotional abuse were by far most reported by people with FND, most often by a parent, and in some cases, by

Table 2.2.4 Historical predisposing factors in the context of family and relationships

Type of life event	Number of cases	Frequency
Childhood or history partner emotional abuse/ parental emotional neglect	20	41%
History of a difficult relationship break-up or estranged partner (in a partner relationship)	10	20.4%
• Loss of parental key figure or important family figure (through death or separation)	9	18.4%
• Childhood or adulthood sexual abuse or assault		
• Childhood or adulthood physical abuse	8	16.3%
• Witnessed or exposure to traumatic event involving other people		
History of being bullied at school	5	10.2%
Financial or sexual exploitation by partners	4	8.2%
High achieving sibling/sibling rivalry	3	6.1%
High parental expectations	2	4.1%

Table 2.2.5 Historical predisposing factors in the context of physical and psychological health problems

Type of life event or experience	Number of cases	Frequency
Personal history of diagnosed mental health problems or mental health services involvement	11	22.4%
Family members with a history of diagnosed mental health issues	9	18.4%
Past suicide attempts or deliberate self-harm	6	12.2%
• Family member with organic illness	5	10.2%
• Childhood hospitalisation		
• Family or personal history of autism		
(Childhood) History of somatoform symptoms prior to FND	4	8.2%
Learning difficulties pre-dating FND	3	6.1%
History of physical disease due to organic factors prior to FND	2	4.1%

an ex-partner. Relationship break-ups and losses were the next most common categories. Past sexual and physical abuse was far less often reported than past emotional neglect or abuse.

Table 2.2.6 shows the more recent precipitating "critical events" that happened nearer in time to the FND and that were hypothesised to have sparked off or "ignited" the FND.

The physical events were often associated with interpersonal issues, for example staff not caring or concurrent traumatic events taking place around the time of the physical event. Although for the person it was clear that the onset of FND took place following the physical event, and therefore it made sense to cognitively link up these two events, it was less clear to patients that

Table 2.2.6 Precipitating critical events of FND

Type of life event	Number of cases	Frequency
Dysfunctional family or partner relationship prior to FND including domestic violence: coercion, assault, as well as partner distancing, estranged family members	18	36.7%
Physical event (e.g. surgery or medical investigation requiring hospitalisation, fall, health problem, pain)	18	36.7%
• Road traffic accident (e.g. car)	8	16.3%
• Job issues (rejection, loss, assault, new job or stress at work)	9	18.4%
• Very busy life schedule (boom Valve)	4 each	8.2%
• Blocked Valve: sudden loss of activities/ loneliness/social network falling apart		
• Exam stress/reduced school results		
Legal, litigation and criminal issues	3	6.1%
• Viral infection	2	4.1%
• Disclosure of sensitive secret with negative consequences		

(1) the interpersonal issues happening around the same time of the physical event in their life or (2) the responses they received from healthcare staff could contribute to the development of the FND.

Layer 2: FND coping triad

STICKY LEFT-OVER FOOD

Three different "sticky strategies" reported by people with FND in child-hood were analysed: a tight Cover (keeping self to self), a boom-and-bust or boom Valve (pushing on/just get on with it) and evidence of any dissociative tendencies in childhood. N = 38 (78%) reported a tight Cover as their "sticky strategy" in childhood. This figure was remarkably similar in adulthood as n = 38 (78%) people still presented with a tight Cover on admission. This sticky strategy was therefore repeated into adulthood after many years. People cited many reasons for adopting a tight Cover as a sticky strategy in childhood:

• Abusive family environment/emotional neglect/strict upbringing and discipline with invalidation in response to emotional expression (n = 18).
• No abuse but family not used to emotional expression ("practical coping and problem solvers"; n = 5).
• Loss of parental key figure at early age and took on parental role in the family unit/not used to speaking about loss (n = 2).

- Patient or family indicated that patient always kept self to self (n = 7).
- Agony aunt of the family unit, "glue" of the unit precluding the person from engaging in emotional expression themselves as no platform available to them (n = 2).
- Non-expression or invalidation of emotions due to cultural reasons (n = 2).
- Invalidation of emotions following release of a secret (n = 1) resulting in subsequent longstanding non-expression of emotions.
- Mental health issues in parental key figure during upbringing prevented emotional expression (n = 1).

The evidence for repetition of the other two strategies was less convincing. Only n = 6 (12.2%) people spontaneously reported a "boom" Valve as their sticky strategy in childhood. Reasons for adopting this strategy included an abusive family environment that made the person push on with activities (n = 1); no abuse but family used pushing on as their dominant strategy (n = 1); and pushing on with care activities as a child (n = 2) or via a busy schedule of sports activities (n = 2). Interestingly, people reporting pushing on as a childhood strategy also invariably reported keeping self to self as a childhood strategy. The number of people presenting with either a boom-and-bust or boom Valve on admission was a lot higher than what was expected on the basis of their use of this strategy in childhood: boom-and-bust, n = 16 (32.7%); boom, n = 2 (4.1%); and the total number of people "pushing on" in adulthood, n = 18 (36.7%). It is possible that the number of patients with pushing on as their childhood strategy was underestimated in the sample. Furthermore, if pushing on or a "boom" Valve is viewed as a precursor to a "bust-after-boom" Valve, it is possible that a higher number of people used pushing on as their main dominant coping strategy at an earlier stage in their FND journey. Surprisingly, early dissociation was reported by only n = 7 people. People with FND cited various reasons for using this sticky strategy in childhood including "keeping myself to myself and cutting off feelings" during bullying experiences at school (n = 1); dissociation used as a coping strategy during a life-threatening event (n = 1); early coping strategy for distressing feelings: approaching emotions in a logical/analytical way: analysing feelings to avoid feeling them (n = 1); and in the context of deliberate self-harm in teenage years (n = 4). Only n = 3 people self-reported "normal" emotion coping childhood strategies, for example having had access to a trusted person and being able to engage in regular emotional expression during childhood. For n = 6 people, their childhood coping strategies remained unclear as no information reported by the patient. The evidence presented here for the robustness of childhood coping strategies over time and repeating into adulthood was strongest for the childhood/adulthood coping strategy of reduced verbal emotional expression.

COVER

On admission, only n = 4 (8.2%) people showed a normal ability to express difficult emotions and thoughts in psychological therapy. The majority of the sample (n = 38; 78%) people with FND exhibited a lack or reduced verbal emotional expression (i.e. a tight Cover). Table 2.2.7 shows the features that made a person's Cover tight. A small subset of people showed an open Cover (n = 7, 14%), characterised by either overexpression and oversharing of emotions, or rude and argumentative comments when distressed. Although this appeared the opposite of a tight Cover, these people tended to experience unspeakable dilemmas or undisclosed secrets that they did not speak about, and therefore exhibited a tight Cover over issues that were core to their problems.

Unspeakable dilemmas ranged from domestic violence, abuse, large demands placed on the patient in the home situation, an unfulfilled wish, sexual preference that was resisted in the family unit, old traumas that were never processed, negative family dynamics and relationships that were not spoken about or else it would greatly impact on the family relationships, perceived failure in a job or school, and severe mental health issues in a close family member that were unprocessed by the person with FND. Unspeakable dilemmas were most often released in therapy or exposed to the psychologist by family members of the patients.

Table 2.2.7 Reasons for a tight Cover in n = 38 people with FND who displayed a tight Cover

Cover feature	Frequency (%)
Reduced assertiveness – not expressing needs to the environment	6 (12.2%)
Masking true emotion with laughter, jokes or expressing positive emotions only	8 (16.3%)
Reports some stress but in relation to low-level daily triggers that did not seem to explain/account for the severe presentation	3 (6.1%)
Functional speech difficulties and FND symptoms interfering with the person from expressing feelings	22 (44.9%)
Social anxiety	N = 11 (22.4%)
Social skills problems	5 (10.2%)
Evasiveness or defensiveness in therapy	7 (14.3%)
Unspeakable dilemma or secret	22 (44.9%)
Oversharing emotions and information (as part of care-eliciting behaviour)	7 (14%)
Glue – balancing other people's emotions in the family unit	2 (4.1%)

NB. Please note that one person could experience multiple reasons for a tight Cover.

VALVE

The most common Valve profile displayed by people with FND on admission was a blocked Valve by two-thirds of the sample. Approximately one-third was classified as experiencing a dysregulated Valve. On rare occasions, people exhibited an overused Valve. It should be noted that a prior "boom" Valve is often a prerequisite towards developing a "bust-after-boom" Valve. Many people with FND from the sample were previously a consistent "boom" pattern, often for many years or even a lifetime. By the time that a person has developed a "bust" after years of "boom", the FND symptoms will have emerged by then. Only one person seemed to have a normal pattern of activity levels (Table 2.2.8).

Layer 3: FND maintenance cycle

THE PRESSURE COOKER CHAIN REACTION: THE FORMULATION

Layer 3 represents the core of the PCM formulation for FND. The search for current triggers (Fuel), beliefs and emotions (Flames), and the strength and intensity of the emotions (Heat), and their relationship with FND (Overpressure Plug) will be key to treatment and resolution of FND symptoms.

FUEL

The Fuel represents a person's current triggers for FND, which could be subdivided into different categories. These categories are artificial and not mutually exclusive. Patients often experienced "multi-triggers", a combination of a series of co-existing triggers that caused FND flare-ups.

PHYSICAL TRIGGERS

Panic attacks, or the catastrophic misinterpretation of physical symptoms leading to high anxiety or an aversive but undefined psychological internal state, fuelled FND in n = 8 (16.3%) patients. A small subset of patients reported physical triggers other than panic attacks and bodily symptoms (e.g. heat, noise, loud sounds, movement, strong smell, bright lights, lack of sleep) as causing their FND symptoms (n = 4, 8.2%).

Table 2.2.8 Frequencies of Valve profiles in n = 49 people with FND

Valve profile	Frequency (%)
Blocked Valve (bust-after-boom)	30 (61.2%)
Dysregulated Valve (boom-and-bust)	16 (32.7%)
Overused Valve (boom)	2 (4.1%)
Normal activity levels	1 (2%)

ENVIRONMENTAL TRIGGERS

Environmental triggers were defined as externally generated triggers that often led to anxiety or a state of elevated arousal that the person with FND was unable to label as an emotion and would lead to a worsening or re-appearance of FND, for example school examinations, college, work-related, housing or legal-related stress. These environmental triggers often felt outside the patient's influence and were reported in n = 6 (12.2%) patients. A small subset of people (N = 4, 8.2%) described that inconsistencies and unpredictable changes to a patient's routine (e.g. time-table, requested food from catering), which suggested to the patient "I don't matter", fuelled their FND symptoms.

INTERNAL TRIGGERS

Internal psychological triggers originate in the individual's belief system and can directly result in FND. For example, persistent worrying led to an overwhelmed state or "generalised anxiety" (if the person was able to label this as anxiety) and worsened FND symptoms in n = 8 (16.3%) patients. PTSD-triggers were detected in n = 10 (20.4%) patients who had witnessed a traumatic event; had vicariously experienced trauma; had been subjected directly to trauma; or had just opened up a "buried" dissociated trauma. PTSD-related triggers could be both internally generated (e.g. flashbacks, nightmares) and externally generated (e.g. seeing a trauma-related news item or a smell) and would lead to a state of discomfort or distress and subsequently to FND.

"EXTERNALLY REGULATED" INTERNAL TRIGGERS

A large subset of people with FND (n = 30, 61.2%) experienced internally generated beliefs and emotions that were subsequently heavily regulated through the social environment. This was typically characterised by an upcoming internal emotional need for psychological safety or validation from healthcare staff. The FND symptoms re-emerged or worsened when a lack of hypothesised psychological safety or distress was present in the healthcare context, due to, for example, anxiety around an approaching discharge date and an associated predicted attachment break; and boredom and lack of ability to self-manage free time with difficult thoughts and feelings intensifying, particularly during weekends that did not involve time-tables; and in crowded social environments (e.g. dining rooms or therapy gyms) where a number of people would gather, often forming an audience.

Unspeakable dilemmas were another type of "externally regulated" internal trigger very frequently observed in the sample (n = 20, 41%). At the start of psychological therapy, a dilemma was not released and often held in over a long period of time, only revealed towards the latter half or end of the treatment, for example family secret, personal secret or unfulfilled wish about a sensitive topic that trapped the person in the situation with FND. Of this group, n = 2 (4.1%) people experienced active longstanding domestic violence requiring safeguarding strongly associated with FND maintenance. Furthermore, another n = 2 (4.1%) patients had already released their dilemma to the environment, prior to starting therapy, but received backlash and lack of acceptance or validation (=rejection) from the environment that subsequently fuelled the FND. For reasons of confidentiality, the specific details of the unspeakable dilemmas are not revealed here.

INTERPERSONAL TRIGGERS

Interpersonal triggers were defined as triggers directly related to other people's behaviours or responses in relation to the person with FND, both perceived and real. The triggers were often characterised by other individuals imposing conditions on the person with FND, for example creating emotional distance, placing demands or seeking proximity to the person with FND. These triggers often originated within the context of dynamics in personal and therapeutic relationships.

A specific set of interpersonal triggers were often associated with a history of complex trauma and a sense of abandonment, rejection or "attachment anxiety". An example of an interpersonal trigger reported and observed in people with FND involved a partner or family distancing or having distanced from the patient already prior to the admission (n = 16, 32.7%). The FND would keep the partner or family member(s) close and caring, even if only practical, to meet an unmet emotional need. There would often be a potential loss, or a threat of loss, of the important person in the patient's life if the FND would improve. Other interpersonal triggers included high conflict or relationship difficulties in the family unit that were directly and acutely associated with more dissociative episodes or other FND symptoms (n = 15, 30.6%), as well as high demands placed on the person with FND from the family, that is, caring responsibilities, with the FND reducing the demands, or the FND acting as a deterrent towards a partner seeking proximity (n = 6, 12.2%).

Making progress in rehab, with the treating team encouraging more independence and praising the patient, was also considered an interpersonal trigger, as this involved the potential for perceived or real social losses if the FND would fully improve, invariably in relation to other people, for example loss of a positive image to other people who may question the nature of the recovery; loss of validation from individuals in the person's environment; loss of a positive self-image (if the FND was a major part of the person's identity); or a loss of mild, as opposed to stronger, demands and responsibilities placed by their environment. Obtaining gains in rehab worsened or caused set-backs in FND in n = 10 (20.4%) patients.

TRIGGERS STRONGLY ASSOCIATED WITH SOCIAL SITUATIONS

Social situations elicited classic social anxiety features and FND symptoms in n = 11 (22.4%) people with FND. The person's cognitions, safety behaviours and physical manifestations upon entering a social situation were often highly suggestive of the condition. Examples of FND symptoms that were triggered by social situations often included motor-type FND symptoms, for example functional tremors and weakness. Social anxiety was not commonly associated with "complex trauma" (or DSM-V Axis II features) and was treated with the CBT model for social anxiety.

SYSTEMIC RE-TRAUMATISATION/RE-TRIGGERS

Slightly over half of the sample (n = 25, 51%) perceived and openly expressed beliefs that revolved around an emotional neglect theme. People would often report not feeling cared for, believed by, receiving empathy, not feeling heard, feeling rejected or singled out by either family members or healthcare staff. Some patients reported witnessing other patients receiving validation or differential (more positive) treatment in comparison to themselves.

Around 41% of all patients (n = 20) spontaneously reported features that were strongly suggestive of systemic re-traumatisation. Occasionally, these beliefs, whether perceived or rooted in reality, could result in a re-emergence or worsening of FND symptoms. For example, n = 15 (30.6%) reported interpersonal difficulties in the family unit that were directly associated with the experience of more FND symptoms.

Flames

People with FND reported a wide range of different beliefs. The thought categories are not mutually exclusive. For example, a person could experience cognitions consistent with social anxiety whilst simultaneously experiencing interpersonal cognitions, for example not feeling heard by staff.

ANXIETY-RELATED BELIEFS

The data showed that the beliefs described by people with FND were consistent with a range of DSM-V Axis 1 conditions. Social anxiety was most reported (n = 11, 22.4%). The social anxiety cycle (Clark & Wells, 1995) was often characterised by openly self-reported cognitions around fear of negative judgements from other people, embarrassment, characteristic safety behaviours (e.g. avoidance of social situations, limited eye contact), anticipatory anxiety before entering social situations and rumination or "post-mortem-ing" after attending social events. Due to the social nature of the ward environment, the features of social anxiety were more amplified, exposed and easier to detect, even in people with FND who did not initially connect well with emotions. The second most common category involved the reliving or re-experiencing of flashbacks of past traumatic events that could be consistent with PTSD (n = 10, 20.4%). However, the quality of these psychological phenomena differed from "acute PTSD". The symptoms of re-experiencing would often emerge after the therapeutic release of an unspeakable dilemma that pertained to one or more remote traumatic events, which due to long-standing reduced emotional expression and dissociation were not previously processed and frequently avoided by the person, maintaining the FND. The process of re-experiencing of these memories, with concomitant emotional expression, was the intervention. Depression rather than anxiety was often the dominant emotion accompanying the release of these traumatic memories. In n = 2 people with FND, a classic PTSD triad with high levels of anxiety, sensory phenomena and hyperarousal was detected following a recent traumatic event. People also described cognitions associated with panic attacks that followed a classic panic cycle (as in Clark, 1986), that is catastrophic misinterpretation of bodily symptoms resulting in FND, often a dissociative episode that terminated the panic loop (n = 8, 16.3%). Occasionally, people named their internal state as panic attacks ("I panicked when I saw we didn't have a session on my time-table"), but these psychological phenomena were not strictly speaking panic attacks as defined in the conventional way. GAD-style worries including rumination associated with anxiety, overthinking, thinking or planning for all the possible worst-case scenarios, devoting a lot of attentional resources and time to worries, as well as worries keeping the person awake at night, were reported in n = 8 (16.3%) people. Health anxiety was described in n = 7 (14.3%) people with FND, often characterised by a strong preoccupation and concerns about physical symptoms, often accompanied by reverberating worries and an "attentional spotlight". It should be noted that there was a qualitative difference between the increased symptom focus as part of health anxiety vs expressing a heightened focus on physical symptoms in a classic FND way. The former is accompanied by typical health anxiety features, for example cognitions about serious illness, reassurance seeking, excessive checking behaviours and high levels of anxiety. The latter type of symptom focus and reassurance seeking behaviours is less often associated with high anxiety and directed towards FND symptoms rather than life-threatening illness. The cognitions revolve around anxiety of not being believed or listened to. Increased symptom focus will be discussed in the Warning light section of this chapter. Psychotic features were rare and reported in only n = 2 (4.1%) of the sample.

Although panic, social anxiety and depression models were most often used in conjunction with the PCM in the treatment of FND, some other CBT models were not utilised (e.g. health anxiety) or less often than would be expected based on the frequency of the cognitions that patients reported (n = 3 were treated with the panic model, but n = 8 reported panic cognitions). There were several reasons for these discrepancies. The beliefs and emotions reported by patients often surfaced in later stages, often months, of therapy, due to either embarrassment around emotional expression or learning to connect with emotions in the context of longstanding dissociation. Furthermore, interpersonal cognitions and attachment anxiety often caused the most distress for patients and appeared to be most strongly related to FND. For these reasons, it was more parsimonious to use the PCM.

DEPRESSION-RELATED BELIEFS: FOCUS INWARDS

A striking observation was the finding of low self-esteem and self-reported confidence issues (e.g. "I'm worthless", self-attacking beliefs) in n = 22 (~45%) people. Other beliefs consistent with low mood and depression included perfectionist thinking or harsh, critical and high standards applied to self, especially compared to standards applied to other people (n = 9, 18.4%), and reports around loss and grief due to the FND, particularly worry around having missed out on many meaningful life activities or having to put life on a standstill (n = 2, 4.1%).

INTERPERSONAL BELIEFS: FOCUS OUTWARDS

Interpersonal cognitions are defined as beliefs experienced by people with FND in relation to other people, most often staff, family and other patients on the ward. This set of beliefs was prominently present in the sample (n = 25, 51%) and frequently associated with anger, frustration, low mood and high levels of "attachment anxiety", that is anxiety around rejection and abandonment rather than "primary anxiety" such as health anxiety or panic, and often accompanied by an acute exacerbation or re-emergence of FND symptoms. During their ward stay, patients reported interpersonal beliefs including not feeling cared for or receiving empathy; feeling let down by other people; not feeling believed; not feeling heard by, listened to, ignored or taken seriously by other people; feeling rejected and fears of abandonment; feeling lonely, emotionally neglected, singled out, not fitting in or being laughed at; fear of being misrepresented and subsequent rejection; fear, worries and hypervigilance about family's well-being, which was viewed as a "safety blanket"; and the perception that other patients were receiving differential and better care or treatment in comparison to the patient themselves.

OTHER NOTEWORTHY BELIEFS

People with FND reported two sets of beliefs that did not fit in existing CBT models but deserve mention. Worries about discharge and transitioning back into the home environment were common in about a third of the sample (n = 17, 34.7%). These worries would often emerge in the final weeks before the due discharge date and were associated with an increase in FND symptoms, for example a sudden re-emergence, high-frequent or more severe dissociative episodes with self-injurious behaviours; speech problems; or motor weakness. In addition, other symptoms could amplify, including physical symptoms (e.g. pain); psychological symptoms (e.g. anxiety, anger, low mood, emotion dysregulation); deliberate self-harm; or an increased frequency in falls. It must be noted that n = 4 (8.2%) people with FND reported a fear of falling. In n = 2 (4.1%) people, the thought contents remained unclear.

EMOTIONS

The most commonly reported emotion was low mood and depression (n = 25, 51%), which interestingly were consistent with the frequencies found for low self-esteem and interpersonal cognitions and appeared to form a cluster. The next most common emotion was anger (n = 12, 24.5%). Social emotions (e.g. guilt, shame, embarrassment, resentment) were only reported by n = 2 (4.1%) people with FND. A substantial group of patients denied the existence of distress (n = 22, ~45%), and did not identify, experience or were evasive about negative emotions and psychological difficulties (e.g. stress, anxiety, low mood, anger) either at present or prior to developing FND, and denied a link between FND and negative emotions, in some occasions presenting as bright in mood throughout the admission. N = 3 (6.1%) people would not deny distress but report low-level anxiety or stress associated with superficial stress triggers, which did not explain the disproportionate impact on FND or which were disproportionate in the context of significant life stresses. Denial occasionally dissipated as the therapy progressed.

Interestingly, the frequency of reports of denial of distress (45%) and low mood (51%) during psychological therapy sessions was roughly similar to the results obtained on the PHQ-9, a quantitative measure. About 43% of patients provided a "0-response" on the PHQ-9 item 2, whilst 58% acknowledged feeling down and depressed. Other related cognitions (items #1 and #6) generated similar percentages (see Table 2.2.9).

Table 2.2.9 Item-level analysis of the PHQ-9 (admission scores)

Item #	Contents	Frequency of 0-response endorsed	Frequency of 1, 2 or 3 endorsed
Item 1	**Little interest or pleasure**	**N = 16 (40%)**	**N = 24 (60%)**
Item 2	**Feeling down, depressed**	**N = 17 (43%)**	**N = 23 (58%)**
Item 3	Trouble sleeping	N = 7 (18%)	N = 33 (83%)
Item 4	Tiredness, little energy	N = 5 (13%)	N = 35 (88%)
Item 5	Poor appetite, overeating	N = 20 (50%)	N = 20 (50%)
Item 6	**Feeling bad about yourself**	**N = 16 (40%)**	**N = 24 (60%)**
Item 7	Trouble concentrating	N = 18 (45%)	N = 22 (55%)
Item 8	Moving slow or being restless	N = 19 (48%)	N = 21 (53%)
Item 9	Thoughts on being better off dead	N = 35 (88%)	N = 5 (13%)

Heat

LOW HEAT: DISSOCIATION

A questionnaire measuring dissociation was not administered. However, questionnaires are subject to bias and social desirability. The ward milieu offered a unique chance for observing dissociation in patient's day-to-day functioning. Interestingly, levels of dissociation were observed. There seemed to be a difference between "not identifying" vs "not able to identify", describe or label the arousal, overwhelming and unpleasant state as a specific emotion.

Qualitative analysis of comments shed light on the difference. A person expressing "I feel rejected/angry but I bury or block out my feelings" suggested active avoidance rather than frank dissociation from emotions, as the person appeared to be aware of experiencing emotions but chose to manage them by actively not engaging with the emotion. Blocking out feelings suggests that the person may acknowledge the existence of emotions to some extent. Other deflection strategies included speaking about other people; redirecting the topic from emotions to physical symptoms; and tangentiality or verbosity that prevented speaking or thinking about emotions. People who were unable to identify emotions reported the following phrases:

- "My mind is not present"
- "I'm easily switched off"
- "I feel cut off from my left side"
- "I'm not here"
- "My body is not my own"
- "My legs are switching off"
- "My brain is going black"
- "Like a black screen"
- "Things go black and glittery"
- "My head feels fuzzy"
- Description of a dissociative seizure as: "The pressure builds in my head and then I don't know what I'm doing"

Other features pointing towards dissociation included the person's observed inability of labelling emotions or relating to emotional experiences; poor emotion knowledge; referring to physical symptoms to describe emotions ("I feel tired", "pain in neck muscles"); restricted range of emotions or only acknowledging some but not other emotions; description of self "as always happy and positive" with euthymic mood; and providing rational and logical descriptions of emotions. People with high levels of dissociation would also frequently report normal scores on mood and anxiety questionnaires despite clear observable signs of anxiety, which did not reflect a patient's psychological state or distress.

Frank dissociative features that significantly "interfered" in psychological therapy and limited the application of CBT models were found in n = 19

(38.8%) patients. Interestingly, most of the highly dissociated patients experienced current motor-type FND as their dominant symptom (57.9%), followed by an equal mixture of motor–FND and dissociative seizures (21.1%). One could argue that a significant motor component was present in n = 15 people with strong levels of dissociation (79%). Functional cognitive symptoms dominated the clinical picture in only n = 2 (10.5%) people with FND. One other person exhibited mostly dissociative seizures, whilst the other experienced functional blindness (5.3% each).

It should be noted that denial of distress did not equal dissociation. A small minority (n = 5 out of 22 people denying distress, 22.7%) presented as highly emotionally dysregulated on the ward.

HIGH-LOW-HIGH-LOW HEAT: EMOTION DYSREGULATION

Approximately n = 24 (49%) patients were emotionally dysregulated, characterised by strong intense emotions that tended to fluctuate often in response to interpersonal triggers. Interestingly, this frequency is consistent with the earlier reported features of low mood and depression (51%), low self-esteem (~45%) and interpersonal cognitions (51%). Emotion dysregulation was associated with motor-type FND in slightly over half of cases (54.2%) and with a mixed motor-type/dissociative seizure picture in 45.8% of patients.

EMOTIONAL INTENSITY: OTHER FEATURES

N = 2 (4.1%) patients showed high levels of anxiety but were not dysregulated, whilst n = 4 (8.2%) patients exhibited flat affect, consistent with severe depression rather than dissociation. Another patient (2%) denied any mood problems and presented as euthymic, but reported moderate-to-severe levels of depression and anxiety on questionnaires. One patient misrecognised high levels of anxiety as anger, due to poor emotion knowledge and similarity in motor signatures such as heart palpitations.

OVERPRESSURE PLUG

Functional neurological symptoms   Table 2.2.10 shows the type of FND symptoms that people experienced ordered from highest to lowest frequency. Figure 2.1.3 shows a histogram of the 10 most commonly observed FND symptoms.

Nearly half of the sample exhibited speech difficulties, frequently characterised by dysfluency and stuttering speech; speech suddenly stopping midway through conversations; or blocked speech during intense emotional experiences. Speech articulation problems occurred, for example dysarthria, slurred speech, reduced speech intelligibility or a slow speech rate. Occasionally, "positive" speech problems could emerge, or the presence of features that do not characterise normal speech: developmental speech sound

Table 2.2.10 Percentages of the four categories of FND symptoms in n = 49 people

FND symptom category	Type of FND symptom	Frequency (%)
Motor	Paralysis or motor weakness	39 (79.6%)
	Tremor, myoclonic jerks, other jerky or ballistic movements	30 (61.2%)
	Speech difficulties	22 (44.9%)
	Dystonia	13 (26.5%)
	Spasms	11 (22.4%)
	Gait difficulties	5 (10.2%)
	Swallowing difficulties	5 (10.2%)
	Balance or coordination difficulties	4 (8.2%)
	Functional ataxia	2 (4.1%)
	Foot drop	1 (2%)
Sensory	Reduced sensation	18 (36.7%)
	Nil sensation/numbness	14 (28.6%)
	Visual changes (e.g. visual field loss, blurred or double vision)	12 (24.5%)
	Paraesthesia, pins and needles, tingling, burning	11 (22.4%)
	Hypersensitivity to external stimuli (e.g. sound, light, touch, weight bearing, pain)	7 (14.3%)
	Altered sensation/altered perception of midline	5 (10.2%) each
	Hearing loss or changes, tinnitus	3 (6.1%)
	No sensation of temperature/temperature dysregulation	2 (4.1%)
Cognitive	Attention, concentration and information processing speed	30 (61.2%)
	Memory difficulties	26 (53.1%)
	Executive dysfunction	16 (32.7%)
	No self-reported cognitive symptoms/no overt cognitive issues on observation	6 (12.2%)
	Self-reported cognitive or brain fog	5 (10.2%)
	Language difficulties: reading problems, word recognition, comprehension	5 (10.2%)
	Post-seizure amnesia/functional amnesia as part of dissociative seizures	4 (8.2%)
	Neurodevelopmental (e.g. dyslexia, dyscalculia)	3 (6.1%)
	Disorientation	2 (4.1%)
	Mild learning disability	2 (4.1%)
	Number processing/calculation	1 (2%)
Seizures	Dissociative seizures present with reduced awareness and responsiveness	27 (55%)
	Dissociative seizures without loss of awareness/ some awareness and responsiveness	5 (10.2%)
	Past dissociative seizures but not current	2 (4.1%)
	Gradually developing dissociative features over time but not developing into full-blown dissociative seizures	2 (4.1%)
	Night-time dissociative seizures; dissociative identity; dissociative wandering/fugue-like states; episodes of loss of consciousness and black-out episodes, suspected for organic reasons	1 (2%) each

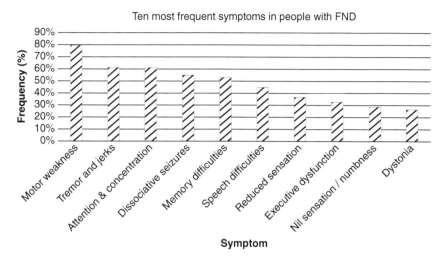

Figure 2.1.3 Ten most frequent symptoms in people with FND.

errors, child–like speech, distorted speech sounds, high-pitched speech and foreign accents. People with FND could also exhibit "negative" speech problems with features missing including episodes of muteness and voice loss; impoverished speech; limited verbal output; low speech volume; or hypophonia.

Reduced or lack of sensation was very common (n = 32, 65.3%), with 28.6% reporting a total lack of sensation, for example in a limb.

Approximately two-thirds of the sample (n = 32, 65.3%) experienced dissociative episodes. There was significant variability in clinical presentation including episodes in between a few seconds to hours long; with and without self-injurious behaviours; with levels in severity of self-injury (e.g. mild bruising to open wounds); with frequency in between multiple times a day to sporadically, occasionally and significantly increasing immediately before discharge; and in semiology (e.g. absences to highly mobile episodes requiring a lot of staff support to protect against self-injury). At times, it was difficult to distinguish between a paroxysmal dissociative episode where the person appeared to retain some awareness vs a motor-type FND relapse. For example, patients would report their "legs giving way" resulting in immobility or collapse on the floor, which could classify as either. Motor-type FND relapses presented with more static symptoms over a longer period of time, often with the person retaining some awareness and responsiveness, for example functional tetraplegia lasting for a few days.

A CLUSTER OF DEPRESSION SYMPTOMS

Cognitive symptoms emerged frequently, either self-reported by people with FND or observed on formal neuropsychological testing and occupational therapy assessments. Domains most commonly affected included attention, memory and, to a lesser extent, executive dysfunction. These findings are consistent with cognitive deficits typically noted in a "depression profile", as well as with the previously described cluster of depression, low self-esteem and interpersonal cognitions involving rejection and abandonment themes.

THE ROLE OF ATTENTION

Interestingly, attention was the most frequently impacted domain in people with FND, with nearly two-thirds of the sample either self-reporting or showing difficulties. In the context of increased self-focused attention on physical symptoms as one of the major maintaining factors in FND, the question arises whether this heightened self-focused attention competes for the same attentional resources that would otherwise be allocated to day-to-day activities. Another factor impacting on attention is mood and anxiety. The "cognitive crowding" effects by increased symptom focus and psychological difficulties may explain the reasons for the high frequency of attentional difficulties in FND.

DISCREPANCY: ASSESSMENT AND SELF-REPORT VS DAILY WARD LIFE

Although a large subset of people with FND self-reported or were formally assessed by a psychologist or occupational therapist as having cognitive difficulties, particularly attention, memory and executive dysfunction, the reported deficits did not always strongly permeate through day-to-day activities on the ward, at least not in the same way as for patients with brain injury (e.g. stroke). Most people were able to spontaneously remember to sign in and out for sessions, and tell the time and exhibited good prospective memory and/or planning abilities for attending sessions. If not accompanied by a healthcare professional, people were often able to independently navigate to sessions to the therapy gym or to a coffee shop nearby, showing preserved wayfinding skills. People demonstrated memory for strategies and techniques learned in sessions, which did not always translate into good carryover of information and techniques between sessions, but this appeared to be due to behavioural and psychological reasons (e.g. resistance towards progress, fear of recovery) rather than cognitive reasons. In addition, most patients were focused and able to remember their medications, which occasionally resulted in disagreements with healthcare providers. At times, patients did not move through self-medication stages; however, this tended to be for behavioural reasons rather than frank cognitive deficits. Nearly all patients showed normal face and name recognition of staff and other patients, and remembered conversations with other people, particularly if these were associated with strong emotions and distress, as part of interpersonal triggers for FND, as well as when staff made promises but did not deliver.

Although a substantial group of patients demonstrated speech difficulties, these tended to be more on the surface, for example stammering or slurring, rather than cognitive-communication disorders as often seen in brain injury. Difficulties with language comprehension (e.g. understanding test instructions) or communicating needs, even if via alternative means (e.g. writing), were rarely affected, with patients often able to provide arguments, and express opinions and viewpoints regarding their care. Writing was observed in diaries, even if a tremor interfered, and people frequently used mobile phones and computer devices without any difficulties, for example to send messages, watch movies or communicate with family.

THE FND-EMOTION LINK

In n = 28 (57%) people with FND, there was a clear association between the presence of negative emotions (or an undefined unpleasant state) and a change in FND symptoms. In this sample, the re-emergence or exacerbation of FND symptoms (e.g. stammer, voice loss, dissociative episode, amnesia, tremors, leg weakness, balance difficulties, functional incontinence, quadriplegia) was strongly linked with periods of increased stressful life events, including an impending discharge and transition; unhelpful interpersonal dynamics on the ward between the patient and staff or other patients resulting in strong emotions; bereavements, difficult messages, relationship or family dynamics outside the ward environment causing distress; anxiety including PTSD flashbacks or social fears; emotional pressure in, for example, physiotherapy sessions; or not feeling listened to causing anger. Of this sample, n = 15 (30.6%) high conflict or relationship difficulties in the family unit were directly and acutely associated with more FND (see the Fuel section).

THE PRESSURE COOKER CHAIN REACTION: EVIDENCE

The group was divided into people where an FND-emotion link was identified vs not identified. Below, the Cover and Valve configurations are displayed for both groups. Both people who identified and did not identify a link exhibited a tight Cover in approximately ~75% of the sample, as well as a blocked Valve in ~50–65% of cases. Irrespective of whether a link was identified or not, no group differences were observed in psychological coping (Table 2.2.11).

MEASURING PCM OUTCOMES: QUALITATIVE CRITERIA FOR CHANGE IN
PCM ELEMENTS

Next, a qualitative analysis was conducted on the outcomes of the rehabilitation programme with respect to the FND symptoms (Overpressure Plug) and the relationship with specific PCM features, in particular the Cover and

Table 2.2.11 Cover-Valve configurations in people with and without identified
FND-emotion link

FND-emotion link identified or reported	Cover difficulties? (Verbal emotional expression)	Valve dysfunctional? (Activity levels)
Yes (n = 28)	Tight: 22/28 (78.6%) Open but abnormal: 5/28 (17.9%) Normal: 1/28 (3.6%)	Bust-after-boom: 16/28 (57.1%) Boom-and-bust: 11/28 (39.3%) Boom: 1/28 (3.6%)
No (n = 21)	Tight: 16/21 (76.2%) Open but abnormal: 2/21 (9.5%) Normal: 3/21 (14.3%)	Bust-after-boom: 14/21 (66.7%) Boom-and-bust: 5/21 (23.8%) Boom: 1/21 (4.8%) Normal: 1/21 (4.8%)

Valve. The following qualitative criteria and attributes were drawn up based
on ward observations and real-life patient examples. NB. These criteria may
be useful in clinical practice to assess a person's functioning, abilities and
skills of the Overpressure Plug, Cover and Valve elements.

CHANGE OVERPRESSURE PLUG: FND RECOVERY?

Near/full recovery:

- **Walking:** Major gains from wheelchair to walking independently unaided/
  or walking independently with minimal reliance on a walking aid (e.g.
  crutch, quad stick) or orthotic, both indoors and outdoors. Ascending/
  descending stairs independently. Independently unaided with transfers.
- **FND symptoms:** Dissociative episodes reduced to 0. FND symptoms
  disappeared or reduced significantly in severity and frequency with very
  few residual or occasional symptoms in response to stressors/triggers but
  easily managed and quickly dissipating with patient quickly becoming
  FND-free. Full functional movement, control and power in all limbs,
  without equipment needs.
- **ADLs:** Independently completing personal and domestic activities without equipment, for example washing and dressing; toileting; simple and
  complex meal preparation; accessing community; using public transport;
  shopping; laundry; and medication management. Functions in the home
  environment without support.
- **Package of care:** No formal package of care on discharge.
- **Recovery curve:** Generally upward trajectory.

Some moderate gains but not fully recovered:

WALKING:

- Made some gains from wheelchair to walking with assistance but not
  consistent and wheelchair still primary mode of mobilising. Able to

self-propel for longer distances mostly independently and outdoors. Ascending/descending stairs with supervision.
- May transfer independently unaided; or with appropriate set up and supervision; or independent with some transfers but Ao1 with others.
- Stepped down from "heavy-duty" equipment (wheelchair) but still dependent on some "lighter" equipment, with frequent rests, for walking and transfers, for example 4-wheeled walker, walking stick and commode.
- Independently unaided/or reliant on lighter equipment for mobility indoors and shorter distances but slow/using wheelchair for outdoor mobility and accessing community to mobilise longer distances.
- May need heavy prompting and no spontaneous use of lighter aids.

FND SYMPTOMS:

- Some FND symptoms improved (e.g. motor weakness), and others may have remained the same (e.g. dissociative episodes). FND reduced in severity or frequency to some extent, but ongoing symptoms fluctuate, for example still using wheelchair when fatigued or in response to stressors.

ADLS:

- Semi-independent", independent in some areas but not in others (e.g. may be independent in personal care, but, e.g., only simple meal planning and preparation in standing for short periods; accessing community in wheelchair; light cleaning activities) with set up, (distant) supervision, minimal or occasional physical assistance from a person or equipment (e.g. perching stool, adaptive cutlery), frequent rest breaks and effortful/time-consuming.

Package of care: Reduced care package following discharge.

Recovery curve: Generally upwards with fluctuations, may be plateauing towards the end.

No or limited gains

WALKING:

- Unable to walk independently unaided, remained in wheelchair or powerchair, and used as primary mode of mobilising. May have practised with limited stepping.
- Difficulties with self-propelling/or on longer distances. May struggle with standing or sitting balance – only for very brief periods, with aids and with assistance of staff.
- Still dependent on a wide range of "heavy-duty" equipment, for example wheelchair, shower chair, self-catheterisation, slide boards and hospital bed.

- Needs ongoing and lots of supervision and assistance. Unsafe to be left alone for mobilising or transfers. In some cases: functional deterioration and discharged with more equipment.

FND symptoms:

- Ongoing symptoms with minimal or no change in frequency and severity.

ADLs:

- Made no or limited gains. Continued and significant dependency in all personal and domestic activities of daily life, requires ongoing physical assistance from at least another person and equipment (e.g. full prompting for medication management; may be able to prepare a simple meal in wheelchair or hot drink with set up and Assistance of one person personal care with shower chair but unable in standing; needing assistance with toileting; often not able to fully participate in outdoor activities such as shopping, accessing the community or using public transport; and not participating in household chores such as laundry and cleaning).

Package of care: Unchanged care package following discharge/high level care package (QDS, care calls four times a day; TDS, care calls three times a day).
   Recovery curve: Follows plateau.

Gains but worse before discharge

- **Walking, FND symptoms, ADLs, on course for no package of care and upward recovery** until discharge was imminent.
- Regression and loss of gains immediately before discharge, for example dissociative seizures reduced to zero during admission but significantly increased again right before discharge.
- Deterioration in mental health with other unhelpful behaviours (re) emerged, for example deliberate self-harm, with in some cases transfer to other ward necessary or additional follow-up in community to manage risks.

CHANGE COVER?

- Tight, not opening up about thoughts and feelings, or expressing emotions. Continued denial of distress, or only labelling positive emotions but not negative. Becoming confused when trying to speak about emotions.

- Strong, active resistance against and/or and persistent unhelpful beliefs in relation to emotional expression. Unwillingness to explore emotions, difficulties engaging with psychological concepts.
- Poor emotion labelling, knowledge or language.
- Deflection each time emotions are explored, particularly towards physical symptoms or exclusively mentioning superficial not core triggers. Not identifying with psychological or emotional explanations for FND, remaining fully focused on physical symptoms.
- Abnormal emotional features present, for example emotions not congruent with reported beliefs, struggling to recognise different levels of an emotion (e.g. feeling scared, frightened both parts of anxiety), naming physical attributes of emotions.

Ajar:

- Willing to explore or able to label some emotions/or to a limited extent. Some emotional expression (e.g. tearfulness, anger) but guardedness or reluctance remains. Person may have ventured into or is experimenting with using other means of emotional expression, for example journaling and art.
- Not releasing or touching only briefly on suspected unspeakable dilemma.
- Abnormal emotional features may still be present.
- Psychological issues remain vague; patient may be attending psychology regularly but not fully engaging. Person may be opening up about past thoughts and feelings but not identifying with current stressors.
- The person may still be attached to physical explanations of FND, show a high symptom focus or prefer a physical over a psychological model for symptoms, but is open to exploring psychological viewpoints further.

Opened:

- Opened up about difficult thoughts and feelings, accompanied by emotional expression in the therapy space.
- Accurately labelling/identifying emotions, able to clearly verbalise thoughts and feelings (=development of an emotion language).
- Applying strategies to help open the Cover, for example assertiveness, reality grounding and developing trusted relationships.
- Opening up about difficult thoughts and feelings during stressful circumstances in the admission or in the family situation, able to regulate emotions without re-emergence or exacerbation of FND.
- Release of an unspeakable dilemma, or opening up about past traumatic experiences, adverse life events, current challenging social situation or family dynamics.
- Generalising skills of opening up about emotions to other staff members or family, particularly to people with trusted and stable (therapeutic)

relationships. Making active and valuable contributions about emotions in group sessions.
- Increased awareness around setting boundaries; recognising when boundaries in relationships are crossed; applying assertiveness skills on day-to-day interactions; and able to assert needs to staff or family without feeling too guilty or uncomfortable.

CHANGE VALVE?

No change to the Valve:

- Not forming peer relationships on the ward. Forming limited or unhelpful peer relationships. Not initiating, engaging or withdrawal from social activities. Declining to participate in ward groups.
- Not engaging or struggling with strategies to support activity levels, for example relaxation, fatigue management, pacing and prioritising. Long periods of inertia if not prompted, especially during weekends.
- Continued demonstration of abnormal Valve profiles, for example over-activity, boom-and-bust cycles or a lack of initiation of enjoyable/social activities.
- No specific plans to make changes in social network, meaningful roles or vocational activities following discharge.

Yes on ward, no plans for outside:

- Forms peer relationships on the ward. Participates in various ward groups or social activities, occasionally with fluctuating engagement, for example exercise, relaxation, art, social meals, baking, gardening, therapy groups, engaged with activity coordinators, quizzes and movie nights. Some evidence of social belonging.
- However, continued reduced social support network with limited or no attempts to increase network following discharge, with little flexibility to increase due to barriers, for example disabilities, geographical location or psychological (e.g. social anxiety, depression).
- Person may have ongoing difficulties independently accessing the community outside of the ward environment for psychological reasons.
- Tentative, little or no self-initiation/reaching out to plan for after discharge despite active prompting, for example not looking into or planning community activities, and remaining dependent on environment for prompting of activities. May express interest in activities but vague plans.
- Unrealistic plans for after discharge, for example overfilled time-table for at home without rest breaks.

Yes on ward and plans for outside:

- Actively participated in social events and ward groups, and formed peer relationships on the ward. Active "ward social life" and "temporary" sense of belonging. No or limited difficulties accessing the community independently. With little guidance or independently organising social events, for example quizzes, movie nights and exercise groups.
- Effective at pacing, planning and prioritising activities to address boom-and-bust cycles and reducing overactivity and the appropriate use of relaxation strategies. Recognition of 'low mood-reduced enjoyable activities' link and behavioural activation.
- Established and consolidated daily routine on the ward including independently attending hospital gym and managing free time over the weekends. Spontaneously engages in leisure activities without prompting.
- Proactive interest in life after discharge that started during admission or active identification of future life goals and meaningful roles with detailed plans of execution and steps to achieve goals. This could involve learning new skills to further enhance independence (e.g. signing up for vocational courses); actively looking for a new hobby, enjoyable activity or sport; searching or completing applications for voluntary work, employment or educational pursuits; growing a social network and making social connections by joining a social group (e.g. choir) or reconnecting with friends; and other meaningful activities that could be smoothly carried over into the home environment. Conversations and agreements with family or workplace around new activity levels and support.
- Creating a realistic activity schedule with balanced daily or weekly routines for after discharge involving productive tasks; sports and exercise; meaningful, enjoyable, social and family activities; and rest breaks and self-care.

These qualitative criteria were used to analyse relationships between FND symptoms, level of verbal emotional expression and activity levels. The analyses were conducted on N = 44 patients, as n = 5 patients either self-discharged or left the unit due to the COVID-19 pandemic (Table 2.2.12).

According to the assumptions of the PCM, the best Cover x Valve configuration is an opened Cover and a Valve that signifies normal activity levels on the ward with future and realistic plans to continue meaningful activities following discharge (in bold). People who nearly-to-fully recovered showed the highest frequencies of this specific configuration (87.5% for both elements), lending support to the PCM. N = 12 (24.5% total sample) out of the 16 people who made a near or full recovery displayed this exact configuration. An additional n = 2 recovered people showed an opened Cover with normalised activity levels on the ward but not firm future plans. This preliminary

Table 2.2.12 Cover-Valve configurations per recovery category (n = 44 people with FND)

Overpressure Plug: FND recovery?	Change Cover?	Change Valve?
Near/full recovery (n = 16, 36.4%)	Tight: 1/16 (6.3%) Ajar: 1/16 (6.3%) Opened: 14/16 (87.5%)	No: 0% Yes on ward, no plans: 2/16 (12.5%) Yes on ward and plans: 14/16 (87.5%)
Some moderate gains but not fully recovered (n = 8, 18.2%)	Tight: 2/8 (25%) Ajar: 1/8 (12.5%) Opened: 5/8 (62.5%)	No: 4/8 (50%) Yes on ward, no plans: 3/8 (37.5%) Yes on ward and plans: 1/8 (12.5%)
No or limited gains (n = 16, 36.4%)	Tight: 11/16 (68.8%) Ajar: 4/16 (25%) Opened: 1/16 (6.3%)	No: 8/16 (50%) Yes on ward, no plans: 6/16 (37.5%) Yes on ward and plans: 2/16 (12.5%)
Gains but worse before discharge (n = 4, 9.1%)	Tight: 3/4 (75%) Ajar: 0% Opened: 1/4 (25%)	No: 2/4 (50%) Yes on ward, no plans: 2/4 (50%) Yes on ward and plans: 0%

Table 2.2.13 Types of pain found in n = 49 people with FND

Body part	Frequency	Body part	Frequency
Lower back	n = 18 (36.7%)	Diagnosis of fibromyalgia or complex regional pain syndrome	n = 3 (6.1%)
Face, neck, throat	n = 6 (12.2%)	Shoulder, joints	n = 7 (14.3%)
Knee	n = 5 (10.2%)	Neuropathic	n = 4 (8.2%)
Legs, feet, ankle, femur	n = 15 (30.6%)	Whole body/ generalised/ undifferentiated "chronic pain"	n = 14 (28.6%)
Arms, wrists, hands	n = 6 (12.2%)	Pelvic or hip	n = 4 (8.2%)
Headaches or migraines	n = 18 (36.7%)	Menstruation pain	n = 2 (4.1%)
Chest	n = 5 (10.2%)		

data shows that if the Cover is opened (normal verbal emotional expression) and the Valve regulated even just only on the ward (normal activity levels), then there is no need for the Overpressure Plug to be engaged (reduced or no FND symptoms).

PAIN

Approximately 92% of people with FND (n = 45 out of 49) reported pain symptoms. Types of pain were as follows (Table 2.2.13).

Table 2.2.14 Fatigue categories in n = 49 people with FND

Type of fatigue	Frequency (n = 49)
General and undifferentiated fatigue	n = 30 (61.2%)
Post-seizure fatigue	n = 5 (10.2%)
Cognitive fatigue	n = 13 (26.5%)
Physical and exercise-related fatigue	n = 9 (18.4%)
Diagnosis of chronic fatigue syndrome or ME	n = 6 (12.2%)

NB. One person could experience multiple types of fatigue.

FATIGUE

Fatigue was reported by nearly all people with FND (96%, n = 47 out of 49). Types of fatigue were as follows. Please note that the fatigue categories are not mutually exclusive (Table 2.2.14).

Layer 4: Medical-contextual

WARNING LIGHT

Increased symptom focus most commonly presented as a preoccupation and persistent verbal expressions around physical rather than psychological symptoms during psychological therapy sessions; despite repeated prompts, patients found it difficult to shift attention away from the physical symptom topic. In line with this finding, most patients who exhibited a high symptom focus during these sessions also rejected psychological explanations for FND. However, people who often spoke about physical symptoms and organic explanations did not invariably reject work with psychology (Table 2.2.15).

POT

Each element was FND SELF CARE acronym (on admission).

F – FOOD FUELLING YOUR BODY

Approximately ~45% (n = 22) of people with FND were found to be continent of bowels (as reported by specialist continence nurses). The most commonly reported gastro-intestinal symptom included constipation (22.4%, n = 11). Less common was gastro-oesophageal acid reflux "heart burn", and food allergies or intolerances (both 10.2%, n = 5). Irritable bowel syndrome was found in 8.2% (n = 4) of the sample. Post-dissociative episode vomiting was reported in n = 2 (4.1%). In terms of vitamin deficiencies, n = 14 (28.6%) people were deficient or low in vitamin D, followed by iron deficiency (n = 7, 14.3%) and folate deficiency (n = 3, 6.1%). Over half of the sample showed a Body Mass Index of 25 or higher (n = 25, 51%).

Table 2.2.15 Manifestations of heightened self-focused attention in n = 49 people with FND

Warning light feature	Frequency (%)
Preoccupation, speaking at length or in great detail about FND symptoms, physical symptoms or medications, hypervigilant monitoring of FND in context of psychological therapy sessions	n = 21 (42.9%)
Strongly focused on organic/physical rather than psychological causes for FND	n = 17 (34.7%)
Writing about/heavily engaging with FND symptoms in a journal or social media blog, presenting with a strong FND identity	n = 10 (20.4%)
Strong inclination towards engaging and working with physical professions over psychology	n = 9 (18.4%)
Frequent mention of new symptoms	n = 6 (12.2%)
Hypervigilant monitoring of patient by family	n = 6 (12.2%)

Table 2.2.16 Sleep features in n = 49 people with FND

Sleep issue	Frequency
Hypersomnia	N = 3 (6.1%)
Insomnia	N = 23 (46.9%)
• Poor sleep hygiene (e.g. going late to bed, getting up late, naps)	N = 4 (8.2%)
• Sleep apnoea	N = 3 (6.1%)
• Restless legs syndrome	N = 1 (2%)
• Insomnia due to patient self-reported psychological difficulties (e.g. PTSD, anxiety)	N = 2 (4.1%)

N – NIGHT REST

Almost half of the sample of people with FND experienced insomnia. Poor sleep could predate the FND but was often amplified due to patients sharing a bay with other patients whom required overnight care. Other reasons for poor sleep included poor sleep hygiene, sleep disorders and psychological difficulties. A thorough sleep evaluation was not undertaken as part of the admission, and this may explain the low numbers of reported causes for the insomnia. In addition, the frequency of sleep disturbance overall may be inflated as patients stayed overnight in a noisy and disruptive ward environment (Table 2.2.16).

D – DRUGS AND MEDICATIONS

People with FND were commonly prescribed and taking a variety of different medications. Nearly all people from the sample were on psychotropic medication. A high frequency of the sample was also on pain relief medications.

Approximately two-thirds of the sample was on vitamin supplementation and medications for gastro-intestinal issues "other" than constipation. Significantly elevated rates were also found for vascular and constipation-relieving medications (Table 2.2.17).

S – SICKNESS AND PHYSICAL ILLNESS

Co-morbid physical conditions were present in the sample although the frequency never exceeded ~30%. The most common co-existing physical

Table 2.2.17 List of medications used by people with FND (n = 49)

Type or reason for medications	Examples	Frequency (%)
Psychotropics	Pregabalin, Amitriptyline, Duloxetine, Fluoxetine, Diazepam, Escitalopram, Aripiprazole, Lorazepam, Sertraline, Venlafaxine, Nortriptyline , Amisulpride, Mirtazapine, Quetiapine, Buspirone	N = 43 (87.8%)
Pain relief	Codeine, Co-codamol, Co-dydramol, Tramadol, Morphine, Naproxen, Paracetamol, Ibuprofen, Diclofenac, Fentanyl, Gabapentin, Aspirin, Topiramate, Valproate	N = 39 (79.6%)
Vitamins and deficiencies	Cholecalciferol, Vitamin D, Calcium, Ferrous fumarate, Folic acid, Fortijuce, Hydroxocobalamin	N = 33 (67.3%)
Other gastro-intestinal	Omeprazole, Lansoprazole, Loperamide, Ranitidine, Buscopan	N = 30 (61.2%)
Vascular risk factors (e.g. blood pressure, cholesterol)	Warfarin, Ramipril, Dalteparin, Bisoprolol, Amlodipine, Propranolol, Atorvastatin, Metformin, Candesartan	N = 21 (42.9%)
Laxatives/ constipation	Senna, Bisacodyl, Docusate sodium, Phosphate enema, Macrogol, Lactulose	N = 21 (42.9%)
Sleep	Melatonin, Zopiclone, Promethazine	N = 14 (28.6%)
Anti-asthma, allergies	Salbutamol, Fluticasone/Salmeterol, Beclomethasone, Flutiform Cetirizine	N = 14 (28.6%)
Hormonal	Desogestrel, Prednisolone, Oestradiol, Levothyroxine	N = 9 (18.4%)
Anti-nausea	Domperidone, Ondansetron, Cyclizine, Hyoscine	N = 7 (14.3%)
Muscle relaxants	Tizanidine, Baclofen, Clonazepam, Solifenacin	N = 6 (12.2%)
Antibiotic	Flucloxacillin, Doxycycline	N = 5 (10.2%)
Bladder	Solifenacin, Bendroflumethiazide	N = 2 (4.1%)
Anti-rheumatic/ anti-inflammatory	Hydroxychloroquine, Methotrexate	N = 1 (2%)

★ Some medications fall in multiple categories.

Table 2.2.18 List of physical health problems encountered in people with FND (n = 49)

Type of physical health problem	Examples	Frequency (%)
Organic musculoskeletal conditions	Sciatica, spinal surgery for discs, degenerative disc disease, polyradiculopathy, cauda equina syndrome, orthopaedic surgery, scoliosis	N = 14 (28.6%)
Vascular risk factors (other than diabetes)	Problems with high blood pressure or blood pressure regulation and treated with medications, elevated cholesterol levels	N = 14 (28.6%)
Organic neurological conditions or features	Evidence of brain injury or mild atrophic changes in the brain on scan, history of meningitis, traumatic subdural haematoma, aneurysm, infarct, peripheral neuropathy	N = 13 (26.5%)
Pulmonological	Asthma	N = 10 (20.4%)
Gynaecological	Problems with menstruation, fibroids, hysterectomy, endometriosis, PCOS	N = 9 (18.4%)
Cardiac	Cardiomyopathy, POTS, history of myocarditis, history of myocardial infarction, atrial fibrillation	N = 9 (18.4%)
Dermatological/ allergies	Acne, dermatitis, psoriasis, allergies	N = 8 (16.3%)
Diabetes	Type 2 diabetes mellitus	N = 4 (8.2%)
Thyroid	Hypothyroidism, overactive thyroid	N = 4 (8.2%)
Auto-immune/ connective tissue rheumatological	Rheumatoid arthritis, Ehlers–Danlos syndrome	N = 4 (8.2%)
Infectious	Past COVID-19 infection	N = 4 (8.2%)
Blood	Eosinophilia, neutropenia, anaemia, thalassaemia	N = 3 (6.1%)
Liver	Non-alcoholic liver disease, cysts, cirrhosis	N = 3 (6.1%)
Past ETOH/substance misuse	–	N = 3 (6.1%)
Cancer (history)	–	N = 2 (4.1%)
Ophthalmological	–	N = 1 (2%)

* Not all physical conditions reported in patients with FND have been listed in the table for confidentiality and privacy reasons that could potentially identify a person, for example rare conditions.

conditions found in this sample of people with FND included organic musculoskeletal conditions, vascular risk factors that are not diabetes, and organic neurological conditions or features (Table 2.2.18).

E – EQUIPMENT

See Table 2.2.19.

Table 2.2.19 List of equipment used by people with FND (n = 49)

Type of equipment	Number of people using this piece of equipment on admission (%)
Wheelchair	31 (63.3%)
Shower chair	18 (36.7%)
Home adaptations (adapted kitchen, wet room, bath lift, raised toilet seat, hoist, stair lift, ramp)	15 (30.6%)
Rails, frames and levers for bed or toilet/grab rails	12 (24.5%)
Frames: Zimmer frame, gutter frame and rollator frame	9 (18.4%)
Powerchair	8 (16.3%)
Commode	8
Walkers: four-wheeled walker	7 (14.3%)
Tilt-in-space wheelchair	6 (12.2%)
Perching stool	6
Boards: Slide board, bathboard	5 (10.2%)
Orthotic (e.g. splint, wrist brace)	4 (8.2%)
Adapted cutlery	4
Adapted car	3 (6.1%)
Pressure relieving cushion	3
Walking stick	3
Crutches	3
Sara Stedy	2 (4.1%)
Mobility scooter	2
Helmet	2
Sunglasses (against oversensitivity to light)	2
Hospital bed	1 (2%)
Riser recliner armchair	1
Self-turning mattress	1
No equipment	1
Pendant alarm	1

L – LIQUIDS AND HYDRATION

Normal continence was described in n = 22 people with FND (~45%), whereas n = 17 (34.7%) experienced urinary incontinence as reported by the specialist incontinence nurses. No information was available on the status of continence in n = 10 (20.4%) people. Urinary retention was found in n = 3 (6.1%) people, with an additional n = 3 people demonstrating large quantities of fluid intake (e.g. water, energy drinks). N = 2 (4.1%) people used a self-catheterisation procedure on a regular basis. N = 5 people (10.2%) experienced urinary tract infections.

F – FIGHT-OR-FLIGHT

It was investigated whether any physical effects of anxiety and emotional distress were self-reported by patients or described by staff in people with FND. The rationale for including this feature in the FND SELF CARE acronym was based on clinical observations of people with FND reporting and demonstrating the physical manifestations of underlying distress but unable to put into words (alexithymia) or connect with the emotional component (dissociation), with otherwise normal medical investigations or cardiological work-up without changes in ECG. In clinical practice, it is important to be extra observant to these physiological effects in the absence of patient self-report of negative emotions or denial of distress, as these may be the only visible indicators of underlying distress. Caution is warranted when interpreting these physical symptoms, which should always take place within a multidisciplinary team setting in the presence of medical professionals, as these symptoms may have both organic and psychological causes (Table 2.2.20).

C – CONTACTS

People with FND commonly have multiple healthcare contacts. This does not automatically mean that the contacts are invariably in the context of FND. On the contrary, as the "S" (sickness and physical illness) section earlier already demonstrated, people with FND often experience co-existing physical and/or mental health conditions that require management or investigation.

The most common recent healthcare contacts prior to the inpatient neurorehabilitation admission in the present sample pertained to A&E visits, which tended to occur in the context of dissociative episodes, for n = 11 (22.4%) people with FND. N = 3 people with FND (6.1%) had been admitted to ITU. People with FND were reviewed by various healthcare professions. Particularly noteworthy for this sample were the frequencies found for healthcare contacts with ENT ("Ear, Nose and Throat", n = 7, 14.3%) and urology (n = 5, 10.2%), which were the next highest of all contacts, and consistent with reports of speech and continence issues as part of the clinical picture.

Table 2.2.20 Fight-or-flight features in n = 49 people with FND

Physical manifestation of potential emotional distress	*Frequency (%)*
Dizziness	N = 9 (18.4%)
Tachycardia, palpitations	N = 8 (16.3%)
Chest pains, tightness in chest	N = 7 (14.3%)
Shortness of breath	N = 5 (10.2%)
Balance issues, unsteadiness	N = 5 (10.2%)
Sweating, clamminess	N = 3 (6.1%)
Tremulousness	N = 3 (6.1%)
Nausea	N = 2 (4.1%)
Tachypnoea (rapid breathing), hyperventilation	N = 2 (4.1%)
Physical restlessness	N = 1 (2%)
Breath holding episodes	N = 1 (2%)

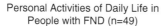

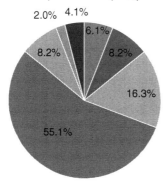

■ Independent with all PADLS
■ Independent with PADLS + equipment / adapted environment
▨ Independent with PADLS + A01 to set up environment
■ A01 to maintain safety whilst completing PADLS
▨ A02 for PADLS
▨ A03 for PADLS
■ No information available for PADLS

Figure 2.1.4 Personal activities of daily life in people with FND (n = 49).

A – APPEARANCE AND ABILITY TO CARE FOR SELF

Activities of daily life can be subdivided into personal and domestic activities.

Figure 2.1.4 shows that the largest subgroup consisted of people who needed physical assistance from one person whilst completing personal care, for example washing, dressing and grooming. Some people with FND were very disabled and demonstrated extra care needs. For example, n = 4 people needed assistance from one person for feeding and drinking (please note that this pertains to act of feeding rather than meal preparation). N = 1 person had overnight care needs and required physical assistance of a person for going to bed at night, as well as for rolling from supine to side lying.

Not all domestic activities of daily life were thoroughly assessed; meal preparation was the most commonly evaluated activity. People with FND struggled to complete domestic activities due to motor-type FND symptoms including upper limb tremors and ballistic movements, as well as fatigue (Figure 2.1.5).

R – RISKS

The following risks were recorded as part of the routine risk assessment process that was organised prior to discharge for every patient in the sample. Figure 2.1.6 shows the 11 most frequently reported risks for people with

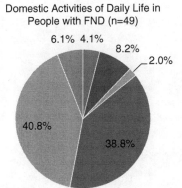

Domestic Activities of Daily Life in
People with FND (n=49)

6.1% 4.1%

8.2%

2.0%

40.8%

38.8%

- Independent for complex meal preparation
- Independent with meal preparation but with environmental adaptations or set up / equipment
- Close supervision of 1 for execution, A01 for planning in the kitchen
- Ao1 for complex meal preparation
- Not completing and fully dependent on others to manage nearly all DADLS activities / or did not participate in DADLS prior to admission
- DADLS not assessed

Figure 2.1.5 Domestic activities of daily life in people with FND (n = 49).

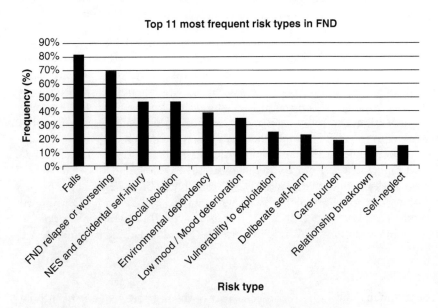

Top 11 most frequent risk types in FND

Figure 2.1.6 Top 11 most frequent risk types in FND.

FND. Falls risk was reported most often and affected the vast majority of patients. This highlights the need for a comprehensive falls risk assessment and profile in FND. Although a past history of FND carries a risk of a future occurrence of FND, it was striking that the risk of FND relapse was deemed high by staff for a large subset of patients (N = 34, 69.4%). Interestingly, this appears to be highly consistent with the n = 33 (67.3%) patients who did not experience a near or full recovery of FND (which was the case for only n = 16, 36.4%). The presence of this risk at discharge stresses the importance of continued follow-up care. The next most common risk involved the risk of dissociative seizures and accidental self-injury (n = 23, 46.9%). This risk pertained to the majority of people with seizures with and without awareness (n = 23 out of 32, 72%).

Interestingly, the remainder of the high-frequent risks mostly involved psychosocial risks, including risks that require comprehensive safeguarding measures (e.g. exploitation, self-harm). It should be noted that the frequent report of psychosocial risks was surprising on a unit with a disproportionate number of "physical" health staff, equipment and services highly focused on physical healthcare, for example medical, nursing, physiotherapists and occupational therapists, in comparison to the minority of staff who were primarily trained or had a strong background in mental health. Although the risk assessments were jointly completed by the team, the psychosocial risks stood out.

Furthermore, the social nature of many of these risks highlights the need for including the direct environment in FND treatment. If the environment has not been involved in treatment or lacks understanding of the formulation around, for example, the risk of environmental dependency (e.g. reciprocal reinforcement playing a role), it is easy to see how this risk can be perpetuated. Table 2.2.21 shows a range of other risks organised by PCM element. Some risks appear to be underrepresented; however, despite the percentage likely not being a reflection of the true frequency, these risks are nevertheless useful to report here to help raise awareness in clinicians working with people with FND and highlight low-frequent but serious risks that if these would emerge would have major ramifications for the person (e.g. medication mismanagement) or the environment (e.g. physical injuries to carers).

E – EXERCISE, MOVEMENT AND PHYSICAL ACTIVITY

See Table 2.2.22.

Layer 5: The Kitchen environment

MODELS (PRIOR TO FND)

Modelling is an important psychological process in FND and may contribute to the development of the condition. It was explored what proportion of the

Table 2.2.21 List of risks encountered in people with FND (n = 49)

Risk	Frequency (%) Total N = 49
Ignition/Fuel	
• Challenging family dynamics following transitioning back home	N = 1 (2%)
Flames/Heat	
• Low mood or mood deterioration	**N = 17 (34.7%)**
• Risk of deliberate self-harm	**N = 11 (22.4%)**
• Emotion dysregulation or anger outbursts	N = 6 (12.2%)
• Risk of passive self-harm (e.g. urinary infection due to poor hygiene)	N = 3 (6.1%)
• Other psychological symptoms (e.g. panic episodes, psychotic symptoms)	N = 2 (4.1%)
Sticky left-over food	
• Lack of confidence to attend personal care activities independently	N = 1 (2%)

Pot

F = Food Fuel	• Accidental risk to body due to limited food/nutritional intake (reasons other than FND)	N = 3 (6.1%)
	• Risk of difficulty eating and drinking due to functional swallowing difficulties	N = 1 (2%)
N = Night rest	• No risks identified or reported by the team	N/A
D = Drugs and medications	• Medication mismanagement (e.g. due to dissociation, functional amnesia, blindness or problems opening medication packets)	N = 6 (12.2%)
	• Iatrogenic damage due to overmedication	N = 1 (2%)
S = Sickness and physical illness	• Skin breakdown (due to incontinence, pressure sores, wearing splint)	N = 3 (6.1%)
	• Pain including analgesic overuse headache	N = 2 (4.1%)
E = Equipment	• Dependency on equipment	N = 1 (2%)
L = Liquids and bladder functioning	• Urinary infections	N = 1 (2%)
F = Fight-or-flight and warning signs	• No risks identified or reported by the team	N/A
C = Contacts	• Failed discharge/return to A&E	N = 2 (4.1%)

Risk		*Frequency (%)* *Total N = 49*
A = Ability to take care of yourself	• Self-neglect due to FND symptoms	**N = 7 (14.3%)**
	• Risk of injuries due to cognitive and physical difficulties in the context of FND impacting on ADLs (e.g. balance issues, poor safety awareness, sustaining burns during cooking during meal preparation)	N = 5 (10.2%)
R = Risks	• Risk of driving accidents if NES occurs during driving	N = 1 (2%)
E = Exercise, movement and physical activity	• Falls, and injuries due to falls (e.g. due to NESs, walking or transfers)	**N = 40 (81.6%)**
	• Deconditioning	N = 1 (2%)

Warning light

• Risk of vulnerability from the environment and breakdown of relationships due to high symptom focus and "overloading" people	N = 1 (2%)

Cover

• Not getting needs met/difficulties setting boundaries	N = 3 (6.1%)
• Risk of reduced ability to express needs verbally or call for help due to FND-related speech problems and communication	N = 3 (6.1%)

Valve

• Risk of accidental injury through over-exertion/self-neglect by not partaking in leisure activities	N = 4 (8.2%)
• Risk of boom-and-bust cycles	N = 2 (4.1%)
• Risk of avoiding activities in the community due to sensory modulation difficulties (sensory sensitivities)	N = 2 (4.1%)
• Risk of returning to pre-admission routine	N = 1 (2%)

Overpressure Plug

• Risk of FND relapse or worsening of FND symptoms	**N = 34 (69.4%)**
• Risk of NES and accidental self-injury	**N = 23 (46.9%)**
• Risk of NES mismanagement by the general public	N = 2 (4.1%)
• Risk of anger, frustration or harm from other people due to nature of FND symptoms	N = 2 (4.1%)
• Risk of child being unattended due to NESs	N = 1 (2%)
• Injury to staff/environment due to NESs	N = 2 (4.1%)

Kitchen

• Social isolation (e.g. due to FND symptoms and disabilities, or social anxiety)	**N = 23 (46.9%)**
• Overreliance on family/support staff, dependency on the environment including care-eliciting behaviours	**N = 19 (38.8%)**
• Vulnerability to exploitation (e.g. sexual, financial)	**N = 12 (24.5%)**

(Continued)

Table 2.2.21 (Continued)

Risk	Frequency (%) Total N = 49
• Carer burden, care breakdown and psychological difficulties in carers including reduced life opportunities due to enmeshed caring and family roles	**N = 9 (18.4%)**
• Breakdown of family or partner relationships/relationship strain (including emotional withdrawal, rejection)	**N = 7 (14.3%)**
• Risk of physical injuries to carers due to moving and handling, helping with PADLS and DADLS, transfers, pushing wheelchair.	N = 5 (10.2%)
• Risk of emotional abuse and coercion	N = 4 (8.2%)
• Risk of harm or verbal/physical aggression from patient to other people	N = 4 (8.2%)
• Vulnerability in the community due to FND symptoms (e.g. when "blacked" out or functionally blind, e.g. to theft)	N = 2 (4.1%)
• Difficulty building rapport with new professionals	N = 1 (2%)
• Risk of splitting teams	N = 1 (2%)
• Risk of disorientation and memory loss for objects in environment due to functional blindness	N = 1 (2%)
• Risk of becoming stuck in a microenvironment	N = 1 (2%)

current sample had been involved in a caring or serving profession or activities that involved a lot of interpersonal contact with people with physical or psychological needs (Table 2.2.23).

THE KITCHEN ENVIRONMENT: FAMILY AND PARTNER RELATIONSHIPS

The current relationships of people with FND were analysed. The most important relationships as indicated by the patient, and who often served as the person's next of kin during the admission, included partners (n = 19, 38.8%), parents (n = 21, 42.9%), and children, siblings and friends (each n = 3, 6.1%). The quality of the relationships could be categorised into six different categories that consisted of various configurations of enmeshed, distanced and normal features. Table 2.2.24 shows the frequencies of these categories in the sample.

Furthermore, analyses of the relationships revealed other noteworthy features. In n = 9 (18.4%) cases, the patient expressed a consistently strong wish for their family not to be involved in treatment. Reasons included a fear of repercussions from the family unit when returning home; not wanting to burden or stress family; or for reasons unclear. Approximately 40.8% (n = 20) of the patients received care from a family member or partner including siblings and children. Interpersonal conflicts in family or partner relationships were reported by ~20% (n = 10) of patients, with n = 2

Table 2.2.22 Movement- and transfer-related features in people with FND (n = 49)

Feature	Frequency (%) Total N = 49
Walking	
Mobilising in wheelchair – but not self-propelling and requiring assistance of one for wheelchair mobility	N = 17 (34.7%)
Mobilising in wheelchair – self-propelled short distances only	N = 1 (2%)
Mobilising via self-propelling in wheelchair	N = 19 (38.8%)
Mobilising in powerchair	N = 8 (16.3%)
Walking ± equipment (e.g. crutch, stick, four-wheeled walker, Zimmer, rollator, pulpit or gutter frame) or assistance of a person but short distances only	N = 14 (28.6%)
Walking independently unaided	N = 2 (4.1%)
Transfers	
Unable to complete most or all transfers independently – needing equipment (e.g. slide board, hoist, Sara Stedy), verbal prompts and assistance or supervision of a person	N = 24 (49%)
Able to complete independent transfers (e.g. high or low pivot, lateral)	N = 11 (22.4%)
Other	
Reduced cardiovascular fitness/exercise tolerance	N = 21 (42.9%)
Reduced ability to stand, e.g. posture, endurance, duration, quality or tolerance	N = 16 (32.7%)
Unable to use stairs independently	N = 9 (18.4%)
Deconditioning	N = 7 (14.3%)
Hypermobility	N = 3 (6.1%)

* Some people who relied on a wheelchair for mobilising were able to walk short distances; the categories were not mutually exclusive.

Table 2.2.23 Premorbid caring roles in n = 49 people with FND

Type of caring role	Frequency (%)
Main practical or "psychological" carer for other family members with mental health difficulties, neurodevelopmental or behavioural issues in family unit	N = 9 (18.4%)
Former teacher, teaching assistant including in special needs, or childcare worker	N = 4 (8.2%)
Former healthcare professional (e.g. nursing, allied health)	N = 3 (6.1%)
Former care professional	N = 3 (6.1%)
Closeness and regular proximity to a person with organic or functional neurological symptoms	N = 3 (6.1%)
Past employment role in healthcare – not as healthcare professional but exposure to healthcare environment	N = 1 (2%)

Table 2.2.24 Relationship profiles in n = 49 people with FND

Pattern	Enmeshment	Distancing	Normal
Enmeshment	**Full enmeshment (Total N = 10, 20.4%)** Enmeshment by all or nearly all key family member(s), for example frequent phone calls, helping out with care **(n = 5; 10.2%)** Enmeshed/ co-dependent relationship with partner (e.g. spending a lot of time together, blurred boundaries; **n = 5; 10.2%)**	**Partial enmeshment (Total N = 13, 26.5%)** Enmeshed or overprotected relationship with one part of the family (or one parent) – distanced, strained, estranged relationship with other part of family (or other parent; **n = 7; 14.3%)**	**Partial enmeshment** Enmeshed or overprotected relationship with one parent – normal relationship with other parent **(n = 6; 12.2%)**
Distancing	–	**Underinvolvement (Total N = 19, 38.8%)** Distancing by all or nearly all key family member(s) such as parental key figures, for example not present for GPMs, not interested in patient's care, not visiting patient, limited phone calls **(n = 9; 18.4%)** Current partner distancing from patient **(n = 2; 4.1%)** Estranged from children **(n = 4; 8.2%)**	**Partial underinvolvement** Normal relationship with one parent – strained or estranged relationship with other parent **(n = 4; 8.2%)**
Normal	–	–	Good and supportive marital or family relationships **(n = 7; 14.3%)**

(4.1%) patients being the victims of domestic violence. Three patients (6.1%) described a lack of "real-life" social support network but a large online support network of followers. Social isolation or a very limited social network was found in n = 30 people with FND (61.2%).

THE SOCIAL FUNCTIONS OF FND: RECIPROCAL REINFORCEMENT

See Table 2.2.25.

SYSTEMIC RE-TRAUMATISATION

Around 41% of all patients (n = 20) spontaneously reported features that could be consistent with systemic re-traumatisation. Patients were not explicitly asked for examples of systemic re-traumatisation, and the frequency is based on spontaneous comments generated by the patients during therapy sessions in relation to their perception of treatment in health services, and in some situations, by their own family. This pertains to both FND and non-FND health service experiences. The following comments were shared by patients:

- Family openly not believing/dismissive of the patient's FND diagnosis.
- Family telling the patient to pull themselves together and start walking.
- Family saying that patient is faking symptoms.
- Being informed that services are unable to help the patient and subsequently leaving the patient alone for an extended period of time to manage FND alone.
- Healthcare services not involved for many years due to lack of awareness of FND.
- Services informing the patient that they are unable to treat FND and subsequently reject the patient from services because of the FND diagnosis.
- Feeling neglected for days and left to own devices on an acute hospital ward with limited input from healthcare staff whilst observing other patients with organic illnesses receiving intensive input.
- Not having felt cared for by hospital staff when admitted to hospital. Self-perceived not progressing well on acute ward as "felt uncared for by staff" in comparison to progress on post-acute ward where the patient felt cared for.
- Being laughed at by staff for my symptoms.
- Being told I can just get up and walk.
- Poor treatment and being subjected to miscommunication by healthcare staff.
- Patient and family treated poorly and in an accusatory manner by healthcare staff.

Table 2.2.25 Reciprocal reinforcement patterns in n = 49 people with FND

Type of pattern reported	Patient behaviours	Family or team response/behaviours	Consequence(s)
N = 7 (14.3%)	Very good engagement with all therapies, for example consistently upward trajectory of progress in rehab, with steady gains, practice of small strategies, without small number of set-backs during admission.	• Staff enjoying working with patient. Team responds positively as unusual for the setting. Team feels confident and not anxious anymore about their own skills and in control about ability to FND management, as confirmed by progress of patient.	• Team spends a lot more time on the patient as patient provides positive emotions about staff's skills and confidence in treating the FND. Other patients less tended to/or avoided. • If set-back, team transiently becomes highly anxious and panicked, often mirroring team's emotions, as team losing confidence.
N = 3 (6.1%)	Depressed patient who engages to a limited extent and makes slower than usual overall progress.	• Team responds deflated and almost mirrors low mood and apathy/lack of initiation of the patient.	• Team disengages and disconnects from the patient's therapy and feels reluctant to put sufficient effort.
N = 10 (20.4%)	Patient openly dismissive about [insert discipline] and hard to engage/whilst only engaging with a subset of other disciplines. Often pro-physical vs anti-psychological, and in a small subset of cases, it is vice versa.	• Patient was progressing fast and not fluctuating in disciplines that are engaged. This made staff happy and encouraging with "walk extra mile", professions drawn in by patient. • Disciplines that are rejected by patient "pull out".	• Heavy focus on (often physical) side of therapy, making it more difficult for patient to engage with/feeding into avoidance and disengagement of (often) psychology. • Psychological issues associated with FND left unaddressed. • Continued firm belief in organic basis of FND and less understanding of FND. Reinforcement and maintenance of FND. • Stronger team split physical (doing well and advocating for patient's progress and to stay in programme) vs psychological (not doing well). Further compounded by engaged disciplines feeling good vs non-engaged disciplines feeling worse

N	Behaviours	Approach: staff	Outcomes
N = 27 (55.1%)	++ care-eliciting and dependency behaviours in front of audience (e.g. bringing frequent crises, self-injury, vomiting, controlled and unwitnessed falls, increase in NES or other FND symptoms, symptom exaggeration, lack of initiation of activities, complaints, oversharing trauma, using heavier equipment than advised, self-sabotage, placing barriers towards progress) – in context of past rejection experiences.	• Approach: staff feeling empathy/compassion and responding to patient care-eliciting behaviours immediately, getting drawn in by patient. • Distancing: staff or family feeling irritated, angry, frustrated or anxious, becoming drained, exhausted and burnt out or very emotionally avoidant, providing practical care only, display of non-verbal signs of frustration.	• Care-eliciting behaviours increase in frequency, as part of intermittent reinforcement schedule. • More dependency and stalling of treatment, not reaching goals, with staff feeling out of their depth, walking the extra mile and longer admissions and risk of institutionalisation. • Self-fulfilling prophecy: staff responding with reduced compassion and less empathy, leading to more rejection from environment (e.g. being short). • Systemic re-traumatisation: staff doesn't believe symptoms becomes dismissive, sarcastic or jokey about the FND. • Diagnostic overshadowing in some cases: not taking the patient's symptoms serious anymore and ascribe everything to FND.
N = 10 (20.4%)	• Special category of care-eliciting behaviours: longlasting or very severe non-epileptic or FND functional weakness episodes lasting for a longer than usual period (at least an hour for NESs and days or weeks for motor-type often quadriplegia) associated with moderate-to-severe self-harm – in the context of past rejection experiences.	• Staff cannot withdraw, due to strong injury risk, staff needing to provide very hands-on protection and support (e.g. prevent head injury and serious self-harm). • Staff emotionally withdrawing (dissociating and mirroring patient's behaviours of NES but lesser form).	• Patient's unmet emotional need of feeling cared for is met. • However, NES continues and increases in frequency. • High dependency on environment continues and no access to practicing alternative more helpful coping strategies. • Staff becomes exhausted and self-fulfilling prophecy: despite physical care, staff withdraws emotionally and encourages discharge => more rejection of patient.
N = 1 (2%)	Not wanting/refusing to set goals.	Team going along with the patient's wishes and resistance.	Team setting smaller goals with less progress over time, stagnation of progress. Increased dependency on the team to direct rehab.

(Continued)

Table 2.2.25 (Continued)

Type of pattern reported	Patient behaviours	Family or team response/behaviours	Consequence(s)
N = 7 (14.3%)	Safety behaviours as part of social anxiety (e.g. avoidance, escape of social situations, limited eye contact, reduced speech production).	**Response #1:** N = 3: wanting to care, gently pushing patient to take a social risk in experiments **Response #2:** N = 4: requesting regular joints for patients with severe SBs (e.g. no speaking, severe FND symptoms emerging in social situation) as staff unable to tolerate discomfort of SBs.	N = 3: patient progressing well, staff enjoying working with patient N = 4: patient exposed to higher and intense level of staffing whilst socially anxious and possibly too quick, with patient feeling highly self-conscious and unable to progress further in therapy.
N = 4 (8.2%)	Playful or overfamiliar behaviours, seeking proximity to staff and forming strong attachments.	Staff going along with it and reinforcing the behaviours/fearful of addressing playful behaviour as to not upset patient's feelings.	Playful behaviours escalating and crossing boundaries, staff becoming frustrated with patient.
N = 10 (20.4%)	Patient not kind to staff, rude manner, constant unhelpful interpersonal dynamics with staff and other patients (e.g. verbal outbursts, irritability, agitation), self-sabotaging behaviours -part of "reject them first before they can reject me" psychological safety behaviours.	Staff not enjoying working with patient, feeling angry and frustrated, or anxious, subsequently reluctant to support the patient.	More unhelpful interpersonal interactions with staff and patients. Increased level of emotional distress for all parties. Disengagement from treatment programme, with patient missing out on opportunities for treatment, maintains FND Self-fulfilling prophecy: more rejection becomes reality.

- Patients not feeling believed or cared for by healthcare staff. Clinician saying "you're making it up".
- Negative hospital experiences with services leaving patient to own devices and not sharing results of medical investigations, with the patient needing to chase for a long period of time.
- Patients signposted to completely inappropriate services for years and missing out on appropriate treatment opportunities for the FND.

These comments are patient self-report and had been corroborated in a small subset of situations by other sources. Even if there was a mismatch between the patient vs staff report, the mere fact that patients reported these instances spontaneously and were invariably associated with negative emotions warrants attention, especially considering past traumatic events associated with emotional neglect and not having felt believed in the context of abusive experiences.

Testimonials: qualitative feedback on the Pressure Cooker Model

The following section will discuss feedback about the Pressure Cooker Model that was provided by people with FND who were admitted to an inpatient rehabilitation unit as part of an intensive treatment programme for FND. Feedback was also obtained from a small group of healthcare professionals working on the same unit. The professionals' feedback was collected following several training presentations on the PCM for staff working with or expressing an interest in FND. This group was heterogeneous and consisted of a variety of professions including occupational therapy, physiotherapy, speech and language therapy, medical, nursing and ward staff. The following tables display feedback on the PCM, organised around five themes.

Theme 1: Increased understanding of FND

See Table 2.2.26.

Theme 2: Educating the environment

See Table 2.2.27.

Theme 3: Multidisciplinary element

See Table 2.2.28.

Theme 4: The pressure cooker itself

See Table 2.2.29.

Table 2.2.26 Comments about increased understanding of FND (theme 1)

People with FND	Healthcare professionals working with FND
The pressure cooker pot was great to learn about and made things so much clearer.	Easy/simple to understand/to follow
I now have more understanding of FND.	Comprehensive explanation
Very helpful in enabling me to understand FND better.	One nurse professional explained that she "now completely understands FND" and there have been requests for more training on the Pressure Cooker Model from nurses since
The PCM helped me to understand [FND] and made a change, I cannot fight what I don't understand. I got a glimmer of hope to fight it, I've got a chance. I came here hopeless, I now go with hope, this [PCM] was the moment.	In response to "How helpful do you think the PCM is in explaining FND to patients, families and healthcare staff?" (0 = extremely unhelpful – 10 = extremely helpful), the following responses were obtained: • 10 (n = 4) • 8–10 (n = 1) • 8 (n = 1) • 7 (n = 1)
It [group therapy programme based on the PCM] has been really interesting and rewarding to understand my illness better. It's provided me with more helpful tools.	

Table 2.2.27 Comments about educating the environment (theme 2)

People with FND	Healthcare professionals working with FND
[Very likely/extremely likely recommend the FND group to a friend or family member]: "so they can understand FND more".	Staff felt that the PCM was very helpful in explaining FND to patients, families and healthcare staff
I have been able to learn about FND and now explain it in great detail to others. I have learned how to describe FND by using the pressure cooker. What each part of the pressure cooker is and how it relates to FND. It is a great way to educate your friends and family in what the FND condition is all about.	
I find it easier to talk to people without it [FND] [now that the person has learned the PCM].	
In relation to FND education of the environment: "staff didn't know and PCM saves explanation" "help people understand to deal with attacks".	

Table 2.2.28 Comments about the multidisciplinary element of the PCM (theme 3)

People with FND	Healthcare professionals working with FND
Helped me to understand that these are the things that make up FND. I didn't get FND, but understood FND after hearing about the PCM, it helped me to start asking questions and it helped me with physiotherapy and occupational therapy. Treating one thing doesn't work, FND governs your brain, your body and things in life. It's not all in your head.	Staff from various non-psychology disciplines indicated that they would highly likely use the PCM when working with people with FND in response to the question "How likely will you use the PCM when working with people with FND?" (0 = extremely unlikely – 10 = extremely likely) • 10 (n = 3) • 9–10 (n = 1)
PCM has helped to understand FND. It pulls everything (physiotherapy, occupational therapy and psychology) together.	

Table 2.2.29 Comments about the pressure cooker itself (theme 4)

People with FND	Healthcare professionals working with FND
Good analogy It [PCM] is in-depth	Good analogy Visual to support understanding Relatable
Once you've applied the strategies, you can understand it [the PCM] better	Enables you to know the bigger picture
I learned the analogy of the pressure cooker. I learned about pacing and not booming and busting, assertiveness, managing symptoms, dealing with anxiety/dissociative attacks, how the environment impacts on me, the importance of having some enjoyable activity and not "a blocked valve". The importance of opening "the lid" and talking with others about how I feel	In response to the question: "Thinking about the presentation and the PCM, would you use any new strategies based on the PCM?" • Encourage them [people with FND] to open up when they feel comfortable (n = 1) • Encouraging patients to talk about their feelings (n = 1) • Yes, be more open to FND patients (n = 1) • More likely to do so now (n = 1) Staff correctly recognised encouraging speaking about feelings as one of the key PCM strategies
Pressure cooker => very good to put yourself in categories. I will look back at it. When I feel down, I will look back at it. Pressure cooker, I have seen what my warning light is	
People have FND because of the lid and the Valve, what can be done about the pot to not make it happen, limit these things	

Theme 5: Negative feedback on the Pressure Cooker Model

- [for improvement]: taking [take] longer to explain the pressure cooker pot.
- Go slower. It is a lot to process.
- Not to throw in the deep end of pressure cooker, as it's hard to get my head around. Breaking down information, not doing everything at once.
- Good analogy, but takes about three to four weeks to understand; it may sometimes be confusing to see which part of FND goes into which part of the PCM. Once you've applied the strategies, you can understand it better.
- The PCM can be quite overwhelming at first but is in-depth, but it eventually sinks in.
- Explaining the PCM in one go is too much, don't rush. Better approach is to use layers and build the pot up.
- Put something up to explain FND, a board devoted to FND. Give a brief description of the PCM and try not to get into detail too quickly.

Research limitations

Descriptive study design

The present descriptive study used a retrospective and non-blinded design. Although these studies have previously been reported in FND (e.g. Speed, 1996), the study was not a gold-standard RCT with an intervention vs control group that could truly test the clinical effectiveness of the PCM. Due to the lack of a treatment-as-usual control group, it was unclear whether the patients would have progressed in similar ways irrespective of the introduction of the PCM. Many confounding independent variables, other than the PCM, could have caused improvement in a subset of patients including the interventions delivered by other non-psychology professions who contributed to the inpatient programme; being temporarily removed from interpersonal triggers for FND in the home environment; and connecting with and expressing beliefs and emotions within the context of naturally developed trusted relationships with peers, therapists and nursing staff, independent from the therapeutic relationship that developed in the context of psychology sessions. In addition, the study lacked follow-up data on patients' long-term progress in the community. Several questions emerge: Were the psychological and physical gains acquired by a subset of patients maintained following discharge, often after returning to the same family environments that likely contributed to the FND? Could psychological gains have emerged following discharge after a period of reflection and distance from the programme?

PCM treatment—related issues

The question arises as to why not more patients achieved near or full recovery, despite each patient having been exposed to the PCM. Apart from the fixed PCM group therapy protocol (findings presented in Chapter 6), the present study did not adhere to a fixed protocol for individual therapy based on the PCM. In practice, this meant that the degree to which the PCM was involved in routine clinical care varied widely amongst patients, which introduced another confounding variable. The variability of PCM involvement emerged as part of individual therapy, for example with 18 patients (36.7%) who were treated with the PCM as their main treatment model, often owing to the high complexity and severity of the FND symptoms, which rendered standard CBT models less useful, whilst another subset was treated with the PCM in conjunction with an evidence-based CBT model ("PCM light" as an adjunct to the main CBT treatment). A small subgroup of n = 9 patients was treated with the PCM both in individual and in group format simultaneously and received a "double dose" of the PCM, suggesting a more thorough immersion in PCM principles (see Chapter 6 for more details). In a subset of patients (n = 20, 41%), PCM principles were used alongside individual therapy for FND family psycho-educational purposes with a focus on the more socially maintaining factors of FND. In addition, not every patient engaged with the model or therapy and outright rejected the PCM.

Another question pertained to the impact of the delivery of interventions other than the PCM (e.g. CBT or non-psychology) on improvement and recovery of individual patients. Due to the wide range of interventions simultaneously offered by multiple disciplines on the inpatient ward, it was difficult to establish the extent to which the PCM played a role in recovery (or deterioration). In this context, it is important to note that many of the ward interventions and activities were inadvertently geared towards managing each of the maintaining factors of FND specified in the PCM. One could argue that throughout the programme, various elements of the PCM were actively treated by multiple disciplines. Table 2.2.30 shows the different interventions offered by non-psychology disciplines categorised by PCM element. It should be noted that joint sessions between psychology and other professions were regularly undertaken. In addition, psychological principles permeated throughout every element, for example attentional shifting, reinforcement, thought challenging, dropping safety behaviours.

Bias

RESEARCHER BIAS

Several biases played a role in this study. All patients who were psychologically assessed and treated by the author were consecutively admitted on the

Table 2.2.30 Multidisciplinary interventions categorised per PCM element

Technique	PCM element
• **Social care:** Addressing housing, safeguarding concerns that directly maintained FND.	Ignition/Fuel
• **Neuropsychiatry:** Medication management to take the edge of mood or anxiety.	Flames/Heat
• **Occupational therapy:** Encouragement of compassion rather than negative attacking statements towards oneself if unable to do certain plans due to fatigue. Promotion of self-managing feelings through leisure and meaningful activities; education on the stress cycle.	
• **Physiotherapy:** Stair practice with reality grounding and attention shifting techniques, positive thinking about the goal, watching negative self-talk, positive reframe of negative beliefs.	
• **Physiotherapy:** Attention shifting techniques to support new movement patterns, normalise lower levels of anxiety on the stairs as a helping attention and walking practice, using sports to divert a patient's attention away from their balance.	Warning light
• **Continence nursing:** Management of bladder and bowel issues (e.g. self-catheterisation).	Pot
• **Dietetics:** Food and fluid intake, vitamin deficiencies.	
• **Pharmacy and neuropsychiatry:** Medication review and ratification. Referrals to other medical specialists for support with other physical illnesses.	
• **Occupational therapy:** Sleep hygiene; equipment review; promoting independence with personal and domestic activities of daily living.	
• **Physiotherapy:** Relaxation/breathing strategies implemented during, for example, movements, stepping, walking practice and standing exercises.	
• **Physiotherapy × occupational therapy:** Video feedback and verbal positive reinforcement when normalised movement and functional tasks were achieved.	
Speech therapy	Tight Cover
• Assertiveness training and role play scenarios for day-to-day interactions and family environments to support setting boundaries, express needs or emotions to other individuals causing distress within relationships.	
• Practice of basic and cognitive-communication skills (e.g. initiation, turn taking; generating socially appropriate questions/ shared topic of interest; conversation maintenance; active listening skills through body language and eye contact; use of facial expression, intonation; things to avoid in a conversation).	
Occupational therapy	Dysregulated Valve
• Management of activity levels and boom-bust cycles via methods (e.g. pacing, prioritising and planning of tasks).	
• Introducing, establishing and consolidating of balanced daily/ weekly routines consisting of productivity, family time, exercise, self-care, rest, meaningful occupations, leisure, enjoyable and social activities.	
Occupational therapy and activity coordinator	Blocked Valve
• Behavioural activation and creating a sense of belonging via social therapy groups on the ward (e.g. breakfast, lunch, arts and crafts group, gardening, sports).	

Technique	PCM element

- Practice of routine that activates behaviour: making a habit out of getting up early and shower, having breakfast.
- Introduction of meaningful activities and re-engagement with past enjoyable activities.
- Graded exposure programme with hierarchy and behavioural experiments to increase confidence in community access, socialising, public transport and shopping.
- Skills assessments to increase motivation to return to work.

Physiotherapy and hospital gym-based staff:
- A mood-enhancing physiotherapy exercise programme or physiotherapy groups organised around dance and music.
- Engagement with social/team sports (e.g. football, darts), mini "assault courses" as part of standing and stepping practice, physio groups with a social element with other patients: standing, fitness, supported exercise group.

Speech therapy
- Removing communication barriers to enjoyable and meaningful activities: interview and presentation practice. Support with behavioural experiments and dropping safety behaviours in the context of social anxiety, for example building confidence communicating with unfamiliar people and in more challenging situations, for example on the phone.
- **Physiotherapy and occupational therapy:** Learning to recognise and monitor for signs of over-exertion.   Overused Valve
- **Occupational therapy:** education and management of physical, cognitive and psychosocial fatigue; energy conservation techniques; relaxation groups that taught reality grounding exercises and breathing techniques: box breathing, passive progressive muscle relaxation, "on the spot" breathing when feeling overwhelmed or in a busy environment. Management of functional sensory difficulties: assessments of sensory profile; sensory programme with craft activities; re/desensitisation programme for altered sensations; strategies to manage any visual or auditory sensitivities.   Overpressure Plug
- **Nursing:** Bed rest schedule.
- **Speech therapy:** Vocal hygiene strategies (e.g. hydration, rest voice when tired or strained, reduce background noise, avoiding strained whispering) that work directly on the functional speech symptoms. Support with functional swallowing difficulties. Video feedback to review and remediate functional speech impairments.
- **Physiotherapy:** Entrainment techniques and use of rhythm to manage tremors directly.

MDT and nursing teams, other patients   Kitchen
- Ward milieu.
- Natural development of trusted and positive friendships and social activities on the ward.
- Exploration of care arrangements: package of care and family.
- Implementation of dissociative seizure guidelines.
- FND family education sessions.

ward. Due to the descriptive and observational nature of the PCM segment of the study, none of the patients were excluded from the analysis. However, the author was the only psychologist treating people with FND without other psychologists available to treat a subset of the patients, due to time and resource issues in the service. Therefore, it cannot be excluded that the qualitative data may have been subjected to researcher bias.

Introducing another FND-specialist therapist into the study with awareness of the ward environment, and having both therapists evaluating each other's data, would have addressed some of the bias. Another way to address researcher bias would be to rely on more objective, quantitative and standardised methods with fixed responses for the assessment of the PCM, as it reduces the subjectivity of the measurements. The majority of the PCM elements were not measured with quantitative standardised measures, only qualitatively with the use of frequency counts. Questionnaires were missing for particularly the elements of Heat (for dissociation), Cover (emotional expression), Valve (activity levels) and Kitchen elements (e.g. family functioning). Other elements were measured with questionnaires that were either not well researched on psychometric properties (DERS-SF) or not researched at all on reliability and validity (Attention to Symptoms). Although the Flames element was represented by two well-studied questionnaires, the PHQ-9 and GAD-7, these measures were crude and did not capture the complexity of some of the beliefs and emotions of people with FND including the fear of recovery and social emotions (e.g. guilt).

SOCIAL DESIRABILITY BIAS

The tendency to provide socially desirable responses on a questionnaire that presents a participant in a more favourable way to other individuals and does not reflect the individual's true internal state is called the social desirability bias. In addition to the impact of dissociation on the reduced report of psychological difficulties on questionnaires, there are also grounds to suspect that social desirability bias may have played a role. The frequency of denial of distress in this sample was high (n = 22, ~45%); social desirability bias could have been one of the reasons. People with FND commonly reported invalidation of emotions by parental caregivers, and it is not surprising that if emotions are strongly associated with weakness, stigma or embarrassment that patients may underreport distress on questionnaires. It should be noted that social desirability bias may also have impacted on the clinician-rated measures potentially inflating a person's neurorehabilitation gains on discharge.

MEMORY RECALL BIAS

To describe early childhood experiences and family functioning, this study relied entirely on patient self-report of often traumatic and adverse circumstances without verification by a second person. Due to the nature of trauma memories, recall can result in the unintentional report of distorted information around these experiences. In addition, the memory trace of events that occurred in childhood may have deteriorated. Some people may have underreported traumatic events due to dissociation, memory suppression and avoidance; not feeling sufficiently comfortable or lack of rapport with the therapist; or shame and embarrassment around the trauma. Other patients may have over-reported events as part of care or sympathy eliciting aspects of their condition in the context of childhood emotional neglect. Reports on family functioning were in most cases only provided by the patient, and a subset did not want their families to be involved during progress meetings. In addition, the perception of trauma events may have been coloured by implicit biases or judgements held by the researcher or influenced by strong emotions from the treating team.

SELECTION BIAS

Selection (or sampling) bias was another type of bias that played a role in the study. Participants were studied as part of a non-random sample. Prior to being put on the waiting list, patients were assessed by a multidisciplinary team and either accepted or rejected from the programme. In addition, some patients were triaged and admitted directly from acute services for the purposes of early intervention or due to the severity of FND. Since the FND symptoms from all patients warranted an inpatient admission, it is reasonable to assume that the patients were at the complex end of FND, which was also evident in clinical practice, for example in relation to the longevity and severity of FND symptoms in some patients, for example 10+-year history of FND, dissociative episodes lasting for hours at a time or quadriplegic motor weakness making the person bed-bound.

Future recommendations

Given the limitations of the current investigation, several recommendations for future studies into the PCM will be described here.

Research design

RCTs remain the gold-standard tool to test the effectiveness of an intervention; hence, a blinded and prospective RCT design where patients are randomised to an intervention group (PCM) vs treatment-as-usual group (not receiving the PCM) is recommended. It is advisable to use a fixed treatment protocol accompanied by process measures (e.g. therapeutic alliance, fidelity and adherence to the implementation of the model), as well as multiple therapists delivering the intervention to reduce bias. Due to the heterogeneity of FND and the impact of dissociation on self-report questionnaires, the use of case analyses would be more informative than the reliance on whole-group analyses, as would be the combined use of patient-rated and clinician-rated measures in research designs. In addition, a repeated-measures design consisting of multiple time-points could reveal useful follow-up data on progress and maintenance of gains following discharge. Another interesting question could be the impact of an "FND prehab" intervention with the PCM on the need for a subsequent full course of psychological therapy. At present, the PCM has only been studied on inpatients who tend to present with more severe, enduring and complex FND. It would be an interesting question to assess the effectiveness of the PCM across the full breadth of patients with FND, for example in different settings (e.g. community, acute), age categories (e.g. child, older adults) and populations (e.g. people with and without a diagnosed personality disorder). As the PCM is predominantly a practical model intended for direct use in patients and practitioners in real-life settings, there is scope for the use of implementation designs or hybrid effectiveness/implementation (E-I) designs (Cully et al., 2012; Curran et al., 2012), which focus on the clinical effectiveness of an intervention and also take into account the methodology needed to deliver and implement interventions in clinical practice – addressing an important limitation of RCTs.

Measurement

Although helpful recommendations for outcome measurement in FND research have relatively recently been published (Pick et al., 2020), it may be useful to consider alternative ideas for the measurement of FND-specific psychological processes in clinical practice. Several thinking and emotional processes that have been uncovered in the PCM study have not thoroughly been studied in people with FND but are nevertheless highly relevant in therapy including the fear of recovery, fear of relapse, feeling cared for, feeling believed, attachment anxiety and abandonment issues, feeling trapped as part of an unspeakable dilemma, and primary distress pre-dating the FND vs secondary distress resulting from FND, in addition to "regular anxiety" associated with panic, social situations, persistent worry and trauma.

SENSITIVE QUESTIONNAIRES

The creation of more sensitive and valid questionnaires that tap into these FND-specific psychological processes, as well as the development of more standardised observation schedules that assess the impact of the environment on FND, including reciprocal reinforcement and systemic re-traumatisation, could be highly informative for clinical practice and furthering the field of FND.

PROCESS NOT JUST CONTENT

The use of systemic, relationship and process measures in research designs could be particularly important in FND, as it reflects core maintaining factors, for example assessment of therapeutic alliance and its impact on outcomes in FND; a more detailed analysis of family relationships and functioning; the level of social belonging or connectedness that a person may feel and its relationship to FND; and gauging the contribution of other professions to a person's gains using the quantification of hours devoted to treatment (e.g. Northwick Park Therapy Dependency Assessment) and patient self-reports.

MIXED-METHODS APPROACH

Eventually, the field may move towards a mixed-methods approach of measuring outcomes in FND, consisting of a combination of both quantitative and qualitative methods, for example standardised questionnaires and methods that can capture more complex change processes that do not lose the finesses of FND by using a PCM assessment on admission and on discharge, and comparing the two.

Summary of Study 2 results: the headlines

This preliminary study on the PCM confirmed earlier reported findings from the literature and revealed several interesting new results that to our knowledge have not yet been reported in the research literature. Overall, the five layers from the model appeared to be accurately reflected in the patient data, although there were differences in how well the data was captured by each layer. Since the amount of data generated by Study 2 was large, the following section will focus on summarising the main headlines and the most interesting results.

Layer 1 (Ignition)

Childhood emotional neglect was reported by 41% of patients. In contrast, childhood sexual abuse was reported by 18% and physical abuse by 16% of people with FND. Findings were consistent with past research on adverse life events in FND, particularly the higher rate of childhood emotional neglect in comparison to sexual and physical abuse (Ludwig et al., 2018).

Layer 2 (The FND coping triad)

The present data showed convincing evidence for the presence of a partial FND coping triad: reduced verbal emotional expression, retrospectively self-reported by over 75% of the patient sample and continued to be maintained over many years into adulthood. Reduced verbal emotional expression in childhood was most often shaped by a challenging family environment during a person's early life and upbringing (47%) and maintained in current circumstances by the presence of an unspeakable dilemma or an undisclosed secret that was often shared towards the end of therapy (45%). Interestingly, people with FND exhibited several physical and psychological features that prevented speech production (and therefore verbal emotional expression) in various ways. For example, functional speech difficulties in ~45% of patients were considered a symbolic and literal representation of reduced verbal emotional expression. In addition, social anxiety was present in approximately 20% of patients and impacted on the person's ability to verbally express emotions to another individual or in social situations.

Layer 3 (The FND maintenance cycle)

INTERPERSONAL > PHYSICAL TRIGGERS

There was significant heterogeneity of different triggers in the sample. However, most often, FND symptoms would flare and amplify in response to interpersonal triggers that were associated with the presence of other individuals in the vicinity of the patient (ranging in between ~30 and 60%). In contrast to interpersonal triggers, physical triggers and panic attacks only accounted for a small proportion of triggers for FND.

A CLUSTER OF DEPRESSION FEATURES

Although the existence of distress was not acknowledged by ~45% of patients, a clear cluster of features strongly suggestive of depression was observed in the sample, with remarkably similar frequencies reported for all these features that tended to hover around the 50% mark. In relation to the *Flames*, which represented a person's emotions and beliefs, low mood and depression was reported by 51% of the sample. Commonly reported beliefs were consistent with depressive features and tended to revolve around low self-esteem (~45%), as well as interpersonal beliefs around rejection, abandonment, feeling uncared for, unheard or not believed by other people (51%). In the context of the Valve (activity levels, which could be considered the "behavioural" component of depression in the PCM), nearly two-thirds of the sample showed a bust-after-boom Valve characterised by significantly reduced activity levels in the person's life that often followed a prolonged period of preceding overactivity. The Pot element revealed sleeping difficulties in ~53%, whereas the Kitchen element showed social isolation in 61% of patients, both features that are common in depression.

Interestingly, this data, which was obtained from the different PCM layers, was remarkably consistent for the entire cluster of depressive features. Uncovering this cluster in the data is important for two reasons. The quantitative, non-significant pre-to-post therapy results found for PHQ-9 scores, as well as their relatively low-grade level of intensity, would not suggest a high incidence of low mood in the sample. However, analysing depression more qualitatively using the PCM revealed a different clinical picture. In addition, theoretical models of FND tend to focus on anxiety-related processes, for example the misinterpretation of bodily symptoms (panic disorder model) and the increased focus of attention on physical symptoms (health anxiety model) leading to FND. However, little attention has been paid in these models to the relationship between depression–related processes and FND, for instance by invoking concepts such as self–esteem, interpersonal triggers, fear of rejection, abandonment and attachment anxiety, which seem to be particularly important for a large subset of patients with a history of adverse childhood events.

PCM PROCESSES

The FND–emotion link was present in 57% of patients where a clear association was observed between the presence of negative emotions (or an undefined unpleasant state) and a re-emergence or exacerbation of FND symptoms. Over half of these instances (54%) were triggered by interpersonal family dynamics. A qualitative analysis on the outcomes of the rehabilitation programme revealed that the ~36% of nearly or fully recovered patients showed an "opened cover" and an "unblocked/regulated valve" in 87.5% of cases each. In contrast, patients who made no or limited gains (also ~36%) had "opened the cover" in only 6.3% and "regulated the valve" in 12.5% of cases. Taken together, these findings lend support to the notion that in order to reduce the risk of FND, verbal emotional expression and activity levels ought to have been normalised. These current findings are consistent with the reported inverse association between emotional expression and FND (Bowman & Markand, 1999; Alsaadi & Marquez, 2005), where better emotional expression improved outcomes in people with FND, whereas unfavourable outcomes emerged for people who were more inhibited regarding self-disclosure and emotional expression (Alsaadi & Marquez, 2005).

Layer 4 (physical facilitating factors: the pressure cooker pot)

Analysis of the FND SELF CARE acronym revealed a range of new and interesting findings that had not been extensively written about in the FND literature and that may provide new suggestions for points of intervention to ensure that a person with FND is in an optimal state for neurorehabilitation.

PHYSICAL SYMPTOMS

Vitamin deficiencies were common in FND, particularly low vitamin D. Approximately two-thirds of the sample was on some form of vitamin supplementation. Over half of the sample showed a Body Mass Index of 25 or higher. Approximately ~43% of the sample were noted to present with reduced cardiovascular fitness. Pain was reported in 92% of people with FND, and this was reflected in the high rates of pain relief medications (~80%). Some of these included medications from the opiate family, which are known to have a propensity towards facilitating dissociation. The frequency of co-morbid neurological features as confirmed by medical and neurological investigations (26.5%) was roughly consistent with the frequency of ~20% recently reported in the literature (Bennett et al., 2021).

FUNCTIONAL STATUS AND DAY-TO-DAY ACTIVITIES

The vast majority of the sample (~92%) used a wheelchair as the primary form of mobilisation. About two-thirds of people (61%) mobilised independently, either via self-propelling in a wheelchair, independently operating a powerchair or walking independently unaided. Only 22.4% of people were able to independently complete transfers. In the context of activities in daily life, people with FND most often needed the physical assistance of at least one person to complete and maintain safety during personal care (~65%). Meal preparation was the most often assessed domestic activity of daily life. About 40% was unable to participate or otherwise fully dependent on other people for domestic activities in daily life, whereas an additional ~40% required physical assistance from another individual to prepare a complex meal. Therefore, approximately 80% of people with FND needed support with meal preparation.

RISK ANALYSIS

Risk analysis revealed the highest risk for falls (~82%). The risk of FND relapse after discharge from the unit was deemed high by staff for a large subset of patients (69.4%), and this was highly consistent with 67.3% of patients who did not experience a near or full recovery of FND. Interestingly, the "top 11" mostly highly frequent risks mostly involved psychosocial risks, including risks that require comprehensive safeguarding measures. The psychosocial nature of many of these risks strongly emphasises the need for involvement of the direct environment in FND treatment to minimise the risks.

Layer 5: The Kitchen environment and social functions of FND

RELATIONSHIPS AND FND

A comprehensive analysis on current relationships of people with FND revealed underinvolvement as the most common relationship pattern where all or nearly all family members were distanced from the patient (38.8%). It was not always clear whether the patient (1) actively rejected efforts from the family or partner to be involved, (2) was actively "distanced from" by the family unit that was primarily driving the schism, or (3) actively rejected the family before they could reject the patient as a psychological coping strategy to protect fragile self-esteem. Many reasons exist for distancing behaviours in either direction including fear of repercussions; not wanting to burden or cause unnecessary stress for the family; not wishing to share the FND diagnosis out of fear for stigma and judgement; and not wanting to be disappointed or feel embarrassed by the family after reaching out would not generate the desired effect of people visiting.

The distancing pattern was followed by a mixed enmeshed/distanced pattern (26.5%) and a full enmeshed pattern, which accounted for 20.4% of relationships. Approximately 40% was cared for by a family member or partner.

RECIPROCAL REINFORCEMENT

Layer 5 revealed a series of reciprocal reinforcement processes on the ward. The most common patterns of reciprocal reinforcement included excessive care-eliciting and dependent behaviours displayed by the person with FND towards the environment. A subset of staff responded with empathy and compassion, whilst another subset responded with distancing behaviours, for example verbally and non-verbally expressing negative emotions in relation to the patient and active avoidance, fuelling the potential for systemic re-traumatisation, a partial reinforcement schedule, and missing opportunities for rehabilitation, as well as preventing learning new adaptive coping strategies.

Other common reciprocal reinforcement patterns (20.4% each) involved splitting behaviours that further compounded existing dichotomies between (often) physical vs psychology disciplines and promoted more avoidance and rejection of psychological support and an exploration and management of psychological contributors to FND, further maintaining the FND; longlasting and severe dissociative episodes that needed excessive safeguarding by staff, in the form of enhanced and long-term physical assistance around risks of self-injury (e.g. headbanging, bleeding wounds) and that perpetuated the seizures; and ongoing negative patient-staff interactions as part of a "reject them first before they reject me" strategy with these interpersonal triggers leading to an increased risk of FND symptoms.

SYSTEMIC RE-TRAUMATISATION

A substantial subset of people with FND (41%) spontaneously reported comments and responses mostly from healthcare professionals and that were characterised by a significant potential to re-traumatise the patient. It is unclear whether that number would have been even higher if patients were actively asked about their experiences in healthcare and/or in their family situation. It should also be noted that this data was not able to demonstrate the direct adverse impact or re-traumatising nature of the comments and responses on

FND symptoms; this was merely hypothesised on the basis of the PCM. This area deserves to become a target for future research.

Acceptability of the PCM

Qualitative feedback by a group of patients and healthcare professionals on the PCM was overwhelmingly positive in nature and suggested acceptance of the model. The feedback revealed a range of themes including the PCM as a helpful aid to increase understanding of a person's FND; the positive role that the PCM played in educating the environment; the utility of the PCM within a multidisciplinary context; the actual features and visual characteristics of the model and how these support understanding of FND; and drawbacks of the PCM. Across all negative feedback, the resounding recommendation of people who predominantly participated in the group therapy based on PCM principles was to explain the PCM at a slower pace with manageable chunks of information on the principles. The relative quick pace of information delivery did not appear to adversely impact on the self-perceived level of understanding FND. None of the participants actively rejected the PCM.

Conclusions

Study 1 highlighted the heterogeneity of the sample and the pressing need to look beyond whole-group analyses during the assessment of therapeutic change in psychological symptoms in FND. Although Study 2 was limited by a range of confounding variables, its results appeared to provide some preliminary support for the potential of the PCM to provide a semi-quantitative, rich description of the psychological, social and biological processes that contribute to the emergence and maintenance of FND, as well as a compelling rationale for adopting a process approach, as outlined in the PCM, to more fully capture the complexity of psychosocial and biological functioning in FND. The inpatient data provided evidence for the existence of the hypothesised elements and processes of the PCM in a sample of people with FND and for the model's utility in a multidisciplinary setting as a tool that is able to incorporate and integrate the different strands of work to guide one coherent treatment plan. Importantly, the findings clearly demonstrated the acceptance of the model by people with FND and their healthcare professionals in clinical practice. These preliminary findings of this pilot study may provide a useful starting point for more scientifically controlled and thoroughly designed future investigations on the effectiveness, feasibility and acceptability of the PCM in different settings of clinical practice.

On a final note, a historical dichotomy exists between quantitative vs qualitative research methods. There are pros and cons to using both methods of investigation in clinical practice in FND, as Table 2.2.31 below highlights.

Table 2.2.31 Quantitative vs "rich descriptive formulation" method in FND

Quantitative method	Rich descriptive formulation method
• Reductionist: simplifies psychological processes to numerical information that loses the finesse, richness and detail of the original data.	• Able to capture FND-specific psychological processes to the fullest extent and which standardised measures of mood and anxiety were not able to detect.
• For example, the PHQ-9 and GAD-7 did not detect FND-specific thought content that greatly impacted on mood and anxiety (e.g. fear of discharge) and did not pick up on FND-specific features of emotional processes in the sample (e.g. fear of relapse, interpersonal cognitions, attachment-type anxiety).	
• Some of the FND-specific psychological processes are hard to operationalise using questionnaires and would not be able to do justice to an accurate description of some key processes in FND, for example reciprocal reinforcement and relationship patterns.	• Able to fully describe more complex relational processes between people with FND and their environment.
• Unable to formulate and make links between various maintaining factors in FND. Information obtained from quantitative measures will likely be more disjointed.	• Described several processes that connected different maintaining factors in FND: reciprocal reinforcement, the Pressure Cooker Chain Reaction, repetition of coping strategies (e.g. sticky left-over food and tight Cover).
• If only quantitative methods would be relied on, the research study would miss out on the discovery of major maintaining processes that contribute to FND: reciprocal reinforcement. Conclusions would have been drawn that would not accurately reflect reality, for example finding significant whole-group neurorehabilitation effects but no psychological effects (i.e. pre-to-post change in PHQ-9 non-significant), whereas in reality, a lot of interesting and clinically significant psychological results were present (i.e. finding a cluster of depression-related features).	• The descriptive study was better able to unearth these complex psychosocial processes. It should be noted that the inpatient ward environment also enabled a comprehensive description of reciprocal reinforcement that would otherwise likely not be found if the study would have been conducted in a community setting.
• As a result, the study has provided an interesting starting point for future studies to build on and further investigate the impact of complex psychosocial processes on FND using more controlled designs.

(Continued)

Table 2.2.31 (Continued)

Quantitative method	Rich descriptive formulation method
• Quantitative methodology enables faster process of data collection and analysis.	• Slower, more laborious process of data collection and analysis, as this takes place during the scope of an admission or the evolution of therapy over time. Requires building a therapeutic relationship and careful behavioural observations.
• Although self-report by patient or clinician-rated observations introduce bias, standardised methods help to control this better than qualitative methods. • However, social desirability bias is an ongoing issue and easy to succumb to when completing questionnaires, especially when denial of distress is present.	• Self-report by patient and an additional layer of interpretation by the clinician introduce another form of bias.

In conclusion, instead of strictly adhering to this historical dichotomy, almost in the same way as the body and mind have been disconnected in FND, the present study findings suggest a hybrid, mixed-methods approach to assessing outcomes in FND that incorporates both quantitative and qualitative approaches towards measuring psychosocial processes and therapeutic change in FND.

3 The principles of the Pressure Cooker Model

Introduction

The PCM consists of 12 elements arranged across five layers. The multi-layered formulation structure aims to capture the psychological, social and biological processes that contribute to the emergence and maintenance of FND. This chapter aims to explore each of these elements, layers and processes of the PCM in more detail, supported by a rationale for inclusion into the model.

Elements

The PCM consists of 12 elements in total. Each element represents an FND-related factor that plays a role in the emergence or maintenance of FND. Figure 3.1 displays the elements and the FND-related concepts that they represent.

In the next section, the elements will be discussed in more detail as part of each layer.

Layers

As can be seen in Table 3.1, past research, predominantly in people with dissociative episodes, has consistently identified a two-layered process of FND.

The elements of the PCM are organised across five layers. The multi-layered formulation structure aims to fully capture the intricacies and psychological processes contributing to the emergence and maintenance of FND (see Table 3.2) and subsumes the classic two-stage process of FND. Each layer has their own specific configuration of elements. The fifth layer of the PCM (social functions) is not similar to the second layer identified in the research literature (secondary gains). In Layer 5, the PCM radically assumes that both the individual and the environment equally contribute to the psychological features of FND as opposed to the common misperception that people with FND are the only group to demonstrate "secondary gains". The twelfth element, "Safety features", representing protective and positive prognostic

DOI: 10.4324/9781003308980-3

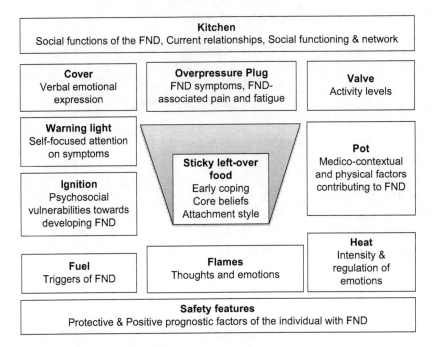

Figure 3.1 Elements of the Pressure Cooker Model.

Table 3.1 Features of the two-layered structure of FND processes

Variable	Layer 1	Layer 2
Functions	FND and distress are internally regulated and supports an individual to quickly and effectively reduce, escape or avoid negative emotions or some aversive internal state	FND and distress are externally regulated via the environment. Once the FND has appeared, secondary environmental gains further maintain the symptoms
Type of regulation	Internal	External
Type of psychological process	Intra-individual	Inter-individual/systemic
Layer # in the PCM	Layer 3	Layer 5

factors in FND, is not positioned on a separate layer. In the following section, we will discuss the elements of each layer in more detail and describe the scientific evidence that supports their existence in the model.

Layer 1: Ignition

The Ignition element describes the factors and psychological history of key life events that set the stage and made a person vulnerable towards developing

Table 3.2 Five layers of the PCM

Layer #	Layer name	Elements
1	Ignition	Ignition
2	The FND coping triad	Cover, Valve, Sticky left-over food
3	The FND maintenance cycle ("Pressure Cooker Chain Reaction")	Fuel, Flames, Heat, Overpressure Plug
4	Facilitating physical factors	Pot, Warning light
5	Environmental and interpersonal factors of FND	Kitchen
–	Protective and positive prognostic factors in FND	Safety features

FND. Ludwig et al. (2018) reported an increased frequency of adverse life events in people with FND in comparison to people without FND, with a higher risk for emotional neglect. Vulnerability factors include the following:

- Adverse early childhood experiences including trauma, abuse and loss.
- Difficult upbringing, circumstances or maltreatment.
- Past significant relationships in adulthood that copy early adverse childhood events.
- Critical incident(s) closer in time to the onset of FND or that immediately precede the emergence of FND.

It is helpful to distinguish between "remote" events in early childhood or adulthood but long before the FND developed and more "recent" critical events that happened later in the person's life but were closer in time or happened immediately before the FND symptoms emerged. Clinically, people with FND often report cumulative exposure to remote and more recent adverse life experiences and interpersonal dynamics prior to the onset of FND, and some of these experiences may still be ongoing in the person's life (e.g. domestic violence, conflict). Table 3.3 displays these adverse experiences, abnormal relationship features and distorted relationship boundaries. It should be noted that a distinction between childhood vs adulthood relationships has not been made as this can be somewhat artificial for the following reasons:

- Although some of these features are reported in childhood relationships and do not necessarily apply to current relationships in adulthood, there is a correlation between adverse experiences in childhood and adulthood, as these experiences make a person vulnerable to experience similar events in adulthood, for example because of low self-esteem and problems with setting boundaries that result in a choice of partners that may inflict trauma in similar ways.
- People with FND may still have relationships in present times with the people that they had relationships with in past times, for example a

Table 3.3 Adverse life experiences and abnormal relationship features in FND

Adverse life experience	Experience or feature	References
Physical abuse and domestic violence	It has consistently been found that people with FND have been the victims of abuse, either in the remote past, recent past or on an ongoing basis. Physical abuse, assault and domestic violence are common in this group.	Lancman et al. (1993), Moore and Baker (1997), Bowman and Markand (1999), Wyllie et al. (1999), Tojek et al. (2000), Malhi and Singhi (2002), Bhatia and Sapra (2005), Thompson et al. (2005), Vincentiis et al. (2006), Thompson et al. (2009), McCormack et al. (2014), Ludwig et al. (2018), Fobian and Elliott (2019).
Sexual abuse	The most common form of abuse reported by people with FND is sexual abuse. Contact with the perpetrator of the abuse has also been noted in connection with the development of FND.	Leslie (1988), Lancman et al. (1993, 1994), Moore and Baker (1997), Bowman and Markand (1999), Wyllie et al. (1999), Tojek et al. (2000), Carton et al. (2003), Stone et al. (2004), Bhatia and Sapra (2005), Thompson et al. (2005, 2009), Vincentiis et al. (2006), McCormack et al. (2014), Ludwig et al. (2018), Fobian and Elliott (2019).
Emotional abuse	Emotional abuse has been less well researched in FND. Bowman and Markand (1999) conducted a comprehensive study and reported various emotional triggers for FND including the following: • Childhood parental rejection that came in several forms including hurtful verbal comments, • Stalking, issuing death threats and vicariously witnessing violence. • Criticism and excessive blaming have also been reported.	Maloney, (1980), Wood et al. (1998), Bowman and Markand (1999), Krawetz et al. (2001).

Interpersonal conflict	Another robust finding, across decades of research in FND, is the presence of interpersonal conflict, distress and communication difficulties in the remote and current environment of both children and adults with FND. Although these features may not reach the threshold of being viewed as abuse or violence, these difficulties have consistently been associated with the emergence and maintenance of FND, for example: • Marital discord • Relationship and family conflicts • Custody battles • Parental conflicts with children • Conflicts around family loyalties • Sibling rivalry • Mismatches between adult independence versus an enmeshed family of origin.	Maloney (1980), Wilkus et al. (1984), Leslie (1988), Lempert and Schmidt (1990), Lancman et al. (1993, 1994), Alper (1994), Speed (1996), Gooch et al. (1997), Moore and Baker (1997), Crimlisk et al. (1998), Bowman and Markand (1999), Wyllie et al. (1999), Tojek et al. (2000), Krawetz et al. (2001), Malhi and Singhi (2002), Carton et al. (2003), Bhatia and Sapra (2005), Vincentiis et al. (2006), Deka et al. (2007), Aamir et al. (2009).
Losses	Loss or a physical separation from a person or group of people, most notably in the form of: • Bereavement • Miscarriage • Divorce or separation • Childhood abandonment and separation from parents • Rejection by peers.	Maloney (1980), Gardner and Goldberg (1983), Leslie (1988), Lancman et al. (1993), Alper (1994), Moore and Baker (1997), Bowman and Markand, (1999), Wyllie et al. (1999), Tojek et al. (2000), Carton et al. (2003), Stone et al. (2004a, 2004b). Goldstein et al. (2020).
Threats of social rejection or loss	FND has been associated with the following life events or circumstances: • Academic pressure • Academic difficulties • Occupational stress • High school graduation • Alcohol abuse by a parent	Alper (1994), Bowman and Markand (1999), Wyllie et al. (1999), Malhi and Singhi (2002), Bhatia and Sapra (2005), Deka et al. (2007), Pick et al. (2019).

(Continued)

Table 3.3 (Continued)

Adverse life experience	Experience or feature	References
	These life circumstances may implicitly have a strong interpersonal component and are connected with the threat of social rejection or social loss. These social threats can involve losing a (positive) parental relationship, exclusion from a social or peer network, loss of rewards or respect.	
Underinvolvement	Relationships of people with FND may be characterised by little involvement or a nearly absent relationship: • Childhood parental emotional neglect is commonly reported in FND as is a lack of affection, attention or action • People with DS perceived reduced levels of care, emotional warmth, cohesion, commitment and support in their families, as well as reduced family interest in political, social and leisure activities • "Distancing" phenomenon, where people with FND experienced difficulties reaching family members.	Leslie (1988), Moore et al. (1994), Bowman and Markand (1999), Wyllie et al. (1999), Krawetz et al. (2001), Malhi and Singhi (2002), Stone et al. (2004a, 2004b), Bhatia and Sapra (2005), Ludwig et al. (2018).
Overinvolvement	A strong investment in the relationship has been noted in the following ways: • Parental overprotection • Presence of a controlling parental figure • Financial and emotional dependence on the family • Significantly higher level of control in the family of origin of people with DS compared to those with ES • Close family members, including partners, parents and children, were carers in a substantial number of people with FND.	Bowman and Markand (1999), Krawetz et al. (2001), Salmon et al. (2003), Bhatia and Sapra (2005), Goldstein et al. (2020).
Adverse physical events	The following physical life events and subsequent triggering of FND symptoms can be associated with threatening cognitions and experienced as highly aversive by people with FND: • Physical events affecting a person's livelihood or bodily integrity: physical injury, surgery, road traffic accidents, military trauma "shell shock" • Other body-related events: physical illness in a close relative, childbirth.	e.g. Parees et al. (2012), Nicholson et al. (2020).

person with FND may still be in contact with a historically emotionally neglectful parent.

- Some of these studies are on child populations with FND. Therefore, the child's childhood relationships are simultaneously their current relationships.

It should be noted that studies investigating past adverse childhood and adult life events in people with FND are limited by confounding variables that may impact on a person's report of these events including memory processes and the different nature of trauma memories; dissociation with people not reporting any events where in fact significant events did happen; and establishing a sufficiently safe relationship with the interviewer that allows disclosure of sensitive information (e.g. Ludwig et al., 2018).

Although many people experience adverse life events and do not acquire FND, and some people with FND do not report adverse life experiences, growing up in abusive family circumstances and parental emotional neglect tends to lower the threshold for subsequent development of FND through their impact on the characteristic maintaining factors of FND, including low self-esteem, depression, reduced verbal emotional expression and the development of dissociative tendencies early in life. Therefore, adverse life experiences on their own are not the full picture in FND; however, they do set the stage and create psychosocial vulnerabilities to develop FND later in life.

Layer 2: FND coping triad

Clinical observations reveal that the vast majority of people with FND, and oftentimes, also their partners and families as they tend to share a similar environment, display a classic triad of psychological characteristics that form the "FND coping triad". Figure 3.2 shows the three elements that make up the coping triad: Cover, Valve and Sticky left-over food.

The FND triad consists of a combination of three PCM elements (see Figure 3.3 for a more simplified diagram). These "pressure conditions" increase the risk of FND:

- Reduced verbal emotional expression and no recourse to regular expression in a psychologically safe and trusted relationship (tight Cover).
- Abnormal activity levels (blocked, dysregulated or an overused Valve).
- Both coping strategies often originate in childhood as early coping mechanisms characterised by the non-expression of emotions, either via keeping the emotions to oneself or cutting the emotions off by pushing on with activities, dissociation or somatisation, and are subsequently repeated into adulthood over many years (Sticky left-over food).

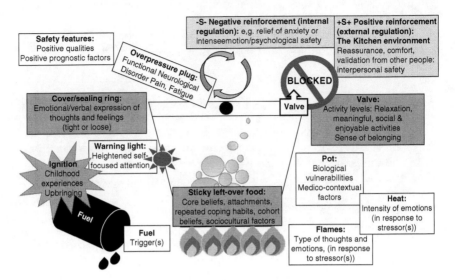

Figure 3.2 Pressure Cooker Model highlighting the FND coping triad.

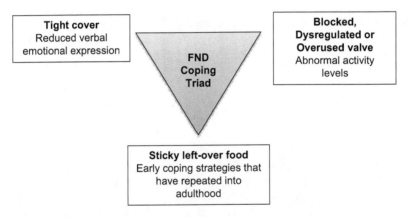

Figure 3.3 Simplified diagram of the FND coping triad.

Coping triad vs coping tetrad

One could argue that the FND coping triad is truly a coping tetrad. Instead of three elements, the tetrad consists of four elements, with dissociation as the fourth element. Dissociative tendencies originate in childhood as a form of coping with adverse circumstances and may culminate in the ultimate form of dissociation: FND. A visual representation of the FND coping tetrad is displayed below (Figure 3.4).

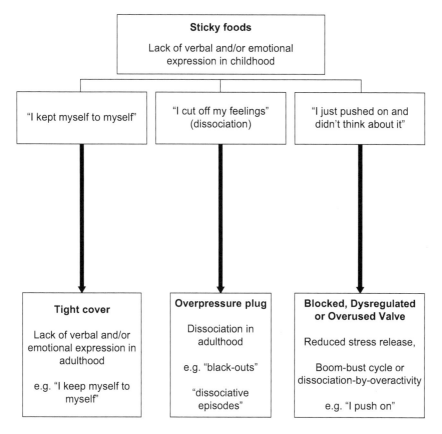

Figure 3.4 FND coping tetrad.

Although both figures could be used in clinical practice to explain the concept of repetition of early coping strategies into adulthood, we would recommend using the triad conceptualisation for several reasons:

• The coping triad is easy to lift out of the model and discuss with the person, as a side-step in therapy.
• The coping tetrad is harder to explain and may cause unnecessary confusion for the person. Dissociation is a complex phenomenon that permeates through all elements of the PCM including Sticky left-over food, Flames, Heat, and the Cover and Valve elements. One could argue that people experiencing a "boom" pattern of activity level (e.g. being constantly on the go without taking sufficient rest periods) is a form of dissociation from emotions. People spending a lot time on activities that absorb their attention (e.g. working, videogaming) means that their attention cannot go to experiencing emotions. In the same vein, people

with tight Covers verbally expressing that they don't feel emotions likely suggests dissociation. Explaining all this information particularly at the beginning of therapy can overwhelm a person with FND.

- The FND coping triad is therefore easier to process, remember and comprehend for people with FND who experience concentration and memory problems.

For these reasons, the book will focus on exploring the FND coping triad. It is up to the clinician and their view on the person's readiness, openness and processing capabilities whether a more complex conceptualisation of the person's coping mechanisms may be indicated. Both conceptualisations are not mutually exclusive, and it may be useful to explain the tetrad towards the end of therapy, as a way of enriching the formulation.

Cover

In the PCM, the Cover is interpersonal in nature and represents the extent and frequency at which a person expresses and verbalises negative thoughts and emotions to other individuals in their environment, in the context of a psychologically safe relationship. A tight Cover would describe an individual that never expresses or verbalises negative emotions, may always maintain a happy front and denies the existence of distress. Somatoform symptoms have been conceptualised as a non-verbal, bodily communication method of distress in an environment or family unit that does not allow verbal expression of emotions and that captures the individual's level of distress (Griffith et al., 1998; Krawetz et al., 2001). A lack or reduced emotional expression has been reported in people with FND (Wood et al., 1998; Bowman & Markand, 1999), as well as functional speech symptoms of a symbolic or adaptive nature that prevent an individual from verbal emotional expression including dysarthria, dysphagia, dysphonia, dysphasia and globus pharyngeus (Maloney, 1980; Moore & Baker, 1997; Crimlisk et al., 1998; Nielsen et al., 2017; Goldstein et al., 2021). Various reasons may exist for a tight Cover.

PERSONAL BELIEFS

Individuals with FND may display reduced emotional expression due to negative personal beliefs and fears around experiencing and expressing negative thoughts and emotions, a past violent history or religious beliefs (Bowman & Markand, 1999; Urbanek et al., 2014; Goldstein et al., 2021).

PERSONAL ABILITY

Alexithymia refers to a reduced ability to provide verbal descriptions of emotions and is commonly observed in people with FND (Demartini et al., 2014). Other reasons that may prevent an individual from verbalising emotions include reduced intellectual or linguistic abilities (Bowman & Markand, 1999) and poor verbal communication skills (Krawetz et al., 2001).

FAMILY SYSTEM

People with dissociative seizures may have been part of a "violent" family that prevented an individual's safe expression of anger (Bowman & Markand, 1999) or anticipate abuse and perceived threat from perpetrators if opening up (Krawetz et al., 2001). Furthermore, childhood family environments may have avoided or punished verbal emotional expression, or minimised the importance of a traumatic event and discouraged the victim to speak about it (Bowman & Markand, 1999; Krawetz et al., 2001). Griffith et al. (1998) described the "unspeakable dilemma" phenomenon in people with dissociative seizures, defined as an unescapable situation that causes a person distress, which cannot be expressed verbally, due to restrictions placed by the environment, which make the person feel trapped. The difficult situation may emerge on various systemic levels including family, social, religious or political. Since a tight Cover is common in people with FND and associated with characteristics shared by the systems that surround the person, for example a family unit, direct environment or culture, it is conceivable that these systems may carry a similar risk of reduced verbal expression.

SOCIETAL AND CULTURAL SYSTEMS

Bowman and Markand (1999) highlighted a possible difference between the genders, with men being more impacted by family and societal expectations that may drive the avoidance of emotional expression in men, particularly of sadness and anger. This played a larger role in men than in women with dissociative seizures. Malhi and Singhi (2002) mentioned that cultural factors may contribute to the maintenance of FND.

THE MIRRORED COVER

The Cover is one of the most important and powerful elements of the PCM. Opening a tight Cover (i.e. verbalising and expressing difficult emotions that were suppressed by the person for a long time) has often improved FND symptoms significantly in clinical practice. Tight Covers are often mirrored in the family system around the person with FND, often for historical reasons; for example, reduced verbal emotional expression may have been a longstanding family coping strategy that has been passed on through generations. Furthermore, a family member caring for the person with FND may not want to upset the person or worries about making the FND worse, and therefore keeps themselves to themselves. In addition, due to caring commitments, the caring family member may not have access to a channel that facilitates expression of their emotions.

Valve

In the PCM, the Valve represents abnormal activity levels. In clinical practice, one can distinguish three types of "valve profile": blocked ("bust-after-boom"), dysregulated ("boom-and-bust") and overused ("boom"). The Valve can be conceptualised as a Valve continuum that ranges from blocked to overused. Each of these Valve profiles will be discussed in turn.

BLOCKED VALVE: BUST-AFTER-BOOM

Blocked Valves are one of the most common activity profiles found in FND and describe a reduced or a complete lack of meaningful, social, enjoyable or relaxation activities in an individual's day-to-day life. Common consequences of FND symptoms are restrictions to activities of daily living including sports, leisure, employment and a loss of social contacts and limited social network that does not go beyond their immediate circle of family (e.g. Lempert & Schmidt, 1990). Patients may spend large amounts of time at home or in bed. This could occur for a variety of reasons including risk of accidental self-injury, physical disabilities, reduced access to the community, anxiety around participating in social situations (e.g. Carton et al., 2003), and the high rates of depression in this group, a condition that is strongly linked to a reduction in activities that provide enjoyment and a sense of achievement. Rates of unemployment or non-participation in education in people with FND were generally high: 42% (Lempert & Schmidt, 1990), 45% (Nielsen et al., 2017), 60% (Walczak et al., 1995), 62% (Moore & Baker, 1997), 66% (Goldstein et al., 2021), 76% (O'Connell et al., 2020), 78% (Bowman & Markand, 1999), 80% (Reuber, 2009), 85% (Petrochilos et al., 2020), 88% (McCormack et al., 2014), 89% (Crimlisk et al., 1998) and 95% (McDade & Brown, 1992). Not being able to work or study leads to a range of consequences. People were found to be socially isolated, lonely and withdrawn from social activities (Nielsen et al., 2020), features that could maintain or further compound an already existing depression in people with FND. Furthermore, substantial levels of welfare dependency have been reported, ranging from 37% (Moore & Baker, 1997) and 40% (Bowman & Markand, 1999) to high rates of 75% (Petrochilos et al., 2020) and 80% (Goldstein et al., 2021). Financial dependence on the family was observed (Krawetz et al., 2001), increasing the potential for further blurring of abnormal relationship boundaries. Employment was highlighted as an important positive prognostic factor for relief of dissociative seizure symptoms (Mayor et al., 2010). It should be noted that on a systemic level, high rates of socio-economic deprivation (51–86%) were described in people with dissociative seizures (Goldstein et al., 2021), as well as low social economic status in families (Deka et al., 2007) and reduced parental education levels (Malhi & Singhi, 2002).

Regardless of whether the reduced level of enjoyable activities pre-dated the FND, is a consequence of the FND, or both, a blocked Valve is a maintaining factor of persisting FND symptoms.

DYSREGULATED VALVE: BOOM-AND-BUST CYCLES IN FND

The Valve can also exhibit abnormal regulation of activity levels over a period of time. A dysregulated Valve refers to a "boom-and-bust cycle" pattern of activity levels, characterised by high peaks and low troughs of activities in daily life. This is different from an overused Valve ("boom" pattern without the "bust"). A typical patient with FND will describe a period of increased, prolonged or sustained high levels of activity, followed by a recovery period characterised by a significantly reduced or total lack of activity. Boom-bust cycles tend to be an inefficient strategy and non-productive for planning day-to-day activities and often contribute to being less active overall (compared to a more paced, even keeled and tolerable level of activity). In addition, a boom-bust pattern is often accompanied by worsened FND symptoms and changes in mood. Boom-bust cycles are frequently observed in clinical practice (Gardiner et al., 2018; Nicholson et al., 2020; Petrochilos et al., 2020).

OVERUSED VALVE: BOOM

People with FND can also be at the other end of the continuum and exhibit an overused valve. People with this valve type are characterised by continuous activity without many rest breaks ("always on the go" "keeping busy at all times") and that deviates from conventional definitions of normal activity levels. Although the research literature does not seem to have picked up on this profile, clinical practice is full of examples of people with FND who experience this pattern of activity level. Reasons that drive this overactive pattern may include dissociation and avoidance of emotions using activities and not being able to tolerate distress during periods of inactivity; strong negative beliefs and emotions about inactivity (e.g. guilt); perfectionist tendencies; low self-esteem and rules for living that drive increased activity levels ("if I work hard and do everything perfect, I can show other people that I'm good enough"); source of the only sense of achievement, accomplishment or emotional containment; difficulties with assertiveness and "saying no" to activities; reduced access to relaxation activities or skills; early coping habit stemming from childhood and family background that feels familiar and containing; and cultural or social background that values "hard work".

Over time, it is not uncommon for boom patterns to evolve into boom-and-bust patterns or eventually "bust" after the initial boom. A classic example is a person who, prior to developing FND, may have had a very active life with a previous overused Valve. They may not have had many stress-coping and relaxing activities to counter-balance the daily stresses; however, they managed to keep themselves going and fare well in life until the stresses started to mount up and the coping mechanisms that were managing the level of stress and were "holding the person together" in order for them to function on a daily basis became less efficient and effective and started to crumble (the "bust" after the "boom"). Another common scenario is a person with FND that was relatively busy with sufficient stress-coping strategies to manage the stress ("boom"). Following a "critical event" (a traumatic or adverse life event, such as a divorce, accident or surgery) or any other reason that blocks their access to their usual high levels of activity, the person's normal stress-coping strategies break down leaving the person stationary in a life that makes them house-bound. This may transform into a blocked Valve ("bust after the boom"), and the person may become very low in mood and experience psychological difficulties due to the reduced activity levels, which previously served as a safety behaviour against experiencing negative emotions.

SOCIAL ASPECTS OF THE VALVE

Since the Pressure Cooker Model emphasises the environment as a key player in FND symptoms, it is important to focus on the social elements of activities and creating a "sense of belonging" as part of treatment in FND. This is underscored by a study that highlighted social isolation, loneliness and withdrawal from social activities in patients with FND (Nielsen et al., 2020). In the clinic, patients often report a longing for more social connection and integration into communities and an important part of therapy is reconnecting the person with social activities. Employment was highlighted as an important positive prognostic factor for relief of DS symptoms (Mayor et al., 2010).

THE ENVIRONMENTAL VALVE

One should not only focus on the Valves of people with FND. In a similar vein, individuals around the person may have blocked, dysregulated or overused Valves. The rationale for discussing environmental valves is that everyone has an inner pressure cooker that contributes to FND. The Valve of a person with FND and that of the family or staff members may sustain the abnormal activity levels on both sides. Therefore, it is necessary to discuss the environmental valve as part of the wider formulation of the person who interacts with the patient with FND.

COMPLIMENTARY VALVES: BLOCKED VS OVERUSED VALVE

Having a close family member with FND and experiencing an abnormal Valve themselves may put this family member at risk of developing FND or other psychological issues, further compounding problems. A typical scenario may involve a person with FND who is house-bound without many activities (blocked Valve). The family member in the same household may be a full-time or part-time carer for this person with FND, may in addition also go to work on a daily basis, and spend some time on their own on a hobby, not only to release stress but potentially also to avoid the person with FND. In contrast to the person with FND who has a blocked Valve, this family member who is always active may experience the complete opposite, that is an overused Valve. Hence, the two types of Valves in the relationship may be complimentary and may become unsustainable in the long run.

MIRRORING VALVES: BLOCKED VS BLOCKED

The family member or healthcare professional caring for the person with FND may drop their own meaningful, social and enjoyable activities, due to significant carer burden, clinical time spend on the patient, fatigue and staying too late at work (if staff member), resulting in blocked Valves for both the person with FND and their environment.

Sticky left-over food

The final part of the FND coping triad, the Sticky left-over food, refers to childhood coping strategies, core beliefs and attachment style. These are rooted in early experiences, often shared by the family of origin, or have been used on a long-term basis within the current family structure. The exploration of these early coping mechanisms is important for understanding current coping styles as these have a high probability of repetition and reinforcement over many years or even decades into adulthood. People with FND often retrospectively report similar childhood and family-of-origin coping strategies (e.g. "I kept myself to myself", "I just pushed on", "we didn't talk about emotions") and repeat these into adulthood. Parental patterns of care and reinforcement processes of illness behaviour in childhood have been implicated in persisting somatic symptoms in adulthood (Benjamin & Eminson, 1992; Fobian & Elliott, 2019). Salmon et al. (2003) reported significantly less expression in the family of origin of people with dissociative seizures, in comparison to people with epileptic seizures. In previous sections, systemic reasons for a reduced or lack of verbal emotional expression were already discussed and included abuse, conflict, punishment and violence in the family environment. This coping strategy served an adaptive and survival function and protected a child from repercussions, retaliation, harm, invalidation and intense negative emotions inflicted by the environment. Wood et al. (1998) explain that the "privileging of somatic over emotional expression" is not a wilful phenomenon within family environments and appear to allude to a more intergenerational passing on of coping mechanisms from the family of origin of the parents, or as part of a process that evolved within the family unit itself. This strategy is adaptive in childhood as it is negatively reinforced by a reduction in distress and serves the rest of the family unit by avoiding negative emotions, as well as protecting the family unit from breaking down.

However, although somatisation may have been an adaptive childhood strategy for coping with family circumstances, it may lose its usefulness in adulthood (Aamir et al., 2009) and may be effective with small stressors, falling apart in the context of large stressors (Wood et al., 1998).

The three top parts of the Pressure Cooker Model (tight Cover; blocked, dysregulated or overused Valve; and Overpressure Plug) each have a counterpart early coping strategy that can be traced back to childhood. People with FND often report three classic childhood coping strategies. All coping strategies involve the non-expression of emotions.

KEEPING SELF TO SELF

People with FND who use this coping strategy often describe phrases such as keeping myself to myself, bottling up emotions or holding it all in. In childhood, this person often describes a lack of a psychologically safe relationship within the family unit or a family environment that would punish or invalidate emotional expression. People with FND who kept themselves to themselves as children tend to repeat this coping strategy and are at a high risk of presenting with a tight Cover in adulthood.

PUSHING ON

This coping strategy refers to ignoring or avoiding negative emotions by getting on with the activities as usual or planning in a lot of activities as a form of avoidance (e.g. sports, any activity that may help escape a difficult home environment). People with this early coping style often describe phrases along the lines of "I just did", "I just got on with the job and didn't think anything of it", "I had a little cry and then pushed on with it" and "I was a very active kid and was always doing sports and spending time outdoors". The "pushing on" coping strategy has a high chance of culminating into either an overused or dysregulated Valve in adulthood (respectively a "boom" or "boom-bust" pattern).

DISSOCIATION

Dissociation is a common occurrence in FND. People with FND who dissociated as children (and theoretically still dissociate in adulthood) often use phrases such as "blotting out emotions", "having a black screen" or "cutting myself off". Some people with FND may have engaged in deliberate self-harm in the past. The spectrum of dissociation is wide and may include subtle forms of dissociation with some people experiencing sleeping difficulties (e.g. sleeping a lot earlier than usual or making long sleeping hours, videogaming) to full-blown dissociative episodes (as well as, e.g., wandering, fugue states) as a complex form of dissociation at the extreme end of the spectrum. Both forms of dissociation may serve the function of cutting off emotions since sleeping or a dissociative episode quickly takes down an intense emotion.

Layer 3: The FND maintenance cycle or "The Pressure Cooker Chain Reaction"

The FND maintenance cycle should be viewed in the same way as a depression "vicious flower" (Moorey, 2010) or any of the maintenance cycles described in the numerous CBT models for anxiety disorders, for example panic (Clark, 1986) or social anxiety disorder (Clark & Wells, 1995). The FND maintenance cycle represents the person's internal regulation mechanism of emotions or an unpleasant state (Figure 3.5).

The FND maintenance cycle ties together four PCM elements and lies at the heart of the model: Fuel, Flames, Heat and Overpressure Plug. After a critical incident (Ignition) marks the onset of FND, a maintenance cycle emerges that perpetuates the FND. The "Fuel" refers to lower level daily triggers, interactions or stressful situations that regularly bring on the FND. The "Flames" under the pressure cooker pot represent negative (automatic) thoughts, emotions, memories or more poorly defined, aversive internal states that are common in FND and are set off by the trigger. This aversive internal state may be characterised by a high, intolerable level of emotional intensity and rapidly fluctuating emotion dysregulation (high Heat); or may be dissociated from and cut-off, with the person reporting a longstanding lack of experience of negative emotions that may pre-date the onset of FND (low Heat).

Helpful ways to manage these emotions can be found at the top of the pressure cooker and include verbal emotional expression (opening the person's tight Cover) and/or by stress release via activities (unblocking, reducing overuse or regulating the valve to release the "steam"). However, due to the

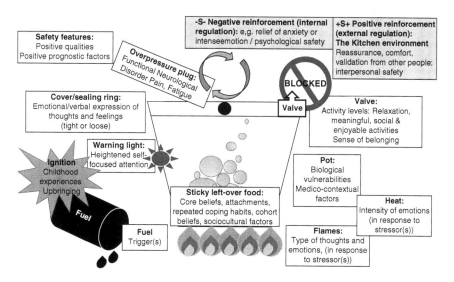

Figure 3.5 Pressure Cooker Model.

FND coping triad, the person has no recourse to these helpful coping habits. As the regular channels are blocked, the person is still left with the aversive internal state. Without these two outlets, the pressure of the emotions (or the aversive internal state) builds up inside the individual (the pot is close to exploding). In people with FND, these emotions find their way out via a third channel at the top of the pressure cooker: the Overpressure Plug, representing bodily FND symptoms, either taking the form of a paroxysmal event (i.e. dissociative episode) or a worsening of static motor-type FND symptoms (i.e. increased motor weakness).

The person quickly and effectively reduces or regulates the aversive internal state following a dissociative episode or worsened functional motor weakness, dystonia or tremor. The FND is a safety behaviour that helps to achieve an internal state of psychological safety (e.g. relief from aversive emotions or an unpleasant state of being; reduced arousal; tiredness that often equals a reduction or absence of aversive emotions). This process negatively reinforces the FND (Skinner, 1963).

In addition to representing the whole spectrum of FND symptoms, the Overpressure Plug also reflects symptoms that are associated "FND after-effects". These after-effects can emerge following a paroxysmal dissociative episode or in connection with worsening motor-type FND symptoms (e.g. dystonia) and include pain, muscle tension and fatigue (McKenzie et al., 2011; Fobian & Elliott, 2019; Nicholson et al., 2020; Petrochilos et al., 2020; Goldstein et al., 2021).

After repeated exposure to these stimulus–response pairings, the emotion–FND link strengthens over time (official notation: S (aversive internal state or distress) → R (FND) → -S- (reduction of distress)) and increases the likelihood of the FND response occurring in future leading to habit formation: the individual acquires the FND response as the main coping habit for distress. Eventually, after many stimulus–response pairings, the person may avoid feeling the distress altogether in response to the slightest sign of stimulus causing it. In the PCM, engaging the Overpressure Plug (OP) represents negative reinforcement (-S-).

It is important to note that the FND symptoms can only emerge in the presence of the FND Coping Triad: reduced verbal emotional expression (tight Cover) and abnormal activity levels (blocked, dysregulated or overused Valve). Layer 2 and Layer 3 should therefore always be interpreted together. The risk of engaging the Overpressure Plug increases when emotions are not expressed verbally and non-verbally in a psychologically safe relationship (tight Cover). This risk further increases when a reduction in meaningful activities is apparent, a boom–bust cycle is present or the person is overactive (blocked, dysregulated or overused Valve). That specific combination of these two risk factors creates the psychological conditions that constitute the highest risk for the FND response to emerge.

The Overpressure Plug can be re-conceptualised as a collection of unhelpful coping strategies, one of which is dissociation or FND, and therefore used in a more broad-based formulation. For people with FND, dissociation may be the primary coping strategy that impacts the most on the individual and the environment, whereas for the surrounding system this tends to take other non-dissociative forms (e.g. excessive caring, reassurance). It should be noted that experiencing FND does not preclude an individual from exhibiting other less-than-optimal coping behaviours (e.g. deliberate self-harm, risk to others) and the PCM is useful in formulating these as well. A comprehensive description of FND will be provided in Chapter 4.

The FND maintenance cycle: research evidence

Past research in FND has indeed identified an acutely or gradually unfolding build-up of an aversive state that coincides in time or is closely followed by an FND symptom. The FND helps the individual to quickly and effectively reduce, escape or avoid the aversive emotion or internal state (e.g. often anxiety, Alper, 1994; Moore et al., 1994; Moore & Baker, 1997; Goldstein & Mellers, 2006; Bautista et al., 2008; Brown & Reuber, 2016) and appears to be maintained by negative reinforcement of the FND (Skinner, 1963).

An inverse association between emotional expression and FND has previously been reported (Alsaadi & Marquez, 2005): better emotional expression improved outcomes in people with FND, whereas unfavourable outcomes emerged with people who were more inhibited regarding self-disclosure and emotional expression. Bowman and Markand (1999) report on a case with dissociative seizures who displayed a combination of a tight Cover (i.e. inability to verbalise anger) and a blocked Valve (i.e. lack of other channels for anger expression). The PCM predicts that improved verbal communication of emotions (opening the tight Cover) reduces the risk of having to resort to using an alternative channel of expression (i.e. the FND and engaging the Overpressure Plug). This was confirmed by a description of a case with dissociative seizures and anxiety in Bowman and Markand (1999) who had not revealed the anxiety in the family environment. Following emotional expression of the anxiety to the environment, the dissociative seizures stopped. Furthermore, Bowman and Markand (1999) describe that their interviews may have served a therapeutic purpose incidentally, as some people with dissociative seizures expressed emotions in relation to a remote trauma in a releasing way, followed by the cessation of dissociative seizures. Elsewhere, Moene et al. (2003) described that the process of expression of "pent up" or "dissociated" emotions could improve symptoms.

Pain has been reported in large number of people with FND (Maloney, 1980; Stone et al., 2010; McKenzie et al., 2011; Fobian & Elliott, 2019; Nicholson et al., 2020; Goldstein et al., 2021), with numbers as high as 94% (Petrochilos et al., 2020). Fatigue symptoms are other highly common symptoms in people with FND (Fobian & Elliott, 2019; Nicholson et al., 2020; Bennett et al., 2021), with fatigue reported in 82% (Stone et al., 2010) and 90% of people with FND (Petrochilos et al., 2020; Goldstein et al., 2021).

Fuel

The Fuel represents triggers that regularly set off FND episodes or worsen FND symptoms. The Fuel and Ignition elements can sometimes be difficult to distinguish from one another, since there is often not a sharp distinction between life events or circumstances that preceded the FND vs still trigger the FND, as was described earlier in the section on Ignition. For clinical and therapeutic purposes, it may be useful to make a distinction between Fuel and Ignition when formulating the FND with a person. Table 3.4 displays the key differences, warranting a distinction between the two in a psychological model of FND:

Although there are significant differences between the Fuel and Ignition elements, there are also commonalities between the two. Both elements trigger off FND. In addition, it is important to keep the social features in mind as both are often associated with interpersonal events that involve other people

Table 3.4 Differences between Ignition vs Fuel

Ignition	Fuel
Events that happened in the more remote past of our lives	Events that happen now and that *regularly* trigger or set off FND episodes (i.e. dissociative seizures) or worsen existing FND symptoms (motor-type FND).
Events happened before the onset of the FND	Events that take place after the FND has already developed – please note that these could be the same events as the events that happened prior to the FND.
Setting events, events that set up the conditions for FND to develop but do not necessarily keep the FND going	Maintaining events, or events that keep the FND going
Tend to be more severe in nature and intensity (e.g. longstanding abuse or conflict in the parental home)	Tends to be less severe in nature and in the moment (e.g. argument)
One big event can set off the FND (e.g. car accident)	Often smaller events set off the FND on a daily or regular basis
Can be a build-up of multiple events over time (e.g. parental rejection, bullied by peers)	Often one discrete event is sufficient to trigger the FND episode
Tend not be modifiable by therapy, for example early traumatic experiences cannot be changed – although your relationship with these events can be changed (e.g. core belief work)	Tend to be modifiable by therapy, for example by identifying daily triggers for FND and subsequently managing these.
Examples: abuse experiences, rejection by parents, bullied by peers, a car accident	Examples: thought, memory or emotion about an accident, low-level environmental stimulus reminding of event

or take place in a social dynamic or situation (e.g. arguments). Table 3.5 demonstrates the full range and wide variety of FND triggers that have been reported by people with FND in research studies or observed in clinical practice.

RELATIONSHIP BETWEEN FND TRIGGERS AND MASLOW'S HIERARCHY

One could view FND triggers as entities that may suggest the existence of unmet needs. Many of the triggers outlined in Table 3.5 can be closely mapped onto Abraham Maslow's hierarchy of needs (Maslow, 1943), as will be highlighted in the following section. Please note that, although only triggers for people with FND will be mapped, unmet needs in FND pertain to both the individual and the environment. A similar hierarchy of needs can be constructed and similarly applied to people surrounding the person with FND.

Esteem. The labels associated with this layer of Maslow's model (e.g. status, respect, recognition) strongly connect to internal beliefs and emotions associated with other people, and are often viewed through a psychosocial or socio-cultural lens, for example, people tend to receive recognition from others rather than actively ascribe recognition to themselves. Status is often seen in relation to other people's statuses.

The opposite of these labels, that is, perceived or real lack of respect, validation, not being believed or accepted, lack of status or recognition of FND as a genuine condition from the "healthcare world", can greatly affect or threaten a person's self-esteem, self-worth and self-identity. These interpersonal triggers can lead to unmet "esteem" needs (e.g. the need to feel believed or respected) causing distress and FND, which the person is not always aware of.

Love and belonging. The concepts on this level of Maslow's hierarchy refer to a sense of "psychological" or "interpersonal" safety in relation to other people in the individual's environment. This need is often reported as unmet in people with FND, for example, by a lack of social connection, belonging or a support network with friendships; social isolation; sense of abandonment, rejection or emotional distancing by other people or social groups including family, partners, healthcare professionals and school peers; as well as challenging dynamics in family settings or personal relationships are all very common occurrences and can act as triggers that directly maintain FND. For example, to meet the need of "love and belonging", FND may contribute to the immediate cessation of a difficult argument and/or elicit a caring response.

Safety needs. This layer represents "physical" and "psychological" safety needs that can be achieved by personal safety from threat or harm inflicted by other people, as well as good health, a job that enables the individual to sustain themselves and dependants, as well as sufficient access to resources.

Table 3.5 Types of triggers for FND symptoms

Trigger	Examples
No trigger	A subset of people with FND will not be able to identify triggers initially. As the person progresses in treatment, most triggers will be identified or reveal themselves over time.
Psychological "internal" triggers	Worries, anxiety or stress, and memories or images, sometimes as part of generalised anxiety disorder or PTSD.
Interpersonal triggers	Interpersonal triggers can be defined as triggers that involve other people and take place in a social dynamic or relationship situation. Bowman and Markand's (1999) results suggest that, at least one trigger for dissociative episodes was interpersonal in nature in the vast majority of their sample (91%).
	• Internal: unmet emotional need for validation, to be noticed, wanting to feel cared for emerges internally, but may not be met by people in the person's environment in that moment. Communication of distress to the environment.
	• External: argument, difficult conversation, witnessing perceived differential treatment of another person.
Multi-triggers	Different symptoms of FND (often dissociative episodes) are triggered by different triggers all within the same person, often a combination of physical and interpersonal triggers:
	• Anxiety of unpleasant state is internally regulated by the dissociative episode
	• External event (e.g. argument in the family home) ceases/is replaced by another external event (e.g. tending and caring response from family) following the dissociative episode.
Re-triggers	Interpersonal triggers that re-trigger an old feeling, memory or thought that was connected to past traumatic events but which tend to be outside our awareness, often in the context of systemic re-traumatisation (e.g. difficult conversation with a healthcare provider).
PTSD environmental triggers ("threat cues")	Low-level triggers in the environment, which were previously neutral and have taken on a threatening meaning since the traumatic event, trigger of the FND symptom (e.g. specific smell or reference to the trauma seen on television).
Bodily symptoms (e.g. as part of a panic attack)	Tingles, funny sensations, dizziness, physical arousal, cold sensations, heart palpitations, some type of prodrome that is misinterpreted "in a catastrophic way" or as described in the ICM or Bayesian formulations of FND, and lead to FND symptoms. Physical exercise, abrupt head movements and alcohol have been reported as triggers (Goldstein & Mellers, 2006; Stone, 2009; Stone & Carson, 2013; Jungilligens et al., 2020).
Physical triggers (not part of a panic attack)	Physical triggers (e.g. heat, noise, bright or flashing lights, sudden movements in objects around the person) found in the environment may provoke FND symptoms, for various reasons:
	• Sensory overload: the physical trigger reduces the threshold for overstimulation, and this unpleasant state elicits FND symptoms
	• Temporary escape and give a "break" from a chronic anxiety state
	• May be masked by an underlying interpersonal trigger.

Many triggers for FND relate to the safety needs outlined in Maslow's hierarchy including:

- Environmental cues (e.g. smells, sights), memories and flashbacks associated with a traumatic event in the context of PTSD-triggers can provoke distress that is managed with FND symptoms.
- FND symptoms may also worsen or become "re-triggered" by interactions with other people (commonly family members or healthcare professionals) due to a real or perceived threat cue that often operates on a more unconscious level and outside the person's awareness, re-triggering early childhood trauma and historic interactions (e.g. not being believed by a parent in the context of abuse).
- Psychological "internal" triggers (e.g. worries, anxiety and stress) may cause a sense of psychological unsafety or uncertainty.
- In that context, it is also important to mention that in rare (or perhaps underreported) occasions, people with FND have been the victims of coercive practices or abuse by a family member that maintained FND symptoms. In these instances, the FND may have different protective functions for the individual, including acting as a deterrent to harm or demands placed by another person, or protecting the individual's psychological well-being by helping to suppress memories about the difficult circumstances.

Other concepts on this level of Maslow's hierarchy are also highly relevant to FND triggers. A subset of people with FND experience panic attacks, health anxiety and a fear of contracting serious illnesses (e.g. heart attack, stroke or cancer). Bodily symptoms can be misinterpreted, leading to distress and FND episodes. Other health-related triggers that cause a feeling of unsafety can revolve around the lack of healthcare resources for FND and difficult relationships with healthcare professionals. Circumstances surrounding a person's employment, including difficult work dynamics or heavy burden placed without access to sufficient stress-coping resources, can act as FND triggers.

Physiological needs. More recently, attention has been drawn to the increased rate of FND symptoms in people who are forced to flee their country of origin to settle in a new country for various reasons including war (e.g. Benabdeljlil, 2022). One could argue that the often-stressful circumstances around finding new ways to meet basic physiological needs (e.g. food and shelter), as well as personal security needs, will understandably contribute to triggering FND. Furthermore, people with FND frequently report physical triggers found in the "physiological environment" (that are not necessarily part of a panic attack or the body, e.g. heat, noise, bright lights). Input from the physical world may cause sensory overloading and overstimulation that elicit FND symptoms particularly if the person experiences chronic anxiety.

Flames

In people with FND, triggers set off beliefs, emotions, memories or any internal states that are aversive in nature (represented by the Flames). These beliefs and emotions have typical characteristics in FND and can be subdivided into beliefs about self, other people, the world and the future.

BELIEFS AND EMOTIONS ABOUT SELF

In the PCM, a distinction is made between primary beliefs and emotions about the self (represented by the outer zone of the flame, as they are more visible, obvious and on the surface in psychological therapy) and interpersonal beliefs and emotions about the self in relation to other individuals (represented by the innermost zone of the flame, due to their hidden features). Primary emotions involve any of the basic emotions (Ekman, 1992), for example sadness, anger or anxiety, and their associated cognitions.

ILLNESS BELIEFS

Given the mind–body interactions that characterise FND, it is unsurprising that a group of commonly encountered beliefs that often lie on the surface in FND and can be a major source of anxiety and distress are thought contents associated with the body, physical symptoms and illness, as has been extensively accommodated in theoretical models of FND (e.g. Brown, 2006; Edwards et al., 2012a, 2012b, see Chapter 1). Increased self-focused attention and thinking biases in the context of bodily symptoms will be discussed in more detail in the section on the "Warning light" below. It may be useful to highlight a specific set of beliefs, termed "illness beliefs", that has often been investigated in people with FND, typically measured with the Illness Behaviour Questionnaire, which taps into a person's health concerns, acknowledgement of psychological features, and the level of denial of life stressors and "conviction" about the condition. Stone et al. (2004a, 2004b) reported that people with dissociative seizures were more likely to ascribe their symptoms to physical rather than psychological variables, as well as to deny life stresses that were not related to the topic of health and attribute problems to the seizures. In another study, people with functional weakness viewed their condition as less likely to be permanent and were more likely to believe in the "mystery" of their condition, in comparison to control participants (Stone et al., 2010). In addition, people with FND believed in the cyclical nature and the major impact of their condition on their lives and psychological well-being.

THE FND-MOOD LINK: CHICKEN OR EGG?

People with FND will also commonly develop secondary beliefs, mood and anxiety symptoms in response to their lived experience of FND symptoms

(FND → mood) and may have a tendency towards reporting these as their main psychological difficulties that in their perception emerged following the onset of FND and did not necessarily precede or are currently driving the FND (mood → FND), occasionally placing emphasis on the correct timeline of events (FND → mood, not mood → FND). In clinical practice, both directions will be important in formulating the maintaining factors of FND.

SELF-ESTEEM

Negative beliefs about the self ("low self-esteem") have frequently been reported and clinically observed in people with FND. Petrochilos et al. (2020) revealed low self-esteem in ~53% of their sample as measured by the Rosenberg self-esteem questionnaire (Rosenberg, 1965). Following treatment, 38% continued to identify with low self-esteem. Interestingly, ~20–25% of people reported high to very high self-esteem, suggesting that the presence of FND did not impinge on people's perception of their self-worth, potentially even enhancing self-esteem, which anecdotally has been reported by patients in therapy sessions. In clinical practice, people with FND generally will perceive themselves as less worthy than others or feeling inferior in some way in comparison with other people ("I don't matter", "I'm worthless"). They often apply harsh and perfectionist standards on themselves, and more realistic standards to other people. People with low self-esteem often experience difficulties with placing and guarding their personal boundaries in their relationships. They may struggle with assertiveness and expressing their needs, often prioritising other people's needs before their own needs. They often do not trust their own decision making and may seek validation in other individuals rather than in themselves. This makes people with FND vulnerable to exploitation, abuse and re-traumatisation by other people. An important clinical observation is that some people with FND and low self-esteem may be particularly sensitive to self-injury in the context of dissociative episodes; the border between what constitutes "accidental" versus "deliberate" may be blurry. Given these serious risks, identifying low self-esteem in people with FND is a crucial part of therapy.

INTERPERSONAL BELIEFS AND EMOTIONS ABOUT OTHER PEOPLE AND THE WORLD

Interpersonal beliefs   Interpersonal triggers are common in FND, as are interpersonal beliefs (i.e. beliefs about other people), which are prominently present, predominantly in the context of healthcare contacts, as well as arising within the family context. Examples of interpersonal beliefs frequently reported by people with FND include beliefs about not feeling believed; not feeling supported or cared for; feeling abandoned, rejected or neglected; not feeling validated, appreciated, treated with dignity, noticed or respected; not feeling heard. These beliefs often originate from past experiences and replicate prior beliefs about a parental key figure, in the context of trauma, abuse, emotional neglect or early abandonment experiences in childhood relationships. The important relevance of these healthcare experiences in the maintenance of FND will be discussed later in detail in Chapter 3.

Social emotions   Interpersonal beliefs are closely associated with the presence of interpersonal triggers and social (or self-conscious) emotions. Social emotions differ from basic emotions in that these are associated with the thoughts, emotions and actions of other people in relation to the person experiencing the social emotion, for example feelings of guilt, embarrassment, shame, jealousy or envy. Although social emotions are a very common occurrence in FND, surprisingly, there is a dearth of studies that have investigated their presence in FND. One recent study explored shame in people with psychogenic non-epileptic seizures (Reuber et al., 2021), with shame regarded as more aversive than guilt. Social emotions and associated beliefs are not always on the surface or readily reported by people with FND. In the PCM, social emotions are represented by the innermost zone of the flame, to symbolise their hidden presence. The psychological therapy process serves the function of raising awareness into and uncovering these deeper beliefs and emotions.

Social anxiety   Social anxiety disorder deserves special mention. Social anxiety cognitions involve the social fear of negative judgements and social rejection from other people and often result in self-conscious feelings, embarrassment and shame. Although social anxiety is not always identified and "flies under the radar", this condition is frequently encountered in clinical practice and associated with the full range of FND symptoms including dissociative seizures (to quickly escape a social situation even though this safety behaviour may attract more unwanted attention in the long run), functional cognitive symptoms ("attentional absences" as a safety behaviour to temporarily retreat or withdraw from an inescapable social situation), motor-type FND (preventing the ability to walk in social situations, or a powerchair serving as a safety behaviour to avoid eye contact and help the person quickly escape a social situation) and sensory-type FND (e.g. functional blindness and eye closure to escape a social situation). Social anxiety in FND can be successfully treated with the CBT model for social anxiety (Clark & Wells, 1995; see Chapter 8 for a case example).

Secondary emotions   It should also be noted that primary emotions can lead to the experience of secondary emotions in people with FND, that is feeling a second negative emotion in response to feeling the original negative emotion. Secondary emotions are often a social emotion such as shame, embarrassment or guilt, for example thinking of oneself as weak and feeling embarrassed about having felt or expressed anger, anxiety or sadness. Embarrassment about psychological difficulties (Carson et al., 2016), as well as negative beliefs about emotional expression (Goldstein et al., 2021), has previously been reported in FND.

Beliefs about the world   People with FND can experience beliefs and emotions that are associated with a sense of psychological or physical threat, and a lack of safety and security in the world. As discussed under the "FND Coping Triad", unspeakable dilemmas (Griffith et al., 1998) have been observed in clinical practice and are often associated with the person feeling trapped in a distressing, unescapable situation that is maintained by the "world" around the person, including family, social, religious or political systems, as well as the person's own appraisals and emotions around the cost and injury to their surrounding systems if the dilemma were to be released to the world. The therapeutic release of the unspeakable dilemma often resolves the FND symptoms.

BELIEFS AND EMOTIONS ABOUT THE FUTURE

A third category of beliefs and emotions often reported by people with FND concerns worries about the future. GAD has been observed in people with FND (e.g. Stone, 2009) and is characterised by persistent and high levels of worry about a variety of different worry topics, often in relation to future events. People with FND frequently experience the following worries about the future (Table 3.6):

Table 3.6 Four types of future worries commonly found in people with FND

Type of worry	Examples
Type 2 FND worries	• Secondary worries about the emergence of dissociative episodes or motor-type FND symptoms resulting in avoidance and restriction of social activities, which stop the person from testing out unhelpful beliefs and maintain the FND.
Fear of relapse	• Forecasting/fortune telling/catastrophising: following discharge from a service, predicting the worst-case scenario ("I'm going to relapse") and lack of confidence and self-efficacy in their ability to cope with life or a set-back.
Fear of recovery	• Worries about the social gains, losses and potential repercussions if the person recovers from FND, which can maintain FND if the balance is tilting towards more negative than positive consequences of recovery.
Fear of falling	• Fear around falling during standing or walking practice, or when stepping down to a lighter form of supportive equipment, which may halt treatment and maintains FND.

EMOTIONS IN FND: CONTENT VS PROCESS

Table 3.7 shows the process features of the beliefs and emotions observed in people with FND. The distinction between content vs process is highly important in FND; the interpretation of thought and emotion *content* without considering *process*, and vice versa, will likely not fully capture the intricacies of the psychological formulation of FND symptoms.

Heat

Heat refers to the intensity of emotions and can be viewed as controlled by a dial on the pressure cooker. People with FND generally experience one of three dial settings. Heat is different from the Flames element, which reflects the contents of emotions (e.g. type of beliefs and emotions), whereas Heat refers to the intensity level of emotions.

LOW SETTING

Dissociation is represented by a low setting in the PCM. Dissociation is a psychological process characterised by a fragmentation between emotion, cognition, memories, awareness, self-identity, language and behaviours and actions, and that may be experienced as a sense of disconnection by the individual (e.g. Carson et al., 2012, for another definition of dissociation). Dissociation in itself is not invariably a pathological phenomenon and occurs in the general population (e.g. daydreaming). FND can be viewed as a complex form of dissociation that lies on the more extreme end of a continuum (i.e. "dissociative seizures"). Dissociation could be viewed as unhelpful when it impacts on a person's day-to-day, social and occupational functioning. Complex forms of dissociation (e.g. FND, dissociative identity, fugue states, wandering episodes) are often triggered by highly stressful or traumatic events that elicit strong and intense emotions but that are deemed intolerable to the individual, on a conscious and more unconscious level of awareness. In response, the dissociating individual cuts off the emotions to not experience the emotion or carry on with normal daily activities. Dissociation can originate in childhood as a protective measure to cope with challenging family circumstances and repeated into adulthood where it may lose its adaptive function over time due to its impact on the person's daily life.

HIGH-LOW-HIGH-LOW SETTING

Emotion dysregulation is another setting on the Heat element of the PCM. A subset of people with dissociative seizures have been found to experience emotion dysregulation (Uliaszek et al., 2012; Brown et al., 2013; Williams et al., 2018) characterised by rapid emotional fluctuations that oscillate between feeling strong, intense emotions and emotional numbness or emptiness;

Table 3.7 Emotion processes in FND

Process	Examples
Alexithymia and other specific emotion characteristics in FND	• Difficulties with identifying, recognising, and labelling emotions. Not being able to provide verbal descriptions of emotions. • A restricted range of emotions with a subset of people reporting exclusively positive emotions whilst denying the existence of negative emotions or stress, sometimes over a lifetime. • Description of emotions using physical features, for example feeling tired or lacking in energy for depression or low mood. • Description of undefined or poorly defined internal states that feel uncomfortable or unpleasant and are often accompanied by heightened physical arousal (e.g. feeling confused, overwhelmed) and do not easily fit into existing CBT models of common psychological problems such as panic disorder, social anxiety disorder, generalised anxiety disorder or depression. • Demonstrating clear outward symptoms of a psychological condition (e.g. safety behaviours and physical effects of anxiety emerge in social situations, likely suggesting social anxiety); however, due to alexithymia or dissociation, the person is not able to describe, "get in touch" or identify with the underlying emotion rendering the use of standard CBT models problematic.
Emotion mix/ inconsistencies in FND	• People may also report a mixture of different emotions all at the same time ("feeling overwhelmed") but are not able to pinpoint the emotions in the maelstrom. • Emotion labels may be mixed up and mislabelled due to similar physical signatures, for example mixing up anxiety with anger. • The emotion is not consistent or congruent with the thoughts, for example labelling emotion as anger but reporting worries rather than hostile thoughts that indicate anger. • "La belle indifference": emotions may not appear consistent with the life situation, for example coming across as happy and smiling despite high levels of disability.
Heterogeneity and variability of beliefs and emotions	• It is important to keep in mind that, clinically, there is a wide variety of psychological conditions associated with FND including health anxiety, social anxiety, panic disorder, PTSD, generalised anxiety, depression, personality disorder, and obsessions and compulsions (e.g. Binzer et al., 1997; Stone, 2009; Carson et al., 2016; Macchi et al., 2021). • Specific psychological difficulties are not necessarily linked to specific FND symptoms; for example, social anxiety has been observed in all "subtypes" of FND.

difficulties labelling and identifying emotions; struggling to settle down following a stressful event; and problems with controlling and coping with emotions on a day-to-day basis often affecting relationships and family dynamics.

HIGH-TO-LOW SETTING

The final setting on the Heat element is characterised by an initial steep or gradually unfolding rise in an aversive emotion, arousal or an undefined internal state that reaches a peak and is subsequently followed by decrease, often culminating in a dissociative episode or worsened FND symptom. The characteristic rise and fall in this internal state is often associated with dissociative seizures and has been widely documented (e.g. Alper, 1994; Moore et al., 1994; Moore & Baker, 1997; Goldstein & Mellers, 2006; Bautista et al., 2008; Brown & Reuber, 2016).

Systemic heat

It should be noted that the concept of Heat is equally applicable to the emotions experienced by people in the system surrounding the person with FND, especially family members and healthcare professionals. As the person with FND experiences an increase in FND symptoms, strong emotions or emotional dysregulation, so does the system around the person often 'surf the same emotion waves' and 'co-dysregulates' with the person experiencing the FND. This form of 'systemic heat' is an integral part of the reciprocal reinforcement process that is a core maintaining factor of FND (explored in more detail in later sections of this chapter).

Layer 4: Facilitating physical factors

Physical symptoms play a central role in FND. Figure 3.6 shows the two supporting elements that make up Layer 4 of the PCM: Pot and Warning light.

Pot

"Mind-body" interactions and physical variables play a central role in FND. Biological vulnerabilities and medical-contextual factors strongly associated with FND are therefore embodied by the Pot element of the PCM. Examples include co-existing medical conditions (epilepsy), sleep difficulties, physical deconditioning, overmedication, healthcare utilisation and equipment overuse (Stone, 2009; Nielsen et al., 2015; Gardiner et al., 2018). Although these medical-contextual factors make up a broad and diverse category, these variables can greatly impact on the psychological formulation, progress, treatment and recovery in people with FND, thus warranting their inclusion in the PCM. Physical variables commonly encountered in FND can be helpfully summarised under the easy-to-remember FND SELF CARE acronym, which consists of the 11 physical and medico-contextual features of the Pot that are important in FND. Table 3.8 details the scientific evidence for adding all the features in

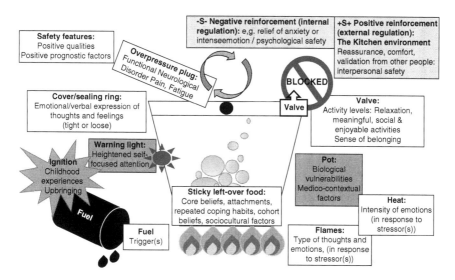

Figure 3.6 Pressure Cooker Model highlighting the facilitating physical factors in FND.

the acronym, as well as additional observations made in clinical practice, but which may not have necessarily been published in literature and are nevertheless important mediating factors in FND. Please note that the FND SELF CARE acronym for the environment will be discussed in Chapter 7.

Warning light

The Warning light refers to the well-documented phenomenon of heightened self-focused attention on bodily symptoms, which constitutes one of the major maintaining factors of FND (Brown, 2006; Van Poppelen et al., 2011; Edwards et al., 2012a, 2012b; Nielsen et al., 2015). People with FND often allocate large amounts of self-focused attention to their body and tend to favour physical, pharmacological and medical explanations and treatments over psychological approaches. In addition to increased self-focused attention, other attentional "abnormalities" have been reported in studies that demonstrated attentional biases to angry facial expressions (Bakvis et al., 2009a, 2009b) and facial emotional expressions in general (Pick et al., 2018) on the pictorial emotional Stroop tasks in people with dissociative seizures. Interestingly, Marotta et al. (2020) found an attentional bias shifted away from sad faces on a dot-probe task in motor-type FND. Other studies reported difficulties with disengagement from emotion categorisations of face stimuli on an attentional task (Gul & Ahmad, 2014), as well as impaired performance on an emotional go/no-go task, which correlated with anxiety, depression and alexithymia measures in people with dissociative seizures (Jungilligens et al., 2020). More recently, Keynejad et al. (2020) reported an attentional

Table 3.8 Evidence for the FND SELF CARE acronym

Letter	Element	Research and clinical findings supporting inclusion in the PCM
F	Food Fuel	**Research findings** • Irritable bowel syndrome is common (Bennett et al., 2021; Stephen et al., 2021). • People with FND report gastro-intestinal symptoms including constipation, irritable bowel syndrome and bladder problems (25%, Crimlisk et al., 1998; 49%, Stone et al., 2010; 30%, Nielsen et al., 2017; Fobian & Elliott, 2019; 55%, Goldstein et al., 2020). Another study reported constipation, loose bowels and diarrhoea in 70% of patients, as well as nausea, gas and indigestion in 66%, and stomach pain in 62% (Petrochilos et al., 2020). • Gastroparesis occurred in ~10% of people with functional dystonia, with patients occasionally needing a gastrostomy tube (Stephen et al., 2021). • Dysphagia was reported in 21% of FND studies in a review (Barnett et al., 2019), also reported by Gilmour et al. (2020) and globus sensation. **Clinical observations** Research on the gut-brain axis has demonstrated a link between the digestive/enteric nervous system and the central nervous system. Many people with FND report gastro-intestinal difficulties, which could play a potential role in FND as part of "gut-brain axis dysfunction" and further compound psychological difficulties. • Co-existing gastro-intestinal difficulties are commonly reported by people with FND, particularly "somatoform" symptoms affecting the gut (IBS); food intolerances and allergies that can pre-date the FND or be perceived as a trigger for FND episodes; constipation; acid reflux requiring medications; faecal incontinence; issues with weight; occasionally gastroparesis. • People with FND may have been on antibiotic medications that negatively impact on healthy gut flora. • Vitamin deficiencies are common including vitamin D, B12 and folate, which further impact on bodily symptoms, brain functioning, thinking skills, psychological functioning and energy levels. It is useful to investigate reversible causes of neuropsychiatric/FND symptoms. • People with FND may be on "polypharmacy" and make poor dietary choices that underlie GI difficulties.

Letter	Element	Research and clinical findings supporting inclusion in the PCM
		• A subset of people with FND will struggle with poor diets and overweight issues that will impact on cardiovascular fitness, pain and other musculoskeletal issues. This may be due to a lack of knowledge on what constitutes a healthy diet, a conscious lifestyle choice or the secondary effects of psychological difficulties (e.g. depression). People may experience weight loss as part of an eating disorder though this is rare.
N	Night rest	**Research findings**
		• Sleeping difficulties were reported in various studies: 62% (Nielsen et al., 2017); 75% (Stone et al., 2010); 80% (Goldstein et al., 2020); and 82% (Petrochilos et al., 2020). Others described sleep disturbance in the majority of people with FND (Bennett et al., 2021).
		Clinical observations
		• Problems with sleep are very common in FND and affect all stages of the sleep cycle, for example falling asleep, maintaining sleep overnight, intermittent sleep, early morning waking and long sleeping episodes (which may be a form of dissociation).
		• A myriad of reasons exist for disrupted sleep-wake cycles in FND including effects of medications; poor sleep hygiene and napping in the day that dysregulates night-time sleep; PTSD-related flashbacks and nightmares, worries, stress or anxiety; depression and its impact on the sleep cycle; sleep as a coping strategy to avoid difficult thoughts, feelings or memories; ingestion of high amounts of caffeinated drinks or alcohol; and sleep and tiredness as "FND after-effects" following a dissociative episode, which prevents a person from feeling difficult emotions and the reinforcing effects this has on FND.
		Sleep conditions are also observed, particularly sleep apnoea requiring a CPAP machine.
D	Drugs and medications	**Research findings**
		• Overmedication is common in people with FND (Bennett et al., 2021) often due to various providers prescribing medications. A reduction in redundant medications is viewed as an important goal (Petrochilos et al., 2020).
		• One study reported that ~57% of people with functional dystonia were frequently prescribed medications such as opiates, opioids and benzodiazepines (Stephen et al., 2021).

(Continued)

Table 3.8 (Continued)

Letter	Element	Research and clinical findings supporting inclusion in the PCM
		Clinical observations • People with FND are often on a long list of medications. These medications can accumulate over years for various reasons including frequent visits to a variety of medical professionals with sparse communication and without an appropriate review by one central person. • "Polypharmacy" and overmedication can be highly problematic since some medications (e.g. opiates) facilitate existing dissociative tendencies and worsen FND symptoms. • Unfavourable interactions between medications can emerge that cancel out or reduce each other's effects or result in harmful side effects. • Occasionally, people use anti-anxiety or sleep medications to quickly stop the underlying anxiety or unpleasant state that drives a dissociative episode or take a sleep tablet to fall asleep as an avoidance strategy and not sit with distress. • There can be problems with substance misuse, for example alcohol or mind-altering drugs. This may be part of a spectrum of dissociative coping mechanisms. In addition, people may accidentally overdose or take an extra dosage that is not prescribed that may lead to adverse effects. • At times, side effects may cause worse symptoms (e.g. analgesia overuse headaches) near the time that the medication dose is due, which can be misinterpreted as a symptom of FND.
S	Sickness and physical illness	People with FND are not exempt from experiencing "organic" illnesses. It is important to note that having (had) personal experience of an organic condition can be a risk factor for developing FND. Furthermore, organic illnesses may be mismanaged (e.g. not adhering to thyroid medications) and cause psychological difficulties (e.g. anxiety or depression), which in turn contribute to FND. **Research findings** • People with FND present with physical symptoms as part of their FND presentation and conditions that are unrelated but may co-occur with the FND. Goldstein et al. (2020) reported that approximately 70% of people with DS self-reported a current co-existing medical problem.

Letter	Element	Research and clinical findings supporting inclusion in the PCM
		• Several 'clusters' of physical conditions can co-exist with FND including spinal problems, joint hypermobility and Ehlers-Danlos syndrome (Bennett et al., 2021).
		• Functional overlay between non-epileptic and epileptic seizures occurs in a subset of people with FND (e.g. D'Alessio et al., 2006; Baroni et al., 2016).
		• Postural Orthostatic Tachycardia Syndrome (POTS) co-existed in approximately 7% of the sample of functional dystonia patients (Stephen et al., 2021).

Clinical observations

- All the abovementioned co-morbid physical conditions have often been observed in people with FND and are subjected to similar "heightened self-focused attention" mechanisms. In this context, it is useful to note that people with Ehlers-Danlos syndrome are sometimes advised to 'pay attention' to their joints which is exactly one of the maintaining factors of FND.
- Occasionally, patients may report a history of somatoform symptoms preceding or concurrent with the FND, as well as a history or past surgeries for musculo-skeletal and spinal problems; medical investigations preceding the onset of FND especially of the abdomen and genitourinary areas (e.g. cystoscopy); and hospitalisations.
- People with FND may experience an exacerbation of their symptoms when contracting flu or colds (and possibly COVID-19 or long-COVID). It is therefore important to avoid and treat the symptoms of these respiratory viruses in order to prevent a negative impact on FND.

Letter	Element	
E	Equipment	**Research findings**

- People with FND often rely or "over rely" on equipment, aids and adaptations, which is generally viewed as unhelpful (e.g. Gardiner et al., 2017; Nicholson et al., 2020) as it could impact on recovery and movement patterns, as well as "secondary" issues such as pain and deconditioning (Nicholson et al., 2020).

(Continued)

Table 3.8 (Continued)

Letter	Element	Research and clinical findings supporting inclusion in the PCM
		Clinical observations
		• People with FND often possess a variety of equipment for support with mobility, personal care, activities in daily living and accessing the community. Occasionally, patients experience severe disabilities, which necessitates the use of "heavy-duty" equipment such as power chairs, tilt-in-space wheelchairs and hoists. Long-term entrenchment and hard-to-reverse home adaptations are common.
		• Psychological factors play a large role in the use of equipment even though this is not always recognised by the person with FND. Equipment can serve as a psychological safety behaviour, become a fixed part of a person's identity, increase confidence and serve social functions.
		• A person with FND may temporarily experience a symptom-free phase, yet the equipment may still be in the home, "just in case", and this increases the risk of it being used when the slightest symptoms re-emerge. Reducing equipment may occasionally cause high anxiety that stops the process of stepping down.
L	Liquids and bladder functioning	**Research findings**
		• Chronic urinary retention has been associated with psychological difficulties and FND symptoms (e.g. leg weakness, loss of consciousness; Panicker et al., 2020; Bennett et al., 2021).
		• Functional urinary symptoms can emerge in FND (28% in Stone et al., 2010; 31% in Nielsen et al., 2017; Gilmour et al., 2020) who mention Fowler's syndrome, a form of urinary retention that has frequently been associated with FND (Hoeritzauer et al., 2016; Gilmour et al., 2020).
		Clinical observations
		• People with FND commonly present with urinary incontinence and occasionally use "invasive" management techniques such as self-catheterisation procedures.
		• Due to the prominence of dissociative or motor-type FND symptoms, issues with continence can be overlooked.
		• Dehydration and in more rare cases, overhydration and excessive fluid intake, has been observed. Dehydration may provide an additional hypothesis for "brain fog".
		• High intake of caffeine and energy drinks can contribute to FND as they may cause palpitations, anxiety and panic symptoms.

Letter	Element	Research and clinical findings supporting inclusion in the PCM
F	Fight-or-flight and Warning signs	**Research findings** • Hypothalamic-pituitary-adrenal axis dysfunction may be a neurobiological marker in FND (e.g. Bakvis et al., 2010; Keynejad et al., 2019). • Bakvis et al. (2010) described increased "basal diurnal cortisol levels" in people with psychogenic non-epileptic seizures particularly in those who reported sexual trauma. • Patients with FND self-reported high levels of biological features that could equally be consistent with anxiety and panic attacks including a racing heart (68%), nausea (66%), dizziness (65%), shortness of breath (63%), chest pain (45%) and fainting spells (44%; Petrochilos et al., 2020). • Discovering prodromes and warning symptoms are deemed essential (e.g. Stone, 2009). **Clinical observations** • People with FND often describe emotions using their somatic characteristics ("I feel tired" for low mood) and often mention physical features or bodily arousal as warning signs of an impending dissociative episode or worsening FND symptom. • The description of physical features of emotions is often in stark contrast with their reduced phenomenological and psychological experience of emotions. People with FND may present with alexithymia, dissociation or denial of distress. • People may experience the full range of the biological signs of depression (e.g. problems with sleeping, appetite, pain, fatigue, apathy) but not making connections with depression. • In a similar vein, a person may accurately describe all the biological features of anxiety (e.g. palpitations, dizziness, nausea, needing to go to the toilet) but not identify this as anxiety.
C	Contacts	**Research findings** • Various reports describe substantial levels of economic burden and healthcare utilisation in patients with FND including in relation to Accidents and Emergency Department (A&E) visits and revisits, hospital admissions, for example on acute stroke and rehabilitation wards, ambulance calls, outpatient or GP home visits and usage of medical diagnostic procedures (e.g. MRI scans, EEGs; see, e.g., Razvi et al., 2012; Nunez-Wallace et al., 2015; Merkler et al., 2016; Stone et al., 2020). One study reported a fivefold increase in average total charges per admission in patients with psychogenic non-epileptic seizures (over 20 years, Ladha et al., 2017).

(Continued)

Table 3.8 (Continued)

Letter	Element	Research and clinical findings supporting inclusion in the PCM
		Clinical observations
		• Increased healthcare "utilisation" has been observed in people with FND. The term utilisation is unhelpful and implies that the cause of these behaviours lies entirely with the person with FND. Despite the negative connotations associated with this term, it remains a fact that people with FND are observed to be frequently in touch with healthcare services including ambulance calls and frequently attending the accidents and emergencies department every time a dissociative seizure emerges.
		• Importantly, healthcare contacts are a source of re-traumatising experiences that impact on the maintenance of FND as will be discussed later in this Chapter under Layer 5".
A	Ability to take care of yourself	**Research findings**
		• People with FND can experience wide-ranging disabilities that impact on their activities in daily living, for example personal care (e.g. washing, dressing, grooming), meal preparation, household chores, employment, caring for dependants and accessing the community to participate in meaningful activities and shopping (e.g. Gardiner et al., 2018; Nicholson et al., 2020).
		• Due to their disabilities, people with FND may experience a sufficiently high level of care needs that necessitates the instalment of a care package for assistance with activities of daily living (e.g. Nicholson et al., 2020).
		• Vroegop et al. (2013) reported that, after correcting for age and gender, people with FND were found to be as disabled as people with neurological conditions. The study also revealed worse health-related quality of life in people with FND than in people with neurological conditions on several Short Form-36 scales including role limitations due to physical problems, social functioning, pain, mental health and "vitality".
		Clinical observations
		• Level of disability and care needs can vary widely between patients and may range from independence to supervision and requiring assistance of one or two people to support personal and domestic activities of daily living.
		• Some patients are cared for by partners and family members, whilst others require a comprehensive care package, with some bed-bound for longer periods of time.

Letter	Element	Research and clinical findings supporting inclusion in the PCM
		• Care activities in personal and family relationships may become enmeshed with blurred boundaries.
R	Risks	**Research/clinical findings**
		• Surprisingly, risks are scarcely described in the research literature on FND, apart from overmedication and equipment overuse. Falls were reported in one-third of a sample with motor-type FND (Nielsen et al., 2017). Chapter 4 will provide a detailed and comprehensive description of risks in FND and will therefore not be repeated in this section.
E	Exercise, movement and physical activity	**Research findings**
		• FND symptoms can greatly impact on mobility, transfers, balance and physical activity (e.g. Nielsen et al., 2017) and result in deconditioning (Nicholson et al., 2020). • Several physiotherapy treatment programmes for motor-type FND reported positive outcomes (Nielsen et al., 2015, 2017; Kim et al., 2021).
		Clinical findings
		• People with FND, in particular the motor variant, may be mobilising in a wheelchair and may have spent long periods without normal movement of their limbs. This often leads to physical deconditioning and wasting of the muscles. The deconditioning can become a problem when a patient with FND does well in psychological therapy (e.g. demonstrates improved emotional expression) but due to the deconditioning remains in the wheelchair and heavily dependent on the environment.
		• Difficulties with mobilisation and physical activity can greatly affect the person's ability to care for themselves, other activities in daily life and access to the community. Problems with movement often cause "secondary" issues, for example social isolation, depression, altered family roles and relationships, and entrenchment and long-term equipment use.
		• Exercise intolerance, muscle deconditioning and reduced level of cardiovascular fitness often drive secondary mood problems.
		• Paying attention to movement is also important for people with dissociative episodes who experience tense muscles or may hurt themselves during the episodes, resulting in a restricted range of movement, or whose presentation may change over time to the motor type of FND.

bias towards somatic interpretations and reduced attentional control in people with FND although these effects were not specific to FND and additionally affected people with chronic fatigue syndrome. Taken together, these research findings suggest that attention, and its association with emotion, is a central concept in FND that is difficult to ignore, thus warranting its inclusion into the PCM.

Layer 5: The social functions of FND ("The Kitchen")

At the end of the '70s, Bruce K. Alexander conducted a series of seminal studies on the impact of the social environment on the development of addiction in rats (e.g. Alexander et al., 1978; Hadaway et al., 1979; Gage & Sumnall, 2019). In his historic experiment, Alexander put two sets of rats in two different cages. One cage comprised an impoverished, socially isolated environment, whilst the other cage was an enriched social environment (a "rat heaven") with lots of socially stimulating activities for the rats and plenty of opportunity to socially connect with other rats. The rats in the impoverished and isolated cage consumed the highest amount of morphine, whereas the rats in the enriched cage were less likely to ingest morphine. These results suggested an important role of the environment in maintaining addiction.

If a social environment has had the dramatic level of impact on a physical process such as morphine addiction in rats, the question arises whether the social environment has the same or an even stronger impact on physical symptoms in "humans" with FND?

Results from the Rat Park experiment heavily challenge existing biological notions on conditions that are thought to traditionally rely on mostly physical processes. These findings do not necessarily suggest that clinicians and researchers should drop biology altogether but instead invite the community to consider a more broad perspective on what was always thought to be a biologically mediated process. Current research in FND has been increasingly slanted towards medical and biological approaches to FND (e.g. Perez et al., 2017, 2021; Keynejad et al., 2019). Although social factors have been implicated in various theoretical models of FND (Edwards et al., 2012a, 2012b), have we sufficiently paid attention in clinical practice to the importance of the environment in the emergence and maintenance of FND? Resource, funding and time limitations aside, the social aspects of FND have largely been neglected or mostly treated as an afterthought in clinical practice.

Layer 3 of the PCM explored the internal regulation function of FND. In this view, FND helps an individual to achieve a state of internal psychological safety. Layer 5 is the final layer of the PCM and consists of the Kitchen element. This element represents the external regulation function of FND and explores the environmental, social and interpersonal maintaining factors of FND.

People with FND do not exist in a social vacuum but have relationships with other individuals from many different social layers (e.g. Asadi-Pooya et al., 2021). A person with FND ("The Pressure Cooker") is encased by a multi-layered social environment ("The Kitchen"). The person with FND has relationships and interactions with the individuals from these systems, which themselves carry their own pressure cookers. The PCM assumes a dynamic interplay between the person with FND and their environment (e.g. Krawetz et al., 2001) and postulates that FND, in part, is a product of emotion dysregulation between the person and the environment that serves to achieve a state of interpersonal psychological safety for each other.

Although originally developed in child psychology, these social layers can be conceptualised by applying Bronfenbrenner's ecological system model (1979a, 1979b) to FND (Table 3.9).

Research on the social aspect of the biopsychosocial perspective in FND has identified a key role for social, environmental and interpersonal variables

Table 3.9 Bronfenbrenner's model applied to FND

System	People and institutions	Applied to FND
The individual		The person with FND
Microsystem	Immediate environment that directly impacts on the person: partners, siblings, parents, children, other extended family, friends, neighbours, health services, religious community, school and workplace	Unhelpful family dynamics or work stresses that may trigger FND, frequent healthcare contacts in the NHS, social isolation and reduced social networks, unemployment, reduced sense of social belonging in a community.
Mesosystem	Interactions within the microsystem	Examples: Referrals between healthcare professionals, communications between family and healthcare professionals involved in the person's care.
Exosystem	Legal system, social care, welfare services, government, mass media, political system	CCGs, care package arranged by social services/local authority, department of work and pensions, benefits system, social media blogs on FND, impact of healthcare funding on FND services.
Macrosystem	Cultural attitudes, norms and values of the culture	Stigma on psychological problems and asking for psychological support, negative attitudes of healthcare towards FND.
Chronosystem	Sociohistorical conditions over time Personal transitions over a lifetime	Loss or divorce in the family home that created a vulnerability to developing FND. Changed and more positive attitudes towards FND, in the context of increased awareness on FND in recent times.

in the emergence and maintenance of FND, for example, in relation to the generation of illness beliefs, health scares in the media and seizure models (Brown, 2006; Edwards et al., 2012a, 2012b; Brown & Reuber, 2016). The next section will provide a series of compelling reasons, derived from the scientific literature, that support a social approach to FND focused on the assessment and treatment of the whole system and not just the person with FND.

The presence of complex trauma ("personality disorder") in FND

People with personality disorder experience interpersonal difficulties with other individuals around them, problematic relationship dynamics, and may respond unhelpfully with intense emotions to interpersonal triggers from the environment. The important role for environmental factors in FND is evidenced by the significant number of people with FND who also carry a diagnosis of personality disorder, particularly with borderline and dependent traits (Stone et al., 2004a, 2004b; Goldstein et al., 2021) or may present with personality traits that do not reach threshold for a full-blown personality disorder diagnosis yet may be prominently present and contribute to marked social and interpersonal difficulties in people with FND (Binzer et al., 1997; Binzer & Kullgren, 1998; Crimlisk et al., 1998; Stone et al., 2004a, 2004b; Pick et al., 2016; Goldstein et al., 2021).

Existence of interpersonal triggers for DS

Anecdotal information from clinical practice often reveals a physical injury, surgery or accident may precipitate the onset of FND (e.g. Parees et al., 2012). At times, both patients and healthcare practitioners quickly and automatically assume that these physical events must have set off the FND. A common interpretation for this link is a "cognitive" ICM or Bayesian-style hypothesis (Brown, 2006; Edwards et al., 2012a, 2012b), for example along the lines of a misinterpretation of sensory input, perhaps due to an activated memory representation or abnormal belief about a personal experience of a physical illness, which then leads to misattribution of FND to the physical illness resulting in an experience of real symptoms. Although this cognitive interpretation is not challenged, clinical practice often reveals contextual and relational factors that have the potential to elicit negative emotions that simultaneously happened around the time of the physical event. People with FND occasionally focus more on the negative way that a healthcare professional may have related to them following an accident or surgery, or the manner in which a patient was treated by staff following a hospital admission, rather than the event or physical injury itself. In addition, interpersonal difficulties in the patient's life at the time of the physical event may play a role. Exclusively homing in on these physical events and the cognitive sequelae that trigger FND without taking into account other more interpersonal and emotional factors may miss the mark in treatment and not fully address the FND.

Interpersonal triggers can be defined as triggers related to other individuals and relationships, and that bring on FND symptoms. The relevance of interpersonal triggers for FND was demonstrated in a study that found interpersonal triggers for dissociative seizures in 91% of participants (Bowman & Markand, 1999).

The undeniable role of family factors in the emergence, maintenance and treatment of FND

A need has been identified to shift the emphasis to the individual with FND within the family environment (Moore et al., 1994) rather than solely focusing on the individual. In line with this notion, many authors suggest the involvement of family members, close relatives and the staff team in the treatment of FND (Maloney, 1980; Ramani & Gumnit, 1982; Leslie, 1988; Betts, 1990; Alper, 1994; Moore et al., 1994; Krawetz et al., 2001).

Authors have provided specific recommendations for the assessment and treatment strategies for the family unit of the person with FND. Figure 3.7 has organised these recommendations around some of the elements of the "Family Pressure Cooker". This figure highlights the importance of family factors in the maintenance of FND.

The consequences of minimal environmental input for outcomes in FND

Interestingly, studies have also shown that focusing the treatment entirely on the individual, with minimal environmental input, may potentially contribute to negative or less-than-optimal long-term recovery rates, at least for people with dissociative seizures. For example, a large study on dissociative seizures by Betts and Boden (1992) showed that at discharge, 63% of the participants achieved complete and 24% achieved partial resolution of their dissociative seizure symptoms, with both of these percentages dropping to 31% and 14% respectively at two-year follow-up. This constituted a substantial 50% relapse rate. In addition, of the 13% of people that did not experience any changes or worsening of symptoms, 34% were worse at follow-up. The authors identified a return to untreated dysfunctional family environments as potentially one of the root causes of dissociative seizures (Betts & Boden, 1992) and described practical problems with carrying out family therapy with most participants, which may have explained the poor long-term outcomes. Another longitudinal study reported favourable but acceptable outcomes at best. Petrochilos et al. (2020) recently published a study on the outcomes of a five-week outpatient multidisciplinary programme for adults with FND. This programme was mostly focused on treating the individual, with a one-off group education session for family and carers that discussed "unhelpful reinforcement of symptomatic movement patterns", "overprotective behaviours"

Kitchen
- Systemic involvement should aim to establish and maintain supportive family relationships (Aamir, Jahangir & Farooq, 2009)
- **Consistency.** Adopt a consistent approach of care from the treating team towards the person with FND and towards supporting the family to support the person (Ramani & Gumnit, 1982)
- **Discharge planning.** Involve family and staff in discharge planning (Ramani & Gumnit, 1982) or invite families and outside agencies to participate in the programme (McDade & Brown, 1992).
- **Continuity of care.** Follow-up meetings with the person with FND and their family (Maloney, 1980), supporting the consolidation of treatment gains following discharge by providing long-term after care and offering the person with FND and their family assistance following discharge via telephone check-ins to maintain therapeutic gains (Ramani & Gumnit, 1982).

Cover	**Sticky left-over food**
<ul><li>Conducting family interviews as a forum that helps facilitate the expression of psychological difficulties in the entire system (Leslie et al., 1988).</li><li>Provide education and interventions that focus on verbal communication skills, conflict resolution and role definition (Krawetz et al., 2001)</li><li>Be aware of an "unspeakable dilemma" within the family unit that maintains the FND (Griffiths et al., 1998).</li></ul> **Family Pressure Cooker of FND**	Review of emotional coping strategies within the family (Bowman & Markand, 1999)

Flames/Heat
Identification of negative responses and stress within the family unit (Maloney, 1980; Ramani & Gumnit, 1982)

Ignition/Fuel
- Systemic involvement should explore the reasons for DS (Moore et al., 1994) and enquiring about a person's system and "contextual contributors" (e.g. marriage, parenting, employment and finances; Bowman & Markand, 1999)
- A focus on early intervention and early involvement of the system in the treatment (Ramani & Gumnit, 1982), to avoid the "behavioural pattern" of dissociative episodes becoming entrenched in life.

Figure 3.7 Elements of the family pressure cooker.

and altered family roles at the very end of their programme. Petrochilos et al. (2020) reported positive outcomes in slightly over 40% of people with FND that were sustained but plateaued over a six-month follow-up period (outcomes showing "much" and "very much" change in 43.6% of participants). This means that more than 50% of the sample showed less than favourable outcomes at discharge and follow-up.

The question arises whether outcomes for people with FND could have been augmented had the environment been actively treated since the start of the programme and during the follow-up period after discharge. This notion is reinforced by the results of an older study by Ramani and Gumnit (1982), which reported the absence of dissociative episodes in 88% of participants after a four-year long follow-up period. It is important to note that in this study the participants were regularly supported with psychological intervention sessions (around 63% of participants) and neurology reviews.

Interestingly, three studies with motor-type FND patients (Speed, 1996; Gooch et al., 1997; McCormack et al., 2014) seemed to generate stronger outcomes than the studies with a dissociative seizure or mixed FND group. One explanation may be the fixed vs paroxysmal nature of the FND symptoms treated, with perhaps motor-type FND more amenable to treatment. However, the intensity and nature of the treatment offered in these studies was characterised by a multidisciplinary inpatient programme based on "environmental" behavioural modification principles. Inpatient rehabilitation environments are often characterised by the presence of a limited number of patients who receive the highest level of daily therapeutic input from multiple disciplines ("low volume, high cost") including psychology, psychiatry, nursing, occupational therapy, physiotherapy, social services, and occasionally, speech and language therapy.

In a multidisciplinary inpatient behavioural modification programme for adults with motor-type FND symptoms that affected gait, Speed (1996) found a significant pre-to-post intervention improvement in ambulation scores of all n = 10 patients. Nine patients were followed up, with one patient followed up monthly by psychology for a year, and two other patients referred onwards for psychological support. Although the difference between pre-intervention vs follow-up ambulation scores was not significant, seven out of nine (78%) of the followed-up participants maintained total independence with ambulation, whereas n = 2 patients experienced a relapse and used a wheelchair. Another inpatient multidisciplinary behavioural modification study involved eight children with motor-type FND predominantly with symptoms of pain, weakness and gait disorder. On completion of the programme, results showed that all children achieved a normal gait and independence in activities of daily living (Gooch et al., 1997). All children and their families were supported with stress and pain management strategies, and the authors identified this treatment aspect as "key" to maintaining gains over time. A more recent study investigated a multidisciplinary inpatient programme for people with severe motor-type FND that used positive reinforcement across all interventions (McCormack et al., 2014). Results revealed significant increases between admission and discharge scores in mobility, activities of daily life and degree of disability and dependence. Good outcomes were found in 73% of participants for mobility, 88% for activities of daily life and 72.7% for degree of disability and dependence. Follow-up data was not available for some of these studies; it is therefore unclear whether treatment gains were retained over time, as anecdotal observations have revealed cases of significant relapse following successful inpatient treatment. In spite of this uncertainty, the results from all of these studies show that a more intensive environmental approach, as well as the presence of systemic support particularly in the follow-up period of an intervention, appears to make a difference to positive outcomes in people with FND. From a clinical perspective, it seems sensible to assume that years of adversity and deeply ingrained emotion regulation and behavioural patterns that often originated in childhood require sufficient treatment intensity and longevity to undo and replace with more helpful strategies.

The important role of behaviourism in FND

Historically, behaviourism has played an important role in formulations and interventions for FND. According to Fobian and Elliott (2019), operant conditioning processes may account for the existence of non-paroxysmal symptoms (e.g. paralysis, anaesthesia) in FND, for example through receiving family support. The most commonly reported behavioural modification approaches are based on the principles of operant conditioning (e.g. Betts, 1990). One example goal of behaviour modification is to attain extinction of the conditioned dissociative seizure response to a "secondary gain" by breaking the link between illness behaviour (i.e. dissociative seizure) and environmental reinforcement (e.g. attention/validation; Alper, 1994). By removing a positive consequence (e.g. attention/validation), the frequency of the unwanted behaviour (dissociative seizure) is decreased. The literature commonly reports on differential reinforcement approaches where the undesirable behaviour is extinguished by discontinuing the reinforcement or providing negative punishment of the unwanted behaviour (e.g. withdrawal of attention/validation) whilst solely reinforcing the desirable behaviour (e.g. verbal praise). Since the removal of a longstanding coping strategy may leave an individual vulnerable, without access to their regular coping strategies, several authors rightfully recognised the need for replacing an unhelpful response that is extinguished (e.g. dissociative seizures) by alternative, more adaptive responses, for example "simple behavioural coping techniques" (Ramani & Gumnit, 1982) and strategies for coping with stress, pain, distraction and imagery (Gooch et al., 1997). The next section will describe the contents of behavioural modification programmes previously used in FND including "antecedents", "behaviours" that are reinforced or punished in these treatment programmes, and commonly used reinforcers and punishers ("consequences").

BEHAVIOURAL INTERVENTION: ANTECEDENTS

Antecedents can be defined as stimuli, situations, events or circumstances prior to the behaviour. In FND, one can conceptualise antecedents as an unmet psychological need of the individual. FND may meet this unmet or emotional need (Alper, 1994; Krawetz et al., 2001; Fobian & Elliott, 2019).

The FND (i.e. behaviour) may therefore support the individual with satisfying this need and acquire a pleasant consequence. Receiving care, comfort, nurture, attention or concern from the environment as a result of FND (Betts & Boden, 1992; Alper, 1994; Moore et al., 1994; Krawetz et al., 2001; Bautista et al., 2008; Fobian & Elliott, 2019) that would otherwise be absent (Moore & Baker, 1997) may satisfy the basic human need of validation and wanting to feel cared for (antecedent). Other examples include obtaining personal control over one's life, individuals and circumstances (Moore et al., 1994) in response to feeling a lack of control (antecedent) or the FND providing a new identity or become part of an individual's identity (Fobian & Elliott, 2019; Klinke et al., 2021) in response to a negative sense of self and low self-esteem. Somewhat controversial, authors have suggested that FND may provide external incentives (Alper, 1994; Moore & Baker, 1997; Fobian & Elliott, 2019).

The FND may also help an individual to avoid, escape, distract attention away or provide relief from aversive antecedent stimuli in the environment including responsibilities, role demands, discipline, conflict, underlying crises in the family unit, high expectations and abandonment by significant others (Betts & Boden, 1992; Alper, 1994; Moore et al., 1994; Moore & Baker, 1997; Krawetz et al., 2001; Aamir et al., 2009; Fobian & Elliott, 2019).

BEHAVIOURAL INTERVENTION: BEHAVIOURS

Table 3.10 lists several behaviours that have been targeted in behavioural modification programmes for people with FND.

BEHAVIOURAL INTERVENTION: CONSEQUENCES

Positive reinforcement

Reinforcement of desired behaviours in people with FND has included the following:

- Verbal praise, positive attention and encouragement (Betts, 1990; Betts & Boden, 1992; Speed, 1996; Gooch et al., 1997). One study used a "dose-response" strategy; the longer the individual was free of DS episodes, the higher the frequency of verbal rewards applied (Betts & Boden, 1992)
- Social warmth" (McDade & Brown, 1992)
- Rewards (Betts, 1990)
- Privileges (Gooch et al., 1997)
- Family/friend visits and phone calls (Gooch et al., 1997)
- A token economy (Alper, 1994)
- Providing "generalised positive reinforcement" across multiple interventions and disciplines (Speed, 1996; McCormack et al., 2014)

Table 3.10 Variety of behaviours subjected to behavioural modification in FND

Positive reinforcement of "desired" behaviours	Negative punishment of "undesired" behaviours
Engagement and progress	**Engagement and progress**
• Making gains and reaching goals (Gooch et al., 1997) • Learning efforts of families (Gooch et al., 1997)	• Engaging in sick role behaviour (Malhi & Singhi, 2002)
Reinforcement of an alternative more adaptive response:	**Punishment of undesired responses:**
• Normal ambulation and successful task completion in physiotherapy (Speed, 1996) • Normal function within the context of functional activities in occupational therapy (e.g. standing during meal preparation; Speed, 1996) • Demonstrating age-appropriate skills (Gooch et al., 1997) • Coping and "healthy behaviour" (Malhi & Singhi, 2002)	• Demonstration of abnormal movement or gait (Speed, 1996) • Expression of pain and weakness, as well as "regressive behaviour and communication" (Gooch et al., 1997)
Positive reinforcement of the absence of the DS:	**Negative punishment of the presence of DS:**
• Time periods that are free from DS episodes (Betts, 1990; Betts & Boden, 1992; Alper, 1994)	• Dissociative episodes (Ramani & Gumnit, 1982; Betts, 1990; Betts & Boden, 1992; Alper, 1994) • Only responding to the FND symptoms to prevent self-injury (Alper, 1994)

Negative punishment

Negative punishers of undesired behaviours have included ceasing the reinforcement of the DS or motor FND symptoms (Ramani & Gumnit, 1982; Betts, 1990; Alper, 1994; Speed, 1996) by:

- Ignoring, withdrawing or withholding attention (Betts, 1990; Betts & Boden, 1992; Speed, 1996; Gooch et al., 1997; Malhi & Singhi, 2002), both by staff and fellow patients (Betts & Boden, 1992).
- Milder forms of ignoring involved staff adopting a "business-like" yet polite manner with minimal attention (McDade & Brown, 1992).
- Structuring a person's milieu (Alper, 1994) and only responding to the DS to prevent self-injury (Alper, 1994).

MODELLING

Modelling is the psychological process of learning behaviours on the basis of observing a model in the environment (Bandura et al., 1961; Bandura &

Walters, 1977). The observed behaviour will result either in reinforcement or punishment from other individuals. If the model's behaviours are followed by reinforcing consequences and observed by the observer, then the likelihood and frequency of these behaviours increase in the observer, a process called vicarious reinforcement.

Bandura's social learning theory appears also highly relevant in FND. Table 3.11 shows that a subset of people with FND have been exposed to "symptom models", either through personal or vicarious exposure to illness, a job in healthcare or media health scares (Alper, 1994; Bowman & Markand, 1999; McCormack et al., 2014; Fobian & Elliott, 2019). In FND, the individual may serve as its own model based on personal history or experience of illness (e.g. epilepsy), which provides an explanation for the comorbidity between DS and ES (Alper, 1994) and is an important risk factor for DS in children and adolescents (Vincentiis et al., 2006). Modelling can also emerge following close contact and observation of other individuals. These personal and vicarious experiences afford learning opportunities for the observation of primary and secondary gains (e.g. receiving comfort, care and attention) and can facilitate the development of dissociative seizures (Lancman et al., 1993; Bautista et al., 2008). Frequencies of symptom models in the environment of people with FND range widely from 28% to 66% (Leslie, 1988; Lancman et al., 1994; Moore & Baker, 1997; Malhi & Singhi, 2002; Bhatia & Sapra, 2005; Deka et al., 2007; Bautista et al., 2008).

It is important to understand the social function of modelling in the context of early childhood experiences. The need for comfort, care, attention and validation is part of the normal human experience. Due to the higher rate of childhood adverse experiences, people with FND often not had access

Table 3.11 Models mentioned in the FND literature

Type of model	References
Family member or friend with neurological, physical or psychological symptoms	Leslie (1988), Lancman et al. (1993, 1994), Gooch et al. (1997), Moore and Baker (1997), Malhi and Singhi (2002), Bhatia and Sapra (2005), Fobian and Elliott (2019)
Another individual with seizures	Bhatia and Sapra (2005), Malhi and Singhi (2002), Bautista et al. (2008), Fobian and Elliott (2019), O'Connell et al. (2020)
Deceased loved one	Maloney (1980)
Ill or dying family member that is cared for	Bowman and Markand (1999)
Exposure to models during multiple hospitalisations	Lancman et al. (1994)
Exposure to models in a (para) medical job role	Crimlisk et al. (1998), Green et al. (2004), McCormack et al. (2014), Fobian and Elliott (2019)
Exposure to neurological disorder in the media	Fobian and Elliott (2019)

to opportunities to develop and practise adaptive coping strategies in order to meet that need, for example using verbal emotional expression. As a result, modelling may be an alternative but equally effective way to meet this basic human need. Modelling provides a different perspective on a phenomenon that is commonly viewed as "attention seeking" or "manipulative" behaviour.

Presence of abnormal features in family and healthcare relationships

Various studies have identified a range of abnormal features in past and current family relationships of people with FND in the context of adverse life experiences that all have the potential to cause significant psychological harm. People with FND often report a history of emotional neglect, parental rejection, interpersonal conflict and communication difficulties, excessive criticism, abuse and trauma, enmeshment, underinvolvement, losses of a relationship or threats to losses, deaths, divorce or some type of separation (e.g. Alper, 1994; Moore & Baker, 1997; Wood et al., 1998; Bowman & Markand, 1999; Krawetz et al., 2001; Stone et al., 2004a, 2004b). For a list of these abnormal features in family relationships, please see the Ignition section and Table 3.3 for more details.

In psychological therapy, people with FND routinely report past and current negative experiences with other healthcare providers. The next section will explore these relationships between people with FND and their healthcare professionals.

MIRRORING PHENOMENON IN FND: ABNORMAL FEATURES IN HEALTHCARE RELATIONSHIPS

People with FND frequently interact with the healthcare system, "permeate" through the full range of health services and therefore will make many, as well as regular, healthcare contacts. Although all systems impinge on a person with FND, the healthcare system that is part of Bronfenbrenner's microsystem is particularly important in FND.

Since the impact of the social environment is core to FND, and the healthcare context is a crucial part of this social reality for people with FND, the question arises what the quality of relationships is between people with FND and their healthcare providers. A large body of research has focused on describing the experiences of people with FND and healthcare staff working with people with FND; however, this has been done in studies that explored the groups separately and have not yet considered a relationship between these two sets of experiences.

HORIZONTAL MIRRORING: PEOPLE WITH FND VS HEALTHCARE PROFESSIONALS

Table 3.12 reveals the existence of six "mirrors" between people with FND and healthcare workers who are compared side by side ("horizontal"). The mirrors represent recurrent themes and responses that are common between people with FND and healthcare workers. The FND mirrors demonstrate the psychological similarities, rather than the differences, between the groups.

Table 3.12 reveals that the negative beliefs and emotions of people with FND are often mirrored and confirmed by the negative responses from the healthcare system. These psychological phenomena contribute to the dysfunctional nature of the relationships between the person with FND and the healthcare system. Given that these phenomena emerge in the healthcare context, it is not unthinkable that these beliefs, emotions and responses, in a similar vein, are detectable in the family system surrounding the person with FND.

Maladaptive person-system cycles in FND: an emotion regulation problem

The notion of a bi-directional relationship between the individual with FND and the environment predicts a reciprocal response from the multi-layered environment towards the individual with FND. These reciprocal responses, emanating from the environment, equally serve a function, in the same vein as FND symptoms. Negative beliefs and emotions driving unhelpful behaviours and responses of the person with FND and the environment may result in harmful person-system interactions and cycles. A particular problem in FND concerns the emergence of dysregulated person-system cycles that maintain distress and contribute to FND. In these cycles, the person and the system co-regulate each other's emotions in a dysfunctional manner. In this view, FND is, at least in part, conceptualised as the product of an emotion regulation problem between the person and the system. FND is therefore maintained by both internal and external emotion regulation mechanisms. For example, witnessing symptoms in the person with FND may cause intolerable discomfort in observers in the environment (e.g. parents and clinicians; Malhi & Singhi, 2002) who, via reciprocal conditioning processes, resort to measures that quickly, effectively and simultaneously reduce their own personal distress and that of the person with FND in the short term but likely unwittingly maintain FND in the long term (e.g. by providing reassurance each time the FND symptoms emerge or worsen, the FND is reinforced and prolonged).

The literature on FND provides some evidence for these dysregulated person-system cycles.

Wood et al. (1998) described another dysregulated person-system cycle where the distress of an individual with FND leads to increased anger, criticism and a hostile response from the family, which further increases distress in the person with FND (and potentially worsens or increases FND symptoms, leading to more anger and hostility). Another cycle pertains to healthcare professionals feeling uncertain and confused about FND (Fobian & Elliott, 2019), which results in the person with FND being passed on between different disciplines (Barnett et al., 2022). Although this avoidance behaviour

Table 3.12 Six FND mirrors between people with FND and healthcare workers

Mirror theme	People with FND	Healthcare workers
Horizontal mirror #1: Patient-staff relationship	People with FND have worries about their relationships with physicians (Wilkus et al., 1984).	Healthcare staff have worries about rupturing the therapeutic relationship, losing patient trust, arguments and offending the person with FND (Adams et al., 2018; Lehn et al., 2019; Barnett et al., 2020).
Horizontal mirror #2: Negative judgements	People with FND overwhelmingly reported worries about negative judgements and invalidation by the environment including being viewed as "crazy" and "seeking attention" (Green et al., 2004; Thompson et al., 2005; Nielsen et al., 2020; O'Connell et al., 2020).	These worries appeared to reflect the views of healthcare staff working with FND who expressed a range of negative judgements using stigmatising and pejorative language about people with FND including referring to this group as "seeking attention", being manipulative, difficult to treat, beyond help, wasting time and resources (Alper, 1994; Harden & Ferrando, 2001; Shneker & Elliott, 2008; Ahern et al., 2009; McMillan et al., 2014).
Horizontal mirror #3: Believing FND symptoms	A common belief held by people with FND related to not feeling believed by healthcare staff (as well as family, friends and society) and worries around the environment believing that the person is "faking" (Ahern et al., 2009; Thompson et al., 2009; Nicholson et al., 2020; Nielsen et al., 2020).	This was mirrored in the healthcare group in one study, with staff reporting worries about the person with FND not believing them (Lehn et al., 2019). However, the majority of studies reported staff to believe that the symptoms of people with FND are fake or not real (Ahern et al., 2009; Sahaya et al., 2012; McMillan et al., 2014), partially or fully feigned (Kanaan et al., 2009, 2011; Edwards et al., 2012a, 2012b), with staff expressing disbelief at the symptoms (Alper, 1994).
Horizontal mirror #4: Lack of support	People with FND perceive a lack of support from healthcare professionals (Nielsen et al., 2020).	The literature reports on unsupportive approaches adopted by healthcare staff towards people with FND: • Poor healthcare (Shneker & Elliott, 2008; Ahern et al., 2009; McMillan et al., 2014; Nielsen et al., 2020).

Mirror theme	People with FND	Healthcare workers
		• Favouring a rushed over a careful approach (Betts, 1990) and treating people with FND in a hostile or rude manner (Ramani & Gumnit, 1982; Green et al., 2004). • Healthcare professionals experience similar beliefs around receiving poor support from their own healthcare colleagues.
Horizontal mirror #5: Rejection and abandonment	A range of studies report that people with FND feel abandoned, dumped or rejected by healthcare professionals (Harden & Ferrando, 2001; Green et al., 2004; Reuber, 2009; Fobian & Elliott, 2019; Nielsen et al., 2020).	This appears to reflect reality in the healthcare field; studies have described: • Abandonment, "dumping" and onward referrals of people with FND to other healthcare professionals (Harden & Ferrando, 2001; Edwards et al., 2012a 2012b; Barnett et al., 2022). • People with FND experience rejection on several levels including avoidance, ignoring and ridiculing by staff (McMillan et al., 2014; Lehn et al., 2019). • Staff believing that people with FND are undeserving of the same care as people with organic conditions (McMillan et al., 2014), therefore singling out and rejecting the person.
Horizontal mirror #6: Negative emotions	People with FND report the following emotions.	Healthcare professionals report the following emotions too.
• Distress, fear and anxiety-related emotions	People with FND report distress and anxiety (Thompson et al., 2009; Nielsen et al., 2020; O'Connell et al., 2020).	Anxiety-related emotions are often reported in the healthcare population including fear, concerns prior to a consultation and worries about making the person with FND worse (Betts, 1990; Monzoni et al., 2011; Edwards et al., 2012a, 2012b; Barnett et al., 2022).

(Continued)

Table 3.12 (Continued)

Mirror theme	People with FND	Healthcare workers
• Anger and hostility	Anger is commonly reported in people with FND (McDade & Brown, 1992; Alper, 1994; Harden & Ferrando, 2001; Malhi & Singhi, 2002; Carton et al., 2003; Green et al., 2004; Ahern et al., 2009; Thompson et al., 2009; Monzoni et al., 2011; Fobian & Elliott, 2019; O'Connell et al., 2020).	Also reported in healthcare staff, particularly frustration and irritation, as well as worries about angering the person with FND (Thompson et al., 2005; McMillan et al., 2014; Rawlings & Reuber, 2018; Fobian & Elliott, 2019; Lehn et al., 2019; Klinke et al., 2021).
• Confusion	Poorly defined feeling of confusion was reported by people with FND, especially around the diagnosis (Carton et al., 2003; Green et al., 2004; Thompson et al., 2009; Monzoni et al., 2011; McMillan et al., 2014; Fobian & Elliott, 2019; O'Connell et al., 2020).	Unsurprisingly, confusion was also found in healthcare workers (Fobian & Elliott, 2019) possibly due to their personal experience of confusion about FND and frequent reports of limited confidence, certainty and self-perceived knowledge in the diagnosis, management and treatment of people with FND (O'Sullivan et al., 2006; Shneker & Elliott, 2008; Ahern et al., 2009; Edwards et al., 2012a, 2012b; McMillan et al., 2014; Fobian & Elliott, 2019; Lehn et al., 2019; Klinke et al., 2021; Barnett et al., 2022). In addition, healthcare workers displayed a tendency to use confusing language, communication and actions that maintained confusion in people with FND and other healthcare professionals, including avoiding the use of the word "functional", using code words, lack of honesty and openness about making or sharing diagnosis and requesting extra medical investigations (Espay et al., 2009; Kanaan et al., 2011; Edwards et al., 2012a, 2012b; De Schipper et al., 2014; Lehn et al., 2019; Klinke et al., 2021).

reduces unpleasant feelings and provides relief for the healthcare professional in the short term, via a negative reinforcement loop, it also increases the likelihood of this "passing on" behaviour re-emerging in future and causing further confusion and feelings of rejection in people with FND, without addressing the underlying problem and receiving the right support, thus further prolonging FND.

If we consider the existence of two maladaptive person-system cycles in one person, one that reinforces (via reassurance) and one that punishes (via hostility and rejection), it is not unthinkable that a partial reinforcement schedule may start to form where the FND symptoms are intermittently reinforced and may be the hardest to extinguish in the long term. Carefully considering these harmful cycles should therefore become a priority in FND care.

Reciprocal reinforcement

The PCM conceptualises these harmful person-system cycles as "reciprocal reinforcement", which is defined as a co-dependent behavioural pattern that is driven by beliefs and emotions and that unfolds in the relationships between the person with FND and individuals in their environment, for example family or healthcare professionals. "Reciprocal" refers to the bi-directional nature of this process, whereas "reinforcement" highlights the rewarding or relieving aspects that maintain this behavioural pattern. The psychological process that drives this co-dependent behavioural pattern between individuals helps to meet each person's psychological needs and reduces distress in both directions. Therefore, both the person with FND and their environment serve as each other's interpersonal safety behaviour. Although the safety behaviours may vary, they all serve the same function and have the ultimate goal of the attainment of a state of psychological safety, characterised by psychological security, validation and acknowledgement. Table 3.13 shows the common reciprocal reinforcement patterns encountered in FND.

The reciprocal reinforcement patterns displayed in Table 3.13 clearly demonstrate that both the person with FND and their environment equally contribute to the maintenance of FND symptoms. Table 3.13 also shows that the inappropriate responses and actions from the environment often cause a normal and logical response from the person with FND. However, the person with FND is faulted, labelled or blamed by the environment for their behaviours and symptoms, despite the joint responsibility, including in the healthcare context (e.g. Robson & Lian, 2017; Bennett et al., 2021; Dosanjh et al., 2021; MacDuffie et al., 2021). The responses described as part of the reciprocal reinforcement process are commonly reported by patients in psychological therapy and always associated with negative emotions. Table 3.13 shows that the emotion co-dysregulation can only be resolved by taking into account the internal states and responses of *both* the individual with FND and the environment, making a compelling case for the use of a hybrid psychological therapy model in FND.

Table 3.13 Examples of reciprocal reinforcement cycles in FND

(S) Internal state	(R) Reciprocal response	(C) For family member or healthcare professional	(C) For person with FND
Person with FND • has FND episode/need for comfort • no access to helpful coping strategies (i.e. verbal emotional expression + pushes on) as not learned in childhood **Environment** • intolerable discomfort witnessing the person's FND episode/distress	**Environment:** Caring/reassurance response	↓ distress, feeling of relief, meets need of comfort of staff and family Caring/ reassurance behaviour strengthened, environment takes away role demands and responsibilities, does everything for the person	↓ distress, feeling of relief, meets need of comfort in person with FND FND response strengthened increased dependency of the person on the environment environment views person as "manipulative" and "draining"
Person with FND • has need for comfort and care **Environment** feels discomfort • anxiety about making person worse, person having set-back, not progressing in therapy • limited confidence about own abilities and knowledge to handle the situation effectively **Environment** may feel need for caring/ overprotection	**Environment:** • Doubles up efforts • Does everything for the person/ taking role demands and responsibilities away	↓ distress, feeling of relief, meets need of comfort of staff/family ↑ meets need of caring/ overprotection of staff/family Doubling up behaviour/doing everything is strengthened	Meets need of comfort and care in person with FND ↑ increased dependency from person on environment, ↓ role demands and responsibilities, environment sees person as "manipulative"

(S) Internal state	(R) Reciprocal response	(C) For family member or healthcare professional	(C) For person with FND
Person with FND • Has episode of FND/in distress	**Environment:** Increased anger, criticism, hostility and negative non-verbal communication from family or professional towards person with FND (invalidation)	↓ anger in professional/ family who opened their own cover by verbally expressing emotions	↑ distress/feelings of rejection/ invalidation person does not feel believed by environment ↓ opening cover about psychological difficulties
Person with FND • Feeling uncertain and confused about FND **Environment** • Feeling uncertain and confused about FND	**Avoidance response:** environment passes person with FND on/dumping behaviour between different disciplines Person with FND branded as "difficult to treat" and "beyond help" **Approach response:** Person with FND seeking reassurance and clarity, "doctor shopping"	↓ aversive feelings of uncertainty and confusion Feeling of relief Avoidance behaviour strengthened	↑ feelings of uncertainty and confusion (↑ feeling abandoned and rejected) Approach behaviour more strengthened in response to more uncertainty and confusion, person branded as "seeking attention", "difficult to treat" and "wasting time and resources"
Healthcare professional: anxious about • mentioning psychology • making patient angry • rupturing therapeutic relationship	**Avoidance by environment:** • avoidance of the word functional • using code words • not honest or open about diagnosis • staff requests extra medical investigations **Approach response:** Person with FND seeking reassurance and clarity	↓ aversive worries and feelings Avoidance behaviour strengthened	↑ feelings of confusion ↑ iatrogenic damage Approach behaviour strengthened Person viewed as "seeking attention" and "wasting time and resources"

Systemic re-traumatisation: vertical mirroring

Although reciprocal reinforcement serves to create a sense of psychological safety in all individuals involved in FND, this interpersonal process can impact negatively on people with FND and their environment, and eventually will maintain the FND. One such side effect is systemic re-traumatisation, which consists of three core ideas: "systemic" refers to the environment; "re" means "again" and refers to the re-triggering of past hurts; and "traumatisation" is the act of inflicting trauma or distress onto someone. Hence, systemic re-traumatisation can be defined as a process where the environment inflicts trauma or distress on an individual by re-triggering old hurts. Systemic re-traumatisation can be viewed as the "unravelled" version of reciprocal reinforcement.

A concerning issue pertains to the potential that healthcare systems have in the ongoing re-triggering of features or memories associated with a traumatic upbringing and early childhood rejection experiences in people with FND. The impact of key parental and caregiving models in early childhood that are associated with trauma and emotional neglect may increase sensitivity to models with similar characteristics in later life and greatly impact current relationships with healthcare staff. As evident from Table 3.13, healthcare professionals frequently experience negative thoughts and feelings about people with FND, which drive unhelpful behaviours, expressed as either verbal or non-verbal, intentional or unintentional, and explicit or implicit. These negative beliefs, emotions and responses filter through interpersonal communications between clinicians and patients and may emulate the responses that people with FND often have been exposed to during their childhood by key family figures, including systematic rejection, chronic invalidation, not being believed, hostility, conflict, lack of support, neglect, abandonment, distress and confusion. This would have likely caused distress, confusion, anger, anxiety and sadness, as well as lay the foundation for the development of core beliefs around being worthless or not good enough.

Therefore, current events that resemble past invalidation (e.g. rude clinician), abandonment (e.g. discharge from a service) and neglect (e.g. reduced sessions or reviews) by their surrounding systems may repeatedly re-traumatise the person with FND and leave them distressed. As the person likely does not have access to the usual channels of verbal emotional expression and other appropriate coping strategies, due to adverse childhood experiences, the FND may be further compounded by these jarring healthcare experiences. Furthermore, openly expressed disbelief at FND may provoke more distress in people with FND, particularly relevant in people who experienced sexual trauma that resulted in disbelief and lack of support from parental figures during their upbringing. The healthcare system has the potential to further prolong these rejection experiences and directly impact on the psychological well-being of a person with FND.

The question therefore arises whether healthcare staff ought to be particularly attuned to the longstanding rejection experiences of people with FND and actively minimise the risk by becoming aware of and actively address unhelpful thoughts, emotions and behaviours towards people with FND. It is therefore imperative to address these often unintentional behaviours produced by the system, due to further harm that can be afflicted to the person with FND, and the strong possibility of prolonging or maintaining their FND symptoms.

Table 3.14 shows that current relationships in the healthcare context often resemble a vertical mirror of early adverse relationships experienced by the person with FND in childhood. The systemic re-traumatisation is characterised by healthcare professionals purposefully or inadvertently recreating copies of childhood relationships that generate similar beliefs, emotions and responses for the person with FND, thus re-traumatising the patient.

Research studies have documented a series of detrimental effects of the negative beliefs, emotions and actions that emanate from dysfunctional interpersonal dynamics between people with FND and their surrounding systems. Furthermore, clinical observations consistently confirm these findings (see Table 3.15).

The quest to stop systemic re-traumatisation: from secondary gains to social functions

The PCM describes the social consequences that maintain FND symptoms (Moore et al., 1994; Moore & Baker, 1997; Bautista et al., 2008; Fobian & Elliott, 2019). Historically, the literature on FND has referred to these consequences as "secondary gains" (e.g. Krawetz et al., 2001; Fobian & Elliott, 2019) and has placed heavy emphasis on the investigation of these gains in people with FND without taking into account their environment. A new terminology is proposed to describe the traditional but outdated concept of "secondary gains" in FND and reduce systemic re-traumatisation. In this book, secondary gains are re-conceptualised as the social functions of FND. Table 3.16 contrasts the defining features of these two terminologies.

Family and team: the social functions of FND

Table 3.17 shows examples of a reconceptualisation of "secondary gains" to the social functions of FND.

Systemic modelling

Historically, modelling has only been described for people with FND (e.g. "seizure models"). However, family and healthcare professionals are equally likely subjected to the same modelling processes. For example, healthcare

Table 3.14 Vertical mirroring: past vs current healthcare relationships in FND

Mirror theme	Past relationships of people with FND	Current relationships of people with FND with healthcare workers
Vertical mirror #1: Relationships marred by unmet needs and confusion	Abnormal parent-child relationships and inconsistencies in caregivers responding to emotional needs resulting in the child feeling confused.	O'Keeffe et al. (2021) reported that a larger number of people with FND than those with multiple sclerosis felt that their needs were not understood by medical professionals. Poorly defined feeling of confusion was reported by people with FND and healthcare workers (Carton et al., 2003; Green et al., 2004; O'Sullivan et al., 2006; Shneker & Elliott, 2008; Ahern et al., 2009; Thompson et al., 2009; Monzoni et al., 2011; Edwards et al., 2012a, 2012b; McMillan et al., 2014; Fobian & Elliott, 2019; Lehn et al., 2019; O'Connell et al., 2020; Klinke et al., 2021; Barnett et al., 2022).
Vertical mirror #2: Negative judgements	Criticism, chronic invalidation by parental key figures/caregivers.	"Healthcaregivers" working with FND expressed a range of negative judgements using stigmatising and pejorative language about people with FND including referring to this group as "seeking attention", being manipulative, difficult to treat, beyond help, wasting time and resources (Alper, 1994; Harden & Ferrando, 2001; Shneker & Elliott, 2008; Ahern et al., 2009; McMillan et al., 2014). O'Keeffe et al. (2021) reported that people with FND felt not treated with respect and dignity by medical professionals.
Vertical mirror #3: Not being believed	Patients often report not having been believed by a parental caregiver in the context of abuse.	Healthcare staff commonly believe that the symptoms of people with FND are fake or not real (Ahern et al., 2009; Sahaya et al., 2012; McMillan et al., 2014), partially or fully feigned (Kanaan et al., 2009, 2011; Edwards et al., 2012a, 2012b), with staff expressing disbelief at the symptoms (Alper, 1994).
Vertical mirror #4: Lack of support	Emotional neglect, lack of emotional and physical support in childhood.	Healthcare staff adopt unsupportive approaches towards people with FND: • Poor healthcare (Shneker & Elliott, 2008; Ahern et al., 2009; McMillan et al., 2014; Nielsen et al., 2020)

Mirror theme	Past relationships of people with FND	Current relationships of people with FND with healthcare workers
		• Favouring a rushed over a careful approach (Betts, 1990) and treating people with FND in a hostile or rude manner (Ramani & Gumnit, 1982; Green et al., 2004) • O'Keeffe et al. (2021) reported that people with FND did not feel involved nor that their wishes and preferences were taken into account in treatment decisions.
Vertical mirror #5: Rejection and abandonment	Childhood abandonment, loss of relationships, by separation or divorce, as well as systematic rejection or being singled out by caregivers, including abusive experiences.	Healthcare staff engages in: • Abandonment, "dumping" and onward referrals of people with FND to other healthcare professionals (Harden & Ferrando, 2001; Edwards et al., 2012a, 2012b; Barnett et al., 2022). • People with FND experience rejection on several levels including avoidance, ignoring and ridiculing by staff (McMillan et al., 2014; Lehn et al., 2019). • Staff believe that people with FND are undeserving of the same care as people with organic conditions (McMillan et al., 2014), therefore singling out and rejecting the person.
Vertical mirror #6: Negative emotions	Interpersonal conflict in parental and family relationships, hostility, distress, high expressed emotion.	People with FND and healthcare staff report distress, fear, anxiety, anger, hostility, frustration, irritation during healthcare contacts (Betts, 1990; McDade & Brown, 1992; Alper, 1994; Harden & Ferrando, 2001; Malhi & Singhi, 2002; Carton et al., 2003; Green et al., 2004; Thompson et al., 2005, 2009; Ahern et al., 2009; Monzoni et al., 2011; Edwards et al., 2012a, 2012b; McMillan et al., 2014; Rawlings & Reuber, 2018; Fobian & Elliott, 2019; Lehn et al., 2019; Nielsen et al., 2020; O'Connell et al., 2020; Klinke et al., 2021; Barnett et al., 2022).

Table 3.15 Detrimental effects of systemic re-traumatisation on people with FND

Detrimental effect for the person with FND	Details and supporting references
Impact on health outcomes	• Adverse effects on recovery, management and treatment of FND (Ramani & Gumnit, 1982; Betts, 1990; Shneker & Elliott, 2008; Ahern et al., 2009; Rawlings & Reuber, 2018; Fobian & Elliott, 2019), including the person receiving poor quality of care, and that directly worsens or impacts on maintenance of FND symptoms and psychological well-being. • Delay the diagnostic process (Fobian & Elliott, 2019) or sharing the FND diagnosis, which prevents early intervention, the person not obtaining the right care, and increases the risk of healthcare utilisation and long-term entrenchment of symptoms, which are harder to undo. • Lack of involvement or active treatment of the environment to work on maladaptive person-system cycles may contribute to suboptimal treatment outcomes or relapse.
Missing opportunities for recovery from FND	Maintains the unhelpful beliefs, feelings and responses that both parties have towards each other, without: • Finding out how each party thinks about each other, not learning about each other's inner worlds. • Any real opportunity for positive change. • Getting to the root of the problem and changing reciprocal reinforcement and systemic re-traumatisation processes, including the uncovering of interpersonal triggers for FND.
Erosion of healthcare relationships and the healthcare system	• Leads to negative emotions and behaviours being projected onto the person with FND and rupture the therapeutic relationship (Harden & Ferrando, 2001), as well as impact on conversations in other ways (Monzoni et al., 2011). • Erodes trust in the healthcare system: patients may be less likely to seek help for physical or psychological symptoms that need immediate medical attention. • Desensitises healthcare professionals to FND: habit formation of reciprocal reinforcement and systemic re-traumatisation. • Healthcare professionals may feel dissonance in relation to upholding positive and professional personal values towards people with FND in the face of challenge by other professionals engaging with stigma (MacDuffie et al., 2021).
Impact on psychological well-being and psychological treatment	• Potential for renewed psychological injury: risks the re-triggering of trauma and memories of past experiences and relationships that are now played out again in a healthcare context (e.g. abandonment, rejection, not feeling believed or cared for, emotional neglect and invalidation), further contributing to FND.

Detrimental effect for the person with FND	Details and supporting references
	• Reduces the likelihood of opening up about psychological difficulties (Ahern et al., 2009) and expressing their emotions, particularly if the person doesn't feel believed and lacks trust. An even tighter Cover further maintains FND.
	• Triple emotion load" and more risk of worsening FND symptoms: additional negative emotions – on top of the (1) emotions that the person is already managing due to FND symptoms and (2) the emotions that drive the FND in the first place.
	• Reduced health-related quality of life (see MacDuffie et al., 2021).
Environmental dependency	• Little confidence of the environment in the patient's ability to cope with the FND symptoms will have a negative impact on the patient's self-confidence and self-efficacy in managing their FND.
	• Environment may stop the patient from engaging with activities: further reduced activity levels (with even a more blocked Valve). Increased dependency on the environment including family, carers and equipment. Missing out on opportunities to practise independent tasks (e.g. preparing meals, personal care).
	• These behaviours can counterproductively become a self-fulfilling prophecy and prevent a patient from practising their skills and testing out that their worst fear of an FND episode or worsened FND symptoms will not take place, further increasing their risk of FND symptoms.
	• Increased carer burden with a risk of reduced quality of life and distress for family members caring for the person.
Stigma	• Lack of emphasis on the social context has the potential to focus on the person with FND as "the problem" and further increase stigma in FND (see Rommelfanger et al., 2017; Klinke et al., 2021; MacDuffie et al., 2021, for a discussion on stigma).
	• People with FND are unfairly and in a one-sided way branded and stigmatised as "manipulative" and "attention seeking" despite the environment playing an active role in the process and the patient never having had opportunities to learn appropriate psychological coping strategies in childhood.
Iatrogenic harm	• Direct iatrogenic harm including too many unnecessary extra medical investigations, referrals, interventions and medications prescribed with adverse side effects, interactions and promoting dissociation (e.g. MacDuffie et al., 2021).
	• Indirect iatrogenic harm as time and effort not spent on other patients from caseload.

(Continued)

Table 3.15 (Continued)

Detrimental effect for the person with FND	Details and supporting references
	• Prevents the search for other means of attaining psychological safety that are less impactful on daily life. The behaviours can prevent a person with FND from the opportunity to learn helpful strategies to address and manage their symptoms. For example, a clinician who experiences anxiety or hopelessness about working with FND may avoid seeing or underdiagnose these patients. The patient may subsequently miss out on appropriate care or treatment sessions that could have helped them manage the FND (e.g. MacDuffie et al., 2021).
Perpetuation of confusion	• As maladaptive cycles and environmental hypotheses are not being tested out, confusion around FND is chronically perpetuated and become entrenched in the person's belief system (e.g. "messages not being passed on from my brain to my body"), which eventually make it more difficult for a psychologist to undo.

Table 3.16 Differences between secondary gains vs social functions in FND

Secondary gains	Social functions
Uni-directional process • Implies that the person with FND is the single "agent" who is acting on the environment. The goal for the person is to gain an advantage from the environment.	**Bi-directional process** • Implies that the person with FND and the individuals from multiple surrounding systems are both agents and are in an interpersonal dynamic acting towards one another in order to gain an advantage. • The psychological features of FND are viewed as the product of an emotion regulation problem between the person and the system.
Intra-individual origins • The process of wanting to obtain a secondary gain originates within the individual with FND.	**Inter-individual origins** • The process of wanting to obtain a secondary gain originates in both individuals (with and without FND) who form the interpersonal dynamic.
Superficial level of analysis • Only considers the person's actions (e.g. rather than underlying reasons for the behaviours.	**Deep level of analysis** Conceptualises gains as behaviours • Views gains as being embedded in a wider system of gains from the environment.

Secondary gains	Social functions
Increases risk of stigma, blame and rejection • Alludes to the idea that the individual may put on symptoms in order to gain some type of advantage. • Stigmatising language with negative connotations, associated with "manipulation", "malingering", "putting symptoms on to seek attention", "sick role" and "monetary" or "financial" gain.	**Suppresses risk of stigma, blame and rejection** • Tries to identify the unmet need behind behaviours. Aspects of FND are viewed as a behaviour that serves a function (e.g. Moore et al., 1994) and that are maintained by psychological conditioning and social learning processes. • Normalises "external regulation" and the social functions of FND as serving a basic human unmet need for receiving care, comfort, attention, being "noted" by another person, validation, belonging, being free from rejection in FND that may not always be met in a helpful way but should still be taken seriously. • Friendly language that does not stigmatise the person with FND.
Language biased towards negativity • Language around "secondary gains" tends to cause immediate negative attitudes, beliefs and emotions in the environment in response to the person with FND (i.e. systemic re-traumatisation; see later section in this chapter). • This is a detrimental consequence for a patient population that has already frequently experienced rejection in early childhood and by the healthcare system in adulthood.	**Language biased towards empathy** • Language around "social functions" elicits compassion and empathy. • Takes a softer and compassionate approach towards the development of unhelpful but understandable behaviours that have social functions in the context of an individual's background of exposure to longstanding rejection experiences. • It reduces systemic re-traumatisation and therefore its impact on the maintenance of FND symptoms.
Always a gain • The term only considers gains as a consequence and is biased towards thinking about positive reinforcement only. It fails to account for wanted losses or the absence of something in the environment, such as FND serving a function to deter another person from seeking proximity.	**Gains but also losses** • Social functions can result in the person obtaining something positive (positive reinforcement) or getting rid of something negative (negative reinforcement).
Individual responsibility • Responsibility for the symptoms and recovery from secondary gains is ascribed to one person. • Treatment is mostly directed to the person with FND.	**Shared responsibility** • Responsibility for the symptoms and recovery is shared amongst all parties involved with the person with FND. • Treatment is directed to all parties – not just the person with FND.

Table 3.17 Social functions and behavioural consequences in FND

-S- (FND takes something negative away from the family or team)	+S+ (FND provides a positive consequence to the family or team)
• Not being able to have sessions with the person as they are recuperating from a dissociative seizure. An "easy way out" to avoid having to work with the person. • FND may take away a sense of emptiness, low self-esteem or a previous lack of identity/purpose in a caring family member.	• Proximity to the person with FND, fulfilling a family member's need to care for the person. • If the person with FND is doing well in therapy after having been disabled, this gives staff confidence about their own skills. • Identity and purpose in life, in the context of the role of carer for sick person.

-S+ (FND takes something positive away from the family or team)	+S- (FND provides a negative consequence to the family or team)
• Family quality time that is separate from caring roles. • Pursuing own life and career goals, as a carer for someone with FND. • Work-life balance may be out of balance due to increased care needed for the person with FND.	• Fluctuations and inconsistencies in FND symptoms may provoke negative reactions from others leading to negative emotions in the family member (e.g. anxiety, embarrassment), as well as in staff who may doubt their skills and lose confidence in treating FND.

professionals may model their responses to other staff treating people with FND. This may have far-reaching consequences for students or early career professionals who start to work with FND patients for the first time. If a student observes a respected healthcare model invalidating a person with FND, then the student may subsequently adopt similar behaviours in their own practice. It is therefore of utmost importance that education and training on reciprocal reinforcement and systemic re-traumatisation processes start early in a degree programme before treatment habits become entrenched and hard to undo, as part of an early intervention.

The focus on positivity in FND: pressure cooker Safety features, the twelfth pressure cooker element

Models of FND, whether clinical or theoretical, generally tend to focus on "pathology" of the individual and emphasise "what's wrong" rather than "what's right". Although from a clinical treatment perspective, it is entirely understandable to highlight unhelpful or dysfunctional thinking patterns, emotion coping strategies and behaviours, the focus on pathology may occasionally feel rejecting and invalidating towards the person with FND. Rather

Table 3.18 Pressure Cooker Model Safety features in FND

Element	Protective factor(s)	Comments, caveats and provisos
Ignition/Fuel	• Healthy early attachments to parental caregivers. • Relatively free from "psychosocial life crises" in the lower levels of Maslow's hierarchy of needs including housing, safety, current/ongoing threats to the person from other people, as well as supportive relationships devoid of interpersonal triggers for FND. • A person's timeline demonstrates a recent onset of FND/short disease duration, as opposed to a longstanding, untreated course of FND, making it more amenable to early intervention.	• Attachment difficulties in the context of adverse childhood experiences are common in people with FND. • Constant psychosocial crises, stressors or a chaotic environment may be an indication that this is exactly the "pressure point" that needs attention. Excluding this type of patient from treatment would be "throwing out the baby with the bath water". Instead, practising crisis management and emotion skills to apply in between sessions may be the appropriate intervention. • In addition, resolving or managing active threats (e.g. abuse, domestic violence, stalking, release of a perpetrator of past abuse into the community) may equal the resolution of the FND.
Flames	• Psychological "mindedness": willingness and engagement with a psychological model of thinking and insight into the maintaining factors of FND including mood–FND link. • Showcasing this engagement by attending and engaging with the contents of the sessions. Good compliance with psychological therapy. • Spontaneous or regular use of psychological techniques (e.g. pacing, expressing emotions). • Demonstrating self-efficacy in addressing symptoms should they re-emerge, for example with having a well-thought plan in place and support in the environment ("FND set-back recovery plan").	• History of psychological difficulties and repeated courses of psychological therapy does not have to suggest that the person has exhausted all therapeutic possibilities and is deemed too complex. People with FND may not have had access to appropriate support for, for example, undiagnosed social anxiety or lack of FND-specialist care. • Ability to label emotions is a protective factor, but this may not be present at the start and may need to be practised during therapy. • Fear of recovery is common in FND. The profile of social gains and losses associated with the FND may reveal how easy or how difficult recovery may be in future.

(Continued)

Table 3.18 (Continued)

Element	Protective factor(s)	Comments, caveats and provisos
	• Able to connect with both positive and negative emotions, as opposed to persistent denial of distress and continuous display of positive emotions. • Lack of the fear of recovery/high motivation towards recovery and clearly demonstrating or active engagement with the steps towards recovery.	
Heat	• The presence of significant emotion dysregulation, interpersonal features and personality disorder does not have to be a barrier towards progressing. In fact, people with personality disorder can be very introspective, psychologically minded, resilient and aware of psychology due to their past experiences in childhood or therapy. • Dissociative features are relatively circumscribed and do not permeate into a wide range of life domains, for example highly frequent episodes during the day, extended sleeping periods. • Absence of polypharmacy with medications that promote dissociation.	• The absence of psychological difficulties is occasionally touted as a protective factor in FND. However, the question arises whether this is a true reflection of a person's psychological functioning. Dissociation and denial of distress are both common in people with FND and may give the false impression of non-existent psychological difficulties.
Pot	• Relatively low care needs in personal and domestic activities of daily life, as well as an absence of significant continence issues that require equipment (e.g. self-catheterisation). • The absence of high levels of entrenchment of equipment or home adaptations. Keen to work on parting ways with equipment including wheelchair. Equipment not strongly associated/part of social identity or positive emotions. • No regular contacts with emergency services or admissions to intensive care units.	• Following medication and equipment review, people with FND may go on to fare well in psychological therapy. • Furthermore, the presence of epileptic and non-epileptic episodes does not always have to signify complexity or be overwhelming for the clinician. Occasionally, people with well-controlled epilepsy for years may suddenly develop new seizures that are strongly associated with psychosocial triggers (e.g. divorce) and found to be functional in nature. A multidisciplinary approach with consistent medical input will be very helpful to distinguish these two clinical entities and reinforce the difference/need for psychological therapy for the functional seizures.

Warning light	• The absence of co-existing organic conditions (e.g. epilepsy) or long history of somatoform conditions (e.g. irritable bowel syndrome), especially since teenage years.	• Heightened self-focused attention that is hard to shift and strong resistance to a psychological model of treatment can be challenging in therapy. However, the actual intervention may be to build a trusted relationship where the person feels psychologically safe to explore this resistance against psychology.
	• Normal focus of attention to symptoms, in contrast to increased self-focused attention.	• Limited or no access to appropriate coping strategies and the presence of "personality disorder" are sometimes viewed as negative prognostic factors in FND recovery.
	• Open towards exploring psychological explanations for FND and mind-body interactions.	• People with FND with more interpersonal features as part of complex trauma may not have had the opportunities to learn these strategies since early childhood. The whole point of therapy is to become skilled at these strategies to reduce the risk of FND.
Sticky left-over food	• Verbal emotional expression is an accepted coping strategy in the family of origin or in the current family unit.	
	• Long-term use of FND-specific strategies (e.g. keep self to self, pushing on, dissociation) in, for example, an older person with FND does not have to mean that the person won't change.	
	• What matters is willingness to change these ingrained coping habits.	
	• Normal self-esteem that is not strongly tied to FND identity.	
Cover	• An ability to verbally express emotions.	• However, initially quiet patients or patients who are reluctant to disclose information, but still attend, may need more time to build a trusted and psychological safe relationship. This may take a considerable amount of time; it is important to be patient.
	• Appreciating the necessity and value of emotional expression in a psychologically safe relationship – even if this is not directly available to the person in their own environment.	• At times, threats to physical safety and relationships can be associated with FND flare-ups, and the FND can disappear after these have been addressed, sometimes as part of releasing domestic violence as "the unspeakable dilemma".
	• Releasing an unspeakable dilemma during therapy.	
	• The ability to set appropriate boundaries and use assertiveness skills.	• Assertiveness problems and the practice of skills are often a major target of intervention in FND.

(Continued)

Table 3.18 (Continued)

Element	Protective factor(s)	Comments, caveats and provisos
Valve	• Supportive social network with a sense of belonging. • Other parts of identity that are not FND-related including an enjoyable job, being part of a community, feeling a sense of social belonging. • Presence of meaningful and realistic life goals following the recovery of FND, "futuristic thinking". • Balanced schedule of leisure, meaningful, employment, enjoyable and social activities. • Meaningful employment, either part-time or full-time.	• Social isolation is very common in FND and addressing this issue, in connection with developing some form of a sense of belonging, can improve a person's mood and FND in major ways. • Many people with FND are unemployed and may be on benefits but would like to find a meaningful occupational role and be part of a workforce with regular contacts with colleagues.
Overpressure Plug	• Relatively short and low-frequency dissociative episodes, as opposed to episodes lasting for hours. • Brief "set-backs" and quick "bounce-backs". • The absence of active deliberate self-harm or severe self-injurious behaviours in the context of dissociative episodes. • Person is believing and accepting of the functional nature of FND symptoms.	• Fast recovery and large gains early on in the therapy may be a red flag and of a brittle nature. • A long duration or chronic relapsing-remitting pattern of FND is often causing hopelessness with patients and clinicians alike. • Long duration of FND does not necessarily mean "chronic" and "beyond treatment". The person may not have had a proper FND diagnosis and no access to FND-specialist resources. • A person not accepting of the functional nature of FND may not necessarily be beyond help; on the contrary, the actual intervention may be helping the person to accept and shift their thinking towards a functional rather than organic cause of FND, within a psychological safe relationship.

| Kitchen | • Good family and social support system that is not colluding with the person; encourages independence; accepting of a psychological explanation for the FND, and is aware of reinforcement patterns that maintain FND.
• Good relationships with partner, family and children, the absence of strong family or negative interpersonal dynamics.
• Treating team aware, sufficiently introspective and able to manage strong negative countertransference towards the patient. | • Normal family functioning" is sometimes suggested as a protective factor but often found to be the core of FND maintenance.
• Enlist the support of the family or system as "FND allies" to help the person and the family members apply their own FND management strategies.
• Social isolation and unhelpful family dynamics may just be the areas that need focus in therapy. |

than fully focusing on pathology, treatment models focusing more holistically on the "psychology" of the person with all its dysfunctional and functional features may be more helpful here. The final element of the PCM involves the Safety features, which represent the positive qualities and positive prognostic factors in treatment for a person with FND.

Table 3.18 lists commonly encountered protective factors for positive outcomes of psychological therapy and recovery in FND. All protective factors have been observed in clinical practice, with some of the listed factors reported in the scientific literature (e.g. Turgay, 1990; LaFrance & Devinsky, 2002; Alsaadi & Marquez, 2005).

4 Using the Pressure Cooker Model in the clinic

Tools, strategies and practical advice

People with FND are encountered in a wide range of mental health, physical health and specialist services. Recent awareness of FND has resulted in a growing number of services dedicated to the assessment and treatment of people with FND. This chapter will share useful questions, tools and strategies that are based on the principles of the Pressure Cooker Model and that can assist you with using the PCM as a practical formulation and treatment model, particularly in busy settings.

FND prehab: before the assessment

The previous chapters have already demonstrated that the area of relationships is core to understanding and treating FND. Keep this in mind at any point during the assessment and treatment process, which starts before the person visits your clinic. Ask yourself the following questions to help you gauge any factors that can impact on engagement and the therapeutic relationship with psychology.

The goals of FND prehab include the following:

- Build trust and set the stage for a positive therapeutic relationship with strong engagement.
- Make the patient feel "heard" and not "hurt".
- Provide the person with the opposite experience of what they have been used to in childhood and healthcare services: care, prediction, control and feeling believed.
- Modelling of good relationships characterised by honesty, psychological safety and object constancy, amongst other relationship features.
- Pre-formulate hypotheses about the FND.

Is the person aware of the referral to psychology?

It is not uncommon for the person with FND to not to be aware of the referral to psychological services. Occasionally, the person may have been aware but felt reluctant and got "swayed" by the referring clinician. This creates a

DOI: 10.4324/9781003308980-4

"false start" for psychological intervention and can limit subsequent engagement. Ensure that the person with FND is on board with the referral or, at the very least, is open to exploring psychology further. Praise the person for attending your clinic despite their reluctance. The fact that they are visiting is a good sign and meaningful. If you find that the person is ambivalent and expresses doubts about psychology, acknowledge these and openly discuss their views, thoughts and feelings during your initial conversation using a compassionate approach.

Does the person have a confirmed, positive diagnosis of FND?

Seek clarity in advance from the referring clinician whether all the necessary investigations have been completed, and a positive FND diagnosis has clearly been communicated to the person, as well as documented in notes and letters, for example the results of video EEG for a confirmed diagnosis of dissociative seizures. This is an important step prior to psychological therapy. If uncertainty remains around the diagnosis, the person with FND may still feel that organic causes have not been excluded. This complicates subsequent engagement with psychological therapy and the acceptance of a psychological perspective on the symptoms, as the person may not identify the need for psychological input for what they believe is an organic condition. Furthermore, it puts the psychologist at risk of not providing a safe service; if doubts exist around the "organicity" of the symptoms, the patient may experience a problem in the sessions that warrants direct medical attention.

Does the person have any other physical and mental health diagnoses?

Occasionally, people with FND may be referred with co-existing organic conditions or a diagnoses that have an organic component or carry a risk of a serious organic consequence including hemiplegic migraine and the risk of stroke; epileptic seizures with concurrent non-epileptic episodes; and spinal problems that produce symptoms and disabilities that may be disproportionate or unexplained on the basis of the original organic problem. It is of utmost importance that no ambiguity surrounds these diagnoses before psychological therapy commences as this will affect the acceptance of a psychological perspective. Furthermore, closer interdisciplinary working with other physical disciplines will be required when managing these conditions due to the risks (e.g. neurologists, epileptologists, physiotherapists).

Some people with FND may have a history of other somatoform symptoms and are known to pain, chronic fatigue, rheumatology, gastro-enterology and urology clinics. A subset of people with FND will have accessed mental health services including community mental health teams, crisis resolution home treatment teams, personality disorder or other secondary care services. Some may be frequent attenders at accidents and emergencies departments. The person may also be connected to social services for a variety of reasons including their package of care and, in some cases, safeguarding issues. Acquiring information on a person's previous mental and physical health history is important for many reasons including their prior experiences of psychological therapy, its perceived effectiveness, acceptance and engagement with psychological models and historic triggers of FND, as well as to inform risk assessments.

Could the person have been subjected to systemic re-traumatisation?

Clinical observations suggest that this phenomenon is commonly reported by people with FND and often rooted in reality rather than perceived or imagined by the person. Be aware that people with FND have often experienced difficult relationships with healthcare professionals. Actively checking in with the person about these experiences may provide clues about beliefs and emotions including feeling abandoned, not believed and not cared for. Use this as a starting point to formulate with the PCM what thought-feelings-behaviour chains may be present.

People with FND who have been referred without their knowledge, have been reluctantly swayed by their referring clinician, or have been discharged from a medical service and then referred to psychology may feel that the referral to psychology is the ultimate confirmation that they are abandoned, not believed and not cared for. Importantly, these experiences may re-trigger negative beliefs, emotions and memories from early experiences. Although discharges are inevitable and a normal part of healthcare services, it is important to keep in mind these vulnerabilities and the impact of prior healthcare experiences, particularly for engagement with psychology.

Invest in the therapeutic relationship before the patient visits your clinic. Actively reach out to the person and leave the service contact details for questions that they may have. Acknowledge and reflect their difficult healthcare experiences back to the person and adopt a compassionate approach by carefully listening to what the patient is communicating to you. In this way, their encounter with your service will provide them with a positive experience and may correct some of the earlier negative experiences.

Could reciprocal reinforcement processes be contributing to the FND?

This phenomenon is a crucial part of PCM theory. At the prehab stage, emphasise the importance of systemic involvement as an integral part of the treatment for FND. Invite the person's closest support circle into the clinic. This could include partners, parents, children, extended family members, friends and other significant individuals in the person's life. At times, the person with FND may be reluctant to invite anyone or there may be a striking absence or disinterest from the family or partner. All situations, whether the system is present or absent, are important to formulate using the PCM.

Does the person understand what psychology entails?

Not every person with FND will have a full understanding of the psychological treatment process, especially in the context of FND. People may come with preconceptions and misgivings about psychology. Before the first appointment, provide an information sheet that debunks common myths about psychology, as well as a one-page "quick fact sheet" on the PCM that details all the maintaining factors of FND (an example is described later in this chapter). Book 2 contains a list of psychology questions and answers.

Assessment

Due to the complexities and multiple layers inherent in FND, it is important to take out sufficient time for an initial comprehensive psychological assessment. A rule of thumb is 1.5 hours with at least 30 minutes for a separate collateral history from a family member, partner or friend who knows the patient well and interacts with them on a regular basis.

In the following section, each element of the PCM assessment will be discussed in great detail and the reader's attention will be drawn to important parts of the assessment. For every element of the PCM, always keep in mind a "social perspective": ask yourself the question "How does the Fuel, Flames, Cover…relate to other individuals in the person's environment?" The PCM assessment form will play a central role in helping you guide your FND assessment. Occasionally, you may feel derailed by the assessment process. During these moments, go back to the PCM and check mentally whether you have covered all elements. This can help you stay on the task. At the end of this section, a practical assessment and formulation template with prompt questions will be provided that can be used in the clinic.

Overpressure Plug

Diagnostic issues

FND is represented by the Overpressure Plug. Confusingly and perhaps reflecting the confusion that often exists amongst patients and healthcare providers alike, FND is known under many different names, some now outdated and controversial. FND has been described with the following variety of names to denote what is essentially the same clinical entity: conversion disorder, hysteria, pseudoseizures, non-epileptic attack disorder (NEAD), non-epileptic seizures (NES), psychogenic non-epileptic seizures (PNES), dissociative seizures (DS), functional non-epileptic attacks (FNEAs), functional motor disorder (FMD), functional cognitive disorder (FCD), medically unexplained neurological symptoms, functional neurological symptom disorder (FNSD), functional neurological symptoms (FNS) and medically unexplained neurological symptoms (MUNS).

Historically, FND was a diagnosis "by exclusion" which increased diagnostic delay, confusion and healthcare utilisation in people with FND. The rate for misdiagnosis significantly reduced in recent years. Due to the increased research and clinical interest in FND, healthcare professionals have become more aware and confident. The diagnosis of FND has now changed into the necessity of making a "positive diagnosis" of FND.

Occasionally, people with FND come to the psychological therapy with confusing diagnostic labels that, upon further exploring, or after several sessions into therapy, may require a reclassification. Common examples that have previously been encountered in the clinic are shown in Table 4.1.

In FND, it is always important to work as part of a multidisciplinary team. If diagnostic doubts emerge during the therapy process, and there are good grounds to challenge the label, for example as it requires a significant change in treatment, it is sensible to check in with the referring or team-related medical professional for a review.

Starting your assessment

Keep your questions as open as possible ("What brought you here today?" "Tell me in your own words what symptoms you experience?" "I have read your notes but I think it's really important to hear from you about your experiences, what symptoms you experience?" "What symptoms bother you

Table 4.1 Common clinical diagnoses in FND with a potential psychological origin

Initial diagnosis	Potential alternative psychological hypothesis
Post-traumatic stress disorder, particularly with clinicians making a hasty link between "traumatic event → FND → must be PTSD"	A different anxiety disorder that requires the selection of another condition-specific CBT model than PTSD, or an underlying depression with rejection themes driving the FND presentation (e.g. the "relational" circumstances surrounding the traumatic event such as treatment in hospital and unhelpful responses from healthcare professionals trumps the actual traumatic event in terms of psychological impact)
Hemiplegic migraine	Dissociative episodes
Restless legs syndrome	Motor features and tremors that are in fact the
Periodic limb movement disorder	symptoms of social anxiety
Dementia	Functional cognitive symptoms
Mild cognitive impairment prodrome	

the most at the moment?"). There are several reasons for keeping the initial question open. It is important to understand a person's current and most bothersome symptoms as people with FND often experience a wide range of physical symptoms and disabilities that impact on their day-to-day life. Furthermore, people with FND have not always felt heard by healthcare professionals. It is important for the person to feel heard by you, particularly if you are a mental health practitioner. You may initially be "at a disadvantage" in the person's eyes and making the person feel heard sets the stage for building a trusted therapeutic relationship. Another reason to keep questions open is to gauge a person's understanding of FND. There can be inconsistencies and discrepancies between what the person and their family understand about the outcomes of medical investigations and the FND ("I had a stroke", "I have tonic-clonic seizures") vs what has been described by the referrer ("functional motor weakness", "non-epileptic seizures").

Some tips if the person generates many symptoms and you feel you are running out of time are as follows:

- **Assure the person** you have read up on their notes and you are aware of some information already. Sometimes people are relieved because they don't have to repeat their whole story again.
- **Ask for permission** to interrupt the person's flow of speech to explore other psychological parts of the assessment.
- **Set an agenda.** It may also help to set an agenda at the beginning of the assessment where you decide both how much time to allocate on exploring physical symptoms and how much time on psychology and the collateral history.
- **Make a symptom list.** Ask the person whether you could both make a list of the symptoms and explore each in turn in more detail.

As the person provides you with an account, try to keep in mind the following categories to help you preserve oversight and not miss crucial details.

Nature of FND: a condition marked by variability

FND can involve the entire neurological system, in the same way as organic neurological conditions do. During the assessment, keep in mind four main categories of FND symptoms: motor, sensory, functional cognitive and seizure. People will often report a mixture of these symptoms and do not neatly fall into a single category, although one category of symptoms will tend to dominate the clinical picture; for example, a person's most prominent FND symptom may be dissociative episodes. Fluctuations and variability on many different levels are a key characteristic of FND. In terms of symptom frequency, a person with FND can experience dissociative episodes on a daily basis or go weeks without symptoms before experiencing a new series of dissociative events, often in the context of a stressful event. In relation to symptom severity, a person with FND may experience manageable motor symptoms that require a walker for mobilising, and on other occasions, severe motor symptoms that renders them bed-bound. FND symptoms can evolve over time ("symptom substitution"), for example from dissociative episodes at the first onset of FND into more motor-type FND symptoms such as tremors and weakness as the condition becomes more chronic. Dissociative episodes can also change "semiology" between episodes or within a single episode, for example beginning with very mobile movements (e.g. rolling over the ground) to immobility towards the end (e.g. shaking). Symptoms in FND often follow a fluctuating nature, and this provides an opportunity and insight into possible triggers. In inpatient settings, tools such as the Functional Behavioral Assessment can be helpful for the assessment of very behavioural presentations of FND, their social functions, setting events, possible antecedents and consequences of FND (O'Neill et al., 1997).

The symbolic nature of FND

Pareés et al. (2012) describe a relationship between the "phenomenology" of physical events at the onset of FND and subsequent symptoms. It can also be helpful to think past the physical features of FND and ask yourself what symbolic or psychological meaning may these symptoms have?

- Lower limb weakness may indicate a lack of physical base and a lack of psychological secure base.
- Functional speech problems may be symbolic for someone with reduced assertiveness and not having a voice in the family setting.
- A tremor may be an expression of underlying anxiety, with a person "literally shaking".
- Loss of sensation may be parallel to not being in touch with or sensing emotions. The lack of physical sensation mirrors the lack of emotional sensation.
- Physical paralysis in the limbs may indicate feeling trapped and psychologically immobilised in a personal situation.

It is important to note that FND symptoms are often confused with other conditions that are qualitatively different nosological entities including somatisation disorder, chronic fatigue syndrome, fibromyalgia, complex regional pain syndrome, factitious disorder, Munchausen's syndrome and malingering, which does not help with beating the stigma around FND, especially in terms of "faking symptoms", "manipulation", "deliberately putting symptoms on or causing these yourself" and "attention seeking".

MOTOR SYMPTOMS

Examples: functional weakness or paralysis of limbs (e.g. hemiplegia, paraplegia, quadriplegia), tremor, jerky or ballistic movements, dystonia (i.e. fixed abnormal posture), spasms, functional gait and coordination disorders, functional tics, speech difficulties (e.g. stuttering, functional voice loss, dysarthria, foreign accent syndrome) and swallowing difficulties.

Common phrases: "My legs are giving way", "My neck is locked", "I feel spasms"

Motor-type FND symptoms tend to be more static and continuously present, for example a tremor that doesn't stop or bilateral leg weakness that is always there (as opposed to more paroxysmal dissociative episodes, that "come and go"). Despite the more fixed nature of motor symptoms, people with motor-type FND symptoms will experience variations in the intensity of their motor symptoms and worsening is often associated with negative emotions, for example a person losing strength in all four limbs in response to an anxiety trigger. The difference between a motor-type "relapse" and seizure-like symptoms can sometimes be difficult to make. Motor-type "relapses" tend to be over a longer period of time (e.g. days or weeks) as opposed to dissociative "relapses" (e.g. few minutes or hours but not days or weeks). In the end, this distinction is not too relevant for psychological therapy as both types of FND symptom are associated with fluctuations in emotions.

SEIZURES

Examples: A lot of names exist to denote the same entity including dissociative episodes, non-epileptic seizures, "hysteria", non-epileptic attack disorder.

Common phrases: "I'm short circuiting", "My brain is going black" "I'm losing consciousness" "I feel a black-out coming up", "I feel locked in, but I can still hear", "I feel trapped in my body".

Dissociative episodes are characterised by paroxysmal symptoms of reduced awareness and responsiveness, occasionally accompanied by movements or a fall, that suddenly come up and then go away. In contrast to epileptic seizures, dissociative episodes are not associated with abnormal electrical activity in the brain, often determined with the gold-standard video EEG investigation. The episodes can vary from brief moments of derealisation and seizure-like episodes without loss of awareness to full-blown dissociative episodes where the person "loses consciousness" and may be unresponsive for hours, with the environment occasionally interpreting these episodes as organic epilepsy and calling an ambulance. Dissociative episodes may last from a few seconds to hours, with some people "dipping in and out" of episodes throughout the day.

Dissociative episodes can be viewed as on a continuum of dissociative behaviours. Dissociation is common in the general population and not pathological in itself, for example daydreaming, motorway hypnosis or "getting lost" in a movie, book or videogame. However, some forms of dissociation can be more problematic due to their impact on day-to-day life and the risks of injury or other untoward events they carry to the individual including wandering episodes, fugue-like states, dissociative identity or amnesia, and spending a long time sleeping.

The following "mini assessment" of dissociative episodes will help to obtain a comprehensive understanding.

ASCERTAIN SEIZURE SEMIOLOGY

Dissociative episodes are characterised by different types of "seizure semiology" with elements of the fight-flight-or-freeze response. It is not uncommon for people to report a mixture of all types (Table 4.2).

ASK FOR DETAILS

Let the person describe their most recent episode or an episode that stood out. You can ask the person and their family to complete a structured FND diary in the session together. At times, patients will report amnesia in relation to dissociative episodes. With their permission, conduct interviews with people who have witnessed the episodes, for example family members or staff, and who can provide a detailed description. Due to their paroxysmal nature, it may be helpful to obtain a frequency: How often does the person experience the episodes, for example daily, weekly or monthly? Try to ascertain any patterns: Do the episodes emerge continuously or are their seizure-free "rest" weeks and what may moderate this? ABC and tally charts may be helpful to determine triggers, responses and frequencies. It is also worth enquiring about other forms of dissociation in the person's life, which will strengthen your hypotheses that the person may use dissociation more generally as a coping habit.

Table 4.2 Commonly encountered dissociative seizure subtypes

Type of dissociative episode	Features
"Tonic-clonic" seizures	Characterised by shaking and thrashing of the body, twitches and jerky movements, occasionally violent and resulting in accidental self-injury.
Collapsing seizures	Seizures characterised by a freeze response: someone might collapse, with their body becoming floppy and going limp. People may present as immobile and lying still in bed or on the floor, or may show a "resting tremor" and stereotyped movements (e.g. softly hitting the abdominal area).
"Absence" seizures	Characterised by often short periods of the person "switching off" whilst still in the upright position or losing strength in neck muscles (e.g. head dropping), for example blank staring, glazed eyes and a lack of blinking.

ENVIRONMENTAL RESPONSES

Enquire how the environment responds to an episode or assists with the person's activities to unearth any reciprocal reinforcement, enmeshed or "distant" patterns. Occasionally, people will experience an episode in the session. These are useful moments to make behavioural observations. Video recordings of the seizures can be helpful too.

RISK ASSESSMENT

Risks are important to consider for all types of FND symptoms but especially for people with hours of violent dissociative episodes, which can result in serious accidental self-injury that is sometimes difficult to distinguish from deliberate self-harm, as well as harm to other individuals in the environment (e.g. physical injury to a family member, leaving young children unattended, driving). A particular tricky risk pertains to individuals who experience both epileptic and dissociative seizures. Management of these risks should always be done within a multidisciplinary setting with medical input.

SENSORY SYMPTOMS

Examples: reduced or altered sensation in the limbs, a spreading sensation throughout the body (paraesthesia), tingling sensations, numbness, dizziness, sensory deficits affecting visual and hearing (e.g. blurry or double vision, functional blindness, tinnitus), altered perception of the midline, hypersensitivity to noise, light, touch, smell, temperature or other external stimuli (hyperesthesia), and increased sensitivity to pain (hyperalgesia).

Common phrases: Not being able to feel your leg, "pins and needles"

In the clinic, sensory symptoms tend to be "secondary" and associated with more "primary" problems of dissociative episodes or motor-type symptoms. It is rarely the main and sole FND symptom except if hypersensitivity to external stimuli is associated with dissociative episodes or functional blindness with the person adopting the identity of a blind person.

FUNCTIONAL COGNITIVE SYMPTOMS

Examples: all cognitive domains can be involved, most often (episodic) memory, but also concentration (e.g. focused or sustained attention, information processing speed), executive functioning (e.g. initiation, planning, organisation, problem solving, mental flexibility), language functions, word finding or reading difficulties, expressive and receptive "functional" aphasia, problems with number processing and calculation, disorientation and confusion, as well as problems with visual and spatial skills.

Common phrases: "I have got a cognitive/brain fog", "my brain feels like cotton wool", "I keep on having memory lapses", "my short-term memory doesn't work", "I struggle to get my words out", "I can't think straight", "I am unable to focus on anything", "I'm confused", "I can't remember what I just said".

Cognitive symptoms are often reported by people with dissociative seizures or motor-type FND (e.g. 60% in Stone et al., 2010; 77% in Nielsen et al., 2017). Although viewed as bothersome, the majority of people with FND will experience cognitive symptoms that tend to play a subsidiary role (or are reported as relatively minor or less disruptive to day-to-day life by patients) in comparison to the often more prominent seizure and motor symptoms which generally cause more disabilities and dependency. In some more unusual cases, however, cognitive symptoms can emerge in an isolated form, as a standalone feature and the main area of difficulty with no, minimal or occasional seizure and motor-type symptoms. A few years ago, Ball et al. (2020) proposed new diagnostic criteria for the "cognitive subtype" of Functional Neurological Disorder: Functional Cognitive Disorder (see Table 4.3).

Some important reflections on these criteria   The proposed criteria for FCD are a valuable starting point, and a lot of hard work has gone into creating this list. When a person with memory problems presents to the clinic, a common question is "What may be the cause of the memory problems?" and the clinician will try to rule out any organic illnesses that can have far-fetching consequences for a person's life, family and future, for example, a neurodegenerative condition. Diagnostic criteria support clinicians with making these important clinical decisions. However, the criteria can also be a source of confusion and are perhaps even marred by some controversy. Below, the caveats for each criterion will be discussed in detail.

Criterion #1 – At least one or more symptoms of impaired cognitive functioning   This criterion states that one or more symptoms of impaired cognitive function will need to be present in order to fulfil it. The assessment of cognitive functions is ideally completed using a neuropsychological assessment that is conducted, analyzed and interpreted by a qualified clinical neuropsychologist with a substantial number of years of training in the field. In the United Kingdom, the necessary neuropsychological qualifications can be checked using a specialist register although the existence of specialist registers will likely vary per country. Please note that clinical neuropsychologists are trained specialists in investigating the relationships between the brain, our thinking skills and behaviours. These tasks are qualitatively different from those executed by a neurologist or neuropsychiatrist. A neuropsychologist will not only consider the test results but also consider the "wider picture" and engage in a process called triangulation, taking into account brain lesions, cognitive difficulties and their impact on day-to-day functioning. Below is an example of frequently probed areas that are important to consider during a neuropsychological assessment:

- History and time course of the cognitive symptoms, for example, are the memory problems "static", "progressive" or changeable depending on life events and stresses ("fluctuating").
  - Nature of the cognitive symptoms and types of symptoms. Ask for real-life examples and go through all core cognitive domains

Table 4.3 Criteria for Functional Cognitive Disorder (Ball et al., 2020)

Criterion #	What it is	Examples
1	At least one or more symptoms of impaired cognitive functioning	Any difficulty in thinking skills that are equally observed in "organic" conditions such as dementia, stroke or traumatic brain injury: Orientation in person, time and location. Remembering names, places, objects and faces; conversations and events; routes and wayfinding. Difficulty focusing on information from conversations, following a movie on television, being able to concentrate on reading a book. Word finding difficulties, making word or speech errors. Remembering the sequence of personal and domestic care activities (washing, dressing, making a cup of tea or preparing a meal). Organising ideas or plans; administrative tasks and "life". Prospective memory: remembering, being on time and finding the way to future appointments or taking medications.
2	Evidence of "internal inconsistency"	A person self-reports memory difficulties or the assessment shows scores that indicate significant memory difficulties, but the memory issues may not greatly impact day-to-day activities as would be expected on the basis of those self-reported or observed memory problems. For example, a person may be able to hold down a challenging job or carry out a normal conversation. These day-to-day activities rely on intact memory abilities and may suggest normal learning and memory functions.
3	A medical or psychiatric disorder does not explain the cognitive symptoms in a better way.	The person does not have something else that can explain the cognitive problems in a better way than the diagnosis of "Functional Cognitive Disorder", for example, Alzheimer's dementia, depression or psychosis. That said, this criterion states that it is possible for a person to have a co-existing condition – in addition to the FND. However, this co-existing condition does not/not fully explain the cognitive symptoms.
4	The cognitive symptoms cause considerable distress or issues in day-to-day life including social, work and other important areas.	The cognitive symptoms prevent a person from taking care of themselves or others/dependants, driving, living independently, taking medications, having conversations with friends, remembering things at work and not being able to be in employment.

including episodic, autobiographical, prospective and semantic memory, attention, language, executive functions, visual and spatial skills (e.g. remembering conversations and appointments, mislaying items, concentration difficulties when watching television or reading a book, wayfinding in familiar and unfamiliar places).

- Enquire about the impact of cognitive dysfunction on day-to-day functioning (e.g. personal care, relationships, employment, driving, activities and access to the community, hobbies and leisure activities, any other cognitively demanding activities, e.g. chairing a sports club).
- Organic reasons for experiencing these symptoms (e.g. prior stroke, medications, pain, fatigue, sleep, any illnesses such as diabetes, kidney, liver conditions).
- Psychological difficulties that impact cognition such as post-traumatic stress disorder, anxiety or depression, relationship and social functioning. Beliefs about self-reported cognitive problems (e.g. memory perfectionism).
- Developmental history (e.g. trauma, dyslexia, conditions affecting the brain), coping strategies, family and psychosocial functioning.
- Premorbid functioning, past educational, occupational and social experiences.
- Determine whether the cognitive difficulties have an organic origin (=brain injury caused by a stroke), a functional reason (=psychological difficulties) or are the result of a mixture of overlapping organic and functional factors.
- If possible to obtain, a collateral history can be very helpful: are there any discrepancies between self-reports and partner or family reports on the cognitive issues?
- The neuropsychological assessment should be part of a wider multidisciplinary team assessment that may also include a neurologist, (neuro) psychiatrist, occupational therapist, physiotherapist, as well as a speech and language therapist.

Criterion #2 – Evidence of "internal inconsistency"   The second criterion focuses on the concept of internal inconsistency (Ball et al., 2020). There may be a discrepancy between moderate or severe self-reported and observed cognitive difficulties and how a person fares in day-to-day life with the cognitive difficulties which do not interfere too much with employment, personal care, doing errands or carrying conversations. Given the severity level of the self-reported or observed cognitive difficulties, a person is expected to experience significantly more problems in daily life only that these problems are not that apparent. In other situations, the person may be able to carry out an activity in daily life without any problems (e.g. hold a fluent conversation with another person) but which heavily relies on intact cognitive functions (e.g. word finding, lexical retrieval of the correct semantic knowledge, grammatical/syntactic abilities, proper planning of speech movements) which the person perceives as deficient (e.g. "severe word finding difficulties"). Several reasons may drive these inconsistencies.

Fluctuating nature of FND

Inconsistencies are bound to emerge if cognitive difficulties are functional by their very nature. Functional memory problems can be driven by many physical reasons including a lack of sleep, medications, vitamin deficiencies and dehydration. For some people, functional cognitive difficulties are strongly connected to psychological reasons or stressful events (that may not necessarily be recognised as stressful by the person). It makes sense that cognitive symptoms worsen or improve (and are therefore "internally inconsistent") depending on the events that come up in a person's life.

Dissociation can make symptoms look inconsistent

If a person experiences functional memory difficulties, it is very well possible that this same individual can have a tough demanding job and continues to be able to socialise with other people yet still reports and experiences major difficulties with remembering on a day-to-day basis at home. Dissociation may explain these phenomena. Some people with FND experience "boom" activity levels and use high levels of activity without rest as an emotional coping strategy. Pushing on with work (or sports) helps some people to avoid, not sit with distress and essentially dissociate from painful thoughts, feelings and memories. Working hard and suppressing emotions or memories as part of functional cognitive symptoms can easily represent different manifestations of the same process: dissociation. This can explain the "internal inconsistency" between reported daily memory problems yet satisfactory job performance. The outward appearance of dissociation is different under different circumstances, but the common denominator remains dissociation. In addition, a job that a person has held down over a long period may have become routine. Activities are automatically executed as part of the job role without much thinking effort or heavily relying on cognitive or memory skills. Hence, job activities may be rather resistant to the memory problems. Finally, if the functional cognitive symptoms are associated with emotional triggers, and these emotional triggers are absent at work but present at home (e.g. family arguments), then it makes sense that the cognitive symptoms inconsistently appear in one area of life but not in the other.

Criterion #3 – A medical or psychiatric disorder does not explain the cognitive symptoms in a better way   The Ball et al. (2020) criteria state that other medical or psychiatric conditions cannot (fully) explain the cognitive difficulties; however, the criteria also do not tell us what hypotheses or causes may underlie these difficulties instead. We have already seen that dissociation likely plays a significant role in functional cognitive symptoms. But why do people dissociate in the first place? Contrary to what the criteria imply, clinical observations often do reveal a strong link between functional cognitive symptoms and underlying psychological difficulties. If these functional cognitive symptoms are severe, for example, in the case of severe memory problems that may render a person completely unable to take care of themselves, adequately function in life and may even warrant a nursing home placement in rare situations, the person may experience severe depression or post-traumatic stress disorder.

Milder functional cognitive symptoms in FND tend to occur as part of a wide range of anxiety disorders that often impact attentional and memory functions, in particular generalised anxiety, social anxiety and panic disorder. Therefore, a "psychiatric disorder" is often perfectly capable to explain the cognitive symptoms. It should be noted that psychological difficulties are not always recognised by the person with FND due to dissociative tendencies and the inability to connect with emotions (but instead are strongly connecting with the physical features of emotions, for example, heart palpitations and tremors suggesting anxiety). An enquiry into psychological difficulties with a person experiencing FND may not yield any valuable information; however, if a person is heavily dissociated from, or embarrassed about, emotions and distress, then it is entirely expected that the person will not report any psychological issues. This does not mean that the person does not suffer from distress and any "denial of distress" should not be taken at face value during an assessment particularly in FND. Please note that the person is not doing this on purpose. Instead, it could be construed as the brain's protection mechanism against experiencing distress or exposing psychological vulnerabilities.

In addition, although a full-blown "medical disorder" should not explain the functional cognitive symptoms (e.g. dementia, stroke or traumatic brain injury), there are certainly a lot of "lower-level" and easily overlooked physical factors in FND that may actively contribute to functional cognitive symptoms, for example, drowsiness-inducing medications and polypharmacy, poor sleep, vitamin deficiencies and dehydration.

Criterion #4 – The cognitive symptoms cause considerable distress or issues in day-to-day life including social, work and other important areas.   For some people, functional cognitive symptoms may feel very stressful and worrying. However, there is also a subset of people who do not seem to experience distress or discomfort in the context of the cognitive symptoms. People may not report any emotions, present as flat in affect or may even be bright in mood despite the cognitive symptoms. For some people, functional cognitive symptoms do not cause clinically significant distress but rather the opposite: the symptoms are the brain's automatic coping mechanism that helps to effectively reduce or remove all of the distress and perhaps help to tolerate a painful reality. Painful and hurtful memories about difficult past traumatic events are pushed into the unconscious and outside a person's awareness using memory suppression. This can present as "functional amnesia" or a memory block and is an effective strategy of the brain to help traumatised people to "more or less" cope in daily life and enables people to take care of themselves and their families, and function at work and in social situations. Relieving the "memory block" and letting those painful memories come through into awareness would be too emotionally overwhelming to bear, and the owner of these memories may fear not being able to cope and lose control. If anything, one could argue that some people are so good and effective at suppressing painful memories that, rather than impaired cognitive functions, this suggests the total opposite: exceptionally strong, above average and enhanced cognitive mechanisms, almost like a form of "super cognition".

Final reflections on the Ball et al. (2020) criteria   The Ball et al. (2020) criteria could potentially pose significant clinical challenges when considering the application of these criteria in a person with FND:

- The idea of "internal inconsistency" may elicit or re-trigger negative thoughts, feelings and perceptions in some people about their **cognitive or memory problems not being real, genuine or believed**, in the same vein as the "general" FND criteria may sometimes do. FND symptoms are often described as neurological symptoms (e.g. tremor or motor weakness) that are *inconsistent* with existing medical or neurological conditions. These powerful beliefs around not being believed are often rooted in past negative healthcare and/or childhood experiences, for example, the experience of a person not believed by a parent in the context of abuse. Beliefs around not being believed can maintain FND symptoms and the question arises to what extent these criteria are clinically useful or even harmful to patients?
- Some psychological issues can fully explain functional cognitive symptoms in people with FND, for example, depression or post-traumatic stress disorder. A diagnosis of FCD does not tell us anything about the connections with emotions, coping strategies (e.g. memory suppression, dissociation) or the wider socio-emotional functions and determinants of cognitive problems even though **emotion features are strongly linked to (cognitive) problems in FND** and the social environment the person is embedded in can greatly impact beliefs and how memory problems are managed (e.g. well-intended family members taking over chores from the memory-impaired person with the person remaining dependent and unable to test out possible "dysfunctional" beliefs around their memory abilities). Furthermore, the criteria do not mention any details about the mechanism of dissociation as a coping strategy even though dissociation plays a key role in FND.
- In line with the comments by Kapur et al. (2021), there is a **flavour of internal inconsistency** amongst the criteria themselves and people may not meet all criteria despite experiencing clear functional cognitive symptoms. Consider the following situation:
  A person self-reports significant memory problems particularly at home or during family interactions (meets criterion #1). There is evidence of "internal inconsistency": despite the severity of the self-reported and objective memory difficulties, as evidenced on neuropsychological

testing, the person is still able to function reasonably well by doing their job, making phone calls, being on time for appointments and meeting up with friends, suggesting intact memory functions (meets criterion #2). The person does not report any medical or psychiatric disorder that can explain the cognitive symptoms (meets criterion #3). In addition, the person may report distress as a result of the cognitive symptoms (meets criterion #4) or, on the contrary, the person is bright in mood and reports being reasonably content in life, in spite of the cognitive symptoms, and the memory problems do not seem to greatly impact work or social activities as stipulated under criterion #2 (and therefore does not meet criterion #4).

In the example above, criteria #2 and #4 directly oppose one another: a person with cognitive problems who is able to work in a cognitively demanding job and/or organises social gatherings demonstrates evidence of internal inconsistency but simultaneously, these preserved day-to-day abilities automatically annul criterion #4.

- The question arises whether the **addition of another diagnostic label** is helpful especially since people with FND tend to have a lot of other illness labels (e.g. fibromyalgia, irritable bowel syndrome, POTS, Ehlers-Danlos) or a complex medical history. It increases the confusion and worries that already often exist regarding the FND diagnosis itself and may add further confirmation of the idea of "I'm complex", "I'm getting worse not better", "I'm beyond help" and potentially induce more feelings of hopelessness about future recovery. Would this label add anything in a clinical sense or for the person's quality of life? Would it make a difference to the treatment approach to FND if people are also diagnosed with FCD? Would it not be better to view functional cognitive symptoms as part of the wider spectrum of FND symptoms, in the name of parsimony?
- A diagnosis of FCD does not tell you what reasons may be driving the symptoms nor does it provide a solution. This is a classic disadvantage of making a diagnosis: it misses the finesses of psychological formulation and does not map out the treatment to help a person overcome their functional (cognitive) symptoms.

The criteria and ideas around FCD are still a work in progress that will undoubtedly be further refined in the future. All in all, the criteria are a useful starting point for trying to understand functional cognitive symptoms. In the following section, we will explore some specific qualitative features of functional cognitive symptoms that can help a clinician to set them apart from the type of cognitive symptoms that tend to be caused by organic conditions like dementia, stroke or traumatic brain injury. We will focus on the cognitive domain of memory because this is probably the most reported functional cognitive symptom by people with FND.

Important aspects of memory features in FND

STRESS, ANXIETY, TRAUMA AND DEPRESSION CAN TRIGGER MEMORY
PROBLEMS

Memory problems can emerge in the context of a wide range of psychological conditions associated with FND particularly in depression, PTSD, complex trauma, generalised anxiety, social anxiety, panic disorder, as well as in other, occasionally encountered, co-existing conditions in FND, for example, obsessive-compulsive disorder, psychosis, bipolar illness and eating disorders.

Memory problems can also be provoked by current emotional events and triggered by interpersonal difficulties in relationships that are not necessarily part of an existing or official psychological condition, for example, not being able to remember a stressful family argument from a few days or weeks ago.

Typically, people may not be able to remember or speak about the emotionally charged events due to the "brain psychologically shutting down" in that moment and causing sudden memory or speech problems. This is involuntary, unconscious and not put on. It is the brain's protection mechanism to guard the individual against overwhelming and painful emotions, a form of coping that helps to keep distressing content away that the person would otherwise experience as emotionally unbearable and unable to cope with.

A DISTINCTION CAN BE MADE BETWEEN PRIMARY AND SECONDARY
MEMORY PROBLEMS

Worries and anxiety can trigger memory problems. For example, a person with social anxiety may forget what to say ("draw a blank", "shut down", "lose train of thought") during a conversation with another person in a social situation. Once the individual becomes aware of the memory problems that are triggered by these social fears, the memory difficulties are further compounded by the development of "secondary" unhelpful beliefs about the memory difficulties, causing additional fear and worries that further impact already existing memory issues. Common memory beliefs include:

- Memory perfectionism about minor lapses.
- Overinterpretation of memory mistakes.
- Increased or excessive self-monitoring of self-perceived memory failures or cognitive errors.
- Development of fixed beliefs around "there is something wrong with my memory" and "my memory is poor" with the person behaving in accordance with these beliefs, for example, by allowing the environment to take over chores or provide extra support (e.g. medication management, always accompanying the person to appointments), which do not afford the individual with opportunities to test out assumptions around poor memory and maintain the memory problems.

NATURE OF MEMORY PROBLEMS: CONSIDER QUALITATIVE AND PROCESS
FEATURES

In order to better understand the nature of memory problems in people with
FND, it can be useful to keep in mind the memory characteristics that are
often associated with organic causes of memory difficulties such as Alzheimer's dementia. The type of memory problems tends to differ in quality for
functional vs organic causes.

Selectivity. Memory difficulties in FND can be situation/time-specific
and selectively associated with periods of emotional distress or stressful
events. For example, people may have lost their memory for a particularly
emotional or traumatic life period in the past that is expected to evoke
high levels of distress, for example, a bereavement, separation, accident or
life-threatening illness. These autobiographical memory gaps are often in
stark contrast with memories from other non-emotional times that remain
unaffected. In addition, in the presence of this retrograde amnesia pattern,
the person may still be able to lay down new memories without evidence
of anterograde amnesia.

A specific type of memory problem that occurs in people with FND in
the aftermath of a dissociative episode is termed "post-dissociative episode
amnesia", which refers to the temporary and occasionally reversible memory
loss for the period of the dissociative episode and the events that may have
precipitated it.

Severity. The memory loss may be so severe that the person cannot
remember anything from that distressing time, with the memory loss
"total" (all memories from that time have disappeared). Less severe amnesia
may be characterised by "fragmented" features (some memories from that
period remain) or "hazy" (only the gist without details is remembered).
In those instances, it is not uncommon for the memory loss to span longer
periods (e.g. weeks, months or years). In rare cases, people may forget their
entire past and identity in the context of dissociative fugue states, even if
completely bed-bound and experiencing other FND symptoms (e.g. functional weakness).

Other qualitative features. Functional memory problems can be temporary and reversible and do not tend to progressively worsen over time
in the same way as in many forms of dementia which result in a gradual
memory decline and permanent memory loss. Instead, functional memory
problems are more likely to fluctuate as and when triggers emerge. Furthermore, memory loss as part of dementia syndromes tends to have insipient
beginnings, whereas memory loss in the context of FND is often marked
by a discrete stressful event. Self-reported memory or cognitive problems and/or "objective neuropsychological deficits" can be significantly
worse than "cognition-in-function" or in memory observed in activities of
"everyday life" ("internal inconsistencies" as mentioned in the Ball et al.,
2020 criteria).

Behavioural observations in and around the clinic visit can be very helpful to help detect these discrepancies. Despite dissociative amnesia, a person may have:

- A good ability to remember their last therapy session and strategies discussed with you.
- Provide a useful personal history with detailed memories about life periods that are not affected by an autobiographical memory gap, rather than vague, gist memories and without relying too much on another person.
- Inconsistencies may emerge around recalling information from the autobiographical memory gap, for example, expressing an explicit inability to remember any details from this epoch yet implicitly providing some detail during other moments of the interview.
- No overt word finding/lexical retrieval difficulties, dysphasia in conversation or problems with communicating needs.
- Good navigation and wayfinding skills including (semi)-independent usage of transport to the appointment.
- Able to find the toilet without or minimal repetition of instructions.
- Normal recognition of your face and name, remembering to sign in and out for appointments and recalling medication lists (or knowing where to find the list in a purse or phone).
- Not showing any confusion, disorientation or repetition of information or questions at any point during the appointment.

Please note that detecting these discrepancies does not mean that the person is "faking" their amnesia or cognitive problems. Nor are these observations intended to "catch the person out" but merely serve to aid your understanding of the nature of a person's cognitive difficulties.

Features on neuropsychological testing. Pay attention to any unusual memory patterns, particularly around inconsistencies. For example, if a person has discordant performance across tests that tap into very similar cognitive processes or exhibits severely reduced scores on all memory tests but performs relatively well on other "non-memory" tests that clearly rely on intact learning and memory functions and/or is able to complete day-to-day activities relying on those same memory processes without any great difficulty, then these could be categorised as inconsistencies. Other features include consistently choosing the distractor over the target stimulus, suggesting potentially preserved memory; better performance on more complex, cognitively demanding tests, in comparison to simpler and less effortful tests (e.g. recall > recognition) which may suggest attentional dysfunction amongst other things or the opposite pattern (e.g. recognition > recall) with retrieval deficits that indicate the successful registration of a memory trace but problems with accessing the information.

Memory difficulties in people with FND can pertain to past autobiographical memories. The Autobiographical Memory Interview (AMI; Kopelman et al., 1990) is worth mentioning here. People with "psychogenic amnesia" show impaired autobiographical memory and variability in their performance on this tool, with a recoverable "often anomalous temporal gradient" (Kopelman, 1993). In contrast, the AMI temporal gradients for people with Alzheimer's dementia and semantic dementia are qualitatively different from each other and from psychogenic amnesia. People with Alzheimer's dementia will show a "typical" temporal gradient with older memories better remembered than more poorly recalled recent memories, whereas people with semantic dementia will show a "reverse" temporal gradient, characterised by preserved recent memories in comparison to the loss of earlier, more remote autobiographical memories (Snowden et al., 1996; Graham & Hodges, 1997).

Please note that these observations are not absolute criteria, not even rules of thumb. These features also do not automatically suggest functional causes or feigning. The assessment of functional cognitive symptoms should always be driven by neuropsychological formulation that provides a holistic view of the person, within a multidisciplinary setting, that is not based on isolated test observations de-contextualised from other sources of information.

A history of avoidant coping. If there is a clear demarcation point after which the memory problems started (e.g. following a bereavement), it can be helpful to enquire about the person's coping strategies and whether/how the grief was processed. If there is an indication that the person has not processed distress or describes avoidant coping strategies ("I just pushed on", "I tried to forget about it"), then this can provide additional indirect evidence for the functional nature of the memory problems. Memory loss can be regarded as an (unconscious) form of cognitive avoidance, inhibition or suppression of distressing psychological material. If an underlying psychological difficulty that is understood to be driving the memory problems (e.g. depression) improves, this will have a positive knock-on effect with memory symptoms improving as well.

THE MECHANISMS OF FUNCTIONAL VS ORGANIC MEMORY PROBLEMS
QUALITATIVELY DIFFER

Organic memory problems can be driven by a brain injury or neurological illness resulting in a (progressive) loss of neurons visible on a brain scan. Although neurons cannot be replaced, new connections can be formed; however, the site of the brain injury will not be the same as it was before the "insult". Functional cognitive problems tend to be driven by psychological factors such as dissociation and suppression mechanisms. Both organic and functional memory problems can also be caused or made worse by physical factors such as dehydration, pain, medications, vitamin deficiencies and poor sleep.

That said, the distinction between functional and organic causes is not always "neat" and the two types of memory problem can overlap. For example, it is possible to have had a stroke resulting in memory loss that is compounded and amplified by psychological difficulties such as post-stroke depression or post-traumatic stress disorder. As another "functional overlay" example, a person may have had an organic condition or treatment affecting their brain (e.g. meningitis, chemotherapy, hydrocephalus, childhood epilepsy) and subsequently develop memory problems. However, it may not be possible to ascribe the memory difficulties entirely to the brain condition or toxic effects of treatment, or may only be partially driven, and the combined result of the brain condition and the "psychological shock" of having had the brain issues. At times, fixed ideas around a brain condition as the natural cause of memory problems may prolong these cognitive difficulties, as people may have resigned to this idea that "nothing can be done" and not test out assumptions around self-perceived poor memory.

ASSESSMENT OF FUNCTIONAL COGNITIVE SYMPTOMS IN FND:
NEUROPSYCHOLOGICAL CONSIDERATIONS

CONDUCT A COMPREHENSIVE HISTORY

A wide variety of factors that are commonly encountered in FND could significantly contribute to the cognitive problems that people with FND experience. The underlying reasons for cognitive dysfunction in a person with FND are very likely heterogeneous and multi-layered. The following list of variables is not exhaustive but may be useful to keep in mind as a "checklist" during the assessment of a person with cognitive difficulties and FND:

- **Brain injuries** are an important cause of cognitive difficulties that can also lead to a disproportionate level of cognitive dysfunction, as part of a functional overlay syndrome.
  - Organic brain conditions may predispose people for developing FND and functional cognitive symptoms later in life through modelling processes, for example, epileptic and dissociative seizures.
  - Some brain conditions impact on cognition in a subset but not in all people afflicted with the condition (e.g. meningitis). However, a person may develop fixed beliefs around the brain condition automatically being the culprit of cognitive dysfunction, which maintain the cognitive symptoms in that individual.
  - Mild traumatic brain injury, a previous concussion/post-concussive syndrome or a whiplash due to a fall, car accident or knock to the head can all cause cognitive dysfunction with functional overlay in some cases.
  - Always ask about the circumstances with regard to the brain injury, "peri-traumatic stress" and any rejection themes that can be linked to early upbringing.
- **Physical illnesses**, in particular hormonal and endocrine illnesses such as hypo- or hyperthyroidism and diabetes that may not be well-controlled or not yet discovered in the person.

- **Excessive symptom focus, pain and fatigue.** Teodoro et al. (2018) argued that these hallmark features of, respectively, FND, fibromyalgia and chronic fatigue syndrome (with the latter two conditions frequently co-existing with FND) all interfere with the efficiency of cognitive/ attentional processing and increase a person's vulnerability to distraction and may create the subjective experience of cognitive difficulties ("brain fog") but also interfere with encoding and memory functions.
- **Underlying psychological distress.** A large proportion of people with FND experience depression and anxiety. Difficult thoughts and feelings can take up a lot of head space, distract and keep a person's mind occupied, affecting people's concentration and memory abilities, in a similar vein to what Teodoro et al.'s (2018) suggested earlier, even if the individual is not aware of these thoughts and feelings, but the brain is actively suppressing unbearable, distressing contents. Table 4.3 displays a few examples of cognitive features found in a variety of commonly encountered psychological conditions in people with FND.

Psychological condition	Effects on cognition
Panic disorder	In panic disorder, the body and mind are in an intense state of alarm and the brain is not able to "think straight" during a panic attack. Although some studies show heightened "attention capture" for panic- or threat-related words in people with panic disorder (Maidenberg et al., 1996; Lundh et al., 1999), interestingly, research has also demonstrated enhanced memory performance for panic- or threat-related words relative to positive and negative words (Cloitre & Liebowitz, 1991; Becker et al., 1994). Increased attention and memory for threat may suggest less cognitive resources for non-threat activities or events.
Generalised anxiety/health anxiety disorder	Persistent worries, including worries about health, capture "limited capacity" attentional resources that stop a person from focusing on other meaningful things in life, such as conversations, tasks or daily activities. People who worry exhibit impaired attentional control, selective attention to threatening information, as well as interpretation biases (Hirsh & Mathews, 2012; Hirsch et al., 2019).
Social anxiety	Social fears upon entering a social situation, where the person can only think and focus on how to "survive" a fear-inducing social event, can greatly disrupt cognition, with people reporting their minds "switching off". Attentional and interpretation biases have been evidenced in social anxiety (Maidenberg et al., 1996; Pishyar et al., 2004; Amir et al., 2005).

(Continued)

Psychological condition	Effects on cognition
Post-traumatic stress disorder (PTSD)	People with PTSD re-experience and have flashbacks about traumatic events that automatically pop up ("involuntary recall"), with the mind trying to suppress or being captured by trauma-related content (e.g. McNally et al., 1993). All these phenomena are bound to cause disruptions to cognitive processes. Trauma memories are known to be qualitatively different from "regular" memories in relation to characteristics such as nowness, vividness, sensory features, as well as defragmentation/disorganisation and the presence of "emotional hot spots" intermixed with other hazier parts of the memory (e.g. Ehlers, Hackmann & Michael, 2004).
Obsessive-compulsive disorder (OCD)	An unusual amount of cognitive resource, focus and sustained attention may be allocated to obsessional thoughts around, for example, doing everything as perfect or keep as clean as possible, or engagement with constant hypervigilance about the environment in relation to contamination fears. Attention, memory, executive functioning and visual perceptual impairments, as well as attentional biases towards threat-related information, have been reported for people with OCD (Muller & Roberts, 2005) including a reduced ability to selectively ignore intrusive thoughts (Clayton et al., 1999).
Depression or low mood	Depression resulting in low energy, lack of motivation and fatigue may contribute to reduced "cognitive energy" or "cognitive fatigue" that is needed to support effective cognitive processing. Forgetfulness, as well as attention, memory and interpretation biases for negative information have previously been reported in people with depression (e.g. Watkins et al., 1996).

- **Interpersonal triggers and cognition.** Cognitive symptoms in FND tend to be viewed as the result of "attentional secondary effects" due to the allocation of attentional resources to symptoms (e.g. Teodoro et al., 2018; Bennett et al., 2021). Attentional features are also a defining characteristic of anxiety disorders which are often encountered in people with FND. However, in clinical practice, people with FND do not always experience or present with "classic" forms of anxiety such as the anxiety seen in panic attacks or social anxiety. It is often evident that people with FND experience another type of more "relational" anxiety, either in addition to or instead of classic anxiety. This attachment-anxiety is strongly associated with the presence of other people and revolves around not only fears but also emotions such as anger and sadness, in connection to abandonment or rejection by, for example, family members and healthcare professionals. Interpersonal triggers including ongoing negative family or partner dynamics, recent arguments and disagreements, as well as healthcare contacts may elicit these attachment fears and can culminate in more severe cognitive symptoms than the typical "attentional fluctuations" in the context of heightened symptom focus, particularly dissociative amnesia and dissociative seizures, which essentially is a temporary "total" breakdown of attentional processes and awareness.

- **Medications.** People with FND tend to be on a lot of medications, also termed "polypharmacy", which can interact and collectively exert unwanted effects on cognition. However, the relationship between medications and cognition in FND is complex. Some medications for depression, anxiety and pain are known to be sedative, "calming" and even dissociating to the brain (e.g. opiates, tricyclic antidepressants). On the one hand, the improvement of mood, anxiety and pain symptoms can greatly benefit cognition. However, these cognitive benefits may disappear altogether if medications make a person too drowsy or "not with it". In addition, some medications are known to cause specific cognitive deficits, for example, difficulties on verbal tasks in people taking the anti-epileptic medication Topiramate (Thompson et al., 2000). In addition, analgesia overuse headaches are not uncommon for people with FND and the combination of medications and pain can jointly exert a double portion of negative effects on cognition. Overdosage on medication can also heavily impact on cognition in people with FND and can happen for a variety of different reasons, including lack of awareness on appropriate medication intake, medication mismanagement in the context of self-neglect, confusion or indeed cognitive difficulties, as well as deliberate self-harm. The opposite should also be taken into consideration: people have been known to stop medications at once due to adverse side effects, but that may require a longer-term tapering regimen, causing subsequent cognitive side effects.
- **Alcohol and substance misuse.** Although mind-altering prescription medications will more likely be problematic as a factor adversely impacting cognitive functioning in people with FND, occasionally people with FND will report coping with anxiety or unpleasant arousal by excessive alcohol intake or cannabis use that quickly and effectively reduces arousal, in the same way as for example a dissociative seizure does.
- **Poor sleep.** Sleeping problems can greatly affect cognition. People may be unable to sleep at all at night, have very little sleep, wake up intermittently, experience sleep apnoea and have a disturbed sleep-wake cycle. Poor sleep can *directly* impact on thinking skills: we may not feel as refreshed or lack energy for the next day. We may not be as alert, focused and cognitively "with it" for our day jobs and activities. In addition, sleeping difficulties can also *indirectly* impact on thinking skills. People

often report feeling worse emotionally after a poor night's sleep, and psychological distress can adversely impact on thinking skills.

- **Food and hydration.** Vitamins and mineral deficiencies occur in FND and can cause memory difficulties, for example, iron or vitamin B12. Furthermore, people with FND may not drink sufficient water or fluids, leading to confusion and a "clouding of the mind". Limited access to the community and a reduced ability for self-care and toileting due to physical disabilities can indirectly impact on cognition if not much support is available to the individual for preparing nutritious meals and managing incontinence by limiting fluids. Some people with FND overconsume energy drinks which may improve alertness and memory functions; however, the downside is that these drinks can also cause palpitations and anxiety symptoms that negatively influence cognition.

- **Form of communicating distress.** One of the most fundamental principles of the Pressure Cooker Model states that people with FND often struggle to express difficult thoughts and feelings verbally and emotionally to another person often lacking safe and trusting relationships, and because of the FND, emotional difficulties and physical disabilities often do not have any recourse to other stress-releasing strategies such as practicing sports and engaging with social activities. With these two channels on the Pressure Cooker Model "blocked", the body becomes the alternative mode of expressing turmoil often more unconsciously than consciously. In the same way, functional cognitive symptoms can represent a method of expressing (or be the direct result of) inner turmoil as the person has no other way to express distress. Therefore, it is important to look beyond "deficit level" and explore the possible functions of cognitive symptoms.

- **A controversial topic: feigning of memory difficulties**....and of course, a very small subset of people may indeed consciously and purposefully put on memory and other cognitive problems for "secondary gain", for example, to receive financial compensation, stand trial or avoid a prison term in the context of a court case. The large body of research on performance validity in FND has, at times, been interpreted in unhelpful ways. Two points are important to mention here for purposes of clarity:

- If memory or other cognitive problems are feigned for secondary gain, the person clearly does not have FND. Feigning in this context is rare, and this entity should not be viewed as similar to FND or FCD.

- However, a subset of people with FND may show either ambiguous or unequivocally low neuropsychological test scores, with reduced scores on multiple performance validity tests which may raise the suspicion of "feigning".

It is important to remember that low neuropsychological test scores, including those on performance validity tests, do not automatically indicate feigning or malingering. Other valid reasons, in the absence of brain injury, that may account for these results pertain to secondary attentional and memory difficulties, for example, due to temporary dissociation and "switching off"; social anxiety as the testing situation is effectively another social situation with a stranger; worries or overthinking about cognitive performance; pain; sedative effects of medications; heightened symptom monitoring that turns attention inwards rather than outwards with people losing focus on the presented stimuli; as well as low energy and cognitive fatigue in the context of depression, as some of these tests require a person to selectively focus for a long time. In addition, neuropsychological test scores on their own should not lead to any firm conclusions about a person's performance.

With low test scores it would be tempting to quickly jump to unhelpful conclusions and make extreme statements such as the person "is faking it", "wants to receive medical attention from healthcare professionals", "has a factitious disorder", "prefers to avoid working or engaging with familial responsibilities" or "currently enjoys or is too entrenched in their life with FND and does not want to give this up".

In all these instances, the lines are often blurry, and one should raise different types of questions instead:

- Let's suppose that each of these situations would be true, what would that tell you about the underlying psychological processes that this person may be experiencing?
- Would it not be important to explore the driving forces behind these neuropsychological test scores in a more nuanced way, moving beyond a superficial level of analysis and making quick inferences?
- Could the person express distress in a non-verbal manner by exaggerating deficits on the tests because it is too hard to speak about feelings to a stranger or anyone in their family?
- What function might these reduced scores serve, does it help to make the person feel heard, validated or convince the healthcare professional to believe the person about how unwell they truly feel because they are often not believed or taken seriously by people close to them?
- What might be so attractive about "attracting medical attention" and could the person's history suggest clues that could have contributed to the development of these behaviours, for example, childhood emotional neglect?
- What may be going on in the person's work, personal or family life that makes cognitive symptoms almost a more desirable state of being, even if "put on" deliberately?
- Does the person possess a high level of suggestibility? Perhaps an initial organic hypothesis (e.g. encephalitis) was entertained but eventually discarded. However, the person has become strongly wedded to an organic explanation as psychological causes would be too embarrassing and shameful to share with their environment and now starts to "behave" in line with the clinical presentation that this organic cause would generate?

Although FND is sometimes difficult to differentiate from factitious disorder, if the person turns out to experience factitious disorder, rather than FND or functional cognitive symptoms, this very fact strongly indicates that the person must feel very unwell, even if not connecting with emotions, and may require longstanding, intensive psychological support to unpick the drivers for these behaviours. If anything, this person needs help rather than rejection.

- **Normal ageing.** FND and functional cognitive symptoms can affect any age, including people of older age. Memory and other cognitive problems can just be part of the normal ageing process. As people get older, the brain ages too. Some cognitive functions start to age already in our thirties, for example, our speed of information processing. A subset of people with functional cognitive symptoms may present to memory clinics as anxious and the "worried well". A person may have a close family member with Alzheimer's dementia, become hypervigilant and worry about their own cognitive functioning and the risk of developing the same condition. A neuropsychologist will be able to determine whether a person's worries about their memory are legitimate concerns, for example, by comparing their assessment results with people of the same age, gender and educational level.

- **Environment.** There are many ways in which the environment and family system can maintain a person's functional cognitive symptoms:

  Recurring interpersonal triggers (e.g. ongoing stressful family interactions, arguments, conflicts, distancing from family members) can lead to more severe symptoms impacting on cognition such as dissociative amnesia and dissociative seizures. The amnesia (or FND) is a protective mechanism against strong, otherwise difficult to tolerate, emotions (internal regulation function of amnesia) and may immediately stop current conflicts or act as a deterrent against the resurgence of future arguments as well as facilitate nurturing responses and positive interactions instead (external regulation function), therefore negatively and positively reinforcing the amnesia. The family's responses increase the future risk of functional cognitive symptoms.

  Social isolation is a frequent issue in FND due to widely varying reasons including depression and lack of initiation; social anxiety and panic attacks; physical disabilities that limit access to the community; interpersonal, emotion regulation or social skills difficulties that interfere with developing relationships; and even coercion by a partner or family member. A lack of social network or regular social interactions stops a person from "testing out" dysfunctional assumptions around poor memory abilities which the person may perceive as significantly more severe than in reality. In addition, not being able to access the community and connecting socially with other people prevents the person from developing alternative coping strategies (e.g. sports, friends) for distress that would reduce the risk of dissociative amnesia.

Occasionally, a person may have experienced a life-threatening or anxiety-provoking condition that has the potential to generate cognitive impairments prior to developing actual functional cognitive symptoms (e.g. meningitis, mild traumatic brain injury or concussion, narrowly escaping a serious car accident resulting in a whiplash) or a person may have a complex medical history affecting multiple body systems that predates the FND (e.g. cancer, diabetes, liver, renal issues). Following recovery or stabilisation of the condition, the person requires ongoing "medical input" with hospital appointments, reviews and medications. This can contribute to the development of a person's "cognitive sick role" that may be maintained not only by the person themselves but also by the partner's or family's perception that the person remains "cognitively ill" and is highly vulnerable and needs care, making them highly dependent on the family. The circumstances around these illnesses will likely have been distressing for all members of the system. The "caring responses" and hypervigilant symptom monitoring from the family may serve different functions, e.g. ensuring that an illness will not happen again to their loved one or managing the family's own distress. Families may inadvertently or unconsciously maintain "the status quo" of the person's illness-family care arrangements. This co-dependency prevents a person from testing out the quality of their memory or cognitive functioning and keeps alive the idea of, for example, a severe memory impairment. Very rarely may suspected secondary gain play a role in maintaining functional cognitive (or FND) symptoms, for example, when a potential advantage exists for family members "to keep" the person ill in the context of a financial allowance that may be the only source of income.

A similar mechanism may emerge with unspeakable dilemmas (Griffith et al., 1998) in functional cognitive symptoms, i.e. a "public" or hidden secret, for example, abuse or domestic violence. Not speaking about the secret maintains the symptoms. The person is stuck in a dilemma as releasing the secret out in the open (and subsequent recovery from symptoms) may have dire, irreversible and far-reaching consequences including a potential threat to well-being; rejection from the social unit; an inability to psychologically tolerate the emotional fall-out and breakdown of the family system by the person or any of the members; the family system losing their bearings and identity. In the person's view, this situation can feel hopeless and escape impossible. The best way to survive and tolerate the pain of an inescapable situation may be memory suppression or dissociative amnesia, since other channels of coping are blocked (e.g. physical disabilities preventing access to the community).

This review shows that the causes of cognitive dysfunction in people with FND are likely multi-factorial in nature and a comprehensive history is therefore essential. Ask about any formal neuropsychological assessment results that are available, and if not, conduct an assessment to differentiate between organic and functional hypotheses of the cognitive deficits. As some dementias may present with psychiatric symptoms in the prodromal stage (e.g. frontotemporal dementia) and it is important to increase diagnostic certainty, it may be helpful to do repeat neuropsychological testing in nine months to a year to exclude a progressive condition. Ensure that you have access to neuroimaging reports that exclude any organic cause for the cognitive problems or clinical presentation. It is worth checking whether the person may have already attended a memory clinic.

Above all, it should be strongly emphasised that a comprehensive neuropsychological formulation led by experienced and sufficiently trained clinical neuropsychologists, embedded in a multidisciplinary team, will be of utmost importance during the assessment and treatment of functional cognitive symptoms in people with FND.

A relatively rare but real occurrence: Severe dissociative amnesia in FND

We should reserve special mention for the manifestation of severe dissociative amnesia as part of extreme psychological distress, for example, severe depression or trauma. Some people's ability to suppress difficult memories will be so strong that this may result in relatively short-lived dissociative fugue states where people may wander away for hours or days, temporarily lose their identity and memories of the past. Other people will develop longstanding severe dissociative amnesia, which may be characterised by forgetting most of a traumatic childhood; a series of parallel life events that have been particularly difficult to cope with using existing but insufficient coping resources; or a distressing life period that has entirely vanished, sometimes covering years or decades. Most people with this type of severe amnesia will be able to function reasonably well in life, with the support of a family or partner. For a small subset of people, the severe amnesia will render them unable to meaningfully participate in day-to-day life, care for themselves with high levels of self-neglect and significant risk of health deterioration, requiring people to be supported with 24-hour care in a nursing home. Chapter 5 will discuss the successful therapeutic journey of a person with severe dissociative amnesia using the principles of the Pressure Cooker Model.

TREATMENT OF FUNCTIONAL COGNITIVE SYMPTOMS

At times, researchers and clinicians view FND symptoms in fragmented and "dissociated" ways. People with FND frequently present with a variety of symptoms, and each symptom may be looked at separately. Entire educational or therapy groups, treatment programmes, as well as specific diagnostic criteria have been developed for one specific subtype of FND. To some extent this is sensible and understandable when planning treatment. A person experiencing dissociative seizures as their sole or main symptom does not likely require intensive physiotherapy sessions in the same way as, for example, a wheelchair-bound person with functional paraplegia may need. Although

FND is heterogeneous and manifests in unique ways for different people, symptoms frequently co-exist that are driven by similar mechanisms. It is more common than not for a person to experience multiple types of FND symptoms at once, for example, occasional dissociative seizures, more static functional weakness, reduced sensation and memory problems or "brain fog". Even if people do not experience these symptoms simultaneously, some people may have been troubled by one specific symptom in the past (dissociative seizures) which have now evolved into a new set of FND symptoms (motor-type FND). Irrespective of the current primary manifestation, cognitive dysfunction is very common in people with FND, most often as an additional, rather than a standalone, isolated symptom. The question arises as to how we treat a person, who, for example, presents with concurrent seizures and memory problems? In the following section, some pointers are outlined that can help you decide what course of intervention may be most helpful:

- **Always start with a neuropsychological assessment and formulation.** As cognitive difficulties will be associated with psychological, biological and social factors in people with FND, your neuropsychological formulation with "fresh" neuropsychological assessment data will be core and guide your (multidisciplinary) treatment plan. Please note that although a neuropsychological assessment is key, a multidisciplinary approach to cognitive symptoms is of utmost importance. For example, a person may be on polypharmacy and the medical team may decide to review these medications to check, amongst other things, whether a person's cognitive functioning improves. In some people, an underlying and clearly defined psychological condition (e.g. depression, PTSD, social anxiety, panic attacks) is evidently driving the cognitive symptoms. It is sensible to address the underlying psychological condition in the hope that resolving these issues will have a knock-on effect on improving cognitive symptoms. Evidence-based CBT protocols can be very helpful especially if the functional cognitive symptoms can be relatively easy incorporated into the formulation, for example, dissociative coping strategies ("I switch my mind off", "I lose awareness") or vacant staring in social situations can be subsumed under the safety behaviours header (rather than as an anxiety symptom) in the social anxiety model. Dropping the functional cognitive symptom as a safety behaviour may mean introducing reality grounding techniques to "switch the mind back on" and "not lose awareness" (see Chapter 8 for more information).
- **If a person does not report distress this does not automatically mean that distress is absent.** People may not report distress for a wide variety of reasons, including dissociation, alexithymia, embarrassment or not wanting to upset and burden loved ones. People with strong dissociative tendencies and alexithymia, or people who experience dissociative amnesia in response to interpersonal triggers, will often poorly fit with existing psychological conditions and their concomitant CBT models. There is no point in trying to shoehorn a person into a CBT model or

actively encourage the person to start identifying emotions especially in people who are not ready to tackle emotional issues.

The Pressure Cooker Model can be a useful "stepping stone", in combination with neuropsychological and other multidisciplinary assessment results, to create an initial formulation of the functional cognitive problems to support psychoeducation on the relationships between interpersonal triggers (Fuel), strong emotions or internal states and the idea of attempting to dissociate from these emotions because they feel highly unpleasant (Flames and Heat), using memory suppression/dissociative amnesia (Overpressure Plug); the impact of physical features such as sedative medications, pain, fatigue, poor sleep and dehydration on cognition (Pot) and heightened symptom focus derailing cognitive processes (Warning light); as well as boom-and-bust cycles that may promote fatigue that contributes to cognitive dysfunction (Valve) and a lack of opportunities for emotional expression in a safe relationship (Cover); and finally, social isolation preventing a person from testing out unhelpful beliefs around poor memory and environmental dependency maintaining memory problems (Kitchen).

- **Psychoeducation on functional cognitive symptoms: other tools.** In addition to the Pressure Cooker Model, the following strategies can be helpful:
  - Offer to carry out joint work with medical colleagues to explore brain scans (whether negative for brain injury or showing injury that cannot explain the disproportionate cognitive dysfunction), neuropsychological test results and the various functions of the brain.
  - It may be helpful to explore the specific features of a person's memory difficulties to highlight their functional nature and the existence of a "memory trace", for example, by:
    - Looking at neuropsychological test scores, e.g. recognition > recall performance, variability and inconsistencies between neuropsychological test scores that point to functional rather than organic amnesia, discrepancies between test scores and day-to-day functions in the person's life or discrepancies between self-reported poor memory and mild deficits on neuropsychological testing.
    - When you highlight any discrepancies between the person's cognitive scores and daily life, ensure to do this in a gentle and compassionate manner, as it can feel confrontational and rejecting. It is important for the person to feel believed, validated and accepted. The goal is not to catch the person out.

Provide more general facts including:

- Fluctuations in cognitive symptoms in response to stress and emotions, as well as maintenance cycles and secondary beliefs about memory (e.g.

the memory problems themselves elicit worries and anxiety, on top of the "original" source of worry).

- The reversible nature of functional amnesia and the fact that "forgotten" memories may not have disappeared completely (are suppressed by automatic psychological mechanisms to protect the individual from hurtful emotions) and can potentially be accessed again, giving hope for recovery.

- How its onset and course tend to differ from a neurodegenerative condition such as dementia (i.e. more likely sudden vs insipient onset, fluctuations vs gradual decline).

- You could consider creating a sheet that captures common cognitive errors and memory lapses in the general population (e.g. walking into a room but forgetting what you needed to do again, searching for your glasses but realising that they are on top of your head, struggling to find your car in a crowded parking lot).

  - The way the environment can maintain functional cognitive symptoms. Increase insight into all these systemic processes. If an "unspeakable dilemma" is suspected that is driving the cognitive symptoms, pre-empt this to allow the person to explore this with you, if such dilemma exists.

- **Adopt a bird's eye view and go beyond "contents" to monitor "the process".** In addition to analysing neuropsychological scores, it is important to explore qualitative features, particularly if functional cognitive symptoms are suspected (e.g. isolated retrograde amnesia, worsening memory problems in response to stress triggers). A multitude of tailored treatments focused on multiple symptoms is probably less recommended, for example, targeting memory problems separately from other FND symptoms. In line with the principles of the Pressure Cooker Model, it is helpful to see any type of FND symptom, including functional cognitive symptoms, as part of the wider spectrum of the often closely related FND symptoms, and formulate this holistically and parsimoniously with the person. Keep in mind any mirroring processes: are you taking on the person's own dissociative tendencies by approaching their FND and cognitive symptoms in a similar defragmented way?

- **Behavioural approaches.** To challenge and test out unhelpful beliefs around self-perceived poor cognitive functioning (often poor memory), it can be useful for the person to create a survey and ask other people in their environment about their own "memory failures" and the meaning they attach to these mistakes – do they jump to conclusions and think the worst of their memories too? What is the worst thing that can happen if you would end up forgetting x, y and z? "Would that be so bad?". Setting up behavioural experiments can help to support the person with acting against dysfunctional beliefs about their cognitive functioning or learning to let go of hypervigilance around memory failures, tolerate the distress of not paying too much attention to memory performance, and lessen the impact of beliefs on the person's mood and memory long term. Behavioural activation that incorporates new social activities that allow the person to establish new friendships and increase sense of social belonging can facilitate the testing out of erroneous self-beliefs about memory performance.

- **Memory diaries.** Ask the person to track their memory functioning on a daily basis for a few weeks, carefully detailing memory lapses, emotions and meanings attached to them (what does the person think of the memory problem, do they think the worst?). It is useful to keep in mind all the reasons for memory problems that were listed earlier. Do the memory problems vary depending on emotional interactions, mood and anxiety levels, quality and amount of sleep, fatigue and pain levels, food and fluid intake, activity levels? The person's family could support with completing the diary if the person struggles to remember or concentrate and "fill in the gaps" in the diary, including noting any instances of "preserved" memory during the day.

- In addition to **normalising the existence of functional cognitive symptoms** as part of FND and memory lapses in the general population, it is important to share with the person that although functional cognitive symptoms may not be that visible or "on the surface" as other FND symptoms such as dissociative seizures and motor weakness, these symptoms can still be anxiety-provoking, bothersome and disrupt day-to-day activities. Experiencing functional cognitive symptoms means that the symptoms are real, genuine, not feigned or done on purpose in any way, and should always be believed by other people.

- **Invest in a therapeutic relationship** as this will be a powerful tool to support a person with functional cognitive symptoms. Although this may not always be possible in an outpatient clinic that assesses and reviews large volumes of patients with cognitive symptoms with varying aetiology, functional cognitive symptoms can be driven by highly distressing causes, for example, unspeakable dilemmas, trauma, abuse, coercion and domestic violence, in people with complex trauma backgrounds characterised by childhood adversity and emotional neglect.

- **Cognitive rehabilitation** could potentially be useful, even though these strategies are commonly used for organic memory problems. Since the person with functional memory difficulties experiences memory problems, regardless of its "organicity", and which impact on their day-to-day life, the person can still benefit from these techniques whilst they are in the process of recovery, for example, with compensatory aids and diary training to support memory, manage daily appointments and create a routine which is psychologically containing. It is also understandable to support the person with adaptations during psychological therapy, for example, written summaries of sessions to enable the person to recall what was discussed in therapy sessions, organise materials in a folder and present information slowly/explain concepts multiple times to allow for sufficient time to process the information – in the same way as you would do with a person with cognitive difficulties due to an organic cause. However, keep in mind that cognitive rehabilitation strategies can potentially reinforce a "sick role" and the idea that something is terribly wrong with the person's cognitive functioning. Always explain the rationale for using these techniques, avoid intensive "drill practice" and aim to phase out the person's reliance on too many of these techniques. The person's cognitive problems are in theory reversible. In the following section, we will explore two more symptoms often experienced by people with FND that can be subsumed under the 'Overpressure Plug' element in the Pressure Cooker Model: pain and fatigue.

Co-existing physical symptoms

Pain and fatigue are highly frequent in people with FND (e.g. Nielsen et al., 2017; Petrochilos et al., 2020; Goldstein et al., 2021). Both symptoms may pre-date the FND. It is not uncommon for people with FND to report a history of chronic fatigue syndrome, fibromyalgia or complex regional pain syndrome. Physical and cognitive fatigue may be driven by a variety of reasons in FND including medication side effects; anxiety, worries and the biological features of depression; high activity levels ("pushing on with activities" as part of a boom or boom-and-bust valve); other physical illnesses due to reduced immunological functioning (e.g. flu); sleeping difficulties; vitamin deficiencies (e.g. low iron levels); poor dietary choices; and dehydration. Most people with FND will also report pain that can affect all body parts. The pain can be a generalised "whole-body ache" or selectively affect a specific limb. Pain can be caused by secondary effects of FND including the (incorrect) use of equipment; abnormal postures and movement patterns; muscle overactivity or tensing to compensate for the weak limb or to suppress a tremor; boom-and-bust cycles and "overdoing activities"; and pain that emerges when the person starts to learn transfers and mobilising.

Post-FND physical symptoms

A specific category of FND-associated fatigue and pain in people with FND deserves mention. Dissociative episodes, particularly the subtype that is characterised by vigorous movements and requires a lot of energy, can result in overwhelming fatigue and long sleeping periods afterwards. The fatigue may function as an extended form of dissociation and a coping strategy to further reduce or cut off strong and unpleasant emotions or arousal. This is problematic since the extended dissociation reinforces the dissociative episode. Post-seizure pain symptoms often stem from prolonged periods of increased muscle tension and overactivity, as well as accidental self-injury.

A note on reactive techniques for FND

Reactive techniques can be defined as self-management strategies that are aimed at helping the person to emerge from a dissociative state (in PCM terminology: blocking the Overpressure Plug). Popular techniques that are often advocated by psychology and non-psychology professionals alike include reality grounding and distraction. Although a subset of people with FND will find these of benefit, people can dismiss these as unhelpful and ineffective. This is not surprising: reactive techniques are occasionally shared "on the cuff". However, they need regular practice and explanation and should always be a part of a comprehensive psychological formulation that provides a firm rationale for their use with the patient. "Superficial-level" reactive techniques on their own are rarely effective and should be used in conjunction with "deeper-level" strategies that focus on all other elements of the PCM, particularly the relational aspects of FND (Kitchen), emotional expression (Cover) and activity levels (Valve), all presumed to reduce the risk of FND.

Ignition (onset of FND, the "why" and "why now?")

The Ignition element refers to remote triggers and critical incidents that have likely contributed to the development of the condition and precede the onset of FND. There are generally three profiles observed in FND. A good treatment strategy is to explore these profiles with the person as part of psycho-education.

Profile #1: Before-and-after

A person may have been healthy and well. Following a critical incident, the person develops FND, for example after a stressful or traumatic life event (e.g. divorce, assault, accident), a physical illness or a medical procedure (e.g. infection, back surgery, cystoscopy). Characteristic features of this profile often include the presence of remote trauma (e.g. adverse childhood experiences) or unhelpful coping strategies developed in the person's early life (e.g. strict upbringing preventing emotional expression and facilitating dissociation), as well as negative interpersonal dynamics or family circumstances around the time of the critical incident that may have played a role in the subsequent emergence of FND (e.g. abrupt manner of a healthcare professional doing a medical procedure, or family dynamics that co-occur with the critical incident). This profile is often associated with themes around rejection, abandonment and not being believed, leading to a clinical presentation of depression.

Profile #2: Out of the blue

People with FND may also report the sudden emergence of a panic attack-like or paroxysmal event, often against a background of chronic life stresses that have cultivated the conditions for these often highly physiologically arousing events to arise. This profile is strongly associated with anxiety presentations. Some of these events may follow a classic panic or social anxiety cycle that self-terminates with a non-epileptic or dissociative episode. This type requires a different course of treatment with the CBT models for panic disorder or social anxiety disorder. See Chapter 8 for more details.

Profile #3: Gradual build-up

Some people have had a lifetime or a longstanding history of abusive experiences in their adult relationships (e.g. domestic violence, coercive relationships) with peak events of particularly difficult moments in their lives. Years of exposure to these destabilising experiences may ultimately provide a vulnerability towards the development of FND symptoms. Another subset of people may experience high levels of stress over many years (e.g. in a demanding job or caring role) without having sufficient access to stress-releasing strategies but they "just get by" and manage to live relatively functional lives. After some time, a tipping point is reached whereby the balance between stressful events and coping mechanisms breaks down, after which FND develops. This profile tends to be associated with clinical presentations characterised by depression.

Time-line exercise

An "experiential" time-line exercise can be very helpful to chart the trajectory of FND (Table 4.4).

When completing the time-line, it is important to carry this out collaboratively and check the person's thoughts and feelings in relation to the events and relationship dynamics. There are three issues to keep in mind. People with FND often report negative experiences with the healthcare system, particularly in relation to feeling rejected and abandoned by healthcare professionals. People with early rejection and emotional neglect experiences may be particularly vulnerable towards being re-triggered by later negative experiences with the healthcare system (systemic re-traumatisation). Furthermore, it is important to not jump to conclusions when encountering someone who experienced a traumatic event as the following excerpt will demonstrate:

> Joe was involved in a recent car accident. He sustained several significant physical injuries as a result including a head injury. He was brought to A&E and received medical treatment. Following discharge, Joe experienced several new symptoms including functional motor weakness, tremor, feeling on edge and sleeplessness. He was diagnosed with post-traumatic stress disorder and referred for a course of psychological therapy. During the re-assessment, Joe mentioned that he was not too bothered about the accident. In addition, Joe's presentation was not fully consistent with classic PTSD symptoms (e.g. flashbacks). In contrast, Joe emphasized that the treatment he received at the hospital and the negative attitudes from the hospital staff had greatly impacted on him. Following

exploration in therapy, it became evident that Joe's hospital experiences had re-triggered difficult memories and feelings around early rejection experiences during his school time. Joe successfully completed his therapy; he became symptom-free and fully participated in meaningful and enjoyable activities.

It is important to keep an open mind and spend multiple sessions to explore the psychological mechanisms that may drive the FND. Take sufficient time to explore and revise a variety of hypotheses, which will either be confirmed or rejected, as more "data" is gathered during therapy.

Other useful tools include Life Events and Difficulties Schedule (LEDS; Brown, 1989) that assesses exposure to psychosocial stressors; Traumatic Life Events Questionnaire (Kubany et al., 2000); or the Structured Clinical Interview for DSM-IV (SCID).

Table 4.4 Example of a time-line exercise

Time-point	Event	Experiences
July 2020	Started A levels	Didn't feel stressed
November 2020	Exams First dissociative episode emerged Brought to A&E by ambulance Admitted to an acute stroke ward Diagnosis of FND by neurologist	I didn't feel too stressed about the exams. It was quite scary to go to A&E, everything happened very quickly. On the stroke ward, some of the staff were a bit short with me and left me for last in the bay after washing all the other patients. The doctor briefly spoke to me and told me he had good news: I didn't have a stroke. I didn't quite get what FND was. I didn't feel believed. Soon after, I was discharged without any equipment or after-care. I felt abandoned
March 2022	Weakness in the left side of my body, pain, self-catheterisation for my bladder problems. Took some time off school Spent most days at home	I went to see my GP but she just prescribed me some meds. I looked everywhere for support for my FND, but there are no services. I feel left to fight on my own
April 2022	Referred by neurologist for psychological support	I didn't realise I had been referred! Felt dumped and discarded by the system. Everybody thinks it's all between my ears
June 2022	First session with my psychologist	I feel suspicious about psychology

Pot

The FND SELF CARE acronym is a useful guide to describe a variety of physical and medico-contextual factors that have been described in the research literature and are commonly encountered in clinical practice, and impact or maintain the FND. Table 4.5 displays a range of helpful strategies.

Establishing the severity of FND

In addition to providing a quick overview on medico-contextual factors, the FND SELF CARE acronym can also help gauge the level of the severity and the impact of the FND on a person's life by inspecting the elements that specifically tap into a person's functional status and day-to-day activities. A person with severe FND will typically experience more difficulties with mobilising, transfers, personal care and domestic activities of daily living, as well as have limited community access. They will likely be seen in multiple departments, with a higher number of healthcare contacts and equipment, have more permanent adaptations to the home environment and may have a care package from social services, with a small subset needing 24-hour care. The severity of the FND will also be reflected in a person's risk profile.

Helpful neurorehabilitation, disability and dependency measures were discussed in Chapter 2.

Risk assessment

Every person with FND and their direct environment needs a multidisciplinary risk assessment and management plan. In the following section, some common and more unusual risks in FND will be described. These risks are divided into three sections: risks associated with the Pot element, those associated with the Kitchen element and risks related to the remainder of the elements. This is due to the disproportionate number of risks associated with the former two elements (Figures 4.1–4.3).

Risk assessment for FND – template

Risk assessment should always be undertaken as an *interdisciplinary* exercise where every discipline makes their contribution within a cohesive, joined-up narrative. In a busy clinical setting, the PCM risk figures below can be a helpful guide to identify the risks for an individual with FND and their environment. Ideally, the risk assessment should be made collaboratively with the patient and their family (Table 4.6).

Fuel

The next series of PCM elements form the "Why still" or perpetuating factors of FND. In the following section, we will consider a myriad of triggers for FND that have commonly been encountered in clinical practice.

Table 4.5 Helpful strategies for assessment of the FND SELF CARE acronym

Letter	Element	Useful assessments and techniques	Good questions to ask
F	**F**ood fuel	Dietician input Continence nursing Review by a medical professional (e.g. "bloods" to check for vitamin deficiencies and reversible causes of FND)	• What's your diet like? Do you eat three meals a day? Do you notice eating a bit more when feeling stressed? Any food intolerances and allergies? Issues with weight that might impact on rehab? Antibiotic use? (gut flora). • Do you open your bowels often? Any difficulties with your bowel movements or stomach? Check for diagnoses of irritable bowel syndrome. • Pay attention to people who are house-bound, socially anxious or are socially isolated: they may not get sufficient vitamin D.
N	**N**ight rest	If sleep issues are significant: use the Pressure Cooker of Sleep Hygiene questions to test out where the "pressure points" are in terms of sleeping difficulties. (A later section of Chapter 4 will highlight an example of using the PCM as a biopsychosocial guide.)	• How has your sleep been lately? Check all sleep stages (e.g. falling asleep, maintaining sleep, early morning waking, long sleeping episodes as part of dissociation) • Any sleep conditions (e.g. sleep apnoea).
D	**D**rugs and medications	Medication review and rationalisation of medications by a neuropsychiatrist	• Check for polypharmacy: What medications are you on and what doses? Could you give me a list? • Check for medication use that is risky: for example as a psychological safety behaviour to quickly get to sleep or end a dissociative episode; as a form of substance misuse; to facilitate more dissociation; taking an extra non-prescribed dose; medication mismanagement during dissociative states; and history of deliberate self-harm using medications.

Letter	Element	Useful assessments and techniques	Good questions to ask
S	**S**ickness and physical illness	Comprehensive medical and mental health records review	• Check the person's medical history for organic conditions (e.g. co-existing epilepsy, spinal problems, joint hypermobility, POTS and Ehlers–Danlos syndrome) and any history of somatoform symptoms, past surgery.
E	**E**quipment	• Physiotherapy and occupational therapy support for, for example, graded "step-down" programmes for equipment use. • Management of fear of falling with behavioural experiments and psychology support	• Get an idea of the role equipment plays in the person's life by making an inventory of the equipment, duration of use, home adaptations and the level of entrenchment. • Explore psychological meaning, social functions and safety behaviours around the use of equipment, particularly if the patient is reluctant to step down (e.g. increases confidence; fear of falling; feeling cared for, noticed, validated by eliciting care or sympathy through the equipment from people; equipment serving as a deterrent from demands placed; worries around people not believing if equipment would be dropped; or is part of a person's identity).
L	**L**iquids and bladder functioning	Continence nursing	• Do you experience any difficulties with passing urine, urinary incontinence or your bladder (e.g. do you self-catheterise, wear pads?). Try to explore the functions of the equipment that is used to manage incontinence. • What beverages do you typically drink? (e.g. watch out for caffeine and energy drinks that cause palpitations).
F	**F**ight-or-flight and warning signs	Pharmacological support "to take the edge of anxiety"	• Does your body often feel on edge? Tell me what parts (watch out for panic disorder symptoms such as a heart palpitations, nausea, dizziness, shortness of breath, chest pain, fainting spells). • Observe whether the person describes emotions using their somatic characteristics and physical features. • Look for objective signs of low mood: tearfulness, withdrawal, motivation and biological signs (poor sleep, eating). • Tell me about any warning signs that you have noticed?

(Continued)

Table 4.5 (Continued)

Letter	Element	Useful assessments and techniques	Good questions to ask
C	**C**ontacts	Medical records review	• Ask the person directly about the number of healthcare service contacts ("Do you ever call an ambulance or visit A&E for your symptoms?"). Often, referrers will volunteer this information, particularly if healthcare "use" is high. • In the context of systemic re-traumatisation, ask the person about their healthcare experiences as these may impact on your formulation of FND. • To measure healthcare resource use: Client Service Receipt Inventory (Beecham & Knapp, 1992).
A	**A**bility to take care of yourself	Occupational therapy support for personal and domestic activities in daily life	• Do you receive any support for daily activities, such as washing and dressing yourself, preparing meals, doing household chores, going on public transport, accessing the community, shopping, childcare? What activities do you need help with on a day-to-day basis? • Do you have carers/a care package in place via social services? How many care calls a day and what do you receive support for? Note down level of support, for example assistance of one or two people, supervision, and for what activities in daily living. • Make sure you check whether partners or family support the person, to what extent, the level of enmeshment, any blurring of boundaries and altered family roles.
R	**R**isks	Team risk assessment	• The next section will review common and more unusual risks in FND. A standard risk assessment template for clinical use will be outlined.
E	**E**xercise, Movement and Physical activity	Physiotherapy assessment	• What's your mobility like? Your transfers and balance (e.g. falls risks)? • Do you exercise or engage with any sports? What has the FND stopped you from doing? What is the person's fitness level?

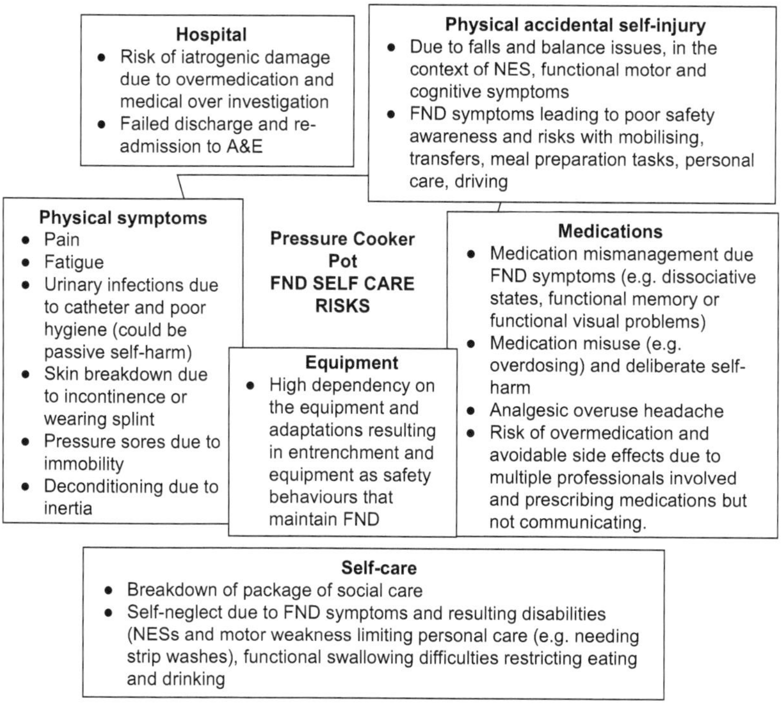

Hospital	Physical accidental self-injury
• Risk of iatrogenic damage due to overmedication and medical over investigation • Failed discharge and re-admission to A&E	• Due to falls and balance issues, in the context of NES, functional motor and cognitive symptoms • FND symptoms leading to poor safety awareness and risks with mobilising, transfers, meal preparation tasks, personal care, driving

Physical symptoms
- Pain
- Fatigue
- Urinary infections due to catheter and poor hygiene (could be passive self-harm)
- Skin breakdown due to incontinence or wearing splint
- Pressure sores due to immobility
- Deconditioning due to inertia

Pressure Cooker Pot
FND SELF CARE RISKS

Equipment
- High dependency on the equipment and adaptations resulting in entrenchment and equipment as safety behaviours that maintain FND

Medications
- Medication mismanagement due FND symptoms (e.g. dissociative states, functional memory or functional visual problems)
- Medication misuse (e.g. overdosing) and deliberate self-harm
- Analgesic overuse headache
- Risk of overmedication and avoidable side effects due to multiple professionals involved and prescribing medications but not communicating.

Self-care
- Breakdown of package of social care
- Self-neglect due to FND symptoms and resulting disabilities (NESs and motor weakness limiting personal care (e.g. needing strip washes), functional swallowing difficulties restricting eating and drinking

Figure 4.1 Common risks in FND organised around the pressure cooker pot.

Emotional triggers

A subset of people with FND will not show any features of alexithymia and will be able to identify and label their emotions without any difficulties. People with sufficient emotion language will report clear external triggers for their FND episodes (e.g. school exams, work-related stress) and describe basic emotions such as stress, worries and anxiety. People with FND may also experience internal triggers. Persistent worrying in the context of generalised anxiety disorder and "anniversaries" of traumatic events (e.g. bereavement) also occur.

Triggers in the context of post-traumatic stress disorder

Some people with FND may have experienced a discrete traumatic event (e.g. car accident) that brought on post-traumatic stress disorder. "Low-level" environmental triggers that previously had a neutral or positive meaning (e.g. smell of cake) may have taken on a threatening meaning due to its association with a traumatic event (e.g. domestic violence incident). Furthermore, environmental reminders of the trauma can cause distress (e.g. seeing a news item on television associated with the trauma topic). These environmental triggers

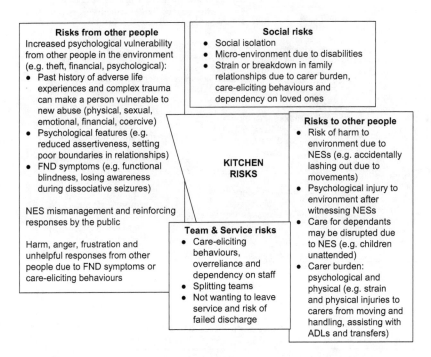

Figure 4.2 Common risks in people with FND associated with the Kitchen element of the Pressure Cooker Model.

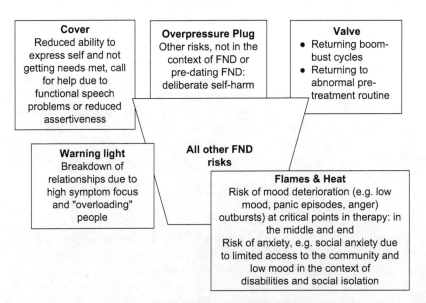

Figure 4.3 Common risks in people with FND in other Pressure Cooker Model elements.

may subsequently set off anxiety or an undefined state of discomfort leading to FND symptoms, which effectively reduces the distress but negatively reinforces the FND as a coping habit for these triggers. Internal stimuli (e.g. trauma memories) are also reported as triggers for FND.

No triggers

Occasionally, people with FND do not report any triggers (and warning signs) for dissociative episodes or motor weakness. This may feel anxiety-provoking and frustrating for both the person with FND and the treating clinician who may struggle to plan treatment. In the absence of triggers, there are several possibilities. Firstly, consider whether a classic panic disorder cycle may be present, characterised by catastrophic misinterpretation of physical symptoms, high levels of anxiety that builds up over a relatively short space of time, and safety behaviours that maintain the panic cycle but may also quickly and effectively terminate it (e.g. with a dissociative episode). Panic attacks tend to come "out of the blue" with no triggers. Chapter 8 will describe the adapted model for panic disorder in FND. A second "no-trigger" hypothesis may be related to a person's reduced awareness of triggers, particularly those of an emotional nature. A subset of people with FND experience alexithymia and dissociation and may not be able to describe and experience emotions, and therefore struggle with identifying emotion-led triggers.

Interpersonal triggers

This type of trigger is characterised by the relationship between FND episodes and other people, often accompanied by social emotions such as guilt, embarrassment and shame, and a sense of abandonment or rejection, or "attachment anxiety". Triggers for FND may include family conflicts, deterrents towards partner seeking proximity, perception of letting other people down or failing them somehow, the perception of witnessing other people receiving validation or wishing to feel supported by other people. Consider also "making progress in rehab" as an interpersonal trigger. Making gains in rehab means "tinkering" with the FND and potential social losses, often losses in relation to other people, including how the person may come across to others if the FND would improve. The section on "Flames" in Chapter 4 will discuss the fear of recovery in more detail.

> Nancy lives with her husband and her three children. She experiences dissociative episodes several times a week. In therapy, Nancy explained that there are often a lot of family arguments in her house. Nancy herself grew up in a conflict-ridden environment. She often feels strong feelings of guilt particularly towards her children growing up in a house full of arguments and feels like she has let her family down. When an argument starts, she often feels a dissociative episode coming up where she will

Table 4.6 Example of a typical risk assessment for a person with FND

Risk	What are the risk factors?	What are the person's pressure cooker safety features? (protective factors)	What can we do to minimise the risk?	What do we do when the risk has occurred?
Risk of dissociative episodes	• Judy has a past history of dissociative episodes. • Judy lives in a family home with a lot of arguments and is used to keep herself to herself.	• Judy is on board with the FND diagnosis and the PCM formulation. Judy engaged well in psychological therapy and made significant gains. • Judy has been able to identify the following triggers: stress related to school exams, arguments in the family home. • Judy has made a Pressure Cooker Fire Extinguisher plan to manage any set-backs that may pop up. • Judy is planning to move out of the family home and live independently.	• Judy will practise her skills regularly, particularly opening her Cover (expressing her emotions) and unblock her Valve (Judy has been attending tennis classes). • Judy will also blow out her Flames (challenge unhelpful beliefs around not feeling cared for).	• In first instance, Judy will apply her Fire Extinguisher plan independently. • If she continues to feel unwell, Judy agreed to contact her GP for further support.
Risk of social isolation	• Judy has social anxiety and finds it difficult to make friends.	• Judy started to reconnect with two past friends and has been enjoying spending time. • Judy has been visiting the tennis club on a weekly basis, is meeting new people and actively works on increasing her social network.	• Judy will keep testing out her social fears by continuing to engage with social activities and dropping her safety behaviours. • She will use her strategies to reduce dissociation, for example reality grounding when the first warning signs of an episode come up.	• Judy will ask a good friend to join her with social activities initially until she feels more confident to go on her own.

Risk of carer burden	• Judy's parents can become highly anxious around Judy, especially when she experiences dissociative episodes.	• Judy's parents have good insight into how their fears drive the reciprocal reinforcement processes between Judy's dissociative episodes and their reassurance and caring responses. Judy and her parents have effectively implemented a seizure management plan together.	• Judy and her parents will all continue to practice their skills.	• Judy and her parents will try to break the reciprocal reinforcement patterns as quickly as possible.

drop to the floor and shake her limbs. After she wakes up from the episode, she will find her family looking worried and crowding over her,
asking her how she feels. The most important thing is that the argument
will have stopped by then, giving Nancy a sense of relief.

In Nancy's situation, she was unable to tolerate her strong feelings of guilt
and her thoughts around letting her family down. The dissociative episode
reduced this uncomfortable state quickly and effectively, which negatively
reinforced the DS as a safety behaviour. In addition, the DS also had the
function of removing something unpleasant in Nancy's environment (the
arguments) and adding something pleasant (sense of feeling cared for by her
family).

   People may not always be able to describe interpersonal triggers as clear-
cut as Nancy's. In contrast, people with FND often struggle with reporting interpersonal triggers, as they tend not to be always that obvious to the
person and the clinician. Although physical triggers may be more on the
forefront and easier to name, interpersonal triggers tend to be more hidden, in a similar vein to the difference between more superficial negative
automatic thoughts vs more deeply hidden core beliefs. Exploring interpersonal triggers for FND often takes the form of detective work in therapy.
At times, it may also be difficult to acknowledge and accept the existence
of interpersonal triggers. For example, FND symptoms may be triggered by
the person experiencing an internal unmet need for validation, psychological
safety or a strong uncomfortable feeling around a lack of being cared for by
another person. Although feeling validated and cared for are basic human
needs, this type of trigger has negative connotations and is often unhelpfully
reframed as "attention seeking" and "manipulative". Due to the stigmatising
responses from the environment (including healthcare professionals) around
these interpersonal triggers, a person with FND and the clinician may find it
difficult to discuss this openly in therapy, due to underlying fears of rejection
and losing the patient. In a similar vein as uncovering more deeply hidden
core beliefs, the uncovering of interpersonal triggers for FND tends to go
through a similar process, which takes place at a later stage in therapy after a
trusting therapeutic relationship has developed and the person feels safe from
negative judgements.

   Try to be as open and transparent to the person with FND about interpersonal triggers, particularly taking into account the fact that a subset of people
will have had adverse childhood experiences, often sexual trauma, where
there was little honesty and transparency and where they may not have been
believed by a parental key figure who failed to act on behalf of their child. A
Socratic method can be useful: "I wonder what you think of the triggers for
the episodes you experience....it seems that the episodes tend to take place in
the gym...have you noticed this too? What do you make of that?" "I wonder
whether you'd be up for exploring this further?" You can use the structured
FND diary for this to look at the "evidence".

Physical triggers

People with FND will often mention physical triggers for dissociative episodes including heat, noise, lighting, physical illness, fatigue and pain. Physical triggers may tell four different stories of FND.

PANIC ATTACKS

Classic panic attacks can be associated with dissociative episodes. The person may experience physical symptoms "out of the blue", for example heart palpitations. The physical symptoms may also present as FND to start with, for example suddenly losing strength in all four limbs in response to a, for the person yet, unidentified trigger. The person just perceives a change in bodily symptoms. These physical symptoms are misinterpreted in a catastrophic manner ("I'm going to have a heart attack, stroke, collapse, die, lose control, another seizure"). Within a short space of time, these catastrophic misinterpretations lead to a high level of anxiety, causing further bodily symptoms that feed into a classic panic loop. In order to cope with the catastrophic thoughts and anxiety, the person engages in a series of safety behaviours, for example breathing or distraction exercises, leaving a situation, and may avoid going places. The difference between a classic panic attack and panic attacks in the context of dissociative episodes is the power that the dissociation has on "closing the panic loop" very quickly and effectively. The dissociative episode stops the loop immediately, which causes negative reinforcement of the FND. In addition, classic panic cognitions may result in "secondary" fears around having another dissociative seizure, which further feeds into the panic loop.

Chapter 8 will discuss the treatment of a case with panic attacks and dissociative episodes in more detail.

TEMPORARY ESCAPE

People with FND who often experience FND symptoms directly in response to a physical trigger such as noise may have developed the FND as a coping strategy that helps them to temporarily escape a state of chronic anxiety, emotional discomfort or distressing warning symptoms (e.g. Stone, 2009).

> Jeremy experiences high-frequent dissociative episodes in response to an increase in environmental noise from cars, people and alarms. This led to Jeremy living a highly restricted life and stopped him from going out to shops and meeting with friends. Each time Jeremy was out and about and an alarm rang, Jeremy instantly experienced a dissociative episode. After several sessions, it transpired that Jeremy was constantly feeling anxious and "on edge", both indoors but particularly outdoors in social situations, which worsened his anxiety exponentially. When Jeremy was introduced

to a social environment and the alarm went off, the dissociative episode took away his heightened anxiety and temporarily gave him "a psychological break" from the chronic state of anxiety he felt, with people from his environment rushing over to support him emotionally and physically. Over time, the dissociative episodes had become an automatic habit in response to the alarm. Although on the surface, alarms seemed to set off Jeremy's episodes, it was the emotional relief and the care from the environment that drove the episodes.

THRESHOLD REDUCTION

Occasionally, a person with FND in response to physical triggers may report feeling generally overstimulated in day-to-day life, often in the context of anxiety, stress and life demands. A physical trigger may further lower the threshold for feeling overstimulated in a person who is already experiencing a heightened state of anxiety. This internal state of increased overstimulation may feel unpleasant and intolerable in the moment. As a result, the person may cope and bring down this state of overstimulation effectively with FND.

UNDERLYING INTERPERSONAL TRIGGERS

Some patients relentlessly focus on physical triggers as the sole explanation for FND ("it was the heat and dizziness that caused the episode") and resist formulating the possibility for interpersonal triggers. What could be going on?

- Some physical triggers coincide in time with interpersonal triggers; however, the person may not be aware of the simultaneous existence of both triggers during an event. In the person's view, the often more visible physical trigger "trumps" the interpersonal triggers as an explanation for the FND. Physical triggers are often more on the surface and straightforward to understand than interpersonal "psychological safety" triggers. It is helpful to explore the interpersonal and social circumstances around physical triggers to help unearth the existence of any interpersonal triggers for the FND and point this association out to the patient. Even if you see a clear connection between FND and interpersonal triggers, the person may not make that connection. Never get into a tug of war with the patient. Instead, build a strong therapeutic alliance that will increase your chances of helping the patient to see what you see.
- Keep in mind that a person may be aware but prefers not to reveal interpersonal triggers, as it makes the person feel vulnerable and exposed, or worried about not being believed ("I'm an attention seeker").
- If the person is wedded to the "physical trigger" formulation, roll with the resistance and reflect this resistance back, to open up a way to explore whether there is room for an alternative hypothesis. Always consider that

this type of trigger can be present, either by itself or in conjunction with interpersonal triggers.

- Don't dismiss the person's view on the FND. This is their reality, and actively challenging their reality may make them feel not believed and worsen your therapeutic relationship.

"Re-triggers"

A special subset of interpersonal triggers for FND are "re-triggers". This type of trigger is particularly pertinent to people with FND that have been exposed to childhood emotional neglect and rejection by (a) parental key figure(s).

RE-TRIGGERING EMOTIONAL NEGLECT

Seemingly "superficial" and "low-key" incidents may re-trigger early experiences of neglect and not feeling cared for. Earlier, we explored PTSD-related "low-level" environmental triggers for FND in the context of a traumatic event ("simple PTSD"). Re-triggers are similar but should be viewed as triggers in the context of more longstanding traumatic events that originated in childhood ("complex PTSD").

Some re-triggered patients may unconsciously and more consciously go into a psychological mode that represents their early adverse childhood experiences. They may relive and replay these experiences, thoughts, feelings and coping survival strategies that they felt at the time. Due to these adverse experiences, they often not had the opportunity to learn helpful strategies to express their emotions (verbal or emotional expression). In addition, a person may "test out" to what extent people in their environment are willing to care for them. All of this may directly amplify the FND symptoms.

> Xavier has lived a lifetime of experiences with abuse and emotional neglect in his family home during which his emotional and physical needs were not consistently met. In his younger years he had developed difficulties with eating and self-harm. Although these coping strategies stopped, he developed FND. Xavier was unable to provide clarity on what may cause his FND symptoms. One day, Xavier reported having a set-back: his dissociative episodes became a lot more frequent and, on top of that, he developed weakness in his legs. Xavier's psychological health had deteriorated significantly; at times he looked very angry, mixed with looking sad and inconsolable. He was unable to function in daily life including caring for himself and dropped all his hobbies. His treating team struggled to identify triggers. When the team got together for a meeting, it transpired that, the week prior to the set-back, Xavier had been promised a phone call from his doctor with newly prescribed

medications. Due to an emergency crisis with another patient, the doctor was not able to get in touch in time which resulted in Xavier not receiving the phone call and the prescribed medications despite the agreement. Soon after, Xavier's symptoms worsened. This was formulated with Xavier in a psychology session. The Fuel consisted of the doctor not getting back to Xavier at the agreed time which made Xavier feel uncared for, angry and low in mood, reliving his childhood abusive experiences. In his childhood, Xavier had not been afforded the opportunity to learn to regulate or cope with his emotions in more helpful ways. Due to his adverse experiences, he had developed trust issues and often felt a lack of psychological safety. He was unable to express his feelings (tight Cover) or release his feelings via activities (blocked Valve) leaving no other way than to express his great distress physically. The worsened FND symptoms helped Xavier to communicate his anger and low mood to the team in the context of not having his needs met yet again, just like in his childhood.

SYSTEMIC RE-TRAUMATISATION

In the example above, the doctor was caught up in an emergency and unintentionally "neglected" or "did not meet Xavier's physical and psychological care needs". The doctor was not experiencing strong emotions, thoughts and responses towards Xavier that needed regulating in the moment.

As discussed in Chapter 3, people with FND are commonly exposed to systemic re-traumatisation, particularly in healthcare environments. The example described above highlights that FND symptoms and their associated emotions can amplify in response to healthcare experiences that bear a resemblance to earlier (often childhood) rejection experiences, particularly perceived neglect by another key figure such as a treating healthcare professional or a current partner. It should be noted that the type of re-triggering in the context of systemic re-traumatisation is different than the example above. Systemic re-traumatisation is the result of a dysfunctional emotion co-regulation process that has gone awry between the person with FND and their environment. Both parties experience strong negative emotions towards one another and attempt to regulate these feelings in unhelpful ways. For example, a healthcare professional feeling anxiety and discomfort about seeing a person with FND may dismiss or discharge the person quicker than normal, which the person with FND may interpret as a rejection that subsequently re-triggers early childhood experiences of emotional neglect and worsens the FND symptoms.

In general, re-triggers of early neglect experiences are not obvious and often require a course of therapy and multiple re-iterations of clinical hypotheses to uncover these links.

"Multi-triggers"

Sometimes a clinician may be left feeling confused and bewildered by a person's constellation of FND symptoms. It is not uncommon for a person with FND to experience separate and co-existing episodes in response to two sets of triggers. A common combination is dissociative episodes due to panic attacks and episodes due to more interpersonal triggers. Each requires a different treatment approach. In Chapter 8 on CBT, a treatment decision tree will be outlined that can guide a clinician with selecting the appropriate model.

Fuel: useful tools

The following section provides questions, strategies and tools that may help you and the person identify their sources of Fuel and uncover triggers for the FND (Table 4.7).

Structured FND diary

People with FND and their family will occasionally provide you with diaries. Although these excerpts can be a helpful window into FND symptoms, another useful tool that can provide information on triggers is the comprehensive structured FND diary (see Figure 4.4).

Ask the person to complete the diary for each FND episode. This could be a "paroxysmal" dissociative episode, which often lasts from a few seconds to hours, or a motor-type FND episode that may last for several days after which the person bounces back. The structured FND diary is less useful for people who experience prolonged "static" motor-type FND symptoms that do not tend to fluctuate significantly, for example longstanding functional paraplegia (Table 4.8).

> Have a think about an FND episode that you remember well, one that stood out to you in some way, or that happened recently. Or think about a time when your FND symptoms got worse. Do you have an episode or time in mind? Try to vividly remember this event. Go through the episode in your mind, frame by frame, unfolding the event scene by scene, like a movie. Try to fill out as many details as you can. Don't worry if you can't remember anything or there are empty spaces on the form. You can ask someone who has witnessed the episode to support you with completing the diary. Some people with FND may struggle to remember their episodes or symptoms and may pick up different features than witnesses. This is not to catch you out but simply to help you get a clearer picture of the episode.

Table 4.7 Enquiries about Fuel: useful points to look out for

Trigger	Details
Stressful events	• Ask whether something stressful or important happened right before the FND emerged. The time-line will be helpful to unearth any relationships between stressful events and FND. However, do not push if the person does not know of any triggering events. • People with FND who are not aware of triggers or dissociate from emotions may find this a frustrating question because they don't identify with stress and can't relate to the emotional experience of stress. • It is also very likely that they have been posed this question on several occasions by different healthcare professionals, who may have linked the FND to stress without any further exploration. Be mindful that pushing for a stressful event may make the person not feel believed.

Fluctuations in frequency or severity	• Asking the question "Do you know what makes your FND better or worse" tends not to be helpful or provide clarity. Discovering triggers for FND is often the reason why the patient visits!
	• Instead: ask the person to describe a dissociative episode or an episode of worsening of motor symptoms that:
	  • Stood out to them because of its severity or meaning
	  • A recent one that is still fresh in memory.
	• If possible, ask a collateral to comment on the fluctuations in the person's FND symptoms.
	• For dissociative episodes, it is useful to look at changes in frequency and severity of the episodes and what factors were associated with these fluctuations, particular times of stress or interpersonal factors in relationships.
	• Motor-type FND is more static than "paroxysmal" DS although worsening of symptoms and relapses are common and it's worth exploring triggers.

Time-line of FND	• Creating a time-line can describe the evolution of FND symptoms and reveal an association between FND and its triggers. • See if an "A-B-A-B design" is present: when the trigger (e.g. argument) is present, the FND worsens. When the trigger is taken out (e.g. no arguments), the FND lessens. When the trigger is re-introduced in the person's life (e.g. new argument), the FND emerges again. That is a strong indication that arguments and FND are associated.
Holidays and other times that mediate symptom frequency or severity	The person with FND should also be asked to identify times or situations when the frequency, severity and intensity of the symptoms changed, as well as times when symptoms disappeared altogether: • Do your symptoms ever go away? When? What characterises these times? Are they stress-free, positive emotions? • It is not uncommon that FND symptoms lessen or may even disappear during holidays, which in most cases represents a time of reduced stress.
Relationships	• Interpersonal triggers are prominent in FND, either as a stand-alone trigger, a multi-trigger or re-trigger. When exploring the time-line, it is a good idea to check whether anything happened in a person's relationships at the time.

Trigger	Details
People, locations	• Pay attention to both family and healthcare relationships and phrases such as "not feeling cared for, believed and abandoned". The FND may be a response to an unmet need in the family context. • During healthcare contacts (please note that the symptoms are real and may be a form of communicating that to the professional). • Crowded places with lots of people (e.g. shopping centre, therapy gym, waiting room, on public transport) vs indoors (e.g. on the couch at home alone). Keep in mind social anxiety and panic attacks. • Only with certain people. • Individual vs group therapy sessions
Time, transitions or changes	• Times of day: morning, early afternoon, late afternoon, at night, weekends. For example, a person may experience dissociative episodes at the end of the day after a stressful workday, as a release. • Times during an inpatient admission or outpatient treatment. Beginning, middle or end of treatment. For example, an exacerbation of FND is common immediately before discharge. • Inpatient settings: for example after a room change, new patient in the bay, delays in care being given or being the last person to be helped in the bay (due to low medical needs compared to other patients). • Important anniversaries (e.g. the passing of a loved one).
Demands	FND symptoms can emerge or amplify: • When demands are placed on the patient in the home environment or relationship/or challenged during a therapy session; during challenging or difficult tasks; asking the patient to do something more complicated as part of therapy (e.g. neurotesting, behavioural experiments, exams, presentations, walking the stairs, increase walking distance, get rid of a piece of equipment). • Before a therapy session leading the person to cancel.
(Reciprocal) reinforcement patterns	• Do you notice a pattern: each time the person experiences an episode or worsened FND (e.g. difficult Maths exam in classroom → dissociative episode), this may be followed by a "reinforcer" from an individual in their environment (e.g. teacher takes out the pupil from the classroom and gives a hot chocolate). Conversely, the teacher may be engaging in a reciprocal reinforcement pattern (e.g. witnessing the episode increases discomfort in other pupils and the teacher. Following removal of the "patient", the system's discomfort reduces).
Check classic CBT cognitions	• This is particularly important when the person does not report any triggers. Explore the panic disorder cycle (Clark, 1986) consisting of bodily symptoms – catastrophic misinterpretation – emotion and the "crescendo of fear". • It is possible that the person does not report fear or anxiety due to the dissociative episode serving as a safety behaviour (which self-terminates the panic cycle as the person often feels very fatigued afterwards).

Question	What happens?	What happens?
Where am I, Who am I with?	On the couch, by myself	At a restaurant, with family
What am I doing?	Watching tele	Eating my meal, then an argument starts
How do I feel? (0 – 10)	Anxious ('8')	Anxious ('10'), sad ('6')
What thoughts, images?	Blank – no thoughts	"Oh no, not again"
Warning signs	Feeling dizzy, sweaty, heart racing, tingles all over	Feeling distant, disconnected from my body and the world
Describe episode (can ask witness)	Fall on the ground, lying still, "frozen"	Fall on the ground, arms and legs are shaking
How long?	About 10 minutes	15 – 20 minutes
How do I feel afterwards? Any emotions?	Tired, drained Anxiety = 0	Tired, drained Anxiety = 2, sad = 0
Thoughts, images?	No thoughts	"What just happened?"
What am I / others doing afterwards?	Go to bed to rest	Argument stops, people are friendly to each other again – relief Everyone is shocked & is focused on helping me
Recovery time	3 days before I'm my old self again	Few hours

Figure 4.4 Structured FND diary.

The Pressure Cooker Chain Reaction

The maintenance cycle of FND is also known as the Pressure Cooker Chain Reaction. It is helpful to keep this chain reaction in mind by trying to link triggers, thoughts, feelings/undefined internal states and the FND in one maintenance cycle. It is possible that a person with FND experiences multiple maintenance cycles; that is, FND symptoms may be linked to multiple but qualitatively different triggers (Table 4.9).

Flames

In the next section, we will discuss useful techniques for managing common unhelpful beliefs and difficulties with emotions experienced by people with FND (extinguishing or blowing out the Flames).

Emotion education

As described in Chapter 3, people with FND often struggle to identify, recognise and label their emotions. Basic emotion education is helpful and can include exploring the different types of emotions (including basic and social emotions) using emotion wheels; identification of beliefs that typically match with the emotion; and their motor, physical and behavioural signatures (e.g. clenching our hands, frowning our face and wanting to attack when feeling

Table 4.8 Structured FND diary: useful strategies and pitfalls

Things to look out for	Pitfalls
Compare the emotion rating before and after the episode: • If there is a significant reduction in emotion or unpleasant state (e.g. from a "9" to a "3"), the episode may have served as a safety behaviour or a strategy that reduces internal distress.	• It is not possible to identify an emotion. • Ascertain whether the person's internal state was negative or aversive in some way. • Label this as an "uncomfortable state", "unpleasant internal state" or anything that the person feels that conveys this state. • Look for the presence of a "pre-to-post episode" reduction in this unpleasant state. • It is possible that the person is dissociated from feeling the emotion.
Check what happened after the episode, particularly if the person reports: • Being very fatigued and sleeping for a few hours. This is post-FND fatigue. When people are tired, they often do not feel a lot of anxiety (=dissociation). • Needing to recover for days or weeks. This may indicate a boom-bust cycle, and it would be worth exploring this further. • Reinforcing responses from the environment ("I got a hug" "I was left alone") • The cessation of a stressful event, for example a family argument that stopped following the episode.	The person does not remember any details of the episode: • This could be due to dissociation. • Ask whether you can check with a witness. • If there is a video available. The person does not identify any triggers: • Consider whether either interpersonal triggers or panic symptoms may be driving the episodes. • Panic cognitions will become clear on the diary "I thought I was going to have a stroke / die / pass out / have a seizure".
People going from one FND episode into another: • Some people with FND will experience a high level of heightened emotion, which may lead a person to experience multiple episodes in close succession. • It may start with one episode that quickly and effectively reduces the emotion. When the person "comes out" and starts to feel the emotion again, they immediately "roll" into a new episode.	The person completes the diary diligently but no clear pattern seems to emerge: • There may be different types of reasons that drive the episodes, for example panic attacks and interpersonal triggers. The diary entries may need a longer time of analysis. • It may be that the actual completion of the diary is serving a function, for example care and validation. • The person may report physical triggers (e.g. feeling hot) but does not describe any anxiety. This may suggest dissociation.

Table 4.9 Two different Pressure Cooker Chain Reactions

Cycle #	Trigger	Belief	Emotion	Response
1	Argument	"My partner may had enough and leave me", "How will I cope?"	Anxiety	Dissociative episode takes away the anxiety (internal regulation) and the argument (external regulation)
2	Sudden physical sensations in the body	Catastrophic misinterpretation "I'm going to have another seizure!"	Panic	Loss of strength in legs, becoming "floppy". Panic loop self-terminates (internal regulation), and my partner cares for me (external regulation).

angry; where in the body do you feel emotion X?). The goal of therapy may just be to analyse these different components of an emotion and subsequently make sense of the emotional maelstrom by teaching the person how to link/integrate an emotion with its physical signature, trigger events and behaviours, as the emotion is dissociated. It can be useful to complete exercises that explore past or present situations that have elicited emotions or an unpleasant arousal state for the individual. Eventually, demonstrating the relationship between emotions and FND is the crux of the PCM formulation.

Normalising emotions

Emotions or their expression are often perceived negatively by people with FND. It is important to reduce the threat of the emotional experience in a person's life. Support the patient with the acceptance of stress and emotional pain as being part and parcel of the human experience and that not the mere existence of stress is the problem, but rather, the way that stress is being managed and released at the top of the pressure cooker will matter. Help the person to become more accepting of emotions by explaining that as humans we are hard-wired to experience emotions and they serve adaptive functions for our survival. It can be helpful to explore what would happen if a person did not experience emotions and what that would mean for day-to-day life. For example, you could explore fight-or-flight scenarios (e.g. imagine walking through the woods and encountering a grizzly bear, tell me what you would do, feel and think? What would happen in your body? List all the physical symptoms) and provide evidence of anxiety as a necessity for human survival. You can cite case studies on people who have difficulties processing emotions and in daily life due to brain lesions (e.g. the amygdala and the fear response, e.g. Feinstein et al., 2011, and the case of SM). Invoking a neuroscientific approach (e.g. LeDoux' model of anxiety and the amygdala; LeDoux, 1996, 2003) may be a helpful way to demonstrate the organic basis of emotions and the fact that each one of us experiences emotions that are anchored in and subserved by the brain. With the Yerkes-Dodson law, show how arousal (which is part of anxiety) can impair performance and functioning in daily life if too low (e.g. fatigue, sleepiness) or too high (e.g. extreme levels of stress impacting on thinking skills like memory and attention). However, explain that humans need a certain level of "optimal arousal" to perform well on a task (e.g. some nervousness during a presentation will sharpen our senses, helps us remember what to say and make us present well).

Interpersonal and rejection themes in FND

Raise your own awareness on uncovering recurrent interpersonal and rejection themes, which emerge frequently in people with FND, that is beliefs and emotions associated with other individuals, in response to interpersonal triggers (e.g. arguments, unmet needs) and often accompanied by the basic emotions of low mood or anger, as well as social emotions (e.g. guilt, shame, embarrassment).

Treating the belief of not being believed by other people

Recent healthcare experiences may echo past traumatic experiences. Explore whether a link can be made between the person's early childhood experiences (i.e. particularly sexual abuse and not being believed by a parental key figure, as well as emotional neglect), their past and current healthcare experiences. Provide psycho-education on the consequences of this vertical mirroring process for both the person and healthcare professional, including maintenance of FND symptoms.

PATIENTS AND HEALTHCARE PROFESSIONALS: DEMONSTRATE
HORIZONTAL MIRRORING

Provide psycho-education on a person's "healthcare Theory of Mind". Almost all people with FND report negative beliefs about the mental states of healthcare professionals *in relation to the person with FND*. People with FND commonly believe that healthcare professionals do not believe them and that people with FND are viewed as putting it on or faking the symptoms. These beliefs cannot be automatically assumed to be "dysfunctional" or "irrational" as these are often firmly rooted in reality, with some healthcare professionals providing "the evidence" with verbal and non-verbal communications. Pushing the person with FND to actively challenge these beliefs could become counter-productive and even dangerous, as it will add to their perception that now the treating clinician too is not believing the person. This specific subset of beliefs is an important area that has often been neglected in psychological treatment but that deserves attention when treating a person with FND. A horizontal mirroring exercise may facilitate normalisation by showing that the thoughts and emotions experienced by the person mirror those of staff and family (you can cite some of the references from Chapter 3 as evidence).

REPARATIONS

It may be useful to read up on healthcare experiences by people with FND and professionals reported in the scientific literature (see Chapter 3). Communicate the findings of this literature to the person with FND and explain how you are intending to treat them differently and positively (see Table 4.10 for an example). The goal of this exercise is to build trust and psychological safety.

THE PCM FORMULATION: THE BELIEF OF NOT BEING BELIEVED AND FND

The PCM can be directly applied on the "belief about not being believed" (Flames), particularly if this belief is clearly linked to an emergence, increase or worsening of FND symptoms (Overpressure Plug). Explore the rest of the elements in the PCM formulation with the person to raise insight into this link. Since the PCM is a hybrid model that equally applies to the environment, it can be a powerful tool to explore the negative beliefs and emotions around not being believed with the person with FND and their family.

OTHER USEFUL TECHNIQUES

The following techniques may be useful for managing the beliefs about not being believed:

- Downward arrow technique to find out what it means for the person to not feel believed by other people. For example, if the person with FND believes that a healthcare provider thinks that the person is faking it and a liar, the person with FND may feel that the worst thing is not being taken seriously, becoming an outcast and rejected by others, and that they don't matter (core belief).
- Distancing techniques and observing the beliefs without interacting with them on an emotional level may help the person accept that opinions about the FND may differ and support the person with distancing themselves from the thought and treat this as what it is: a thought. In a way, this is almost a form of adaptive dissociation. Encourage the person to use this type of dissociation more adaptively in this situation but that it is important to toe the line of dissociation.

Table 4.10 Treatment strategies to manage patient worries about healthcare professionals

Common worry from people with FND about healthcare professionals	Healthcare professionals treating people with FND
1 Staff don't believe me	1 "Symptoms are real". Acknowledge that a lot of people in healthcare express doubts at the reality of FND symptoms. However, emphasise that you and the team 100% believe the person's symptoms are genuine and real. "They are happening in front of me, they are real".
2 Worries about negative judgements from staff, for example crazy, faking, seeking attention	2 Acknowledge that you are aware that some professionals may make all kinds of unhelpful assumptions about FND including that people "are faking, seeking attention, waste time, difficult to treat, beyond help…" but that you don't endorse any of these ideas. If you do inadvertently make them feel this way, tell the patient to honestly let you know.
3 Perceived lack of support from staff	3 Mention that you are aware that professionals in the past may not have treated the person with FND well by being rude and unkind but that you are here to provide a supportive approach focused on positive interactions.
4 Worries about relationships with staff	4 Express that healthcare professionals too worry about their patients not believing them and the patient losing trust, by saying the wrong thing.
5 Confusion about diagnosis	5 Tell the patient that there is a lot of confusion about FND amongst healthcare professionals as they experience limited confidence in the diagnosis, management and treatment of FND and they have low self-perceived knowledge on FND. In a way, we are all similar.

- Assertiveness techniques: If the person's environment actively challenges the genuineness of the FND symptoms, practising assertiveness skills in role plays and developing an FND narrative that the person can use with their environment may be helpful.
- Occasionally, the belief of not being believed can be challenged to check whether an alternative interpretation is possible (e.g. healthcare

professional doing a joint with another colleague may not immediately suggest that I'm not believed). Behavioural experiments to break the Flames-Overpressure Plug link would be appropriate in these situations.

Treating the belief about abandonment and not feeling cared for

People with FND who possess strong beliefs around abandonment often report a variety of phrases that indicate these beliefs including "people don't care about me", "nobody cares", "I'm a nobody", "I have been abandoned by the healthcare system", and core beliefs around "I'm unlovable" and "I'm not worth it". Beliefs around not feeling heard or not feeling listened to (by healthcare professionals or family members) are strongly associated with beliefs of not feeling cared for and are one of the most commonly encountered interpersonal beliefs in FND.

If the person allows you to, always explore early childhood experiences and watch out for experiences that contributed to the development of these beliefs, particularly parental emotional neglect, longstanding rejection and abandonment by important figures in other significant relationships, and school bullying experiences. Furthermore, in parallel, explore the person's current relationship dynamics, as well as recent healthcare experiences. Try to make a link between all these childhood and adulthood experiences ("have you ever felt like this before?"). It is possible that past experiences of feeling neglected and abandoned by caregivers re-trigger the same feelings during rehab and may halt an intervention. For example, a person whose emotions have been dismissed and who has been pushed to keep working or caring for family members in childhood despite feeling ill themselves (and therefore has been emotionally neglected) may be newly re-triggered in a rehab session when heavily encouraged to walk whilst feeling unwell with FND, pain or fatigue. It is important to note that people do not always identify childhood emotional neglect or strict and emotionally avoidant parenting as such ('I have never been abused, I have no trauma') or may minimize emotional neglect ('It wasn't that bad' 'lots of parents were like that').

COMPASSION FOR THE SOCIAL FUNCTIONS OF FND

If the FND symptoms may serve to meet an unmet need for validation, being noticed and cared for (external regulation function of FND), it is important to explore this social function of FND in a gentle and compassionate manner with the person and their direct environment. If the social function of FND is not addressed, the FND is likely to persist. Emphasise to the person and their environment that the need to feel cared for is a basic human need and nothing to be embarrassed or frustrated about. The person needs support to meet this need in more helpful ways (e.g. verbal expression). You could pre-empt the often scathing perceptions around care-eliciting behaviours in FND and emphasise that these behaviours have functions that exist to serve an unmet need.

In addition, in case of adverse childhood experiences people have likely not learned what constitutes normal caring behaviours, in terms of both providing and receiving care. This can be expressed in overstepping boundaries around caring behaviours; for example, the person with FND may be "overcaring" and become overinvested in caring activities for other people, whilst holding loose personal boundaries and a low threshold for accepting uncaring behaviours from other people. It is therefore important to share with the person that these aberrant caring patterns are not held against them since they have simply not learned and practised normal caring patterns whilst growing up. A good technique for increasing insight into these skewed standards is to explore with the person what caring standards they hold for themselves vs people in their environment, in the same way for people with perfectionist beliefs.

THE PCM: ADDRESSING RECIPROCAL REINFORCEMENT

The PCM can be a very helpful tool to formulate the internal regulation function of interpersonal triggers (e.g. seeing a peer spending more time with another person) and social emotions (e.g. envy, "attachment anxiety" – which is different from the anxiety in the context of social situations, health or panic attacks). The attachment anxiety can be experienced as intolerable and directly lead to FND (dissociative episodes), as this effectively and quickly reduces the anxiety for the individual in the moment.

In addition, creating a hybrid formulation that incorporates the "being cared for" vs "caring for" reciprocal reinforcement patterns and their relationship with FND maintenance will be key to demonstrate that interpersonal triggers not only have an internal but also an external regulation (or social) function. If the care theme is prominent, any reciprocal reinforcement patterns need to be addressed to have a chance at full recovery from FND.

Illness beliefs

The (Brief) Illness Perception Questionnaire (e.g. Broadbent et al., 2006) can be helpful to obtain a quick snapshot of a person's illness beliefs. However, if the focus on illness and symptoms is strong, and associated with health anxiety or panic disorder, check whether the CBT models for health anxiety (Salkovskis et al., 2003) and panic disorder (Clark, 1986) may fit better with the person's cognitions and clinical presentation, which would trump the use of the PCM. See Chapter 8 for a case description.

Illness beliefs often co-exist with heightened self-focused attention. It may be useful to raise insight into the person's heightened self-focused attention and recommend attention shifting techniques. However, these techniques tend to be more superficial, in the same vein as reality grounding techniques are for acute dissociative symptoms. To truly bring about a shift in a person's thinking about illness and reduce symptom focus, behavioural experiments are likely needed, as well as determining the root cause of the illness beliefs by either applying the CBT for health anxiety model or the PCM in psychological therapy.

Illness worries can easily cause another set of worries: Type 2 worries about FND. For example, a primary illness worry ("I'm going to have a stroke") may result in a dissociative episode. This may evolve into secondary illness worries ("I'm going to have another seizure") on top of the original illness worries, which may amplify the FND symptoms even more. The best way to manage Type 2 worries is to address the underlying cause: the Type 1 worries and their link to FND.

Chicken or egg? The FND-mood link

At times, patients may acknowledge psychological factors but only in response to the FND symptoms ("The FND has caused me to feel anxious, depressed, angry – before the FND I never experienced this"). Acknowledge the link in the FND → mood direction; however, also gently explain that it is common in FND for psychological symptoms to both pre-date and emerge following the FND symptoms. You can use a PCM formulation to explain this. Even if the person is resistant to accepting the mood → FND link, *any* dialogue on the link between FND and emotions will be a helpful start.

Attachment anxiety vs anxiety

The rejection theme is very prevalent in people with FND. Rejection tends to be rooted in childhood, often starting with parental emotional neglect, rejection from one or both key parental figures, abandonment by a parent (e.g. absence following divorce) or bullying experiences at school. Due to these adverse rejection and neglect experiences in childhood, people with FND develop negative beliefs around people rejecting, ignoring, disrespecting or abandoning them including a heightened sensitivity to outright rejection or towards subtle cues that may signal rejection (e.g. another person's facial expression or talking to someone else with the person perceiving this as rejection). These beliefs may result in an increased anxiety for rejection and abandonment in relationships, including relationships with healthcare professionals, which can be conceptualised as an "attachment anxiety".

It should be noted that people with FND who experience deeply ingrained beliefs and intense anxiety around interpersonal rejection also frequently experience low self-esteem and self-attacking beliefs that have been internalised because of the adverse childhood experiences. This poses risks from their environment including exploitation, abuse and re-traumatisation in new dysfunctional relationships, in order to prevent their worst fear of rejection from happening. In addition, people may use "crisis survival" strategies to protect their self-worth at a high cost and resort to rejecting or keeping other people at a safe distance before they can reject the person, resulting in limited social networks and lack of opportunities to test out their rejection beliefs. Due to adverse childhood experiences, people with FND may not always had the opportunity to regulate their emotions in more adaptive ways and over time have learned to regulate their emotions and access validation via the environment where the FND symptoms may serve an additional function of eliciting care and validation. Another complication in people with FND with a central rejection theme is dissociation. This is a coping strategy that often originates in childhood as a consequence of adverse experiences and repeats into adulthood. People with FND may not be aware of the fear of rejection, attachment anxiety and the way that the unmet need is met by the FND symptoms.

This type of "attachment" anxiety tends to have a very different quality to "regular" anxiety such as social anxiety, panic, health anxiety, "simple" PTSD, obsessions and compulsions. The treatment approaches differ substantially between these two types of anxiety. Attachment-type anxiety in people with FND is more suited to longitudinal formulations (e.g. Beck Judith, 1995) with an embedded maintenance cycle (e.g. PCM or vicious flower of depression, Moorey (2010)), whereas regular anxiety tends to be more suitable to condition-specific CBT models.

Unspeakable dilemma within a system: being trapped

An unspeakable dilemma is characterised by secrecy and a situation, which, if the unspeakable dilemma would be revealed and "out in the open", it may likely have consequences and ramifications for the person in question, as well as for the family unit or relationships that they are part of. The person feels trapped in the situation with no perceived realistic way out. An example includes abuse or a social function of FND that has not been revealed. In this context, it is important to keep in mind potential safeguarding and risk issues to the person.

At times, FND may start in response to anxiety around a stress-trigger that is relatively small and manageable (but is big for the person), for example a perceived failure at school or work. Subsequently, FND becomes triggered by a wider range of stressful situations with the FND becoming heavily entrenched in day-to-day life, for example with the family or system around the person heavily invested in caring, the accumulation of a large number of equipment, irreversible home adaptations, a comprehensive package of care and an FND identity that reaches into social networks. The person may feel psychologically and physically trapped in this situation and becomes hopeless about departing from the situation. It is important to provide a person who is suspected to be in this situation, a "face saving" way of escape.

Classic CBT cognitions

It is common for people with FND to experience co-existing psychological conditions such as health anxiety, social anxiety, generalised anxiety, panic, and more rarely, obsessions and compulsions. A subset of people with FND will experience classic beliefs and cognitions that fit with existing condition-specific CBT models. The FND symptoms they experience will neatly fit into these models, particularly under the label of safety behaviours. During the assessment, it is important to look out for those cognitions because they will determine the treatment approach (CBT model vs PCM). A multitude of evidence-based models exist for many different psychological conditions. It is therefore strongly recommended to use condition-specific CBT models when encountering the cognitions and features that belong to specific psychological conditions such as social anxiety and panic disorder. CBT intervention in people with FND is not much different than CBT for people without FND and consists of similar techniques including behavioural experiments, fear hierarchies of gradually more anxiety-provoking situations and the encouragement of dropping safety behaviours.

It may not always be clear whether an underlying psychological condition is present that can be treated with an evidence-based CBT model. Some people with FND may find it difficult to verbalise or understand their beliefs because they may have been invalidated in childhood. The therapy may feel stuck as beliefs are hard to identify for the person and the psychologist is struggling to plan the next steps. With patients where an underlying psychological condition is suspected or who may tick the boxes of multiple conditions, a helpful technique may be to (perhaps counter-intuitively) provide some direction and "to start bringing up" the various classic cognitions that belong to the different models, to gain a bit more clarity on the thought contents, for example:

> People may experience all kinds of bothersome thoughts and feelings. For example, some common worries include persistent worries (GAD), worries about being judged by other people / feeling self-conscious in social situations (social anxiety), worries about having a stroke, heart attack or a life-threatening illness (panic, health anxiety), seeing or believing things that other people may not (psychosis), beliefs around rejection and losses (depression), trauma memories (PTSD), obsessive thoughts and so on. Does any of these ring true for you or feel familiar? Which of these stand out to you? Shall we explore the ones that feel the most applicable to your situation? Don't worry, these beliefs are really common in the general population and there are good treatment options available.

It is beyond the scope of this book to go through every CBT model for each of these types of anxiety in FND. Chapter 8 will provide more details on when and how to use CBT models alongside the PCM. It will also demonstrate that some CBT models can be morphed into "PCM+" models that accommodate for the specific maintaining factors of FND, particularly environmental reinforcement, whilst preserving the evidence-based principles of the classic CBT models.

Fear of relapse

For some people with FND, their course of illness can follow a waxing and waning pattern. Table 4.11 displays common risk factors for actual relapse found in clinical practice.

Table 4.11 Clinical risk factors of relapse in FND

PCM	Details
Ignition	• History of multiple relapses of FND. • Longstanding complex trauma history that started in childhood and repeated into adulthood, with ongoing strong rejection and care themes, which have not been fully managed through multiple long-term treatment programmes and mental health hospitalisations.
Fuel	• Approaching the end of therapy or discharge from service (due to attachment break or stress of not being able to cope without therapist, or both). • Increased stress in life and not having access or not fully have consolidated helpful coping strategies (e.g. verbal emotional expression). • Upcoming anniversaries of difficult life events (e.g. bereavement, divorce).
Flames and heat	• Strong belief and fears around the relapsing-remitting character of FND whilst not holding on to any beliefs around the reversibility of the condition: "I'm going to relapse and I won't be able to cope", "FND is a fluctuating condition and I will have to learn to live with this condition for the rest of my life". • High levels of anxiety around discharge. • Not fully buying into the psychological formulation of FND.
Sticky left-over food	• Strong negative core beliefs that persist and despite active work on challenging negative core beliefs/building positive core beliefs; the person continues to greatly struggle with this process.
Pot	• High level of entrenchment in equipment and hard-to-reverse home adaptations. • Future planning around disabilities and not focused on recovery (e.g. thinking about disability adjustments at work or study without believing FND will improve). • Strong need to keep holding on to equipment as psychological safety behaviours.
Warning light	• Continued high focus on physical symptoms that has not abated following a course of psychological therapy. • "Systemic hypervigilance": heavy monitoring of FND symptoms by environment that fosters continued co-dependency and reluctancy to part ways with this.
Cover	• Emotional expression not consolidated – and does not constitute the dominant coping strategy in the social environment to which the patient is returning.

(Continued)

Table 4.11 (Continued)

PCM	Details
Valve	• Significant social isolation and limited social network, or a social network that consists of remote and irregular social connections, or only with other people with FND.
Kitchen	• Family not on board with strategies/or not involved in therapy/family having similar coping strategies as the premorbid FND patient but not changed.
Overpressure Plug	• Long history of FND symptoms (though be aware that some people may not have had access to appropriate specialist support for years and are "FND treatment naïve").
	• Long history of organic and/or other functional somatoform symptoms that pre-date the FND.
Safety features	• Protective factors against relapse include good insight into the PCM formulation, consolidated strategies and a supportive/helpful family and social environment that is on board with the formulation.

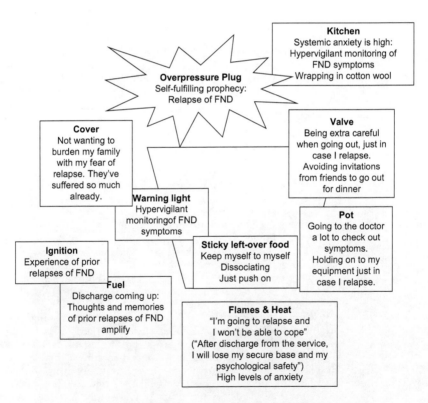

Figure 4.5 Pressure Cooker Model formulation of the fear of FND relapse.

Self-fulfilling prophecy of FND relapse: a PCM formulation

The problem with people's fears and beliefs of relapse is that these can become a self-fulfilling prophecy where their most feared worst-case scenario becomes reality. A "pressure cooker of FND set-back" may look like Figure 4.5.

If the person with FND expresses a fear of relapse (and importantly: if there is palpable, strong systemic anxiety around relapse), it will always be helpful to formulate the fear of relapse and the association with recurrent FND symptoms. This formulation can guide the steps of intervention to prevent actual relapse by tackling each element of the PCM. This can culminate in the co-development of a "pressure cooker explosion emergency plan" between the person with FND, their family and the clinician to focus on prevention of relapse or on an emergency plan for if the relapse does happen. Please note that it is strongly recommended that the person's environment formulates their own systemic fear of the person's potential relapse using a similar hybrid PCM formulation applied to themselves.

Fear of recovery

Many people with FND will experience, often hidden, fears around recovery. This seems counter-intuitive as FND can be a very disabling condition. This type of fear is often driven by a lack of perspective on what a future could look like if the FND did not exist, particularly if the person experienced FND for several years, where they lost all hope and their minds have not gone near the idea of recovery. In addition, FND can have strong social gains, whilst recovery from FND could result in social losses including the FND identity, support and relationships with carers (see Table 4.12).

Table 4.12 Social gains and losses in FND recovery

Social gains of recovery from FND	Social losses of recovery from FND
More independence without the restrictions of disabilities will make it easier to access the community, grow my social circle, gain new friendships, develop more social connections and a sense of belonging in a community. I will also have more time as getting round in a wheelchair/or needing equipment often takes more time. I will be able to find a home without adaptations or live on my own	Losing friendships with carers Losing proximity to someone I deeply care about, for example a family member who supports me with washing and dressing.
Finding new parts of my identity that is not mostly focused on FND. Going on a journey to discover who I am without the FND and enriching my identity.	Losing my identity as a person with FND. Who am I without FND?

(Continued)

Table 4.12 (Continued)

Social gains of recovery from FND	Social losses of recovery from FND
Increasing my self-esteem in other ways and not being defined by FND. Being defined by a range of other personal qualities and features is a less risky strategy for my self-esteem than being defined by one feature, the FND, only.	Losing my self-esteem. FND and equipment may give some people new confidence to fare in the world and establish relationships, being part of a community, being valued, validated and respected. Without FND, I may lose this and this may impact on someone's self-esteem.
Gaining less practised but more helpful coping strategies: • Expressing my emotions to other people • Hobbies, interests Finding new routines with new exciting activities that my disabilities previously prevented me from doing, such as driving without adaptations and taking on any job role that I can, it will "open up my world" and help me live life to the full. Reducing risk of injury and less impact on daily living (e.g. if I don't experience dissociative episodes). People asking less questions about what's wrong with me and why I need equipment.	Losing a well-established coping strategy: • How will I cope with difficult thoughts and feelings when I recover from FND? • Will I be able to cope? Losing stability and routine in my life. • FND gives predictability (e.g. carers coming in three times a day). • Being in a "small world" that gives me a feeling of control over my life circumstances, perhaps the control that I have never experienced before. Experiencing a threat to how I am perceived socially and risking rejection and expulsion from a social group: • for example, how will I explain my recovery from FND? • will people believe me or judge me again? Maybe even more than when I had FND?
Gaining a new identity as someone who has overcome FND and can support others who are experiencing FND in that process and live life to the full.	Losing my position being part of the FND community as a "patient", "warrior", "fighter", losing my sense of belonging to a community, losing potential friendships that I have in "followers" on social media, in this case the FND community.
Family gains: • What new roles in the family unit will I take on? • Underlying family problems contributing to the FND may be finally addressed by addressing the FND	Family losses: • What will other family members lose if I recover from FND? Think about losing control over you. • Would there be resistance from my environment when I recover? • Will the family destabilise because roles have now changed? If FND is the glue keeping the family together: will peace disappear? • Would my partner, family, friends or bosses expect more of me if I recover from FND and place more heavy demands and responsibilities on me?

FEAR OF RECOVERY: POTENTIAL INDICATORS

It is important to be gentle and compassionate towards this situation. A person with FND and their family may not be fully aware of the social gains and losses of recovery. In addition, a person who is more conscious of this dilemma may feel "paralysed" between gains and losses, leaving them stuck in a status quo about whether to move towards or away from FND recovery, in part because of predicted major consequences for the social system and high anxiety. Moreover, the person may not be "moving" for reasons that are less associated with the fear of recovery but, for instance, may be more due to emotional neglect experiences often being re-triggered, which prevents FND recovery. This would require a different therapeutic approach (i.e. exploring traumatic experiences) than the former situation (i.e. behavioural experiments to test out beliefs about social fears).

Fear of recovery can greatly impact on actual recovery, and it is important to recognise the clinical signs that may suggest this. The following observations may indicate a potential fear of recovery. The presence of these clinical features does not automatically mean that the person fears recovery but warrants further monitoring and exploration (Table 4.13).

Table 4.13 Potential indicators of fear of recovery in FND

Theme	Details
Goal setting	• Not progressing in therapy or rehabilitation: not reaching goals or reaching goals initially but followed by a plateau. • Slow progress on goals or "just" reaching goals. • Difficulties establishing goals or mentioning vague goals that are harder to measure. • Selective goals: preference to work selectively on one type of symptom (e.g. dissociative episodes) and expressing feelings of indifference towards addressing other symptoms (e.g. mobility and motor weakness), often associated with equipment such as a wheelchair.
Positive view on equipment	• Describing positives about having FND or advantages around holding onto equipment; for example, the wheelchair helps to access the community, as opposed to staying in a micro-environment, receiving certain privileges. • People with a fear of recovery may be dismissive of the idea that a piece of disability equipment may elicit friendly responses, support, care and validation from the environment. • A person who is in the process of recovery may be oscillating between using a piece of equipment/wheelchair some of the time vs walking at other times, which may almost be representative of an internal battle between not recovering vs recovery.

(Continued)

Table 4.13 (Continued)

Theme	Details
Persistent inability to identify FND triggers	• An inability to identify triggers for FND is normal. However, if this persists after several therapy sessions and suspected triggers are heavily dismissed, then this may indicate a fear of recovery.
Strong beliefs around not recovering	• Some people mention having been informed by healthcare professionals of the chronic nature of their FND and associated this with unlikely recovery, especially if they have experienced FND over many years with little improvement in their symptoms. People may strongly hold onto this idea and repeatedly mention their lack of belief in recovery.
Lack of alternative plans or goals	• A person fearing recovery may not be able to describe clear or any goals for when the FND would not exist, and "live in the moment" without displaying any futuristic thinking. The person may struggle to come up with the steps/have loosely or vaguely defined steps to achieve goals.
No social sense of belonging/ no strong supportive relationships or allies	• The person may not have strong, supportive alliances in their system, or lacks a sense of belonging to a group or community. They may not experience a "psychologically safe haven" with encouraging allies.
Unspeakable dilemma	• An unspeakable dilemma can maintain a fear of recovery, as releasing the dilemma into the open may have damaging consequences for the person and their environment.
Safety behaviours	• Occasionally, people may struggle to progress in rehab and fear recovery because of the prospect of losing their safety behaviours; for example, learning to stand and walk again may make a person feel more self-conscious about their body or would mean losing a coping strategy for anxiety (e.g. the wheelchair may help prevent a person having to look other people in the eye; hence, losing this equipment would mean losing a strategy).
Living well using adaptations	• Over a long time, some people may not see the benefit of recovery from FND as they have been very well adapted to the FND with a range of equipment, adaptations and services in place for support. In terms of functional status, recovery from FND may not be significantly different than living with FND; a person may be able to access the same activities. The social functions of FND, particularly feeling cared for, may push towards living with adaptations whilst away from recovery and losing those social functions.
Strong FND identity	• A person may have adopted a strong FND identity and efforts to tinker with this identity (e.g. progress in rehab, meeting goals) may be met with resistance due to the social fear of losing the identity when recovered.
Positive view on FND by the environment	• The environment around the person may indicate contentedness with the outcomes gained so far, even if this suggests ongoing or residual FND symptoms. This may suggest a reciprocal reinforcement process and warrants further exploration.

FEAR OF RECOVERY: PREPARATORY WORK

People's fears around recovery can be very strong, and it can severely halt therapy progress and recovery in FND. We need to consider the fear of recovery as a social construct that is strongly associated with social gains and losses. Building a strong therapeutic alliance between the patient and the clinician will be very important in this regard. Normalise the fear of recovery and openly acknowledge to the person that this fear can be a difficult and highly sensitive topic to discuss because their social network and the "general population" may firmly believe that it is logical for everyone to want to recover from a disabling condition. Praise the person for their willingness to openly explore this with you and ensure that the person knows that you are not rejecting or abandoning them for experiencing this fear. For some people, this may be a large barrier to overcome that, once expressed, provides a sense of relief. Emphasise that exploring the fear of recovery is the actual start of the intervention and the first step in FND recovery as you both work on strengthening your secure psychological base to explore what a life without FND might look like. Be patient as letting go of the fear of recovery does not happen overnight. Allow time for this process to unfold and for the person to get used to the idea of recovery. It is possible that a person's mind has not gone there yet, maybe for years. Finally, raise insight into your own potential fears about the person's fears of recovery: how would you feel if the person did not recover from FND? Would that say something about your own therapeutic skills and reduce your confidence as a clinician, perhaps impact negatively on your clinical track record? In other words: ask yourself what your social gains and losses may be if the person would recover vs not recover, and whether you can unearth a reciprocal reinforcement process between yourself and the person with FND.

FEAR OF RECOVERY: ASSESSMENT TEMPLATE

A good starting point can be the assessment template below. Identify any psychological safety behaviours that may stop a person from recovering. What are the main reasons for the fear? What social gains and losses are at stake? The table on social gains and losses may be helpful to share with the person as a guide. When completing this exercise with the patient, emphasise that some questions will feel difficult and challenging to answer and can cause strong emotions (e.g. frustration, anxiety, anger, shame and embarrassment). Further emphasise that the worksheet is not designed to convince the person that they are in conscious control of their own recovery and that they are doing this to themselves, on purpose or are consciously putting on FND. The goal of the worksheet is to help a person think about routes towards recovery and how to address some thoughts and feelings that may stand in the way of recovery (Figure 4.6).

After completing the worksheet, check in with the person on how this process was for them and what beliefs and emotions came up. When identifying

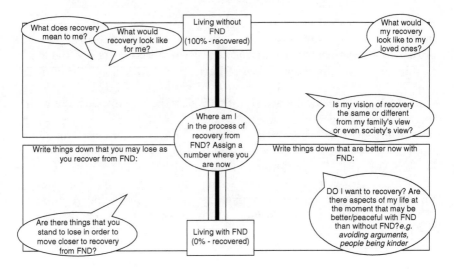

Figure 4.6 Fear of recovery worksheet.

social gains and losses, it can be helpful to focus on the long-term gains of recovery (e.g. increasing their social network, being able to work and getting around more quickly without a wheelchair and having to plan their journey) in favour of the short-term losses (e.g. losing their identity as an "FND warrior", social rejection from their environment). The short-term losses may often feel insurmountable and highly anxiety-provoking, whereas the long-term gains of recovery may feel less attractive and more time-consuming. To overcome the fear of recovery, the person should start to feel that tolerating the distress around their short-term losses will feel manageable and less threatening than they initially believed.

PCM FORMULATION: FEAR OF RECOVERY AND FND SYMPTOMS

It is always useful to apply a PCM formulation on the fear of recovery and demonstrate any relationship with FND symptom maintenance. If a fear of recovery is suspected with the patient, externalising the problem and sharing this pre-populated PCM formulation could start a dialogue (Table 4.14). After seeing the formulation, ask the person whether they think they may experience a fear of recovery and what parts of the PCM may be most applicable and maintaining their fear of recovery?

Once you have mapped out the fear of recovery and its relationship to FND, the "positive pressure cooker of recovery" may help you find strategies to help move the patient along on the continuum towards recovery. The following PCM formulation template will demonstrate some useful strategies. The entire template with ideas can be shared with the person (Table 4.15).

Table 4.14 Fear of recovery: a Pressure Cooker Model formulation

---

Kitchen
Worsening FND symptoms cause more rejection in my environment
(self-fulfilling prophecy): "She's putting on more symptoms, you see?"

Tight Cover
Embarrassed and ashamed
to speak about my fears
with anyone. Keeping
my fear of recovery to
myself.

Overpressure Plug
Old habits kick in:
My fear of recovery
feels intolerable
and uncontrollable:
Dissociation and FND
symptoms worsen.

Blocked Valve
Standing at the crossroads
and pondering about
what to do activity-
wise: Not knowing
what meaningful
activities I'll be able to
fill my days with when
recovering further and
not able to take steps
to explore this as I feel
frozen with fear. Status
quo/staying the way I
am feels psychologically
safe and emotionally
containing.

Warning light
FND symptoms worsen as
my fears about recovery
are building up.
Focusing more on the
symptoms.

Sticky left-over food

Dissociation as an early
childhood coping habit

Pot
Sleepless nights
Holding on to my
equipment, afraid to
step down, despite
recommendations.

Ignition
Past rejection experiences
(e.g. bullied, singled out
by parent)

Flames and Heat
I experience the following social fears:
• Fear that people will think I've faked it. Will my
family and friends understand the change and how
will they respond?

Fuel
Making some progress in
rehab/treatment. People
in my social circle
and at work giving
me puzzled looks and
openly questioning my
FND.

• Fear of recovering further: What will I tell people
about how I recovered?
• Fear of rejection and being shunned by people.
• Fear about losing my identity and about what's
next in my life.

Safety features
I am aware of my fear of recovery and have shared this fear with my therapist and
people close to me. That's a first step in my recovery from FND.

LOOSENING BELIEFS AROUND THE FEAR OF RECOVERY: DEVELOP AN FND
RECOVERY PLAN

Make a collaborative recovery plan with the person with FND, that is, ideally, shared with their family. Keep in mind that the fear of recovery is a sensitive topic for both people and their families alike. It is therefore important

Table 4.15 Positive Pressure Cooker Model of recovery from fear

Kitchen

- Help the person find an ally in their environment. Educate the person's environment on FND and ask what support they can provide/what barriers they need to drop (e.g. break the cycle of reciprocal reinforcement, encouragement of emotional expression) to help the person move along towards recovery.

Overpressure Plug

Behavioural experiments may be useful for:

- Helping to drop a piece of equipment that is held on to but not needed, for example for a day in the week, to start with.
- See what people's reactions are. Worse or better than expected? Did their biggest fear come true? Is it worth building on this?

Cover: Expressing fears

Encourage the person to find a non-judgemental person to discuss their fear of recovery with in private (e.g. a psychologist, GP, friend, family member they trust)

Warning light

Is the fear of recovery impacted by the association with their FND identity? How can the identity be diluted from FND? For example, identify interests, hobbies, personal qualities.

Sticky left-over food

Are there any negative core beliefs that drive the person's fear of recovery (especially around rejection and abandonment)?

Ignition

Is it possible that the person's fears are being re-triggered (by former rejection experiences)

Fuel

Help the person develop assertiveness skills to manage difficult questions from their environment in response to their recovery.

Valve

- **Day and week schedule.** Start thinking about what the person's days and routine may look like once recovered, in terms of activities that they can't do but would like to (e.g. driving, employment, sports). Explore what feelings come up during the discussion.
- **Pre-work/intermediate steps.** Can they make any preparations, for example if the person would like to pick up a study: looking out for colleges or courses. When going back to work, exploring voluntary roles first.
- **Realistic time-line.** Keep in mind the boom-and-bust cycle and encourage the person not to overdo it. At the same time: set some goals to keep them going. It cannot feel too comfortable that they are not moving forwards or too uncomfortable that sets the person up to fail but needs a middle ground.

Pot

Encourage the person to discuss with their healthcare providers what equipment may be dropped to move towards recovery, if there is any "intermediate" equipment they may need to rely on, any exercises that they can do and a medication review. Close collaboration from an interdisciplinary perspective is essential here.

Flames and Heat

- Help the person define their top 3 of biggest fears around recovery. You can glean from the social gains/losses table.
- Challenge the person's beliefs around social rejection and disbelief about their recovery. Would this be worse from the responses that they are experiencing now?

Flames and Heat (continued)

- Write and rehearse a script and uses role plays for practice.
- Depending on the person's wishes, the script can contain basic information about the biopsychosocial factors of FND.
- Practice answers to personal, sensitive and other tricky questions, as well as hostile responses and coping habits to deal with the emotional aftermath.
- Re-direct the questioning person's attention to FND resources or "boomerang" by explaining that the PCM is for everybody's use – not just the person with FND.

- An anonymous survey may help to test out their biggest fears and judgements from other people about FND recovery. Is the response always negative or could the response be the opposite? (person seen as a survivor or warrior who could help other people with FND?). Even if the judgements are realistic: should that stop the person in their recovery?
- Pressure cooker explosion emergency plan: if the person's most dreaded scenario of not being believed does take place: What steps can they take to cope?
- Plan a behavioural experiment to test out the person's biggest worries and fears and drop some safety behaviours (e.g. equipment), to get a glimpse or preview of what life without FND may feel like.
- Visually imagine with the person what a future life without FND will look like. How can the person make "the unknown" more known? Go through each PCM element and explore what each element will look like without FND, for example what social activities will they do, what daily routine, what job (Valve), who would they regularly speak to about difficult thoughts and feelings (Cover), what strategies will they use to manage triggers (Fuel). Complete a PCM formulation template with these questions and the person's responses.
- If they would like to go back to the person they were, ask them to describe what that previously looked like, for example walking without difficulties, healthy sleep routine, having a job, in control of stress and worries, feeling happy, big social network and more in control of dissociation. This will help the person plan their goals.

Safety features
Identify the person's and family's safety features.
How can these be used to facilitate FND recovery?

to gauge the situation first and tread carefully to prevent causing any unnec-essary "social injury" to the person with FND. There may be significant shame and embarrassment associated with sharing the fear of recovery with loved ones. In addition, some people with FND prefer to keep their families removed from the therapeutic process, particularly if recovery would mean significant social losses; and if their recovery would likely be met with sys-temic resistance due to reciprocal reinforcement processes; or cause strong negative emotions, social judgements and responses towards the person with FND that would cause psychological harm.

Below is an example of part of an FND recovery plan. Viewing an actual plan and "a way out of FND" may help the person to see that recovery is possible. It will be helpful to explore what steps elicit the highest fears or reluctance, or feel insurmountable? (check the value they assign to how far removed they are from recovery). Explore what the person can do about making these steps feel less big and how their environment can help with this process. Finding an ally in the social system around the person with FND, with their consent, will be the most favourable situation to keep the person on track towards recovery (Table 4.16).

If the person is open to exploring an FND recovery plan, collaboratively complete their current PCM and their future PCM. Make a comparison between their current PCM (with FND) and their future PCM (without FND). Compare current vs future PCMs for every element in the model. Help the person to think about the steps and activities that they could under-take to move from current to future PCM. Emphasise to the person that this does not mean that they must at all costs act on these steps. In a transparent manner, explain that this plan is intended to loosen their beliefs around their fear of recovery and will help identify areas of strength and areas that need more attention. If they would like to act on the plan, offer your support, but explain that it is their decision in the end. The person needs to "own" the plan, be self-motivated and be fully behind it, and not be coaxed on their journey by the clinician.

Fear of falling

A common fear of people with FND is the fear of falling, which can occa-sionally occur in people with dissociative episodes, but will be more of an issue for those with motor-type FND that affects transfers, standing and walking. Several factors have been identified that may increase the risk of falls in people with FND, which can be categorised as physical, psychological and FND-specific factors.

Physical factors include a history of multiple falls; reduced use of a limb and compromised ability to break a fall; lack of knowledge on equipment use; not wearing appropriate footwear; pain and stiffness; fatigue; dizziness; problems with balance; and muscle wasting.

Table 4.16 Example of an FND recovery plan

Element	My current pressure cooker	How far on the FND recovery spectrum? 0–10	Steps to move from current PCM => future PCM	My future pressure cooker
Ignition/ Fuel	I don't know what my triggers are	2/10	• Identify triggers using the structured FND diary • Remove triggers once I've got a better idea, for example using reality grounding techniques when I feel an episode coming up.	With strategies I will be able to recognise my triggers and control my dissociative episodes
Flames	I worry about being rejected and abandoned by my family and friends, who may think I'm exaggerating my condition and won't believe me.	3/10	I will take the plunge and challenge my beliefs around rejection with behavioural experiments whilst dropping my safety behaviours including my walking stick. I will "downward arrow" myself to find out the meaning behind my fears of not being believed. I will try to distance myself from the thought. This is just a thought.	I will be able to tolerate the discomfort that comes with my fears of rejection and abandonment by using my coping techniques (downward arrow and distancing).

Psychological factors include feeling "psychological pressure" if the person is aware that other people are waiting for them resulting in rushed movements and transfers; feeling self-conscious about walking in front of other people in the context of social anxiety; confusion, disorientation, memory, concentration, or any other cognitive difficulties ("brain fog") that emerge in the context of co-existing psychological conditions or the FND; not feeling psychologically safe or cared for and a tendency to regulate emotional distress via the environment, which can sometimes result in a higher frequency of falls; not feeling own base both psychologically and physically; and impulsivity. Another important psychological factor that may increase falls risk in a person with FND is a fear of recovery that often unconsciously interferes with progress and may bring treatment to a grinding halt. The falls may symbolise a sense of psychological powerlessness, perceived lack of control or an anticipated lack of social/healthcare support when the person starts to make sufficient physical gains during their recovery journey that warrants discharge from the service, but which comes with a "high price", i.e. a simultaneous loss of any social gains that are attached to the FND (e.g. compassion from the environment, an "identity"). FND-specific factors play a role as well, for example dissociative episodes; any form of dissociation that is not a full-blown dissociative episode ("absences", "switching off"); having had falls in the context of dissociative episodes; functional blindness or visual problems; and oversensitivity to environmental stimuli as part of FND. Given this long list of factors that impact on falls risk in FND, it is important to do a comprehensive falls risk assessment.

Protective factors against falls: fire safety blanket

In addition to variables that increase the risk of falls, several protective factors have been identified that reduce the falls risk in people with FND.

These can be subdivided into physical and psychological factors. Examples of protective physical factors include no history of (recent) falls or low frequency of falls without serious injuries; good adherence and comprehension of transfer, standing and walking techniques and taking the right precautions when initiating movements; regular practice with success and spontaneous use of strategies as recommended by physiotherapist or occupational therapist; using appropriate equipment and footwear; physiotherapist has observed good movement in the body part affected with FND or strong muscles (e.g. "good core strength" and "strong leg muscles") that makes it less likely for the person to fall; strong arm muscles that could help when the person loses their balance; environment free of spillages and hazards; good knowledge of energy conservation techniques (e.g. resting on a perching stool); not on medications that may cause drowsiness, fatigue or difficulties with balance; and the absence of brain injury.

Protective psychological factors include the person not engaging in risky or impulsive behaviours with good safety awareness; good engagement in psychological therapy that helped the person to find psychological safety, feel their base and improve confidence; intact cognition that is not impacted by dissociation, low mood or anxiety; not feeling psychologically pressured or rushed by the environment; and the absence of functional visual difficulties.

The falls risk and protective factors can be pitted against each other in an "evidence for" (insert the risk factors) vs "evidence against" (insert the protective factors) table that tests out the belief "Given my physical symptoms, I will fall down". This should help loosen the beliefs around fear of falling, particularly if physiotherapist-led and reinforced by the entire multidisciplinary team.

Behavioural experiments

Occasionally, FND symptoms are driven by panic attacks. The person may misinterpret physical symptoms in a catastrophic way ("I'm going to fall", "I'm going to have a seizure" – and subsequently fall if that is part of the seizure semiology). The person may hold on to people, furniture, equipment or other objects in their environment (e.g. sit back in the wheelchair, hand-held 1:1 support, falls sensory monitors, alarms), as psychological safety behaviours, which maintains the panic symptoms and reinforces the FND. In this situation, it can be helpful to teach the person reality grounding techniques to nip early dissociative features in the bud and drop safety behaviours for as long as is possible in that moment. It can also be useful to compare with situations where the person had similar physical symptoms but without the accompanying catastrophic misinterpretations and which did not result in falls or seizures (e.g. on the treadmill in the gym). Irrespective of whether the person experiences falls as a result of panic symptoms, dissociation or other fears, behavioural experiments carefully planned in conjunction with physiotherapists or occupational therapists will be key to help progress a patient with fear of falling in rehab.

PCM formulation: fear of falling

The following PCM formulation demonstrates how a person's fear of falling can maintain FND symptoms. The PCM formulation can be very useful to formulate and plan subsequent treatment to address the fear of falling. Explore the formulation with the person and which areas to tackle first. Behavioural experiments combined with the use of reality grounding techniques may be helpful to break the "Flames-Overpressure Plug" link (Table 4.17).

USEFUL QUESTIONNAIRES

Commonly used questionnaires to obtain a quick snapshot of a person's thoughts and emotions and to assess progress in therapy include the following: Clinical Outcomes in Routine Evaluation (CORE-34 or CORE-10; Barkham et al., 2001); Patient Health Questionnaire (PHQ-9; Kroenke et al., 2001); Beck Depression Inventory (Beck et al., 1961); Generalised Anxiety Disorder Scale (GAD-7; Spitzer et al., 2006); and Beck Anxiety Inventory (Beck et al., 1988; Beck & Steer (1990)). Although it may seem less useful to administer questionnaires in people who present as highly dissociated, it is advisable to proceed with doing this as people with FND may initially display "0" responses on nearly all questions that may change into the acknowledgement of significant distress following psychological therapy. This effect, discussed in the next section, may actually signify progress in therapy as the person is becoming more connected with emotions.

Table 4.17 Fear of falling: a Pressure Cooker Model formulation

---

Chaotic kitchen

People around you are very afraid too
that you will fall again and protective of you,
and won't let you walk or transfer on your own, are always on "standby"
just in case you might fall

Tight Cover

Not speaking about your fear, keeping it to yourself, or expressing a lot of worries, with your family worrying with you.

Overpressure Plug

FND keeps going: Fear of falling stops you from trying and practising techniques.

Every time you try to stand you feel high anxiety around falling down, which you dissociate from, resulting in a loss of balance, feeling weakness and reduced sensation in your legs ("can't feel my base"). You engage in the following safety behaviours: quickly sitting in the wheelchair, holding on to the double bars for support.

Blocked Valve

The fear of falling has gripped you, you are not doing your standing or walking practice. You prefer to stay indoors or only practise your walking indoors. Lack of a sense of belonging, being part of a community.

Warning light

You are very focused on the risk that you may fall during standing or walking practice.

Sticky left-over food

Dissociation was your coping strategy in childhood.

Pot

You hold on to equipment as your psychological safety blanket.

Ignition

You have memories of having had falls before and sustained injuries.

Fuel

Your physiotherapist feels you are ready and you are both thinking about trying to stand or walk

Flames

You experience reduced confidence in your walking.

Anxiety, fear of falling and sustaining more serious injuries his time.

As you started to take first steps and you are moving different types of muscles, body sensations may feel new and different, and you may "misinterpret" these new sensations as threatening or signs of impending FND.

Heat

You are starting to cut off your anxiety. The world around you feels a bit unreal, you are getting dizzy.

Safety features

Favourable falls risk profile
Many protective factors against falling

Heat

In this section, we will discuss the different clinical manifestations of the Heat element in FND.

High heat: emotion dysregulation

A subset of people with FND experience emotion dysregulation (e.g. Uliaszek et al., 2012; Brown et al., 2013). Useful questionnaires to assess emotion dysregulation include the Difficulties in Emotion Regulation Scale (Gratz & Roemer, 2004; Kaufman et al., 2016) and the Inventory of Altered Self-Capacities (Briere & Runtz, 2002). The Personality Assessment Inventory (Morey, 1991) contains scales that may suggest emotion dysregulation. More subjective tools to measure the intensity of emotions (including undefined, unpleasant internal states that the person may not be able to label as emotions) may be an emotion thermometer that runs from 0 to 100°C or visual analogue scales (0, "not feeling anything at all" − 10, "most extreme level of emotional intensity"; 0%–100%, or any system according to the person's preference).

Extreme heat: emotion co-dysregulation

It is important to note that the family and healthcare system around the person with FND often experience similar variations in emotional intensity ("systemic heat"), for example in response to witnessing a person with FND unwell with a dissociative episode. This is the driving force behind reciprocal reinforcement patterns, which can only be broken if the system's Heat is addressed in a similar way as the person's Heat. Therefore, a formulation will only fully capture the FND if it considers both the person and their environment.

Low heat: dissociation

Various features may indicate dissociation in a person with FND. The history and observations may provide important clues to dissociation.

LANGUAGE

During therapy sessions, dissociative features may become evident in the language that the person with FND uses, for example phrases such as "I blot out my emotions", "I cut my emotions off", "I bury my feelings". People may also report that they have never experienced stress and firmly hold onto this belief. This may be reflected in "0 responses" on questionnaires (see below). Physical descriptions of emotions ("I felt tired" and "I felt my chest tightening") can also suggest dissociation or alexithymia.

COGNITION AND BEHAVIOUR

In the context of cognitive processes, people may report having no memory of important life events, traumatic events, their entire life or parts of their past including a full retrograde amnesia without anterograde amnesia, and dissociated identity ("Who am I?" and "I am not Jane"). Certain behaviours may indicate dissociation including a dissociative episode in response to an emotional topic during your session and reports of a longstanding history of dissociation and trauma in childhood. People may also report fugue-like or wandering states lasting for several hours or days and that are often associated with memory loss, as well as vacant staring episodes.

PSYCHOLOGY VS PHYSICAL DISSOCIATION

The way people with FND approach a multidisciplinary team may also provide some insights into the level of dissociation, particularly if people prefer to work with more physical healthcare professionals but reject or are reluctant to work with psychological disciplines. People who experience dissociation may not connect with work on emotions because it feels foreign to them. Instead, they may favour physical treatment approaches, as this is the "currency" that they identify with better. It should be noted that the "physical over psychological" preference may be driven by other reasons, which are not necessarily dissociation, for example a preference to avoid exploring emotions as people may not experience much confidence in their ability to tolerate the distress that would emerge if they would stop avoiding emotions. Other reasons may involve the stigma and prejudice around acknowledging emotional distress, as well as fear around the level of severity of physical symptoms.

QUESTIONNAIRES

Questionnaires that tap into dissociative features may be useful to administer including the Dissociative Experiences Scale – II (Carlson & Putnam, 1993) or the Impact of Events Scale – Revised (Horowitz et al., 1979; Weiss & Marmar, 1997). Although inspection of the contents of a questionnaire can be helpful and may reveal a score that reaches the threshold for abnormal levels of dissociation, it can sometimes be more useful to make a distinction between "content" vs "process".

HEAT STRATEGIES

Assessment   A helpful way to assess "Heat" is the use of diaries. A dissociation diary can not only help track the frequency of dissociative episodes, but also shine a light on activities that may suggest but may not have been previously identified as dissociation (e.g. hypersomnia, sports activities that go on for too long, hours of videogaming, reading or wandering), as well as moments during the day that the person may "switch off" and "feel fuzzy-headed" but not experience full-blown FND symptoms. Keeping a diary can help raise the person's insight into their level of dissociation and determine whether the dissociation is excessive and standing in the way of life. Before starting a dissociation diary, it is helpful to create a shared definition of dissociation to ensure dissociative features are recognised by the person.

In a similar vein, diaries can be used to track mood swings. Ask the person to track their mood for a week and record possible triggers, associated thoughts, behaviours, activities and the physical manifestations of the emotion. Importantly, ensure that FND symptoms are tracked to check whether there is an association between FND and mood swings.

THE PRESSURE COOKER OF DISSOCIATION: PSYCHO-EDUCATION

People with FND and their families are often not aware or have a vague idea of the concept of dissociation. Although the PCM is a model for FND, the different elements of the PCM can be used creatively as a "biopsychosocial guide", to ask a series of questions and provide answers about a phenomenon important in FND. The biopsychological guide approach will work well with people who are able to distinguish the different pressure cookers from one another. Biopsychosocial guides can also be used for Q&A's about sleep and emotions. Book 2 will describe a few more practical examples (Table 4.18).

Table 4.18 Pressure Cooker Model of dissociation

Kitchen

Q: What are the social functions of dissociation?
A: Someone with a dissociative episode may express and communicate their distress to the environment through dissociation, especially if they haven't got any other coping strategies. Dissociation may also act as a deterrent to the environment, for example to stop an argument.

Cover	**Overpressure Plug**	**Valve**
Q: What sorts of language and phrases might a person who dissociates, use? **A:** "Things feel distant", "I feel like I'm out of my body" **Q:** What are some common verbal expressions that may suggest dissociation? **A:** "I'm switching off", "I feel spaced out", "I feel disconnected from the world".	**Q:** What does dissociation look like? How does dissociation manifests in terms of our behaviours? **A:** We can experience a dissociative episode. Dissociation is on a spectrum of behaviours, other examples include sleeping long periods, "getting lost" in a movie or a book, "motorway hypnosis" and daydreaming.	**Q:** How can dissociation impact on daily life? **A:** Some people are "busy bees" and always keep themselves busy at every moment of the day. This can be a form of dissociation. If you push on or are always absorbed in activities, you don't have to think or feel difficult emotions.

(Continued)

Table 4.18 (Continued)

Warning light

Q: What happens to a person's attention when they dissociate?

A: Dissociation is the opposite to "paying attention and being focused". It can impact negatively on our attention and distract us during activities (e.g. driving a car, cooking a meal).

Sticky left-over food

Q: Does dissociation originate in childhood? Can it repeat into adulthood?

A: Some people who experienced difficult events in childhood can develop dissociation to cope with very traumatic circumstances, as it was protective for their feelings. Dissociation has its origins in childhood and can repeat over time and many years to become your main coping strategy.

Pot

Q: Are there any risks of dissociation? Is dissociation dangerous?

A: Yes, if you dissociate a lot and are cooking a meal or drive a car you may risk an accident. Some people mismanage their medications.

Q: How about medication, what is their relationship to dissociation?

A: Some medications can make you vulnerable towards dissociation, for example opiates.

Q: Are there any biological and physical factors that can make you more prone to dissociation?

A: Lack of sleep, drinking alcohol

Ignition/Fuel

Q: Who dissociates and do people with some experiences dissociate more? What triggers dissociation?

A: Everyone dissociates! (e.g. daydreaming). Dissociation can be triggered by difficult thoughts, feelings and memories.

Flames

Q: What happens to our emotions when we dissociate? What is the relationship between dissociation and emotions?

A: Dissociation is a coping strategy and can help manage strong emotions by cutting them off so you don't feel them.

Heat

Q: Are there any levels of dissociation? Do some people dissociate more or to a higher degree than others?

A: Some people do it more often than others, and some people experience stronger levels than others. A good way to measure dissociation is to complete the Dissociative Experiences Scale.

Safety features

Q: What are some of the protective factors for dissociation?

A: Learning and practising reality grounding techniques. Having knowledge about when dissociation is happening including more subtle forms (e.g. long sleeping episodes).

DIALLING UP THE HEAT

Although reality grounding, emotional awareness and emotion education strategies can be a helpful start to support a person in learning "to get back in touch" with their emotions, it is important to keep in mind that dissociative tendencies in people with FND often originate in childhood and are repeated over many years into adulthood. Dissociation may be a highly practised and automatic skill. The person may have had a lifetime of dissociation and not connected with emotions in a long time. Clinicians that recommend "off the cuff" reality grounding techniques may find variable effectiveness in people with FND, with some dismissive of any strategy ("I tried that and it didn't work" and "That didn't work either") leaving the clinician to feel frustrated and hopeless. Reality grounding techniques may be too superficial to manage the dissociation. Instead, psychological therapy that addresses the root causes of the dissociation will likely make the difference, particularly if interpersonal triggers, relationship difficulties and family dynamics are managed that drive dissociation.

A process approach to questionnaire interpretation in FND

In the clinic, comparisons between pre-therapy and post-therapy scores are important for gaining an understanding of the level of therapeutic change. We may calculate "clinical significance" using a statistical formula (e.g. Jacobson & Truax, 1991). In the ideal world of psychological therapy, clinicians wish to see clinically significant scores on pre-treatment questionnaires moving towards the non-clinical ranges on discharge, following the completion of a course of psychological therapy. This may not always be the case for people with FND. However, that does not automatically mean that the therapy has failed.

Often, questionnaires are interpreted quantitatively. We may quickly glance over the items scores and calculate a total score, which we compare with a norm group. Although this is helpful, in people with FND, it is important to consider both content and process. Occasionally, a compassionate approach that explores the functions of "questionnaire response behaviour" will be far more insightful. For example, the non-communication of distress on questionnaires may be doing exactly the opposite, namely, communicating something important about the person's emotions and distress. Table 4.19 reviews some common "process" patterns found on questionnaires completed by people with FND.

In addition to questionnaires, it should also be noted that homework "process analysis" can be helpful in FND. Homework may play into dissociation. For example, asking the person to carefully track emotions using weekly thought diaries or FND symptoms in tally charts may be a good start; however, it is important to monitor the "process" aspects: Is the person not avoiding emotions by approaching them in an intellectual or dissociated manner?

Table 4.19 Questionnaire processes in FND

Response pattern	Details	What might it indicate?
0 response pattern	• No endorsement of emotional items but high endorsement of physical items on questionnaires. • Extremely low total scores. • Scores seem inconsistent with the level of disability and psychosocial circumstances.	**Dissociation and alexithymia** • Extremely low scores or "0" responses on questionnaires are sometimes referred to as "denial of distress", an unhelpful term that implies that people with FND purposefully may not admit to experiencing emotions, whereas in fact they may not be aware of emotions. • Low scores may indicate high levels of dissociation and alexithymia. From an early age, people with FND may have learned to dissociate in the context of traumatic experiences and have lost touch with their emotions where they struggle to label, describe and experience emotions. Completing a questionnaire about emotions may be a foreign experience for people with FND. **Shame and embarrassment** • High levels of shame and embarrassment about experiencing and acknowledging negative emotions can be present, particularly in people with FND who experienced high levels of invalidation, criticism and punishment in response to emotional expression in childhood. People may hold firm beliefs around emotional expression including "expressing emotions makes me look weak" "admitting that you want to hurt yourself is weak". **Deterrent and avoidance** • Low scores may also serve the function of acting as a "deterrent" for needing psychological input. People with FND may experience negative emotions (and not dissociate from the emotions) but may be reluctant to work on this area, preferring to work on the more physical aspects of rehabilitation. If a person with FND has had a longstanding history of avoiding speaking about emotions, and avoidance is a fixed part of their coping repertoire, asking them to complete a questionnaire about emotions may cause high levels of anxiety and discomfort, resulting in an approach intended to protect their inner emotions. In addition, questionnaires are sometimes completed in the presence of, or with support from partners or family if the person's FND symptoms may prevent them from completing questionnaires (e.g. functional blindness, functional cognitive problems) and this may influence a person's responses.

Response pattern	Details	What might it indicate?
Low to high scores paradox	• Pre-questionnaire shows a low score in the non-clinical range. At discharge, the score is suddenly high and clinically significant.	**Increased insight into emotions** • Although a seemingly contradictory phenomenon, due to dissociation, alexithymia, avoidance or negative beliefs around emotional expression, a person with FND may display low scores at the start of therapy. • However, following a completed course of psychological therapy, the person may have confronted avoidant patterns, become more aware of dissociation, found strategies to recognise and experience emotions better, and developed a more compassionate view towards experiencing emotions, subsequently reflected in higher scores on discharge. In this context, paradoxically, higher scores on discharge questionnaires are a sign of progression rather than regression. **Attachment break** • Another important reason for this questionnaire pattern may include the desire to not be discharged from the service. It does not automatically mean that people with FND purposefully exaggerate scores on questionnaires to avoid discharge. In contrast, a more likely view is that this is genuine distress around breaking an attachment and a trusted therapeutic relationship with a compassionate clinician. Within the context of an emotionally neglectful childhood, elevated scores reflecting great distress on discharge are understandable and expected.
Extreme scores	• Pre- and post-therapy questionnaire scores are clinically significant, in the high or extreme ranges.	**High levels of distress** • High scores on mood questionnaires often reveal that a person is struggling with psychological difficulties. Exaggerated scores can also be a tool for the person to communicate or convince the clinician of their distress. • At times, extreme scores endorsed on the questionnaires may not entirely be reflected in a person's functioning who may present as functioning relatively well, for example able to get up, prepare a meal and spend time with friends. It is important to note that, irrespective of these discrepancies, people with FND may endure great levels of distress, even though this may not be evident on observation of their day-to-day activities. Scores on mood questionnaires may also greatly fluctuate within a short space of time, further indicative of dysregulation.

(Continued)

Table 4.19 (Continued)

Response pattern	Details	What might it indicate?
Choosing two responses	• Response choice difficulties	• Some people struggle with choosing between discrete and opposite response categories and circle both options. For example, people with FND who experience an unstable sense of self may inadvertently reflect this in their questionnaire responses, for example choosing both "disagree" and "agree" on the item "I'm inclined to feel that I am a failure" from the Rosenberg self-esteem scale.

As discussed earlier, people with FND may occasionally dismiss strategies that a clinician recommends. If strategies are consistently dismissed, it is important to consider whether an underlying process or social function may be driving the "behaviour", for example resistance against adopting a more psychological approach to FND or an unmet need that may spur on more care and validation from the clinician.

Sticky left-over food

The Sticky left-over food element of the PCM affords a good opportunity to explore early experiences, family history of relationships and past family coping mechanisms. It is not uncommon for people with FND to report a difficult upbringing characterised by emotional neglect, losses and abuse. Due to the sensitivity of these experiences, a careful approach should be adopted when exploring early upbringing with people with FND. "Can I ask you a few questions about your upbringing?" Occasionally, it may be better to reserve these questions for a later time, when you have started to build a therapeutic relationship and the person with FND trusts you.

Sticky left-over food: interview questions

Useful questions to ask are based on the existing research literature and clinical observations (Table 4.20).

Sticky left-over food: strategies

PSYCHO-EDUCATION ON STICKY-FOOD MECHANISMS

Provide the person with psycho-education on the three most common coping strategies in FND: keep self to self, pushing on and dissociation. Help the person with FND to uncover their own childhood coping strategies and link these in with current adulthood coping strategies, within the PCM framework

Table 4.20 Sticky left-over questions with clinical examples

Topic	Questions	Examples and comments
Birth and formative years	• Where were you born and raised? • Stability and predictability of the family environment Consider the following: • Moved around a lot? Unsettling and destabilising? Was it better not to make new social connections and friendships in light of the prospect that these relationships would likely soon be broken again? • Different culture? How are emotions and psychological difficulties expressed or viewed in this culture?	Jane's father was in the armed forces. Her family of origin lived abroad and moved around a lot. Her father was also very strict. Jane learned not to express her emotions, as any verbalisation of emotion was punished. She also learned to manage problems on her own rather than confide in friends, and not create strong attachments, because she knew she could lose these friendships soon. Ron's parents emigrated to the UK from eastern Europe. In his family of origin, emotions and psychological difficulties are seen as a weakness and not openly expressed.
Family structure	Make a genogram; who was in the family? • Biological parents • Step-parents and step-siblings in the context of divorce • Absent parental figures • Care provided by grandparents and reasons	Kate's parents split up when she was three years old. Her parents each met a new partner. Kate grew up in a family of five siblings consisting of three biological and two step-siblings. Her biological father was sporadically in touch, whilst her step-father was quite strict and distant with her, probably more than with his biological children.
Parent and sibling relationships	• Quality of relationships in the family of origin: who closest to/distant? • Alliances and difficult relationships • Emotional needs were met? • The magnitude of the family unit and whether perceived level of emotional support was reduced	Rae is from a large family of 8 and one of the oldest. From a young age onwards, she has been involved in caring for her younger siblings, almost "like a second Mum". Her parents did not always have the opportunity to spend time with Rae. She learned to cope with difficult feelings on her own and became very self-sufficient.

(Continued)

Table 4.20 (Continued)

Topic	Questions	Examples and comments
Family coping	• How did members of their family of origin cope with difficult thoughts and feelings? What was the main way of coping in the family unit of origin? Did everyone share the same coping strategy? Were problems shoved under the carpet or discussed more openly? What was the level of expressed emotion at home and were there a lot of negative emotions and conflicts? Any childhood traumatic events (e.g. abuse, losses, separation, serious illness in the family) and how did the person and family cope? Did the family of origin feel psychologically safe? • Pay attention to: non-expression of emotions, punishment, ridicule and invalidation of emotions, pushing on and ignoring emotions; dissociation. • Unhelpful intergenerational coping mechanisms are not uncommon in FND. People may mention longstanding, rigid patterns carried through generations.	• Questions to help elicit historical information about early coping mechanisms include how did the person cope with difficult thoughts and feelings when they were younger; if they experienced a distressing event as a child (e.g. hurt their leg, an accident or a poor mark at school), how did they usually cope; did they have regular access to a trusted person in a psychologically safe relationship in whom they could confide and express their emotions freely? • Link this with current coping mechanisms: how do you cope with difficult thoughts and feelings now? Have early childhood coping mechanisms repeated into adulthood? (particularly non-expression of emotions, "pushing on"/ boom-bust patterns).
School period	• History of being bullied at school • Social networks at school • Also consider work bullying	• People with FND commonly report bullying experiences at school. During these bullying experiences, people report developing dissociation as a coping strategy to "survive" these moments.

Topic	Questions	Examples and comments
Critical events (during upbringing)	• Parental emotional neglect and active rejection of the child. • Trauma and abuse: sexual, physical and emotional, and the level of secrecy and not being believed. • Explore coping mechanisms of the person with FND and the family members around that trauma (e.g. did some family members deny the existence of the abuse?) • In this context: Explore healthcare experiences and the level that the person with FND felt believed or not believed by the professional?	• Belle confided in her psychologist and expressed that, as a child, she had been abused by a family member. After disclosing her secret to her mother, she was punished and "never to speak about this again". Her mother did not believe Belle. • Fast forward to the future: Belle has developed FND and finds herself at her GP practice. The doctor is not very sympathetic to Belle and advises her "to relax more" "because it's all in her head". Yet again, Belle finds herself not being believed by people in her environment.
Attachment and Attachment breaks	• Significant losses particularly of parental key figures, including through death, divorce or separation • Moves • Looked after by the system and taken into care • Multiple partners • Start hypothesising about attachment style: for example avoidant, anxious–ambivalent	• Dean was taken into care at age 14 years, following neglect by his mother. Dean and his siblings were separated. Since he was a teenager, Dean had to learn to fend for himself. Dean recently met his girlfriend. The relationship has been full of turmoil, and Dean often worries about being abandoned by his partner. During those times, he notices that the FND symptoms amplify.
Ongoing family dynamics	• Continuous conflicts, arguments and strife between parents and/or siblings in the family of origin. • Level of expressed emotion and enmeshment.	• Grace grew up in a "house full of arguments", which caused her great distress. • Grace is married with two children. Her family is always bickering with each other. One day, Grace could not tolerate the arguments anymore, and collapsed on the floor with a dissociative episode. Her family immediately stopped bickering and tended to Grace, stroking her hand and reassuring her with kind words.

(Continued)

Table 4.20 (Continued)

Topic	Questions	Examples and comments
Symptom models	• Illnesses in the family: physical, neurological and mental • Autism and the potential for undiagnosed autism in the patient • Cultural aspects to caring and whether the person with FND was required and expected to care for others? • Past job roles in health or social care?	• Ron's mother was ill, and he was expected to care for her at all times. Resisting this would be viewed as culturally unacceptable, even though Ron was making long hours at college, and booming and busting with his activity levels. This created a vulnerability for Ron to develop FND.
Core beliefs	• Start hypothesising what core beliefs may have emanated from these early experiences and how this fits your formulation.	• Sally's father singled her out, but none of her siblings. She couldn't do anything right in his eyes. Over the years, Sally developed very low self-esteem and strong beliefs around worthlessness.

(e.g. the relationship between Sticky left-over food: "I kept myself to myself as a child"; and a tight Cover: "I still keep myself to myself").

"PRE-EMPTING" TECHNIQUE

Psycho-education on how early invalidating childhood experiences can lead up to FND can also be helpful. Patients sometimes ask questions such as "how does your childhood link in with FND?" "What sorts of events and experiences can lead to FND?" "What does my childhood have to do with FND?" The following technique may be particularly helpful for people with FND who have not opened up about their childhood or where the clinician feels that they do not have a good handle on what may be going on for the patient, that is what remote setting events and critical incidents could have contributed to the FND.

Nina has been experiencing dissociative seizures and high levels of dissociation in other life areas. For this reason, she has been accessing psychological therapy sessions for a while. Both Nina and the psychologist feel that they have made little progress. The psychologist feels a bit left in the dark about what has made Nina vulnerable to developing FND and has not been able to establish a firm psychological formulation with Nina. It has been challenging to build a therapeutic relationship with Nina who tends to keep herself to herself and has been guarded. Although there was no obligation, Nina has not been forthcoming about her childhood and never speaks about her parents or her childhood, only to indicate that "it was great" "I've had a normal childhood" "I don't understand how I have become this way given that everything was fine in my childhood". The psychologist noticed that Nina mentioned "childhood" a few times and may be "signalling" that perhaps she may want to speak or disclose something childhood-related but that fear, embarrassment or another emotion is holding her back. One day, Nina asked the psychologist why people dissociate. The psychologist decided to provide Nina with psycho-education on the link between early adverse childhood experiences, dissociation and FND. She explained that people who have been through tough times in childhood develop crisis survival strategies to cope with difficult circumstances especially the strong negative emotions that these events can elicit. The psychologist explained that difficult events may include physical, emotional and sexual abuse, emotional neglect, invalidation, never being listened to, being criticised, constant conflict and arguments in the home. At this point, Nina welled up and shared a difficult childhood memory. She said "you started to bring up these events" "that's how I realised this is important". This point in the therapy felt as a pivotal moment for both Nina and her psychologist.

NORMALISE

Normalise early childhood coping strategies, by explaining that there is a time and place for all of these strategies and that the use of these strategies does not automatically indicate poor coping. For example, temporarily keeping yourself to yourself during a heated argument may actually prove to be helpful and not further aggravate an already volatile situation. In addition, since dissociative tendencies are common in FND, the occurrence of dissociation in the general population and the normalisation of this phenomenon (e.g. daydreaming) should also be highlighted.

FOSTER A COMPASSIONATE VIEW

Some people with FND feel guilty and highly critical of themselves for having developed these coping strategies in childhood and their continued use in adulthood. Focus on the adaptive nature of these early strategies: "what worked well then (in their childhood) may not work so well now". At the time, bottling emotions up or temporarily cutting emotions off was a helpful and adaptive strategy as the person with FND may have avoided worse consequences (e.g. invalidation, punishment, mistreatment, abuse, conflict, violence, retaliation or repercussions) or was able to tolerate intense negative emotions over a period of time. The strategies may have been negatively reinforced by a reduction in distress within the family unit and may have served the rest of the family unit by avoiding negative emotions and protecting the family unit from breaking down.

REFRAME AND CHANGE

Reframe the person's early coping mechanisms as adaptive survival strategies that may have been developed under difficult and highly stressful circumstances and teach the person to view themselves as a survivor (a victor not a victim). However, encourage change, as in present times, these strategies lost their usefulness (Aamir et al., 2009). You could share the following list.

Holding in emotions, pushing on or dissociating often:

- Stops the person from living their best life/their life to the full.
- Stops the person from engaging with the life activities that they prefer and choose.
- Make them miss out on the world and make the world miss out on them.
- Costs time; for example, some dissociative episodes may take a long time to settle or recover from. This time you won't get back and is forever lost.
- May create dependency on the environment.
- Make a person not deal with the painful emotions but avoid them.
- May make the person lose touch with their emotions, not feel or experience them and being unable to label them.
- In addition, dissociative episodes as part of the FND may also cause accidental self-injury and harm to the individual.

POSITIVE QUALITIES LOG

Low self-esteem is very common in FND. Psychological assessment and therapy should therefore always be attentive to the signs and features, for example boundary violations, validation of self-worth through other people and not accepting compliments. Core belief work may entail the challenging of negative core beliefs and building positive core beliefs.

A positive qualities log is a useful tool, from both a content and a process point of view. Content-wise, it is important for the person to identify positive core beliefs to support self-esteem. However, watch carefully how the person approaches this task and pay attention to the following:

- Any delays or "failing" in completing the task.
- Or the opposite: "racing" through the task and not being able to sit with the distress that it elicits.
- Attempting the task but struggling to generate any positive qualities or evidence.
- Minimising positive qualities/or the evidence that supports the qualities. Not fully owning the qualities.

- Fully relying on other people for generating positive qualities rather than coming up with some qualities on their own.
- Negative personal qualities permeating through the task.
- Generating a wide range or unusual number of positive qualities but with "surface-level" evidence that suggests that the person may not have entirely internalised these qualities.

For people with FND, the process of completing this task is often more informative about their self-esteem levels than finding qualities. The "journey" rather than the actual "goal" may be more interesting to analyse with the patient, for example in demonstrating low self-esteem at work by highlighting that the person's strong negative core beliefs may repel positive evidence/qualities.

Cover

Verbal emotional expression is one of the most important elements of the PCM and together with activity levels (Valve) represents "the alternative response to FND"; for example, self-initiating conversations about feelings in a trusted relationship during difficult moments in life is a more helpful form of internal regulation as opposed to regulating emotions via FND. It is therefore important to focus and practise strategies for both these elements to help reduce the risk of FND.

A comprehensive analysis of a person's level of verbal emotional expression will often shine a light on the underlying reasons that drive FND symptoms. Table 4.21 shows useful questions that can help explore a person's "Cover".

Cover strategies

Strategies that can be used to support a person with opening up a tight cover will be discussed next.

THE THERAPEUTIC RELATIONSHIP: YOUR BIGGEST TOOL IN FND

The distinction between content vs process commonly emerges in FND. The process of attending and engaging in psychological therapy sessions, as well as the process of establishing a trusted and psychologically safe therapeutic relationship with another person, is probably the pillar of FND treatment and one of the major assumptions of the PCM. Exploring barriers to emotional expression, as well as the act of emotional expression (e.g. tearfulness, anger) and opening up about difficult thoughts, feelings and memories within that safe space without running the risk of rejection, abandonment or invalidation, will often be one of the most meaningful interventions that will make significant shifts and gains in FND. A classic

Table 4.21 Useful "Cover" questions

Topic	Questions
Sharing thoughts and feelings	• With whom does the person with FND share their inner thoughts and feelings? (e.g. partner, family, friends). Do they have at least one psychologically safe and secure relationship that allows healthy expression of emotions? Can you gauge whether this relationship(s) is helpful or hurtful to the person? Look out for a tight cover. • Does the person have access to this relationship on a regular basis? Is this face-to-face, online? • Importantly: Is this a safe and trusted relationship? Does the person feel heard and understood?
Past and current family factors	What was the level of emotional expression in the person's family of origin? Watch out for strategies such as: • Not speaking about emotions • Everybody keeping themselves to themselves • Shifting emotions "under a rug or a carpet" • Negative consequences for engaging in the act of emotional expression (e.g. punishment, invalidation) • High expressed emotion, either resulting in the person engaging in the same strategies (overexpression of emotions, a loose Cover) or the opposite (keeping themselves to themselves, a tight Cover). What is the current level of emotional expression in the family or in the relationship (tight cover?) • Are there strong personalities in the family, where the more sensitive member feels more silenced?
Social anxiety	• Explore whether classic social anxiety cognitions are present, particularly worries about being negatively judged by and fear of rejection by others when expressing emotions.
Reduced assertiveness	• A tight Cover may also be reflected by ongoing difficulties with expressing needs to the environment (not being able to and always letting other people's needs ahead of the person's own needs, i.e. assertiveness issues), or difficulties with tolerating the distress that emerges when a need is finally expressed.
Cultural factors and societal pressures	• Some people may come from cultural backgrounds where emotional expression is unacceptable and viewed as a weakness.
Symbolic representations	• Watch out for symbolic representations of a tight Cover, particularly speech difficulties, which may physically prevent a person with FND from expressing their emotions.
Beliefs about EE	• Questionnaires include the Berkeley Expressivity Questionnaire (Gross & John, 1997), Emotion Regulation Questionnaire (Gross & John, 2003), Emotion Beliefs Questionnaire (Becerra et al., 2020) and Beliefs About Emotions Scale (Rimes & Chalder, 2010).

example is traumatic experiences that have been suppressed or dissociated from for a long time, and have become unbearable to hold for the individual, often in relation to a critical incident, resulting in FND symptoms. For a clinician, it can be difficult to weigh up whether to practise coping strategies first or whether to "allow" the person to express these traumatic memories without necessarily having had practice in helpful strategies. Preventing the person from doing so, because they may not "be ready" or fully equipped with coping strategies, especially in a condition like FND where people have often been rejected or not believed by their environment, can be detrimental, as it may copy their early childhood experiences. Chapter 5 (Case 1) will discuss the treatment with the PCM of a person with FND with exactly this type of presentation.

A THERAPY PROTOCOL FOR EMOTIONAL EXPRESSION

- Formulate with the patient where the difficulties with emotional expression come from (i.e. adverse invalidating childhood experiences that prevented emotional expression).
- Encourage the person to identify, label and express emotions, particularly anger, frustration, low mood and anxiety.
- Plan a behavioural experiment to apply these skills (e.g. an interaction with another person). If the person is very fearful, you can practise role plays first.
- Explain that people with tight Covers will often stop themselves from expressing emotions. Explore what the drawbacks might be (i.e. sitting with the distress on your own, turning it "inwards". The tight Cover will subsequently increase the risk of engaging the Overpressure Plug and maintains the FND).
- As part of therapy, help the person to learn to express their feelings without the emotional expression being followed by "punishment" or invalidation. Normalise emotional experience and expression. Bust any myths "expressing anger does not mean I'm being aggressive. I am able to express anger in a way that is acceptable and necessary to meet my emotional needs". You may need to encourage the person.
- Help the person to sit with the "aftermath" of emotional expression. This state of discomfort can be even more difficult to tolerate for a person than the actual "act" of expression, especially people who have been severely invalidated. Help them identify and label the "after-effect" emotions and apply strategies to sit with the distress in the moment for as long as possible.
- Help the patient to generalise this skill to people outside the clinical space.
- Reflect their feelings back and praise the person for expressing emotions afterwards (reinforcement).

RELEASING THE UNSPEAKABLE DILEMMA

A subset of people with FND will carry an unspeakable dilemma that is tightly associated with the persistence of FND. If an unspeakable dilemma is suspected, but the person does not feel that the therapeutic relationship is sufficiently safe to express it "out in the open", the clinician can pre-empt the presence of unspeakable dilemma in FND, in general, and highlight that the release of such a dilemma is often associated with the subsequent resolution of FND symptoms. If a person feels ready to release the unspeakable dilemma, the therapist can facilitate the process of releasing the dilemma and the associated, often strong, emotions and negative beliefs that come with it. In some cases, the unspeakable dilemma may form a risk to the person or other people and will need safeguarding.

PRACTICAL SKILLS TRAINING

Psycho-education on assertiveness, skills training with role plays and behavioural experiments help the person tolerate the discomfort that often arises with using assertiveness skills, as well as managing the aftermath or fall-out in the environment. Social skills training may benefit people with FND and autism features, or people with FND with longstanding adverse childhood experiences who may find it difficult to relate to other people and may not have had opportunities to practise social skills.

Valve

Strategies for blocked, overused and dysregulated valves

Start the assessment of Valve functioning by asking the person and their environment to keep separate daily activity logs for a few weeks to establish the Valve profiles in the person with FND and individuals in their environment. On the basis of the data, ask your clients to classify their Valve profiles. With all profiles, it is important to explore the psychological meaning of these activity levels: What functions do this serve? (e.g. reducing anxiety, raising confidence levels, assertiveness problems, dissociation, pressure from the environment) (Table 4.22). In addition, how balanced is the person's activity schedule in terms of meaningful, occupational, enjoyable, family and friends, rest and relaxation, social connectedness and daily routines?

Warning light

Heightened attentional focus on physical symptoms is one of the maintaining factors of FND and has been incorporated in major theoretical models of FND (e.g. Brown, 2006; Edwards et al., 2012). Attention shifting strategies have often been proposed to manage these increased levels of attention in patients.

Table 4.22 "Valve" strategies

Valve type	Strategies
Blocked Bust-after-boom	**Unblocking the Valve:** • A gentle behavioural activation programme with enjoyable activities and mood-lifting exercises (allowing for physical disabilities) to start with. Emphasise to the patient that they may not feel like doing any activity, but that starting is the key, and the feeling will follow. • Ask yourself whether, in addition to lifting mood, these activities have the potential to create a sense of social belonging, a sense of purpose in the world and a sense of achievement? Creating "connection" is an antidote against "rejection". • Is the person socially isolated and is there scope and a wish to help the person increase their social network? Do they need skills, for example assertiveness, social skills? • Be gentle and compassionate around friendships and social networks as some people may feel embarrassed and may "mask" low activity levels or limited networks. For example, it may be important to explore the frequency of encounters with friends; geographical distance whether friends are close by; modality of meeting friends (e.g. face-to-face, online, part of an internet forum); only FND friends or more heterogeneity in friendships with non-FND friends; and the quality of friendships: "sensible" vs harmful friends, especially since people with FND can present with low self-esteem and become victims of boundary violations or even coercion in relationships. • What are the barriers to accessing the community and social belonging? (e.g. social anxiety, depression, disabilities that may need physiotherapy and OT support). • An occupational therapy assessment can be very helpful for exploring any meaningful activities and vocational rehabilitation, for example employment, education.
Dysregulated Boom-and-bust	**Regulating the Valve:** • Pacing schedule. Provide psycho-education on the boom-and-bust cycle and explore any pros and cons of adhering to abnormal activity patterns for the person. Often people will not realise that they "lose" more time with the peaks and troughs that is so characteristic of boom-and-bust cycles and "win" more time if they would apply a pacing schedule instead. Ask the person to start a pacing schedule with low, tolerable levels of activity and to sustain these levels throughout the week. • Explore any psychological barriers to achieve the "even keel" (e.g. thoughts around feeling "lazy" or "not very productive" wanting to do more and going over the allocated time spent on an activity).

(Continued)

Table 4.22 (Continued)

Valve type	Strategies
Overused Boom	**Relieving the Valve:**
	• Help the person identify relaxation or enjoyable activities that they can build in that are not "another activity in the schedule" but support with genuine stress release. This could mean "no activity". Which activities can be dropped? How does the person feel about that, what thoughts come up?
	• Carry out behavioural experiments with a reduced activity schedule. Ask the person to track difficult thoughts and feelings that will likely come up and practise strategies to help the person tolerate the discomfort and "sitting with the distress" whilst not being as active.
	• Challenge unhelpful thoughts around activity reduction ("I'm lazy") and highlight the positives of relaxation (e.g. the mind and body need restoration).
	• Explore any negative emotions that may sustain a person's activity levels (in particular, guilt if not sufficiently active) and link these with early experiences.
Systemic strategies	• Explore the environmental valve: what do activity levels look like in the person's environment? (e.g. mirrored, complimentary). Raise awareness into the interactions between the valves.
	• If the relationship is enmeshed and co-dependent, encourage "me-time" for both individuals where separate activities are pursued.
	• Recruit a sensible ally in the person's network. Allies can be very useful to prompt the person with FND if they "overdo" or "underdo" activities.
Questionnaires	Canadian Occupational Performance Measure (Law et al., 1990)

Although these invaluable techniques certainly have their place in treatment approaches for FND, this section will highlight that heightened self-focused attention, in addition to being a crucial cognitive process directed at physical symptoms in FND, permeates through many other psychological and social areas of FND including the explanations that a person may adopt on the origins of FND; the level of the person's engagement with psychological treatment; the impact on surrounding systems; and symptom focus being a part of identity. As Table 4.23 shows, heightened symptom focus is commonly observed in clinical practice and can manifest in a myriad of ways.

Measurement

Several published scales exist that measure concepts strongly related to increased self-focused attention including awareness, consciousness,

Table 4.23 Various manifestations of heightened symptom focus in FND

Area of increased symptom focus	Details
Preoccupation	• Preoccupation in thinking, speaking or reading about physical symptoms, and devoting most of the conversations to physical symptoms, for example in psychological therapy, or spending time on FND websites or social media blogs.
Inflexibility in thinking	• Rigidity in thinking including a difficulty disengaging from speaking about physical symptoms and quickly re-engaging, even after several prompts.
Physical > psychological	• Expressing a strong preference to physical explanations over psychological formulation of FND, persistently seeking organic explanations even if these have been excluded. • Better engagement with physical over psychological treatment, for example focusing or emphasising the physical aspects of treatment and minimising the role of psychological factors.
Hypervigilance	• Hypervigilance on physical symptoms and bodily sensations, for example symptom checking behaviours, body scanning, hypervigilant monitoring of bodily functions (e.g. blood pressure) or warning signs (e.g. upcoming dissociative episode). • Systemic hyperawareness and symptom focus by partners or family members, which mirror the patient's heightened attention on physical symptoms (e.g. hypervigilance or "being on the outlook" for signs of an impending dissociative episode).
Environmental markers	• Attentional focus on physical symptoms is manifested in the person's environment, for example equipment, house adaptations, medications and care.
Reassurance seeking	• Reassurance seeking for physical symptoms, culminating in frequent doctors' appointments and visits to accidents and emergencies.
Identity	• Identity may be mostly defined and absorbed by FND.

perception and vigilance associated with bodily processes or physical symptoms. Examples of these scales include the Scale of Body Awareness (Hansell & Mechanic, 1991; Hansell et al., 1991); Body Consciousness Questionnaire ("Private Body Consciousness Subscale", Miller et al., 1981); Body Perception Questionnaire (Porges, 1993); Body Vigilance Scale (Schmidt et al., 1997); and Body Awareness Questionnaire (Shields et al., 1989). Although these scales can be useful in clinical practice, for example to assess pre-to-post change in attentional focus after a course of therapy, the most useful information on a person's increased self-focused attention is probably gleaned from behavioural observations using Table 4.23 as a guide.

The Warning light: resolving the physical vs psychological dichotomy

Heightened focus on physical symptoms is one of the maintaining factors of FND. However, could this notion be reversed by re-conceptualising the heightened physical symptom focus as a reduced focus on psychological symptoms that is maintaining the FND? This dichotomy, favouring a physical over a psychological focus, mirrors the classic dissociation between the experience of physical symptoms in the body without the ability to identify with or relate to the concomitant emotional experience that is commonly observed in FND. As a result of this dichotomy, the person with FND and the clinician can have diametrically opposing explanations for FND. This can lead to frustration, anger, hostility and resistance and the feeling of "stuck-ness" in therapy. Below are various strategies outlined that may help ease the resistance and resolve the dichotomy.

EXPLORE UNDERLYING PSYCHOLOGICAL REASONS FOR THE DICHOTOMY

The heightened focus on physical symptoms may be an expression of underlying psychological variables. For example, dissociation and alexithymia are common; people with FND do not always identify with or recognise psychological processes and give preference to physical explanations, which are simply easier to understand and to relate to. With time, psycho-education on dissociation, psychological therapy that addresses the root causes of dissociation, and the practice of reality grounding techniques may resolve some of these issues and support the person towards identifying more psychological viewpoints. Furthermore, due to adverse childhood experiences, cultural beliefs and mental health stigma, people with FND may experience shame and negative beliefs about psychology, for example "if you need psychology you are weak", "psychology is for people who are not strong enough to deal with life and can't cope". To explore the underlying reasons for the dichotomy further, use the mind-body split therapeutically in psychology sessions ("I noticed that we have been exploring your physical symptoms for some time now, have you noticed that too, what do you make of that? What do you think of psychology / how would you feel about exploring some common psychological features of FND?").

LISTEN OUT TO POOR PAST EXPERIENCES WITH PSYCHOLOGICAL TREATMENT

A heightened focus on physical symptoms may be driven by poor experiences with psychology. A subset of people with FND will have accessed psychological treatment before. However, these experiences may not always have been positive for the person. It is not unheard of that, unbeknownst to them, the person has been referred to a mental health professional and receives an unexpected invitation letter in the post. This can lead to the person feeling a loss of control, not believed and abandoned by the referrer – all features that people with FND may have been exposed to during their upbringing. It is always sensible to explore past experiences with psychological services. Good questions to ask:

- Was there a click with the clinician?
- Was the therapy effective in addressing the FND/co-existing psychological difficulties? What aspects were particularly helpful in the person's view?
- What was the treatment modality? (e.g. CBT, DBT or psychodynamic approaches)
- How long was the therapy and in what service (e.g. IAPT vs secondary care). Could the therapy have been too brief to bring about change in the person's symptoms?
- Was the therapy conducted by FND-specialist workers?
- Did the person with FND feel believed, understood, heard? Does the person feel like this at present, with you exploring these past therapy experiences with them? This will help engagement.

NORMALISE PSYCHOLOGICAL THERAPY

Psychology is often viewed as negative, not just by people with FND, but also in the general population. Some of the useful strategies listed below can help normalise psychological therapy:

- "Psychological problems are not unique to FND but actually very common in society, including problems with mood and anxiety".
- "Instead of thinking about psychological therapy as fixing a person's mental health, we can look at it from a different angle: therapy is about learning new, more helpful life skills that we may not have had the opportunity to learn in the past".
- "Psychological therapy can help you learn new life skills that can be at your advantage in other life areas, for example in your job, university studies or relationships". "Think about what a head start you will have if you actively practice your psychological coping techniques when you have to do an exam later on".
- "Once you have learned psychological life skills, you will know of them for the rest of your life and they won't run out like medications do" "You can even teach others, like a friend with anxiety, about some of the skills you've learned in therapy, such as the fight-or-flight response".
- "When you are hungry, you have a bite to eat, when you feel thirsty, you take a sip of water…but when we experience a dip in mood or feel scared we don't tend to think about helping ourselves". "Physical healthcare is important, as is psychological healthcare!"
- "There are a lot of celebrities, stars and famous people that have experienced psychological difficulties, can you name a few?" "They did a great job on

television / singing / acting despite experiencing a difficult patch". "Do you think any of these may be a positive role model to you?"

- "I believe everybody could benefit from psychological therapy – not just people with FND".
- "Nowadays people are more open about psychological issues, and it has become more accepted to seek psychological support". "There is a lot more access to psychological therapy than there used to be", "Would you like me to signpost you to useful websites about therapy X, so you can have a read?"
- "The Pressure Cooker Model views FND is a product of the person x environment". Emphasise that the PCM theory views FND as driven by psychosocial factors that are shared by the person and their environment. It therefore looks at a shared responsibility for the recovery from FND and advocates that psychology is necessary for everyone involved in FND including partners, family and clinicians.

MOVE AWAY FROM A DICHOTOMY => TOWARDS INTEGRATION

Throughout the years, psychology and the more physical and medical disciplines have significantly diverged or have been pitted against each other. This has created a false dichotomy between the mind and the body. Despite more awareness in recent years, this dichotomy remains alive in the minds of both clinicians and people with FND: "If we cannot find any physical explanation for the symptoms, then it must all be psychological". In psychological therapy, it can be helpful to move away from this dichotomy:

- "Let's move away from what causes this, irrespective of whether your symptoms have a physical or psychological cause: you are not feeling well, let's see how we can help you feel better?" "Is it helpful to try to solve a big question like that whereas we can already start working on how to make you feel better again?"
- Explain that people with "hard" "physical" brain conditions such as Parkinson's disease or multiple sclerosis frequently experience emotional difficulties, which can be directly the result of the brain changes and a response to difficult circumstances. There is not much point making a distinction between the mind and the body; it is better to treat the person in a holistic manner by taking into account both physical and emotional aspects of the condition. In the same way, physical and psychological disciplines collaborate with each other and take into account the physical symptoms and psychological difficulties that FND brings.
- Explore whether a person with FND experiences confusion between multiple dichotomies: physical vs psychological; believed vs not believed; and real vs fake. Psychological symptoms or therapy are often viewed as people not being believed and faking their symptoms, whilst physical

symptoms or physical treatment is seen as "I'm believed" "my symptoms are real". However, the question is not whether symptoms are believed or real. The question is not even about whether FND is psychological or physical: the condition stands at the crossroads between mind and body and both aspects need to be treated, for example mood, anxiety and unhelpful ways of relating to other individuals, but also deconditioning, learning a new movement pattern and stepping down from equipment.

"DE-THREATENISE" PSYCHOLOGY

Psychology is often seen as separate and generating higher levels of psychological threat to the person than "physically" oriented disciplines such as medicine, physiotherapy and occupational therapy, which can feel more psychological safe to the person. Historically, psychology is surrounded by myths and threatening associations: "Psychology means that it's in between my ears", "Psychological therapy is about digging into painful and traumatic memories". People are not always aware that there are a lot more physical aspects to psychology than is generally assumed. As a clinician, focusing on the relationships between psychology and physical features may reduce the threatening meaning of psychology and can be done without having to deny or compromise on psychological principles. There are several strategies:

- "Psychology means it's in between my ears". That is technically correct: in the end everything, including the brain, is in between our ears. All our cognitive, emotional, behavioural and physical functions originate from the same brain including eating, drinking, walking, writing, running, speaking, seeing, hearing, navigating, sleeping and thinking, feeling, planning, understanding, remembering, predicting and controlling our emotions, impulses and behaviours.
- It may be helpful to invoke neuropsychological principles into this discussion and provide easy-read scientific references about important brain-behaviour relationships that support these functions, for example LeDoux' (1996) model of the fear response and the amygdala. The fight-or-flight response is another example of tight relationships between psychological and physical features.
- Challenge any inaccurate beliefs and perceptions that the person may have about psychology and provide the person with a sense of control: "Don't worry, we won't be digging into your early experiences and opening up traumas". "However, for the treatment of FND, we have found that it can be useful to talk about your upbringing". "So if you would like to talk, the door is always wide open but at your pace, I want you to feel that you have the reins in your hands". Provide the person

with a fact sheet on the positives of psychology and debunk myths (Book 2 has a list in Chapter 1).

- Offer an "escape clause": explain that you are keen to support the person but offer an exit "Why don't you give it a go for one or two sessions and see how we get on?" Throughout the session, check with the person how they think the session is going. Remember: if a patient shows up for your session, that is a gain and meaningful.

MAKE THE PERSON FEEL "HEARD" NOT "HURT": TRANSPARENCY IS KEY

Avoid a tug of war   A person's resistance against a psychological perspective on the FND can result in two unhelpful strategies in psychological therapy: a tug of war and collusion. A psychologist may attempt to actively convince the person of their psychological formulation. Even if it is completely clear and the psychological formulation makes complete sense, it is important to let go of the battle. It is best not to push the psychological formulation and actively fight the person's views. Creating a tug of war risks the person not feeling heard or believed and will make you lose the patient. Keep in mind that the goal is a shared formulation, not a formulation that has been created by yourself and subsequently imposed on the person with FND. This creates a power differential and may further push the person away from considering psychological principles. The process of building a trusted therapeutic relationship and arriving at a shared formulation between the patient and the clinician during the therapy journey may be the actual intervention.

AVOID COLLUSION

Letting go of the battle does not mean communicating false information and colluding with the person. It simply means standing back from the resistance. Ensure that you continue to communicate a positive diagnosis of FND and do not align with the patient by colluding and, for example, stating the FND is caused 100% by physical factors, out of anxiety of "losing" the patient. FND has a strong psychological component that maintains the condition on several levels, and it is important to not lose sight of these factors. Going along with the patient would not help the person's recovery journey.

COMMUNICATE THE RESISTANCE

A helpful strategy is to notice and communicate the observed resistance in the moment and explore its meaning with the person, for example "I notice from your expressions that you may be unsure about what we just discussed? Would you feel comfortable sharing more about this with me?" What are the reasons that the person is holding on so strongly to their own physical explanations and views on the FND?

Psychological formulation of the resistance, in both directions, may not only provide an insight into the drivers underlying the resistance for the person and the manner in which we as clinicians respond to that resistance; it may also be key to understanding the maintaining factors, as the hybrid PCM formulation below will highlight. As part of a transparent therapy process, it is possible to share this hybrid formulation with the patient (Tables 4.24 and 4.25).

Kitchen

Although this can be a neglected area in clinical practice, understandably due to time, resource and funding limitations, a clinician has many good reasons to focus treatment on a person's Kitchen environment.

- A large subset of people with FND experience significant interpersonal triggers for their symptoms within the context of their social environment, personal relationships and family unit.

Table 4.24 Person with FND about the psychology service

PCM element	Example
Ignition	Experience of emotional neglect and not being believed by parental key figure
Fuel	Letter for an invitation to psychology service
Flames	"They think it's all in my head", "No one believes my symptoms" "My neurologist has abandoned me"
Heat	Dissociation, not in touch with my emotions. The idea of psychology and emotions is foreign and uncomfortable
Sticky left-over food	"I'm different", "I don't matter" Childhood coping strategy of dissociation, keeping myself to myself, due to emotions dismissed or invalidated
Pot	Feeling unpleasant physical symptoms of anxiety in my body including palpitations, hyperventilation, feeling dizzy
Warning light	Increased self-focused attention on the physical symptoms I feel, I can't stop thinking about my FND symptoms
Cover	Reduced verbal emotional expression, I prefer to keep myself to myself. Showing emotions makes me vulnerable
Valve	Blocked valve: reduced activity levels, no sense of belonging, unable to test out my beliefs about psychology with other people
Overpressure Plug	Continued or amplified resistance against psychological explanations. Not addressing psychological factors of the FND will likely maintain the FND
Kitchen	Clinician encounters the person with FND for the first time and notices the resistance against psychology and the heightened symptom focus

Table 4.25 Clinician from the psychology service about the person with FND

PCM element	Example
Ignition	Experience of working in a generic psychological therapy service that occasionally encounters and cares for people with FND.
Fuel	I have been treating a person with FND for a few sessions in my clinic. No matter how hard I try, the person with FND seems resistant to my psychological explanations of FND and displays a heightened symptom focus. It has been hard to shift the person away from physical explanations to exploring a psychological formulation.
Flames	Worries emerge around "How will I cope?" "The person is not budging", "What if the person self-discharges?" "I will look like a poor clinician" and "my colleagues may think I'm not up to the job". Fear of failure, frustration and low self-confidence.
Heat	High levels of internal distress about the situation.
Sticky left-over food	"I'm not good enough as a clinician". Low self-esteem about my abilities to manage this patient.
Pot	Sleepless nights, feeling funny and butterflies in my stomach on the day that the person is visiting the clinic for our session.
Warning light	Heightened attentional focus on the resistance, putting in a lot of energy and focus on trying to "shift" the person away from physical explanations.
Cover	Not speaking to the person with FND about the strong resistance in the moment, too afraid to mention it as I fear losing the patient from my caseload.
Valve	Boom and busting with my caseload. Feeling deflated after having seen the person and needing to "recover" from the resistance. Not planning in any other patients the rest of the day.
Overpressure Plug	• Colluding with the person that there are significant changes in the central nervous system, which have not yet been demonstrated/being less transparent with the information from the referrer that may make the person defensive or rejecting. • Avoiding contacting the person to plan in a few more sessions. • Resisting the person's resistance: not letting go of your psychological formulation and trying to push it on the reluctant patient.
Kitchen	Colluding with the person, avoiding contact and pushing the formulation on the person reduces my own anxiety about my skills as a clinician.

- FND is a two-step process: In addition to an internal regulation function, FND has social functions that provide external regulation of emotions. The system may (inadvertently) engage in reciprocal reinforcement and systemic re-traumatisation processes that maintain the FND, for example apply unhelpful reassurance responses to a dissociative seizure, which may create psychological safety for both the person with FND and individuals in their environment.
- The recruitment of allies from the person's system is crucial for FND recovery and for the maintenance and consolidation of treatment gains in the long run. An ally can support and encourage the person with FND with applying strategies and implementing treatment plans.
- People with FND tend to have small social networks, are often socially isolated and may lack a sense of belonging to a social group. Treating the person in isolation may not generate the expected results during the therapy and may facilitate set-backs after discharge because goals are not linked to the social environment.
- A "broken system" to which a fully recovered person may return to after completing treatment more than likely will need support and treatment as well. Viewing FND as a systemic condition and treating the entire unit to which the person belongs and has strong ties with will help reduce relapse and maintain treatment gains following discharge from the service.
- Simultaneously focusing on the person and their environment takes away the emphasis of FND as "the problem of the person". The PCM assumes that FND is, at least in part, the product of emotion dysregulation between the person and their system. From this assumption flows the idea that recovery of FND is a joint venture between the person and all individuals in their environment.
- A stronger focus on the environment will help the patient and clinician not miss any crucial and maintaining factors that may pose a threat to the person with FND, for example domestic violence and other safeguarding concerns, or create difficult life circumstances for people caring for the person with FND, particularly young carers who have had to make sacrifices.
- Importantly, a recognition of our own contribution to the FND in the sessions will help identify and further reduce any maintaining factors of FND.

Kitchen assessment

Although the Kitchen element may overlap with the Sticky left-over food, the two elements differ in other ways (Table 4.26).

Quick Kitchen assessment

If you have not got the time, several quick techniques can be useful to make a start with mapping out the person's Kitchen environment including creating

Table 4.26 Differences between "Sticky left-over food" and "Kitchen" elements of the PCM

Sticky left-over food	Kitchen
Family of origin	Current family or social situation. Maps out caring arrangements and level of enmeshment between family vs caring roles
Does not tend to explore beyond family system	Looks at current interactions with multiple systems: family, healthcare
Links early experiences to/how these give rise to core beliefs and rules for living	Makes connections between early relationship patterns and current re-triggering events, uncovering potential systemic re-traumatisation
Often one perspective about their personal history (person with FND) resulting in a single PCM formulation	Often multiple perspectives on current personal history (person with FND and significant others) resulting in multiple PCM formulations and information on reciprocal reinforcement processes
Techniques are aimed at understanding early experiences, relationships and past coping mechanisms and how these culminated in FND	Techniques are aimed at supporting and remediating current experiences, relationships and coping mechanisms to reduce or stop FND

a *genogram* of the current family structure ("Who is in your family?" "What are their names and ages?" "What position are you in terms of age?" e.g. middle child), strength of the relationships ("Whom are you closest / less close to?" describe the reasons), quality of the relationships ("Who do you get on best with?" "Are there any conflicts?") and care arrangements ("Does anyone help you out with care?"). Another useful technique is to map out the system with a concentric circle diagram. Ask the person with FND to position each family member, as well as their friends, social network and any other key figures (e.g. supportive grandmother) on the map according to emotional distance from the person. This will provide a brief snapshot of the person's system and a start for hypothesising about potential systemic influences on the FND.

Comprehensive Kitchen assessment

Table 4.27 contains useful questions to ask a person with FND and their family, if there is more time available in your assessment.

Kitchen treatment techniques

It is beyond the scope of this book to provide a detailed description of family therapy approaches, and it would not do justice to the already available knowledge and literature on this topic. However, since the PCM assumes that

Table 4.27 Guiding questions enquiring about family functioning in FND

Topic	Useful questions to ask
Questionnaires	• McMaster Family Assessment Device (FAD; Epstein et al., 1983)
	• Beavers Self-Report Family Inventory (SFI; Halvorsen, 1991)
	• Family Adaptability and Cohesion Evaluation Scales (FACES; Olson et al., 1978)
	• Family Strengths Scale (Olson et al., 1982) – to assess "Pressure Cooker Safety Features"
	• The Circumplex Model of Family Systems (Olson, 1989)
	• Inventory of Altered Self-Capacities (IASC; Briere & Runtz, 2002)
Current partner and family relationships	• Can I ask you some questions about the people in your life?
	• Are you in a relationship? Who is in your family? Make a "current" genogram of the family structure. Include extended family members if they play an important role or cause stress
	• Establish how the person with FND perceives the quality and attachments of these relationships
	• Try to obtain a collateral history, this is very important. If this is not possible and the person's "important people" are absent and not engaged with the person's FND care, explore reasons
	• Are there any absent key figures and what are the person's thoughts and feelings around that? (e.g. partner divorced the person and left the family). Formulate the absence of key people in the person's life in your sessions, as well as any reluctance to involve people close to the patient in the treatment, as this may provide important clues to where to target treatment
Systemic stressors	• This may have been addressed in the Fuel part of the assessment
	• Find out if any current family stressors are present that serve as interpersonal triggers for the FND, particularly conflicts and arguments in relationships, mental health issues in family members
Systemic/family cohesion	• What does a typical day in the family look like? Family activities? Or is everyone minding their own time?
	• Aberrant patterns of cohesion, boundaries and communication in terms of style (enmeshment, distance, interpersonal conflict) and members (some members especially close, distant or completely absent).
	• What are current the alliances in the family? Who doesn't get on?
	• Coping strategies of the family unit or in the relationship: How are emotions and difficult thoughts managed? Are they expressed, spoken about? What are the individual members' stress-coping strategies?

(Continued)

Table 4.27 (Continued)

Topic	Useful questions to ask
Family roles and identities	• Who gets on with whom (e.g. mother and younger brother), who is more like whom (e.g. father and myself are similar in personality)? • Who provides the "glue" in the system and "keeps the unit together" and "balances the emotions" of all members but neglects their own emotion coping. If the person that represents the glue would be removed, would this lead to system breakdown of relationships? • Family roles and identities before FND vs after FND. • If FND would not exist anymore or reduced, what would the family roles look like? Is the person with FND somehow keeping the family together via a sick role? What would be the cost of the switch for the family unit as a whole? Do you think the family unit will be happy?
Caring arrangements	• What do the caring arrangements look like? Is there a package of care or is a loved one caring for the person with FND? How long has this been the case? What is the level of involvement, does it include personal and intimate care? • Is there enmeshment between family vs caring roles? • Are there young carers present? Do they need support?
Carer burden	• How does the person caring for the person with FND feel and manage in life? Have they got quality of life, occupational balance, dropped hobbies? (Valve). • Questionnaire to measure carer burden: Zarit Burden Interview – Short Form (Bédard et al., 2001).
Current social network	• Who is in your social network? • List the number of people that are meaningful to the person with FND: Who are they, how long have you known them for? Do you meet up with friends? How regular? • Who is helpful/supportive and who is not so helpful? (note: person, family and clinician perceptions may differ). What is the quality of these relationships? • Look out for signs of social isolation and the family or partner comprising the person's only social system and source of social interactions. • Concentric circles exercise: Map out a person's social network with a circle diagram that depicts people closest, a little further away and farthest away from the person with FND. Identify helpful allies for treatment and less helpful people that may adversely impact on FND recovery.
Wider social situation	• How is the person with FND faring in life? Are there social pressures, stressors or challenges, for example in terms of socio-economic status? • Are they connected to and actively involved with social media? Does this environment provide validation?

Topic	Useful questions to ask
Systemic re-traumatisation: Healthcare relationships	• Explore the process of FND diagnosis, what type of experience this was for them, sense of being believed, sense of grievance or injustice, feeling marginalised, invisible, not believed. • How would they describe their relationship with individuals in the healthcare system? • To assess stigma in the context of systemic re-traumatisation: Implicit Association Test, Stigma Scale for Chronic Illness.
Reciprocal reinforcement: Management FND symptoms	• What happens in the environment when the person experiences FND symptoms? How does the family or partner behave around the person with FND? Occasionally, FND episodes can happen in the clinic and are a good way to make these observations • How does the partner or system respond to dissociative episodes? • What are their thoughts, feelings and behaviours in response to FND (whether paroxysmal or static symptoms)? Does it provoke anxiety, anger, frustration? Or the opposite: is the FND serving a need for the family system? • Are there any other behaviours observed, for example "baby-ing", distancing • Start loosely identifying reciprocal reinforcing cycles using a behavioural analysis
Insight and awareness into FND	• What is the family's insight into FND? • Family or partner perceptions of FND: Do they believe the person with FND? Are they accepting of the diagnosis, searching for organic explanations or rejecting and ridiculing FND? • Explore views about the person with FND: Do they think it's all the patient or does the family contribute to FND? Is the patient blamed for FND and seen as "the problem"?

the system around the person with FND plays an integral role in the maintenance of FND, the most important systemic strategies that have worked in the clinic will be shared here.

SOCIAL FUNCTION(S) OF THE FND AND CARING

Keep in mind that FND can have a range of social functions in a relationship or family unit. The social functions of FND are *always* bi-directional and part of an interpersonal dynamic and should never be treated as uni-directional "secondary gains" that a person with FND applies to their environment. An important reciprocal pattern of responses that people with FND and individuals in their environment commonly experience is the FND response (person with FND) <= vs => Caring response (environment).

The following social functions of FND have been encountered in people with FND:

- To feel better: to feel cared for, to feel heard, be noticed, be treated with respect or feel validated by people. "FND helps me to feel heard" "I'm visible" "people take more care".
- To elicit empathy and sympathy.
- Deterrent from something difficult or unpleasant in the environment, for example negative judgements or comments from other people, an argument, demanding tasks, unwanted intimacy or proximity from another person.
- Or the opposite: a need to feel proximity to someone else and bringing or keeping someone closer who has been quite distant, for example being closer to someone during personal care and preventing "abandonment".
- Communication of distress or expression of emotional pain to other people; for example, a physical expression of anxiety (such as a tremor or a non-epileptic episode) may express anxiety better than words, as well as make more impact (e.g. witnessing a dissociative episode can feel harrowing for the environment).
- Communication of a symbolic message, emotion or situation to others: functional voice loss and speech problems may reflect the emotions around "not having a voice" in the family unit (e.g. being dismissed).
- Increasing the person's confidence in social situations and accessing the community, for example "going out and about in a wheelchair and being able to do activities". FND can also serve as a "social" safety behaviour, for example sitting in a wheelchair and not having to make eye contact.
- Providing a sense of control over the person's life situation; for example, dissociative episodes can stop arguments and conflicts in the home or help the person find out whether people truly care about them.
- Expressing distress in ways that are more socially acceptable and less stigmatised: experiencing physical symptoms is less "frowned upon" by society than experiencing distress or mental health problems.

The following social functions of caring have frequently been encountered in the system around people with FND:

- Caring for the person may reduce the carer's own anxiety and discomfort at witnessing the person's FND symptoms and distress and, importantly, the discomfort of the person with FND.
- Some carers may feel embarrassed or ashamed of the person's symptoms (e.g. dissociative episodes in public places causing crowds to form), and the care response will quickly reduce these symptoms.
- The carer may feel compassion, sympathy and sadness for the person and wants to express these feelings through caring activities.

- In the same way as FND can form a large part of the identity in people with FND, the FND can become part of a carer's identity by creating dependency in the person with FND. The caring activities may provide the carer with a new role, identity and purpose in life.

- Some people may not have had much emotional and physical care in early life, missed out on care, were not supported and neglected, or otherwise have not been validated and appreciated by their parental caregivers or other family members in childhood. The family may now make this up by engaging in excessive guilt-driven caring.

- FND families often showed reduced verbal emotional expression and may not know any better. A carer may show their affection through caring, a more practical rather than an emotional way, by meeting a person's care needs with washing, dressing, preparing meals and accessing the community.

- Some carers experience a fear of abandonment from the person with FND and keep the person close by creating dependency, limiting the person's movements and preventing other people to seek proximity to the person with FND. This can be for protective purposes, for example worries about the person not receiving the correct care from healthcare and social care systems and wanting to do a better job. This can also be for control purposes and, in rare instances, may have a coercive nature. In this regard, the importance of meeting the person with FND *separately*, in addition to meeting together with the coercive family member, cannot be emphasised enough.

- Carers may experience high levels of worry and anxiety around their lack of knowledge and confidence about managing FND in the moment, particularly when symptoms do not seem to abate (e.g. "am I doing the right thing during the dissociative episode?"). Carers may intuitively believe that excessive caring is naturally helpful, and this may be evidenced by the short-lived symptom relief that caring will likely bring to the person with FND and the carer; however, the carer may feel anxious, on edge and hypervigilant around when the next episode will take place and will therefore increase caring efforts as a preventative measure.

The lines between what constitutes FND and caring are very blurry. The PCM views FND as a systemic condition that affects the person with FND and their close environment in equal amounts. In a sense, one can say that "the entire system is afflicted with FND" and "FND is an expression of underlying difficulties in relationships and emotions". Although the person with FND is bearing the brunt of experiencing the actual symptoms of FND, the FND is entirely mirrored in the system around the person in a non-FND way: by caring and reciprocal reinforcement patterns. One can also ask the question whether, at least in some cases, it is the person with FND that is caring for the person without FND, for example when the "carer" experiences fears of abandonment from the person with FND and prefers to keep the person close via caring. In this way, although not immediately obvious, the roles are reversed: the person with FND may meet the stronger unmet needs of the "carer" almost to a greater extent than the "carer" is meeting the needs of the person with FND.

FND EDUCATION SESSIONS: RECIPROCAL REINFORCEMENT

The social functions of FND, caring responses and any other understandable but possibly unhelpful behaviours that maintain FND and that are imposed by the system can be explored using hybrid PCM formulations applied to the person with FND and their direct environment. Once these reciprocal reinforcement patterns have been elucidated, the formulation will guide the subsequent treatment. Often, the act of sharing the hybrid formulation with the family or staff team will serve as the intervention. The following section will highlight some commonly used tools in FND practice.

SYSTEMIC RE-TRAUMATISATION: APPLICATION OF THE PCM

The PCM is very well placed to address the impact of systemic re-traumatisation on FND. Although the formulation may not necessarily directly manage the unhelpful behaviours of the individuals that inflict the systemic re-traumatisation on the person with FND, it can provide a helpful narrative for the person for understanding worsening FND symptoms in the context of unknown and puzzling interpersonal triggers. The PCM formulation also provides avenues for intervention, for example challenging unhelpful (not irrational, as they are rational) thoughts, as well as identify and manage FND prodromes to reduce the impact on the FND (Table 4.28).

RELATIONSHIP TRAINING

A common problem in FND families is the lack of verbal emotional expression as a coping strategy, which is often part of a longstanding, life-long and sometimes intergenerational pattern of coping. Although a 12-session course of psychological therapy will not completely reverse these often ingrained coping habits, a helpful start can be made by increasing the person's and family's insight. FND family meetings are a powerful tool at the disposal of the psychologist. Therapy sessions can be used to practice emotional expression skills in the moment within a safe space. Sometimes, the person with FND may need emotional support and modelling experience from the psychologist to express difficult thoughts and feelings to another family member, where the psychologist has a facilitating and mediating role that enables the person with FND to express their emotions and can help the person manage the aftermath or backlash following the act of emotional expression. Another useful technique is helping the person with FND to express the adverse emotional impact and hurt that other family members' thoughts, feelings and

Table 4.28 Pressure Cooker Model formulation of Systemic re-traumatisation

Kitchen

- The seizures show the healthcare professionals how unwell I am.

Cover

- I don't really talk about my feelings with my partner and I don't have a close friend whom I can trust. People may abandon me if I show them my true emotions.

Overpressure Plug

- Experienced a dissociative episode at the end of the consultation. Frequency and severity of the episodes have increased since the consultation and I'm doing a lot worse.

Valve

- Blocked Valve: the seizures stop me from going out in the community and meeting my friends. I have had to cancel socials.

Warning light

- I'm worried about the dissociative seizures and how this is affecting my life. I can't stop thinking about my recent relapse and I'm searching for a lot of information on the internet to help myself.

Sticky left-over food

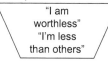

"I am worthless"
"I'm less than others"

In childhood, I mostly kept to myself

Pot

- I stopped exercising because of my seizures, causing my mood further to drop.
- My partner has called an ambulance and I've visited accidents and emergencies a few times to get support for my seizures, since I'm not getting help anymore.

I feel funny and weird sensations in my body, I am afraid I feel another seizure coming up.

Ignition

- Childhood adverse experiences of longstanding emotional parental neglect.

Fuel

- Interpersonal "re-trigger": healthcare professional making the consultation review very brief and subsequently discharging me from the service. The professional was rushed and short with me in their approach.

Flames

- I feel abandoned and left to my own devices".
- The healthcare professional's attitude and manner towards me reminded me of my parents when growing up. I've been re-triggered and experience the same difficult thoughts and feelings right now as when I was a child.

Heat

- I can't really describe the feeling, it's just not very nice. Things around me feel unreal, as if I'm detached from the world.

Safety features

I've been attending my psychology sessions regularly. My partner is supportive.

responses may have had on them (e.g. family members frequently dismissing the person or arguing) and worsened the FND.

SOCIAL BELONGING

People with FND often have a reduced sense or lack of social belonging to communities other than their own family. It is not uncommon for a person's social network to be limited to their direct family environment. This situation not only maintains the limited social network but also creates more dependency and burden on the family unit, which ultimately maintains FND (through the "blocked Valve"). It is therefore important to identify psychological, physical and social barriers that prevent a person from venturing out and making social connections outside the family home.

ENMESHMENT

Enmeshed relationship patterns between the person and the caring family members are not uncommon and can result in blurry boundaries between family vs caring roles; increased carer burden; lack of breathing space and pursual of own life goals for the carer; lack of proper "family or couple quality time" as opposed to "care time"; and in the end: FND symptom maintenance. In a sensitive manner, explore the concept of "enmeshment" with the person and their family. Clinicians can feel surprised to hear that family members respond with relief once the topic has been broached as it can often feel as "the elephant in the room". This does not mean it will be easy to separate the family from caring roles as both the person and family member's needs are often met by each other via reciprocal reinforcement patterns. Another barrier towards role separation is "saying no" and setting boundaries when the person elicits care and the carer is likely to succumb to care requests. Only a systemic approach will be able to support the family in learning to become assertive towards the person with FND and tolerate the discomfort of assertiveness.

FND GUIDELINES

In order for a behavioural intervention to work, seizure guidelines should be implemented in a consistent and predictable manner by the environment. If these are not consistently applied and only intermittently reinforced, a much harder to extinguish partial reinforcement schedule may emerge which may make it more difficult to extinguish the FND. Therefore, when drawing up seizure guidelines, check the following:

- Are the person and family both on board with the psychological formulation and rationale behind the guidelines? Do they understand the formulation?

- Some family members may feel unsure about the often counter-intuitive practices (e.g. disattending, withdrawal of care) towards their loved ones. This state of uncertainty may provoke inconsistent application of the guidelines. Pre-empt and acknowledge these common beliefs and emotions but emphasise that not applying the guidelines will hurt the patient more, for example reduced ability to perform activities of daily life independently, maintain dependency, lack of pursuing constructive life goals, prevent the person from accessing opportunities for learning more adaptive emotion regulation strategies, intermittent reinforcement and FND symptom maintenance.
- What barriers may emerge during the implementation of the guidelines? (e.g. environment's distress or guilt as part of reciprocal reinforcement). Will the partner or family struggle with role changes, relationships and increased independence once the FND improves?
- Do they have an understanding of more serious consequences for the FND if they adopt intermittent reinforcement? Provide psycho-education on all behavioural concepts including basic principles of reinforcement, schedules, extinction bursts and the need to continue despite temporary worsening of the behaviours.
- What are the family's attitudes towards the FND? Is there evidence of systemic re-traumatisation that could maintain the seizures?

Formulation

Based on your initial information gathering, complete a PCM template. There are many ways to go about this. If you haven't got much time in the clinic:

- Try to get at least a "minimum data-set" covered in your PCM template consisting of the pieces of information listed in Table 4.29. Complete a layered formulation on your own about the person with FND using the quick prompt questions.

If you have more time available:

- Complete a formulation with the person, and if there is time and it feels appropriate, with their family member at the end of your session. Try to uncover any reciprocal reinforcement patterns between the two formulations.
- Ask members in the MDT to complete their own "environmental" formulation in response to assessing and treating this person. Formulate the "environmental" responses under the Overpressure Plug.

Brief Pressure Cooker assessment template

See Figure 4.7.

Table 4.29 Brief pressure cooker assessment template

Kitchen

Reciprocal reinforcement: How does the system normally respond to the FND? What may drive their responses?
Systemic re-traumatisation
Social functions of FND and modelling processes
Social isolation and specify social network
Current relationships and quality of relationships with special attention to enmeshment, conflict and distancing

Cover

- Do they have a trusted person with whom they can safely express their thoughts and feelings on a regular basis?
- Make an initial assessment about what makes the cover tight in this person.

Overpressure Plug

- Specify current most bothersome symptoms including frequency, severity and impact on daily life (if many symptoms, ask for a top 3 most disabling symptoms)
- Hold in mind the four categories: motor, seizures, sensory and cognitive
- Fatigue, pain
- Patient and family's perception and understanding of FND and view on its mechanisms particularly whether they believe the FND-emotion link

Valve

- Specify the valve pattern: bust-after-boom, boom-and-bust, Boom
- Typical day: what do you do? How do you relax, enjoy yourself?
- Meaningful activities: education, work, life roles, sense of belonging and purpose
- Have you stopped doing anything due to the FND?

Warning light

Based on your initial conversation, can you say something about physical symptom focus? Pay attention to speech, acceptance of psychological factors for FND, connectedness with social media. Is there "systemic hypervigilance" on the symptoms, that is family preoccupied with FND, level of supervision and focus on symptoms?

Sticky left-over food

> Hypothesize about potential core beliefs

- Early relationships with parents, siblings and parenting style.
- Early childhood and family of origin coping strategies: how did you or your family cope with difficult thoughts and feelings as a child/ in response to stressful events?
- Keep in mind the three classic FND coping strategies: Pushing on, keep self to self, hiding or avoiding emotions, and any indication of early dissociative tendencies.

Pot

Keep in mind the FND SELF CARE acronym, in particular:

- Warning signs for FND symptoms
- Interdisciplinary risk assessment
- Details of care packages and equipment
- Other somatoform symptoms (e.g. irritable bowel syndrome, continence issues)
- Impact of FND on personal and domestic day-to-day activities: How has the FND impacted on personal care, accessing community etc.).
- Medications and physical illnesses.

Kitchen

Ignition

- Childhood adverse events. Think about the five childhood/adulthood relationship and adverse childhood event patterns in FND: (1) conflict, (2) enmeshment, (3) distance, emotional neglect and rejection experiences (parental, school and later relationships), (4) abuse and (5) loss.
- Time-line: Onset of FND, surrounding events and emotions/ beliefs about these experiences, particularly in healthcare.
- Specify pattern: gradual build-up (stress but no sufficient resources), "before-and-after", for example traumatic event or surgery.

Fuel

- Ask for an example dissociative episode/ worsening of motor-type FND symptoms that stands out to the person or the most recent one.
- Fluctuations in frequency and severity of FND symptoms, and possible triggers.
- Keep in mind emotional and interpersonal triggers: family interactions and psychological safety.

Flames

- Previous experiences with psychological therapy and healthcare experiences. Look out for systemic re-traumatisation and common interpersonal cognitions: not feeling cared for, not being believed, not feeling heard and feeling abandoned.
- Test out the models for the different psychological conditions (e.g. panic model, social anxiety, depression) to see if the cognitions are a good fit for a condition-specific CBT model rather than the PCM. Be aware of safety behaviours and physical symptoms (e.g. lack of eye contact, tremor), even in the absence of a reported emotion (e.g. social anxiety).
- Any indications of a fear of recovery from FND, including social gains and losses.

Heat

Dissociation
- Check for evidence of dissociation: language, behaviours, cognitive events that are indicative, for example "everything feels distant", zoning in/out, functional amnesia.
- What is your take on the person's emotion language? Any odd features to the reported emotions? (e.g. intellectualisation, labelling emotions as physical events, thoughts not consistent with feelings).
- Emotion regulation
- Evidence of emotion dysregulation, rapid oscillations between emotions, and any wider "complex trauma" symptoms, for example relationship difficulties, deliberate self-harm.

(Continued)

Table 4.29 (Continued)

Kitchen

- If you can: identify
  a Pressure Cooker
  Chain Reaction by
  linking triggers,
  thoughts, feelings/
  undefined internal
  states and the FND in
  the maintenance cycle
  of the PCM.

Safety features

Positive prognostic factors and personal qualities, for example:

- Accepting of a psychological formulation of FND, or some acknowledgement of psychological factors that contribute to FND.
- Supportive personal or family relationships that are helpful rather than hurtful/ not maintaining FND, and on board with the diagnosis and role of psychosocial factors in FND.
- A stable, social network with supportive friends.
- Some ability to identify, label and express emotions, introspection/psychological mindedness.
- A recent onset of FND rather than a chronic course, with minimal equipment, entrenchment or a care package. Includes the absence of a history of premorbid long-term somatoform conditions preceding the FND, for example chronic pain, ME.

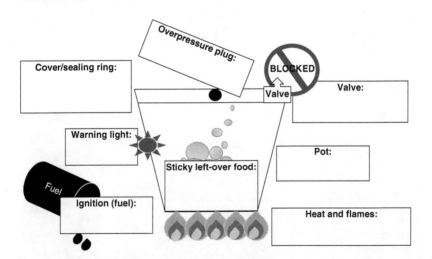

Figure 4.7 Empty Pressure Cooker Model formulation template.

Creating an initial PCM formulation

After you have gathered all your information, use the layered formulation below with prompt questions to create an initial formulation of the FND. Keep in mind that this is your starting point. As you gather more information during the therapy process, your hypotheses may change. In the sections on "Managing Formulation Fear and Frustration" and "Progressive hypothesising in FND" later in this chapter, we will explore some thoughts and strategies to help you manage this occasionally challenging hypothesising process.

Layer 1: Were any traumatic events in childhood and adulthood relationships or ways of upbringing disclosed (in particular emotional neglect) that made the person vulnerable towards developing FND? What is your hypothesis about the person's early childhood coping mechanisms?

Layer 2: Is the FND coping triangle present? Have early childhood coping mechanisms repeated over time into adulthood? (i.e. keep self to self, pushing on and dissociation/cutting emotions off).

Layer 3: What is your hypothesis on the internal regulation mechanism of the FND? How does the person with FND reach psychological safety? Are they able to label and identify emotions? Keep in mind that interpersonal triggers may not be obvious at this stage. Pay attention to cognitions around not feeling cared for, not being believed and the fear of recovery.

Layer 4: What do you make of the person's symptom focus and its impact on engagement with psychology? Do any of the medical-contextual factors contribute to FND? Go through the FND SELF CARE acronym and tick off any relevant factors. Ensure you cover the risk assessment section as this is part of your standard assessment.

Layer 5: What is your hypothesis on the external regulation mechanism of the FND, what may be the social functions of the FND? Can you outline any interpersonal safety behaviours between the person with FND and their environment?

Person's formulation of FND

It is important to check the person's own personal theory on what they think caused the FND to develop and their views on maintaining factors particularly psychological and environmental. This is helpful for the following reasons:

- "Hearing" the person and demonstrating to the person that you take them seriously. Remember, many of these patients have not felt believed – both in childhood and in adulthood.
- Checking their insight and understanding of FND and determining whether they are aware of the maintaining factors of the FND.
- Check their "psychological mindedness" and awareness of psychosocial factors, as well as their level of dissociation and focus on physical symptoms.
- Observe the presence and size of a discrepancy between the person's vs clinician's formulation.
- Work towards reducing that discrepancy to make it a shared formulation in a collaborative way. Sometimes arriving at a consensus on the PCM formulation = FND education and the intervention. You are effectively

using the therapeutic relationship as a means to help the person manage the FND.

Hybrid pressure cooker formulation template

See Table 4.30.

Multidisciplinary formulation

The PCM can be a powerful tool to help create a joined-up and psychologically driven formulation of the FND. Although all elements in the PCM are associated with psychological and social features, Table 4.31 demonstrates how the different elements in the PCM can simultaneously be linked to the different professions that are often involved in the multidisciplinary treatment of FND.

Pressure Cooker quick fact sheet on psychology and FND

Do not assume that, just because FND and emotions are closely linked, a person who arrives in your clinic will have up-to-date knowledge on what psychology entails. It is good practice to share some quick facts on the role of psychology in FND.

- Some of these facts can sound familiar to a person. This is particularly important to people with FND because they often hear that they are too complex, beyond help, nothing else can be done, or they feel not believed, cared for and branded as "attention seeking". It creates trust in you as a clinician who can take on the FND and will make them feel heard by you, helping to build a positive therapeutic relationship from the start.
- Exploring these facts can also provide reassurance to the person, for example if they are worried about not having found any triggers for the FND yet.
- Highlighting the important impact of the environment may help the person feel less heavy about accessing psychology. After all, the FND is a shared problem, a "condition of an unwell system" and therefore both the person and their close environment have a shared responsibility for recovery from FND.
- You can use this space to emphasise that you believe the person and their symptoms. Another way is to pre-empt any qualms about accessing psychology for FND, that you are aware that people immediately think of psychology that "it's in between your ears" "faking it" and "put on" but that this is not how you work or what you think.
- Keep the PCM in mind when sharing quick facts on psychology in FND, in the same way as you would when "testing out a CBT model" to check

Table 4.30 Examples of PCM configurations for the person, family and healthcare professionals with FND

PCM element	Maintaining factor in FND	Person with FND	Family RE: person FND	Staff RE: person FND
Ignition	Remote trigger(s) • Early childhood • At a later stage in adult life just before the onset of FND ("critical incident")	Examples: emotional neglect, abuse, car accident, domestic violence.	Background of family conflicts and negative interpersonal dynamics.	Past healthcare experiences with non-abating symptoms in FND, "difficult, heart sink patients".
Fuel	Current trigger(s) • Set off regular episodes or symptom fluctuations following FND onset	Staff member not speaking to the person, giving looks.	Witnessing symptoms of the person with FND.	Person with FND does not progress in session, branded as "therapy-interfering" behaviours.
Flames	• Negative beliefs, emotions, memories • Poorly or undefined unpleasant internal states	Feeling neglected and rejected by another individual.	• Worries about how to help the person. • Feeling distressed seeing the person in distress.	• Beliefs around feeling de-skilled in FND – anxiety, confusion, shame. • Negative beliefs about person wasting time – anger, frustration, feeling drained.
Heat	• Intensity of emotion • Rate of fluctuation of emotion or internal state • Emotion dysregulation	Intense and strong feelings that fluctuate on a daily basis (=emotion dysregulation).	Intense anxiety and discomfort when witnessing an FND episode.	Strong negative feelings about the person before entering a session.
Overpressure Plug	• FND symptom (patients) • Unhelpful coping strategies towards the person with FND by staff or family	Dissociative episode or worsened functional tremor when in close proximity to this person who is neglectful in the person's view.	• Quickly reassuring the person, to reduce person's and own personal distress. • Family overinvolved or underinvolved with the person with FND.	• "Therapist-interfering" behaviours: Open expressions of stigmatising thoughts, shorter sessions or being late for sessions, avoiding the person.

(Continued)

Table 4.30 (Continued)

PCM element	Maintaining factor in FND	Person with FND	Family RE: person FND	Staff RE: person FND
				• Unable to control negative facial expressions/ emotional coldness towards person. • Staff unusually invested in the person's treatment, doubling up efforts.
Cover	Verbal expression of beliefs and emotions	Not expressing emotions	Not wanting to worry the person/therefore not expressing emotions.	• Not expressing emotions in a helpful way "unconstructive venting". Lack of reflective space
Valve	Abnormal activity levels. The extent to which meaningful, enjoyable, relaxation and social activities are reduced, dropped or dysregulated in a boom/bust cycle	• –Blocked: Not participating in enjoyable activities • –Boom–and–bust/ dysregulated: Overdoing activities, followed by a recovery period with no meaningful activity.	• –Blocked: dropped all hobbies, family members only taking on caring duties without respite. • –Dysregulated: boom–and–bust cycle, becoming less efficient managing care for person • –Overused: overactivity.	• Blocked: staff feeling too drained, cancelling hobbies and social activities after work. No work-life balance. • Dysregulated: staff booming and busting themselves, or "boom" constantly on the move and high rate of sickness absences.
Sticky left-over food	Early and repeated coping strategies	• Kept self to self • Pushing on	Same family coping: everybody keeps self to self/pushes on	Not used to speaking about own difficult feelings that come up in response to the person

	System (social functions of FND)			
Kitchen		Social function of FND: Receiving care, comfort, concern from family and healthcare system.	Reciprocal reinforcement: aimed at reduction of family's distress witnessing the FND (e.g. reassurance).	Reciprocal reinforcement: reduction of staff's distress witnessing the FND (e.g. reassurance).
Warning light	Heightened self-focused attention to FND symptoms. Omnipresence of FND in the person's life.	Heightened self-focused attention on symptoms. Many pieces of equipment and frequent healthcare contacts reminders of FND and disabilities.	Heightened attention or systemic hypervigilance around person with FND, "tiptoeing," "24 surveillance" in case of a seizure.	• Person with FND is frequently on staff's minds. • Staff cannot stop thinking about person with FND after hours. • Person with FND gets discussed a lot during meetings and "eats" into other patients' time slots.
Pot	Biological vulnerabilities (FND SELF CARE acronym)	Poor sleep hygiene. High caffeine intake causing palpitations. Polypharmacy.	Ignoring own health and lack of self-care strategies.	Main carer of person with FND/doing overwork on a regular basis. Risk of retaliation to the patient.
Safety features	Positive factors for a good prognosis and recovery from FND	Accepting of psychological formulation and prominent role of psychosocial factors in FND.	Supportive towards the person with FND, acceptance of psychology.	Regular reflective space, mental health workers present to support MDT, willingness to open up about beliefs and emotions re: patients.

Table 4.31 Multidisciplinary adaptation of the Pressure Cooker Model

---

Kitchen

- Social care—support with reducing care package and family work: facilitation of safe and smooth discharge.

Cover
- Psychology: Verbal emotional expression in psychological therapy sessions.
- Speech and Language Therapy: video feedback of functional speech for remediation purposes; assertiveness skills training; increasing awareness into the emotion-speech link.
- Social care: Safeguarding for victims of coercive control, which often presents with "tight Covers".

Warning light
- Physiotherapy input for attention shifting/distraction techniques to reduce heightened self-focused attention.

Sticky left-over food
- Psychology: history of early childhood coping strategies and family coping, core belief work.

Overpressure Plug
- Psychology: strategies for reality grounding and tolerance of discomfort and distress before progressing into full-blown FND symptoms.
- Neurology: Management of functional neurological symptoms, including functional dystonia, Botox injections.
- OT: sensory profiles, fatigue management.
- Physiotherapy: pain management.

Pot
(FND SELF CARE acronym)
- **Food fuel:** Dietetics: Advice on food choices, vitamin intake, sufficient hydration to prevent "clouding of the mind".
- **Night rest:** Psychology: Addressing adherence problems to medications, sleep hygiene. Neuropsychiatry: pharmacological management of sleeping difficulties.
- **Drugs and medications/sickness and physical illness:** Neuropsychiatry: review and rationalisation of long lists of medications with interacting side effects. Reducing medications that may promote dissociation (e.g. opiates).
- **Equipment:** Occupational Therapy and Physiotherapy for equipment review and plan for stepping down.
- **Liquids and Bladder functioning:** Continence nursing: advice on management of bladder and bowel incontinence.
- **Fight-or-Flight and Warning signs:** Neuropsychiatry and Psychology input for, for example, taking the edge of severe anxiety symptoms and identification of warning signs.
- **Contacts:** Liaison with services outside MDT.
- **Ability to take care of yourself:** OT assessment and practice of self-care, personal and domestic activities of daily life, for example grooming, personal care.

Valve
- Psychology x Occupational Therapy to address boom-bust cycles, pacing techniques, planning of meaningful enjoyable, relaxation and social activities, behavioural activation.
- Physiotherapy: Walking practice to enable better access to the community and social activities.
- Nursing: Planning bed rest in between activities.

Kitchen

| | • **Risks:** Team assessment of the patient's risks. |
| | • **Exercise, movement and physical activity:** Physiotherapy: increasing cardiovascular health, graded exercise programmes. |

Ignition/Fuel

Flames/Heat

• Psychology, neurology and neuropsychiatry: initial assessments may reveal a remote history of difficult events and relationships, as well as a critical incident that set off the FND.

• Psychology and Physiotherapy or Psychology and Occupational Therapy sessions for setting up behavioural experiments and challenging unhelpful thoughts around fear of falling, support for tolerating distress in the run-up to a dissociative seizure.

• Neuropsychiatry: Pharmacological support to take the edge of intense emotions.

Safety features

In the same way that the entire team contributes to an assessment of risks to the person with FND, the team can create an assessment of the positive prognostic factors.

whether it fits. This will help you prompt your memory and not forget any facts (see Figure 4.8).

• Explain that stress and stress triggers are normal occurrences in daily life. However, due to the FND coping triad, the person with FND has no recourse to appropriate coping habits to release this stress at the top of the pressure cooker, for example by verbal emotional expression (opening the person's tight cover) and/or by constructive stress release via activities (unblocking, reducing overuse or regulating the valve). The goal of psychological therapy is to work on the person's and the environment's pressure cookers.

• Most importantly, keep observing whether the person feels heard or hurt. The role of providing these facts is education, but foremost, making the person feel heard and "set the stage" for psychology in a positive way.

• You can print this figure out and give this to the person and their family to ponder over, as part of homework. Ask them to read it and bring it in the next session, provide a space to discuss questions, ask what elements stood out to them and which ones they would like to work on, and ask whether they have any goals in mind (e.g. "to find my triggers", "to stop pushing myself so much", "to identify emotions") (Figure 4.9).

FND formulation fear and frustration

Imagine yourself in the following situation: You may initially not know what may be going on for a patient, and as the therapy progresses and you are not seeing any significant results or improvement, you are becoming anxious and frustrated. You feel that the therapy process is derailing under your watch and you start to unravel yourself. You feel anxious and embarrassed

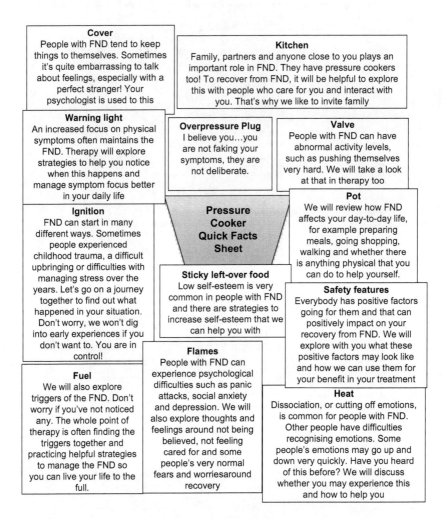

Figure 4.8 Quick fact sheet on the Pressure Cooker Model.

and start doubting your skills. This is a good moment to take stock and apply the PCM on ourselves. Table 4.32 displays some common scenarios in the FND clinic.

Managing formulation fear and frustration with the PCM: top tips

EXTINGUISH YOUR FLAMES

- **Normalise your fears and frustration.** This sounds cliché, but FND is a multi-layered condition that poses many complexities to the therapy process and is bound to ignite thoughts and feelings within the professional.

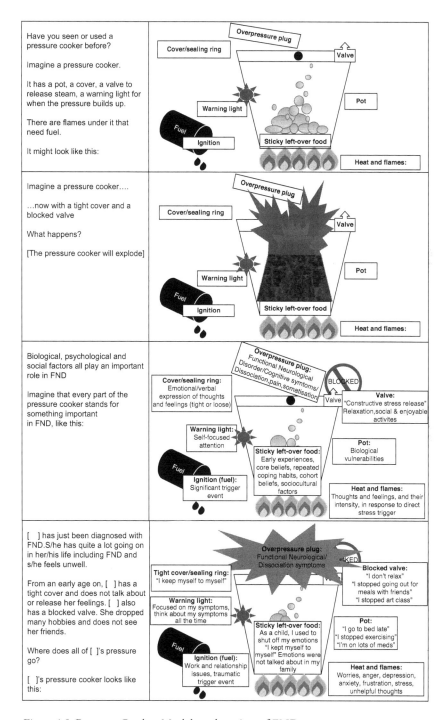

Figure 4.9 Pressure Cooker Model explanation of FND.

Table 4.32 Pressure Cooker Model of formulation fear and frustration in FND

Kitchen

Social functions of your own unhelpful behaviours:
- To find your own psychological safety during the therapy process.
- To stop feeling de-skilled and low in self-confidence about your clinical skills.

Reciprocal reinforcement: Your unhelpful behaviours, even though they create psychological safety, are contributing to the person's FND, for example non-verbal communications filtering through, which the person with heightened rejection sensitivity (rightfully) interprets as a rejection, further amplifying the FND symptoms.

Fostering systemic re-traumatisation

Due to countertransference, the risk of causing emotional hurt to the patient increases, even through non-verbal communication of your true feelings.

Cover

- Keep self to self about how you feel about your formulation skills and the lack of progress the patient is making in therapy.
- Carrying your own unspeakable dilemma: wanting to share your thoughts on interpersonal triggers with the patient but unable to do so for fear of the aftermath.
- Unconstructive venting about the patient to your colleagues or displacing negative emotions to other people in your personal life.

Overpressure Plug

Unhelpful, psychological safety behaviours in response to the person with FND:

- Shortening sessions.
- Pairing up with another colleague to "share the burden" without giving the patient the clinically needed one-to-one time.
- Non-verbal retaliation, tit-for-tat behaviours towards patient increase, for example distancing and coldness.
- Trying to discharge the person earlier as you don't feel you're getting anywhere.
- Putting the blame for lack of progress on the patient.

Valve

- Blocked "bust-after-Boom" pattern: staying at home, feeling drained and backing out of social, relaxation or sporting activities.
- Boom-and-bust cycles with longer periods of recovery needed.
- Boom: Going to extra mile, over and above for one particular patient, in comparison to other patients on your caseload.

Warning light

- High attentional focus on the person at the expense of other patients you are treating in your clinic.
- Reassurance seeking with other professionals.

Sticky left-over food

Low confidence about your "clinician self-esteem"
Impostor syndrome flares-up

Pot

- Feeling physically sick and nauseous every time you are going to see the patient.
- Increased sickness absence at work.

Kitchen

Ignition/Fuel	Flames	Heat
• Person with FND and/or family doesn't accept the formulation, with high levels of resistance against psychology – even though it's "crystal clear" to you. • Formulation remains unclear, even after several sessions. Family of the patient thinks you are not doing a good enough job to help the patient. • Person displays several "therapy-interfering" behaviours, for example hostility. • Person brings in crisis after crisis each time and you don't get to the "real" work. • Person gives you triggers for FND but these remain superficial, symptoms don't improve and you know that interpersonal triggers are driving the condition but there's no way of sharing this with the person. • You keep on "formulation hopping".	• Frustration, anger about the person not following or accepting your formulation, and "messing you about". • Anxiety or embarrassment about "not knowing", "cracking the patient" "I'm not getting anywhere with this person" and resulting lack of confidence and doubts about your skills. • Frustration, anger and anxiety about being on the receiving end of it. • Frustration about not getting anywhere with the patient and feeling de-skilled and loss of control. • Feeling trapped in therapy, wanting to share your thoughts and formulation on interpersonal triggers with the person but too anxious about "taking the plunge" for fear about losing the patient. • Anxiety and embarrassment: not wanting to come across as unprofessional or unskilled about not really knowing what's going on with the person, and any admission to struggling may say something about your own skills as a psychologist.	• You may start mirroring the person and take over the person's dissociative tendencies or become as internally dysregulated. You may mirror the loss of control that a person in crisis may feel.

Safety features

I'm trained in applying psychological principles.
I have been managing an FND caseload for some time
Some of the patients I have treated have improved and made progress.

- **Challenge your own thinking with observable facts:** if the person is attending, no matter what levels of resistance and hostility, the person is present and that is meaningful.
- **Reframe your thoughts:** When an emotion comes out in therapy, consider this as a positive development, especially with patients who have been dissociating and not been in touch with their emotions for a long time.
- "Therapy-interfering" behaviours (TIBs) may emerge during the therapy process. Examples of TIBs include patients not attending or cancelling sessions, late arrivals, "psychology not helping" and openly resisting psychology, increased number of falls or near-misses, worsened FND symptoms and increased dissociative seizure frequency. Instead of seeing TIBs as a problem, **fully embrace resistance** and other TIBs as an opportunity to start hypothesising about the functions of the FND, incorporate into the formulation and use therapeutically.
- **An increase in TIBs suggests that you may have hit on something important:** you may be pressing an important button that is the crux of your therapy and is what maintains FND even if it is not clear what this may be. If we think of the therapy session as the Fuel and the Overpressure Plug reflecting an increase in FND symptoms or more TIBs, it is time to start hypothesising about the steps that lie between these two elements and complete the PCM assessment template: what information do you have on hand about the person that can help you complete the empty boxes in the PCM formulation? Think about a tight cover, blocked valve, adverse childhood experiences and coping strategies. Feed this formulation back to the person, even if half-completed, and ask the person to help you make sense of the formulation together. Reflect on the function of the TIBS; for example, tinkering with an existing coping strategy (FND) may cause turmoil as the person is resisting letting go of a well-established coping habit with nothing to replace it yet.
- **Be ready to embrace patient crises.** Some people with FND may experience a continuous barrage of events in their personal lives outside the therapy space that impact on the person's engagement with therapy. Treat these psychosocial crises as crucial information that help your formulation and enable a person to directly practise their skills.
- **Practice self-compassion:** patients not making progress does not immediately say anything about the state or quality of your clinical skills. The patient may not have been ready for therapy. Keep in mind that the therapy experience you provided, no matter how brief, may have planted a seed. Some patients need time to digest psychology and may come back with new insights at a later point in time.

TIME TO OPEN YOUR OWN COVER

The supervision space is a good place to explore formulation fears; however, it may feel somewhat psychologically unsafe to discuss with a supervisor or a manager that may also be doing your appraisal, feeding into worries about "not being able to manage the case-load". Keeping your cover tight about formulation fears is not recommended either; this unspeakable dilemma should be released. Organise regular reflective group sessions with other members of your team or other FND specialists to explore your fears and discomfort.

BLOCK YOUR OVERPRESSURE PLUG

Therapy is a process that is driven by patient and therapist. Raise insight into your own "therapist-interfering" behaviours, for instance by keeping a reflective diary or discussing this with colleagues, and monitor how your own TIBs may contribute to the issues in therapy. Reflect on their impact on maintenance of the FND, for example, regularly shortening your sessions with the person may deprive the person from vital opportunities to learn and consolidate alternative, more adaptive coping skills. In addition, therapist-interfering behaviours maintain therapy-interfering behaviours, and vice versa; for example, a person with FND not progressing in therapy may lead to a sense of hopelessness and shortening of therapy sessions in the therapist, which may then be perceived by the patient as rejection, further halting progress and maintaining FND.

BRING ORDER INTO YOUR KITCHEN

Clinicians are not immune to reciprocal reinforcement and experiencing a need for psychological safety during therapy. Let's suppose the patient is holding on tightly to physical triggers of FND, not entertaining the existence of interpersonal triggers, dismissing your strategies, resisting your psychosocial interpretation of the FND, or hostile. All these instances may make you tread carefully and withhold you from sharing any further suggestions or observations to the point that you are both stuck in a therapy status quo. The question arises whether you are mirroring the patient and holding on to your psychologically secure base that is halting the process? Ask yourself whether it is time to venture out from your secure base and take a positive risk in therapy, whilst simultaneously not fearing the discomfort that comes with the aftermath this may cause in the therapeutic relationship? In the end, no matter how psychologically uncomfortable, moving on from a status quo will ultimately provide the patient with the best chances for recovery.

ACTIVELY IDENTIFY THE PATIENT'S SAFETY FEATURES

Treatment of psychological difficulties is often focused on "pathology" and "problems". We may lose sight of the fact that every person possesses personal qualities and positive features that helps their recovery or helps a clinician move someone through their recovery journey. Specify protective and positive factors of the person with FND, their family and of yourself. Have you ever actively reflected on your own "safety features" in the therapy process?

Formulation hopping

Therapy can be a destabilising experience for both the person and healthcare worker involved in the treatment of FND, resulting in high levels of anxiety, discomfort and frustration. These emotions may result in hopping between formulations; that is, a patient may present with a range of psychological difficulties that may fit multiple models. An initial model is selected but becomes "defunct", and the therapist hops onto another one. Formulation hopping could be interpreted as a failing of the therapist…however…is that truly the case? In the next section, we will reflect on the quadrilinear process of therapy in FND.

The initial formulation may be a conduit to the core formulation:

- Sometimes focusing on a superficial problem may uncover a deeper layer of the core problem that is driving the maintenance of FND: relationships and interpersonal triggers. This uncovering process, via more "superficial" problems, may be a necessary step to take before getting to treating the core of the problem. The PCM can be a good starting point for an initial formulation.
- The therapeutic process, particularly in FND, is sometimes about the establishment of a trusted and psychologically safe relationship; the end goal may not be about "addressing social anxiety", and both patient and therapist may not even be aware of that. As therapy progresses, it becomes evident that the social anxiety formulation is a tool or conduit that helps both patient and therapist to work on what is really pressing: relationships and the act of relating to another person.
- Keep in mind that therapy is a dynamic process and may not follow the regular rules of, for example, standard CBT treatment of panic disorder, no matter how fitting the initial formulation may be. The process is often not linear in FND. Instead, you are actively collaborating as a team, constantly revising hypotheses, as new information is revealed to you in the course of the therapy. Establishing a trusted relationship, with all its bumps, hurdles and roadblocks, whilst you are remaining "object constant" may be the actual treatment. From this secure base, the patient may feel more confident to subsequently reveal the core matter to you.

Ask yourself: Is this more about me?

- Be willing to flexibly abandon an initial hypothesis that you are wedded to. Reflect on what it means to let go of your original hypothesis: do difficult thoughts and feelings about your own skills emerge? Is it psychologically safe to hold onto your first hunch and psychologically unsafe to venture out?
- Be also willing to ride the wave of quadrilinearity and let go of any linear and standard conceptions that you may have about "standard therapy" in FND. Learn to tolerate the distress of quadrilinearity and re-formulation! Sometimes this is more about you than the patient.

SELF-COMPASSION

- You have to start somewhere and it's ok not to get it right immediately.
- Treat what's most prominently present and affecting the patient. This may indeed be social anxiety as the patient is not coming out of their home. You are doing the right thing to focus on that most pressing problem first.
- Don't be too hard on yourself if you need to abandon your initial formulation and you engage in subsequent formulation hopping. Instead, fully embrace the process of progressive hypothesising as an essential journey that you and the patient are on to achieve their recovery.
- Practice acceptance about not being able to avoid simultaneously entertaining two hypotheses to explain the presentation. Relationships are often a vulnerable area in FND, the therapeutic relationship has to develop over time, and interpersonal triggers are often not revealed immediately.

Progressive hypothesising in FND

See Table 4.33.

Treatment

This section will discuss helpful treatment strategies. Remember that as a clinician treating people with FND, you will be representing a crucial part of the person's kitchen environment, much in the same way as the person's immediate family and other significant people in their life.

Reverse systemic re-traumatisation: heard or hurt?

People with FND have often experienced childhood adverse experiences that may have included not being believed by a parental caregiver or another important key figure in the family. The fear of not being believed about FND is real. At times, patient's families may not believe them, repeating earlier experiences. Make every effort to communicate to your patient and their families that you believe their symptoms. It is a rare occurrence that people with FND malinger; hence, this cannot be a viable reason not to believe them. It is also important that you believe in this yourself, it needs to be genuine. Heard and hurt are homophones, but from a semantic point of view, they could not be further apart (Table 4.34). Before you start, ask yourself: with my comments and behaviours, would the patient feel heard or hurt?

Assessment = intervention

The last point in relation to dividing the assessment over multiple sessions may not be feasible in clinical practice due to time and resource issues. However, one can make the argument that the actual assessment is the intervention if

Table 4.33 Stages of progressive hypothesising in FND

Stage in psychological therapy	Examples
Initial formulation of the person and the environment with FND based on assessment results	Initial hypothesis: "dissociative episodes = panic attacks".
Implementation of the treatment plan Testing out your initial hypothesis	Sharing the FND-adapted panic formulation with the person. Based on the panic formulation, you suggest behavioural experiments dropping safety behaviours, psycho-education on the fight-or-flight response that the person subsequently implements.
Re-formulation New incoming data doesn't (entirely) fit with the initial hypothesis but fits equally or better with an alternative hypothesis. The initial hypothesis tends to be an internal regulation hypothesis (reduction of unpleasant internal state by FND) whereas the alternative hypothesis tends to be an external regulation hypothesis (FND is mediated by interpersonal triggers in the environment).	The panic treatment has reduced the person's dissociative episodes but these continue to persist. Is it possible that other reasons drive the FND? • Initial hypothesis 1: panic attacks explain the dissociative episodes. • Alternative hypothesis 2: dissociative episodes take away an unpleasant interpersonal trigger, that is an argument, powered by reciprocal reinforcement from the environment. • Mixed hypotheses 3: both hypotheses can explain the full picture of dissociative episodes in that person.
Re-implementation Keep testing out both hypotheses during the therapy with data. Entertain the possibility of one vs two hypotheses explaining the dissociative episodes.	Treatment focuses on both the panic model and panic strategies, as well as couple's sessions in parallel to unearth and address the triggers for arguments and eventually the FND.
Consolidation of evidence base for initial, alternative or both hypotheses Keep testing out both hypotheses during the therapy as new data streams in.	As the therapy progresses, implementation of panic and couple's strategies are effective in reducing the dissociative episodes. You are becoming more confident that both hypotheses explain the FND.
Firm up conclusions of the best fitting hypothesis for the FND	The final conclusion is that the dissociative episodes are driven by both panic and interpersonal triggers.

it achieves the goal for the person to feel heard, believed and cared for and understand FND through these means. This experience may be new for the person, in the context of not having felt heard during their upbringing, and later during healthcare appointments and in unhelpful personal relationships. Establishing a safe and trusted relationship this way will enable and give the clinician permission to push the person further and achieve better outcomes. Although it may feel as if the assessment overspills into the treatment, it may be a good "investment" for better progress later in therapy and you can legitimately view the assessment as the intervention. Relationships is a core topic in FND treatment.

Modelling: providing the opposite experience

The PCM greatly emphasises the social functions of FND. As clinicians, we are part of the person's social environment, and therefore, we need to take into account the fact that people with FND often report a difficult or traumatic upbringing and subsequent adverse experiences in adulthood. As a clinician, it is important to reflect and connect with the features of these past relationships as they can play out in your therapeutic relationship. Below the features of experiences from childhood or past personal relationships in adulthood will be listed that have often been reported by people with FND in therapy. Beside the feature, the "antidote" will be named and you will learn how to incorporate this antidote in your own clinical practice. Take this opportunity to model a good relationship through the therapeutic relationship.

Childhood rejection and being singled out during abusive or bullying experiences: Dishonour, humiliation, degradation, and treated as worthless

Antidote: Unconditional positive regard, minimising rejection experiences, dignity

Use the therapeutic relationship to show the person unconditional positive regard. Remain compassionate, calm and validating, irrespective of the person's negative feelings and responses towards you (e.g. anger, dismissing strategies you suggest). This may require a lot of effort, particularly if the person is heavily defended against psychology or even hostile. This is a great opportunity to show the non-judgemental character of a psychologist.

To minimise rejection and singling out a person *again*, it is also a good idea to emphasise one of the core principles of the PCM and reciprocal reinforcement: FND is a problem that everyone contributes to including the "patient", family, friends and healthcare staff. Therefore, every member directly in relation to the person with FND carries a responsibility towards recovery. The recovery process does not just pertain to the individual but the entire system.

Lack of trust, incongruity and insincerity

Antidote: Build trust, congruence, genuineness

Does your expression and demeanour towards the person with FND match the honest thoughts and feelings you experience? Are you authentic? This is a very important concept in FND as many healthcare professionals have presumptions and negative attitudes towards people with FND that may inadvertently and unwillingly permeate through communications. Ask yourself whether there is any evidence that you may not be authentic with the person, for example are you engaging in behaviours towards the person that are

Table 4.34 Clinical examples of "feeling heard" vs "feeling hurt"

Feeling heard	Feeling hurt
I believe you, your symptoms are not deliberately put on.	(Inadvertently) making the person feel with verbal and non-verbal language as if you don't believe them: being short with the person, deep sigh, rolling your eyes.
Your symptoms are real. Acknowledge the reality of the person's symptoms ("your symptoms are happening right in front of me/I can see your symptoms, of course they are real, no doubt about that") but simultaneously highlight the absence of an organic reason ("your symptoms are real though not caused by an injury to your brain – different than for someone with a stroke or MS" "However, you should know that it does not make your symptoms less valid or important, they just have a different origin").	Keep on hammering that the video EEG has come back negative/that the MRI is clear and there is nothing organic about the symptoms.
I won't judge you or your condition, I can see that having FND has been difficult for you. I know that people don't always like to see a psychologist because of the stigma and often think that this means that they are not being believed, but I'm here to help you. Would you mind me explaining a bit more and tell you what we do here? I'd really appreciate your time.	Psychology is the core treatment for FND, it's a psychological condition. Without psychology, you are unlikely to make many gains. Better attend the psychology sessions for your own good.
I know that a lot of people with FND have had difficult experiences in the healthcare system, especially with not being believed. Maybe you have had more of these experiences outside healthcare. I would like to give you a different experience.	Not affirming, acknowledging and engaging with their difficult experiences in healthcare but brushing over it during the assessment.
If there is anything that I say or do that makes you think I don't believe you or makes you feel unheard, would you please be able to let me know? How will I know? Don't worry about speaking up, I want to make sure that we are on the same page, we are a team.	Not repairing a potential rupture in the therapeutic relationship due to the person not believing you that you believe them.
There is a lot to explore and I want to make sure that I hear your views, thoughts and feelings in the best way possible: shall we take our time and continue with the rest of the questions next time?	Pushing on with questions.

opposite to the Rogerian principle of genuineness? A good way to find out is to apply the PCM on yourself.

Be patient and keep in mind a person's background, in terms of both early experiences and systemic re-traumatisation: building trust takes time. Allow yourself to focus the first few sessions on engagement rather than "therapy". Consider engagement building the actual therapy, as relationships are often a vulnerable area in FND. A person who is engaging with you is making gains:

with gradual trust, they may learn to express their feelings better, maybe even for the first time. Therefore, time is never wasted on working on engagement in FND.

Emotional neglect: lack of compassion, empathy and feeling cared for

Antidote: Compassion, empathy, care, collaboration and appropriate boundaries.

A caregiver may not have met the physical and emotional care needs of the person with FND in childhood, "leaving the person to their own devices" without support. As a clinician, emphasise the opposite by cultivating a sense of collaboration and togetherness. Showing a willingness to collaborate and care for the person whilst remaining compassionate, regardless of their resistance against psychology, raises your chances of improved collaboration and acceptance of a psychological perspective in the future. A subset of people may have had a physical diagnosis for many years before it switched to FND (e.g. epilepsy) and may be going through an adjustment process. Show empathy for the person, actively imagining what it must feel like standing in the person's shoes, in the context of stigma on mental health and the way it can elicit anger. A history of emotional neglect may also result in a high level of care-eliciting behaviours and dependency on the environment. Emphasising a more equal relationship by setting boundaries and encouraging independence can be very powerful. Helpful phrases include the following:

- "You are not feeling well, how about we try to find ways to help you feel better, even if these are psychological?"
- "I'm on your team, on your side" "I'm team [insert name of patient]".
- "You know yourself best, I know a few psychological strategies, why don't we team up and see how far we get?"
- "I can see that this is really upsetting to hear for you, I would like to help you work through this, shall we do this together?"
- "We are on a journey together. Not me doing things to you. We are working through the FND together, as a team".
- Communicate that you care for the person's needs from a therapeutic point of view "I really want to support you and help you reach your goals, live life to the full".
- "I feel that you have a lot of amazing talents and skills that have been suppressed by the FND, I look forward to supporting you with living your life to the full".

Poor role models for emotional coping and relationships – chronic invalidation and criticism around emotional expression: negative emotions, hostility and conflict in the family home

Antidote: Validation of emotions

Some people with FND experience high levels of dissociation and suppression of emotions, which may come out during the therapy process: they are learning to open up the cover of their pressure cooker. Reflect the expression of negative emotions back to the person. Praise them for expressing their emotions in that situation.

- "I think you have done really well in the session today, opening up about difficult thoughts and feelings to a stranger is not easy".
- "I notice that you are upset, would you mind sharing with me what you are thinking and maybe feeling?"
- Ask for permission: "Are you willing to share what you just felt / together have a go at identifying what you felt?"
- Resolving conflicts in a compassionate way whilst you show the person "I'm here with you, I'm holding this".
- If there is a rupture in the therapeutic relationship, use this therapeutically to explore this together with a view of learning how to mend.

Making promises but never delivering

Antidote: Being dependable and reliable

People with FND may report having had an inconsistently available parent (e.g. a parent promising to pick up their child but not doing so on a systematic basis). It is of utmost importance that when you promise, you deliver. What may seem like a small comment "I will call you later this week" but a crisis has come through which prevented you from contacting the person, or "Please complete this homework and we will discuss next week" but not doing so may have a major impact on and "re-trigger" an individual that has been through these adverse childhood experiences.

Childhood abandonment or a loss of an important person through death or separation

Antidote: Object constancy, careful handling of discharge and endings.

People with FND report abandonment experiences in childhood and (perceived) abandonment as part of later healthcare experiences. Examples include discharge from services, referrals not crystallising, results from investigations not shared, but also cancellations and holidays.

In this day and age with long waiting lists and high pressures to discharge, it is important to consider what this may mean to a person where a parental key figure has "discharged" from the family of origin. Keep in mind that some people with FND have had long journeys in the health system, often characterised by short bursts of treatment, for example a time-limited three week rehab programme, a course of psychological therapy sessions, perhaps another course in a different modality, "islands" of allied health input. The common denominator between these experiences is often starting a relationship with a stranger, feeling more comfortable and validated with the clinician, and a subsequent break in the attachment, which feeds into a life-long rejection theme for some people with FND. Occasionally, this may be misinterpreted as "doctor shopping" and the patient blamed where in fact the system is contributing in major ways by the structural problems of services and clinicians unaware of FND.

If a person with FND is due to be discharged from a service, keep in mind common themes associated with abandonment around low self-esteem, rejection, not feeling cared for and attachment anxiety. Discharge can be considered as another break in attachment (think about a person having being taken into care or lost a parent). It is not uncommon for FND symptoms and distress to become amplified before a discharge date, which is often directly associated with a sense of abandonment as well as fears around lacking confidence and ability to cope with symptoms on your own (without the attachment figure present). Use this therapeutically and formulate with the person what is happening for them. Offer one or two booster or check-in sessions following discharge. You can also agree to space out the sessions in later stages of the therapy to ease the transition after discharge from the service.

Unpredictability

Antidote: Prediction

Prediction and holding onto a routine may be psychologically containing, especially if unpredictability was common in childhood. Examples of preserving prediction in therapy include providing a fixed weekly therapy slot that is not tampered with, setting an agenda and giving an advanced warning of an upcoming discharge or clinician leave.

Not being believed and secrecy by a key family figure, for example in the context of abuse.

Antidote: Transparency and honesty

- Acknowledge to the patient that you are aware that some healthcare workers wrongly believe that FND patients fake symptoms or put them on. Communicate with the person "I believe you", "I know you are not making your symptoms up".
- The formulation is sometimes a difficult truth to share particularly when it involves interpersonal triggers and the FND being part of a psychological safety behaviour. However, with a trusted therapeutic relationship, these "uncomfortable truths" can ultimately be shared for the benefit of the person's recovery. More importantly, these communications are characterised by honesty and do not mirror a person's background.
- Don't battle with the person, even if you think you are right. Battling is different from gently challenging. By battling you are effectively saying to the person: "I don't believe you and what you say, here's how it is".
- Pre-empt the widely held view that accessing psychology may mean that the person does not feel believed.

- Be mindful that as a clinician you may make things worse when pushing a formulation that a patient does not identify with; for example, the person experiences social anxiety with obvious physical features and safety behaviours but is dissociating from the emotion. The worst thing is to push that formulation onto the person. The formulation may be completely true and correct in your mind but pushing may mean not believing the person. Instead of tackling the social anxiety, the intervention becomes centred around raising insight into the dissociation from anxiety whilst ensuring the relationship stays intact.
- Trickery is not acceptable. Don't say that FND is all organic where in fact it is not. Don't use code words in letters as this may remind someone of the secrecy that used to surround sensitive topics in childhood.

Lack of well-defined boundaries in the family of origin: overinvolvement and enmeshment

Antidote: Setting boundaries, even if boundaries are pushed against

A subset of people with FND will have experienced or still experience enmeshed relational patterns within the family unit. Modelling relationships with appropriate boundaries may be a very important therapeutic experience for a person used to enmeshment. Examples include ending your sessions on time, setting boundaries around the emergence of severe FND symptoms, and in the context of deliberate self-harm and other behaviours that interfere in major ways with therapy or rehabilitation, for example functional tremor or dissociative episodes stopping progress in a session or stalling therapy. Contracts around disattending those symptoms, stopping the sessions or deferring to the week after, as agreed and signed by patient and clinician, can be helpful. Boundary setting may also be important for colleagues who may struggle with setting boundaries or when family members are overinvolved with the person's care, for example ensuring that the person with FND has their own confidential space that is not violated by requests from the "family carer".

Placing and adhering to appropriate boundaries is crucial in therapy. Even if misperceived as rejection, experienced as highly aversive by the patient and heavily pushed against (e.g. person may become rejecting to you), boundaries provide psychological containment and a sense of predictability, particularly if these boundaries are consistently reinforced during next sessions whilst you remain kind, respectful, gentle, compassionate and caring towards the person, who will receive this as "the clinician is not rejecting or abandoning me". This is a powerful tool to build trust and strengthen your therapeutic relationship with the person.

> At the end of an assessment or therapy session, always ask yourself the question: Have I created a space of psychological safety that enables the person with FND to feel heard, validated and respected?

PCM treatment techniques

The section below provides a snapshot of useful treatment techniques for FND. Book 2 will discuss these techniques in a more comprehensive manner; however, a few will be highlighted below.

Principles of reinforcement: a person-friendly explanation

See Table 4.35.

Behavioural experiments in FND: what to look out for

A core part of FND treatment is often the undertaking of behavioural experiments (BEs). There are several similarities between the structure of BEs conducted in psychological conditions such as social anxiety and panic disorder, and those conducted with FND patients, for example:

- Identification of the person's worst-case scenario, beliefs and emotions.
- Identification of safety behaviours that maintain the distress.
- The idea of tolerating an emotion or an internal state of discomfort without resorting to the use of safety behaviours.

However, in spite of these similarities, some crucial differences exist that are worth mentioning.

Safety behaviours are often the FND symptom

In a regular BE, the safety behaviour to be dropped is often dropping avoidance or escape of situations, or not using distraction techniques, for example dropping the use of breathing exercises or counting exercises during a panic attack. Safety behaviours to be dropped in FND are often the actual FND symptom. For example, a person asked to "drop" a dissociative episode or functional leg weakness equals the person learning to tolerate the underlying distress and discomfort for a gradually increasing period of time without the emotion being followed by the response (FND). Keep in mind that helping the person to drop this safety behaviour (FND) will remove, especially for some people, a longstanding and ingrained coping habit that comes natural to the person. Ensure that you help the person with selecting and practising a competing response that can replace the FND (i.e. the top parts of the PCM will be key in this process, including verbal emotional expression and adjusting abnormal activity levels).

Safety behaviours can be introduced

Reality grounding techniques are often introduced in BEs with FND patients. Although they are commonly considered safety behaviours in

John's dissociative episodes

- **Trigger/Before the seizure:** John has an argument with Sally. He starts to feel more and more unwell: an unpleasant feeling is building up and is becoming more intense. He experiences tingling, a headache and sweating all over his body.

- **John thinks:** "Oh no, here we go again, another seizure!"

- **John's emotions:** He can't define the feeling but what he does know: it's unpleasant and strong.

- John has the seizure

- **After the seizure:** John feels drained and tired. Since he feels fatigued, he does not experience the unpleasant feeling anymore. The argument with Sally has also stopped.

- He goes to bed for a nap

- John's aversive internal state ➜ seizure ➜ relief from the unpleasant state (and the argument)

- John's seizure took away something unpleasant (=internal state + argument)

Table 4.35 Explanation of reinforcement principles in the context of dissociative episodes

How dissociative episodes sometimes work

Suppose you have a headache. Taking a painkiller (=coping strategy) takes away something unpleasant (=headache) and you feel relief.	John feels unwell and has an argument. John's seizure (=coping strategy) took away something unpleasant (=feeling unwell + argument) and gave him relief.
Next time you have a headache, you'll likely use the same coping strategy again (=taking a painkiller) – as it worked well in the past.	Next time John feels unwell/there is an argument, he'll more likely have a seizure, it gave him relief last time.

regular experiments, they are not automatically assumed to be safety behaviours in FND experiments. In order to "drop" a dissociative symptom as the safety behaviour, a person is often required to introduce reality grounding techniques to do exactly that, that is, emerge from the dissociative state.

Behavioural experiments beyond anxiety

Although regular BEs tend to be used in the context of treatment of anxiety disorders, such as panic or social anxiety disorder, BEs and hierarchies in FND are not exclusively intended for anxiety but are applied on a wider spectrum of emotions including social emotions such as guilt. Furthermore, alexithymia and dissociation often prevent the person with FND from being able to identify and label emotions. A BE in FND is still applied to undefined emotions or an "unpleasant internal state" (which often is anxiety but not always).

Behavioural experiments in social context

Although in regular BEs, people can act as safety behaviours (e.g. a person with social anxiety who only goes shopping with other people), the social context, attachments and relationships with other people are often the core focus in BEs for FND, even in situations where clear-cut anxiety is identified. The relational "uncoupling" process between a person with FND and their environment as part of the BE and tolerating an uncomfortable internal state can be the intervention.

Example: a guilt hierarchy

> Angela feels high levels of a mixture of anxiety and guilt when she has to ask people in her environment for support or act in an assertive manner by stating her needs, particularly if these are violated or overridden by others. Angela worries about burdening or letting other people down. When she finds herself in these situations, Angela feels her guilt building up quickly, almost like a "crescendo of guilt". This is subsequently followed by FND, i.e. functional bilateral leg weakness with Angela collapsing on the floor. Following the episode, it takes several days for Angela to recuperate from the FND. Angela's psychologist suggested that they work on creating a "guilt hierarchy" consisting of a graded step ladder of interpersonal situations that elicit guilt to varying degrees, running from 0% guilt to 100% guilt, with 10% incremental steps in between. In the same way as with a regular anxiety hierarchy, Angela gradually worked her way up the hierarchy by trying to drop her safety behaviours by not avoiding the interpersonal situation and using her reality grounding techniques to nip the leg weakness in the bud when the first warning signs appeared.

Paradoxical reinforcement

When managing a dissociative episode, a tension often arises between intervening with the episode in the moment vs disattending by withdrawal of care and "leaving the person to it". A commonly used intervention technique in these situations is reality grounding, for example helping to re-orient the person to where they are and what is happening; mentioning that the person's fight-or-flight response is "in overdrive" to help understand what may be happening in their body; and using the five senses to ground the person in their surroundings ("tell me 5 things you can see, 4 things you can hear...."). Although reality grounding techniques in response to dissociative symptoms could help to "get the person back" and therefore reduce their FND symptoms/dissociation in the short term, intervening in the moment simultaneously risks paradoxically reinforcing FND symptoms in the long term. The person learns that when they experience an FND symptom and this is followed by meaningful reinforcement (e.g. an act of care by a staff member who helps to apply reality grounding strategies), this increases the likelihood and frequency of the FND symptom to re-emerge in future.

How can we help the person to cope with dissociation and FND whilst at the same time not reinforce the FND? There are generally two approaches to resolving this tension: a quick shift vs slow wean.

"Quick shift" approach #1

In a quick shift approach, reality grounding techniques are regularly and intensively practised in advance with the person when they are in an emotionally settled state, feeling relatively well or seizure-free. The moment a dissociative episode emerges, staff or family members follow a strict behavioural model. An agreement is made in advance with the person around the procedural aspects of the intervention, for example, "when you start to experience a dissociative episode, in first instance try using your reality grounding techniques" "if the episode gradually unfolds or persists, we will ensure that you are safe from harm by helping you to lay down on a flat surface and reduce your risk of injury but we will cease all other care, e.g. not speak to you or provide reassurance, hold your hand." If possible, subsequently increase physical distance, disattend the FND (i.e. stop any form of reinforcement) and have the person manage the situation entirely on their own. A quick shift approach would work with someone who exhibits FND symptoms where the person may not be able to engage in a conversation and is at risk of no or minimal injury (where they can be safely left alone for a period of time), or with a person who has agreed to pursue this line of intervention with you and with whom you have co-developed seizure guidelines for the environment to follow.

What could be the problems of a quick shift approach for patients that are
less severe?

A quick shift approach may feed into rejection and abandonment concerns for the person, especially if introduced too soon without a fully established and trusted therapeutic relationship. The intervention may feel as too harsh and counter-intuitive for both person and environment resulting in a loss of faith in the treatment and problems for the environment in managing their own strong emotions or distress around disattending. This may lead to an inconsistent application of the principles. When people are unsure about the quick shift approach, the behaviour may become intermittently reinforced, which makes it harder to extinguish the behaviour over time.

In order to cope with "the quick shift", the person may learn or temporarily rely on other unhelpful coping strategies that helps them to avoid experiencing negative emotions (e.g. distraction techniques), whereas what they truly need is to experientially go through the process of learning to sit with and tolerate the discomfort of their unpleasant internal state rather than escape with distraction or FND.

FND may be a person's longstanding and entrenched coping strategy that has been learned and consolidated over many years of practice. They may not have had access or opportunities for learning other stress-coping strategies.

Asking a person to drop their familiar coping habit overnight may be a tall order, and it is unrealistic to expect this to happen quickly and smoothly. The person might find it difficult to part ways with FND because of its reinforcing internal and external regulation functions as it is helping the person (1) with reducing anxiety quickly and effectively, and simultaneously (2) enabling them feel validated and supported by the environment. It will take a considerable amount of time to undo ingrained patterns of coping. A quick shift approach may feel too brittle and unstable; the person may easily fall back on the FND as a coping habit again. It is therefore important to offer a reasonable and meaningful alternative response that can "compete with the FND" as a coping habit. Examples of alternative responses to FND include expressing emotions in a psychologically safe relationship to another person ("opening the cover") or via constructive activities (unblocking, regulating or alleviating the valve) rather than expressing them via the body, as well as feeling and experiencing emotions ("staying with them", slowly turning down the temperature of the Heat) rather than avoiding or escaping them via FND. This alternative and competing response needs to be practised over a period of time in order to consolidate, as with any new skill that needs to become a more automatic habit.

"Slow wean" approach #2: from co-regulation to regulation

In contrast to a quick shift approach, a slow wean may be a more appropriate and softer approach to managing FND symptoms. The slow wean approach consists of series of phases:

Preparatory phase

1 Teach and practise alternative emotion regulation skills with the person, for example reality grounding to apply when the first signs of an episode start to emerge; verbal emotional expression and labelling of emotions; or regular constructive stress release via enjoyable activities. The person needs to practise these skills regularly and particularly when not currently in a heightened overwhelmed state, which impairs cognitive functioning, for example learning new knowledge and laying down new memories.
2 Establish with the person what their warning signs are: Is there anything happening in their body or mind that tells them an FND symptom or dissociative episode is about to emerge or worsen? (e.g. motor tremor). Make a list of warning signs. Provide explanation on the fight-or-flight response. (If the person does not report any warning signs, which is common, ask for a witness to comment or make behavioural observations if possible.)

Co-regulate with the person: apply the strategies together initially

3 In the beginning, use the already regularly practised "early warning phase" or more adaptive emotional regulation skills with the person

when they start to dissociate or experience FND symptoms, to help them apply the skills "in the moment", especially if they have not done that before. The person needs to have a chance to practise with another person who has knowledge and experience of these skills and can guide them and problem-solve any issues that pop up. You could do that a few times with the person so that they "get the hang of it".

Move from co-regulation to independent regulation and application of skills

4   Timing is important: there comes a moment where you need to decide that it would be useful for the person to slowly start the independent regulation of their emotions and find psychological safety on their own – without your presence. Be open and honest about that moment and explore any barriers to "cutting the cord".

5   Explain the rationale to the person with respect to independently managing the FND symptoms as tapping into their own coping skill-set and without having to rely on another person, who may not always be around. Agree on a time that this process of "disconnecting from the person" and independent practice with applying strategies on their own will start, once warning signs emerge or the episode has started to progress so that they are prepared.

Encourage the person to start to consistently apply independent regulation

6   A prompt may be helpful: a quick phrase once the person starts dissociating or an FND episode is imminent: "pick a strategy that you're going to use now" and then stop the verbal support. You can have a visual display of coping strategies that you show them – without verbal support.

Once the person starts to independently regulate and apply their skills

7   Drop the prompt altogether: you can drop the "quick phrase"/visual display of strategies and don't say anything. This will help to build confidence in the person and give them an opportunity to practise their skills without the environment jumping in.

8   Once the person with FND has started to regularly apply the coping skills for FND on their own accord, the key is to keep practising and consolidate the skills.

9   Praise and reinforce each time the person uses their newly acquired and more adaptive coping strategies.

Advice

•   These phases may not follow a strict sequence and are intended as a rough guideline to help make a start with managing the FND. Some people may skip phases or prefer to stay longer in one phase.

- The process may stall or the person's symptoms become temporarily worse (as part of an extinction burst), particularly once you start to distance yourself from "co-regulating the person's emotions" and transition towards independently practising strategies: the person that practises the skills with the patient may inadvertently serve as a psychological safety behaviour. Sometimes, the biggest issue is family or staff tolerating their own emotions as it feels counter-intuitive.
- Allow for trial and error: the strategies may not work or not work immediately since new habits are being formed that need time and effort to consolidate and become more automatic.

Hybrid pressure cooker treatment plan

If we operate under the assumption that FND is caused by both the person and the environment, then the best way to assess and treat FND is by taking into consideration the biopsychosocial processes of both sides and avoid a solitary focus on just the person with FND. Although time and resource pressures in the healthcare system often prevent a more systemic approach to FND, the key to an effective and optimal (rather than suboptimal) intervention in FND revolves around the relationships between the person and their environment, often the missing piece of the FND-puzzle. Your PCM formulation of the person and environment with FND will guide your treatment plan.

What are other advantages of adopting a hybrid treatment approach?

- Seeing hybrid formulation and treatment plans side-by-side on paper can be an eye-opener and provide major insights into the maintaining factors of FND to the person with FND and their environment. These plans instantly demonstrate what the pressure points are and what needs to be done to relieve the pressure.
- It will also help recruit the environment as an "FND ally" in recovery.
- It shifts the "blame" for FND away from the person with FND, thus reducing the risk of reciprocal reinforcement and systemic re-traumatisation, which are two maintaining factors of FND. The hybrid plan inherently stipulates that both the person and their environment are responsible for the person's recovery.
- A description of the exact details in the treatment plan will serve as a reminder as to what everyone's role in FND recovery involves and hold everyone accountable to the plan – especially important in situations of high distress, which can greatly impact on thinking skills. Every participant will have clearly outlined roles and responsibilities and their part to play in FND recovery.

It should be noted that in day-to-day practice, it is not always possible to include "the other person" in a hybrid plan for various reasons including patient reluctance of involving their family; not wanting to burden family; or unwillingness of family to participate and engage with the plan. These situations can potentially halt or adversely impact the recovery from FND in other ways (Table 4.36).

Rather than going through each of the PCM elements, you can also opt to create a hybrid PCM treatment plan that makes use of the five-layer structure of the PCM and describes what each person's roles and responsibilities are on each layer (Table 4.37):

Table 4.36 Hybrid PCM treatment plan by Element

Elements	Person with FND	Person close to the person with FND
Overpressure Plug	**What does the FND look like?** I have dissociative episodes and no feeling or strength in my left arm and leg. I also experience pain in my limbs and a brain fog.	**What do my unhelpful responses look like?** I am involved with caring for my partner who feels unwell with FND. Sometimes, I take a lot of tasks out of her hands and won't let her do personal care or chores. I always keep an eye out and make sure that there is always one other person with her, 24 hours a day.
Ignition	**What events in my life created the vulnerabilities towards developing FND and what do I need to take into account?** My early experiences of emotional neglect. In my childhood, I have not had the opportunities to learn how to cope with difficult thoughts and feelings. I probably need to be mindful of when I am using my "old" coping habits (like keeping myself to myself and dissociation – which were useful and protective whilst growing up but have lost some of its functions at present).	**What events in my life created the vulnerabilities towards my unhelpful responses and what do I need to take into account?** I grew up in a caring and compassionate family. Caring for my partner is really important. Not doing things for her in the household/not being there for her makes me feel uncaring towards her. I know that if I want my partner to become more independent, I have to allow my partner to do some tasks for herself, without me intruding or helping.
Fuel	**What triggers the FND?** I have identified several triggers: (1) physical symptoms in my body such as dizziness, heart racing, sweaty palms, muscle pain, and feeling distant and cut off from the world and (2) interpersonal triggers, particularly arguments with family members or when I feel left alone in the household and difficult thoughts and feelings come trickling in.	**What triggers my unhelpful responses?** Whenever my partner experiences an episode, I drop everything and run to her to reassure her and hold her hand. I now know this feeds the episodes and I should be standing back and let the episode run its course.

Elements	Person with FND	Person close to the person with FND
		Ways I can cope with stopping my unhelpful responses: • If I spot the first signs of a dissociative episode in my partner, I will keep her safe from harm and can direct her to reality grounding exercises but I will stand back after that. • Tell myself that standing back will help my partner better and beat the FND than not standing back. I am actually helping her to recover from FND by not feeding it. I will think about all the enjoyable things we will be able to do once she recovers from the episodes/or if the frequency goes down again, for example visiting the sea side, shopping, spending quality time with family. • If I feel conflicted, I will tell myself that this is normal and that it's ok to not feel ok about this approach. I will not give myself a hard time if I stray from the treatment plan.
	Ways I can cope with my triggers: For trigger (1): I know this is like a panic attack. I will tell myself it's my fight-or-flight response in overdrive and it's a natural biological response. I will use my reality grounding techniques to bring myself back and connect myself with the world again and tolerate the discomfort, to nip any dissociative episode in the bud. For trigger (2): during an argument, the same physical symptoms appear. I will try to label my emotions to help me connect with them. If I start to experience my first warning signs, I will immediately use my reality grounding techniques. I will tell my family not to rally around me or reassure me in any kind of way, because this feeds into the episode. I can also try to extract myself from the argument temporarily until things have calmed down ("the 20 minute rule").	
Flames	**What type of thoughts and feelings do I experience? What can I do about them?** I don't really feel anything to be fair. It's all one big blank screen for me. The best thing I can do is to continue with practising my emotion labelling exercises. I will ask my partner for help to complete these exercises together.	**What type of thoughts and feelings do I experience? What can I do about them?** I often worry about my partner whether she's overexerting herself and frankly that she will have another fit if she overdoes it. I will write down my worries in a worry diary.

(Continued)

Table 4.36 (Continued)

Elements	Person with FND	Person close to the person with FND
Heat	**How strong do my emotions get? What can I do to take it down – without FND?** • I feel an overwhelming feeling coming up that I can't really describe. It's very unpleasant and I just want to escape it as quickly as possible. • I will try to "surf the emotion-flame" as long as possible and sit with the discomfort of that feeling until it starts to reduce again. As much as I feel very comfortable having my partner around me, to keep an eye out, I will let them know to stand back a bit more.	**How strong do my emotions get? What can I do to take it down – without resorting to my unhelpful behaviours?** • Pretty strong! I feel highly anxious about the prospect of episodes emerging in my partner and I'm always on the outlook for signs. • Although this feels incredibly difficult, I need to control my own anxiety and ask myself whether I'm helping or hurting my partner. My anxiety and own ways of coping (e.g. hypervigilant monitoring of seizure signs, taking things out of her hands) contribute to my partner's FND.
Sticky left-over food	**How did I cope with emotions as a child and have these coping strategies repeated into adulthood?** • Kept myself to myself, "I just did" • I still tend to keep myself to myself although I feel more comfortable expressing emotions to my partner.	**How did I cope with emotions as a child and have these coping strategies repeated into adulthood?** • Same, I kept myself mostly to myself and that is still the case. That was the way we coped in my family of origin, very practical. My partner and I make more of an effort to check in with each other's feelings although it still feels a bit strange, as we're not really talkers by nature.
Warning light	**Am I quite focused on the symptoms, such as talking about them a lot, or looking them up on the internet, hypervigilant monitoring?** • I do speak a lot about my symptoms and consult Dr Internet almost on a daily basis, as my symptoms tend to be changeable. I like to spend time on FND fora for peer support.	**Is the system around me, my family or loved ones, on the look-out for my symptoms? What can I do to change this?** • Yes, I am always near my partner, just in case she has a fit or needs my help with an activity at home. I make sure there is always someone around in the house "24 supervision".

Elements	Person with FND	Person close to the person with FND
	• I will engage a bit less with FND online and during conversations and re-direct my attention away by doing something creative or work in the garden. • My partner will help me raise insight into my self-focused attention. Whenever I talk too much about my symptoms, they will point this out to me.	• I will stand back more and try to meet up with lost friends so that I'm not always around in the house. My partner's treating team has reassured me that it is safe to leave her on her own for periods of time during the day. I started to rekindle some old friendships.
Pot	**Are there any biological factors that make me vulnerable to FND? What are my warning signs?** • I drink a lot of caffeine and I am not a great sleeper: I have trouble falling asleep and wake up multiple times at night. I will try to observe better sleep hygiene and cut down on caffeine which can give me palpitations and may contribute to the episodes. • Feeling distant and cut off from the world is often a big warning sign for an episode.	**Or that start to impact on me due to the caring?** • I've started to feel quite tired recently. Like my partner, I am a light sleeper and suffer from insomnia. We tend to go to bed at night at different times and drink coffee after dinner. We are going to trial going to bed at roughly the same time everyday and cut out caffeine.
Cover	**Do I speak to someone about difficult thoughts and feelings on a regular basis? Do I have a trusted and safe relationship(s) where I can express my emotions without feeling invalidated or embarrassed?** • I speak to my partner a lot about the FND and my symptoms but not really about difficult thoughts and emotions. We are in the process of trying to change that and slowly started practising. It's feels a bit weird but we know that this is the key to fewer dissociative episodes.	**Same question** • Although we're both not great talkers, we have started to open up a bit more to one another about emotions. My partner struggles identifying what she feels and I help her make sense of her emotions.

(Continued)

Table 4.36 (Continued)

Elements	Person with FND	Person close to the person with FND
Valve	**Can I say anything about my activity levels, in terms of meaningful, productive, enjoyable, rest and relaxing, and social activities? Am I bust-after-boom, boom-and-bust, or boom?** • I'm a "bust-after-boom" for sure and have not much on in my daily schedule of activities. I can try to plan in an enjoyable activity a day and stick to it. • My partner is a boom and is always on the go. He needs to slow down. I am going to actively tell him to go out with his friends/do his football and have some "me-time".	**Can I say anything about my activity levels, in terms of meaningful, productive, enjoyable, rest and relaxing, and social activities? Am I bust-after-boom, boom-and-bust or boom?** • I'm definitely a "boom" and always on the go. I hold down a job and I do some of the care for my partner, it's quite full on. We are each other mirror images for sure. I feel guilty leaving my partner on her own and I worry she won't manage the seizures without me. • I will make an effort to see my friends once a week. I will tell myself "if I want to be a good carer to my partner, I need to care for myself first and not burn out".
Kitchen	**What are the social functions of the FND? Are these impacting on the FND?** • The episodes help me to cope with difficult and strong emotions in the first place. The episodes are coping strategies that help me feel less uncomfortable in the moment and they quickly take away those unpleasant feelings. Yet, in the long run, these strategies are not helpful, for example they stand in the way of living my life to the full. • The episodes are also very effective in helping to stop arguments at home. Instead of people shouting, everyone stops, holds my hand and is kind to me, which feels like a relief. Yet, this is not a long-term strategy to use. • My family can help me use my strategies, and they can help me by communicating better with each other.	**What are the social functions of the caring responses? Are these contributing to the FND?** • Although it's well-intended and understandable, I know that my overinvolvement in my partner's care will only make her more dependent. Caring for my partner also manages my own anxiety; I just want the seizures to stop as quickly as possible because I don't want to see my partner in distress. Maybe it's more about me sometimes than about her!

Elements	Person with FND	Person close to the person with FND
Safety features	**What are my positive qualities, what do I have going for me that can help tackle the FND?** • I'm motivated to get better from the FND and engaged with the treatments.	**What are my positive qualities, what do I have going for me that can help tackle the FND?** • I'm committed to helping my partner get better from the FND even if that means withholding my own reactions and leaving her to it. I am fully on board with the treatment.

Table 4.37 Hybrid PCM treatment plan by Layer

Layer	Person with FND	Person close to the person with FND
#1	**What made me vulnerable to developing FND in the first place?** • Strict upbringing • Emotional neglect, witnessed domestic violence • Our family was more into practical and problem-solving solutions than speaking about emotions.	**What made me vulnerable towards developing some of the unhelpful responses to the person?** (*please note: everyone will have vulnerabilities – not just the person with FND*). • I come from a caring family and not being vigilant to the seizure makes me feel guilty or anxious. • My family was neglectful and I vowed to never do that to a future partner. • I've not always been nice to my partner/mistreated them/worked really hard and not paid much attention, I feel I have to pull out all stops to ensure they are ok.
#2	**The FND Coping Triad** *What does the triad look like in terms of the Cover, Valve and Sticky left-over food? What can you and your family do to change this?* • For example, I share a lot of my emotions, maybe too much, but I don't share how I truly feel about the issues that I'm grappling with (making the Cover still tight rather than loose). My Valve may be "bust-after-boom", I used to be very active but mostly spend my days indoors and had to stop working because of my symptoms. Sticky left-over food-wise, me and my family of origin always kept emotions to themselves. The circumstances did not allow me to express emotions.	**The Coping Triad that contributes to FND and to my own psychological well-being** *What does your triad look like, and like the person with FND, can you delineate the Cover, Valve and Sticky left-over food? Do you see any similarities or differences? What can you learn from each other?* • For example, I'm not a talker (tight Cover) and never have been (Sticky left-over food). I don't have any other means to release what I feel inside (blocked Valve). It looks like me and my partner are more similar than I thought! We share the same coping strategies. It's not an "FND thing", it's a thing that affects all of us.

(Continued)

Table 4.37 (Continued)

Layer	Person with FND	Person close to the person with FND
	• => I guess we need to open our Covers a bit more and unblock both of our Valves: a daily "emotion" check-in with each other, telling my partner what's really bothering me, and some more me-time separately from each other.	• → We should make more of an effort to talk about our emotions, it will be tough, as I'm not really used to it, but if it helps to reduce the FND, then I'm willing to try. It may help me to view emotions differently/more positively as well.
#3	**The Pressure Cooker Chain Reaction**	**The Pressure Cooker Chain Reaction**
	• *What does the PCCR look like in the context of FND symptoms? Describe the Fuel, Flames, Heat and Overpressure Plug.*	• *What does the PCCR look like in the context of unhelpful behaviours that contribute to the FND? Describe the Fuel, Flames, Heat and Overpressure Plug. For example, witnessing a seizure/ distress in my loved one (Fuel) I feel highly anxious (Flames and Heat), and as a result, I tend to be hypervigilant and watch them all the time (Overpressure Plug). I don't have time for hobbies or meet friends because I feel anxious and guilty leaving my partner on their own (blocked Valve) and don't express this to my partner because I don't want to hurt and burden them (tight Cover).*
	• *Looking the PCCR, what steps can you take to break the links between elements? For example, can you take away the Fuel and temporarily remove yourself from a difficult interpersonal situation; blow out the Flames by challenging difficult thoughts; tame the Heat of the Flames by tolerating and sitting with the distress a bit longer; use grounding or relaxation techniques to reduce the impact of a functional tremor or nip a dissociative episode in the bud, block the Overpressure Plug directly?*	• *Looking at the PCCR, what steps can you take to break the links between elements? For example, leave my partner alone for some parts of the day knowing they have the strategies (block the Plug), challenge my own thinking (they are attending therapy regularly and working on their problems, this is more about me; I can care even better if I practice some self-care first; blow out the Flames), spend some time outside the house with my friend whom I have not spoken to in ages (unblock the Valve).*

Layer	Person with FND	Person close to the person with FND
#4	**Facilitating physical factors**	**Facilitating physical factors**

#4 — Person with FND

Facilitating physical factors

What physical factors from the FND SELF CARE acronym contribute to the FND? Can we change anything about these physical factors?

- For example, urge my partner not to call an ambulance or go to A&E each time a dissociative episode appears, request a medication review from my GP, psychiatrist or neurologist.
- I can invite him to join my physiotherapy sessions so he sees what I do and can encourage me to apply my strategies at home.
- We both have poor sleep hygiene, so we need to develop a better sleep routine, we can encourage each other to do that and hold each other accountable if it doesn't work out how we planned!

#4 — Person close to the person with FND

Facilitating physical factors

What physical factors from the FND SELF CARE acronym contribute to the FND and what is my personal FND SELF CARE acronym "assessment"? Can we change anything about these physical factors?

- I can help my partner by not always calling an ambulance and encourage them to not use their wheelchair as often. I can become their close ally that actively supports her in the process of stepping down equipment, by attending her physiotherapy appointments together and taking on board the advice. This will greatly help recovery from FND.
- My personal FND SELF CARE acronym shows me that I have an issue around poor sleep hygiene and lack of exercise that doesn't help my health and fitness levels.

#5 — Person with FND

The FND Kitchen and Social functions of FND

What are the social functions of my FND symptoms and how does my partner or family contribute to the problem? What can I do to manage this better?

- My partner is always around and feels like my "safety blanket". Without my partner, I feel lost and unable to manage the seizures on my own. The social function of the seizures is keeping him close, as my safety blanket, it feels very comfortable and secure – and totally understandable, as it's something that I've not experienced in my childhood.
- Although this feels really tough, I will ask him to stand back a bit more, so I can learn to manage the seizures on my own. I need to have the opportunities to practice, as I really would like to become seizure-free one day and venture out on my own – without needing to rely on others for support.

#5 — Person close to the person with FND

The FND Kitchen and Social functions of FND

Take a good look at your own situation: Is there evidence a "systemic anxiety" or "hypervigilance" present and have reciprocal reinforcement processes been identified that contribute to the maintenance of FND? How can these be managed better?

- Yes, I am anxious around my partner experiencing seizures and I watch her continuously. That does not give her much confidence that she could potentially manage the seizures on her own and makes her more dependent on me, if I'm always hanging around. They may get more anxious too, if they see me freaking out. All of this keeps my partner's FND going.
- I can try to stand back more/ spend time with my friends outdoors, even though it feels counter-intuitive. I need to tolerate my own distress!

Hierarchy of needs

See Figure 4.10.

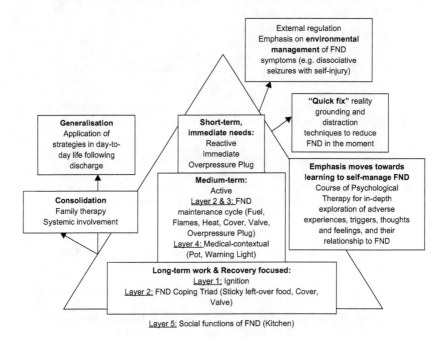

Figure 4.10 Hierarchy of treatment needs in FND.

5   Clinical applications of the Pressure Cooker Model

Case studies

One of the most attractive features of the PCM is the practicality of the model and the relative ease of clinical application in a condition that is commonly viewed as complex and anxiety-provoking in clinical practice. Fully immersed within the PCM perspective and terminology, Chapter 5 will discuss the therapeutic journeys of four distinctive patients with a wide spectrum of FND symptoms. Importantly, it will equally highlight the journey of the system around the person that ultimately contributed and maintained the FND in all these patients and make a strong case for the need to address both person and system during the treatment of FND.

Case study 1: The system is sick...everybody's ill...and FND is a Person × Environment condition: a hybrid application of the Pressure Cooker Model

This first case study will describe the bumpy road that an FND journey can bring and the significance and utility of the PCM formulation in understanding and improving the impact of these bumps on recovery.

Background

Thomas was a 53-year-old male and married with three children. In 2015, he developed FND after learning that a close family member had narrowly survived a car accident. Thomas accessed a year-long course of psychological therapy for post-traumatic stress disorder (PTSD), which failed to improve his psychological well-being and his FND symptoms. He was subsequently referred and admitted to a specialist inpatient unit for an intensive multidisciplinary 12-week programme. Thomas' inpatient medical and therapy team established that, apart from FND, he did not fully meet criteria for an Axis I or II disorder, including PTSD, a diagnosis that was ruled out on two further separate occasions during the admission.

Presenting problems

Thomas experienced a variety of functional motor, sensory, cognitive and dissociative symptoms, alongside other somatic symptoms (see Table 5.1).

DOI: 10.4324/9781003308980-5

Stroke was ruled out as a cause for his symptoms, and investigations revealed no additional disorders. This led to a diagnosis of FND in 2018, based on positive clinical signs. The severity and frequency of his symptoms fluctuated, with "good and bad days", and two- to three-week periods with minimal symptoms. Thomas presented with severe levels of anxiety, low mood, tearfulness, avoidance and a lack of initiation; his FND symptoms worsened during heightened emotional states, supporting a link between emotions and FND. The symptoms significantly impacted on Thomas' day-to-day functioning. He was unable to walk, care for his family, communicate with people or access the community. Thomas stopped all his hobbies and withdrew from social activities. His home was fully adapted to his disabilities; Thomas relied on equipment and his family who offered high levels of support with personal care. He was at risk of falls during mobilising, holding his balance and transfers, and accidental self-injury due to FND symptoms.

Psychosocial history

Thomas grew up in a military family, as the eldest child with one younger brother and a sister. Due to the nature of his father's job, the family lived abroad. His upbringing was characterised by unpredictability; the family moved around regularly, often informed about an impending move at short notice. Thomas' mother suffered from a chronic cardiac condition and provided limited child care. From the age of 10, Thomas became the main carer of the family. Thomas did not recall many positive childhood memories; he described a strict upbringing with emotionally avoidant parents who frequently disciplined the children and failed to respond to their physical and emotional needs. Whilst growing up, Thomas coped with difficult feelings by *"just pushing on"* and *"putting everything into a box"*. Thomas subsequently left the family and met his wife, with whom he raised three children. Although Thomas successfully held down several managerial job roles, he decided to become a full-time caregiver for his own and his extended family. His premorbid functioning was described as independent, outgoing, active, organised and "always on the go", with a rich social life, family holidays and regular football games that helped him to release stress. Following the family member's accident, Thomas' personality changed drastically; he became fully dependent on his environment for his physical and emotional needs.

Assessment

Thomas was assessed by his multidisciplinary treating team consisting of psychology, physiotherapy, neuropsychiatry, occupational therapy, speech and language therapy, dietetics, social work and nursing. Staff-rated neurorehabilitation measures revealed scores of 99/210 on the UK Functional Independence Measure and Functional Assessment Measure (UK FIM+FAM; Turner-Stokes et al., 1999) suggesting high levels of dependency for basic daily activities, personal self-care, toileting, transfers, mobility and communication. Scores also suggested difficulties with social interaction, emotional status, adjustment, problem solving and concentration, reflecting the features of depression. On the Neurological Impairment Scale (NIS; Turner-Stokes et al., 2014), Thomas obtained a score of 20/50, suggesting several physical and cognitive impairments. Thomas self-reported mild anxiety and depressive symptoms on the Hospital Anxiety and Depression Scale (HADS scores 10; Zigmond & Snaith, 1983), which appeared incongruent with his highly distressed presentation on the ward. These scores were likely driven by Thomas' dissociative tendencies and his negative beliefs around emotional expression. An assessment of his personality features was discontinued as the questions often triggered non-epileptic episodes.

Initial formulation of depression

Thomas' difficulties were initially formulated using a longitudinal formulation of depression (Beck Judith, 1995) with an embedded "hot cross bun" that also covered the Six Cycles Maintenance Model ("vicious flower" of depression; Moorey, 2010) (Figure 5.1).

First bump on the road: initial engagement

During the first weeks of his admission, Thomas' engagement with psychological therapy was poor; he either declined sessions or struggled to wake up in response to prompts at the time that his sessions were due. After waking up, he instantly exhibited a non-epileptic episode. Following active encouragement, Thomas would eventually attend sessions; however, the symptoms greatly impacted on engagement and progress in psychology. The Personality Assessment Inventory was discontinued after several attempts due to severe fatigue and non-epileptic episodes triggered by questions such as "I feel I have let everyone down". Thomas' attempts to speak about feelings and past events, or his upbringing would frequently result in acute conversion FND symptoms that precluded him from speaking or writing down his thoughts and feelings, including non-epileptic and vacant episodes; slurred, blocked or incomprehensible speech; and tremors, gross motor movements and motor weakness. These FND symptoms were frequently observed to be accompanied by high levels of affective dysregulation, extreme tearfulness and anxiety, perceived lack of control over the FND and losing his sense of self and identity. He was unable to label these thoughts and feelings. The FND and emotional symptoms often led to early termination of therapy sessions, both by Thomas and staff. To manage these symptoms, Thomas attempted to apply various anxiety management techniques in the moment including breathing exercises, meditation, grounding and distraction techniques; however, the effectiveness of these strategies was variable and worked in the short term only or not at all. The FND symptoms continued to significantly interfere

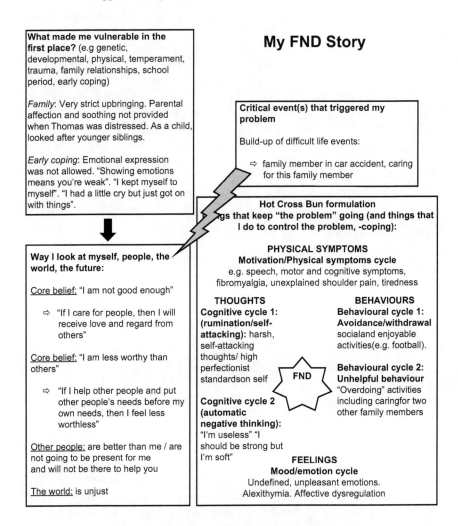

Figure 5.1 Longitudinal formulation of depression.

with therapy sessions, and the focus of treatment shifted towards "crisis man-agement" of FND symptoms rather than the intervention as mapped out by the psychological formulation. Across disciplines, members of Thomas' treating team observed minimal progress and persistence of FND symptoms. During physiotherapy, Thomas was described as "non-compliant" and at best able to mobilise for a few metres with a frame before indicating being too fatigued to carry on. Occupational therapy sessions focused on fatigue management; however, Thomas often returned to bed immediately after sleeping for large parts of the day. In speech and language therapy sessions, Thomas struggled with practising communication strategies and was using assisted communication with writing. At this stage, Thomas was started on a treatment course with anti-depressant and short-term anxiolytic medication. The multidisciplinary team questioned whether an inpatient admission was the appropriate treatment pathway for Thomas, and the possibility of early discharge was actively entertained.

Thomas' Pressure Cooker Model assessment

As Thomas' engagement and progress across all disciplines were poor, the PCM was subsequently introduced to help re-formulate his difficulties and support his engagement with psychological and other therapies. Table 5.1 shows how the results from the initial multidisciplinary assessment were categorised according to each element of the PCM.

Pressure cooker re-formulation of Thomas' difficulties

Using the information from the PCM assessment template and the psychological assessment, Thomas' FND symptoms were re-formulated using the layered system of the PCM.

Table 5.1 Thomas' multidisciplinary Pressure Cooker Model assessment

Kitchen

Enmeshed, overprotective and overcaring family system

Cover	Overpressure Plug	Valve
Reduced verbal expression of beliefs and emotions in trusted relationships. Does not speak to partner about emotions. Expressed negative beliefs about emotional expression (e.g. "emotions are weak").	*FND:* speech difficulties, limb and trunk weakness, tremor, ballistic movements; non-epileptic episodes; memory and concentration deficits. *FND after-effects:* shoulder pain, muscle tension, physical and cognitive fatigue. *Behaviours:* No suicidal ideation/self-harm.	*Current (Blocked).* Withdrawal from social, enjoyable, meaningful and relaxation activities (e.g. football). Poor awareness of the mood-activity link. *Past (Dysregulated):* Boom-and-bust cycle: overdoing caring activities. Difficulties maintaining appropriate boundaries around caring.

(Continued)

Table 5.1 (Continued)

Pot

Food/Fuelling your body: Vitamin D deficiency, gastro-intestinal issues.

Night rest: 24-hour sleep episodes, night-time waking

Drugs and medications: fluoxetine, prednisolone, inhaler.

Sickness and physical illness: respiratory infection, breathlessness, high blood pressure.

Equipment: motorised wheelchair, home fully adapted to disabilities with stair lift, raised toilet, shower seat, hospital bed and frame for walking indoors.

Liquids and hydration: Urge incontinence, normal fluid intake.

Fight-or-flight: Physical effects of anxiety and distress present – tachypnoea.

Contacts: 5× emergency and ITU admissions, with quick discharges. Reviews by cardiology and pulmonology

Appearance/ability to care for self: unable to care for self independently, assistance of one person for personal care (e.g. washing, dressing, meal preparation), domestic tasks.

Risks: accidental self-injury due to FND symptoms, self-neglect, dependency, falls during mobilising, holding balance and transfers.

Exercise and movement: Walking, standing and all transfer types affected. Severely reduced cardiovascular fitness, exercise intolerance.

Warning light

Heightened self-focused attention to FND and bodily symptoms, for example high focus on breathing difficulties

Sticky left-over food

Family coping strategies: lack of verbal emotional expression. Emotions were invalidated. FND triad: early childhood coping strategies repeated into adulthood.

Ignition

Build-up of adverse life events. Car accident family member.

Fuel

(1) Stressful family dynamics

(2) Occasional reminders of the accident, for example seeing a similar topic on television

Flames

Beliefs: Rumination and heightened sense of responsibility for accident. Negative self-perception regarding managing poor family dynamics and FND. Unrelenting, high perfectionist standards on self.

Emotions: Poor psychological awareness of emotions/thought-feelings link.

Heat

Discrepancy between Thomas' self-report on emotional distress (denial) vs staff report (high distress observed in Thomas), suggesting dissociation.

Rapidly fluctuating aversive state that quickly reached a high intensity for Thomas.

Layer 1: Ignition

Thomas' adverse early experiences gave rise to negative core beliefs around worthlessness and low self-esteem. Thomas developed a set of conditional assumptions or "rules of living" that helped him to live his life whilst compensating for his self-perceived "shortcomings". He internalised that caring for people and putting other people's needs ahead of his own would result in receiving love and acceptance from others, making him feel less worthless. Thomas' dysfunctional beliefs were deeply ingrained; he was unable to generate positive qualities about himself. His system of core beliefs and conditional assumptions enabled him to fare well in his life until he experienced a stressful life event where a close family member became a victim in a road traffic accident. It was hypothesised that the family member's accident re-triggered Thomas' negative belief system and made him feel low in self-esteem and out of control, as he was unable to prevent the accident from happening, despite being in close regular contact with this family member and major caring efforts.

Layer 2: the FND coping triad

During his strict upbringing, Thomas was not able to safely express emotions as his parents strongly disapproved and punished emotional expression with harsh discipline, invalidation and rejection ("showing emotions means you're weak"). Thomas avoided these negative consequences by learning to regulate his emotions by "keeping emotions to self" and "pushing on" with activities that helped him to dissociate from emotions (sticky left-over food inside the pot) by way of negative reinforcement. The lack of opportunities to practise emotional expression as a child impacted on his ability to verbalise emotions and resulted in poor emotional communication skills. Thomas' early childhood coping habits, as well as his negative personal beliefs around emotional expression and the need to sustain high activity levels, persisted into adulthood and were reinforced over decades. Throughout his life, these childhood coping habits were effective in managing difficult thoughts and feelings in relation to his upbringing; other adverse life events that happened later in adulthood; and family discord, until the road traffic accident happened, an event "one too many": his coping habits were insufficiently capable of managing all of the distress. Thomas kept emotions to himself and did not verbally express his feelings about the car accident (cover tightly sealed to pot, coping habit 1). Furthermore, Thomas dissociated and avoided feeling emotions by pushing on and absorbing himself in daily tasks, not releasing stress via enjoyable, relaxing or social activities (blocked valve, coping habit 2). In addition, Thomas often prioritised other people's needs ahead of his own, frequently overdoing caring activities that followed a boom-and-bust cycle pattern (dysregulated opening and closing of valve, coping habit 3).

This classic FND coping triad, consisting of early abnormal coping habits, reduced verbal emotional expression and abnormal activity levels, is commonly found in people with FND.

Layer 3: FND maintenance cycle

Adverse childhood events and the accident (Ignition) represented the remote setting events and critical incident that created a vulnerability for Thomas to develop FND. Thoughts, feelings, memories and reminders of the family member's accident, as well as unhelpful family dynamics (Fuel), triggered an aversive internal state characterised by poorly defined emotions (Flames), which was high in emotional intensity (Heat). This re-activated Thomas' early coping habits (Sticky left-over food): he was unable to verbally express these emotions in a trusted and safe relationship (tightly sealed Cover) or release the emotions via meaningful activities and engaged in boom-and-bust behaviour (blocked/dysregulated Valve). With both of these channels blocked, the risk of the FND response increased. To prevent an explosion ("psychological breakdown"), Thomas engaged an alternative channel for releasing his "steam": the aversive emotional state was immediately followed by a behavioural response (FND episode, Overpressure plug), which quickly and effectively removed these aversive stimuli providing relief: Thomas reported feeling tired immediately after an episode, and his intense feelings ceased to exist temporarily. This provided negative reinforcement of the FND symptoms. After repeated stimulus-response pairings, the S (internal distress) → R (FND) → -S- (reduction in distress) link was strengthened over time and increased the likelihood of the FND response occurring in the future leading to habit formation: Thomas had now acquired the FND response as the main coping habit for managing negative emotions. Thomas reported several "FND after-effects" including severe fatigue, pain and muscle tension.

Layer 4: Facilitating physical factors in FND

Thomas displayed heightened self-focused attention directed towards his bodily symptoms (Warning light), which maintained his symptoms. Thomas' fragile pot showed "ruptures", that is medical-contextual factors that negatively impacted on his mood, cognitive functioning and the FND, including vitamin deficiencies, reduced cardiovascular fitness, respiratory problems and night-time waking. Prolonged sleeping episodes stopped Thomas from experiencing intense emotions. Frequent hospitalisations and overreliance on equipment and family for care and transfers reinforced Thomas' low self-efficacy beliefs; he lost confidence in managing the condition by himself.

Layer 5: Social functions of FND

Thomas had a longstanding history of caring for other people including his family of origin, his current family and two ill extended family members. The caring activities provided some internal reinforcement and helped Thomas to feel less low in self-esteem and more in control, over the short term, consistent with his conditional assumptions. However, the caring activities maintained his negative self-image in the long term as he was unable to test out the hypothesis that people in his environment would still provide him with unconditional love and acceptance even if he would withdraw from the caring activities. Furthermore, his caring experiences afforded Thomas with opportunities, through vicarious reinforcement, to observe illness models receiving positive reinforcement from the environment in the form of comfort, care and attention. Due to the high rate of childhood adverse experiences, Thomas did not have opportunities to develop and practise adaptive coping strategies (e.g. verbal emotional expression) in order to meet his basic human need for comfort and care. Therefore, the FND was an alternative but equally effective way to meet his unmet emotional need. In addition, an FND episode also helped Thomas to avoid or escape aversive stimuli in the environment through negative reinforcement, for example family conflict, abandonment by his family or a psychology session.

Course of psychological therapy

Thomas attended 20 individual psychological therapy sessions. The PCM predicted that regular verbal expression of emotions (opening the Cover) would reduce the risk of Thomas' FND response (not using the Overpressure plug), consistent with studies reporting inverse associations between verbal emotional expression and FND (Bowman & Markand, 1999; Alsaadi & Marquez, 2005). It was further hypothesised that normalising activity levels by increasing enjoyable and meaningful activities (Valve unblocked), as well as reduction in boom bust cycles (regulated Valve), in combination with improved verbal emotional expression, would further reduce the risk of Thomas' FND.

Building stable foundations: engagement and socialisation to the PCM

The PCM was introduced to provide psycho-education on the FND maintenance cycle and to raise Thomas' insight into the FND-distress link, without initially delving into past experiences. The components and mechanisms of the PCM formulation were collaboratively explored ("what happens with a lot of Ignition, hot Flames, tight Cover and a blocked Valve?" and "it may come out as FND, pain and fatigue via the overpressure plug"). At a later stage, the psychological formulation was further built up by embedding the FND maintenance cycle into the following longitudinal Pressure Cooker Model formulation (Figure 5.2).

My early experiencesmade me vulnerable to FND
- I had a very strict upbringing with lots of unpredictability.
- Parental affection, comfort and validation was not provided when I felt distressed.
- My Mum had a chronic illness andwas away from home.
- As a child, I was the main care provider for my younger siblings.

My core beliefs
- "I am not good enough" / "I'm unlovable"
- "I am less worthy than others"
- Other people: are better than me / are not going to be present for me and will not be there to help you

Ignition: What sparked off the FND
- I had a life-time of difficult childhood and adult life events
- Critical incident: Family member in a car accident

My rules for living
- "If I care for people, then I will receive love and comfort from others"
- "If I help other people and put other people's needs before my own needs, then I feel less worthless and more in control"

Pressure Cooker Model Formulation (Maintenance Cycle)

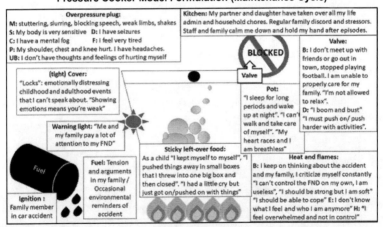

Figure 5.2 Pressure Cooker Model embedded within the longitudinal formulation.

Pressure Cooker Model formulation (maintenance cycle)

In spite of his distress, Thomas tolerated longer and more regular psychology sessions. In parallel with these psychological gains, Thomas' therapeutic alliances, treatment compliance and progress towards goals slowly and gradually improved across all disciplines. After Thomas was socialised to the model, each PCM element was addressed during the psychology-driven intervention, similar to plucking the petals in the vicious flower formulation of depression (Moorey, 2010).

Stopping the ignition and emptying the Fuel

Thomas identified longstanding and unpredictable family crises as an important trigger for FND. He felt a great responsibility for the crises, which often caused him distress and made him self-critical. Thomas was encouraged to create some distance and increase his non-judgemental acceptance of these highly emotive family situations, rather than become absorbed by the events and directly addressing the crises in the moment, as Thomas had often done in the past. He practised with sitting and tolerating the distress. To cope with triggers that could not be easily removed, Thomas also learned to make use of more practical problem-solving strategies. For example, he abdicated some of the responsibility by allowing a family member to manage the dynamics. He also managed "smaller" stressors in more practical ways (e.g. obtaining external support for household chores).

Extinguishing the Flames

Prior to a non-epileptic episode, Thomas often described a poorly defined and overwhelming internal psychological state. Basic emotion education helped him to identify and label his confusing feelings particularly anxiety, sadness, guilt and embarrassment. A prominent feature was the presence of relentless self-critical thoughts, rumination and feelings of guilt especially about the accident, family dynamics and his self-perceived inability to manage the FND. Using cognitive restructuring techniques, Thomas developed a more balanced viewpoint and self-compassion ("I am starting to control the FND: I walked a few steps and I am engaging in therapy"). Thomas exhibited a strong tendency to apply strict standards on himself compared to his family. Although he struggled with letting these double standards go, Thomas practised with setting more realistic standards for himself.

Dialling down the Heat

Thomas was fearful about future situations that he felt unable to control and predict, especially poor outcomes of family crises and future FND set-backs. To help Thomas with regulating his emotions, he outlined several "emergency coping" plans by vividly imagining worst-case scenarios and naming coping skills that he could use if the events would occur. For highly emotive situations that he could not easily escape or solve immediately, and that could potentially elicit an FND episode, he practised skills that helped him sit with the distress for longer. For example, he distracted himself with an activity or used his five senses for reality grounding to nip the gradually evolving symptoms in the bud before a full-blown episode would develop. These strategies helped to facilitate longer tolerance of the aversive stimulus (distress) and increase the delay between the aversive stimulus (distress) and the response (FND).

Opening the Cover

The core part of Thomas' psychological treatment focused on practising the skill of verbal emotional expression. Thomas felt ashamed about showing distress and not being able to control the FND. After the therapeutic relationship grew stronger, Thomas was able to express his thoughts and feelings about "lower level" distressing situations during his admission, for example feeling anxious and vulnerable whilst attending a pulmonology clinic for investigations. After practising with these "lower level" situations, he was able to express his emotions about the family member's accident that set off the FND. This cascaded into Thomas identifying a range of other emotionally distressing events that happened in the years prior to the accident and that he had not disclosed to anyone ("locked secrets"). A subsequent "unlocking" process of these past stressful events took place during which Thomas vividly described and skilfully expressed his emotions about the events, followed by a period of relief afterwards – in the same way that FND would have provided him with relief. Thomas generalised these skills and was regularly praised for expressing his emotions to other staff.

Unblocking and improving regulation of the Valve

Thomas' insight into the link between low mood and reduced activity was raised. As part of behavioural activation, he was encouraged to engage with social activities, therapeutic groups and former physical hobbies (e.g. football and gardening). Thomas learned about his boom-and-bust pattern of caring activities that often resulted in long periods of inertia and low mood during the recovery phase. Thomas' strong negative beliefs against taking breaks and engaging in relaxation activities were challenged. He used assertiveness skills to manage strong feelings around placing boundaries on caring activities in response to environmental demands.

Blocking the Overpressure Plug

In order to reduce the risk of FND (using the Overpressure Plug), longer-term work during Thomas' admission focused on improving verbal emotional expression (opening the Cover) and normalising activity levels (unblocking/regulating the Valve). However, as Thomas was in the process of learning and consolidating these new coping strategies, he continued to occasionally experience non-epileptic episodes that needed "unlearning" and needed strategies "in the moment". To further "unlearn" this entrenched habit, he practised using short-term strategies for rapidly escalating symptoms, including actively experiencing and sitting with the distress; reality grounding; distraction; and breathing exercises. These techniques aimed to facilitate longer tolerance of the aversive stimulus (distress) and increase the delay between the aversive stimulus (distress) and response (FND), with the ultimate aim to extinguish FND. Stopping a non-epileptic episode in its tracks also helped to prevent post-FND fatigue, pain and prolonged sleep that Thomas often experienced after an episode and that stopped him from feeling emotions.

Releasing and dissolving Sticky left-over food

After working through the PCM maintenance cycle, the focus in therapy shifted towards embedding the cycle within a longitudinal framework; Thomas explored the relationships between his early experiences, core beliefs and rules of living, and the subsequent development of FND later in life. Thomas was highly self-critical about having developed coping habits in childhood that he continued to use in adulthood. To foster more self-compassion, Thomas learned that his early coping habits served highly adaptive functions during his upbringing to survive and cope with challenging and unpredictable family circumstances, minimise negative emotions and avoid repercussions from the family unit. In present times, these habits lost some usefulness as they increased the risk of FND and prevented Thomas from fully living and enjoying his life. Although Thomas felt unworthy of praise (i.e. one of his negative core beliefs) and he struggled to tolerate the strong feelings that emerged in response to praise on his positive qualities from his environment, he reluctantly identified a few positive personal qualities on a log to help build positive core beliefs including being kind, caring, organised, strong-willed and creative.

Switching off the Warning light and healing ruptures in the pot

Thomas became aware of the way heightened self-focused attention on his bodily symptoms maintained the FND. An experiment showed that when engrossed in an enjoyable task and distracted, thereby reducing self-focused attention, his FND symptoms lessened. Thomas practised several attentional shifting techniques. A multidisciplinary approach towards ameliorating Thomas' biological and medical-contextual factors impacted positively on his mood and FND symptoms (see later section in this chapter for more details on the multidisciplinary techniques used on all PCM elements).

Kitchen environment

Although the ward milieu was supportive and validating, with daily predictable routines and a familiar treating team, Thomas' family and team showed overprotective tendencies towards him. Behavioural observations and ABC charts revealed that Thomas' non-epileptic episodes were immediately reinforced with reassurance and care. The PCM formulation was shared with Thomas' environment to increase understanding of the social functions and maintaining factors of the FND. Behavioural guidelines encouraged Thomas' environment with the consistent withdrawal or withholding of care and comfort following his non-epileptic episodes. "Disattending", or removing a reinforcing consequence contingent upon the behaviour (i.e. FND), aimed to reduce the frequency of the behaviour. To provide an "alternative competing response" following the removal of Thomas' usual coping strategy of FND, and consolidate his new skill, regular practice of verbal emotional expression was encouraged in therapy, in the family unit, and between Thomas and staff that he had developed trusted therapeutic relationships with.

Second bump on the road: residual symptoms

Despite significant improvements, Thomas continued to experience mild FND symptoms and residual anxiety, which triggered strong negative emotions in staff and family. The question arose whether the emotions and responses from the environment contributed to the persistence of Thomas' symptoms. The PCM formulation was therefore re-applied to individuals in Thomas' environment. The Overpressure Plug represented a broader spectrum of behavioural responses that included, but was not limited to, FND.

Layer 1: Ignition

The initial symptom presentation of the FND, either in the family unit or during his new arrival on the ward, was regarded as the critical incident that created a vulnerability for the family and the team to develop unhelpful responses towards Thomas.

Layer 2: the FND coping triad

Interestingly, Thomas, his family and team shared the same coping triad: reduced verbal emotional expression about their anxiety and self-perceived ability to manage Thomas' symptoms (tight Cover) and pushing on with caring activities for Thomas at the expense of sufficient rest periods (blocked/dysregulated Valve). These coping habits were longstanding in both environments (Sticky left-over food). Thomas and his family used these "intergenerational" coping habits over many years. Staff on the unit consisted mostly of physical health professionals who, historically, were not familiar with regular psychological reflection to help facilitate verbal emotional expression of their beliefs and emotions; the impact of the patient's behaviours on their own mental health and self-confidence; or the impact of their own behaviours on a patient's recovery.

Layer 3: FND maintenance cycle

Thomas' non-epileptic seizures, as well as his contemporaneous tearfulness and emotion dysregulation (Fuel), triggered high levels of distress and low self-efficacy beliefs in the family and team about their own skills and ability to manage the FND (Flames and Heat). To reduce their own distress and remove the trigger (i.e. Thomas' episode), the environment engaged in caring and reassurance "safety" and "escape" behaviours (Overpressure Plug), which quickly reduced Thomas' symptoms and the environment's distress simultaneously, providing short-term relief by negative reinforcement but maintaining the anxiety and caring behaviours in the long term.

Layer 4: facilitating physical factors in FND

Thomas' FND symptoms were doubly reinforced: he was strongly focused on his symptoms; however, his family and team displayed even higher levels of attentional focus and overt hypervigilant monitoring to prevent and manage his FND episodes, further increasing Thomas' heightened self-focused attention.

Layer 5: the social functions of FND

Reciprocal reinforcement

The final layer describes an interpersonal maladaptive cycle between Thomas and his environment that caused triple negative reinforcement of his FND and fully explained the persistence of his symptoms. Thomas reduced his distress internally following the FND response (process 1). The FND episode, however, simultaneously increased distress in his environment resulting in an immediate caring response. This removed the trigger (the FND episode) and therefore the environment's distress (process 2). The external caring response further reduced Thomas' FND episode and distress, providing him with extra relief on top of the relief already obtained via internal emotional regulation (process 3). Thomas' emotional need continued to be met internally via FND and externally by the environment via the caring response, which also managed the environment's own emotional needs. This "reciprocal operant conditioning" process perpetuated the FND and distress in both Thomas and his environment, and prevented him from practising more adaptive coping strategies (verbal emotional expression) and testing out that everyone's worst fear of an FND episode may not take place. The next few figures demonstrate three emotion dysregulation cycles that emerged between Thomas and his direct environment (Figures 5.3–5.5).

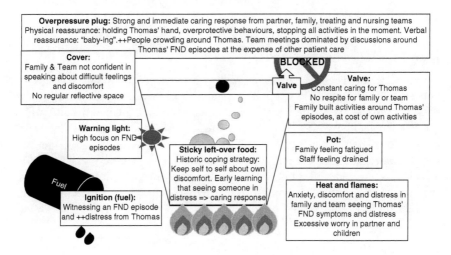

Figure 5.3 Emotion dysregulation cycle 1: person with FND ⇔ family and treating team dyad.

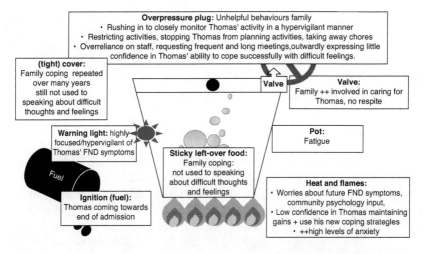

Figure 5.4 Emotion dysregulation cycle 2: person with FND ⇔ family dyad.

Systemic re-traumatisation

Thomas felt greatly distressed about past experiences with healthcare professionals who did not understand the diagnosis and management of FND. His experiences mirrored those commonly reported by healthcare professionals who describe anxiety, frustration, anger and confusion, as well as a lack of understanding and confidence in diagnosing and managing FND (e.g. Ahern et al., 2009; Edwards et al., 2012; Fobian & Elliott, 2019).

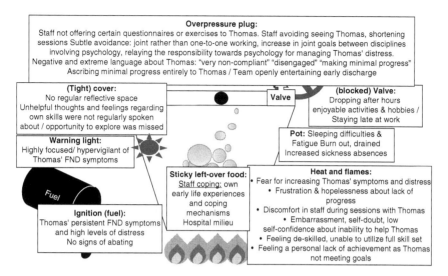

Overpressure plug:
Staff not offering certain questionnaires or exercises to Thomas. Staff avoiding seeing Thomas, shortening sessions Subtle avoidance: joint rather than one-to-one working, increase in joint goals between disciplines involving psychology, relaying the responsibility towards psychology for managing Thomas' distress. Negative and extreme language about Thomas: "very non-compliant" "disengaged" "making minimal progress" Ascribing minimal progress entirely to Thomas / Team openly entertaining early discharge

(Tight) cover:
No regular reflective space Unhelpful thoughts and feelings regarding own skills were not regularly spoken about / opportunity to explore was missed

Valve

(blocked) Valve:
Dropping after hours enjoyable activities & hobbies / Staying late at work

Warning light:
Highly focused/ hypervigilant of Thomas' FND symptoms

Pot: Sleeping difficulties & Fatigue Burn out, drained Increased sickness absences

Fuel

Sticky left-over food:
Staff coping: own early life experiences and coping mechanisms Hospital milieu

Ignition (fuel):
Thomas' persistent FND symptoms and high levels of distress No signs of abating

Heat and flames:
• Fear for increasing Thomas' symptoms and distress
• Frustration & hopelessness about lack of progress
• Discomfort in staff during sessions with Thomas
• Embarrassment, self-doubt, low self-confidence about inability to help Thomas
• Feeling de-skilled, unable to utilize full skill set
• Feeling a personal lack of achievement as Thomas not meeting goals

Figure 5.5 Emotion dysregulation cycle 3: person with FND ⇔ treating team dyad.

These negative beliefs, emotions and responses have likely led to "systemic re-traumatisation" in Thomas' situation with detrimental consequences to his care. Due to his neglectful childhood, Thomas had limited access to useful coping strategies. Encountering an anxious and confused healthcare professional who lacks confidence and knowledge in treating FND may have driven the professional to avoid or abandon Thomas and other patients with FND, which temporarily reduced their own aversive emotional state. However, these systemic rejection behaviours are negatively reinforced, increasing their risk of re-occurrence. In response to the professionals' rejection behaviours, Thomas felt confused, angry, abandoned and not believed. Thomas became even more reluctant to disclose psychological difficulties and attempted to seek more reassurance and clarity for his physical symptoms. This resulted in several years of seeking and accessing treatments, which failed and caused him prolonged psychological distress, before his unexplained symptoms were finally diagnosed and treated appropriately. As in Thomas' situation, a distressed and confused system may interpret a patient's reassurance seeking behaviour as "attention seeking" and "difficult to treat" leading to more systemic avoidance behaviours, which in turn may repeat or re-trigger memories of traumatic early childhood rejection experiences. The person with FND, still without useful coping strategies and confused, becomes re-traumatised and blamed by the system. These maladaptive interpersonal cycles between people with FND and the healthcare system adversely impact on the recovery, management and treatment of FND and can result in a delay of the diagnosis, ruptured therapeutic relationships, iatrogenic damage with medical investigations and overmedication, as well as entrenchment of symptoms that become more difficult to reverse over time (Ahern et al., 2009; Fobian & Elliott, 2019) – all of which Thomas had experienced.

Shared interdisciplinary treatment plan: pressure cooker skills

See Table 5.2.

Outcomes

Throughout his admission, Thomas participated in a collaborative goal-setting process. Admission and discharge scores on psychological and neurorehabilitation measures were compared, and involved calculation of the Reliable Change Index (RCI; Jacobson & Truax, 1991).

Table 5.2 Neurorehabilitation techniques used by non-psychology professions in Thomas' multidisciplinary treatment classified into each PCM element

---

Kitchen

Establishing trusted therapeutic relationships with Thomas and supporting him with emotional expression, disattending non-epileptic episodes.

Cover	Overpressure Plug	Valve
Speech therapy: Assertiveness skills. Education on functional speech–emotion link. Supported communication techniques	• *Physiotherapy:* Tapping techniques for tremor elimination. Shoulder exercises for pain. • *Occupational therapy:* Fatigue management and relaxation. • *Speech therapy:* Video feedback for functional stutter.	*Occupational therapy:* Shop visits for increased access to the community, reconnecting with former hobbies and interests (e.g. football). Pacing strategies to break boom-and-bust cycles. *Nursing:* Bed rest break schedule. Development of daily and nightly routine on the ward.

Pot
- *Physiotherapy:* Practice of indoor and outdoor walking. Standing and grasp exercise to increase fitness.
- *Occupational therapy:* Practice with personal care, transfers, chores and meal preparation. Sleep hygiene. Equipment review.
- *Medical:* Rationalisation of medications. Muscular review. Vitamin supplementation.
- *Nursing:* Support to practice independent self-medication.
- *Dietetics:* Establishing a daily bowel routine with nursing.

Warning light
Physiotherapy: Distraction techniques to divert attention away during walking practice.

Sticky left-over food
The entire multidisciplinary team helped Thomas with uncovering his positive personal qualities with the log that he kept.

Ignition/Fuel
Social work: Support with managing family dynamics.

Flames and Heat
Medical: Anti-depressant and anxiolytic medication to support Thomas' mood and anxiety symptoms.

To understand the relationship between psychological difficulties and FND

Thomas spontaneously reported the "locked" Cover as an important PCM element. He was able to describe the PCM maintenance cycle and the inverse relationship between FND and verbal emotional expression. Thomas accepted that the bottom parts of the PCM (i.e. Ignition and Flames) would "always be there" and that tolerance of some degree of stress is required as part of the normal human life experience. However, he was able to change the quality, presence and intensity of the negative emotions and relieve FND symptoms by changing ways of regulating emotions at the top (e.g. verbal emotional expression, behavioural activation, pacing). Although Thomas received new distressing family news and became fearful of another FND episode, he completed a behavioural experiment that tested out the effectiveness of his new coping strategies: Thomas expressed his emotions to a select group of staff that he had built strong alliances with and continued to participate in meaningful activities on the ward. After managing his distress with his new PCM strategies, he did not experience FND.

To open the Cover and to unblock and regulate the Valve

On admission, GH became distressed by noticing the word "psychology" on his time table and was hard to rouse for psychology sessions. At discharge, he had attended and engaged with a full course of psychological therapy. Thomas demonstrated increased confidence and skill in expressing his emotions through writing and speaking. Although he initially bottled up his emotions all week to reserve their release for psychology sessions, towards the end of his admission, this skill generalised outside the psychological therapy space to other non-psychology staff. Thomas engaged with meaningful, social and enjoyable activities that created a sense of belonging and achievement, for example football and gardening. He initiated the planning of social activities for after discharge. His group attendance increased from zero to five groups. Thomas' long sleeping episodes ceased, and as he consistently applied his pacing schedule, his boom-and-bust cycles stopped.

To improve Thomas' psychological and physical symptoms

On the HADS, his level of anxiety and depression dropped from mild to normal (seven and four, respectively). Clinical reliable change was found for depression (RCI = 2.31) but not for anxiety (RCI = 1.21). On observation, Thomas was brighter in mood with substantially reduced episodes of tearfulness. His NIS score reduced from 20/50 to 9/50 (RCI = 3.0), suggesting a reliable change. Although his cognitive impairments disappeared and his non-epileptic episodes gradually reduced in frequency and severity, he continued to experience residual functional weakness, pain and fatigue.

To improve Thomas' functioning in day-to-day life

On the UK FIM+FAM, Thomas' score increased from 99/210 to 195/210, suggesting a reliable change (RCI = 3.2) and indicating near or full independence on most day-to-day activities. Thomas was independent with personal care, preparing a meal and mobilising unsupervised with a walker over a long-distance indoors. He returned home with a reduced care package and relied on fewer pieces of equipment. Figure 5.6 shows the breakdown of Thomas' UK FIM+FAM scores on the Motor items. The largest improvements in his motor functioning were observed for personal care, particularly grooming, bathing and dressing, as well as for mobility and various types of transfers.

On Cognitive items, Thomas demonstrated the largest improvements on writing and speech intelligibility, consistent with a reduction in his FND symptoms. In addition, substantial improvements were found on scales that tapped into aspects of depression that tend to be affected in these areas, including social interaction, emotional status, adjustment to limitations, problem solving and concentration (see Figure 5.7).

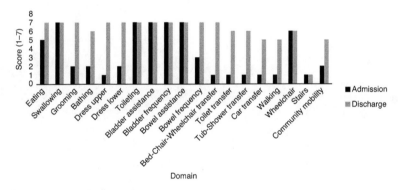

Figure 5.6 UK FIM+FAM score breakdown (Motor).

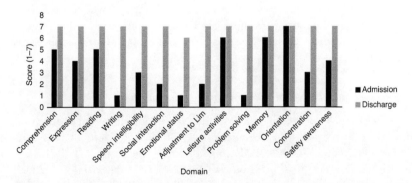

Figure 5.7 UK FIM+FAM score breakdown (Cognitive).

To improve MDT emotional functioning

On admission, the emotional load experienced by staff in response to Thomas' presentation and symptoms was categorised as high, indicating "severe emotional load" "requiring active intervention to support or relieve staff" on the Northwick Park Therapy Dependency Assessment. At discharge, the emotional load reduced significantly to none, suggesting "no load at all, staff look forward to sessions".

Follow-up

Following his discharge, Thomas was referred to a community neurorehabilitation team. He did not meet the criteria, and his psychological care was abruptly suspended. The referral rejection increased his and his family's distress who felt unable to cope and consolidate the gains that he had made during his admission. Approximately six weeks following discharge, Thomas was reviewed by his treating team. The FND symptoms had partially returned. His emotional well-being had deteriorated, although not to the level that he presented with when initially admitted to the ward. He continued to participate in activities of daily life. These suboptimal outcomes replicate past findings of substantial relapse rates in FND and highlight the detrimental impact of re-introducing the patient to a largely untreated family environment that was likely core to the FND (Betts & Boden, 1992).

Case study 2: caught in a brain fog: a tale of social connection

Background information

Alex was a 67-year-old female who had been diagnosed with FND several years prior to her admission to an inpatient treatment programme. Her symptoms predominantly involved severe amnesia and some slight functional motor problems. The dystonia symptoms were minor, in comparison to the "brain fog" that she described, and did not significantly impact on Alex' ability to walk independently. She was able to mobilise on the ward with a Zimmer frame and required assistance of another person due to her amnesia rather than the dystonia. Alex was unable to function without significant amount of help from her support worker for activities in daily life including personal care, preparing meals, doing her household chores, paying bills and taking care of finances, shopping and accessing the community. Due to the amnestic symptoms, Alex was unable to continue with the job in a local shop that she had greatly enjoyed for many years, particularly the social interactions with the customers. At one point, Alex' amnestic symptoms became so severe that a diagnosis of possible dementia was given. She was under dementia services for over a year. The amnesia necessitated a prolonged stay in a local nursing home. After several months, Alex was referred to and assessed by an outreach team and subsequently referred to a specialist rehabilitation unit to receive treatment aimed at reducing her day-to-day care needs.

Presenting issues

During her initial time on the ward, Alex presented as "not with it" and was not fully orientated in time and place. She was kind and soft-spoken. In response to interview questions, Alex provided limited answers. She did not spontaneously generate conversation. Alex did not make eye contact and was mostly sitting hunched down. It was difficult to obtain a comprehensive history and ascertain a time-line of events that may have led up to the FND. Alex struggled with verbalising her main difficulties, from both a physical and a psychological perspective. She was unable to label her feelings and provided vague descriptions of emotions "I don't know what I feel". Although she expressed some doubts and uncertainty about her treatment goals and the reasons for her admission, Alex indicated that she wanted to "find my emotions again". The psychologist was struck by the lack of social connection and belonging in Alex' life. She did not describe any significant relationships and appeared to live in a social vacuum. Alex was rarely in contact with her adult children. In addition, ward staff did not observe Alex to have any regular visitors. It also proved to be difficult to establish a next-of-kin contact person for regular updates on Alex' progress in rehab. Eventually, Alex suggested her ex-partner as the link person throughout her admission. The team's impression was that Alex seemed to be on the world on her own, devoid of any regular social contact with other people, apart from occasional contact with health services and nursing home staff.

Neuropsychological assessment

In the past, Alex had undergone several investigations to explore whether her amnesia may be driven by organic reasons. Her brain scans were found to be normal and did not reveal any significant neurological changes that suggested an incipient dementia process. As part of her initial work-up on the unit, she agreed to participate in a brief neuropsychological battery. The results of this neuropsychological assessment showed severe impairments across all cognitive domains. She was unable to sustain her attention for long periods of time. Although Alex exhibited a significantly slowed speed of information processing on a classic test of attention, she was found to have relatively preserved speed of processing of meaningful sentences, demonstrating intact sentence comprehension abilities. She performed well with word retrieval if a meaningful sentence structure was provided but struggled on other language-based tests that required her to retrieve single words on fluency and naming tests. Her performance did not improve on a semantic association test that circumvented the need for naming. Poor visuo-spatial perception and constructional abilities were noted. Alex' memory difficulties spanned both short-term and long-term memory domains, as well as verbal and non-verbal modalities. Her verbal short-term memory was impaired, as was her learning, remembering and recognition of a list of words, meaningful stories and a complex figure. Recall was generally as impaired as her recognition abilities. Interestingly, an "island" of preserved cognitive ability was found on a test of response inhibition, suggesting that Alex appeared to have relatively good skills in suppression of irrelevant information, consistent with the hypothesis of her amnesia serving as a suppression mechanism of "irrelevant" (intolerable) thought and emotion content. Although Alex' neuropsychological test results on their own suggested severe memory and cognitive decline, this was not fully reflected in her day-to-day functioning on the ward and in therapy sessions. Alex was able to recognise people's faces and names without any difficulties; sign in and out of the ward when attending sessions without any observed memory or visuo-spatial perception difficulties; and attended her sessions on time, always finding her way to the correct location. Her language and communication were observed to be fluent and without any paraphasias. The team felt that Alex' cognitive difficulties appeared to be more consistent with a functional than organic origin.

Initial formulation: severe depression

Alex was not able to verbalise any thought content or describe her emotions. She characterised her mental state as "blank" and a "brain fog". Although this provided some additional complexity in relation to the initial interpretation and formulation of her psychological difficulties, it was evident that Alex presented with a wide range of "biological" features that appeared to be highly consistent with the maintaining factors of depression. Furthermore, Alex reported subtle and subclinical psychotic-like experiences, predominantly a hallucination of a supportive person whom she perceived on a continuous basis. Alex did not report feeling distressed by this person. In contrast, she described this person as positive and a source of comfort. It was hypothesised that Alex may be experiencing depression, potentially with psychotic features. Alex' psychological difficulties and FND symptoms were initially formulated using the Six Cycles Maintenance Model ("vicious flower" of depression; Moorey, 2010) (Figure 5.8):

The "goodness-of-fit" between the vicious flower formulation and Alex' difficulties was acceptable at best. Depression-related psychomotor slowing could possibly account for some of Alex' motor-type FND symptoms. Her amnestic symptoms were subsumed under the two cognitive cycles and hypothesised to function as a mechanism to suppress negative thought content that was as yet inaccessible in therapy and potentially involved rumination, self-attacking and automatic negative thoughts. This preliminary formulation was a good starting point; however, it failed to fully capture the intricacies

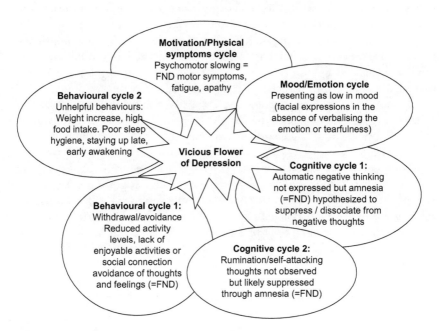

Figure 5.8 Vicious flower formulation of depression.

of Alex' complex presentation. Although the model was able to accommodate Alex' amnesia as a suppression method for difficult thoughts and feelings, the contents of her internal psychological world remained unidentified. Alex greatly struggled to verbalise her thoughts and emotions due to high levels of dissociation and alexithymia. Depression was indirectly inferred based on Alex' biological features, outward appearance and behaviours, but it was unclear whether she truly experienced classic depressogenic cognitions or emotions. Any standard CBT model for depression (Beck Judith, 1995; Moorey, 2010) fell short in psychological therapy as there was no thought content to work with. Therefore, the vicious flower formulation served as a rough estimation and initial narrative of Alex' psychological difficulties. The formulation was not collaborative; upon sharing the formulation, Alex passively acquiesced.

Initial pressure cooker assessment: switching from content → process → content

Several weeks into her admission, Alex' overall progress in the inpatient programme was viewed as minimal. Alex' psychological and physical difficulties remained unchanged in quality, and she struggled to achieve even the smallest of goals. The team felt that her rehabilitation did not seem to "come off the ground". The vicious flower formulation had been useful in the process of initially formulating the relationship between emotions and FND; however, it was a loose hypothesis that needed updating, particularly in the context of therapy progress halting across multiple disciplines simultaneously. Although the two cognitive cycles in the model were unidentified to a great extent, the model was accurate in suggesting that the amnesia, Alex' most prominent FND symptom that stopped her from functioning in day-to-day life, was covering or suppressing some form of intolerable internal psychological state (e.g. thoughts, emotions or memories) that her mind and body were actively resisting against and that could not yet see the light. The vicious flower formulation was subsequently abandoned, and Alex' difficulties were re-formulated using the PCM.

Table 5.3 shows the PCM assessment of Alex' difficulties. The formulation was completed with information that was known about Alex from past medical records, current hospital notes and the scarce details that Alex had shared in the sessions. Please note that the text in italics represents the core information that was uncovered later during the therapeutic process following the introduction of the PCM. Since the start, Alex had been participating in weekly one-to-one individual psychological therapy sessions. She was subsequently invited to attend a course of intensive group therapy with other people with FND, in parallel alongside her individual therapy sessions. The group heavily leaned towards psycho-education of FND and explored each element of the PCM (see Chapter 6 for a detailed description of the group). As the group therapy progressed, Alex started to slowly connect with people and established new relationships with fellow patients in the group. She started to build more trust in her therapeutic relationships. After a few sessions, Alex revealed in the group that she had gained an understanding of FND and that this was an "eye opening" experience for her. In addition, Alex explained that she felt "treated like a human" and "heard" by the group. The flatness in Alex' presentation disappeared; she gained confidence and became more talkative, and was smiling and making appropriate jokes. The positive group therapy experience had a knock-on effect on Alex' progress in individual psychology and non-psychology therapy sessions, culminating in the release of an unspeakable dilemma. The social environment, positive friendships and the sense of belonging that the group therapy afforded her represented a pivotal moment that drastically changed Alex' progress in rehab.

Initial attempts at working with *contents* using a standard CBT model had failed. After investing in *process* by introducing Alex in a social group therapy environment that collaboratively aimed to learn about FND together and provided a sense of belonging, it was possible to switch back to *contents*. The temporary departure from contents and shift towards process enabled the release of the psychological brakes that were blocking Alex and the team from accessing thought content and allowed Alex to learn more about FND and eventually release her unspeakable dilemma that maintained the FND.

Re-formulation

Layer 1: Ignition

Alex reported a largely normal upbringing with loving parents. Her siblings were high-flyers and developed stable families of their own whilst Alex worked hard to hold down a modest job and was twice divorced. These childhood

Table 5.3 Alex' Pressure Cooker Model assessment

Kitchen environment

- Estranged, very distant relationship with adult children from a previous marriage. No visits to hospital.
- Recent separation and complex relationship with ex-partner in Alex' view, with exploitative features. Team felt that Alex was vulnerable and at risk of financial exploitation.
- Alex was socially isolated and did not experience "a sense of belonging" anywhere. Social support network was very limited to a neighbour that she occasionally was in contact with.
- *Systemic re-traumatisation: Alex was told by healthcare professionals that "it was all in my head" and did not feel believed. Alex' current team initially "babied" her but started to become frustrated for failing to see progress despite their efforts, feeding into Alex' rejection beliefs.*

Overpressure Plug

- Functional amnesia
- Other functional cognitive symptoms including problems with concentration, multi-tasking, planning and problem solving, slowed speed of information processing and high level of distractibility.
- Dystonia, gait difficulties, psychomotor slowing and impaired balance, but relatively minor in comparison to prominent cognitive difficulties.
- Reduced sensation and lower limb weakness, Alex was "unable to feel her physical base", which was almost a symbolic representation of not having a psychological base.
- Fatigue and pain.

Cover

- Initially "tight Cover": Did not have trusted relationships or a significant person in her life to open up to regularly about emotions. In the process of divorcing partner and lost usual "buddy" to speak to.
- Problems with assertively expressing her needs.
- *Unspeakable dilemma about circumstances leading up to FND subsequently remembered and released in therapy.*

Valve

- Blocked valve, bust-after-boom pattern: Previously very active in the community, held down job she loved, engaged in hobbies. Then bust accompanied by lack of enjoyable, leisure, exercise, other meaningful activities and social isolation. Has not accessed community for a long time.
- Unemployment due to functional amnesia. Gave up much-loved job. Due to giving up her job as a shop assistant as a result of the FND, she had also lost her daily conversations and social interaction with customers.
- Furthermore, the functional memory problems stopped her from engaging with hobbies.

Kitchen environment

Warning light

Alex displayed a heightened self-focused attention on her symptoms and regularly presented with new physical symptoms

Sticky left-over food

Core beliefs:
I'm a failure.
I'm not worthy and less than others. People will let you down.

Pot

- Unable to take care of herself or perform activities in daily life without assistance including medication management, washing, dressing, preparing meals and household chores. Lives in a nursing home.
- Physiotherapy assessment revealed slow walking speed, unable to stand tall, ascend/descend stairs and reduced exercise tolerance. Independent with transfers.
- Equipment included a Zimmer frame.

Early childhood coping strategy:
Keep self to self

Ignition

- Self-reported trauma-free childhood, which was uncorroborated by significant others. Reported a good relationship with both parents and sisters. Parents had a good marriage. Siblings went on to become highly successful in their careers and formed stable families. Alex was divorced and reported being happy with her job, even if this was not viewed as "high-flying" as her siblings. Death of father was difficult but normal grief reaction.
- *Re-formulation Ignition: "Perfect storm" of a multitude of triggers culminating in a suicide attempt and fuelling the FND: Recent divorce, children not wanting contact or understanding the FND, family arguments, not feeling heard and mistreated by people, "not living a life" but merely existing.*

Flames

- Alexithymia – unclear what emotions she felt. Poor emotion labelling. Vague descriptions of emotions.
- *Low self-esteem beliefs: "I'm a failure, I don't matter", with self-attacking beliefs.*
- *Feeling trapped in the situation and not knowing how to escape.*

Fuel

- Lack of communication in the context of difficult relationship with children and ex-partner.

Heat

- "Low heat": high levels of dissociation, appeared flat in affect.

Safety features

Alex was willing to attend and engage with the rehabilitation programme.
She was friendly and kind and, with time, able to build new friendships with fellow patients, as well as therapeutic relationships with staff.

and later adulthood experiences gave rise to Alex' negative core beliefs about herself including *"I'm a failure"* and *"I'm less worthy than other people"* and created a vulnerability towards developing FND. The critical incident in Alex' life was a "perfect storm" consisting of a combination of three key life events: Alex' most recent and second divorce, her estranged children not wanting contact, and the suicide attempt that did not reach the goal of ending her life, further fuelling Alex' feelings of failure.

Layer 2: the FND coping triad

Alex displayed the classic coping triad often found in FND. She repeated her early childhood coping strategy of "keeping myself to myself" (Sticky left-over food) into adulthood (tight Cover) and experienced a complete reduction of meaningful and occupational activities in her life (blocked Valve: bust-after-boom pattern).

Layer 3: FND maintenance cycle

The Fuel for Alex' psychological difficulties and FND symptoms consisted of interpersonal triggers: her frantic efforts to re-establish contact with her estranged children but not managing in reaching that goal. Throughout her admission, Alex' children refused to visit and were not involved in the therapy or goal planning process. Alex experienced this as a major rejection, and this re-triggered her core beliefs of failure and worthlessness (Flames). Another trigger for the FND was Alex carrying an "unspeakable dilemma" with her without having a safe forum to express the dilemma (Fuel). The unspeakable dilemma consisted of her self-perceived failure to be "successful" in her personal and work life and the shame that she experienced about the suicide attempt (Flames). Expressing this dilemma to people around her would risk further rejection (tight Cover). Alex found herself psychologically trapped in an impossible situation where the personal cost of not expressing the dilemma vs the social costs of expressing the dilemma to her environment were felt to be equal and causing an intolerable psychological state (Heat) in Alex that she was oscillating between and could only manage with FND. The functional amnesia (Overpressure Plug) served as an emotional survival strategy that helped Alex to feel "psychological safety" and stop the oscillation between these two intolerable states. The amnesia served as a coping strategy to dissociate from the strong, intolerable emotions caused by the unspeakable dilemma. Note that the "perfect storm" of difficult life events triggered the FND but was not the core maintaining factor that perpetuated the functional amnesia. The maintaining factor was Alex' internal battle with her thoughts and feelings that were temporarily inaccessible due to the amnesia. In addition, Alex reported reduced sensation, impaired balance and lower limb weakness, which prevented her from feeling her base, which was almost a symbolic and physical expression of

Alex not feeling a secure psychological base of safety with any individual in her immediate environment.

Layer 4: medical-contextual

Several medical-contextual factors contributed to the functional amnesia and motor symptoms including Alex' low back pain and fatigue. Due to the functional amnesia, Alex was unable to manage her own medications and care for herself without assistance.

Layer 5: the Kitchen

Alex reported that, in the past, her symptoms were not believed by her children and healthcare professionals. As a result, she felt a lack of confidence in expressing her thoughts and feelings to other people, out of fear of being rejected (systematic re-traumatisation). Reciprocal reinforcement patterns that maintained the FND were frequently observed on the ward. Alex was soft-spoken, kind and mobilised slowly whilst being hunched over with a Zimmer frame. This often elicited compassionate responses from her direct environment, including "baby-ing", using child-like almost patronising speech, and a high level of encouragement from staff during therapy sessions. The baby-ing and strong encouragement were the opposite to what Alex was used to and had a reinforcing effect on her mood and concept of self. After many years of feeling unheard, Alex finally felt validated by her environment, a feeling that she had not experienced in a long time. However, the team also started to become frustrated at seeing a lack of progress despite relentless efforts and slowly disconnected from Alex' treatment resulting in a thinned-out time table. This fed into Alex' rejection beliefs and the maintenance of her FND symptoms.

The pillars of treatment: creating a secure base

There were several crucial components to Alex' treatment for FND:

- Building the therapeutic relationship with the psychologist and other staff members involved in her rehabilitation, as well as forming new friendships with fellow patients. This resulted in Alex experiencing the opposite of what she had experienced prior to developing FND: validation, respect, kindness, compassion, being noticed and valued, and encouragement by "someone who was cheerleading me".
- The development of these relationships with various staff members and fellow patients created trust, a sense of social belonging and a psychological secure base, in the same way that young children develop attachments to a parental key figure who subsequently provides a secure base from which to "explore the world". Alex developed attachments to the staff

and patients, and a sufficiently safe secure base that facilitated the release of Alex' unspeakable dilemma to another person without the threat of being rejected.

- The psychological process of going on a collaborative journey to "get the story of FND straight", and like a detective, in a joint process uncovering the different events, thoughts and feelings that led up to the FND.
- Psycho-education on the mechanics of FND, with Alex developing a firm understanding of the psychosocial maintaining factors.
- Putting into practice techniques of the different elements of the PCM (see Table 5.4 below for more details).

Outcomes

On discharge, Alex' amnesia had fully cleared up, further lending support to a functional cause of her memory problems. Qualitatively, her depression had lifted and she was appropriately bright in mood. Alex developed

Table 5.4 Alex' multidisciplinary treatment organised by PCM element

Kitchen

- The compassionate ward milieu and group therapy space helped Alex with developing friendships on the ward and establishing positive therapeutic relationships with staff.
- Group therapy programme helped Alex to experience a long-lost feeling of validation, being heard and feeling respected by other people. The group also provided her with a sense of belonging and education on FND.

Cover: Release of the unspeakable dilemma in psychology sessions:	**Overpressure Plug**	**Valve**
	• In addition to the FND group, Alex also participated in a cognitive rehabilitation group ("memory group") to support her with strategies to manage the amnesia.	Joint Psychology × OT sessions helped Alex to plan a daily routine, rediscover her interests and engage with meaningful and enjoyable activities that could be carried over after discharge in her community (behavioural activation)
• Alex expressed and described the difficult events and circumstances that led up to her suicide attempt in vivid detail, as well as her thoughts and feelings connected to these events.		
• Sensory grounding and distraction techniques were helpful for Alex to feel her base again.	Alex also participated in multiple ward groups including relaxation, art group, gardening, memory and the pressure cooker group
• Made active and valuable contributions to the group sessions.	• Physiotherapy supported Alex with walking techniques and facilitating a gradual step-down on equipment.	
• Practice of assertiveness skills	• Fatigue management, energy conservation and relaxation strategies were practised with OT.	

Kitchen

Warning light

Alex was highly focused on her physical rather than psychological symptoms and would initially only speak about her FND features, pain and fatigue. However, she learned to interpret this heightened symptom focus in the context of her psychological formulation and slowly shifted her attention away towards psychological mechanisms.

Sticky left-over food

Psycho-education on the FND coping triangle was provided.

A positive qualities log helped Alex to uncover her positive core beliefs and achievements.

I'm kind and I like to help other people. I'm a survivor and a worthwhile human being. I'm just as worthy as other people.

Pot

Physiotherapy sessions on the treadmill. Alex also walked independently indoors and outdoors using a walking stick.

OT supported Alex with strategies to help her with ADLs including washing, dressing, planning and preparation of a hot meal, as well as independently accessing the community in unfamiliar environments and on public transport.

Ignition/Fuel

Psycho-education on vulnerabilities towards the development of FND including the impact of early childhood and later adulthood experiences, negative core beliefs, as well as interpersonal and relationship triggers.

Alex was able to delineate her triggers that sparked off the FND on a daily basis including internal (thoughts, feelings and memories around the unspeakable dilemma) and external triggers (children not wanting contact).

Flames

Psychology sessions and emotion education sessions helped Alex to become aware, uncover, process and express thoughts and feelings that maintained the FND.

By the end of therapy, Alex reported increased confidence in managing difficult thoughts and feelings should they re-emerge in future.

Heat

Through the course of psychological therapy, Alex started to reconnect with her emotions again and allowing the intolerable thoughts, feelings and memories to come through.

Safety features

The ward milieu and MDT supported Alex in discovering her "safety features" including her consistent motivation and engagement in the rehab programme, as well as her ability and social skills in establishing relationships.

a social network of peer relationships on the ward. Her walking improved significantly. She was able to mobilise independently and unaided. Alex became independent in personal and domestic activities of daily life including preparing a complex meal with minimal assistance. She experienced increased confidence in using public transport on her own to local shops with supervision. Alex continued to receive ongoing support for the management of her medications and the risks around her past medication overdose, particularly during the transitionary period from the unit to the supported accommodation that she was discharged to.

Table 5.5 shows Alex' results on self-reported and clinician-rated questionnaires. Although the data collection was patchy, due to time and resource limitations on the ward, the scores provided some idea of Alex' initial psychological and physical functioning. Interestingly, at discharge, Alex' scores on the mood measures increased, suggesting severe levels of depression, the core focus of her psychological treatment. This score was not regarded as alarming as it was consistent with Alex connecting with her emotions, specifically her sadness around leaving the ward and her social network behind.

Case study 3: FND for a decade: a whirlpool of chronic FND symptoms

Reason for referral

The next case study will describe the assessment and treatment of a 40-year-old male ("Gabriel") with a complex medical history and a confirmed diagnosis of longstanding FND that had lasted for more than a decade. Gabriel experienced a wide range of physical, cognitive and emotional symptoms, which severely impacted on his day-to-day activities and quality of life. Due to the complex overlay of organic and functional features, as well as the severity of his symptoms and disabilities, Gabriel was admitted for a period of intensive rehabilitation on an inpatient ward. Given the severity and longevity of Gabriel's symptoms, the goals for admission were initially modest and aimed

Table 5.5 Alex' scores on psychology and neurorehabilitation questionnaires

Questionnaire	Pre-admission	Post-admission
HADS-depression	10 (mild)	11 (moderate)
HADS-anxiety	9 (mild)	11 (moderate)
PHQ-9	8 (moderate)	17 (severe)
GAD-7	7 (moderate)	10 (top end of moderate)
ATSQ	19/35	–
DERS-SF	57 (z = 1.91 above mean)	–
Rosenberg's self-esteem	6	10
UK FIM+FAM (Motor)	80/112	No information/missing data
UK FIM+FAM (Cognitive)	58/98	–
UK FIM+FAM (Total)	138/210	–
Neurological Impairment Scale	14/50	–
Barthel Index	16/20	–
Rehabilitation Complexity Scale	12/22	–

at "coping" and disability management rather than a "cure", with a focus to reduce FND symptoms and Gabriel's care needs.

Background information

A time-line of Gabriel's complex medical history

On admission, Gabriel presented with a significant medical health history. Table 5.6 shows the time-line of events:

Gabriel and his family had never sought help for the FND symptoms due to the potentially life-threatening nature of his previous medical conditions that needed urgent attention and treatment and that had masked and put the FND symptoms "on the backburner" for many years. Other reasons for the delay in diagnosis included the lack of familiarity and awareness with healthcare professionals on FND symptoms, as well as the lack of FND-specialist services in his local area.

FND features

Gabriel's FND symptoms consisted of a mixture of dissociative seizures, sensory and motor-type FND symptoms. Gabriel's seizures were confirmed as "non-epileptic" following a video telemetry investigation. During seizure

Table 5.6 Gabriel's FND time-line

Time-point	Significant health events
14 years ago	• Diagnosis and treatment of lymphoma • Underwent several cycles of chemotherapy • Resulting in recovery and remission.
13 years ago	• Onset of FND – after completing treatment for lymphoma • Gabriel experiences occasional bouts of tingling and weakness in his legs, which in Gabriel's view were his first FND symptoms.
Five years ago	• Gabriel sustains a mild head injury following a fall from the stairs, recovers to some degree following initial hospital treatment, subsequently develops a post-concussive syndrome
Present – five years ago	• Following the mild head injury, Gabriel's FND worsens significantly. • Fluctuating tingling and leg weakness cause walking difficulties and require Gabriel to mobilise in a wheelchair, Gabriel also develops dissociative episodes, retrograde amnesia and a speech disturbance. • Gabriel undergoes various medical investigations, including video telemetry and an MRI, which all come back negative. Gabriel is subsequently diagnosed with FND.
Present	• Gabriel is unable to function and "withdraws from life". • Inpatient admission for intensive rehabilitation for FND.

episodes, Gabriel often reported "losing consciousness" with reduced responsiveness, disorientation and confusion. The motor-type symptoms resembled Gabriel's "unconscious" dissociative seizures but were characterized by intact awareness and an inability to suddenly feel his legs or walk. Gabriel's FND episodes were described as unpredictable; without any apparent triggers; and often lasting for a few hours at a time before self-terminating. Other bothersome physical symptoms included urinary incontinence, headaches, pain and fatigue.

Functional cognitive symptoms

In addition to these more overt FND symptoms, Gabriel reported a large autobiographical memory gap for the period following his recovery from the life-threatening conditions, treatments and hospitalizations. The onset of his amnesia was sudden and clearly demarcated by the concussion. In Gabriel's own words, "after the fall, I just forgot everything", "everything went over my head", "I just switched off from life". Although rehabilitation staff observed normal day-to-day memory abilities, Gabriel reported problems with learning and remembering new information, concentration, organizing his thoughts and initiating activities. Gabriel and his family had not noticed any gradual decline in his cognitive functioning, more a fluctuating course, characterized by "peaks and troughs". Occasional dissociative seizures resulted in post-episode amnesia for the seizure or the triggering events leading up to the seizures. Neurological reviews failed to find any organic causes or neurological changes on Magnetic Resonance Imaging, Computerized Tomography and lumbar puncture investigations. Gabriel's memory problems and seizures were attributed to functional causes. Gabriel did not report any history of mental health problems; a family history of dementia; alcohol and drug misuse; or vitamin deficiencies.

Mood

Prior to his admission, Gabriel only spent his time indoors and had not accessed the community for months. His only social interactions consisted of those with his family and carers. Gabriel was unable to participate in meaningful life roles including work, sports and hobbies. On arrival to the ward, Gabriel kept himself mostly to himself and hardly interacted with peers and staff. Gabriel was often found resting in bed for long periods. He needed intensive day and overnight care which involved assistance of multiple staff members for personal care, toileting, overnight bed repositioning, transfers and feeding. Occasionally, Gabriel was seen out of bed and mobilized in a wheelchair for brief periods. However, he was unable to self-propel or walk, with reduced sitting tolerance and severe fatigue. Although Gabriel did not report any form of distress, his mood scores suggested moderate levels of depression and mild anxiety. Gabriel mostly endorsed physical items on the questionnaires, and in conjunction with his behavioural presentation which suggested depressive symptoms, it was thought that Gabriel may be experiencing dissociation.

Initial neuropsychological rehabilitation formulation

Due to the physical healthcare setting, Gabriel's difficulties were initially formulated from a cognitive neurorehabilitation perspective that summarised his multidisciplinary assessment. Table 5.7 shows this integrated biopsychosocial formulation mapped out on Gabriel's physical, cognitive, emotional and social difficulties.

Neuropsychological assessment: Initial hypotheses

Gabriel's medical history was highly complex and revealed a wide range of notable factors that could impact on the integrity of his brain, cognitive and

Table 5.7 Schematic representation of the Oliver Zangwill Centre biopsychosocial formulation framework

Family and social support (key relationships)	Brain pathology (neuroanatomical changes)	Premorbid factors
Gabriel is a married father with two adult children. His wife is his full-time carer, with his children occasionally chipping in with care activities.	• Multiple cycles of chemotherapy for lymphoma. • Mild head injury. • No significant brain pathology noted on imaging; MRI scan came back clear. • Polypharmacy.	Gabriel had several hospitalisations and "heavy-duty" treatments for life-threatening illnesses. History of longstanding challenging interpersonal dynamics with specific family members resulting in domestic violence.
Cognitive impairment Memory problems particularly retrograde amnesia Post-seizure amnesia High distractibility and concentration difficulties.	**Mood, affect and behavioural symptoms** Mostly physical items endorsed on mood and anxiety questionnaires, with suspected depression. Unable to identify emotions, features of possible dissociation. Appears low in mood, based on behavioural indicators (i.e. apathy, no self-initiation of behaviours or activities) and biological features.	**Physical** Intermittent episodes of functional paraplegia Fluctuating right-sided weakness, balance issues Stammering speech Tingles in the legs, reduced sensation Sleeping difficulties Fatigue, joint pain Urinary incontinence Weight issues

(Continued)

Table 5.7 (Continued)

Insight	Communication	Losses
Due to the amnesia, severe apathy and communication difficulties, it was difficult for Gabriel to formulate and communicate his thoughts about the FND and his physical difficulties Lack of "systemic insight" of family into FND.	Speech disturbance (e.g. resembling developmental errors, halting and stammering speech)	Job role – unemployed for many years Lack of social network, no other social contacts apart from family, loss of all other friendships. Loss of role of father and husband. Loss of leisure activities, no hobbies or interests

Functional consequences
Assistance of two people for washing and dressing (wheeled commode)
Unable to prepare and complete meals, household chores, shopping, accessing the
community, dispensing and administering medications
Unable to mobilise (wheelchair-bound but unable to self-propel)
Assistance of two for bed positioning and transfers (using Sara Stedy equipment)
Unable to drive or work
Fully adapted house for disabilities including a wet room, a stair lift and a
hospital bed.

behavioural functioning. To unpick all these potentially contributing factors, a thorough description of each of the hypotheses will be outlined in the section below.

Lymphoma and Chemotherapy.   Hodgkin lymphoma can be associated with cognitive difficulties in people treated with chemotherapy including in the domains of attention, executive functioning, as well as learning and memory functions (e.g. Fayette et al., 2017; Trachtenberg et al., 2018; Magyari et al., 2022). Although Gabriel had since long recovered from lymphoma, his body had been exposed to multiple cycles of chemotherapy. Most chemotherapeutic agents fail to pass the blood-brain-barrier (Angeli et al., 2020); however, neuroimaging studies have found brain changes following chemotherapy including in the grey and white matter, cerebellum, basal ganglia, prefrontal gyrus and Broca's area, an area important for speech production (e.g. Saykin et al., 2003; Tannock et al., 2004; Silverman et al., 2007; Ahles et al., 2012). Although one study failed to find group differences between patients who were "on" and "not on" chemotherapy (Donovan et al., 2005), other neuropsychological studies identified wide-ranging deficits across all cognitive domains including in verbal and visual memory; attention, working memory and information processing speed; visuospatial skills; verbal fluency and language; mental flexibility, go/no go tasks and (psycho)motor function (Wieneke & Dienst, 1995; Van Dam et al., 1998; Schagen et al., 1999; Ahles et al., 2002; Castellon et al., 2004; Shilling et al., 2005; Stewart et al., 2006; Fardell et al., 2011; Jim et al., 2012; McDonald et al., 2013; Hermelink et al., 2017; Vitali et al., 2017), despite "high-normal" estimated premorbid intellectual abilities (Wieneke & Dienst, 1995). It should be noted that many studies investigating chemotherapy-related cognitive dysfunction focus on breast cancer patients, with deficits reported as mild (Matsuda et al., 2005; Stewart et al., 2006; Hermelink, 2015; Hermelink et al., 2017) although cognitive impairment following chemotherapy can persist in a subset of patients (Ahles et al., 2002; Castellon et al., 2004; Tannock et al., 2004; Boykoff et al., 2009; Fardell et al., 2011) with an adverse impact on quality of life and disabilities (Tannock et al., 2004; Matsuda et al., 2005; Vitali et al., 2017). Longitudinal outcome studies demonstrated cognitive decline in a subset of chemotherapy patients (Shilling et al., 2005 – even pre-dating chemotherapy: Wefel et al., 2004), although cognitive deficits were deemed subtle (Collins et al., 2009; Jim et al., 2012) with significant improvements over time (Shilling et al., 2005; Collins et al., 2009). The origins of chemotherapy-related cognitive dysfunction are complex and not solely ascribed to its neurotoxic effects and generally viewed as the result of "biopsychosocial" factors including genetics, cytokines, hormones, medications, cancer stage, prognosis, comorbid medical conditions, menopause, radiotherapy, chemotherapy dose, surgery, anesthesia, psychological burden and distress, disruption to life, fatigue, as well as social and behavioural variables (Tannock et al., 2004; Hurria et al., 2007; Boykoff et al., 2009; Hermelink, 2015; Vitali et al., 2017). With Gabriel's medical history in mind and findings from the research literature, could it be possible that chemotherapy had caused residual cognitive effects?

Post-concussive syndrome. Gabriel had also fallen from the stairs and sustained a mild head injury with post-concussive syndrome. No loss of consciousness was reported at the time although Gabriel had been experiencing ongoing memory symptoms since the fall. Brain scans did not reveal any injuries. The neuropsychological research literature suggests that, post-concussion, people can experience cognitive problems in the domains of attention, processing speed, reaction time, working and long-term memory (Iverson et al., 2004a; Iverson et al., 2004b; Iverson et al., 2012; Collie et al., 2006; Sterr et al., 2006 though see Vander Werff & Rieger, 2019). However, in the majority of people who may be "transiently" affected by a concussion, sequelae do not persist (e.g. Bigler, 2008).

Functional neurological disorder. The following section will summarise the neuropsychological findings for the two subtypes experienced by Gabriel, i.e. dissociative seizures and motor-type FND. Although the results do not clearly suggest a characteristic neuropsychological profile for either subtype, the following conclusions can be drawn based on the available case-control studies. Attentional difficulties are common in both subtypes especially on cognitively more demanding tasks with an "executive" component. Information processing speed was generally slowed in motor-type FND patients (e.g. Almis et al., 2013; O'Brien et al., 2015; Huys et al., 2020; Vechetova et al., 2022). Verbal and visual memory have sparsely been investigated in FND, although slightly more often in motor-type FND patients. Results show subtle deficits on some memory performance indicators (e.g. Almis et al., 2013; Heintz et al., 2013; Brown et al., 2014; Vechetova et al., 2022). Language functions are the least examined area of cognition. Normal object naming abilities were reported on the Boston Naming Test in motor-type FND patients (Voon et al., 2013). Visual and spatial skills were rarely examined but appeared intact in both subtypes (Voon et al., 2013; Pick et al., 2016; Pick et al., 2018; Leon-Sarmiento et al., 2019). In general, normal executive functions were reported for people with dissociative seizures though the evidence base is small. Executive functions were far more often researched in people with motor-type FND yielding highly variable results, even within one neuropsychological task (for example the Trail Making Test; e.g. Brown et al., 2014; O'Brien et al., 2015; Van Wouwe et al., 2020; Hamouda et al., 2021; Vechetova et al., 2022).

Experimental neuropsychological tasks measuring emotion-attention interactions (e.g. emotional Stroop tasks) were far more commonly investigated in dissociative seizures. Results suggested the presence of attentional biases in response to emotional face stimuli in people with dissociative seizures (e.g. Bakvis et al., 2009a; Bakvis et al., 2009b; Pick et al., 2018) in the presence of intact basic facial perception (Pick et al., 2016) and normal performance on a neutral Stroop task (Bakvis et al., 2009). An attentional bias away from sad faces was found in people with motor-type FND (Marotta et al., 2020). Interestingly, when looking beyond the level of "deficits" what stood out in this literature review was the extent of the variability in test results within and across cognitive domains. Although the body of neuropsychological evidence on deficits in people with functional cognitive symptoms is less well developed than the research for the other two FND subtypes, neuropsychological studies suggest mixed findings widely ranging from increased, but non-significant, rates of verbal memory and executive functioning deficits in people with co-existing depression (Bhome et al., 2019); "sub-threshold deficits" on letter fluency and digit cancellation tasks (Wakefield et al., 2018); objective deficits in attention and verbal memory (Schmidtke et al., 2008); and at least one affected cognitive domain on neuropsychological testing in 73% (Bhome et al., 2019). Subjective memory difficulties persisted in 87% at follow-up (Schmidtke et al., 2008). In addition, people with functional cognitive symptoms showed an impaired perception of their own memory performance ("metamemory" or "memory self-efficacy") on a functional memory disorder questionnaire in the presence of normal performance on verbal memory, processing speed and intellectual tasks (Metternich et al., 2009; see also Wakefield et al., 2018; McWhirter et al., 2020).

Polypharmacy.   Over the years, Gabriel's FND had mostly been "forgotten" by the healthcare system. According to Gabriel, healthcare professionals that treated him often lacked awareness on FND. Gabriel had accumulated a long list of medications, with some possessing sedative and dissociation-inducing effects (e.g. opiates), and that could potentially adversely impact his memory functions and level of alertness.

Pain and fatigue.   In their systematic review, Teodoro et al. (2018) described widespread attentional dysfunction across FND, fibromyalgia and chronic fatigue syndrome. The authors argued that the hallmark features of each condition – increased self-focused symptom focus, pain and fatigue, respectively – all interfere with the efficiency of cognitive/attentional processing that increases vulnerability to distraction and disrupt attentional, encoding and memory functions. Together with "memory perfectionism", overinterpretation of cognitive failures and increased self-monitoring for cognitive errors, this creates the subjective experience of cognitive difficulties ("brain fog"). Gabriel was diagnosed with severe FND and reported symptoms of joint pain, fatigue and poor sleep causing daytime somnolence. In line with Teodoro et al. (2018), these features could all interfere with Gabriel's efficiency of cognitive/attentional processing and increase his vulnerability to distraction.

Depression.   The influence of psychological variables on Gabriel's presentation was also considered. Video telemetry had already confirmed the dissociative rather than organic nature of Gabriel's seizures. There was a suspicion that Gabriel was suffering from depression and had not fully processed his emotions around his illnesses especially considering Gabriel's comment about not remembering his previous hospitalisations that suggested potential dissociative tendencies and unresolved emotional processing. The periods around Gabriel's investigations, diagnoses and aftermath of the conditions were expected to cause high levels of emotional distress. However, Gabriel did not report feeling distressed nor could he indicate any triggers in his life that could make him feel distressed although he did allude to unhelpful family dynamics. He did not present as particularly tearful or anhedonic, and was unable to identify any helpful coping strategies, but acknowledged that at times he overate on sweet and processed foods. In addition, even though the contents of his thoughts and feelings were largely unclear and Gabriel "denied" the existence of low mood, despite his moderate PHQ-9 score, there were a range of "indirect" pieces of evidence that would possibly increase the risk for depression. For example, Gabriel's life lacked meaningful and enjoyable activities. Not only did his physical disabilities create high dependency needs that prevented him from taking care of himself, his family and his household, Gabriel was also unable to access the community and engage in work, social, leisure or sports activities. He could not identify "what ticked him", including any hobbies, interests or passions. His social network was limited to his immediate family only and he had lost contact with his once tightly knitted former friendship group. In addition to his health, Gabriel had incurred several other losses including his role as the "head" and provider for his family, a much-loved job and his ability to drive a car. On observation, Gabriel presented with apathy and exuded a sense of hopelessness without any futuristic thinking. As neuropsychological studies of people with depressive symptoms have demonstrated deficits, particularly in the domains of memory, speed of information processing and executive functioning (e.g. Zakzanis et al., 1998; Hammar & Ardal, 2009; Rock et al., 2014; Mohn & Rund, 2016), it was hypothesised that perhaps an underlying depression was driving Gabriel's memory difficulties.

Atypical dementia.   An alternative "wild card" hypothesis of possible dementia was also considered. Gabriel's age was far below the (even presenile) age range expected for dementia and he did not report (young-onset) dementia in his family history. However, he demonstrated consistent problems with expressive speech, often with stuttering and halting, as well as a sweet food preference, accompanied by psychological and behavioural difficulties (e.g. apathy). Could this be the prodromal stage of a rarer form of neurodegenerative illness, for example, frontotemporal dementia? After further deliberation, a dementia hypothesis was not actively entertained, as Gabriel's symptoms were characterised by a sudden rather than insipient onset; with a brain scan that was negative for atrophic changes; without evidence of gradual cognitive decline; and with the presence of selective memory problems fluctuating in response to stress triggers. However, for the purposes of a comprehensive investigation, it was important to "keep all options open" to ensure a full understanding of Gabriel's functioning.

To investigate and disentangle these hypotheses further, Gabriel agreed to participate in a neuropsychological assessment which aimed to explore the nature of his self-reported amnesia and to what extent organic or functional influences were able to explain Gabriel's clinical presentation, in particularly his memory difficulties. Irrespective of the driving forces underlying Gabriel's clinical presentation, the neuropsychological assessment also intended to obtain a view on Gabriel's current strengths and difficulties to help inform his rehabilitation programme and gauge the potential impact of his cognitive difficulties on multidisciplinary sessions. If the neuropsychological assessment would point towards more functional reasons for Gabriel's amnesia, then in conjunction with the MRI results, this would provide strong converging evidence for Gabriel to consider a psychological formulation for his difficulties, which would potentially help increase his engagement with subsequent psychological therapy.

Behaviour during testing

Gabriel engaged well throughout most of the neuropsychological assessment, apart from visibly struggling on memory tasks. He could not remember having done a subset of the tests. Both Gabriel's expressive and receptive language functions were unimpaired, with normal fluency in conversation. Neither speech and grammatical abnormalities nor semantic or phonological paraphasias were observed. He was able to understand and follow all test instructions. His stammering episodes and motor weakness did not impact any of the verbal and motor aspects of the testing. Gabriel's results on a performance validity test were well above the cut-off score and suggested that Gabriel's neuropsychological test performance was likely an accurate reflection of his true cognitive abilities

Test score observations

Closer inspection of Gabriel's test scores revealed several interesting findings. A defining characteristic of Gabriel's neuropsychological test results was variability and inconsistency in performance across tests. Gabriel appeared to demonstrate less difficulty on complex and cognitively demanding tasks in comparison to other less effortful and simpler tasks, e.g. normal working memory in the presence of abnormal short-term memory. There was a lack of converging evidence on tests measuring similar concepts, e.g. widely diverging performance on two visual information processing speed tests. Furthermore, on several tests assessing information processing speed skills, Gabriel showed a wide variability in performance and response times, ranging from normal to significant cognitive slowing. However, he performed in the superior range on a complex "higher order" executive functioning test that relied on quick and accurate "lower level" information processing under time pressure, or he would have likely not been able to perform well on this "higher order" test, suggesting that there was little converging evidence to make a case for slowed information processing speed. In a similar vein, Gabriel struggled with processing simple sentences, but this did not seem to impact his good performance on a "higher order" verbal memory test that relied on these "lower level" basic skills.

Neuropsychological assessment: conclusions

In a nutshell, Gabriel's neuropsychological testing revealed subtle cognitive dysfunction. Gabriel's current intellectual functions fell in the average range and were in keeping with his premorbid intellectual abilities, educational and occupational history. He showed mild difficulties with focused attention. In contrast, Gabriel's information processing speed was not universally slowed. Across verbal and visual memory tests, Gabriel's performance was characterised by problems with the retrieval of information rather than with encoding or storage. On recognition tests, Gabriel's memory performance significantly improved to near-perfect. For example, Gabriel's inability to recall any visual design stimuli and ever having done the test in the first place initially suggested that his memory trace had "vanished". However, Gabriel's memory performance subsequently benefitted and normalised with retrieval cues and structure, suggesting that he was able to encode and lay down a visual memory trace earlier but struggled to access the visual information. There was some mild executive dysfunction, only pertaining to cognitive flexibility but with relatively preserved response inhibition. Gabriel exhibited intact verbal, visual and spatial skills. Overall, Gabriel's severe self-reported levels of amnesia did not mirror his "mild cognitive impairment" on objective neuropsychological/memory testing and suggested functional causes.

Qualitative observations

A qualitative analysis of Gabriel's amnesia strengthened the notion of a functional cause for Gabriel's memory difficulties.

Selectivity.   The nature of Gabriel's memory loss seemed to pinpoint to a strong and selective association with events that are expected to evoke psychological distress, including life-threatening illness, surgeries, hospitalisations; psychological therapy sessions that explored highly emotive topics and involved the disclosure, as well as emotional release of distressing life events; and challenging interpersonal family dynamics that Gabriel had alluded to. Furthermore, Gabriel's memory symptoms were not continuously present but, instead, showed a tendency towards fluctuations. His memory symptoms ameliorated when the distress settled, with distraction, or with expressing his thoughts and identifying emotions ("opening the cover"). Distraction often improves functional symptoms and is a key strategy in treatment programs for FND.

Autobiographical memory.   Gabriel reported an unusually long autobiographical memory gap that was characterised by a self-reported "total" and sudden loss of memory for all past life events following the start of his health problems. The sudden rather than insipient nature of the amnesia, in the absence of gradual decline over time and the consistent lack of an organic correlate on neurological investigations, suggested that dementia was unlikely, even a more atypical form. Even though the Autobiographical Memory Interview (Kopelman et al., 1990) was not conducted, an anecdotal analysis of Gabriel's life-time memories suggested an absence of a "temporal gradient" normally found in different types of dementias, for example, Alzheimer's (poor recall of recent vs relatively spared recall of remote events) or semantic ("reverse gradient": better recall of recent vs poorer recall of remote memories). Gabriel's temporal gradient of autobiographical memories resembled more of a U-shaped parabola (recent and remote memories spared with a memory gap for a long period in the middle). Furthermore, although he reported being unable to remember even snippets from his time of sickness when directly asked, Gabriel was able to spontaneously conjure up some memories from that time when attention was not drawn on them.

Day-to-day memory functioning.   There was a strong discrepancy between Gabriel's self-reported memory symptoms and his deficits obtained on neuropsychological testing and his day-to-day cognitive abilities. Despite Gabriel self-reporting severe amnesia affecting years of life events as well as problems learning and remembering new information (hence both a retrograde and anterograde amnesia), his neuropsychological deficits were generally mild and did not reflect this severity level. Several observations on the ward suggested normal learning and memory functions. Apart from when in a dissociative state with reduced awareness, Gabriel was able to consistently lay down new memories, from the moment that he arrived on the ward including:

Table 5.8 Ward observations of Gabriel's day-to-day cognitive abilities

Type of memory	Gabriel's examples
Orientation	Intact orientation in person, time and place.
	Remembering the location and name of the hospital, as well as the reason for his admission.
Episodic memory	Preserved recall of faces and names of staff and patients.
	Remembering to sign in and out on the ward, occasionally even reminding absent-minded therapy staff.
	Able to watch and remember the story lines of movies on the ward television or relevant information broadcast on the radio (e.g. current political affairs).
	Gabriel was able to learn and successfully apply his rehabilitation strategies across all multidisciplinary disciplines. He spontaneously initiated the use of distraction strategies during walking practice without any prompts. Rehabilitation therapists noted good carry-over between sessions and a consistent demonstration of faultless memory for rehabilitation strategies.
Prospective memory	Good memory for future sessions and always on time waiting for his next session at the correct location, without a need for prompting. Gabriel was very organised and able to use his timetable effectively.
Semantic memory	Gabriel showed good knowledge of a wide range of gardening plants and skills.
	He recognised all the food items and different types of mealtimes on the food menu sheet without needing explanation. Gabriel was able to follow all procedures around the usual sequence of steps of how to order take-away food and what types of food exist.
	Often self-initiated and independently organised social gatherings and ward activities (e.g. quiz nights) without much staff support. Gabriel did not need explanation about generating quiz questions that often tapped into semantic knowledge.
Topographical and spatial memory	Good wayfinding and topographical orientation, from sessions in the gym to his bedspace, venturing out to meet his family outside the hospital, finding the coffee shop without any difficulty or getting lost.
Implicit and procedural memory	Occupational therapists were not concerned about Gabriel's intact "cognition-in-function" abilities around washing, dressing, toileting and grooming.
	In physiotherapist sessions, Gabriel was able to learn new gait patterns and use equipment. He was able to 'step up' and progress in his walking practice by learning to ascend/descend a full flight of stairs without any evidence of memory problems.

The inconsistencies between Gabriel's self-reported severe amnesia in the presence of mild objective neuropsychological deficits were in line with studies on functional cognitive symptoms (Metternich et al., 2009; see also Teodoro et al., 2018; Wakefield et al., 2018; McWhirter et al., 2020). The discrepancy between Gabriel's subjectively reported poor memory and intact "day-to-day memory" was consistent with the notion of internal inconsistency in the context of FCD criteria, as defined by Ball et al. (2020). When reviewing in more detail, Gabriel appeared to only partially fulfil the criteria for FCD. He exhibited the symptoms of impaired cognitive functioning, based both on Gabriel's own self-perception and on observation of mild deficits on neuropsychological testing, with clear evidence of "internal inconsistency". However, it appeared that a "psychiatric disorder", depression, was able to explain Gabriel's cognitive symptoms. Although the cognitive symptoms caused issues in day-to-day life at home, including preventing Gabriel from taking care of himself, working, driving and socialising (which were also driven by family factors), the symptoms did not emerge on the ward and were clearly situation specific. In addition, the cognitive symptoms did not cause considerable distress to Gabriel. On the contrary, his distress was reduced as a result of his effective ability to suppress memories. If anything, the cognitive symptoms were almost helpful and stabilised Gabriel's mood. The question arose whether the dissociative amnesia was truly a cognitive "deficit" and not merely a "strength" that supported Gabriel with surviving his hopeless situation.

Type of amnesia.   The features of Gabriel's amnesia were unusual and striking. His memory loss followed a retrograde amnesia pattern. In addition, Gabriel demonstrated retrograde amnesia in the absence of anterograde amnesia. His non-epileptic episodes appeared to be driven by emotional triggers and invariably resulted in post-episode amnesia for the seizures and the events leading up to the seizures.

Heightened self-focused attention.   Across all disciplines, it was observed that Gabriel's symptoms significantly reduced on distraction. When Gabriel focused his attention on the neuropsychological tests, his memory, speech and motor difficulties disappeared. He remembered the test instructions without the need for repetition or correction. As the therapeutic relationship strengthened and Gabriel developed a sense of psychological safety that allowed him to disclose the details of sensitive events from his past, his stammer soon disappeared, and he developed good conversational ability with clear expression of thoughts during psychological therapy sessions. Similarly, his physiotherapists showed Gabriel that, once his attention was diverted, he was better able to mobilise. In line with contemporary theories of the important role of heightened self-focused attention on symptoms in FND (e.g. Edwards et al., 2012), this was further converging evidence of the functional nature of Gabriel's presentation.

Multidisciplinary investigations. Physiotherapy consistently described Gabriel's motor weakness as functional, whereas speech and language therapy assessments revealed that Gabriel's pattern of expressive language difficulties were more likely to fit with a functional than an organic cause. In addition, Gabriel's brain was rescanned following an episode of reduced awareness, to ensure nothing sinister had appeared given his complex medical history, and this reconfirmed that Gabriel did not show evidence of a brain injury. All multidisciplinary investigations of Gabriel's cognitive, seizure, motor and speech symptoms converged and were unanimously consistent with a functional cause.

Conclusions

His neuropsychological assessment suggested that Gabriel's memory problems and FND were probably consistent with a longstanding depression, including:

1 Gabriel's **neuropsychological profile** of variable and inconsistent attentional, memory and executive functioning deficits was consistent with a depression profile (Zakzanis et al., 1998; Hammar & Ardal, 2009; Rock et al., 2014; Mohn & Rund, 2016), and possibly reflected the "misallocation" of his cognitive resources to the fluctuating nature of the waxing and waning of his stream of negative thoughts and feelings, consistent with Teodoro et al. (2018), even though Gabriel's thought contents were initially inaccessible due to prolonged dissociation.

2 Gabriel's **distinctive pattern of memory problems**, including recall rather than recognition deficits, as well as his amnesia selectively affecting emotional events in the presence of preserved memory for non-emotional events.

3 His **PHQ-9 score** of 12 suggested moderate depression. On this mood questionnaire, Gabriel strongly endorsed physical rather than psychological features, with Gabriel struggling to identify and label emotions, consistent with dissociation. It is possible that the severity of his depression may have previously gone unnoticed due to "dissociative amnesia".

4 Although Gabriel did not present as tearful or anhedonic, a **behavioural analysis** of his mood revealed several "biological" and behavioural features in line with depression including apathy and lack of interest in activities, psychomotor slowing, pain, fatigue, overeating and poor sleep – in addition to social isolation.

5 **Unprocessed emotions** in the context of his complex medical history and ongoing family triggers without any identifiable access to helpful coping strategies (e.g. sports, friendships and a safe trusted relationship to help emotional expression) likely cultivated the conditions for Gabriel to develop depression.

6 As will become evident at a later stage, the **reversible nature** of Gabriel's memory difficulties, previously observed in depression (Rabins &

Nestadt, 1985), was further evidence of the functional cause of amnesia. This was perhaps the biggest piece of evidence for the functional nature of Gabriel's amnesia: the fact that following multidisciplinary treatment, all of Gabriel's functional symptoms, including his memory problems, had dissipated and he made a full recovery from FND, therefore adding further weight to the functional hypothesis for his amnesia.

Re-formulation using the Pressure Cooker Model

A standard CBT model for depression was difficult to apply since Gabriel did not identify with low mood or reported any depressive cognitions. Therefore, Gabriel's FND and psychological difficulties were formulated using the PCM (Table 5.9).

Table 5.9 Gabriel's PCM formulation

Kitchen

- Enmeshed family system, Gabriel's wife is registered as his main and full-time carer whilst other family members occasionally "chip in". Gabriel was highly dependent for all activities in daily life. Certain family members prevented Gabriel from undertaking any activities, for example shopping, cooking, social activities.
- Reciprocal reinforcement: when Gabriel experiences a worsening of amnesia, non-epileptic episodes or leg weakness, the family rallies around him to provide maximum support and prevent Gabriel from undertaking any activities at home or outdoors.
- Query around coercive control, as well as physical and emotional domestic violence, that was followed up after his discharge.

Cover	Overpressure Plug	Valve
• Unreleased unspeakable dilemma about his tumultuous family situation and feeling trapped in a hopeless situation with no view of escape. Keeping himself to himself and not having a person to express his emotions to. • Functional speech problems without swallowing difficulties. • Speech disturbance was symbolic of Gabriel's inability to express his thoughts and feelings and not having a voice within the family unit.	• Functional amnesia • Non-epileptic episodes with reduced awareness and post-episode amnesia. • Intermittent episodes of fluctuating functional bilateral leg weakness characterized by intact awareness and an inability to suddenly feel his legs or walk. • Reduced sensation and tingles in the legs • Pain in the back • Fatigue	• Prior to developing FND, Gabriel used to be "boom": always on the go, various jobs that he enjoyed, active social life. • At present, Gabriel displays a bust-after-boom profile: apathy, no self-initiation and complete reduction in enjoyable and social activities. Unemployed and on benefits. • Lack of social network. His only interactions are with immediate family members. Gabriel lived indoors and had been house- and bed-bound for years.

Warning light
- Lack of information on Gabriel's self-focused attention.
- However, the FND was highly entrenched with the system around him showing hypervigilance and completely in charge of managing Gabriel's symptoms.

Sticky left-over food
- Low self-esteem, lack of self-belief and self-efficacy around coping with FND.
- Retrospectively reported coping strategies from childhood and in family of origin: "just pushed on", "kept self to self" and "hid my emotions" in response to stressful events (avoidant coping).

Pot
- Significant medical history requiring invasive treatments and admissions to intensive care.
- Polypharmacy including several medications that facilitate dissociation.
- Biological and behavioural features of depression.
- At risk of falls, environmental dependency, medication mismanagement due to amnesia.
- Highly entrenched with equipment: wheelchair- and mostly bed-bound, house adaptations.
- Reduced cardiovascular functioning, muscle wasting and deconditioning.
- Poor sleep, continence issues.

Flames
- Unable to identify, label, feel and connect with emotions. Poor emotion language: describing sadness as "tiredness".
- Outward appearance of severe depression based on behavioural indicators: complete inertia/apathy, loss of appetite, poor sleep.
- Inconsistent with mood questionnaire results: minimal depressive and anxiety symptoms reported.

Heat
- High levels of dissociation, with prolonged vacant staring episodes throughout the day.

Ignition
- Relatively normal upbringing without obvious adverse or traumatic childhood experiences. Attended mainstream school without additional learning support.
- Years of unresolved problematic interpersonal family dynamics, with several members experiencing mental health issues requiring active support and admissions.
Domestic violence (physical and emotional).
- Critical incidents: Past history of lymphoma and mild head injury.

Fuel
- Mostly interpersonal triggers: complex, problematic relationships with recently escalated interactions within the family unit.
- Marital relationship had deteriorated significantly.
- Attempts at walking elicit a fear of falling down.

Safety features
Although severe apathy initially limited Gabriel's engagement, he showed a willingness to attend all sessions and practise in between sessions. He was pleasant in interaction and staff enjoyed working with Gabriel and seeing his steady upwards progression in rehab.

Layer 1: Ignition

Gabriel's psychosocial history demonstrated several factors that made him vulnerable towards developing FND and depression. Although Gabriel did not report any trauma background, the main coping style in his family of origin in response to stressful events involved dissociation ("pushing on" "hiding emotions"), as well as keeping self to self. Pushing on with activities was also viewed as a form of dissociation, as it stopped Gabriel from having to sit with the distress and connecting with emotions. Gabriel married young and disclosed a longstanding history of a coercive marital relationship and dysfunctional family dynamics prior to the development of his first FND symptoms.

Layer 2: the FND coping triad

Gabriel's childhood dissociative tendencies had repeated into adulthood. As a result, Gabriel coped with the challenging circumstances in his family situation by dissociation. Throughout most of his life, dissociative coping served Gabriel well until he experienced a series of emotionally overwhelming critical events in the context of life-threatening health conditions and invasive treatments, which rendered his previous coping strategies as insufficient to manage the higher-than-normal levels of distress emanating from these events.

Layer 3: the Pressure Cooker Chain Reaction

The unravelling of his usual coping strategies in response to high stress levels sets off a maintenance cycle characterised by the development of a more extreme form of dissociation to manage the distress: FND. The functional amnesia, dissociative seizures and post-seizure amnesia (Overpressure Plug) helped Gabriel to suppress and avoid experiencing intolerable, strong and negative emotions, thoughts and memories (Flames and Heat) related to his illnesses and interpersonal triggers in his family situation (Fuel). The lack of verbal release of his emotions (tight Cover) and the chronic inertia maintained by his physical disabilities and overbearing family members that did not afford Gabriel with any opportunities to undertake activities independently (blocked Valve), in combination with his low self-esteem and lack of self-belief in his abilities to manage the FND, increased the risk of Gabriel regulating his internal distress with FND. Gabriel's memory suppression and dissociative episodes (which temporarily suppressed memories) from this painful reality were an internal emotion regulation mechanism to tolerate the unbearable feelings of hopelessness, low mood and lack of meaningful roles, activities and life goals. It should be noted that Gabriel demonstrated a good ability to inhibit and suppress "irrelevant" information as evidenced on neuropsychological testing. These cognitive strengths likely facilitated his already existing memory suppression tendencies and problems retrieving information including painful memories. In a similar vein to the functional amnesia, Gabriel's other FND symptoms appeared to have a specific meaning. Given the strong links between the body and emotions, Gabriel's inability to feel parts of his body (sensory symptoms) corresponded to his inability to feel and connect with his emotions. Gabriel's functional speech problems were almost a symbolic reflection of his physical inability to verbally express emotions and physically mirrored his absence of a voice in the family unit. The relationship between Gabriel's FND symptoms and emotions was confirmed on multiple occasions by the re-emergence of FND in response to stressful family interactions, as well as the dissipation of FND following management of emotions evoked by these events. For example, after learning to apply his new psychological strategies during a relapse of FND following a distressing interaction, Gabriel expressed his emotions in a one-to-one conversation with staff. Within a few hours, sensation and strength returned in his legs and he was able to walk again without aids.

Layer 4: facilitating physical factors of FND

Gabriel's heightened self-focused attention, pain and fatigue further increased his vulnerability to attentional distraction that interfered with the efficiency of his cognitive functioning, as described by Teodoro et al. (2018), impacting on memory functioning and creating Gabriel's subjective experience of severe memory difficulties. Furthermore, Gabriel's longstanding dissociative tendencies were further facilitated and amplified by chronic polypharmacy, which resulted in significant sedation, dissociation, cognitive dysfunction and long sleeping episodes. His sudden motor weakness and urinary incontinence could be part of the fight-flight-or-freeze response in relation to underlying anxiety and stress during challenging family interactions. Due to the chronic nature of his FND, Gabriel had developed secondary consequences to his immobility including muscle wasting and deconditioning that needed professional input. High levels of longstanding entrenchment, a lack of involvement of any services, an absence of regular reviews of Gabriel's FND symptoms and equipment, coupled with his fear of falling, prevented Gabriel and his family from an opportunity to step down equipment and testing out beliefs around his ability to manage without equipment.

Layer 5: the social functions of FND

Gabriel's FND symptoms served an external function: the worsening of his FND, whether this was in the form of amnesia, non-epileptic episodes, post-episode amnesia or leg weakness, resulted in his family ceasing any arguments and strife on the spot and, instead, provided Gabriel with support, kindness and care. Therefore, Gabriel's symptoms were both negatively and positively reinforced by the environment. The FND symptoms served as a deterrent against the resurgence of family conflicts and effectively and quickly removed unpleasant emotions and interpersonal triggers from his environment, therefore reinforcing their re-occurrence in the future. The family's enmeshed relationships and excessive caring behaviours in response to Gabriel's FND symptoms also revealed a darker side. Not only did it remove their own discomfort and distress at seeing Gabriel unwell, the caring behaviours and systemic hypervigilance made Gabriel highly dependent on his environment for meeting his physical and emotional needs. The suspicion arose that Gabriel's physical disabilities and lack of independence were to some extent actively maintained by a subset of people in his environment who preferred Gabriel to stay at home and prevented Gabriel from undertaking meaningful activities, pursuing hobbies and a job, making social connections, and accessing the community on his own. Gabriel felt trapped in a hopeless and inescapable situation without any view towards a resolution. The thoughts and feelings of this unspeakable dilemma (Griffith et al., 1998) and a lack of opportunities to express his emotions further fed into Gabriel's distress and FND. Gabriel's recovery from his amnesia and FND would likely generate major emotional consequences for the family system that would risk falling apart. His family inadvertently or unconsciously kept "the status quo" of Gabriel's illness ⇔ family care arrangements in place as the emotional fall-out would not be psychologically tolerated by any of the members. This hypothesis was confirmed by Gabriel's removal from his home environment and admission to the unit. This helped break down ingrained reciprocal reinforcement patterns. It should also be noted that Gabriel's past medical conditions, which threatened or had the potential to threaten his life, understandably caused high distress in him and his family, creating a sense of alarm and urgency. However, the aftermath of these potentially life-threatening conditions and associated continuing care may have "overshadowed" the potential impact of Gabriel's FND symptoms.

ENVIRONMENTAL INFLUENCES ON THE MAINTENANCE OF DISSOCIATIVE AMNESIA

Functional cognitive symptoms, including dissociative amnesia, are often viewed as an "internal" problem impacting on processes that are mostly located in the individual's own psyche and dysfunctional belief patterns. This was certainly applicable to Gabriel's situation. Gabriel shared fixed ideas about his memory including the belief that his memory was "extremely poor" even though this was not mirrored by his mild deficits found on an objective neuropsychological assessment. In addition, Gabriel held a fixed illness belief around the concussion and chemotherapy as the automatic and irreversible causes of his memory problems, given their potentially life-threatening nature and temporal association. His subtle cognitive inflexibility probably contributed to these fixed ideas. However, functional cognitive symptoms are equally maintained by the individual's environment as Gabriel's case will demonstrate with the following examples:

- Environmental triggers (i.e. stressful family interactions) were the predominant recurring triggers for Gabriel's dissociative amnesia as it increased his vulnerability to attentional distraction interfering with the efficiency of his memory processes and activated his tendency towards memory suppression and dissociative seizures.
- His hypervigilant and restricting family stopped Gabriel from accessing the community and building a social network. His social isolation prevented Gabriel from "testing out" assumptions around his self-perceived poor memory and developing alternative coping strategies (e.g. sports, friends) for distress that would reduce the risk of dissociative amnesia.
- Gabriel's complex medical history and ongoing "medical input" for these conditions (rather than the FND) contributed to the development of a sick role that was primarily maintained by his family's perception that he remained ill and needed care. Gabriel's family had taken on many caring responsibilities including medication management and engaged in hypervigilant symptom monitoring. This took away any opportunities for Gabriel to become more independent and update his erroneous beliefs about his memory, for example, by allowing him to manage or at least partially help him to self-administer his own medications and review the "evidence" that he is capable of remembering, even if a little. This dependency prevented Gabriel from testing out the quality of his memory functioning and kept alive the idea of a severe memory impairment.
- The lack of insight that Gabriel and his family had into all these systemic processes further maintained his memory problems.

Intervention

Table 5.10 shows Gabriel's psychological and multidisciplinary intervention that was guided by his PCM formulation.

Extinguishing the fear of falling

Although Gabriel progressed well in his psychological therapy sessions, Gabriel's physical rehab journey started to halt due to his fear of falling during walking and stair practice. A joint Psychology × Physiotherapy collaboration was undertaken to help Gabriel overcome his fears. Gabriel's fear of falling was formulated using the PCM (Figure 5.9).

Table 5.10 Gabriel's multidisciplinary treatment organised by PCM element

Kitchens

- FND family education sessions on identifying interpersonal triggers in the family environment and reciprocal reinforcement, for example stop reassurance.
- Family encouraged to facilitate independence, withdraw support and take positive risks in terms of activities in daily life, for example Gabriel preparing simple meals.

Opening of Cover

- Building a trusted and therapeutic relationship that provides a secure base and a platform to regularly express emotions. Skills of verbal emotional expression were practised within the therapy space.
- Adverse life events were processed using these new skills.
- New "Cover" skills generalised to other staff members with Gabriel opening up about difficult thoughts and feelings.
- Unspeakable dilemma and distressing secrets that he had been holding in for years about his family situation and marriage was released.
- Although speech disturbance improved as verbal emotional expression improved, speech therapy supported Gabriel with additional "challenging" communication techniques.

Overpressure Plug blocked

"Set-backs" during Gabriel's admission were formulated to demonstrate the mood-FND link, for example a dissociative episode with total amnesia following a particularly difficult psychology session where Gabriel had disclosed a "secret".

Unblocking of Valve

- Bust-after-boom became boom-after-bust: Gabriel started to build new relationships with staff and peers, engaged in enjoyable and social activities on the ward, frequently walked outdoors with family, participated in exercise groups, created a sense of belonging.
- Psycho-education on the mood-activity link (behavioural activation).
- Occupational therapy input supported Gabriel with exploring meaningful life roles and employment that he could pursue once discharged back to the community.

Strengthening the pot

- Physio × OT: practice with transfers, walking, personal care, domestic activities (e.g. preparing a meal, go on public transport and shopping for groceries), movement retraining, stepping down equipment, fatigue and pain management.
- Exercise programme and fitness group improved Gabriel's cardiovascular status and lifted his mood.
- Psychology × Physiotherapy: Fear of falling on the stairs initially stopped Gabriel from dropping equipment but with joint sessions, he overcame his fears, using a series of behavioural experiments, reality grounding and distraction techniques.
- As the depression lifted, his cognitive functioning improved and he independently managed his own medications with a step-down programme facilitated by the nursing team.
- Techniques to identify warning signs for worsening FND or dissociative episodes and apply reality grounding techniques to nip the FND in the bud before it progresses to a seizure.
- Medications were reviewed and rationalised by neuropsychiatry.
- Continence nurses supported Gabriel with his bladder issues.

Warning light

- Gabriel did not show a particularly high level of symptom focus; however, his family did and were hypervigilant around him ("systemic hypervigilance").

Sticky left-over food

Positive qualities log and social interactions on the ward supported Gabriel with building his self-esteem.

Psycho-education on repetition of coping strategies over time

Ignition

- Psycho-education on the relationship between Gabriel's early coping strategies (keeping self to self), subsequent coping with these strategies when he encountered adverse experiences later in life, and the culmination into FND.

Fuel

- Gabriel gained insight into daily, distressing interpersonal triggers for the FND including recently escalated family interactions.
- Set-backs were linked to triggers; for example, Gabriel experienced a very brief FND relapse in response to a difficult interaction with his family.
- Practical solution of managing triggers for FND: a subset of the family moved out permanently of Gabriel's home. This removed challenging interactions and created more peace in the home environment. The enmeshed family structure ceased to exist in this way.
- Due to a complete reduction in his care needs, Gabriel's marriage improved.

Flames

- Psycho-education on the relationship between (1) low mood-FND and (2) the mechanism of FND.
- Exercises supporting emotion identification and labelling.
- Challenging unhelpful thinking around self-managing and coping with FND by reflecting on "evidence" of achievements and progress in rehab, as well as successfully having managed set-backs using strategies learned in rehab.

Heat

- Therapy sessions provided space to help Gabriel with reconnecting with his emotions following years of dissociation.
- Reality grounding exercises during walking and stair practice.

Safety features

Gabriel remained very engaged with his rehabilitation journey and showed significant futuristic thinking making post-discharge plans.

Techniques were based on the Pressure Cooker Falls formulation and included the following:

Dialling down the heat and strengthening the pot

Gabriel was encouraged to practise reality grounding techniques prior to trying out a motor task, for example watch his breathing, and become aware of his body and his physical surroundings (e.g. listen out to all the sounds he can hear). Gabriel was instructed to actively feel the physical ground under his feet (his base). Participating in fitness group and leg strengthening exercises helped Gabriel not only from a physical perspective but also to feel more confident that his legs would be able to hold him up.

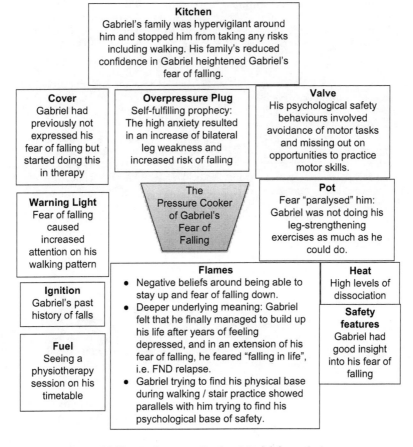

Figure 5.9 Fear of falling: a Pressure Cooker Model formulation.

Extinguishing the Flames

Try to label and rate his anxiety before cutting the emotion off. Think about the end goal of the practice: to go on the stairs in his house and reframe the stairs as something positive: practising gratitude for the stairs and how it is holding him up and taking him to places. The goal for Gabriel was to become aware of his fear and gently bringing himself back to the task at hand without negative self-talk. Positives of low-level anxiety were also shared with Gabriel: it can sharpen our senses and concentration levels and help us perform the motor task even better.

Switching off the Warning light

When doing the actual motor task (e.g. walking, stairs), Gabriel was encouraged to shift his attention outwards to his physical environment: feel the ground under his feet and name objects and sounds he could see and hear.

Outcomes

Gabriel overcame his fear of falling and eventually walked freely without any assistance of people or equipment. Table 5.11 shows Gabriel's results on outcome measures.

Mood

Gabriel's score on the mood questionnaire showed a clear pre-to-post therapy improvement; at discharge, he did not report any depressive symptoms. There were no behaviours that indicated the presence of depression: Gabriel was fully engaged with the ward programme and did not miss any session; he self-initiated personal care, social and other meaningful activities; and established solid therapeutic and peer relationships. Interestingly, Gabriel's normal levels of self-esteem rose to high at the end of his admission, suggesting that

Table 5.11 Gabriel's scores on psychology and neurorehabilitation measures

Questionnaire	Measures	Admission	Discharge
PHQ-9	Depressive symptoms	12/27 (moderate)	0/27 (minimal)
GAD-7	Anxiety symptoms	8/21 (mild)	0/21 (minimal)
Rosenberg's self-esteem	Self-esteem	24/30 (normal)	30/30 (high)
ATSQ	Self-perceived self-focused attention	25/35	7/35
Work and Social Adjustment Scale	Impairment in day-to-day functioning	27/40 (moderately-severe)	0/40 (subclinical)
UK FIM+FAM★	Captures the level of disability and dependency		
• Motor		43	112
• Cognitive		68	98
• Total		111/210	210/210
Modified Barthel Index★	Functional independence in activities of daily living and mobility	7/20	20/20
Neurological Impairment Scale★★	Measures a variety of physical, cognitive, affect, communication and behavioural impairments	23/50	2/50
Rehabilitation Complexity Score★★★	Care needs	13/22	6/22

★Higher scores suggest more independence; ★★higher scores suggest more severe impairment; ★★★higher scores mean more care needs.

he felt more than confident about himself. This was reflected in qualitative observations. His increased confidence was expressed in him exhibiting futuristic thinking and exuding the confidence to start planning a new life already during admission. Gabriel flourished and found his identity back.

FND symptoms

Gabriel made a full recovery from FND with respect to all four subtypes of his FND symptoms. In the context of his cognitive features, Gabriel had not been asked to participate in repeat neuropsychological testing, due to the short time that had elapsed since the last assessment, with the potential impact of practice effects in the absence of alternate forms. However, qualitatively, Gabriel's amnesia for distressing events, thoughts, emotions, memories and stressful interactions disappeared. He did no longer display the symptoms of functional amnesia and he had become seizure-free since many weeks. He regained full strength, function and sensation in both of his legs, without evidence of motor-type FND symptoms. His pain levels reduced and he felt more energetic. His sleep returned to normal.

Functional outcomes

By the end of his admission, Gabriel was walking independently unaided. He did not need the wheelchair or walking aids for any mobilisation or transfers, neither for indoors or outdoors. Gabriel was able to ascend and descend stairs without experiencing a fear of falling. He was fully independent with all personal and domestic activities of daily life including personal care; planning and preparation of simple and complex meals; shopping; laundry; and medication self-management. Gabriel independently accessed the local community around the hospital. He identified interests, set up a balanced routine, and engaged with meaningful activities on the ward such as art and gardening group. Gabriel made friendships with fellow patients and created his own social network on the ward. During his admission, Gabriel already started to plan for his life outside the hospital, demonstrated futuristic thinking and rekindled old friendships. Gabriel was eventually discharged without any equipment or care package.

Gabriel's case clearly demonstrates that a chronic course of FND does not automatically suggest that recovery is impossible.

Case study 4: surfing the flickering Flames of FND: a behavioural application of the Pressure Cooker Model

Background information

Rob was a 19-year-old young male who experienced dissociative episodes that lasted in between one and four hours, with an average seizure duration of approximately two hours. Rob's episodes emerged for the first time when he was at secondary school where he was bullied by his peers. The dissociative episodes were so severe that Rob stopped going to school. Rob's parents sought help from the school and health services to manage the episodes, as these started to impact on his day-to-day activities in major ways. Rob was referred for an intensive inpatient rehabilitation treatment programme and was admitted for five months. Although Rob's case was severe, his situation is unfortunately not unheard of in the community. Learning about Rob's case may benefit patients and families who are currently struggling to access appropriate support.

Pressure Cooker assessment

Information gathering

A series of interviews was conducted with Rob, his parents, siblings and the staff (1) to gain a better understanding of each element of the PCM, (2) to formulate hypotheses about the FND and (3) to conduct a comprehensive risk assessment (see Table 5.12). Tally charts helped to determine the frequency and duration of the episodes whilst ABC charts were useful for uncovering potential triggers ("A" – antecedents), and describe the semiology of the dissociative episodes ("B" – behaviour) and responses from the environment to the episodes ("C" – consequences).

Table 5.12 Rob's PCM formulation

Kitchen

- *Family and Social structure:* Family of five, with Rob the middle sibling. No social network outside family unit. Rob did not leave the house and mostly lived indoors, except for attending hospital appointments.
- *Reciprocal reinforcement:* Environment was highly anxious around Rob and lacked confidence with respect to managing Rob's episodes. This resulted in an enmeshed pattern: every time Rob experienced an episode, staff and parents, who felt highly anxious about Rob injuring himself and generally witnessing the "violent" episode, ran to Rob as quickly as possible to provide him with verbal and physical reassurance for hours. *Social function:* The environmental reassurance helped to terminate Rob's episodes eventually. In addition, the reassurance also reduced the environment's distress, as people felt they were taking constructive action to help Rob calm down his distress and the episode that helped to calm down the environment's distress simultaneously.
- However, Rob's episodes were reinforced by the overinvolvement. He did not have opportunities to learn new, alternative coping strategies and became very dependent on his environment.

(Continued)

Table 5.12 (Continued)

Cover	Overpressure Plug	Valve
• Initially, Rob expressed being very unsure about psychology. He cited difficult past experiences with psychologists and did not find them useful. • Fear of rejection when expressing emotions, reduced assertiveness. • Kept himself mostly to himself and did not regularly express his feelings to another person in a safe and trusted relationship – not in the family or social setting. • Rob was often known as "the clown" and made a lot of jokes. Although his outward appearance suggested high levels of self-confidence, inside, his self-esteem was low and he endured social situations with great distress. The jokes were a safety behaviour.	• Dissociative episodes lasting for hours. Functional motor weakness, tremors and numbness in all four limbs. • Deliberate/accidental self-harm during episodes. • Post-episode fatigue resulting in Rob sleeping for long periods afterwards, serving the function of dissociation from difficult emotions. • Post-episode muscle and body pain due to self-injury and tensing up of the muscles during the episode.	• Blocked Valve: Rob had dropped all hobbies, no other meaningful activities, no sense of belonging to any community • Valve overuse (Valve complimentary to Rob's): Staff spent copious amounts of time and effort caring for Rob resulting in exhaustion and burn-out at the expense of care for other patients and staff's own meaningful activities as part of a healthy work-life balance.

Warning light	Sticky left-over food	Pot
• Rob was highly focused on the dissociative episodes and other physical symptoms (not on emotions) and would speak constantly about it during therapy sessions, as well as to other staff and patients who felt overwhelmed by his narratives and started to avoid and reject him. • Environment was hypervigilant around Rob and "on the edge" in case he had another dissociative episode.	Core beliefs: I'm worthless • Early childhood coping strategies: • Not speaking about difficult thoughts and feelings. Although his family encouraged Rob to express emotions, he mostly kept himself to himself. • Keep pushing on with lots of activities at school and college.	• Rob's sleep was disrupted due to the long sleeping episodes after an episode during the day. • Polypharmacy: Rob was on a lot of pain medication including opiates that facilitated dissociation. • Rob had access to a lot of equipment and needed at least two people to support him with personal and domestic activities of daily life. His family was heavily involved in care activities.

- Cutting off emotions during bullying episodes to "survive" the hurtful events.
- Risks included accidental self-injury, deliberate self-harm (of which the line was sometimes blurry), systemic re-traumatisation by staff who started avoiding and rejecting Rob.

Heat
- Rob displayed significant mood swings. On some days, he was bright in mood whilst on other days low in mood and feeling empty, with suicidal and self-harm thoughts.
- Rob also had a tendency to dissociate.
- He did not exhibit "emotion lingo"; staff felt Rob was alexithymic. Rob would often use the physical features of emotions to describe how he felt.

Ignition
- Emotional neglectful and abusive parents who did not meet his physical and psychological needs. Rob was exposed to difficult events in his childhood, taken into care and adopted at age 8. Bullied at primary and secondary school. Rob struggled to focus in class.
- Critical incident: Rob trained at college to become a chef, but due to the pandemic, all lessons were initially discontinued and thereafter online with a significantly reduced time table and no practicals. He lost his entire social network.

Fuel
- Rob indicated that feeling hot and light sensitivity fuelled the dissociative episodes.
- Staff had a different view on Rob's triggers: Dissociative episodes were more common during (1) quiet times after a subset of staff had gone home and fellow peers would retire to bed early, without much social activity in the evenings; (2) in social situations particularly in the gym where Rob was challenged in physiotherapy and occupational therapy sessions that aimed to increase his independence. Seizures never occurred during psychology sessions, which took place in a confidential space on a one-to-one basis.

Flames
- During therapy, Rob struggled to label or identify his emotions – only that it felt unpleasant and uncomfortable.
- Staff suspected that during "alone" time, Rob was grappling with difficult thoughts and feelings creeping in.
- In between dissociative episodes, Rob also displayed classic safety behaviours and features of social anxiety, for example avoiding eye contact, not initiating spontaneous conversation, "hiding" in the background.

Safety features
Although Rob's dissociative episodes were highly frequent and severe, in between episodes, he showed insight into his situation and a willingness to change. He was pleasant in interaction. In the past, Rob trained to become a chef and his teachers felt he was talented with great potential to further his career in this area. Rob showed a great passion for cooking.

Initial formulation

Based on the data, the following hypotheses were formulated about Rob's dissociative episodes.

Layer 1: Ignition

Rob had a difficult early start in life. During his early childhood, Rob was exposed to traumatic events and not afforded the opportunities to learn how to self-regulate his emotions with useful strategies (e.g. emotional expression), as well as relate or connect emotionally and socially to people, and feel psychologically safe in a trusted relationship. It was hypothesised that Rob had likely developed a range of negative core beliefs about himself ("I am unlovable" "I'm worthless"), people ("people will just disappoint and abandon you") and the world ("the world is a hurtful place"). On a day-to-day basis, Rob's rules for living included pushing on with lots of activities at school and college, "to prove his worth" and "be validated and loved" by his environment. A critical incident, that is the pandemic causing a significant reduction in teaching and loss of social connections, stopped Rob from having access to his usual coping strategies (i.e. pushing on with activities and connecting socially with friends), which laid bare and challenged his core beliefs. These conditions cultivated the emergence of a maintenance cycle with FND.

Layer 2: FND coping triad

Rob's childhood and teenage years were riddled with hurtful rejection and abandonment experiences, which set the stage for the development of Rob's protective coping mechanisms to manage any distress from rejections that could emerge in the future. These "traditional FND" coping strategies originated in his childhood and included (1) dissociation during bullying episodes to "survive" the hurtful events, (2) pushing on with activities (which not only resulted in praise and validation from parents, teachers and peers, but also served as a form of cutting off emotions, as "always being on the go" prevented Rob from having to sit with distress), and (3) keeping self to self. Despite his family encouraging Rob to speak about his thoughts and feelings, Rob did not ever express negative emotions to other people and presented with a "jokey" exterior. All three FND coping strategies had repeated over many years into adulthood.

Layer 3: FND maintenance cycle "The Pressure Cooker Chain Reaction"

Rob's dissociative episodes were an extension and almost an amplified version of his longstanding tendency towards dissociation. As a result of the pandemic, and the consequences for his educational and social life, Rob was experiencing an unusually high amount of distress, which he was unable to appropriately manage. There were two types of *Fuel* in his Pressure Cooker Chain Reaction: (1) *re-trigger:* "alone" time in the evenings with virtually no social or rehabilitation activities planned that increased the risk for difficult thoughts and feelings to creep in without any means to control them (Rob did not have a social support network apart from his family and would often feel lonely), and (2) *interpersonal trigger:* entering a social situation. These triggers caused Rob to feel a state of internal discomfort and arousal that was gradually increasing in intensity but that he was unable to identify and label, other than using its physical signature and its emotional valence ("my heart's racing, my chest hurts" "negative and unpleasant"; *Flames and Heat*). It was hypothesised that Rob's internal state was likely associated with attachment anxiety, beliefs around abandonment and a fear of rejection. Being left on his own bore a similarity to past "emotional neglect" situations and re-triggered old feelings and hurts, similar to the feelings that he experienced during his school years and the pandemic when society was locked down and he had no access to his usual coping strategies and social connections with peers. Rob found it hard to self-manage his time. In social situations, Rob had also developed a heightened sensitivity towards social clues of rejection and he was believed to experience a profound fear of negative judgements, abandonment and social rejection, in case Rob would say something improper in social situations that may not be well received by others (NB. Rob was generally not inappropriate in his interactions, even when engaging in safety behaviours; however, he worried about coming across that way to others).

Rob was experiencing a lot of turmoil and emotion dysregulation with strong, intense emotions; however, the top parts of Rob's pressure cooker were malfunctioning: Rob had no recourse to his usual stress-coping strategy of pushing on with activities at college and with peers, at home and in the evenings on the ward (blocked Valve) and although he had access to people around him who encouraged and would facilitate verbal emotional expression (e.g. family and staff), Rob did not feel sufficiently secure to express his emotions, mostly out of fear of rejection. Given that Rob's two channels for expression were blocked in his pressure cooker, the only channel that was left for emotional release of his turmoil constituted dissociation. This presented itself in augmented form as full-blown dissociative episodes, as well as in post-episode fatigue. Rob's dissociative episodes tended to last for long durations, often resulting in prolonged sleeping episodes following each seizure. These sleeping episodes helped Rob to cut off his emotions for even longer parts of the day. The dissociative episodes and subsequent long recovery time quickly and effectively helped Rob to internally regulate his emotions and reduce his discomfort. However, this created a negative reinforcement loop that increased the risk of episodes in the future.

A second Pressure Cooker Chain Reaction maintenance cycle that revolved around classic social anxiety features was also present. Rob had developed social anxiety due to his longstanding rejection experiences. Although his dissociative episodes were driven by various types of anxiety, that is

"attachment anxiety" and social anxiety, on the basis of tally charts on seizure frequency, the team observed that Rob's seizures appeared to be mostly
fuelled by "quiet times" in the evenings and weekends and that seizures were
less likely to emerge in social situations, for example during sessions in the
gym. It was therefore decided to mainly focus on the management of Rob's
evening seizures and put potential treatment of social anxiety temporarily on
the backburner.

Layer 4: Facilitating physical factors

Several physical factors compounded Rob's psychological difficulties and
FND symptoms. His dissociative tendencies were further facilitated by the
long sleeping periods following the dissociative episodes, as well as by the
opiate pain medication. The sleeping episodes resulted in a secondary effect
and a vicious cycle: due to the seizures during the day, Rob struggled to fall
asleep at night. His sleep deprivation started to affect Rob's rehabilitation
during the day and intensified his mood problems and ruminative thinking.
In addition, Rob was very well adapted with a lot of high-level equipment
and semi-permanent home adaptations including a state-of-the-art power
chair, a wet room and a built-in stair lift at home, as well as a four times a
day care package to support Rob with personal care and meals – in addition
to care support from his family. He needed at least two people to support
him with day-to-day activities. These physical factors reinforced Rob's FND
symptoms; whenever he had a "bad" day he could easily fall back on the
power chair as a safety behaviour and the 24-hour supervision schedule that
Rob was subjected to reinforced the notion that he was heavily disabled;
prevented him from learning more adaptive coping strategies; and did not
help him test out whether he could carry out activities more independently
on his own.

Layer 5: the social functions of FND (the Kitchen)

Not only did the dissociative episodes support Rob with regulating his internal
state of discomfort, it was also hypothesised that the episodes helped him to
regulate his emotions directly via his environment, driven by a strong need
to find psychological safety with other people rather than by self-regulation
and self-soothing strategies. The dissociative episodes were characterised
by a dual external regulation function: (1) the environment quickly sought
proximity towards him and reduced Rob's state of internal discomfort, and
simultaneously (2) met his need to feel validated, cared for and noticed ("I
matter"), reaching a state of psychological safety and providing him with the
acknowledgement that people were present for him, available and attentive to
meet his psychological needs, and truly cared for him.

Rob's need for psychological safety was strongly rooted in his longstanding
history of rejection and lack of a psychologically secure base in his early years.

Although Rob's adoptive family was enmeshed in his well-being and care, his family clearly showed the best intentions; they were emotionally warm, loving and caring towards him, with mutual respect and validation. During his admission, his parents and siblings were Rob's biggest advocates and cheerleaders. However, there were two specific points in his life that boosted Rob's self-esteem in ways that his family was not able to achieve, and made him feel particularly valued and noticed by other people: (1) attending his college and being praised for his achievements by his parents, teachers and peers alike (and for the first time: not being bullied and rejected) and (2) his admission to the inpatient unit – again a nurturing and caring environment that was geared towards helping Rob to thrive in his life.

His admission to the unit drastically changed circumstances for Rob. The full-on ward programme offered a busy schedule with rehabilitation, creative activities, film nights, and cooking, gardening and fitness sessions, all embedded within a social environment. In contrast to his past rejection experiences by peers, Rob started to develop friendships and felt accepted. The dissociative episodes initially resulted in compassion and care from his environment. Since Rob had not commonly been exposed to these positive responses by individuals outside his family unit throughout most of his life, these new experiences were highly reinforcing and met Rob's unmet need for psychologically safety on the ward, increasing the frequency, as well as the duration of his dissociative episodes.

RECIPROCAL REINFORCEMENT: INTERPERSONAL PSYCHOLOGICAL SAFETY

Both reciprocal reinforcement and systemic hypervigilance were evident: staff, family and patients on the ward felt highly anxious and uncomfortable at witnessing Rob's FND symptoms and distress, and responded promptly and consistently with verbal and physical reassurance, as well as with "tiptoeing behaviour" around him to ensure that he was safe at all times. These responses reduced not only Rob's distress but also the environment's own discomfort. Both Rob and the staff were stuck in a continuous "reciprocal reinforcement loop".

SYSTEMIC RE-TRAUMATISATION

The dissociative episodes happened daily for prolonged periods of time and started to take its toll on the staff treating Rob. Although the dissociative episodes resulted in Rob's environment seeking proximity to him, and Rob feeling psychologically safe as a result, over time, this coping habit had started to unravel and lost its effectiveness in reaching that internal state of relief. Some staff members became avoidant and short with Rob, and limited interactions with Rob, whilst others called in sick. The dissociative episodes started to create the opposite to the environment seeking proximity and

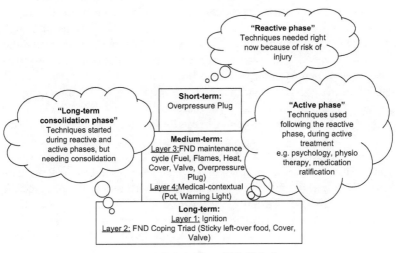

Figure 5.10 FND hierarchy of needs.

became a self-fulfilling prophecy that led Rob to feel rejected by staff (i.e. systemic re-traumatisation), exactly the thing he tried to avoid at all costs.

Intervention

See Figure 5.10.

Phase 1: short-term and reactive strategies: dissociative episode management

The dissociative episodes were the most urgent symptom that needed to be addressed, for the following reasons:

- Rob was at high risk of sustaining accidental injuries to his body, particularly to the head.
- The episodes started to impact on Rob's rehab. Due to the prolonged episodes, he was missing sessions and, in addition, spent long periods in bed with post-DS fatigue and muscle pain.
- The length, frequency and severity of the episodes were draining to staff who started to burn out and increased sickness absence. The severity of the episodes was emotionally impacting on staff who experienced a variety of emotions including anxiety, sadness, anger and frustration. In addition, other patients missed out on sessions because staff was pulled to help out with Rob's episodes, which left patients frustrated and angry, and made staff feel guilty.

- The emotional impact on other patients who were upset at seeing Rob's episodes and did not understand their dissociative (as opposed to organic) nature.
- High level of reinforcing behaviours towards Rob that were observed in staff and family (e.g. physical reassurance, hugging) and remained unaddressed, which maintained the dissociative episodes.

Implementation

A behavioural management plan was drawn up and shared with Rob, his family and his treating team. The goal of the behavioural management plan was to extinguish the FND as a strategy to feel psychologically safe by consistently disattending the dissociative episodes ("Block the Overpressure Plug") and gradually replacing the dissociative episodes with alternative, more helpful coping habits, that is verbal expression of emotions ("Opening the Cover") and releasing the feelings of discomfort using activities ("Unblock the Valve"). It was hypothesised that if Rob would engage with emotional expression and normalisation of his activity levels, Rob's risk of dissociative episodes would significantly reduce. In the beginning of his treatment, Rob was not able to control the episodes by himself and felt powerless; hence, the environment played a large role initially in the management of the episodes.

NEGATIVE (BEHAVIOURAL) PUNISHMENT OF UNHELPFUL RESPONSES

During the dissociative episode
His treating team was encouraged to consistently withhold the caring response that had been contingent on the dissociative episode behaviour. In this way, the dissociative episode was not followed by the reinforcing consequence (caring response), helping to extinguish the behaviour. Verbal or physical reassurance was withheld in response to Rob's episodes. A minimum number of staff was allowed at any point during the episode.

Safety
Rob's risk assessment revealed a range of risks including risk of self-injury. As Rob was moving and rolling over the floor, it was imperative to protect his head and body against serious injury. This was the only time that staff would provide Rob with physical support. His head was supported with pillows to soften the blows. His bedroom and treatment rooms were padded with soft fabrics and cushions to protect his head and body from sharp edges. All sharps and objects that could potentially cause him injury were removed including equipment (e.g. getting his hand stuck in the wheelchair spokes, hitting his head against the foot plates). His mattress was lowered on the floor to reduce the risk of Rob falling out of his bed on the floor or getting stuck in between the bed rails.

Dignity

The team attempted to preserve Rob's dignity as much as was possible by closing the curtains, trying to gently move him into a single room away from other people, using opaque screens that occluded the view. People, apart from staff assigned to support Rob, were asked to leave the situation and not crowd around but to leave him to it. In addition to protect Rob's dignity and stop the reinforcement of the episodes from the environment, these measures also protected other patients and staff from the "emotional harm" and psychological injury of witnessing the episodes.

Post-FND episode

Rob and the team agreed on a sign that indicated that he was coming out of the dissociative episode: Rob opening his eyes. To prevent immediate reinforcement of the episode, Rob was given "down time" where he was given sufficient time to get up on his own without people present, to increase the delay between the behaviour (dissociative episode) and consequence (asking how Rob is feeling = compassion, empathy and care). During "down time", the team did not check in immediately with Rob's mood or provide verbal reassurance, refrained from engaging in non-urgent physical care following an episode, or provide Rob with a cup of tea or food, as this would directly reinforce the FND. Physical care that could wait was postponed. The team waited before a significant amount of time had elapsed, at least one hour. Furthermore, Rob was not left on his own all day, as this could have been seen as harsh and punitive, and feed his rejection fears. It was important to have an open conversation and follow up on the dissociative episode by encouraging the helpful response of "emotion talk".

Systemic support

With Rob's consent, his formulation was **shared with the people closest to him** including family and staff caring for him to educate on the mechanisms of FND including reciprocal reinforcement. The team and his family learned that Rob's episodes were a way of coping to meet a basic human need that applies to everyone, not just people with FND. His environment was supported with coping with their own **conflicting feelings around withholding the caring response**, which felt counter-intuitive to family and many staff and which resulted in an inconsistent application of the treatment strategies. His team was informed about potentially worse consequences (i.e. partial reinforcement schedule). Not applying these "harsh" strategies would not help Rob to live his life to the full as it reinforced and prevented him from learning useful strategies that were more adaptive and did not hurt him physically. His environment was also educated on **fine-tuning** their behavioural **responses** towards Rob. Some staff had interpreted the withholding response too literal and left Rob to his own devices almost immediately after he started to experience a seizure and left him with little supervision or check-ins. Part of the problem that contributed to staff leaving Rob quickly was their compassion-fatigue and burn-out after having managed several of his daily and prolonged seizures. **Compassion was cultivated** in the team for Rob's problems and him not doing this on purpose or "faking it" in the context of longstanding emotional neglect. The team was supported with toeing a fine line between not reinforcing the episodes whilst not avoiding and taking so much distance from Rob that it was veering into rejection. **A regular reflective space to air feelings** around witnessing the severe nature of the episodes and the emotional impact on the team was also organised. Furthermore, to support staff morale and faith in the effectiveness of Rob's intervention, an explanation about the **extinction burst** ("behaviour may get worse before improving") was provided to help the team maintain confidence in the model even if Rob's FND symptoms seemed to get worse.

Re-formulation, re-negotiation and re-implementation
In spite of these measures, Rob's dissociative episodes continued to emerge. Due to the risks of self-injury, Rob had to often be physically protected by staff. However, this opposed the principles of withholding reassurance (from a behavioural perspective), as the act of physically protecting and "holding" Rob was meeting his psychological need of feeling safe, and directly reinforced and maintained the episodes.

In addition, Rob felt highly distressed and inconsolable about the perceived "harshness" of the measures proposed in the treatment plan. The treating team agreed with Rob. Due to the severity, entrenchment and length of time that Rob experienced the episodes as a coping strategy, and Rob not being able to access and consolidate other helpful coping strategies at short notice, the treatment was renegotiated with Rob and adjusted to a more graded approach. Rob felt heard by the team and this strengthened his trust in the therapeutic relationships and the treatment.

Rob agreed that during an episode, he would try to minimise the risks of serious self-injury, whilst the risks of him sustaining lighter injuries were deemed acceptable (e.g. bruises on his arm). Two staff members would stay in close proximity to him but not physically or verbally reassure him. It was shared with Rob that persisting risks of serious injury would suggest that the inpatient unit was likely not the appropriate environment for him and that he would risk discharge from the programme. The team acknowledged Rob's difficulties and expressed their willingness and commitment in helping him; they emphasised to Rob that they would want him to stay and help him to live his life to the full again. Rob felt heard and contained by the team setting boundaries.

As agreed with Rob, the distance between him and staff was gradually increased to staff staying behind a curtain or opaque screen, with staff not visible to Rob. In later stages, only one staff member would be present outside Rob's room and sufficiently far away outside his visible range. Eventually, Rob was on intermittent observations throughout the hour, which eventually stopped as the episodes ceased to exist.

POSITIVE (BEHAVIOURAL) REINFORCEMENT OF HELPFUL RESPONSES

Rob's inclination was to externally regulate his emotions via the environment. Removing his well-rehearsed coping habit of dissociative episodes would leave Rob in a vulnerable position without any alternative coping strategy to regulate his emotions. Therefore, the treatment focused on supporting Rob to connect with strategies to help internal regulation of his emotions. The strategies were viable "competing" alternatives that replaced the unhelpful response (FND), for example speaking about feelings, reality grounding, distraction techniques and doing a vigorous exercise on the stationary bike. Whenever Rob used these helpful responses, he was directly verbally praised by his team, as well as during progress and family meetings. In addition, the absence of episodes was reinforced with praise.

DIALLING DOWN THE HEAT OF THE FLAMES: TOLERATING STRONG EMOTIONS

In psychological therapy, Rob was supported with uncovering and managing the triggers for dissociative episodes ("Fuel"). Although Rob initially reported physical triggers such as heat and light, as the therapeutic relationship grew stronger and Rob started to feel more in touch with his emotions, Rob's fear of rejection about disclosing interpersonal triggers that were driving the dissociative episodes reduced. Rob identified several triggers including feeling psychologically unsafe when spending time on his own with difficult emotions and experiencing a strong need to connect socially with other people; his deep-seated fears of rejection and seeking proximity and validation to other people to appease these fears; and witnessing other patients receiving care that prompted Rob to feel unsafe and rejected.

Rob learned to self-manage "alone" time, either by trying to surf and psychologically tolerate the flame of rapidly increasing negative emotions on his own; or by distracting himself temporarily from the emotion by engaging with creative or sports activities; or by finding a staff member to speak about his discomfort or negative emotions. Emotion mapping exercises helped Rob to identify and label his feelings, as well as learn about the different aspects of emotions including their functions and physical features.

OPENING UP THE COVER: EMOTION TALK

The most important helpful response was practising emotion talk including regularly expressing thoughts and feelings and labelling emotions in one-to-one chats with people that Rob trusted. The "emotion talk" response competed directly with the FND. Rob was encouraged to express his emotions during psychological therapy and seek out non-psychology staff he had built a trusted therapeutic relationship with to express his thoughts and feelings. Rob was creative and encouraged to express his thoughts and feelings in another acceptable way, including art and recording them in a diary, since Rob did not have much experience with this coping strategy and experienced strong fears of rejection.

POT: RECOGNISING WARNING SIGNS

Rob also learned to recognise the warning signs of an impending episode, including feeling confused and out of touch with reality. He learned reality grounding techniques and explored these early dissociative symptoms and their connection with negative emotions including sadness about feeling alone, fear about being rejected and envy in relation to other patients receiving care.

RELEASING STICKY LEFT-OVER FOOD

Rob learned about the relationship between his adverse childhood experiences and his core belief of feeling worthless. He participated in a positive qualities exercise. Rob struggled to initiate the exercise, and it took several weeks for him to engage with it. His reluctance was explored throughout therapy, including in the context of his strong core belief repelling any evidence that he was not worthless. Eventually, Rob asked staff to help him to identify positive qualities and collect evidence that supported these. Towards the end of the admission, Rob continued to find this exercise very difficult.

UNBLOCKING THE VALVE

At the start of his admission, Rob's Valve was completely blocked, which pre-dated the FND, but was further complicated by the impact that the dissociative episodes had on his activity levels. Once the episodes reduced in frequency, Rob was able to identify and engage with enjoyable, meaningful, social and physical exercise activities to release his emotions in alternative and more helpful ways.

ROB'S COPING GRAPH

Gradually, Rob's dissociative episodes reduced in frequency, whilst simultaneously his use of alternative coping skills increased in frequency. During the treatment, there were three "pressure points" (marked as **X**s in Figure 5.11):

- In response to the treatment approach, Rob's dissociative episodes initially worsened ("extinction burst") before a reduction was observed.
- In the middle of his treatment, there was a point where Rob exhibited equal "use" of both dissociative episodes and emotional expression (where the lines cross in the figure). This was a sensitive point where Rob easily defaulted into dissociative episodes as a main way of coping.

With increasing trust in his therapeutic relationships, continued practice of emotion talk and participation in enjoyable activities, Rob eventually managed to pass this vulnerable crossing point and further consolidate his helpful coping strategies.

• Before discharge to the community, Rob's dissociative episodes increased in frequency, whilst he simultaneously opened up about his fears around impending discharge. Later in Chapter 5, the PCM formulation on Rob's discharge fears will be shared.

Phase 2 re-formulation: social anxiety work using PCM

The frequency and severity of Rob's dissociative episodes gradually reduced over time. Eventually, Rob became seizure-free. By that time, it had become apparent that Rob was experiencing a strong fear of social situations, which was almost masked by the gravity and urgency of the dissociative episodes. Although Rob's participation in the enjoyable and social activities of the ward programme increased, the team noticed safety behaviours consistent with social anxiety. It should be noted that the team still felt that the episodes had the function to meet a more "attachment-based" psychological safety need from people in the environment; however, another function of the dissociative episodes was simultaneously hypothesised: the dissociative episodes acted as a safety behaviour that quickly and effectively brought down Rob's social anxiety. The original PCM formulation remained applicable and paved the way for Rob to learn to label his anxiety and understand additional maintaining mechanisms of the FND. This initial formulation was subsequently

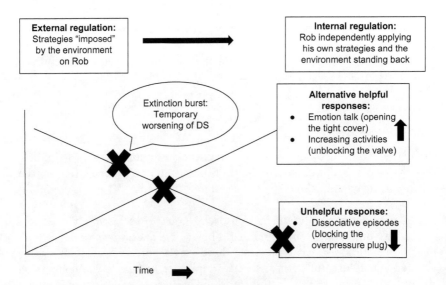

Figure 5.11 Time course of dissociative seizure management.

merged with a classic social anxiety model (Clark & Wells, 1995), which enriched Rob's formulation and planned out a new layer of treatment.

Figure 5.12 shows the social anxiety model (Clark & Wells, 1995) merged with the PCM, which helped to account for the rapid, self-terminating nature of his anxiety by the dissociative episodes and simultaneously explain other safety behaviours that did not necessarily terminate his anxiety immediately. Upon entering a social situation (Fuel), Rob experienced his worst fear of being judged negatively by other people, which caused him high levels of anxiety (Flames and Heat) that he did not express (tight Cover) and led him to engage in a range of safety behaviours (Overpressure Plug) to prevent his worst fear from happening. In order to break the link between his beliefs, feelings (Flames) and safety behaviours (Overpressure Plug, which needed to be plugged), Rob created a graded hierarchy of feared social situations (unblocked his Valve) and engaged in a series of behavioural experiments where he tried to drop his safety behaviours to test out his worst-case scenario of being judged and rejected. Situations included going out shopping to a nearby shopping centre, making a phone call, saying something in the team meeting and making a presentation about his favourite topic to a select group of staff.

ROB'S POSITIVE PRESSURE COOKER TO REDUCE SOCIAL ANXIETY

This hybrid model is psychologically driven, which means that each element represents a psychological component important in social anxiety and FND

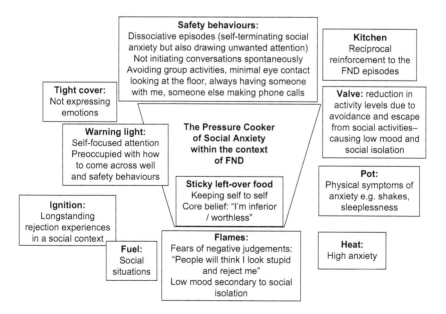

Figure 5.12 Pressure Cooker Model formulation of social anxiety.

but it should be noted that each element also reflects the work that was done by the entire multidisciplinary team who contributed to Rob's social anxiety treatment. Figure 5.13 shows the PCM formulation.

Outcomes

On discharge, Rob's neurorehabilitation measures all showed major gains. Despite these achievements, Rob continued to experience clinically significant symptoms of low mood and anxiety on the PHQ-9 and GAD-7, respectively. Furthermore, his level of emotion dysregulation became more pronounced over time. Qualitatively, Rob's confidence in social situations

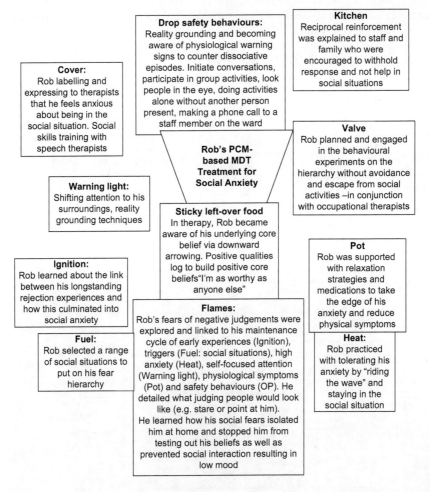

Figure 5.13 Pressure Cooker Model–based multidisciplinary treatment for social anxiety.

had slowly grown and this was also reflected in the increase in his self-esteem score, which fell just below the cut-off point for healthy levels (see Table 5.13).

Formulation, formulation, formulation!

Although Rob's dissociative episodes gradually reduced and eventually disappeared as he progressed through his admission, the episodes re-emerged towards the end of his admission with a vast approaching discharge date on Rob's radar. On multiple occasions, Rob expressed that he did not want to be discharged from the unit. The hospital had become a place of psychological safety for Rob, and this was formulated with him using another PCM formulation (Figure 5.14).

Rob agreed to collaborate on a "stay psychologically safe" plan based on the elements of the PCM (Table 5.14).

Table 5.13 Rob's scores on psychology and neurorehabilitation measures

Questionnaire	Measures	Admission	Discharge
PHQ-9	Depressive symptoms	21/27	17/27
GAD-7	Anxiety symptoms	13/21	15/21
ATSQ	Self-perceived self-focused attention	22/35	20/35
Rosenberg's self-esteem	Self-esteem	4/30	14/30
DERS-SF	Emotion dysregulation	Total: 51/90, mean: 2.83, $Z = 1.4$	Total: 65/90, mean: 3.61, $Z = 2.6$
UK FIM+FAM★	Captures the level of disability and dependency		
• Motor		60	110
• Cognitive		42	80
• Total		102/210	190/210
Modified Barthel Index★	Functional independence in activities of daily living and mobility	10/20	20/20
Neurological Impairment Scale★★	Measures a variety of physical, cognitive, affect, communication and behavioural impairments	25/50	7/50
Rehabilitation Complexity Score★★★	Care needs	17/22	9/22

★Higher scores suggest more independence; ★★higher scores suggest more severe impairment; ★★★higher scores mean more care needs.

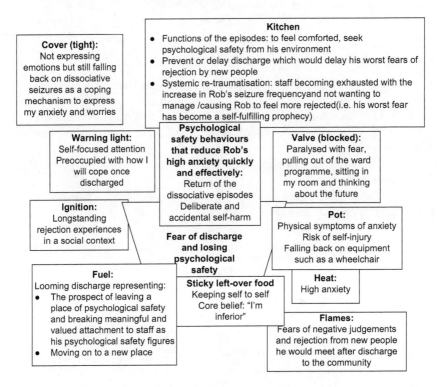

Figure 5.14 Fear of discharge: a Pressure Cooker Model formulation.

Table 5.14 Rob's psychological safety plan

PCM element	Strategies for staying psychologically safe
Ignition/Fuel	• Accepting that the "bottom parts" of the pressure cooker are inevitable in day-to-day life, and "part and parcel" of the human life experience: Some Fuel, Flames and Heat we are not able to remove, for example a looming discharge date. In those circumstances, we have to learn to sit with the distress rather than avoid. • However, we can change our relationship to the triggers, thoughts and feelings, surrounding challenging events such as a discharge from a safe place. • Accept and learn to tolerate a state of psychological unsafety before we reach psychological safety. Reminding ourselves that we may appreciate psychological safety even more once we have worked through a period of feeling psychologically unsafe in life. • Looking at the positive aspects of moving to a new dwelling, for example meeting new friends, starting an independent life, able to make your own rules.

PCM element	Strategies for staying psychologically safe
Flames/Heat	• Normalising anxiety about moving on and the uncertainty about what was awaiting him when living in the community. • Accepting that a degree of anxiety and discomfort needs to be tolerated in life by every one of us. • Not seeing the increase in dissociative episodes as a set-back. Instead, reframing it as a learning point and an opportunity to re-apply newly learned coping strategies.
Sticky left-over food	• Keep reminding yourself of your positive qualities – including an additional one: successfully engaging with the treatment programme and working through various "bumps on the road". Rob learned that "it's OK to fall" but it is the way we get back up again that matters.
Pot	• Do not immediately fall back on the wheelchair, remind yourself that the wheelchair is a safety behaviour, and if you really need to use the wheelchair: limit the time in the wheelchair as much as possible and focus on the goal of trying to get up on your feet sooner rather than later.
Warning light	• Distract yourself from unhelpful thoughts about the seizures and remind yourself that you have coped well managing the seizures during the admission: in a hospital environment with strangers. If you can manage an inpatient unit, you have a high chance of being able to manage the community. To "snap out" of my negative thoughts, I am going to cycle on my bike.
Cover	• Keep practising your skill of emotional expression with a person you trust and feel safe with – even though it may feel scary because of my fears around rejection. I know that opening my cover is the key to reducing FND.
Valve	• Already during my admission, I pre-planned an activity schedule ("behavioural activation") by actively searching for social and enjoyable activities in the community where I am going to be discharged to. With a plan in mind, this will help me to engage with activities quickly and unblock my valve.
Overpressure Plug	• I will remind myself that if I (1) open my cover and (2) unblock my valve, consistently and regularly, I will (3) greatly reduce the risk of my dissociative episodes rearing their head again.
Kitchen	Staying in touch after discharge: • "Booster" check-ins with the psychologist to check how I am doing several weeks after my discharge to the community. • Review appointment with the consultant. • Stopping by to "show off" my positive improvements to the staff and spending some time on the ward.

Table 5.15 describes this common scenario and other "pitfalls" of dissociative episode management and solutions that can help address hurdles.

Pressure cooker afterthoughts: pitfalls of dissociative seizure management

Table 5.15 Pitfall scenarios during the management of dissociative seizures

#	Scenario	Solutions
1	The episodes were well managed for a while but suddenly re-appeared or suddenly increase in frequency and/or severity.	• Check whether there may be new stress-triggers, for example impending discharge from the service, a new psychosocial life stressor. • Incorporate this into your formulation and share this with the patient.
2	The person with FND is quite mobile during the episode. • Leaving the person physically unsupported will mean that they are at significant risk of accidental or deliberate self-harm. • However, supporting the person (e.g. protecting their head from injury by stopping their head from touching a hard surface) means I will be reinforcing the episode. How should I manage?	• It is relatively unusual for a person to experience episodes so severe that they are at risk of significant self-harm. However, these episodes do occur and people do hurt themselves. • The management of this type of severity requires very close multidisciplinary team working. • Perform a team risk analysis on how to reduce any impact of the episode, for example: • Removing environmental hazards (sharp edges, furniture). • Temporarily setting up a safe bed space (mattress on the floor). • Additional temporary equipment (helmet to prevent brain injury). • Shortening the dissociative episode (the administration of medications by the medical team – although this may not always be successful). • Using a person's high levels of suggestibility to stop an episode *"OK, on the count of 3-2-1/ in 5 minutes' time your seizure will stop"* and then actively start engaging in the actions that signify that the seizure has stopped (e.g. start cleaning up any items that were accidentally hit during the episode/ask the person what their next activity is and disattending that the seizure happened). • Frequent rotation of staff to manage the episodes due to the emotional and physical burden. • Discussion with the patient afterwards that dissociative episodes of this calibre may not easily be managed in the current environment or by current services and that discharge may be needed as the environment/service is not doing the symptoms any favours but are making them worse instead. Simultaneously ensure that this is not delivered as a "threat" or "if/then style statements" (if you keep having episodes, we will discharge you), as this would be hurtful and counter-productive.

#	Scenario	Solutions
3	The strategies are not working.	• Habits need time to unlearn and to be replaced with more adaptive coping strategies. This is not an overnight solution. • Find out whether the strategies are consistently implemented by the person and the environment. In particular, pay attention to whether a partial reinforcement schedule may be at work (intermittent reinforcement). • Some strategies are very counter-intuitive (withholding reassurance), and people may be reluctant to consistently apply them. • Find out whether the episodes are inadvertently reinforced, for example offering a cup of tea and a chat immediately after an episode. • Formulate, formulate, formulate! Go back to the drawing board and ask yourself: "is my formulation right?" You may need to gather more information.
4	The person heavily resists/their family don't accept the management plan for the dissociative episodes and accuse the team of being harsh and punitive.	• Collaborate with the patient and family, and help the patient to own the plan. • Organise regular family meetings to support with answering any questions about seizure management and FND; reflect with the family on the counter-intuitive nature of the strategies and the need to prevent reciprocal/intermittent reinforcement; and give the family praise for adhering to the plan. • It is possible that emotions such a guilt play a role in resisting the treatment? • Highlight the reinforcing nature of caring responses and how this maintains FND, and use a hybrid PCM formulation plan. Explore what the person and family would like: continue like this or recover from FND? Sometimes, these needs may be opposite with the person feeling reluctant about recovery but the family wanting recovery.
5	The environment becomes frustrated and angry at you for disattending the episodes (e.g. in a public space like a waiting room, shopping centre or in a hospital bay with other patients).	• Skill up the person and family on what to say to members of the public, for example practising a script. • A dissociative episode card that briefly describes not to call emergency services can be helpful. • It may help when the person themselves explains what happened and show that they are alright after the episode.

Final thoughts and recommendations

The case studies described in this chapter showed that the PCM was able to formulate and treat a series of heterogeneous and complex patients with FND. The model provides a suitable alternative for clinicians who encounter a patient with psychological features that cannot easily be accommodated within traditional CBT models. Due to its relative simplicity, the PCM could play a role in early intervention in busy departments (e.g. accidents and emergencies, stroke wards and first seizure clinics) by providing newly diagnosed patients and their families with initial FND education using the model. The early introduction of psychology may reduce the risk of a patient feeling "dumped", rejected, not believed or "faking" symptoms when referred onwards for psychological therapy. Furthermore, this chapter demonstrated that the PCM can also serve as a psychology-driven multidisciplinary model since the elements of the PCM represent the various disciplines commonly involved in the treatment of FND. The model was capable of integrating multidisciplinary findings into one cohesive formulation of FND and facilitating collaboration by mapping out a clear pathway for treatment. This chapter has hopefully demonstrated that the PCM shows promise as a new practical model in the clinic that can increase awareness on the systemic maintaining factors of FND and positively impact on patient care and patient-provider relationships, and further optimise healthcare outcomes in FND.

6 Pressure Cooker Model adaptations for different populations with FND

FND is an umbrella term that covers a wide range of symptoms. The heterogeneity in symptoms that is so characteristic for FND is also reflected in the many different subgroups of people that FND can affect including the full age range from children, adolescents, people of a working age to retirees and older adults, as well as people with different levels of cognitive ability; and people with co-existing neurological or neurodevelopmental problems (e.g. organic epilepsy and autism). Chapter 6 will show that the PCM is a versatile model that can be applied in different subpopulations of FND. We will explore various configurations and adaptations of the PCM for common "co-morbidities" in FND and draw the reader's attention to the specific features of FND in each subgroup.

Children, adolescents and young people

FND has frequently been reported in child and paediatric populations (Raper et al., 2019; Weiss et al., 2021; Paleari et al., 2022; Vassilopoulos et al., 2022). CBT has shown great promise as an effective treatment for FND in a pilot study with children (McFarlane et al., 2019). More recently, "psychologically informed" physiotherapy approaches have been championed and found to be effective for children and adolescents with FND (e.g. Gray et al., 2020; Kozlowska et al., 2021; Kim et al., 2022). Interestingly, Kozlowska et al. (2021) described a range of systemic factors impacting on children and families with FND, including stigma, reduced empathy and an "outdated culture of care", which appear to bear strong similarities to the issues invariably encountered in adults with FND and which have been extensively discussed in other chapters of this book. The current section will highlight FND-specific features detected in children and young people with FND, arranged by each PCM element, and explore the clinical application of the PCM in an adolescent with FND (Table 6.1).

Example case: dissociative episodes and functional tremor in a young person with generalised anxiety disorder

Chloe was a 17-year-old female with approximately a ten-year history of FND since middle childhood. Chloe experienced moments of brief

DOI: 10.4324/9781003308980-6

Table 6.1 FND-specific features encountered in children and adolescents with FND

Kitchen environment

- Reinforcement by the school system. FND awareness is often lacking in systems that children frequently interact with.
- Models in the home environment, for example a parent or sibling with an organic illness, with the child learning to meet an unmet need for, for example, validation or feeling noticed, through modelling processes. In addition to the presence of "symptom models", are other FND-specific features present, particularly reduced verbal emotional expression and abnormal activity levels?
- Social functions of the FND in the family unit or classroom: Does the FND communicate an unmet need that is being met via the FND through reciprocal reinforcement processes? (e.g. FND may act as a deterrent towards peers refraining from bullying the person or against heavy demands placed on the child who is otherwise unable to cope, or it may elicit care and validation from their peers or family that would otherwise not be present, helping the person to "fit in" and increase their self-esteem due to the validation).
- Is the child exposed to systemic re-traumatisation by peers and school staff, which, on top of the original triggers for FND, may further exacerbate the clinical picture?

Cover

Keep self to self

Likely similar coping strategies as parents. Useful to ask parents about their way of coping with emotions and judge concepts such as "psychological mindedness", "level of introspection" and any features of intellectualisation, alexithymia or dissociation.

Valve

It is not uncommon for a child or adolescent with FND to have (had) a lot of hobbies, after school activities and high-achievement focus sports activities ("boom" or "bust-after-boom" valve) without many rest breaks or breathing space.

Overpressure Plug

Although all types of FND symptoms can emerge in children and young people, dissociative episodes are a common occurrence.

Keep in mind that deliberate self-harm may occur as a form of "passive" self-harm in the context of accidental self-injury during dissociative episodes. The distinction is not always clear-cut. In the case of self-injury that results in significant injuries and harm to the body (e.g. head banging, lots of facial injuries close to the brain, broken bones or (re)-opened wounds) requiring frequent medical treatment, it is important to raise suspicion of active self-harm.

Warning light

Hypervigilance from the environment can be a big issue for this age group, due to the many systems that children and adolescents are embedded in including the family unit (e.g. parents and siblings), school (e.g. teachers and peers) and sports/leisure clubs.

Watch out for altered or adapted routines at the home that "tip-toe" or are highly adapted to the person with FND

Sticky left-over food

Core beliefs: I'm different (e.g. when struggling with subjects) I'm not good enough (e.g. reduced grades)

Pot

History of physical illness or somatoform symptoms such as irritable bowel syndrome or past hospitalisations in childhood.

Ignition/Fuel: common triggers of FND for children and young people

- Exam stress
- Not being able to keep up due to undiagnosed learning difficulties, dyslexia, dyscalculia or language delay for other reasons.
- Sibling rivalry
- Victim of school bullying and problems in friendships
- Parental pressure and high expectations for the child, for example in school grades and sports.
- Issues and conflicts in the parental relationship, significant family dynamics
- Abuse, neglect and unspeakable dilemmas
- Look out for an unmet need that is not verbally expressed by the child, for example in the context of parental emotional neglect and needing psychological safety.

Flames and Heat

High levels of anxiety can be present, as well as perfectionist thinking and dissociation. Look out for the level of emotion language and dissociation. In their sample of children with FND, McFarlane et al. (2019) found "subthreshold" emotional and behavioural features on questionnaires, despite the observation of clinical anxiety and depression, which may indicate the presence of dissociation.

Safety features
- Factors for positive treatment outcomes identified by Turgay (1990) in n = 137 children, adolescents and their families with FND included
- Patient features: Younger age, absence of psychological difficulties, presence of "healthy" personality features
- Treatment factors: insight, adherence/compliance to treatment, early intervention
- Systemic factors: normal family functioning, family accepting psychological perspective on the FND, team experiencing positive feelings towards the child and family

---

dissociation that could culminate in longer lasting full-blown dissociative episodes, although these happened on rare occasions. Chloe's dissociation mostly consisted of "zoning out" and feeling confused multiple times a day. Chloe displayed other dissociative features including spending hours of her time sleeping, playing videogames and "getting lost" in watching movies. The FND symptoms greatly impacted on Chloe's day-to-day functioning. She was unable to continue in full-time education and became socially isolated; her only interactions were with her immediate family (Table 6.2).

Table 6.2 Chloe's Pressure Cooker Model formulation

Kitchen

- Social functions of FND: Chloe was supported by parents, school staff and peers, who would not place demands or reject her but instead were caring, compassionate and respectful.

Cover
- Chloe maintained being very open about her difficult thoughts and feelings; however, in reality, Chloe's level of verbal emotional expression was reduced. Her worries emerged only in the latter phase of therapy when trust was built in the therapeutic relationship.

Overpressure Plug
- Dissociative episodes at school and brief moments of "zoning out" in therapy.
- (Other dissociative phenomena: sleeping, playing videogames and "getting lost" in watching movies)
- Functional tremor

Valve
- Bust-after-boom: previously very busy and highly active, both intellectual and sports pursuits. In the last year, Chloe became withdrawn; she played videogames and got lost in watching movies for long periods during the day, with dissociation as the hypothesised underlying function of these activities.

Warning light
- High focus on symptoms, with the symptoms changing weekly. When staff suggested ways to cope, Chloe put up barriers.
- High attentional focus on worry thoughts

Sticky left-over food

> Keep self to self,
> Pushing on and
> Dissociation

"I'm worthless"/low self-esteem. "If I work very hard, I will feel good about myself"

Pot
- Long sleeping episodes including power naps during the day, suggesting dissociation.

Ignition
- Family supportive, but parental pressures to achieve high grades.
- Background of having been a victim of bullying.
- Critical incident: Episode of deliberate self-harm in response to feeling overwhelmed with different responsibilities and demands, in the context of busy life

Flames
- Chloe's worries pertained to a wide range of different topics:
- School and putting pressure on herself to obtain the highest possible grades during exams.
- Future job and career opportunities
- Family members and their health
- Friendships
- Finding a romantic partner and starting a family in future

The worries were subjected to many different worry processes leading to more worries.

High achiever and perfectionist at school and sports.

Fuel

- Worry thoughts were the main triggers of dissociative "zoning out" episodes, with the anxiety expressed in a functional tremor.

Evidence of suicidal ideation on mood questionnaire but deemed low risk due to lack of plans, futuristic thinking and positive protective factors.

Cognition: The results from a neuropsychological assessment were unremarkable.

Heat

- High levels of anxiety which Chloe dissociated from.

Safety features

Variable engagement, Chloe was suggestible, peers had impact on her engagement with the therapy programme.

Layer 1

Several historic factors made Chloe vulnerable towards developing FND symptoms later in life. In childhood and as a young person, Chloe had been exposed to high demands and relentlessly high standards from her parents regarding her school and sports achievements. For many years, she was also systematically bullied at school by her peers. In response to these experiences, Chloe developed several adaptive coping strategies to "survive" the hurt and rejection that would ensue if she did not produce good enough school results or the rejection by her peers. These adverse childhood experiences helped Chloe to develop three main coping strategies since childhood including keeping herself to herself, pushing on with sports activities and tireless studying, as well as dissociation via deliberate self-harm (superficial cutting).

Layer 2

Chloe's FND coping triangle consisted of the three main FND coping strategies that were present since a young age (Sticky left-over food) and were repeated into 'teenhood': keeping herself to herself resulted in reduced verbal emotional expression (tight Cover), pushing on continued as a well-developed habit of constant and high levels of activity (an "overactive valve") for many years until "the bust" emerged after "the boom" (the valve became blocked), and finally, deliberate self-harm as a form of dissociating from strong emotions morphed into a different form: FND.

Layer 3

Internal regulation function of the FND: the Pressure Cooker Chain Reaction started with an internal psychological trigger, that is worry thoughts (Fuel) that were put on an imaginary "thought conveyor belt" and further processed by "worry mechanisms" including rumination, thinking about all the worst case scenarios, worries jumping from topic to topic and worrying extra in the hope that this would somehow prevent bad future outcomes (Flames). These processed worries were simultaneously subjected to high levels of self-focused attention (Warning light) and gradually grew into a highly unpleasant internal state (Flames) that Chloe was unable to identify or label due to alexithymia and dissociation (low Heat). The worries and unpleasant state continued to build internally and reached a "worry boiling point", which required Chloe to act on expressing them (or the imaginary Pot would explode). However, without recourse to helpful ways of expression (reduced verbal emotional expression and activity levels; tight Cover and blocked Valve respectively), Chloe had no other choice than to express her worries via dissociation: zoning out and a functional tremor that represented the physical expression of her anxiety. The dissociation temporarily removed worry triggers and a highly unpleasant internal state for Chloe by negative reinforcement; however, the subsequent relief from worries reinforced dissociation as a coping habit. Furthermore, after Chloe came out of her dissociative state, new "Type 2" worries about how she had come across would feed back into the Fuel, adding secondary worries to an already large reservoir of primary worries, further feeding into the maintenance cycle.

It should be noted that Chloe's current Pressure Cooker Chain Reaction was not dissimilar to the way she historically coped with unpleasant emotional states as a young person. She described having felt overwhelmed (Flames) in response to past worries about various responsibilities and demands (Fuel) which she did not speak about (tight Cover) or released via helpful activities (blocked Valve) and that culminated in a serious episode of deliberate self-harm (Overpressure Plug). Although the deliberate self-harm episodes had stopped, they had been subjected to the same Pressure Cooker Chain Reaction and were "replaced" by FND.

Layer 4

In addition to the zoning out episodes, sleeping (as well as playing videogames and "getting lost" in watching movies – listed under the Valve element) helped to reduce Chloe's worries by negative reinforcement.

Layer 5

The zoning out and full-blown dissociative episodes appeared to have a social function: following these episodes, Chloe was supported by parents, school staff and peers, who would not place demands or reject her but instead were caring, compassionate and respectful. This provided positive reinforcement of the dissociation and increased its frequency in future.

Treatment

Chloe's psychological therapy was based on the PCM formulation (Figure 6.1).

Outcomes

At discharge, Chloe endorsed minimal levels of psychological difficulties on questionnaires, except for on a worry measure. Qualitatively, she presented as settled and greatly looked forward to the future. Although her worry levels remained substantially elevated, Chloe felt in control of self-managing her worries (Table 6.3).

Chloe achieved complete remission of her FND symptoms and went on to live an independent and happy life following discharge, without any known relapses.

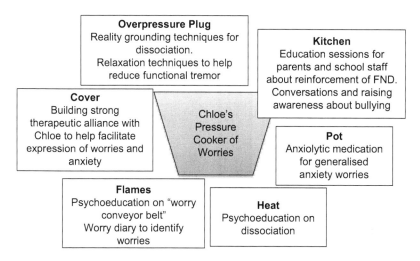

Figure 6.1 Pressure Cooker Model strategies for Chloe's persistent worries.

Table 6.3 Chloe's psychology questionnaire results

Questionnaire	Measures	Admission	Discharge
PHQ-9	Depressive symptoms	27/27 (severe)	4/27 (normal)
GAD-7	Anxiety	21/21 (severe)	3/21 (normal)
HADS–A	Anxiety	12/21 (moderate)	6/21 (normal)
HADS–D	Depression	11/21 (moderate)	2/21 (normal)
DERS–SF	Emotion dysregulation	Not administered	Total: 51/90, Mean: 2.83 Z = 1.37
Penn State Worry Questionnaire	Worries	58 (moderate worry, at the top range, nearly reaching high worry)	49 (moderate worry)

People with FND and learning difficulties

There is not much known in the scientific literature about co-existing learning difficulties or disabilities in people with FND, in part because the presence of learning disabilities is often used as an exclusion criterion in research studies. A few studies described a co-occurrence of dissociative episodes and learning disabilities (e.g. Duncan & Oto, 2008; Baslet et al., 2010) or learning problems (e.g. Plioplys et al., 2014; Doss et al., 2017). Furthermore, case studies highlighted a relationship with learning disabilities in, for example, adolescents with dissociative seizures (Silver, 1982) and in a case series with Amish adolescent girls with limb weakness that rendered them bedridden where the majority of the girls experienced problems at school "or learning disabilities" with three girls repeating a school year (Cassady et al., 2005). Duncan and Oto (2008) highlighted clinical differences between people experiencing dissociative episodes with vs without learning disabilities including fewer people with a history of sexual abuse and a higher frequency of people with emotional triggers associated with the episodes in the FND group with learning disabilities. It should also be noted that a subset of people with dissociative episodes present with concurrent epileptic seizures, which can greatly impact on the brain and may result in cognitive dysfunction or learning disabilities.

From a PCM perspective, learning difficulties can lower the threshold for developing or experiencing FND symptoms. For example, people with learning disabilities may find it harder to describe or express their emotions due to verbal communication difficulties. In addition, co-morbid physical disabilities and epilepsy may prevent a person from accessing the community, which can impact on activity levels. In addition, people with learning problems may have been or are still exposed and subjected to higher rates of school bullying and victimisation, which may be triggers for FND symptoms.

Simplifying the Pressure Cooker Model: a social story of FND

Although the PCM elements are all equally important variables that help explain the emergence and maintenance of FND symptoms, it is not helpful to push this on people with FND who may experience problems with understanding and remembering the elements and the psychological processes that maintain the FND. The goal is to collaborate with the patient to create a mutual understanding of the FND, not to shoehorn the person into the PCM. In the next section, we will discuss several adaptations to the PCM that may foster greater understanding of FND in a person with learning problems. One of these adaptations, the use of social stories, can be a powerful technique to build and share a complex psychological formulation.

Owning the FND narrative

Keep in mind that people with learning disabilities – with or without FND– may not have had a voice. Encourage the person to take ownership of the social story by asking them to select the pictures, language, colours, type font and the format they prefer. Although care plans are sometimes shared without the person's involvement, for example when the dissociative episodes are severe and need immediate treatment, it is good practice to have the patient "on board" with the formulation. Explore and ask the person for permission whether they would like to take the lead with your assistance to share their social story with other people including parents, friends, school staff and hospital staff.

Externalise the FND

At times, a social story about FND can feel threatening to the person. Linking the social story on FND with the person's interests or a person they admire, for example a movie character or a positive role model, can be helpful. Instead of focusing the social story on the person with FND, use the character to explain FND.

Use accessible language

Simplicity is the key. Irrespective of a person's level of cognitive functioning or learning difficulty, in first instance, keep the model basic and stick to only a few elements that stand out to the patient or that are the most important maintaining factors of the FND. Presenting the PCM as a whole is not recommended especially for people with slowed speed of information processing, difficulties with focused attention, remembering concepts, problems with language comprehension or executive-organisational issues. Be mindful that a person may be at risk of attentional overload and become cognitively overwhelmed with the details, particularly if a lot of elements are presented at once.

Social stories are dynamic: focus on the relationship

The creation of social stories in FND is a dynamic process. As the person learns more about the maintaining factors of FND, more elements can gradually be added in to build the PCM and enrich the formulation. Keep in mind that relationships and interpersonal functioning remain core to FND including in people with learning problems, and maybe even of specific importance in people with learning problems who have a history of exposure to bullying and victimisation. Occasionally, it may not be about the contents of the social story, but it may actually be about the process of engaging with the person on a joint project that impacts positively on FND symptoms, particularly if the person is made to feel heard, validated, noticed, accepted and treated with respect, which may not be their usual reality.

Strengths-based social stories

If the person does not connect with "paperwork" for the social stories or experiences significant levels of visual or language difficulties due to a developmental condition (e.g. dyslexia) or site of the brain injury (e.g. left temporal lobe), use other creative materials that link in with the person's cognitive strengths. Describe the PCM using materials that a person prefers to use: painting, drawing, clay, laminated emotion coping cards and "live" building of a pressure cooker. Videos and reels can be helpful; however, keep in mind that some maintaining influences of the FND are found in the positive reinforcing effects of social media.

The following section will describe an example of a social story formulation based on the PCM. As can be seen, several PCM elements have been removed to facilitate the person's understanding of the formulation (Figure 6.2).

Social story element	Comments
I have black-outs	(Overpressure Plug) Describe the FND symptoms that the person experiences. Incorporate words used by the person that refer to the FND.
During a black-out, I can: • Fall to the floor • Have shakes • I may not hear sounds or see you	
The episodes stop me from: • Going to school • Taking care of myself • Going out shopping	(Pot) Describe the impact of the FND on day-to-day functioning for the person.
During the black-outs, I sometimes hurt myself. I may get bruises and muscle pain	(Pot) Describe any physical risks to the person
Sharing my story will help to stop the black-outs	"I have black-outs and I'd like to tell you about them, so you know what to do when they happen"
The black-outs are like a boiling pot	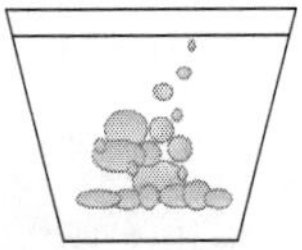
The pot has flames under it. The flames are my thoughts and feelings	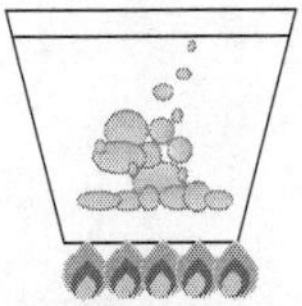
This is my first flame:	 "I feel scared going to school"

Figure 6.2a Example of a Pressure Cooker Model–based social story adapted for FND.

My second flame is:	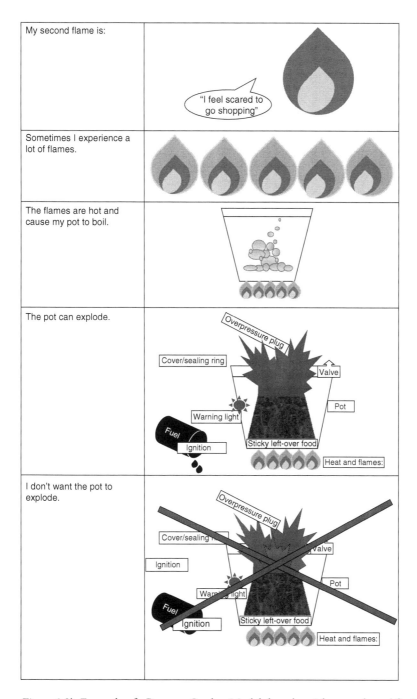
Sometimes I experience a lot of flames.	
The flames are hot and cause my pot to boil.	
The pot can explode.	
I don't want the pot to explode.	

Figure 6.2b Example of a Pressure Cooker Model–based social story adapted for FND.

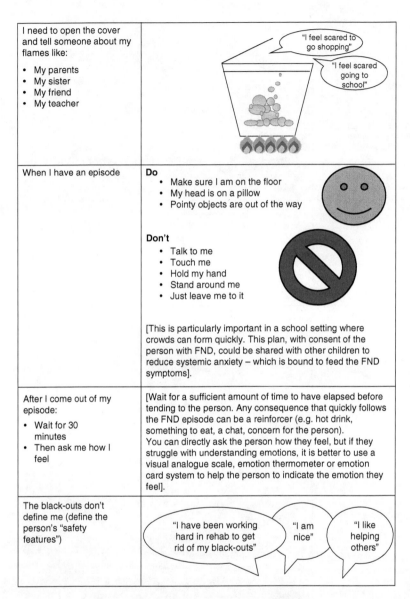

I need to open the cover and tell someone about my flames like: • My parents • My sister • My friend • My teacher	"I feel scared to go shopping" "I feel scared going to school!"

When I have an episode	**Do**
	   • Make sure I am on the floor
	   • My head is on a pillow
	   • Pointy objects are out of the way
	
	Don't
	   • Talk to me
	   • Touch me
	   • Hold my hand
	   • Stand around me
	   • Just leave me to it
	
	[This is particularly important in a school setting where crowds can form quickly. This plan, with consent of the person with FND, could be shared with other children to reduce systemic anxiety – which is bound to feed the FND symptoms].

After I come out of my episode: • Wait for 30 minutes • Then ask me how I feel	[Wait for a sufficient amount of time to have elapsed before tending to the person. Any consequence that quickly follows the FND episode can be a reinforcer (e.g. hot drink, something to eat, a chat, concern for the person). You can directly ask the person how they feel, but if they struggle with understanding emotions, it is better to use a visual analogue scale, emotion thermometer or emotion card system to help the person to indicate the emotion they feel].
The black-outs don't define me (define the person's "safety features")	"I have been working hard in rehab to get rid of my black-outs" "I am nice" "I like helping others"

Figure 6.2c Example of a Pressure Cooker Model–based social story adapted for FND.

Adaptations that are normally used in psychological therapy for people with learning difficulties or cognitive problems equally apply to people with additional FND symptoms. Figure 6.3 shows strategies that may be particularly useful.

Functional overlay patients: FND+

Occasionally, people with FND may present with functional overlay. The overlay bit is the FND in the context of another often longstanding organic condition. A common type of functional overlay in FND is the combination of epileptic and non-epileptic seizures (Table 6.4).

Epileptic and non-epileptic seizures

Since childhood, Esther has experienced organic epileptic seizures. She has been under the care of an epileptologist for yearly reviews. For a long time, the epilepsy had been managed well on anti-epileptic medications and her seizures were under control. Esther functioned well in life; she had a small family, held down a part-time job and was able to drive, go shopping and spend time with friends. Recently, the relationship with her partner broke down and they mutually agreed to separate.

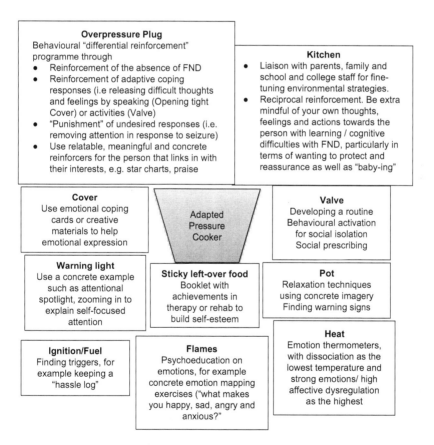

Figure 6.3 Pressure Cooker Model adaptations for people with FND and co-existing learning or cognitive difficulties.

One day, the seizures suddenly re-emerged and over time became more frequent. The seizures would often emerge at home or at work during stressful and emotionally overwhelming situations. After a big seizure, Esther would often have to recuperate for days. She was unable to fulfil her daily duties and became depressed. The epileptologist ordered several video-EEGs which captured Esther's seizures and the results came back consistent with a diagnosis of non-epileptic seizures. In the referral letter to a psychologist, the epileptologist noted that Esther seemed overwhelmed with the stressful demands of her life.

Complex trauma ("personality disorder")

A subset of people with FND show features consistent with personality disorder. Rates vary widely; Binzer et al. (1997) reported a frequency of personality disorder in their sample of motor conversion inpatients as high as 50%. Although research studies tend to use a dichotomous categorisation ("personality disorder present or absent"), in clinical practice, personality features in FND are better understood as existing on a continuum (Table 6.5):

Table 6.4 Esther's Pressure Cooker Model formulation

Kitchen environment

Look out for environmental patterns of reinforcement.

- *Hypervigilant monitoring: Parents checking in daily and sometimes multiple times a day.*
- *Esther's household and shopping chores have been taken over by parents and neighbours. They won't let her do anything, even though she would like to do a few chores.*
- *Reciprocal reinforcement: Esther's epilepsy team has been ordering extra medical investigations.*

In addition, it is important for a treatment team to be able to describe and distinguish between organic vs functional neurological symptoms as these emerge and to be able to discuss any doubts (Klinke et al., 2021).

Cover	Overpressure Plug	Valve
• "Tight cover"	Describe the semiology in detail (in close collaboration with the medical team) what the differences and similarities are between the NESs and ESs (non-epileptic episodes and epileptic episodes).	• Bust-after-boom pattern:
In between episodes, Esther did not express her feelings and often said "I'm fine" "I'm not stressed"		• Due to the separation, a lot of the childcare and household demands fell on Esther's shoulders.
During episodes, Esther was not able to express any emotions even though she seem to demonstrate the features of anxiety		
	• Esther's NESs: immobile in bed but shaking.	
	• Duration varies between five and 20 minutes.	

Kitchen environment

Sticky left-over food

Core beliefs:
Due to my
epilepsy, I'm
different.
People will let
you down.

Warning light

- For the person, it may be difficult to accept the non-epileptic nature of the seizures. Due to their medical experiences in the context of epilepsy, their belief system and personal theory of the seizures may be strongly geared towards organic explanations.
- Ensure that there is an unambiguous diagnosis of NES from an epileptologist or neurologist and that this has been clearly communicated to the person.
- If possible, Joint medical × Psychology sessions can be powerful to explore a more psychological explanation for some of the seizures.
- *Esther engages in hypervigilant monitoring for epilepsy symptoms. Esther is adamant that something is seriously amiss, and the causes are organic in nature. Esther has been making videos of the episodes and showing this in therapy sessions.*

Ignition

Make a time-line of the epileptic and non-epileptic seizures. Check if there is a trigger event that marked the sudden onset of NES, as well as a correlation between stressful life events and the NES episodes. Find out about the history of epilepsy and what the environment's responses were (e.g. validating, caring).

- *Esther grew up in a family with significant traumas in her personal background.*
- *Esther's sports achievements were a protective factor.*

Fuel

- *Recent separation which is still a difficult time for Esther.*

Pot

- The Pot element will be key here, particularly:
- Reviewing warning signs and triggers for NESs to help differentiate between the two conditions.
- Close collaboration with the medical team is vital.
- Be careful about diagnostic overshadowing in both directions: considering a NES if it is an ES can result in catastrophic consequences. Vice versa, considering ES if it is a NES can lead to harmful effects and iatrogenic damage.
- *On anti-epileptic medications.*
- *Many A&E visits but false alarms.*
- *Esther noticed a specific profile of warning signs for NESs that is different from the profile she has when experiencing epileptic seizures.*

Flames and Heat

Comprehensive psychological assessment and formulation to check for (trauma), stresses, common coping strategies found in FND (e.g. reduced emotional expression, boom-bust) and personality features.

- *During therapy sessions, Esther did not seem to be in touch with her emotions and denied any distress.*
- *Whenever Esther experienced the first warning signs in her body that alerted her to an impending episode, Esther was not able to label the emotion she felt and became immobile with vacant staring.*

NES = non-epileptic seizure; ES = epileptic seizure; FND = functional neurological disorder.

Table 6.5 Wide spectrum of personality features in FND

Dual diagnosis of FND and personality disorder	People with FND who have been officially diagnosed with a personality disorder, often with the personality disorder preceding the FND.
Diagnosis of FND and high suspicion of personality disorder	People who display the features of a personality disorder but have not sought help or received a formal diagnosis.
Subthreshold personality features	People who exhibit subthreshold personality features that may meet some, but do not fully meet the criteria of a personality disorder but are still significantly impacted by the features on a daily basis.
Interpersonal features associated with FND, without personality disorder features	People whose FND features emerge or worsen in response to interpersonal triggers but who do not meet criteria for a personality disorder
No personality disorder or features	People with FND whose symptoms are strongly tied to an "Axis I" disorder, for example social anxiety, panic disorder.

In clinical practice, particularly in inpatient settings, the most common personality features encountered will fall into Cluster B and C, that is most often emotionally unstable and dependent, with occasionally narcissistic or histrionic features. The PCM can incorporate the behaviours, beliefs and emotions associated with these features, for example care-eliciting and dependency behaviours often displayed by individuals with a dependent personality. Rather than "personality disorder", the PCM uses the term "complex trauma" to indicate repeated trauma that often started in childhood and carries on into adulthood.

Generic PCM complex trauma formulation

Figure 6.4 displays a generic PCM formulation with features that are encountered in clinical practice with individuals with FND, a complex trauma background and ongoing complex psychosocial circumstances that seem to perpetuate the FND.

As can be seen from Figure 6.4, the PCM is able to incorporate the features characteristic of complex trauma and demonstrate the relationship between complex trauma and FND.

The PCM of complex trauma and FND

Table 6.6 provides recommendations to help build your PCM formulation of complex trauma in FND, followed by a case study.

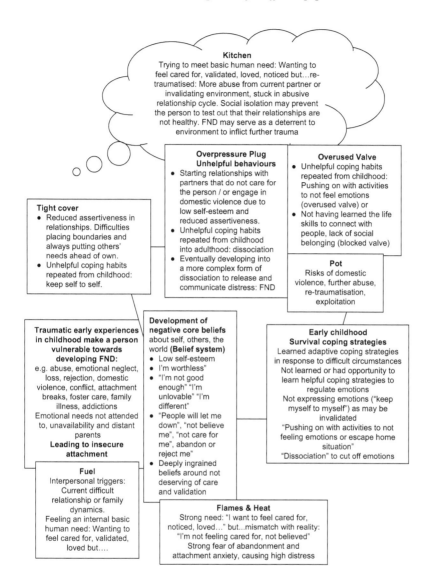

Figure 6.4 Generic Pressure Cooker Model formulation of complex trauma.

Case study: dissociative episodes and motor-type FND symptoms in a person with FND and complex trauma

Background information

Leah was a 21-year-old female with FND that started after she contracted a non-life threatening virus that required a hospital admission. Soon after this admission, Leah developed stroke-like symptoms including black-outs,

Table 6.6 Pressure Cooker Model formulation adapted for complex trauma

Kitchen environment

- Spend more time and make a detailed analysis of the person's "kitchen environment", including their relationship history and current relationships, as well as interpersonal difficulties, as these will be core.
- The therapeutic relationship may be more intense and unstable, mirroring the person's relationships outside therapy.
- Group therapy and interactions with other people with FND: How does the person function?
- Think about the function of the FND, as well as the "wider function" of all "unhelpful" coping strategies considered together: care-eliciting, validation, proximity. Can one function parsimoniously explain the presentation that includes FND?
- FND may have the specific social function of proximity in the context of a "pervasive and excessive need to be taken care of" and can lead to "fears of separation" where the FND may stop the separation from another person.

Cover	Overpressure Plug	Valve
• People can have a very tight cover and keep themselves to themselves. • However, the opposite has also been observed, a "loose Cover": oversharing of emotions, and this can serve the function of validation of the emotions from the environment. Alternatively, it can also be a way to distract from deeper problems. • Assertiveness problems in people with dependent features and "difficulty expressing disagreement with others", as well as violation of boundaries to obtain support and nurturance.	• Interpret the Overpressure Plug as a broad category consisting of a pool of unhelpful strategies or ways of emotional expressions of distress, of which FND is one, and deliberate self-harm may be another one. • The Overpressure Plug is often more changeable and fluctuating. It is possible that, in time, one unhelpful coping habit (e.g. self-harm, binge eating) is replaced by another unhelpful one including FND.	• Due to emotion dysregulation, unstable relationships or care-eliciting, the person may be highly prone to a blocked Valve, social isolation and lack a sense of belonging because their environment does not want to interact with them • In the context of dependent features, people may have initiation difficulties and are unable to participate in independent activities.

Kitchen environment

Warning light
Heightened self-focused attention towards FND symptoms is common

Sticky left-over food

Core beliefs:
-I'm worthless
-People can't be trusted or will let me down

Pot
Watch out for other past and current "unhelpful but understandable" ways of coping including:
- Eating disorders
- Substance misuse
- Hypersomnia
- Deliberate self-harm/ suicide attempt(s)

Risk of deliberate self-harm vs accidental self-harm as part of FND may be blurred.

Strong fears of being unable to care for themselves impacting on activities in daily life.

Ignition

Fuel
- Interpersonal triggers will be more likely in this group of people with FND, and therefore, an analysis of interpersonal triggers will be key to the formulation.
- For example: validation, being noticed, arguments.
- Variation and fluctuation in FND symptoms will likely be associated with interpersonal events and dynamics with other people, and their associated emotions.
- Due to attachment difficulties, endings (e.g. discharge from a service) can be traumatic and need to be handled sensitively. FND symptoms can increase before discharge, in the context of "frantic efforts to avoid abandonment".
- The concept of systemic re-traumatisation is particularly important here: people with trauma backgrounds, especially sexual, may have been in situations where they were not believed by a parental key figure.

Flames and Heat
- Previous mental health contacts, particularly crisis and secondary care services, as well as longstanding therapies such as dialectical behaviour therapy or mentalisation-based therapy.
- Emotion dysregulation including anger outbursts and rapidly oscillating/fluctuations in emotions.
- More severe levels or expressions of dissociation including dissociated identity and wandering/'fugue' episodes.

---

dystonia, leg weakness and distorted speech. Following thorough medical investigations, Leah was given a positive diagnosis of FND and subsequently admitted for a period of inpatient treatment.

In the first few weeks, Leah's FND symptoms dominated the clinical picture. Leah mobilised using a wheelchair. Her psychological symptoms were present to some degree but relatively mild. Although Leah had been in a series of troublesome and abusive relationships that involved frequent police involvement, and had frequently engaged in acts of deliberate self-harm in the past, she reported feeling happy and content in her current relationship. She identified the FND and "strong emotions" as her only psychological difficulty in life. Leah exhibited a pattern of "high service receipt", which included longstanding individual and group therapy, involvement of mental health crisis services, and being listed as a frequent attender of the accidents and emergencies department.

Initial hypothesis: post-traumatic stress disorder vs depression

Leah reported often waking up in a panic with flashbacks about the many years of abuse she had endured in the context of her early childhood and later romantic relationships. She also described high anxiety in the context of social and crowded situations. After further exploration, Leah's flashbacks were characterised by ruminative features about past painful memories and associated with low mood rather than anxiety. In addition, Leah did not present with overt avoidance or hypervigilant behaviours. Therefore, a hypothesis of PTSD felt less likely to fit with Leah's presentation. The question arose whether depression would be a viable alternative hypothesis since Leah also displayed many features including severe levels of depressive symptoms on mood questionnaires, repeated rejection experiences from significant people in her life, ongoing worries about rejection, and social isolation and the complete lack of a social network apart from her partner and immediate family.

The vicious flower of depression

Leah's difficulties were initially formulated using a combination of the longitudinal formulation of depression (Beck Judith, 1995) and the Six Cycles Maintenance Model (Moorey, 2010) embedded within (also known as the vicious flower) (Figure 6.5).

As can be seen in the table below, Leah's vicious flower contained a wide range of petals that covered the Six Cycles Maintenance Model (Moorey, 2010) (Table 6.7).

Treatment: the virtuous flower against depression

Leah's vicious flower formulation guided her subsequent intervention for depression (Table 6.8).

A conundrum of inconsistencies

With Leah's discharge vast approaching, the team reported feeling puzzled by her presentation and behaviours on the ward. Despite Leah's major achievements in rehabilitation, occupational and physiotherapists started to observe

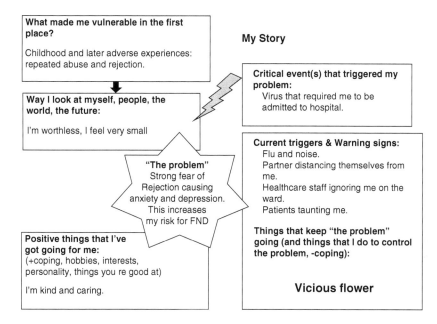

Figure 6.5 Longitudinal formulation of depression.

Table 6.7 Leah's vicious flower formulation of depression

Cognitive cycle #1 Automatic negative thinking	Cognitive cycle #2 Rumination/self-attacking	Mood/emotion cycle
• Negative beliefs around emotional expression. • Pushing away/suppressing difficult emotions and thoughts. • Thinking errors: "Jumping to conclusions", catastrophising, fortune telling.	• Being hard on myself, self-attacking and putting pressure on myself.	• Episodes of tearfulness and low mood. • Putting on a happy face, so I won't get rejected.

Vicious flower of depression

Behavioural cycle #1 *Withdrawal/avoidance*	Behavioural cycle #2 *Unhelpful behaviour*	Motivation/physical symptoms cycle
• Withdrawal from social and enjoyable events. • Reduced assertiveness	• Reassurance seeking with loved ones to make sure they have not abandoned me. • Pushing people quickly away before they can reject me.	• Problems with sleeping • Binge drinking and eating

Table 6.8 Leah's virtuous flower formulation against depression

Cognitive cycle #1	Cognitive cycle #2	Mood/emotion cycle
• *Automatic negative thinking* • Challenge negative beliefs and think about the advantages of regular emotional expression including communication strategies to improve speech intelligibility that was affected by FND. • Tolerating difficult thoughts and feelings longer. Actively releasing emotions instead of pushing them away. • Psycho-education on thinking traps.	• *Rumination/self-attacking* • Core belief work on developing positive core beliefs and self-compassion. 	• When I feel distressed, I tell myself it's OK to not look happy.
Behavioural cycle #1 *Withdrawal/avoidance* • Psycho-education around the relationship between reduced activity levels, lack of enjoyable activities and low mood. • Behavioural activation with social and enjoyable activities to help increase positive emotions including exercise programme, accessing community and social ward groups with occupational therapy and physiotherapy colleagues. • Practice of assertiveness skills in FND family education sessions.	**Behavioural cycle #2** *Unhelpful behaviour* • Group therapy for FND, learning not to push people away and develop new, positive relationships/friendships. Giving people a chance. • Use a calling schedule to help feel more in control and contain reassurance seeking.	**Motivation/physical symptoms cycle** • Sleep hygiene • Medical advice around overeating and alcohol misuse.

various "near-miss" risky behaviours, with Leah appearing to put herself in harm's way despite clear instructions, as well as an increased rate in falls during sessions. Staff also reported more pronounced emotion dysregulation and tearfulness, as well as a range of "hyperactivating" behaviours (e.g. Mikulincer & Shaver, 2003) including developing a provocative, interpersonal manner of relating to staff, and frequent oversharing personal and sensitive information. Leah expressed an increase in suicidal ideation and a plan to act on these urges, requiring risk management. Post-discharge planning of activities was slow and stalled.

Several inconsistencies were also noted. Leah was socially very active and outwardly enjoying being the centre of social events, without any obvious physical signs of anxiety, which seemed inconsistent with her reports of social anxiety, although the team still entertained the possibility that she had been enduring the social situations with distress. In addition, Leah's physical gains heavily fluctuated, particularly towards the end of her admission. On some days, she was bed- and wheelchair-bound, whereas on other days she mobilised without any equipment. At discharge, Leah was highly distressed and her symptoms had amplified requiring an alteration in her care package. Table 6.9 displays a re-formulation of Leah's difficulties that incorporated these new observations.

PCM complex trauma re-formulation

Table 6.9 Pressure Cooker Model re-formulation of Leah's FND and psychological difficulties

Kitchen

Behaviours and FND elicited care from the environment; however, the behaviours also resulted in a self-fulfilling prophecy:

people were feeling drained and wary of interacting with Leah, which directly fed Leah's rejection fears and ultimately resulted in real-time rejection. This created a partial reinforcement schedule making the FND even harder to extinguish

Cover	**Overpressure Plug**	**Valve**
• Oversharing of intimate details but keeping unspeakable dilemma to self.	FND: black-outs, dystonia, leg weakness and distorted speech	• Bust-after-boom Valve: "pushing on" with activities was a form of dissociation. Unable to sit with distress.
• Reduced assertiveness in relationships when boundaries are crossed.	**Other unhelpful behaviours:** Deliberate self-harm	• Currently blocked Valve: lack of enjoyable activities and social isolation.
• Reduced speech intelligibility.	Binge drinking	

(Continued)

Table 6.9 (Continued)

Kitchen

Warning light
- High levels of symptom focus: new symptoms emerged on a weekly basis and often in response to newly admitted patients with the same symptoms.

Sticky left-over food

Core beliefs:
"I'm different"
"I'm worthless"
"I'm unlovable"

Childhood coping strategies repeated into adulthood:
Dissociation, pushing on, keeping myself to self

Pot
- High level of entrenchment with equipment including wheelchair, irreversible home adaptations, with more planned in future.
- Reduced cardiovascular fitness, problems with sleeping.

Flames
- Worries about partner rejecting and abandoning her.
- Attachment anxiety.

Ignition
- Parental emotional neglect, with regular physical and emotional abuse.
- History of having been a victim in multiple abusive relationships.
- Critical incident (later revealed): close friends abandoning Leah, around the same time as the infection that required hospitalisation.

Heat
High levels of emotion dysregulation and frequent tearfulness. Associated with FND set-backs

Fuel
Triggers were associated with an increase in all FND symptoms:
1. Physical triggers, for example flu or noise
2. Interpersonal triggers, for example
   (a). Distancing behaviours from the partner not being in touch, even though Leah attempts to make contact.
   (b). Witnessing other patients making better progress and receiving praise and validation.
   (c). Leah's perception of healthcare staff and patients either ignoring or taunting her.
   (d). Not having needs met for validation and being noticed by other people.

Safety features
Leah attended all her sessions, although engagement was variable. Leah was kind and social to other patients and staff.

PCM team formulation

Due to the strong thoughts, emotions and behaviours of the team towards Leah, it was felt that a standalone PCM formulation of Leah's difficulties would not fully capture her presentation, behaviours and their relationship to the FND symptoms. Therefore, a hybrid patient × team PCM formulation was applied following a reflection session, to help with understanding the confusing presentation (Table 6.10).

Table 6.10 PCM hybrid Patient × Team formulation of Leah's FND and psychological difficulties

---

Kitchen

- Co-dysregulation between Leah and her environment: patient and environmental distress reduce, resulting in relief. However, intermittent reinforcement from the team in response to Leah's behaviours poses a risk to these behaviours becoming harder to extinguish over time.

Cover
- Team engages in regular unconstructive venting but does not discuss their own "unspeakable dilemma" around feelings of failure and low self-confidence in skills to manage Leah's symptoms.
- Reduced assertiveness with none of the team members addressing Leah's unhelpful behaviours and dysfunctional interpersonal dynamic with the team.

Overpressure Plug
- Environment responds with attention, validation, care, soothing to stop hyperreactive behaviours as soon as possible.
- Shortening or avoiding sessions, unhelpful non-verbal behaviours displayed towards Leah.
- This mixture of behavioural 'reinforcement' and 'punishment' causes even more confusion in Leah.

Valve
- "Boom" Valve: staff spends a lot of time, effort and extra unplanned sessions on Leah's rehabilitation and managing the FND and behaviours, at the cost of caring for other patients.

Warning light
- Team highly focused on Leah's increased FND symptoms and lack of progress in rehab.

Sticky left-over food

Team's confidence in managing Leah's symptoms is low: negative team core beliefs

Pot
- Team risk of retaliation towards Leah increased (e.g. avoidance of sessions).
- Team struggling with self-care including nourishment. Sickness absence increased.

Flames/Heat
- In response to Leah's FND and emotion dysregulation, the environment feels distress and discomfort.
- Team reaches an internal state of "psychological unsafety".

Ignition/Fuel
- In response to interpersonal triggers and feeling minimised, rejected and worthless, Leah has an increased need for comfort, soothing, care, being noticed and validated.
- However, due to invalidating upbringing and later abusive experiences, Leah has limited access to self-soothing and is dismissive of internal strategies: Leah was unable to effectively use her own self-soothing strategies including opening the cover and unblocking valve.

(Continued)

Table 6.10 (Continued)

• Staff experiences a strong need to terminate the FND and Leah's behaviours as soon as possible.	• No access to external soothing either: usual "comforter" (partner) absent.
• Despite intense rehabilitation, staff starts to question their own abilities to treat Leah.	• Leah starts to communicate her needs externally by physically expressing through the FND. Leah seeks proximity to staff and elicits soothing from environment to manage internal distress.
• Feelings of failure and powerlessness.	• **Hyperreactive strategies:**
	• Black-outs/FND
	• Regular expression of deliberate self-harm
	• Increased rate of falls. Using wheelchair.
	• Expression of sadness, tearfulness and pain
	• Overt panic attacks
	• Provocative style of relating to staff
	• Inappropriate oversharing of personal information
	• Team witnessing Leah's FND symptoms, her ongoing internal distress and tearfulness, including worsening motor-type or dissociative episodes.

Safety features
Leah engaged well with plans for risk management.
Although Leah's behaviours caused considerable psychological "unsafety", the
   team had established positive working relationships with Leah.

Layer 1: Ignition

Since childhood, Leah experienced a series of adverse traumatic and rejection events that created a vulnerability towards the development of insecure
attachment, negative core beliefs and FND later in life.

Layer 2: the FND coping triangle

Leah's coping triangle mirrored the team's coping triangle.

Sticky left-over food

Leah kept herself to herself and used dissociation as her main coping strategies,
which was reflected in pushing on with activities and deliberate self-harm.
Historically, her treating team tended to push on with activities and was not
used to emotional expression or reflection on psychological processes.

Tight Cover

Both Leah and her team overshared sensitive information in their own ways.
Leah presented with loose boundaries and shared intimate details with people

she barely knew. It was hypothesised that the practice of oversharing served two functions: (1) to elicit care and validation from her environment and (2) to distract from deeper matters, in particular Leah's unspeakable dilemma that she kept to herself. The team behaved in a similar way and resorted to unconstructive and highly negative venting of frustrations and anger amongst each other in relation to the contents of Leah's sessions and her behaviours.

On the surface, both displayed a loose Cover. However, although Leah and the team expressed emotions, both parties did this in an unconstructive manner and did not speak about what was truly at the heart of their problems: an unspeakable dilemma that was yet unreleased, a "secret" that had the potential to result in a state of internal psychological unsafety and rejection from their immediate environment, and that was predicted to result in emotions too intolerable to manage. For Leah, the unspeakable dilemma was an unexpressed secret that she had carried with her for many years, whilst for the team, the dilemma comprised the anxiety, doubts and lack of confidence about their own skills in managing Leah's FND and behaviours, which seemed to amplify rather than ameliorate as rehabilitation progressed. Opting to keep the unspeakable dilemmas private seemed the better alternative.

Furthermore, both parties experienced reduced levels of assertiveness. For Leah, this emerged in personal relationships, whereas the team felt uncomfortable addressing the boundary violations in response to Leah's provoking behaviours. In a similar vein to Leah's reduced speech intelligibility, the team's ability to communicate with Leah had become blurred by the "noise" of Leah's behaviours.

Complementary Valves

Leah's reduced activity levels (blocked Valve) contrasted with the team's over-activity levels ("boom" Valve). The more Leah withdrew from the ward programme and displayed hyperreactive behaviours during sessions, the harder the team worked to get Leah "back on board" by putting major efforts in sessions and planning in extra sessions. These two complementary Valves maintained each other's activity levels in unhelpful ways.

Layer 3: the Pressure Cooker Chain Reaction

Interpersonal triggers (Fuel) caused Leah a chronic state of "psychological unsafety" and strong fears of abandonment that resulted in heightened distress (Flames, Heat #1). Her impending discharge and the prospect of (1) losing her sense of social belonging by parting ways with the validating, largely non-rejecting environment that she had grown comfortable with in the past months and, (2) returning to her pre-admission social isolation with no firm plans in place to change this quickly further increased her turmoil (Flames, Heat #2). Due to the lack of opportunities for learning helpful coping strategies and multiple rejection experiences in childhood (Sticky left-over food), Leah kept her most bothersome beliefs and emotions ("unspeakable dilemma") that had the potential to result in rejection, mostly to herself (tight Cover). She stopped engaging with some ward social activities and spent her time in bed. As a result, her emotions could not be released in other meaningful ways (blocked Valve). With both Cover and Valve blocked, this created an increased risk of FND (Overpressure Plug), thus resulting in fluctuating symptoms.

The lack of psychological safety felt by Leah was mirrored in the team's sense of psychological safety. Leah's behaviours elicited strong doubts and reduced confidence in skills managing the symptoms, especially given that the team did not observe the positive effects of their efforts on reducing Leah's symptoms (Flames, Heat). The team was unable to reflect on these thoughts and feelings (tight Cover), which contributed to overactivity (boom Valve), eventually resulting in unhelpful behaviours towards Leah, including shortening or cancelling sessions (Overpressure Plug).

Layer 4: facilitating physical factors of FND

Hypervigilance was a common theme. Leah was highly focused on her symptoms, with new symptoms emerging regularly, which the team responded to with more hypervigilance. Furthermore, the team's sickness absence rates increased, which resulted in a reduced number of sessions for Leah, as less staff was available to support her. At a psychological level, this further fed into Leah's beliefs around rejection as this was reminiscent of her childhood emotional neglect.

Layer 5: the social functions of FND

RECIPROCAL REINFORCEMENT

Strong reciprocal reinforcement patterns maintained Leah's FND, hyperreactive behaviours and the team's caring, soothing and validating behaviours that served to stop Leah's hyperreactive behaviours and emotion dysregulation as soon as possible. These reciprocal strategies were highly effective as it helped everyone to quickly and effectively reach a state of psychological safety. However, over time, an increase was observed in the frequency of the reciprocal behaviours, due to their reinforcing and relieving effects.

SYSTEMIC RE-TRAUMATISATION

Although the reciprocal behaviours were effective in reaching psychological safety in the short term, the behaviours lost their effectiveness in the long term. The environment experienced increasingly more frustration and anger with Leah's hyperreactive behaviours and started to feel drained. As a result, the sickness absence rate increased, and the team ignored and avoided Leah at all costs, leading to a reduced number of sessions, prematurely ending sessions, less one-to-one time in group sessions, lots of joint sessions to "share the burden" and unhelpful non-verbal behaviours displayed towards Leah. This unhelpful dynamic became a self-fulfilling prophecy: Leah felt minimised, worthless and rejected again.

The FND maintenance loop had now closed: the environment had taken on the role of becoming an interpersonal trigger for Leah's FND symptoms through the same distancing behaviours and not having her needs met for validation, exactly as Leah had experienced in her childhood and relationships. This re-started the PCM maintenance cycle all over again. In response to the team's distancing behaviours, Leah developed more emotion dysregulation, FND symptoms and hyperreactive strategies, which served as an interpersonal trigger for the team to display more distancing behaviours. Eventually, Leah and her environment served as each other's interpersonal triggers.

PARTIAL REINFORCEMENT

The team's paradoxical pattern of responding towards Leah, that is simultaneously validating and rejecting, risked the development of a partial reinforcement schedule. Due to the intermittent reinforcement provided by the team, Leah's behaviours became even harder to extinguish in the long run.

This case study demonstrates that the use of two PCM formulations in the treatment of a person with complex trauma is exceptionally important.

Therapy progress and outcomes

Leah thrived in the inpatient environment. At discharge, Leah fully recovered from her FND symptoms; she regained normal movement and the use of her legs. The dystonia improved significantly, as did her speech, which was fluent with minimal changes to speech intelligibility. The dissociative episodes reduced in frequency and severity. Qualitatively, Leah's confidence had increased and she reported having a positive outlook on her future. By the end of the admission, Leah was an active member of "ward life" and engaged in many social and enjoyable activities. Table 6.11 shows Leah's results on psychological and neurorehabilitation outcome measures. Despite making major physical gains, Leah's psychological functioning remained severely impacted. She continued to experience high levels of emotion dysregulation and endorsed clinically significant mood and anxiety symptoms on questionnaires. Qualitative observations showed that Leah was highly anxious and struggling to leave the ward to start her new life.

Autism and FND

Attention has recently focused on the interesting relationship between autism and FND. For example, studies have reported dissociative seizures in children with autism (Miyawaki et al., 2016; McWilliams et al., 2019). Nisticò et al. (2022) investigated the overlap between the two conditions in a sample of people with FND, ASD and healthy controls. The vast majority of people

Table 6.11 Leah's scores on psychological and neurorehabilitation measures

Questionnaire	Measures	Admission	Discharge
PHQ-9	Depressive symptoms	25/27	22/27
GAD-7	Anxiety symptoms	21/21	20/21
ATSQ	Self-perceived self-focused attention	32/35	31/35
DERS-SF	Emotion dysregulation	Total: 77/90, mean: 4.28, Z = 3.73	Total: 75/90, mean: 4.17, Z = 3.55
UK FIM+FAM*	Captures the level of disability and dependency		
• Motor		83	106
• Cognitive		64	89
• Total		147/210	195/210
Modified Barthel Index*	Functional independence in activities of daily living and mobility	14/20	17/20
Neurological Impairment Scale**	Measures a variety of physical, cognitive, affect, communication and behavioural impairments	17/50	4/50
Rehabilitation Complexity Score***	Care needs	13/22	9/22

*Higher scores suggest more independence; **higher scores suggest more severe impairment; ***higher scores mean more care needs.

with ASD reported an FND symptom, with tactile hypersensitivity, vulnerability for developing functional weakness and paraesthesia.

Table 6.12 shows that both conditions share many overlapping and distinct features. Although there are overlapping features between the two conditions, the underlying reasons for the symptoms are likely very different, with FND driven by psychological or trauma features, and with ASD, it is part of the symptom presentation and due to neurodiversity.

Case study: dissociative episodes and functional motor weakness in a person with Asperger's syndrome

Background

Stephen was a 28-year-old male on the autism spectrum who developed FND just before he was due to starting a new job. Suddenly, Stephen found

Table 6.12 Overlapping features in people with FND vs ASD

FND-specific	Overlapping features	ASD-specific
• As part of a dissociative episode, for example vacant staring and reduced awareness. • As part of social anxiety disorder and safety behaviours, which may make the person look odd but which serve the function to cope with distress in social situations. • As part of personality disorder and difficulties relating to other people.	Problems with reciprocal and social communication, abnormal social interactions.	**DSM-V criterion for autism (2003) A1:** "Deficits in social-emotional reciprocity".
• Can be due to safety behaviours in the context of social anxiety or as part of functional visual loss. • Not all people with FND will have this symptom, and it is likely the minority.	Abnormal eye contact	**DSM-V criterion for autism (2003) A2:** "Deficits in nonverbal communicative behaviours used for social interaction". One of the defining features of ASD and likely found in the majority of people with ASD.
• As part of personality disorder and difficulties relating to other people and adverse childhood experiences and not having had opportunities to learn relationship and emotion regulation skills.	Relationship skills	**DSM-V criterion for autism (2003) A3:** "Deficits in developing, maintaining, and understanding relationships".
• Repetitive movements can take place in the context of a tremor or dissociative episode • Balance difficulties and falls are common, for example in people with motor-type FND.	Motor stereotypies/ clumsiness	**DSM-V criterion for autism (2003) B1:** "Stereotyped or repetitive motor movements, use of objects, or speech".
• A subset of people with FND has experienced childhood adverse experiences characterised by unpredictability and their physical/psychological needs met on an inconsistent basis.	Preference for routine	**DSM-V criterion for autism (2003) B2:** "Insistence on sameness, inflexible adherence to routines, or ritualized patterns or verbal nonverbal behavior"

(Continued)

Table 6.12 (Continued)

FND-specific	Overlapping features	ASD-specific
• Heightened focused attention on physical symptoms (Edwards et al., 2012).	Heightened attentional focus on a subject matter	**DSM-V criterion for autism (2003) B3:** "Highly restricted, fixated interests that are abnormal in intensity or focus".
• In clinical practice, hypersensitivity to external stimuli (e.g. sound, light, touch, weight bearing, pain) has been reported. Hypersensitivity to noise may set off a dissociative episode in a subset of patients with FND. Underlying reasons may more likely be interpersonal triggers or "low-level" environmental triggers in the context of PTSD. • Other sensory phenomena have also been reported including reduced sensation or numbness is a common symptom reported by people with FND, often in combination with functional motor weakness, for example in the legs. • Sensory processing difficulties have been reported in FND (Morgante et al., 2011, 2018; Ranford et al., 2020).	Sensory sensitivities	**DSM-V criterion for autism (2003) B4:** "Hyper- or hyporeactivity to sensory input or unusual interests in sensory aspects of the environment". Part of autism presentation and reported in Riquelme et al. (2016).
• FND symptoms can originate in childhood and carry through into adulthood; however, it is generally rare for people with FND to present with longstanding symptoms since childhood. Bennett et al. (2021) reported that FND appears rare before the age of ten years. People with FND may occasionally report having experienced other somatoform conditions in childhood, for example chronic fatigue or migraines.	Developmental course	• **DSM-V criterion for autism (2003) C:** "Symptoms must be present in the early developmental period (but may not become fully manifest until social demands exceed limited capacities or may be masked by learned strategies in later life)".

FND-specific	Overlapping features	ASD-specific
• In addition, FND tends to be more often observed in adult patients, although there is a possibility of underdiagnosis in child samples.		• Neurodevelopmental and ASD features emerge in childhood (although it is possible that in an older cohort of people the ASD was diagnosed in adulthood, despite the presence of features in childhood).
• Social isolation has been reported (e.g. Gardiner et al., 2018) and appears highly prevalent in FND as observed in clinical practice for many reasons including problems accessing the community due to disabilities, social anxiety, depression. • FND also impacts on employment and activities in daily life.	Major impact on social networks, employment, and personal as well as domestic activities of daily life.	• **DSM-V criterion for autism (2003) D:** "Symptoms cause clinically significant impairment in social, occupational, or other important areas of current functioning".
The co-occurrence of FND and learning disabilities or learning problems has previously been reported in a small number of studies (e.g. Silver, 1982; Cassady et al., 2005; Duncan & Oto, 2008; Baslet et al., 2010; Plioplys et al., 2014; Doss et al., 2017).	Intellectual difficulties can occur	• **Although DSM-V criterion for autism (2003) E** specifies that "These disturbances are not better explained by intellectual disability (intellectual developmental disorder) or global developmental delay", it should be noted that intellectual difficulties can occur in ASD.
• Alexithymia has been described in FND (Myers et al., 2013; Demartini et al., 2014; Sequeira & Silva, 2019). • Mechanism tends to be driven by dissociation and having dissociated from emotions for a long time, losing touch with emotions.	Alexithymia and difficulties recognising emotions including (1) the inability or reduced ability to describe emotions in words, identify, label or experience emotions, (2) a tendency to describe emotions in terms of somatic features (e.g. palpitations for anxiety, or feeling tired)	• Alexithymia has been described in ASD (Milosavljevic et al., 2016; Nicholson et al., 2018; Poquerusse et al., 2018; Kinnaird et al., 2019).

(Continued)

Table 6.12 (Continued)

FND-specific	Overlapping features	ASD-specific
• A subset of people with dissociative seizures have been found to experience emotion dysregulation (Uliaszek et al., 2012; Brown et al., 2013; Urbanek et al., 2014; Williams et al., 2018)	Emotion dysregulation	• Emotion regulation difficulties have been described in ASD including by Samson et al. (2014), Cai et al. (2018); Joshi et al. (2018), Mazefsky et al. (2018), Neuhaus et al. (2019), Conner et al.(2021).
• Patients with functional motor disorders demonstrated reduced interoceptive accuracy in comparison to healthy controls, although with similar awareness levels (Ricciardi et al., 2016, 2021). Koreki et al. (2020) found people with dissociative seizures exhibiting lower interoceptive accuracy than healthy controls. • Pick et al. (2020) reported lower interoceptive accuracy scores in FND, as did Williams et al. (2021) who showed lower levels of interoceptive sensitivity in patients with FND than in healthy controls.	Interoceptive awareness	• Abnormal interoception has been associated with ASD (Quattrocki & Friston, 2014; Mul et al., 2018), though see Nicholson et al. (2018). People with ASD were found to show a slight tendency towards 'hyporeactivity' in interoception (DuBois et al., 2016).
• Reports of ToM deficits in FND have surfaced, which demonstrate ToM deficits on classic tasks including False Belief Task, Faux Pas Recognition Test, Reading the Mind in the Eyes Test (Silveri et al., 2022). • People with FND display heightened self-focused attention. The self-focus may come at the expense of focusing on other people, in particularly their thoughts and feelings. This has certainly been observed in clinical practice.	Theory of Mind and mentalisation skills	• One of the defining features of ASD and likely found in the majority of people with ASD.

FND-specific	Overlapping features	ASD-specific
• It should be noted that FND co-exists with personality disorder (e.g. Binzer et al., 1997), which has been associated with ToM deficits (Nemeth et al., 2018). • An interesting strand of research found the opposite: superior ToM features in people with borderline personality disorder (Arntz et al., 2009; Franzen et al., 2011), as well as "hypermentalisation" (or excessive ToM skills; Normann et al., 2019).		• ToM deficits have been reported in a range of classic studies with people on the autistic spectrum: Frith (1994), Happe and Frith (1995), Baron-Cohen et al. (1997), Tager-Flusberg (2007), Baron-Cohen (2000, 2001).
• Epileptic seizures in the presence of non-epileptic seizures emerges in 10–13% of patients (Krumholz & Niedermeyer, 1983; Lesser et al., 1983; Meierkord et al., 1991; Benbadis et al., 2001). Higher rates of co-morbid epilepsy and PNES in 10–40% of people from tertiary epilepsy centres; Pillai and Haut (2012). • In their study, Pillai and Haut (2012) found a higher prevalence of frontal seizures in people with ES and PNES, whereas temporal seizures were more common in the ES without the PNES group. • Kutlubaev et al. (2018) noted that the frequency of epilepsy in people with PNES is 22%; however, vice versa, the frequency of PNES in patients with epilepsy is 12%.	Concurrent conditions can emerge in both conditions: • Organic epilepsy • Learning difficulties or disabilities • Psychological conditions such as depression, panic attacks, obsessive-compulsive disorder	There is an increased risk of epilepsy in autism: Tuchman and Rapin (2002), Canitano (2007), Levisohn (2007), with a frequency of up to 20% children with either condition (Tuchman & Cuccaro, 2011).

(Continued)

Table 6.12 (Continued)

FND-specific	Overlapping features	ASD-specific
• Neurodevelopmental changes, if these emerge, are more likely part of the influence of childhood trauma and PTSD, which occurs in FND and can impact on neurodevelopmental processes, as well as the structure and functioning of a person's brain (e.g. Creeden, 2009; Herringa, 2017), affecting similar neurological areas that support the stress response (Perry et al., 2018).	Neurodevelopmental changes	Neurodevelopmental changes are present since birth. However, people with ASD are not exempt from traumatic experiences, in the same way as people with FND are not immune from other physical conditions that can impact on the brain such as organic epilepsy.
• Some people with FND will have siblings or parents with current or past FND/somatoform symptoms. However, the development of FND is likely due to learning and modelling experiences rather than genetics.	Familial links	• There can be a genetic link in ASD. Parents or siblings of the person with ASD may have ASD themselves, which is diagnosed or may have gone undiagnosed but features still present.
• Bullying history is common in FND, and this can lead to a person "missing out" on opportunities to make friends and practise social skills, as well as feeling emotionally neglected, rejected and abandoned. Not specifically a basic "deficit" in recognising social cues.	Early experiences: Bullying history and problems making friends during school period	• Bullying history is also present in people with ASD and in the same way as in FND can lead to missed opportunities to make friends and practice social skills. • However, problems with picking up social cues driven by neurodevelopmental and neurodiversity reasons will also underlie these reduced social skills.

himself unable to swing or feel his legs. He was able to call for help, and an ambulance took Stephen to the emergency department as he was suspected to have a stroke. After some investigation, an organic cause was excluded and Stephen was subsequently diagnosed with FND. He spent the following three weeks recovering on a stroke ward. After discharge from the hospital,

Stephen continued his recovery at home although his symptoms did not subside immediately. Stephen struggled to mobilise and care for himself independently in his home environment, including washing, dressing, cooking meals and doing household chores. He temporarily put employment on hold for six months. Eventually, Stephen regained his ability to walk. The sensation in his legs gradually returned a few weeks later. He was able to return to a part-time working pattern.

During the assessment, Stephen reported intermittent episodes of functional lower limb weakness with reduced sensation, about one to two times a week. He described the pattern as "a few days on, a few days off". Stephen was unable to identify any triggers for these episodes. The fluctuating nature of the FND symptoms impacted greatly on his day-to-day activities and employment, and had taken its toll on his relationship. Since Stephen did not have a care package in place, he was completely reliant on his partner to provide him with personal care and support during FND "set-backs". Apart from his job, Stephen stopped all his social activities and the couple mostly spent time at home, which often caused tensions in the relationship.

PCM assessment

A comprehensive history was obtained from Stephen and his partner. Table 6.13 shows how the information obtained from the assessment was categorised under each PCM element.

Table 6.13 Pressure Cooker Model assessment incorporating Stephen's ASD features

Kitchen

- Social "external" function of FND: Stephen's partner was heavily involved in caring activities, particularly during intermittent episodes where Stephen's care needs were at their highest level.

Cover	**Overpressure Plug**	**Valve**
• Usual coping strategy: not expressing emotions, keeping self to self. • Social skills difficulties, abnormal eye contact and boundary violations that impacted on conversations with his partner.	• Motor-type FND: Functional weakness and numbness in the lower limbs, with episodes of double incontinence. • Clumsiness as part of ASD contributed to overall presentation. • Occasional anger outbursts ("I just blow up").	• Bust-after-boom: used to be very active in previous full-time job role and social life with many enjoyable activities and sports. • Following the development of FND, Stephen became more socially isolated but still able to hold down part-time job. • Very limited social network.

(Continued)

Table 6.13 (Continued)

Warning light	Sticky left-over food	Pot
• When Stephen shifted his attention away from his symptoms and "didn't think about it", the FND disappeared.	"I'm different" "I don't fit in" Low self-esteem Stephen's early childhood coping strategy: keep self to self and "just getting on with it".	• Described emotions in terms of bodily symptoms "I'm tired". • Bladder and bowel incontinence that accompanied the intermittent episodes of motor-type FND. • Difficulties sleeping. • Unable to perform activities in daily life during an episode, but back to normal functioning as symptoms resolved.

Flames/Heat

- Stephen initially denied the existence of any anxiety, sadness or worry.
- Alexithymia and a reduced ability to label emotions were noted.
- Later in therapy, the following beliefs and emotions were identified with Stephen and his partner:
1. "I'm going to be left on my own by my partner and I won't be able to cope ⇔ 'attachment' anxiety, fear of abandonment, sadness, anger".
2. Physical symptoms of emotions fed into panic cognitions: "I'm going to have an episode!" ⇔ secondary anxiety and intense panic built up within a short space of time.
3. Fear, anger, feeling unsettled causing blow ups.

Ignition

- Longstanding rejection experiences, in the context of history of having been bullied at primary and secondary school. Stephen never felt he fit in.
- Enmeshed parents who were overinvolved, always in "protection" mode and advocating for Stephen.
- ASD features: childhood experiences of not picking up on social cues and difficulties recognising emotions, struggling to make friends, often felt socially isolated.

Critical incident

- Start of a new job.

"High heat"	Fuel
High levels of rapidly oscillating emotion dysregulation: some days bright mood, other days anxious, angry, tearful but unable to label or identify these feelings	1. Relationship triggers and perceived abandonment, for example arguments with partner causing intense fear but unable to recognise emotion as fear. 2. Physical symptoms associated with emotions under (1) are felt by Stephen but unable to label this as belonging to fear. 3. ASD-specific triggers: changes in routine, people communicating too much with Stephen, arguments in relationship due to not picking up on social cues

Safety features

Attended therapy sessions on a weekly basis.

Engaged well with the contents of the sessions and practised skills in between sessions.

Couple's sessions were successful with partner on board.

Formulation

LAYER 1: IGNITION

There were three notable factors in Stephen's childhood, adolescence and adult experiences that set the stage for Stephen to develop FND later in his life.

1 Due to the ASD, Stephen struggled within the realm of social functioning and interactions, for example pick up on social cues, recognise and verbally describe emotions, as well as make appropriate eye contact during social interactions with peers. These made Stephen vulnerable towards experiencing emotional difficulties.

2 Life-long victim of bullying and rejection experiences, and the accompanying fear of abandonment.

3 Enmeshed, overinvolved parent-child relationship that fostered a strong dependence on caregivers, as well as loose, undefined emotional and physical boundaries between him and his parents.

Stephen's life-long bullying and rejection experiences gave rise to core beliefs around being different, "not fitting in", worthlessness, being unlovable and other people abandoning him. The prospect of starting a new job with new colleagues and routines (critical incident) greatly unsettled Stephen, particularly about whether he would fit in and could cope with the changes in routine that the new job would bring. The critical incident set off an unpleasant internal state that Stephen found hard to identify and to cope with.

LAYER 2: THE FND COPING TRIANGLE

Stephen's main psychological coping mechanism appeared to be keeping himself mostly to himself and "just getting on with it". Since childhood, Stephen did not have access to the tools, knowledge and social skills to express his emotions, in the context of ASD neurodevelopmental features, but also due to the "social sequelae" of ASD of having missed out on social opportunities for emotional expression with peers. In addition, the enmeshed pattern of relationships within his family of origin made Stephen less willing to share private information and he preferred to keep emotions to himself. Over time, his early coping strategy of keeping himself to himself repeated into adulthood and was partly motivated by his fear of rejection from his partner.

LAYER 3: THE FND MAINTENANCE CYCLE: THE PRESSURE COOKER CHAIN REACTION

After the FND was "ignited" by the critical incident, other stress triggers came to the surface that set off Stephen's intermittent motor and continence symptoms. Two sets of triggers were identified: interpersonal and physical. Arguments with his partner (Fuel) triggered perceived and imagined fears of abandonment, attachment anxiety and an emotional maelstrom, which Stephen did not manage to settle quickly (Flames, Heat, #1). Although Stephen struggled to identify the underlying emotion, he did experience the physical symptoms of fear, which were misinterpreted as a sign of an impending FND episode, causing further strong, unpleasant feelings (i.e. anxiety, Flames, Heat, #2). As Stephen did not regularly express his emotions to his partner or other people in his environment and did not possess much emotion language (tight Cover) whilst not being engaged in any social and enjoyable activities (blocked Valve), the only channel left for expressing his distress was his body (episodes of functional weakness and numbness, Overpressure Plug). This provided immediate negative reinforcement of the unpleasant internal state that he felt, increasing the frequency of these episodes in future. The FND had taken on an internal regulation function: Stephen's panic and fears reduced immediately after the FND set in and created a state of internal psychological safety.

LAYER 4: FACILITATING PHYSICAL FACTORS

In addition to the functional weakness and numbness, Stephen also experienced bladder and bowel incontinence. This was interpreted as playing a part in Stephen's general "freezing response" in the context of his triggers and anxiety.

LAYER 5: THE SOCIAL FUNCTIONS OF FND

Stephen's symptoms helped him to stay in proximity to his partner, to assuage one of his biggest fears and to "prevent" his partner from abandoning the patient. Stephen often experienced FND following arguments. In response to witnessing the FND, his partner worried about having pushed him over the edge and became kind and caring, placating Stephen in an attempt to prevent further worsening of the symptoms. Therefore, both Stephen and his partner were stuck in a reciprocal reinforcement pattern and co-regulated each other's feelings to reach a state of interpersonal psychological safety.

Over time, a pattern of systemic re-traumatisation developed from his partner. Stephen's heightened rejection sensitivity, his tendency to overinterpret neutral signs as abandonment (e.g. his partner and friend leaving a room) and Stephen becoming quickly panicked and dysregulated resulted in an increase of proximity seeking behaviours towards his partner. Stephen's partner felt "trapped" in the home and became resentful, which resulted in avoidance of interactions and spending time with Stephen. Stephen's biggest fear of being abandoned started to gradually develop into a self-fulfilling prophecy.

Treatment: positive pressure cooker of FND

See Table 6.14.

Table 6.14 Stephen's multidisciplinary treatment based on the PCM formulation

---

Kitchen

- Education on the features of autism to the treating and nursing team, who were becoming increasingly frustrated with Stephen and risked unhelpful behaviours towards Stephen.
- Prediction: staff was encouraged to when making promises to the patient, "to deliver". For example, "your medications will be reviewed later by the doctor at this time" with the doctor indeed visiting Stephen at the agreed time.
- Guidelines on how to manage the intermittent episodes of FND to help the environment respond appropriately and reduce reciprocal reinforcement and systemic re-traumatisation.
- Couple sessions to gain a better understanding on the relationship between interpersonal triggers and FND, the concept of interpersonal psychological safety and support with undertaking more social events.

Cover	**Overpressure Plug**	**Valve: Routines**
• Coping cards with emoticons to indicate to other people how Stephen was feeling on the day without them having to ask him. • Started speaking to partner about feelings (occasionally).	• Psycho-education on the emotion-FND link. • Reality grounding techniques • Physiotherapy	• Upset over minor changes in daily routine: it was difficult to keep the therapy schedule the same as much as possible on a weekly basis; however, care was taken to prepare Stephen in advance so that he knew what to expect in a new week. The sessions that were possible to keep the same, were kept the same.

(Continued)

Table 6.14 (Continued)

• Informing staff that Stephen didn't like to spend too much time communicating with staff and to keep it as brief as possible. • Modelling and practice of social and assertiveness skills in sessions. Learn about social boundaries.		• Special interests were incorporated into the rehab programme. • Care was taken to invest in developing a therapeutic relationship, using the interests and taking into account the impact of attending goal planning meetings and rotational staff/staff that cover in sickness absence.

Warning light
• Reduce heightened self-focused attention on physical symptoms by noticing with Stephen when the symptom focus was high and shifting towards speaking about psychological topics.

Sticky left-over food

Psycho-education on the link between early childhood and repeated adulthood coping strategies.

Pot
• Bladder and bowel regime was adapted: collaboration with nursing team on continence issues and agreed plan with Stephen, incorporating his wishes, even though it was not what would be recommended under normal circumstances but would also not hurt the person's care or have a harmful impact on care for other patients, was feasible within the restrictions of the ward environment, and would promote rehab and recovery of FND. It had a positive effect: Stephen's distress about the sequence of activities involved in the regime reduced significantly.
• Sleep hygiene methods.

Flames/Heat
• Emotion education, practice "getting in touch with emotions", verbal descriptions, emotion labelling and reality grounding.

Ignition/Fuel
Reduce triggers for FND:
• Education on the relationship between interpersonal triggers, thoughts, feelings, behaviours and FND, with emphasis on attachment anxiety and fears of abandonment.
• Helping to recognise and have an open dialogue with Stephen about interpersonal triggers for FND who subsequently opened up and acknowledged their presence.
• Management of ASD triggers: When routine changed, this was shared with Stephen far in advance. Some "me" time with curtains closed around bed and put in a quiet bay for sensory sensitivities.

Outcomes

At discharge, Stephen obtained scores that fell within the normal or sub-clinical ranges on most psychological measures. On his qualitative feedback measures, Stephen indicated that "every session, I feel great and it makes my life and my family life a joy". He was "extremely satisfied" with his therapy experience and felt that it was helpful in managing his symptoms, particularly "talking helps" and "talking about your problems helps to become a better person" (i.e. opening the cover). He also indicated that "keeping busy, enjoying life, talking whenever possible" were his most helpful coping strategies (i.e. unblocking the valve, opening the cover). He noticed a 100% complete improvement of the FND (Table 6.15).

Internet therapy with the Pressure Cooker Model

The advance of digital technology in modern times, particularly in the light of the COVID-19 pandemic, has revolutionised the online delivery of psychological therapy. Recent studies have investigated virtual modalities of psychological treatment for people with FND (e.g. Jones et al., 2021; Lin & Espay, 2021). The PCM is a model that can be used online. The following section will describe an n = 1 case study of online "iPCM Therapy for FND".

> Lydia was recently diagnosed with dissociative episodes. She lives in a remote area with limited transport links and no provision of FND services in her locality. Lydia decided to seek online support to help her manage the episodes. Following an initial online consultation with the

Table 6.15 Stephen's scores on psychology questionnaires

Questionnaire	Measures	Admission	Discharge
CORE-34 (Total score)	Psychological distress	57 (moderate)	3 (healthy)
HADS-A	Anxiety	9 (mild)	0 (normal)
HADS-D	Depression	8 (mild)	0 (normal)
Work and Social Adjustment Scale	Impairment in day-to-day functioning	20/40 (moderately severe)	0/40 (subclinical)
ATSQ	Self-perceived self-focused attention	N/A. no data available	7/35
FFMQ-SF (Five Facet Mindfulness Questionnaire – Short Form)	Self-perceived attention and awareness of emotions	N/A. no data available	Only clinically significant subscale was "Non reactivity to inner experience"
DERS-SF	Emotion regulation	N/A. no data available	None of the subscales were clinically significant

psychologist, it became apparent that Lydia's episodes were mostly driven by anxiety, both in social situations and indoors "out of the blue". Lydia's Pressure Cooker Chain Reaction showed that her triggers mainly included bodily symptoms ("a funny feeling") that she heavily focused on and that Lydia misinterpreted catastrophically ("I'm going to have a seizure"). Lydia was unable to label or express the feeling that was connected with it and only described these in physical terms ("I feel my chest is tight, sweating, feel clammy and fidgety") and emotional valence ("It doesn't feel good"). The emotional pressure and physical arousal built up, to a "boiling point" where it became intolerable. This was followed by a dissociative episode which removed the unpleasant state that Lydia was feeling but reinforced the dissociation as a coping habit and a psychological safety behaviour. Lydia slept for hours afterwards and felt relief but the episodes increased in frequency. Due to the episodes, she had dropped many of her hobbies and stopped seeing friends.

Using the PCM, Lydia and the psychologist created a shared formulation that they both felt explained Lydia's episodes. Lydia engaged well with a remote series of behavioural experiments and reality grounding practice that were based on the PCM.

Table 6.16 shows the results on a qualitative questionnaire that Lydia was asked to complete as part of her treatment. As the therapy was delivered digitally, the psychologist wanted to assess Lydia's perception of the therapeutic process and its impact on Lydia's understanding of FND and the PCM. At discharge, Lydia obtained a score of 1 on the PHQ-9 and a score of 0 on the GAD-7.

Table 6.16 Lydia's responses on a digital therapy experiences questionnaire

Question asked	Response
Your views on the iPCM Therapy for FND/Black-outs	
How satisfied are you with your experience of iPCM Therapy for FND? (1. extremely dissatisfied to 7. extremely satisfied)	7. Extremely satisfied
How helpful was iPCM Therapy for FND in managing your symptoms? (1. extremely unhelpful to 7. extremely helpful)	7. Extremely helpful
Because of iPCM Therapy for FND, my symptoms have: (1. completely deteriorated to 7. completely improved)	7. Completely improved
Anything about iPCM Therapy for FND that could be improved? Please explain.	N/A (Lydia did not have any comments to make)
How likely would you recommend iPCM Therapy for FND to a friend, family member or someone else with FND? (1. extremely unlikely to 7. extremely likely)	7. Extremely likely
Details: Found it to be very helpful and could recommend it to anyone who was dealing with something similar.	

Question asked	Response
On a scale from 0 to 10 (where 0 is the worst possible rating and 10 is the best possible rating), **how would you rate the following?**	
• Understanding the therapist/contents/what was discussed during the sessions	10/10
• Your understanding of FND and the black-outs following iPCM Therapy for FND	10/10
• Information and explanation of the psychological strategies over the internet	10/10
• The speed with which things were discussed online	8/10
• Understanding the homework materials that were sent to you over email without a face-to-face conversation to go through the homework first	10/10
• Helpfulness of these homework materials that were sent to you over email	9/10
• Practicing psychological strategies on the basis of the instructions/explanations given online	10/10
• Your ability to express your thoughts and feelings, and share your ideas and experiences over the internet	9/10
• Your level of comfort and feeling at ease using the computer to talk about sensitive and personal issues	9/10
• The extent to which a therapeutic relationship could be built with the psychologist over the internet that enabled you to open up	9/10
• The extent to which iPCM Therapy for FND has helped you to feel better about yourself	10/10
• Your level of safety with talking about personal issues over the internet, in terms of safety on the web	9/10
• Quality of the internet connection	7/10
• Image quality on the webcam	7/10
What has been the impact of iPCM Therapy for FND on your FND symptoms and day-to-day life? (On a scale from 0 to 10, where 0 is the worst possible rating and 10 is the best possible rating): **Impact of iPCM Therapy for FND on:**	
• The black-outs	9/10
• Your mood	10/10
• Your work/study activities	9/10
• Doing things at home (like cleaning, shopping, cooking)	10/10
• Your social life and leisure activities	9/10
• Your relationships with other people	10/10

Positive aspects of internet therapy ('iPCM') for FND

Accessibility

Physical disabilities can be severe for some people with FND requiring specialist hospital transport that may not readily be available. A person may also be socially isolated and unable to rely on a support network to help with transport. In addition, in more remote areas, FND services can be particularly scarce and internet therapy will provide a viable treatment option to the person.

The Kitchen environment

The home environment may facilitate the use of a hybrid model of the PCM with the patient and individuals close to them who live in the same house. In addition, remote sessions can provide better access to "significant others" and provide a good view of the person's living circumstances and interpersonal triggers, including what happens when the person with FND experiences an episode and what responses this elicits in the environment (i.e. reciprocal reinforcement), as well as the level of hypervigilance and insight into FND in the system, and any abnormal relationship patterns (e.g. enmeshment, conflicts) that may contribute to FND, as well as the level of dependency. Furthermore, an ally may be easier identified who can directly help implement the intervention.

Negative aspects of internet therapy ('iPCM') for FND

Cover issues

Verbal emotional expression is an important part of treatment with the PCM in FND. However, the home environment may limit this crucial process due to various circumstances that may be encountered including coercive control by a person living in the same household; lack of privacy around discussion of sensitive issues; and the discomfort and distress of releasing an unspeakable dilemma that may pertain to people in the household, which may render this process impossible and therefore maintains the FND.

Relationships

Although remote sessions may provide a window into a person's living circumstances and family behaviours around the person with FND, it may be more difficult to establish a trusted and psychologically safe therapeutic relationship over the internet, which may exactly be the core issue already for a lot of people with FND that is further complicated by remote sessions (Table 6.17).

> Lydia provided the following informative feedback around the abovementioned topics including a few potential issues with online therapy.

Despite some of its limitations, online therapy for FND appears to be a viable and alternative option if face-to-face therapy is not available to the person.

Table 6.17 Lydia's feedback on another qualitative questionnaire

Theme	Question asked	Response
Accessibility	Name the positive aspects of iPCM Therapy for FND for you?	"Good option as I don't live nearby FND services. Convenient and affordable. Easily accessible. Would have had to travel from my hometown to the nearest clinic otherwise".
Negative aspects	Name the negative aspects of iPCM Therapy for FND for you?	"Personally, didn't have a major problem but I imagine it can be frustrating if there are technical problems".
Cover issues	Was there anything that you couldn't say or do because of the limitations of doing iPCM Therapy for FND?	"Not really, showing materials face-to-face may have been easier/helpful".
Relationships	Do you think that it is feasible and acceptable to do iPCM Therapy for FND for all sessions online including the initial assessment online? Please explain.	"I think it is better to have the initial assessment face-to-face as you already have an idea of the person".
Relationships	If the option was there and realistic, would you have chosen face-to-face sessions over online sessions with iPCM Therapy for FND? Please explain your reasons.	"Yes, I would have chosen face-to-face sessions if realistic". (consistent with findings from Jones et al., 2021).
Relationships	Did you miss anything in the iPCM Therapy for FND sessions that face-to-face therapy sessions would have given you?	"Human contact".

Group therapy

A small number of intervention studies have focused on group therapy approaches in FND, either as part of a wider treatment programme alongside individual therapy (e.g. Moene et al., 1998; Bullock et al., 2015) or in the form of a group therapy clinic dedicated to people with non-epileptic episodes (Libbon et al., 2019). Groups were either focused on psycho-educational elements of FND (e.g. Chen et al., 2014; Cope et al., 2017) or characterised by a more 'experiential' group programme that included social skills training and creative therapy (e.g. Moene et al., 1998). Groups were informed by a variety of different psychological therapy modalities including cognitive-behavioural therapy (Conwill et al., 2014; Cope et al., 2017), dialectical behaviour therapy (Bullock et al., 2015), psychodynamic (Barry et al., 2008), hypnosis (Moene et al., 1998) and 'eclectic group psychotherapy' consisting of a mixture of behavioural and psychoanalytic approaches (Metin et al., 2013). The majority of the groups treated people with non-epileptic seizures rather than people with motor-type FND symptoms. Some group studies reported positive outcomes for people with FND as a result of group participation including reduced seizure frequency or severity, as well as improved walking, psychological well-being, illness beliefs, dissociative tendencies and activities in daily life (e.g. Moene et al., 1998; Barry et al., 2008; Chen et al., 2014; Conwill et al., 2014; Bullock et al., 2015; Cope et al., 2017; Senf-Beckenbach et al., 2022).

The PCM is a versatile model that can be used in individual therapy and as part of group work in FND. There are many advantages of setting up group therapy for people with FND including the following:

- Hitting the core of FND: relationships and interpersonal functioning. Group therapy will help becoming aware of the interpersonal triggers of FND, which are more likely to surface in a group context and offer members to practise communication strategies directly and improve relationship and social skills, such as assertiveness.
- Offering people with FND an opportunity to meet other people with FND and reduce social isolation.
- Addressing service needs and long waiting lists.

Although group therapy can be a very powerful experience for people with FND, it also poses its unique challenges. The following section will focus on exploring some of these difficulties that have been observed in clinical practice. These are not meant to deter clinicians from running groups for people with FND. Quite on the contrary: if these challenges are managed carefully and in line with the psychological formulation, the challenges can be turned into powerful positive experiences and opportunities for learning and practising skills for the individual group members, as well as for the facilitators (Table 6.18).

Group processes

Group therapy can be organised on the basis of a wide range of variables. Table 6.19 displays some important variables that need to be taken into account when organising a group for people with FND.

Pressure Cooker Group Therapy: findings from a pilot study

A group therapy protocol was developed based on the PCM and implemented in a small group of inpatients with FND. The protocol covered every

Table 6.18 General and FND-specific difficulties in groups and management
strategies

PCM element	Difficulties	Management strategies
Ignition	• Shared experience of trauma and adverse life experiences may be very powerful in a group setting. • Oversharing of traumatic life events in group context may serve an unmet need to feel validated and feel psychological safety. • At times, "stand-offs" may happen in relation to severity of trauma and graphic details shared risking re-traumatising other patients. • People with a history of parental emotional neglect may find it particularly challenging to be part of group therapy. "Competition" for validation from the group may emerge if a member witnesses validation of another group member, in the context of past history of parental emotional neglect or abuse.	• A degree of sharing experiences can be therapeutic, especially "being in the same boat". This is a unique feature of group therapy. • However, high levels of oversharing and "stand-offs" may derail the group process. • It is recommended to incorporate this into the group rules and draw a person's attention to the rules whenever it happens. This is to protect both the person and the group. • Sharing difficult memories is clearly meaningful to the person. Offer a one-to-one space to discuss this, to ensure the person is heard, does not feel rejected, and it won't cause overspill into the group context. • Remember that it may also be the first time that a person with FND has shared their personal story with other people ("not keeping themselves to themselves"), which may previously have not been listened to, dismissed or rejected by important people in their life. • Always formulate any "competition" behaviours and increase in FND symptoms with the person. • Emphasise collaboration skills around helping or doing something for another person, or allowing another person to be the centre of attention in a specific session, as well as supporting group members in praising and encouraging other group members.
Fuel	• Keep in mind that interpersonal triggers are very common in FND and have a higher risk of emerging in a group context.	• Make a note of when FND symptoms worsen in the group context and feed this back to the person in a one-to-one context. Use this therapeutically and incorporate this into the formulation.

(Continued)

Table 6.18 (Continued)

PCM element	Difficulties	Management strategies
	• Group therapy can be powerful in FND to unearth these interpersonal triggers, which otherwise may have remained hidden. • Hence, introducing a person with FND into a group context is likely a necessity in treatment, especially if interpersonal triggers have not yet been uncovered or individual therapy may be stuck.	• Support the person in becoming more aware of these interpersonal triggers and encourage them feeding this back to you.
Flames	• Lack of language for emotions • Denial of any distress • Social anxiety is common in people with FND and may cause a person to not engage and participate in group discussions	• Focus on emotion education, language and functions, use therapeutically • If social anxiety is present, attending the group and participating in group discussions could be used as goals and in behavioural experiments.
Heat	• High levels of emotion dysregulation or dissociation in the group setting	Events around loss of control over emotions that arise within the group context can be formulated and used therapeutically to practise skills in perception, identification, expression and appropriate control over emotions.
Sticky left-over food	• Low self-esteem is common in people with FND • Repeated FND coping strategies may be observed in action during the group process including dissociation, pushing on/boom-bust cycles and keeping self-to-self.	• To increase confidence in a group member, ask the group member to co-lead or lead one of the sessions, with support of the facilitators, as part of their therapy.
Pot	• Overmedication may greatly impact on the level at which people process and remember information, engage with the group processes and lower the threshold for dissociation.	• Risk assessments and management plans prior to group entry will be useful.

PCM element	Difficulties	Management strategies
	• Some risks may increase in the group setting, for example worsening of FND symptoms, taking over new symptoms that other people experience, relationship breakdown, splitting teams.	• Joint working with other professions can be a good way to incorporate some of the Pot elements (e.g. group sessions focused on meal preparation as part of a social event, exercise to improve cardiovascular fitness, or education on medications by a pharmacist or medical professional).
Warning light	• Open rejection of psychological concepts • Heightened focus on physical symptoms may be prominently present: preference to talk a lot about physical symptoms at the expense of psychological symptoms, with all members chiming in. • Members may be in various stages of acceptance of psychological factors in maintaining FND.	• Allow for some exploration of physical symptoms. After all this is what is bothersome in day-to-day functioning and members need to feel "heard not hurt". • However, bring this to awareness and explore heightened self-focused attention as a maintaining factor of FND. • Diaries to record instances of heightened self-focused attention. • Divide the group session in a 50–50 physical-psychological discussion of features.
Cover	• Keep self to self and not sharing thoughts and feelings in the group setting, as the default coping strategy and therefore not contributing to the group discussions. • Strong personalities in the group with opinions that may adversely impact on other members or prevent others from opening up about emotions. • Regular interrupting or interfering with (negative) comments when strategies are discussed or during, for example, relaxation exercises, derailing the group process.	• Remind group members of the house rules and boundaries. • Address communication issues with the specific group members in a one-to-one chat in a compassionate way and use this therapeutically, to practise emotional expression in a psychologically safe environment. • Formulate the interfering behaviour: what need may the person want to meet? • Have a pre-group conversation with the person in a non-judgemental and compassionate way. They may not be aware of the behaviour and if they are, being open and honest about a tricky subject will create trust, even if this is resisted initially. • Use this situation as a platform to practice assertiveness skills with group members that are less vocal and confident or struggle to express a difference in opinion.

(Continued)

Table 6.18 (Continued)

PCM element	Difficulties	Management strategies
Valve	• Pushing on as not able to sit with distress (e.g. doing homework tasks very quickly focusing on contents rather than process). • Boom–bust cycles in terms of doing homework tasks, inconsistency in completion. • Complete withdrawal and disengagement from the group.	• Highlight the importance of pacing and "doing a little, every day". Use homework tasks as a medium to illustrate the principles of pacing. • Creating a sense of social belonging to improve group cohesion. • Explore whether the withdrawal and disengagement serve an unmet need.
Overpressure Plug	• Dissociative states and full-blown non-epileptic episodes and worsening of FND symptoms may be a behavioural manifestation to meet an unmet need for care and validation from the environment, or a way to regulate anxiety in the group setting (or both). • Some FND symptoms can complicate group processes, for example functional speech difficulties.	In the situation of a full-blown non-epileptic episode, decisions need to be made about the best approach, based on formulation and the group's wishes and needs: • Taking the person out may reinforce the episode as the person is supported one-to-one and may be viewed as special, or the opposite, feel as punitive to the person. • In addition, other patients may respond with worse FND symptoms in response to seeing the person being taken out of the group context, further derailing the group process. • Keeping the person in the group may disrupt or halt the group process and will interfere with care for other patients. • Important to discuss this in a one-to-one session and agree on a clear plan for management of the non-epileptic episodes. • Incorporate into group rules, jointly discussed and determined by the group.
Kitchen	• Modelling processes may take place in the group context: copying or "synching" symptoms	• The emergence of these symptoms would provide a good opportunity for psycho-education on the relationship between modelling processes in the environment and FND symptoms.

PCM element	Difficulties	Management strategies
	• "Acutely" with multiple members experiencing dissociative episodes at the same time. • "Gradually" with one member developing the same symptom as another member, for example functional weakness, flashbacks, dissociative seizures, dizziness.	
	Relationship difficulties and interpersonal dynamics in the group: Splitting between facilitators. • Forming subgroups that may negatively impact on group dynamics with other members feeling left out and rejected. • Unhelpful dynamics between individual group members (e.g. arguments, negative comments). • Members overpowering/ taking over group discussions • Boundary violations (e.g. oversharing of personal information).	• In case of splitting, it is important to discuss this on a one-to-one basis with the person who is splitting, in a empathic way. Emphasise the unity of the team. In addition, group facilitator reflection meetings should be organised to analyse the dynamics, increase awareness and implement strategies. • Mediation meetings between individual group members can be used therapeutically and serve as a practice ground to acquire better communication skills and improve emotional expression. • One-to-one meetings and re-iteration of group rules with permission of members to bring this to the overpowering individual's awareness when it happens. This may also serve to practise assertiveness skills.
	• Systematic re-traumatisation by facilitators or group members/reciprocal reinforcement by other group members in case of a dissociative episode	• Dissociative seizure management can be a useful topic of discussion in the group with the person owning their formulation and explain to other group members the process of reciprocal reinforcement.

element of the PCM. People with FND participated in the group therapy also attended individual psychological therapy sessions alongside the group. After each session, participants were asked to gauge usefulness and enjoyment levels of the group on a visual analogue scale and provide a rating between zero and ten (running from "not at all useful/enjoyable" to "very useful/enjoyable"). The means and standard deviations of these ratings are

Table 6.19 Variables in group therapy for people with FND

Structured	Unstructured
• Patients follow a strict sequence of sessions with fixed topics, which can be containing for people who experience high levels of emotion dysregulation. • The inflexibility may be a drawback, particularly if the group has a need to discuss specific topics that are not on the list or wants to spend more time on a given topic.	• Patients bring in what stands out to them, agree on the topic and the PCM element is chosen to work on (open, inpatient groups) • Sense of agency and control over a psychological topic, may make it less threatening • However, some topics that are important for the group's needs may end up barely being discussed (psychological processes) in favour of topics that the group identifies better with (FND and physical symptoms). • In addition, the group may be experienced as "loose sand" and make patients and staff feel uncontained.
Open	**Closed**
• Patients are invited to attend at all stages of the group cycle, even if the group has already started, and can stay for a prolonged period of time. • The constant "movement" of people entering and leaving the group will not support group cohesion in the same way as a closed group would and impact on emotional expression and therapeutic self-disclosures. In addition, "group leavers" may amplify abandonment issues in FND; people have commented on feeling abandoned when a group member left.	• Separate group cycles facilitate better group cohesion and more likely create a psychologically safe space for emotional expression and managing endings.
With one-to-one support	**Without one-to-one support**
• Useful for exploration of sensitive topics that would be too threatening to release in the group setting and would make a patient vulnerable. • The group setting can be a powerful tool that facilitates the release of an unspeakable dilemma or helping stuck patients "to move" in individual therapy. • Waiting list pressures and lack of staff resources within an overburdened healthcare system may preclude this option.	• The threshold for important self-disclosures, in particular, unspeakable dilemmas, will likely increase if only the group setting is available. • Unhelpful behaviours are harder to address if there is no individual forum available and may be very exposing in a group setting.

High intensity
- Drill practice can lead to "group fatigue" and "cognitive overwhelm" in a group of people with often co-existing anxiety and depression that impacts on cognition.
- Boom-and-bust cycle due to intensity within a short space of time, which is one of the maintaining factors of FND.

Low intensity
- Spaced practice is recommended as it improves retrieval of information and reduces an important maintaining factor in FND: the (boom)-and-bust cycle.

Family involvement
- Family triggers are very common in FND and missing out on opportunities to explore these will leave a crucial "gap" in treatment.

No family involvement
- Some people with FND may not be in contact with family members who have distanced themselves. It will be difficult to involve these people into the group and emotionally hurtful to observe other patients having their family members participating.
- However, the majority of patients will have people in their environment that in one way or another contribute to maintaining the FND.

Educational ("Contents")
- The majority of people with FND and their families will have a reduced or lack of awareness on FND. An educational element is crucial.

Experiential ("Process")
- Relationship and interpersonal triggers are at the heart of FND. An experiential format will be a powerful medium to bring about changes.

---

displayed in Table 6.22. Two group cycles were run in succession using the same protocol that covered every element of the PCM. However, the groups were not entirely identical, as some of the feedback obtained from participants in cycle 1 was implemented to improve the quality of cycle 2. One of the drawbacks identified by participants in cycle 1 involved the speed and amount at which the information was presented; therefore, changes were made to cycle 2 to meet these needs. This resulted in removing some sessions from the original protocol (without removing discussion around any of the PCM elements; all elements were preserved in the second cycle) and repeating specific sessions at the request of the participants to help them process the information more accurately.

Patients

The following tables show the background demographic and clinical information on the small sample of nine people with FND that participated in the

PCM group therapy. The questionnaire data was patchy at best; scores were missing on a number of measures for a variety of reasons, which precluded data collection including early discharge and unable to "catch" the person in time for final scores; the pressures in a busy clinical environment and lack of time and resources; and a change in the data collection system that resulted in data loss (Tables 6.20 and 6.21).

Pressure Cooker Model Group therapy protocol

See Table 6.22.

Table 6.20 Demographic and clinical characteristics of the group therapy sample (n = 9)

#	Cycle	Gender	Age	Admission length (days)	Disease duration (months)	FND symptoms
1	1	F	25	84	49	Functional paraplegia, paraesthesia, reduced sensation, non-epileptic episodes
2	1	F	58	81	34	Speech difficulties, functional weakness, reduced sensation, functional cognitive symptoms
3	1	F	32	83	50	Speech difficulties, functional weakness, dystonia, tremor, spasms, hyperalgesia, brain fog, non-epileptic episodes
4*	1	M	43	79	335	Speech difficulties, tremor, spasms, functional weakness, reduced sensation, non-epileptic episodes
5**	1	F	21	83	145	Tremor, spasms, non-epileptic episodes
6	2	M	39	49	195	Dystonia, tremor
7	2	F	28	69	171	Dystonia, spasms, swallowing difficulties
8	2	F	37	126	46	Functional paraplegia, reduced sensation
9***	2	M	47	43	35	Tremor, functional weakness

*Left the group after session #4, due to early discharge against team's recommendations, and attended for a total of n = 4 sessions only;**entry in session #7, attended a total of n = 9 sessions;***entry in session #4, attended a total of n=6 sessions, early discharge.

Table 6.21 Neurorehabilitation and psychology questionnaire scores for the group therapy sample (n = 9)

#	Cycle	Gender	Neurorehabilitation pre-therapy	Neurorehabilitation post-therapy	Psychology and mood pre-therapy	Psychology and mood post-therapy
1	1	F	Motor: 58 Cognitive: 55 Total: 113 NIS: 14 Barthel: 11 RCS: 12	Motor: 93 Cognitive: 85 Total: 178 NIS: 7 Barthel: 15 RCS: 14	PHQ-9: 7 GAD-7: 7 ATSQ: 19/35 DERS-SF: 38 Rosenberg: N/A	PHQ-9: 10 GAD-7: 8 ATSQ: 25/35 DERS-SF: 56 Rosenberg: N/A
2	1	F	Motor: 80 Cognitive: 58 Total: 138 NIS: 14 Barthel: 16 RCS: 12	No neurorehabilitation discharge scores	PHQ-9: 8 GAD-7: 7 HADS-depression: 10 HADS-anxiety: 9 ATSQ: 19/35 DERS-SF: 57 Rosenberg: 6	PHQ-9: 17 GAD-7: 10 HADS-depression: 11 HADS-anxiety: 11 ATSQ: N/A DERS-SF: N/A Rosenberg: 10
3	1	F	Motor: 83 Cognitive: 64 Total: 147 NIS: 17 Barthel: 14 RCS: 13	Motor: 106 Cognitive: 89 Total: 195 NIS: 4 Barthel: 17 RCS: 9	PHQ-9: 25 GAD-7: 21 ATSQ: 32/35 DERS-SF: 77 Rosenberg: N/A	PHQ-9: 22 GAD-7: 20 ATSQ: 31/35 DERS-SF: 75 Rosenberg: N/A
4	1	M	Motor: 72 Cognitive: 77 Total: 149 NIS: 20 Barthel: 13 RCS: 13	Motor: 88 Cognitive: 77 Total: 165 NIS: 15 Barthel: 15 RCS: 14	PHQ-9: 8 GAD-7: 10 ATSQ: 25/35 DERS-SF: 41 Rosenberg: N/A	No psychology discharge scores

(Continued)

Table 6.21 (Continued)

#	Cycle	Gender	Neurorehabilitation pre-therapy	Neurorehabilitation post-therapy	Psychology and mood pre-therapy	Psychology and mood post-therapy
5	1	F	No neurorehabilitation admission scores	No neurorehabilitation discharge scores	PHQ-9: 27 GAD-7: 21 HADS-depression: 11 HADS-anxiety: 12 ATSQ: N/A DERS-SF: N/A Rosenberg: N/A	PHQ-9: 4 GAD-7: 3 HADS-depression: 2 HADS-anxiety: 6 ATSQ: 30/35 DERS-SF: 51 Rosenberg: N/A
6	2	M	Motor: 74 Cognitive: 62 Total: 136 NIS: 15 Barthel: 16 RCS: 9	Motor: 107 Cognitive: 97 Total: 204 NIS: 1 Barthel: 20 RCS: 9	PHQ-9: 8 GAD-7: 16 ATSQ: 32/35 DERS-SF: 46 Rosenberg: N/A	PHQ-9: 2 GAD-7: 1 ATSQ: 10/35 DERS-SF: 26 Rosenberg: N/A
7	2	F	Motor: 58 Cognitive: 75 Total: 133 NIS: 21 Barthel: 11 RCS: 15	Motor: 77 Cognitive: 84 Total: 161 NIS: 14 Barthel: 12 RCS: 15	PHQ-9: 6 GAD-7: 1 ATSQ: 10/35 DERS-SF: 30 Rosenberg: N/A	PHQ-9: N/A GAD-7: N/A ATSQ: 12/35 DERS-SF: 27 Rosenberg: N/A
8	2	F	Motor: 49 Cognitive: 49 Total: 98 NIS: 14 Barthel: 10 RCS: 11	Motor: 100 Cognitive: 93 Total: 193 NIS: 11 Barthel: 20 RCS: 11	PHQ-9: 7 GAD-7: 10 ATSQ: 9/35 DERS-SF: 49 Rosenberg: N/A	PHQ-9: 15 GAD-7: 5 ATSQ: N/A DERS-SF: N/A Rosenberg: N/A
9	2	M	Motor: 30 Cognitive: 57 Total: 87 NIS: 26 Barthel: 7 RCS: 14	Motor: 59 Cognitive: 70 Total: 129 NIS: 25 Barthel: 8 RCS: 14	PHQ-9: 9 GAD-7: 13 ATSQ: 29/35 DERS-SF: 62 Rosenberg: N/A	No psychology discharge scores

Table 6.22 Pressure Cooker Model: a group therapy protocol

#	PCM element focused on	Title of group session	Themes and contents	Usefulness (mean ± SD rating)	Enjoyable (mean ± SD rating)
1	All of the PCM	Welcome to the Pressure Cooker Group!	• General introduction on FND group therapy • Group rules, management of FND episodes in the group setting • Brainstorm about habits (e.g. examples and characteristics of habits) and linking to FND as a coping habit.	Cycle 1: 9.3 ± 1.5 (n = 4) Cycle 2: 8.7 ± .64 (n = 3)	Cycle 1: 6.8 ± 2.4 (n = 4) Cycle 2: 8.6 ± .61 (n = 3)
2	All of the PCM	Goal setting and putting the plug back on FND	• Introduction and brief overview on the PCM. • Brainstorm on the PCM: which element stood out or was remembered most? • Completion of a PCM formulation as a group task on a vignette description of FND. • Goal formulation (e.g. reducing frequency of FND episodes, mood goals and long-term goals)	Cycle 1: 8.6 ± 2.4 (n = 4) Cycle 2: 8.9 ± 1.0 (n = 3)	Cycle 1: 9.7 ± 0.6 (n = 4) Cycle 2: 7.4 ± 3.1 (n = 3)
3	All of the PCM	The Power of the Pressure Cooker Model formulation	• Completion of the PCM formulation on two vignettes with FND. • Completion of your own PCM formulation about a recent stressful situation or a stressful situation from the past that stood out (individually).	Cycle 1: 8.8 ± 2.5 (n = 4) Cycle 2: N/A	Cycle 1: 10 ± 0 (n = 4) Cycle 2: N/A

(Continued)

Table 6.22 (Continued)

#	PCM element focused on	Title of group session	Themes and contents	Usefulness (mean ± SD rating)	Enjoyable (mean ± SD rating)
4	Pot, Flames	Body talk: What happens in our brains when we feel?	• LeDoux (1996, 2003) model of fear, the amygdala and the fight-or-flight response, adaptive functions of fear. • Psycho-education on panic attacks: the concept of the fight-or-flight response in overdrive in panic attacks, classic panic cognitions (including "I'm going to have a seizure"), and the relationship between panic and FND. Vignette of a person with FND and a panic attack and points of intervention to stop dissociative or motor-FND episodes. • Strategies to manage warning signs of start of FND episode (e.g. dizziness, heart palpitations).	**Cycle 1:** 10 ± 0 (n = 4) **Cycle 2:** 8.2 ± 1.7 (n = 4)	**Cycle 1:** 10 ± 0 (n = 4) **Cycle 2:** 8.4 ± 1.7 (n = 4)
5	Fuel, Ignition	Coping with triggers of FND: emptying my fuel/ stopping the Ignition	• Rationale for exploration of triggers for better management of FND. • Three different Ignition stories: before-and-after, gradual build-up and out-of-the-blue. • Psycho-education and group brainstorm on common triggers of FND (e.g. thoughts, feelings, physical symptoms, flashbacks, upsetting memories, dissociation, interpersonal situations including arguments and rejection by healthcare professionals) and the existence of multiple triggers of FND in one person: for example panic and arguments. • Playing detective and looking for clues: how to complete a structured FND diary for a recent episode or one that stood out. Looking out for times and situations when FND symptoms increase in frequency, intensity or disappear/re-emerge.	**Cycle 1:** 10 ± 0 (n = 3) **Cycle 2:** (session #1) 9.7 ± .58 (n = 3) Session #2 10 ± 0 (n = 3)	**Cycle 1:** 10 ± 0 (n = 3) **Cycle 2:** (session #1) 9.4 ± 1.1 (n = 3) Session #2 9.8 ± .29 (n = 3)

6	Flames, Heat	Tackling our Flames ("Blowing out our Flames")	• Emotion education exercises: (1) types of basic and social emotions, as well as (2) exploration of functions of emotions (e.g. communication, build relationships, make decisions, not repeat behaviour that harms others, avoid danger and survival, drive and motivation) • Difference Flames (contents) vs Heat (intensity of emotions) • Strategies to help tolerate an unpleasant emotion or internal state and how this relates to FND.	**Cycle 1:** 10 ± 0 (n = 3) **Cycle 2:** $9.5 \pm .61$ (n = 3)	**Cycle 1:** 10 ± 0 (n = 3) **Cycle 2:** $9.2 \pm .74$ (n = 3)
7	Flames, Heat	Turning/dialling down the heat of emotions: My fire extinguishers	• Illustration with a vignette about how worries and anxiety can stand in the way of rehab and progress. • Exercises to "turn down the heat": making a Pressure Cooker emergency plan with the imagined worst-case scenario (e.g. discharge from rehab and FND relapse) and what coping strategies/helpful responses/problem solving skills would the person use? • Exercises to "change your flames": psycho-education on worries and worry processes (e.g. rumination, snowballing, negative self-talk "I won't cope", thinking about all worst-case scenarios in advance and running through each of them). • Relationship between worries and FND; how worries build up and cause anxiety; and the FND temporarily taking away worries. Type 1 and Type 2 worries in FND ("I worry about another seizure", "my attacks make me look strange").	**Cycle 1:** 8.3 ± 3.5 (n = 4) **Cycle 2:** (session #1) 7.5 ± 2.7 (n = 4) Session #2 $9.7 \pm .38$ (n = 4)	**Cycle 1:** 8.8 ± 2.5 (n = 4) **Cycle 2:** (session #1) 7 ± 3.7 (n = 4) Session #2 $9.7 \pm .38$ (n = 4)

(Continued)

Table 6.22 (Continued)

#	PCM element focused on	Title of group session	Themes and contents	Usefulness (mean ± SD rating)	Enjoyable (mean ± SD rating)
8	All of the PCM, with an emphasis on Flames	My pressure cooker emergency plan: coping with discharge	• Worry remedies: keeping a diary, worry scripting, worry zones, postponing worries, enjoyable activities to distract from worries. • Other common Flames in FND: health worries, thinking errors, traumatic memories • Session focused on biggest fears for after discharge. • Recap on: making a pressure cooker emergency plan • What can you change in your own pressure cooker? (e.g. take away the fuel, turn down the heat of the flames, work on sticky left-over food and positive qualities, opening the cover, unblock valve, build a social network). • What top three rehab skills have been helpful so far? What have been your top three achievements in rehab? • Exercise: complete a pressure cooker emergency plan for your own situation.	**Cycle 1:** 8.8 ± 2.5 (n = 4) **Cycle 2:** N/A	**Cycle 1:** 8.8 ± 2.5 (n = 4) **Cycle 2:** N/A
9	Cover	Opening the Cover: letting loose of difficult thoughts and feelings	• Exploring what the Cover represents in the PCM (e.g. verbal emotional expression) • Reasons why we need to communicate feelings to other individuals; effective strategies for communicating feelings with others; things that can go wrong when communicating feelings.	**Cycle 1:** 7.8 ± 4.4 (n = 4) **Cycle 2:** (session #1) 9.4 ± .85 (n = 2)	**Cycle 1:** 7.9 ± 4.2 (n = 4) **Cycle 2:** (session #1) 9.1 ± 1.3 (n = 2)

(Continued)

| 10 | Warning light, Heat | ATTENTION! ("Switching off our Warning light is switching off the FND"). | • Discussion of a classic feature in FND: a tight Cover (e.g. keep self to self and reduced assertiveness) and the relationship with FND. Strategies to help open a tight cover (e.g. increase social network, challenge negative beliefs around emotional expression, practice assertiveness skills, tolerate discomfort around opening up).
• Warning light (heightened self-focused attention) as a maintaining factor of FND ("too much attention") and how it manifests in FND (e.g. checking body, thinking or speaking a lot about symptoms). Discussion of strategies to turn off the warning light including distraction techniques.
• Discussion of dissociation ("too little attention"), its functions (to cut off from experiencing strong intense emotions), childhood origins, examples, phrases ('zoning out', feeling numb, things don't feel real), normalising dissociation and compassion for dissociation as a helpful childhood strategy to survive in difficult circumstances but with a view to change, as dissociation and FND as a stronger form of dissociation, may be less helpful in the present.
• Discussion of reality grounding techniques: Stage (1) when warning signs come up; Stage (2) to prevent further escalation of FND once symptoms have appeared; Stage (3) to get back in the "here-and-now" after FND has settled. | Session #2 8.9 ± 1.0 (n = 3)

Session #3 9.8 ± .35 (n = 3)

Cycle 1: 10 ± 0 (n = 3)

Cycle 2: (session #1) 9.5 ± .92 (n = 3)

Session #2 9.8 ± .45 (n = 4) | Session #2 8.5 ± 1.5 (n = 3)

Session #3 9.8 ± .40 (n = 3)

Cycle 1: 10 ± 0 (n = 3)

Cycle 2: (session #1) 9.8 ± .29 (n = 3)

Session #2 9.9 ± .30 (n = 4) |

Table 6.22 (Continued)

#	PCM element focused on	Title of group session	Themes and contents	Usefulness (mean ± SD rating)	Enjoyable (mean ± SD rating)
11	Valve	How regulating your Valve will help you release your pressure	• Discussion of the valve element and the relationship between activity levels, stress release via activities, with FND. • Exploration and management strategies for the three types of valve: (1) Blocked Valve: psycho-education on the mood-enjoyable activities link. Breaking the vicious cycle with behavioural activation and building positive experiences. (2) Dysregulated valve: psycho-education on the boom-and-bust cycle and discussion of a vignette with a pacing exercise. Comparison boom/bust vs paced activity schedules. (3) Valve overuse: "Pushing on", how it helps to avoid or dissociate from emotions; its origins in childhood; strategies to slow down "stop and think, sit with distress".	**Cycle 1:** 10 ± 0 (n = 4) **Cycle 2:** 9.5 ± .56 (n = 4)	**Cycle 1:** 10 ± 0 (n = 4) **Cycle 2:** 9.6 ± .57 (n = 4)
12	The Kitchen	The Big Kitchen Clean-up: Helpful and unhelpful features of the environment in FND	• Focused on the impact of the environment and responses from individuals on maintenance of FND. • Discussion of different types of Kitchens: (1) someone constantly checking the pot (characterised by systemic hypervigilance, continuous reassurance), (2) messy, chaotic kitchen (characterised by interpersonal triggers and the powerful impact of an FND episode on responses from the environment, e.g. stopping arguments and providing care instead) and (3) kitchen attended every once in a while but pot left on its own to cook (person kept safe but left alone during an episode to ride it out).	**Cycle 1:** 9.3 ± 1.5 (n = 4) **Cycle 2:** 8.8 ± 1.6 (n = 3)	**Cycle 1:** 9.3 ± 1.5 (n = 4) **Cycle 2:** 8.6 ± 2.3 (n = 3)

13	Sticky left-over food	Getting unstuck: Sticky left-over foods		Cycle 1: 9.2 ± 1.4 (n = 3)	Cycle 1: 9.1 ± 1.6 (n = 3)
			• Discussion of the external regulation function of FND and normalising the basic human need to receive empathy, feel validated, cared for and have needs met by other people.		
			• Discussion of different reinforcement learning processes in FND including double reinforcement and partial reinforcement.		
			• Systemic re-traumatisation examples (e.g. "it's all in your head", people not believing symptoms) and group discussion around the central theme in FND: "not being believed".		
			• Psycho-education on the relationship between early experiences, childhood coping mechanisms, core beliefs and cultural factors. Definition and functions of core beliefs, as well as the existence of positive and negative core beliefs. Strategies to challenge negative core beliefs and build up positive core beliefs.	Cycle 2: 10 ± 0 (n = 2)	Cycle 2: 10 ± 0 (n = 2)
			• Discussion of three classic coping mechanisms in FND, repeated from childhood to adulthood: pushing on, keeping self to self, and dissociation.		
			• Cultivating compassion for repetition of childhood coping mechanisms as a survival strategy in difficult circumstances that worked well in childhood but lost some of its function in adulthood (e.g. causing injuries).		

(*Continued*)

Table 6.22 (Continued)

#	PCM element focused on	Title of group session	Themes and contents	Usefulness (mean ± SD rating)	Enjoyable (mean ± SD rating)
14	Pot	Taking care of your body: biological vulnerabilities to FND	• Discussion of physical aspects of FND in two ways: (1) Healing or managing tears or vulnerabilities of our pots (taking medications on time), (2) Strengthening our pots (doing exercise to help muscles). • Topics of discussion included sleep hygiene; exercise for physical and mood reasons; rationale for good nutrition; psycho–education on vitamin deficiencies and physical symptoms; dehydration and clouding of the mind; gut health and mood; alcohol, drugs, coffee and its impact on psychological processes (e.g. dissociation, palpitations and panic); management of organic illnesses (e.g. diabetes); and medication issues in FND (e.g. analgesia overuse headaches, polypharmacy, medications facilitating dissociation).	**Cycle 1:** 6.7 ± 2.9 (n = 3) **Cycle 2:** 10 ± 0 (n = 2)	**Cycle 1:** 8.3 ± 2.9 (n = 3) **Cycle 2:** 10 ± 0 (n = 2)
15	All of the PCM	Puling everything together	• Final session: PCM formulation meeting that focused on pulling all elements together with participants completing their own PCM models individually.	**Cycle 1:** 9.6 ± .70 (n = 3) **Cycle 2:** N/A	**Cycle 1:** 9.4 ± 1.1 (n = 3) **Cycle 2:** N/A

Qualitative feedback

At the end of each cycle of the group, people with FND were asked to complete a feedback form that gauged their personal views and reflections on the group therapy. The questionnaire consisted of eight questions in total. Five out of nine people were able to complete the questionnaire.

QUESTION 1

Question 1 asked how satisfied people were with their experience of the group (on a scale of 1 – extremely dissatisfied to 7 – extremely satisfied). Most people indicated to be "7 – extremely satisfied" (n = 4), and only one person mentioned being "5 – slightly satisfied". Comments included the following:

- "It's very good as everyone in the group experiences FND, good to be around the people who experience it, as they know how you feel (similarities). Good to get strategies and learning about triggers".
- "It has been really interesting and rewarding to understand my illness better. It has provided me with more helpful tools".
- "I have found the FND group a great help to me. I have been able to learn about FND and how to explain it in great detail to others".
- "I have better knowledge and understanding of FND from attending the group, and how best to deal with it".
- "Too much information given too quickly".

QUESTION 2

Question 2 asked the participants how helpful the group was for them in managing their symptoms and in what way? (on a scale of 1 – extremely unhelpful to 7 – extremely helpful). Responses to this question were variable and ranged from people feeling the group was not very effective ("3 – slightly unhelpful", "4 – neutral/not sure", "5 – slightly helpful") to more positive ratings ("6 – mostly helpful" and "7 – extremely helpful").
  Comments included the following:

- "It's helped in some way managing some symptoms but not others, e.g. leg weakness. Haven't had FND symptoms since the group. Black-outs are not frequent".
- "Sometimes, after some of the groups, I can have more symptoms because I have been thinking about it so much".
- "Didn't do anything. But has made me more comfortable".
- "I have learnt techniques and ways to control my symptoms and to recognise them".
- "FND group has given me a lot of information and techniques for if certain symptoms arise and I would know how to deal with them".

QUESTION 3

For Question 3, participants were presented with a scale running from 0% (no improvement of symptoms at all) to 100% (complete improvement of symptoms), and asked "how much have your symptoms improved because of the group?" Give your rating here ...%. Ratings were as follows: 0% (n = 2), 10%, 85% and 100%. The two people that provided a 0% rating indicated "I now have more understanding of FND" and "as my main symptom are spasms, I feel this was mainly improved by strengthening my core".

QUESTION 4

Question 4 was a statement with multiple-response options: "Because of the group, my symptoms have deteriorated/not changed/improved (on a scale of 1 – completely deteriorated to 7 – completely improved)". Three people indicated that their symptoms stayed the same and did not change as a result of the group. One person's symptoms slightly improved, whereas another person achieved completely improved symptoms due to the group.

QUESTION 5

Question 5 asked what people learned in the group that was useful? Comments included the following:

- "I learned about the pressure cooker, very good to put yourself in categories. I will look back at it. When I feel down, I will look back. I have seen what my Warning light is".
- "The pressure cooker pot was great to learn about and made things so much clearer".
- "Pot" (NB. it should be noted that this participant experienced tremors that greatly affected their writing abilities).
- "I have learned how to describe FND by using the pressure cooker. What each part of the pressure cooker is and how it relates to FND".
- "I learned the analogy of the pressure cooker. I learned about pacing and not booming and busting. Assertiveness. Managing symptoms. Dealing with anxiety/dissociative attacks. How the environment impacts on me. The importance of having some enjoyable activity and not a "blocked valve"".

QUESTION 6

Question 6 enquired about which coping strategies people found the most helpful? Distraction techniques were overwhelmingly mentioned (n = 4) and included listening to music, trying to watch films, breathing techniques and thinking of the five senses "(smell, sight, hearing, taste, touch)", and creating the FND Survival Kit to collate all useful strategies in one place. One person specifically highlighted the importance of opening "the Cover" and "talking with others about how I feel".

People were also asked whether anything about the FND group could be improved. Three people indicated that the group went too fast and there was too much information presented simultaneously: "Break down the information, not doing everything at once. Not to throw [people] in the deep end of [the] pressure cooker", "take longer [time] to explain the pressure cooker pot" and "just go slower, to understand FND more, it is a lot to process". Other people mentioned "I think every individual that takes part in the group should start from the beginning and not come in halfway through as it can be difficult to catch up" and "nothing I can think of – possibly more focus on spasms".

Question 8 asked how likely people would recommend the group to a friend or family member? (on a scale of 1 – extremely unlikely to 7 – extremely likely). All five people unanimously indicated "7 – extremely likely" as their response. Some comments included the following: "Helped me – it helps reduce symptoms so it doesn't happen as often as it did at home", "It is a great way to educate your friends and family in what the FND condition is all about" and "very helpful in enabling me to understand FND better, and it was good to have the support network of other people in a similar position".

Group therapy: reflections

The group was mostly focused on FND education and less on relational or experiential features. From a psycho-educational point of view, the group protocol *contents* are important, particularly in a condition such as FND that causes high levels of confusion. People with FND and their families often lack information and awareness on FND which the group can provide. However, it is equally important, if not more important, not to lose sight of the *processes* in FND group therapy. The experiential aspect hits at the core of the psychosocial difficulties in FND. It is possible that the group may have produced better outcomes and generated more positive feedback if the more relational features would have been incorporated.

Group therapy: learning lessons for the future

During this pilot group therapy project, it was evident that certain important themes and maintaining factors of FND were missed or lightly touched upon in the initial group therapy protocol. The following recommendations may be helpful to add in a future PCM-based group protocol.

Missed opportunities

Although the group was heavily focused on psycho-education for FND, some topics that deserve attention for future inclusion include the discovery of individual "safety features" or positive prognostic factors and qualities that help recovery in FND, to help shift attention away from "what is wrong" with the patient and support people with low self-esteem, which is common in FND. In addition, more basic information on FND, the diagnostic process, FND as an umbrella term that covers many different types of symptoms and the different existing terminologies for FND, may be helpful as this was not always clear and occasionally halted the process of accepting a more psychologically driven perspective on FND.

Exploring underlying undercurrents and "things left unsaid"

Fears that are commonly not talked about in therapy, require a gradual process of uncovering in therapy sessions and are often associated with shame and embarrassment in FND include the fear of recovery and its associated social gains and losses; fear of relapse and the increased risk of it becoming a self-fulfilling prophecy; and fears around not being believed, not being cared for and not feeling heard. All these fears are vital topics to address as these have the potential to maintain FND.

Environmental considerations

The group protocol consisted of only one session on environmental factors in FND at the very end. However, in light of the major impact of the environment on symptom maintenance in FND, it is highly recommended to spend more time on this important area, with a particular emphasis on reciprocal reinforcement, systemic re-traumatisation and the discussion of FND thinking traps that are common to people with FND and their healthcare workers to illustrate the similarity rather than dissimilarity between the two groups. Although service infrastructures do not always allow for this, it is also strongly recommended to run groups for both people with FND and their environment alongside and that also regularly interact with each other, given that interpersonal triggers contribute to FND.

Content…and process

The group protocol was mostly focused on education ("content"). However, relationships are a core topic in FND. Incorporating content and process features equally in future groups may further improve outcomes. Practising skills experientially in the group can help develop more positive relationships in day-to-day functioning and expose vulnerabilities in the process of "relating". Group processes that may be useful include helping others; co-design group projects between service users and facilitators; and repairing ruptures in relationships in and outside the group. A challenge in FND group therapy is not to succumb to exclusively adhering to a protocol especially during times that facilitators feel anxious or rattled in some way. It is advisable for staff facilitating a PCM group to regularly complete their own PCM formulations to raise insight into processes that they may contribute to and adversely impact on group dynamics and on FND symptom maintenance of the individual group members.

FND aftercare: a forgotten area

Endings, transitions and maintaining gains are often a difficult area in FND. In addition to educational elements, the group setting often provides a lot of containment, familiarity and social support that will likely not continue in the same form after a group ends. This is a particular problem for people with FND who often feel socially isolated and lack a sense of belonging. Making the transition from group therapy to independent self-management of FND in the community without the support of a regularly facilitated group cannot take place without the development and instalment of a sense of social belonging and making social links in the community outside the group, a process that has ideally already started whilst in the group. Due to time, funding and resource constraints in health services, it is not always possible to offer continuous less intensive support to monitor a person's progress and gains. However, offering post-group booster sessions may be helpful to problem-solve any issues.

7 Pressure Cooker Model complex case discussions

In previous chapters, we have seen that the PCM is a versatile model that can be used with people with different subtypes of FND, their families and within a multidisciplinary team context where every element represents one or more non-psychology disciplines. In this chapter, we will review the use of the PCM as part of complex case discussions. This commonly consists of a PCM formulation of the person and the family with FND. In addition, a PCM formulation can be drawn up for each member of the team separately, or for the team "as a whole". Importantly, an additional aim for Chapter 7 is to highlight the similarity rather than the dissimilarity between people with FND and any individual in their environment, further strengthening the notion of FND as a systemic condition.

Background

In the same way as each person with FND will have an individualised hierarchy of treatment needs, the team treating people with FND will have their own hierarchy of team needs. Considering the team you are in, it will be helpful to think about the layered formulation and identify which layer of the PCM currently needs the most attention for your team to address any challenges (Figure 7.1).

A hybrid model of FND: rationale for a team approach

Figure 7.2 shows the rationale for using the PCM to explore team-level processes that contribute to the maintenance of FND.

Pressure cooker complex case discussions: a radical new approach to FND

Supporting people with FND on their journey towards full recovery requires the surrounding systems to make radical changes to current care practices for people with FND. This radical change in thinking starts with invoking

DOI: 10.4324/9781003308980-7

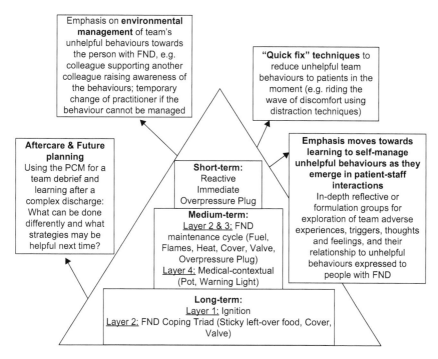

Emphasis on **environmental management** of team's unhelpful behaviours towards the person with FND, e.g. colleague supporting another colleague raising awareness of the behaviours; temporary change of practitioner if the behaviour cannot be managed

"Quick fix" techniques to reduce unhelpful team behaviours to patients in the moment (e.g. riding the wave of discomfort using distraction techniques)

Aftercare & Future planning
Using the PCM for a team debrief and learning after a complex discharge: What can be done differently and what strategies may be helpful next time?

Short-term:
Reactive
Immediate
Overpressure Plug

Medium-term:
Layer 2 & 3: FND maintenance cycle (Fuel, Flames, Heat, Cover, Valve, Overpressure Plug)
Layer 4: Medical-contextual (Pot, Warning Light)

Emphasis moves towards learning to self-manage unhelpful behaviours as they emerge in patient-staff interactions
In-depth reflective or formulation groups for exploration of team adverse experiences, triggers, thoughts and feelings, and their relationship to unhelpful behaviours expressed to people with FND

Long-term:
Layer 1: Ignition
Layer 2: FND Coping Triad (Sticky left-over food, Cover, Valve)

Layer 5: Social functions of FND (Kitchen)

Figure 7.1 Hierarchy of team needs in FND.

complex case discussions. Table 7.1 shows the differences between regular vs "Pressure Cooker Model"–based complex case discussions.

The team's own pressure cooker

A useful and productive complex case discussion requires focus on the person with FND and on their family. However, of equal importance is the team's willingness and ability towards looking into "the mirror of FND". There is nothing unique about the pressure cooker of FND: every person, with or without FND, has their own individual pressure cooker. The PCM is not a model of pathology of the individual but, rather, a model of systemic pathology. In the following section, we will take a closer look at the team's Pressure Cooker Model using the same layered system that is applied to the "person and family with FND".

Layer 1: Ignition

A large body of research has demonstrated a wide range of vulnerability factors that contribute to the development of FND at a later stage in life,

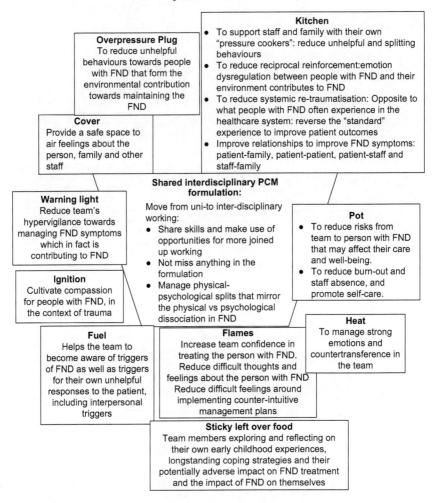

Figure 7.2 Rationale for the use of hybrid models in FND treating teams.

for example trauma, a difficult upbringing (e.g. harsh parenting, emotional neglect) or other adverse childhood and adulthood experiences (e.g. domestic violence inflicted by a partner). Vulnerability factors also exist in the staff and services that treat people with FND. We can consider FND as a safety behaviour, and in the same way, a team will have adopted their own safety behaviours, which in a similar vein will be driven by vulnerability factors that have contributed to the development of these team safety behaviours – and occasionally to FND itself, as healthcare professionals are at an increased risk of developing the actual condition. Table 7.2 demonstrates that the Ignition element in a person with FND is highly similar to the Ignition of the team treating people with FND.

Table 7.1 Complex case discussions in FND

Regular complex case discussions	*The pressure cooker way*
Reactive	**Continuous**
• Invoked when a person with FND is stuck in therapy or displays challenging behaviours that the team has difficulty managing.	• Complex case discussions are regular and considered an essential part of the person's treatment regimen.
One formulation	**Multiple formulations**
• Emphasis is on "the patient" often resulting in a formulation of the patient, with the environmental factors playing a subsidiary role.	• Focus is on the person with FND, family and team, resulting in multiple formulations that interact with one another.
Patient is mostly responsible for recovery	**Shared responsibility for recovery**
• Strategies are mostly focused on supporting the patient applying the strategies rather than the individual team members applying strategies on themselves.	• The PCM assumes that both person and system equally contribute to and are therefore both responsible for recovery in FND.
	• Strategies that emanate from the formulations are for every participant involved in FND including the person, family and team.
Complex case discussion	**Complex case discussion**
• To support a person's treatment.	• Part of the actual treatment = "the intervention".
Less emphasis on joined-up working	**Emphasis on joined-up working**
• Not geared towards generating a multidisciplinary formulation.	Yields an integrated formulation that incorporates multiple disciplines involved in FND:
	• Model naturally lends itself for an integrated formulation and joined-up working.
	• Lowering the threshold towards joined-up working.

Layer 2: the team's FND coping triad

In the same way as people with FND and their families do, the team treating people with FND can exhibit a similar "FND team coping triad" consisting of the following:

Sticky left-over food

• Individual staff member's own (potentially adverse) childhood experiences, early coping mechanisms, attachment and personal core beliefs have repeated over time (e.g. I'm not good enough, low confidence in managing patient's symptoms, not trusting other team members, and reduced verbal emotional expression or dissociative tendencies since childhood).

Table 7.2 Ignition element in people with FND and their healthcare professionals

Ignition elements	Person with FND	Team treating FND
Upbringing and personal history	Person's childhood upbringing in their family of origin	• Team's "upbringing" and the way it has historically coped with stress including with "difficult patients", service pressures, conflicts between individual team members, the level of neglect of or tending to the team's emotional needs. • Individual members' upbringing and historic stress-coping mechanisms. • The history of the healthcare milieu "the way things are / have always been done in the service" and that may unlikely or difficult to change (e.g. service structures, referral pathways, services with a physical vs a more psychiatric focus on FND, rotational staff).
Attachment	Insecure attachment as a result of adverse childhood experiences	• Team's attachment to the person with FND; to the FND patient group as a whole; and the attachment between individual team members may be insecure (anxious-ambivalent, avoidant), particularly if there is anxiety and frustration about working with the person with FND or amongst colleagues. • The existence of historically stronger attachments between certain disciplines as opposed to others, for example physiotherapy and occupational therapy. • Historically weaker or more anxious-ambivalent attachments between physical and psychological disciplines, possibly mirroring the patient's ambivalence or reluctance towards psychology.
Lack of psychological way of thinking and helpful emotion coping	Person may have learned to dissociate from emotions from an early age onwards and not had the opportunities to learn adaptive and helpful emotion coping strategies	• Lack of a psychological-driven model in FND services, which may not have been regularly exposed to a psychological way of thinking or a reflective space, due to a lack of psychologist (community neurorehabilitation teams) and time (long waiting lists), or may be heavily dominated by biological models.

Ignition elements	Person with FND	Team treating FND
Adverse experiences causing strong emotions	Traumatic experiences, conflict and arguments in the home, oppression, rejection, invalidation	• Historic adverse experiences with people with FND and their families: complaints or threat of complaints, heightened emotions and hostility towards individual team members. • Level of pressure on the team at a senior management level.
Critical incidents that sparked off the FND or safety behaviours	Accidents, surgeries, illnesses, trauma, divorce, work stress	• Service or environmental changes, for example staff members leaving their post but vacancies not refilled leaving a gap in the service, the COVID pandemic necessitating a new way of working.
Gradual build-up of stresses without recourse to balanced stress–coping strategies	Gradual build-up of life stresses with the person unable to cope over time resulting in the development of FND	• Gradual build-up of stresses in the team that trigger safety behaviours, for example challenging patient-mix on the ward or a heavy caseload over a prolonged period of time.

- Team core beliefs (we're not good enough managing the patient, we are imperfect when it comes to working with FND).
- Team's historical way of coping when it's under pressure. The team's survival coping strategies when under high pressure, for example in health-care context "keep self to self", "just pushing on", "bowing out of the process" and "sickness absence".

Cover

The Cover in the hybrid PCM represents the extent to which the staff (or family member) speaks or expresses their true personal thoughts and feelings about the person with FND in psychological safe and trusting relationships with other people.

A TIGHT COVER: KEEPING SELF TO SELF

Healthcare professionals working in the field of FND and family members may keep their worries, anxiety and frustrations about the patients and their progress in therapy to themselves. This may be due to a personal longstanding coping strategy of reduced verbal emotional expression that the staff member takes into the work place. In addition, an often fast-paced work atmosphere with oversubscribed clinics and waiting list pressures can afford little time for staff members to express feelings or may even be punitive towards expressing emotions due to unhelpful ideas around expression, which may limit opportunities for emotional expression. Moreover, the service infrastructure with limited "psychological mindedness" in a team may not be appropriately set up to incorporate regular reflective practice groups that facilitate expression of negative thoughts, feelings and behaviours related to patients, and there may not be any time available with "admin time" consistently favoured over reflection, or low staff morale leading to frequent cancellation of reflective sessions.

UNCONSTRUCTIVE VENTING

A lack of a reflective practice space in a service that regularly sees people with FND may become problematic. Team members may get into the habit of openly "inadequate venting" practices instead of constructively releasing difficult inner thoughts and frustrations in a psychologically safe reflective space. Examples include sarcasm, bashing and ridiculing of patients, each of which can contribute to systemic re-traumatisation and FND. Although venting is technically speaking a form of "opening one's Cover", this type of venting is deemed unconstructive and characterised by excessive negative expressions about the person, which "infects" other team members.

In the same vein as people with FND, a tight Cover in healthcare professionals may increase the risk of using their Overpressure Plug (i.e. unhelpful behaviours exhibited by staff members towards people with FND, e.g. hostility, passing on to other services). These unhelpful behaviours are detrimental to staff's psychological well-being and resilience, and can have major adverse consequences for a patient's treatment including systemic re-traumatisation.

Valve

The Valve represents the activity levels that people with FND and the individuals in their direct environment have adopted.

In the same way as people with FND can display abnormal activity levels in their day-to-day life, individual team members can exhibit their own abnormal Valve profiles that will adversely impact on their work-life balance. The same three Valve profiles that have been uncovered in people with FND have equally been observed in the clinic. A *blocked Valve* is common and may include consistently cancelling planned enjoyable, social, relaxing or other meaningful activities after work or in the weekends, with "paralysing inertia", resulting in an insufficient stress release and a potential impact on the quality of other relationships for the person caring for the patient with FND, whether that be a staff or family member. Occasionally, taking yourself out of the equation when it comes to attending social or enjoyable events will be a helpful strategy, particularly with big case- or workloads during the day that require down time. However, a chronic lack of social belonging and connecting with communities over a long period is not only problematic for people with FND but can equally become troublesome for staff and family members resulting in secondary mood problems such as depression.

A *dysregulated Valve* may be characterised by healthcare professionals or family members booming-and-busting themselves leading to periods of high work or care activity intermixed with regular staff absences in the service and inefficient working patterns over time. *Valve overuse* has frequently been observed in healthcare settings with workers taking on caring duties without any form of respite, being "constantly on the move" or "pushing on" with clinical and administrative activities, sometimes after hours. Due to the complex needs of a subset of patients with FND, overdoing caring activities for one patient (who may display a high level of care-eliciting behaviours towards the clinician) at the expense of care for other patients who are more in the background and do not elicit as much care is not uncommon. A bust-after-boom Valve can develop as a result and represents staff burn-out or compassion fatigue in both healthcare workers and family members who have "succumbed" to the carer burden that FND may bring.

As was discussed in Chapter 3, the Valve is "social" in nature. The patient's Valve may exactly copy, mirror or complement the staff or family member's Valve.

Layer 3: the team's Pressure Cooker Chain Reaction

Systemic Fuel

In the same way as for a person with FND, a Pressure Cooker Chain Reaction starts with the Fuel, which is represented by the presentation and behaviours of the person with FND ("the trigger" for the team). Figure 7.3 displays common situations involving people with FND that have served as triggers for the team's "safety behaviours", which will be discussed below.

Flames and Heat

In the same way that people with FND experience unhelpful beliefs and emotions about themselves and their healthcare professionals, people working in the field of FND will report similar psychological phenomena. For an extensive discussion about healthcare professionals' thoughts and emotions about patients with FND, the reader is referred to Chapter 3. The chapter explored healthcare professionals' thoughts and emotions about the person with FND without reference to themselves. The current section will focus on healthcare professionals' thoughts and emotions about *themselves in relation to the person with FND*. Other terms that may capture these psychological features more fully include "FND Theory of Mind", "FND self-esteem" or "FND self-efficacy" in the context of managing and treating the FND.

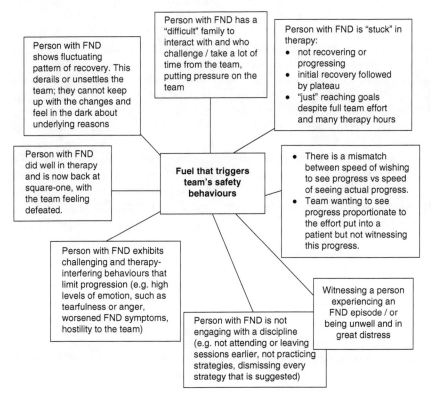

Figure 7.3 Examples of systemic Fuel.

We will now turn to common cognitions and emotions reported by healthcare professionals about themselves in relation to people with FND (Table 7.3).

Heat

The thoughts and emotions experienced by healthcare workers about people with FND, or about themselves in relation to the person with FND (e.g. own abilities and skills to manage FND), will have a level of emotional strength. In a similar vein to people with FND, healthcare workers have a Heat button that can be dialled up or down.

LOW SETTING

Dissociation is common in the general population. However, in healthcare environments with high levels of dissociation experienced by the patients, the healthcare professionals treating those patients may start mirroring similar

Table 7.3 FND Theory of Mind–type beliefs and emotions reported by healthcare professionals in FND

Common beliefs	Emotions
I am not able to utilise my full/usual set of skills (e.g. standard CBT models, physiotherapy techniques). I am not doing my work with FND patients in a perfect manner as I would with other types of patients. "I'm imperfect" [when it comes to working with FND].	Frustration, anxiety
I worry that the person is not making the gains that I normally see in people with more organic presentations such as stroke/brain injury/or psychological presentations (e.g. depression/panic disorder)…"I must be doing something wrong", "I'm not good enough". "The patient is at fault and being difficult".	Low mood, anxiety, anger, frustration
Reduced self-efficacy, I feel de-skilled, I doubt myself, I am not confident, I question my own abilities about managing FND. I don't know what I'm doing. My confidence levels are low in managing the patient's FND.	Low mood, anxiety, frustration
I worry that the person relapses, experiences a set-back or shows fluctuations in symptoms during my treatment *[and that this will say something about me, that I am an incapable clinician]*.	Fear, anxiety
The person has not achieved their goals/the person still has FND/the person had a set-back/the person's FND symptoms are not abating…I have not achieved anything either. "I must get the person better or else I have not achieved anything in treatment".	Embarrassment, shame, frustration, anger, sadness
My actions are making/going to make the person worse (e.g. withdrawing support to promote independence).	Guilt, anxiety
The person is doing well with my other colleagues but not in my sessions, what's going on?	Anxiety, anger, envy, embarrassment
I feel distressed seeing the person in distress.	Anxiety, sadness

tendencies and cut off negative emotions. Dissociation in these settings does not have to be a pathological phenomenon to the same extent as patients may experience it and can be highly protective. For example, a healthcare worker's caseload will show some variability of complexity, with some patients engaging and progressing well, whereas other patients, often those with severe interpersonal difficulties that greatly impact on the therapeutic relationship and FND presentation, may not always show the expected trajectory of recovery. Situations where dissociation may be adaptive include days with very full caseloads and highly complex patients who elicit strong and intense emotions or patients who may experience extreme levels of emotionality perhaps projected onto the clinician who will have to "hold", "tolerate" and "absorb" these emotions in the moment. During such moments, cutting off the emotions to not experience the emotion temporarily can be highly adaptive for the clinician's psychological well-being and preserve their ability to carry on with therapy. In addition, since people with FND share a family environment, it is not surprising that they may share coping strategies including dissociation.

Although using dissociation as a temporary coping strategy is not unhelpful, in the same way as for patients who dissociate, the moment that dissociation starts affecting personal and work relationships, social and occupational functioning, or any other meaningful activities in the daily life of the clinician, or starts invading into life and taking lots of time, this will likely have adverse rather than protective effects on the healthcare worker.

HIGH-LOW-HIGH-LOW SETTING

Emotion dysregulation emerges in both people with FND and individuals in their environment including strong, intense emotions, as well as difficulties settling down following witnessing of the FND episode. This is termed emotion co-dysregulation, which can be seen as the precursor stage that eventually leads into the reciprocal reinforcement that often effectively manages the systemic co-dysregulation but perpetuates the FND symptoms in the long run.

HIGH-TO-LOW SETTING

The characteristic rise and fall in aversive emotions, arousal or unpleasant internal state during a patient's dissociative episode is not dissimilar to the rise and fall experienced by healthcare professionals witnessing the episode, in the context of the mirroring of the emotions connected to an FND episode as part of reciprocal reinforcement processes. Clinicians witnessing an FND episode, particularly those who are less experienced or versed in the field of FND, will likely connect strongly with the symptoms and distress displayed in the patient and will feel a need to regulate their own thoughts, emotions and responses in relation to the symptoms. As a result, clinicians may feel a similar "rise and fall" in distress, as the person with FND experiences during and after a dissociative episode.

Overpressure Plug

We have seen that the Overpressure Plug represents the symptoms of FND. The PCM considers FND as an understandable but unhelpful form of coping with difficult thoughts and emotions, because it stands in the way of living life to the full. Healthcare professionals are not any different from people with FND: they too can exhibit understandable but unhelpful forms of emotional coping habits, particularly in the absence of verbal emotional expression and abnormal (work) activity levels, which are all too common in healthcare contexts. As a result, the Overpressure Plug can be broadened as a concept and viewed as a more general plug of the system around the person with FND that subsumes a collection of understandable but unhelpful ways of coping, responses and behaviours from the system that are directed or expressed towards the person with FND and that maintain the FND. The system's unhelpful responses are driven by negative beliefs and emotions, in the same way as negative beliefs and emotions will drive FND symptoms in a person with FND.

There are many different terms that can be used to describe the Over-pressure Plug element in healthcare workers including therapist-interfering behaviours, countertransference, defence mechanisms, coping strategies or unhelpful behaviours. The PCM prefers to use the term "psychological" or "interpersonal" safety behaviours, in the same vein that people with FND exhibit safety behaviours, to make the models as similar as possible. Figure 7.4 reviews common safety behaviours in the context of FND services, as observed in healthcare professionals and family members.

Layer 4: the team's facilitating physical factors

Biological vulnerabilities and medico-contextual variables of the team treating people with FND play an important role in FND maintenance, in a similar vein to people experiencing the FND.

Pot

In much the same way as people with FND, each individual team member will have their own **FND SELF CARE acronym** since it equally applies to the individuals in the system around the person with FND (Table 7.4).

Warning light

The allocation of a high amount of attentional resources to a patient's physical symptoms, particularly if the FND is severe or unusual in nature, may be replicated by individuals in the person's direct environment, as a form of "systemic hypervigilance". This can lead to the *triple reinforcement* phenomenon, which can be defined as a reinforcement process that is driven by three sources: the heightened attention that a person with FND applies on their own physical symptoms, amplified by the hypervigilant focus on the person's symptoms from healthcare workers and family members alike. The team's hypervigilance on FND symptoms may express itself in many ways, for example tip-toeing around the person to ensure that dissociative episodes do not emerge or the family member ensuring their presence near the person and carefully monitoring symptoms in case the episodes appear and they can nip the episode in the bud or prevent the person from self-injury. Healthcare workers may also display similar hypervigilant behaviours around the person, particularly if gains are believed to be fragile and in danger of tipping over into worsening of the FND symptoms at any minute, for example during

Abandoning care plans • Problems with fidelity and staying true to treatment models and care plans, particularly in the face of worsening FND or behaviours, contributing to prolonging the FND • For example, not following a behavioural plan and providing physical and verbal reassurance as reinforcement because it feels otherwise counter-intuitive.	**Trickery**, lying to the person with FND, for example telling the person you have another appointment, you need to call someone, or need to do admin, where in fact you may have a break.	**Reinforcing the power differential** • Patronising the person with FND. • "Baby-ing" the person using childish language and behaviours you would use when interacting with children • Taking on "teacher" mode and forcing the person with FND into a "child" mode • Adopting a parental role in interactions with patient (e.g being extra firm with the patient). • Family members and team openly expressing little confidence in the patient's ability to cope successfully with difficult emotions and managing the FND.
Using negative labels, extremely aversive language to denote the person including as manipulative, "severe FND that is beyond help", "non-compliant", "disengaged", "making minimal progress" "faking it" "crazy" "seeking attention" "time-wasters" "difficult to treat" "beyond help") – and ascribing all the "blame" for treatment failure on to the patient.		

Overprotective behaviours Restricting a person's choice of activities and increasing dependency on the environment (e.g. doing a chore for the patient which could have been done by the patient or closely monitor the patient's activity and symptoms in a hypervigilant manner).	**Team's safety behaviours**	**Tinkering with sessions** which impact negatively on the person with FND but positively for the clinician: • Shortening duration • Reducing frequency • Delaying the moment to start session • Doing a lot of joint sessions to spend as little one-to-one time with the person and not driven by underlying clinical rationale.
	Discharge or strongly encouraging early discharge of a "difficult patient" from the service because the person with FND is not making progress quickly enough.	

"Tit-for-tat" retaliation and rejection behaviours towards the person with FND: • Being short, unpleasant, rude or hostile with the person. • Rushing approach towards people with FND but not towards people with organic conditions ('singling' out, differential treatment). • Paying extra attention to a different patient on purpose and ignoring the person with FND. • Non-verbal language that strongly suggests 'I reject you'. Staff unable to control negative facial expressions / emotional coldness towards person with FND.	**Uni-disciplinary working: Team defragmentation** Members focusing exclusively on their own disciplines without much interdisciplinary communication, collaboration, joint working, absence of inter-disciplinary treatment goals, poor attendance at team meetings

Figure 7.4a Common team psychological safety behaviours in FND.

significant time–points such as an imminent discharge. Another common example is the staff member who becomes drawn into long conversations about physical symptoms each time the person with FND has a session and which can detract from other more pressing issues or topics. Other examples of heightened attention on the patient frequently found in clinical practice include the person with FND often being on staff or family members' minds;

- **Direct avoidance:** Ignore or avoid the patient (e.g. ignore patient on the ward, not greeting, not make an appointment with the patient, passing the patient on to another colleague, "dumping" the patient onto another service, discharge patient from the service)
- **Subtle avoidance:** doing lots of joint rather than individual one-to-one sessions to 'share the burden', not re-scheduling the patient if the patient misses a session in the same way the clinician would do for a patient with organic illness.
- Sickness absence to avoid seeing the patient, causing frequent incomplete multidisciplinary teams.

Team splitting
- Individual members of multidisciplinary team are getting drawn in by patients resulting in a split between disciplines
- Classic split between physical vs psychological disciplines where person with FND engages well with the more "physical" disciplines than with psychology

Team's safety behaviours

Going the extra mile / above and beyond, with staff or family overinvolved or unusually invested in the person's treatment, over the top caring for the person, sometimes at the expense, or taking time and resources away from care for other patients.
- Giving patient high levels of reassurance and empathy, or extra attention in groups, planning in extra sessions.
- Physical and verbal reassurance during a dissociative episode, strong and immediate caring response from the family and team: comforting the patient, hand-holding, patting on the back
- Accommodating the patient, doing things for the patient that you wouldn't do for other patients, 'doubling up efforts' to help.
- Team meetings dominated by discussions about the patient at the expense of other patient care.

Cynicism & Sarcasm
- Becoming cynical, judgemental and generalizing of the patient or patient group (e.g. 'all patients with FND are like this, here we go again').
- Staff openly expressing negative feelings about the patient in unproductive and stigmatising ways, for example in team meetings, with other team members, and negatively impacting on other colleagues working with the person.

Bargaining with the patient (e.g. patient needs to take medications but is reluctant making the staff member bargain and trying to encourage the patient to take the medications). Convincing the patient for a long period of time to join a session / carry out an activity.

Figure 7.4b Common team psychological safety behaviours in FND.

staff being unable to stop thinking about the person with FND after hours; as well as discussing the person endlessly during team meetings and "eating" into other patients' time slots. Hypervigilance may come at a great cost for other members in the family system; for example, "24-hour supervision" imposed by the family automatically means that the "supervisor" will be restricted in their own activities in life.

Layer 5: the team Kitchen

All these team safety behaviours have a range of different social functions that can cause an increase in unhelpful behaviours that perpetuate FND and result in other adverse consequences (Table 7.5).

Table 7.4 FND SELF CARE acronym of healthcare professionals working in FND

Letter	Represents	Details
F	Food fuel	Skipping lunch at work, eating an unhealthy and unbalanced diet without nutrients to save time, weight gain, consuming high-calorie foods.
N	Night rest	Unable to fall asleep or intermittently as worrying too much about the patients. Early morning waking due to feeling depressed about the complexity and emotional burden of the job.
D	Drugs and medications	Drinking alcohol more regularly, taking extra anti-anxiety tablets to self-medicate to cope with stress due to increased carer burden or work stress. Drinking too much caffeine or energy drinks.
S	Sickness and physical illness	Contracting more colds and flu, not taking care of yourself, feeling drained and burnt out, high levels of sickness absence and high staff turnover. Ignoring own health check-ups and lack of self-care strategies.
E	Equipment	In the same way as people with FND may sometimes become highly dependent on equipment and walking aids, a clinician can rely too much on their own standard "therapy equipment" and classic tools during the treatment of FND without using a flexible approach, due to anxiety about the patients and achieving psychological containment by reaching out to familiar tools.
L	Liquids and bladder functioning	Not hydrating yourself, not drinking enough water during the day or taking a break for a cup of tea.
F	Fight-or-Flight and Warning signs	Fight-or-flight response in, for example, healthcare workers: feeling heart palpitations, sweating, "funny feeling in the gut", butterflies when looking at how much work still needs to be done or before meeting a patient with FND.
C	Contacts	Visiting the GP more often because you feel unwell yourself. Developing somatoform/physical symptoms yourself (i.e. risk of development of FND symptoms is somewhat elevated in healthcare workers due to exposure to "symptom models").
A	Ability to take care of yourself	Neglecting yourself: not putting much effort into taking care of yourself or in your appearance.
R	Risks	Risks towards the patients with FND, for example systemic re-traumatisation. Risks towards the service if staff absences exhibit a more chronic pattern with staff attrition, other staff becoming overburdened and at risk of burn-out as they may need to carry some of the sick staff member's caseload, and patients with FND missing out on opportunities learning and practising new coping strategies that is intended to reduce FND symptoms.
E	Exercise, movement and physical activity	Dropping exercise classes due to fatigue, carer burden or overwork, reduced cardiovascular fitness in carers or professionals.

Table 7.5 Functions and consequences of team psychological safety behaviours

Team psychological safety behaviour	Functions	Consequences for care of people with FND and staff well-being
Abandoning care plans	• A coping strategy that helps a staff member to tolerate the distress of witnessing FND episodes. • Reduces the uncomfortable feeling that staff is rejecting the person with FND by withholding reassurance.	• Reciprocal reinforcement and maintenance of FND • Staff will not see how FND may decrease because they cannot get past the extinction burst where behaviour temporarily worsens. • Staff may have lack of coping strategies to manage the distress of witnessing FND episodes – abandoning care plans will prevent them from practising to tolerate this distress longer.
Trickery	• Placing boundaries by the staff member may be interpreted by the person with FND as "rejection". • Withholding the truth to not "hurt" the person with FND reduces discomfort in the staff member.	• Staff member does not learn to tolerate their own discomfort in placing boundaries and will struggle doing this with other people. • Lack of ethical approach to work: withholding the truth may have taken place in the person's early upbringing.
Reinforcing the power differential	• Provides the staff member with a sense of control and psychological containment over the FND, reduces their own feelings of loss of control in the situation.	• Systemic re-traumatisation: Person may feel patronised and rejected. • Due to a preserved and amplified complementary therapeutic relationship, the person with FND regresses even more, more dependency. • Person prevented from opportunities to independently practise adaptive coping skills.
Negative labelling, extremely aversive language	• External locus of control reduces discomfort in staff around own capabilities and skills in managing FND. • Blaming the person for lack of progress in therapy is less threatening to self-confidence and self-worth than "admitting" you are out of your depth.	• Systemic re-traumatisation: open communication of these labels to the person may re-traumatise the person and lead to feeling more rejected and not believed, in a similar way as during adverse childhood and adult life experiences. • Non-verbal communication driven by these labels instil a sense of hopelessness in the team that trickles down to the person with FND.
Going the extra mile/above and beyond	• Reduces anxiety and discomfort when the person with FND is not doing what you want or predict in a session.	• Overinvolved or overprotective caring reinforces FND.

(Continued)

Table 7.5 (Continued)

Team psychological safety behaviour	Functions	Consequences for care of people with FND and staff well-being
	• Reinforces the belief that we are helping to preserve the therapeutic relationship at all cost (clinician not wanting to be rejected or viewed as a poor clinician). • Convinces us that we will continue seeing upward progress in the person, in the light of the fluctuating nature of FND (as it may otherwise tell us we are poor clinicians).	• Burn-out in staff due to overwork and the mental energy this takes. • Negative impact on other patients in the clinic or ward who may miss out on care or may notice the extra effort that you put into the patient and feel rejected, increasing the potential risk of FND in other patients. • May restrict a person's choice of activities and increases dependency on the environment. • Takes away a person's belief in their own sense of agency; it reduces confidence and self-efficacy to manage their own FND.
"Tit-for-tat" retaliation and rejection behaviours	• Staff feeling rejected by the person with FND and unable to control their responses. • Driven by having been hurt/feeling rejected by the person with FND.	• Systemic re-traumatisation: the person feels rejected again, and this feeds into earlier rejection experiences.
Discharge or encouraging discharge	• Reduces anxiety, frustration and discomfort around not being able to manage the person with FND. • It is less threatening to staff self-confidence to discharge a person who is not progressing than keeping the person in the service and having to witness your lack of skill in "controlling" the person's FND.	• Disrupted attachments in a patient population that is already exposed to this to a higher degree. • Extra stress for patient and staff with managing endings and potential amplification of FND symptoms in the face of new broken attachments. • Increased emotional burden on person with FND when arriving at a new service: building new therapeutic relationships and having to get used to new team members with opening up and telling life story again.
Tinkering with sessions	• Form of avoidance or escape from the patient. • Reduces internal discomfort in staff. • Sharing emotional burden by doing lots of joint sessions.	• Rejection sensitivity in this group may be high and the person may feel "cheated" out of sessions leading to feelings of rejection and abandonment, particularly when comparing themselves with other people with FND attending the service. • Person misses out on full treatment and opportunities to practise new skills to address FND.
Team splitting	• Mirrors the person's split between psychological vs physical reasons for FND.	• Preserves and strengthens the mind-body distinction and rejection of psychological principles.

Team psychological safety behaviour	Functions	Consequences for care of people with FND and staff well-being
	• Splitting can emerge in different ways: • Within teams (multiple disciplines pitted against each other) • Between staff team vs person/family with FND. • Between staff team vs patients. • Factions within the patient group.	• The underlying psychological issues of FND are not addressed and the FND is maintained. • Disagreements between disciplines about the treatment plan resulting in the patient missing out on care. • RR: The non–split-off team members may further reinforce the split, due to their own lack of confidence in skills and anxiety about working in FND. The non–split-off position becomes evidence for the team member's good skills and reduces anxiety where in fact … • Patients may notice the poor integration of the team further reinforcing team splitting. • The issues can become apparent to the patients who may not ever had good role models of relationships and are now confronted with a similar situation, eroding trust in the treatment team.
Uni-disciplinary working: team defragmentation	• Stress-coping technique that creates psychological containment and a feeling of safety to hold on to something that is familiar to you, work with the disciplines you are familiar with during times of stress.	• Poor attendance at goal planning meetings may make the person with FND think it is because of them and feel more rejected. • Poor communication between disciplines, crucial clinical information may be missed, eroding patient care. • Repetition of clinical activities further burdening the patient who may already experience high levels of fatigue. • Uni-disciplinary working can reinforce splitting (and vice versa) between disciplines as disciplines working in silo and not in joint sessions have reduced awareness of what is being communicated between patients and other disciplines. • Lack of knowledge and awareness of each other's work and missing information can lead to disciplines unnecessarily challenging rather than collaborating with each other, including conflicts, clique forming and relationship breakdown.

(Continued)

Table 7.5 (Continued)

Team psychological safety behaviour	Functions	Consequences for care of people with FND and staff well-being
		• The lack of team cohesion may reinforce negative and potentially distorted views about other disciplines as due to a lack of integration and communication, hypotheses about each other are not being tested out.
Sickness absence	• Avoiding work to avoid the person with FND leads to a reduction in anxiety or frustration in the staff member.	• Staying away from work due to safety behaviours can result in a gradual mental check-out, leading to low staff morale, high staff turnover and longer waiting lists that are not cleared.
		• Due to staff absence, the remaining subset of team members becomes overburdened with work: risk of stress, burn-out, sickness absence and resentment in the rest of the team.
		• Incomplete MDTs become particularly problematic; for example, a patient in psychological therapy who is improving psychologically has further progress halted due to deconditioning and a lack of physiotherapist to learn helpful walking patterns. A person with FND may be attending a physiotherapy programme and suddenly emotional difficulties escalate but there is no psychologist in the team.
Direct/subtle avoidance	• Avoidance reduces own anxiety or anger felt towards the patient.	• Patient may perceive your avoidance or absence as rejection or abandonment, feeding into FND symptoms.
		• Patient loses out on crucial training and practise opportunities for coping skills.
		• Perpetuates your own negative beliefs and adverse feelings further eroding your care towards the patient without addressing or testing these out (systemic re-traumatisation).
Bargaining	• Reduction of aversive emotions.	• Strengthens the unhelpful bargaining behaviour in clinicians and the care-eliciting behaviour of patients.
		• Can take a lot of time – time not spent on other patients or clinical duties.

Team psychological safety behaviour	Functions	Consequences for care of people with FND and staff well-being
	• May make a clinician feel powerful or flattered and good about themselves as they manage a "difficult patient" who eventually "budges" because of the clinician's "skill".	• In the longer term may feel very effortful and draining to the clinician who may avoid the patient or become reluctant to provide care. Bargaining is not a sustainable strategy to convince a person.
Cynicism and sarcasm	• Rejection of the patient to feel better about yourself where in fact you may feel very de-skilled and low in confidence.	• Increases risk of systemic re-traumatisation. Even if these clinician behaviours take place outside the patient-provider relationship, non-verbal communication may still permeate through interactions. • May infect other staff members to treat people with FND in a similar way. • Could be a sign of burn-out.
Strong, selective patient-clinician attachments	• Patients and clinicians may form strong attachments with each other making the clinician feel good about themselves and "flattered" and the patient "contained". • In the end, it often serves as a strategy for reducing anxiety on both sides.	• Perpetuates false sense of confidence in clinician and psychological containment in patient. • Does not teach either clinician or patient more helpful ways of relating and anxiety-reduction techniques. • These selective attachments may risk splitting of teams, where some members are overvalued at the expense of other undervalued team members. • Other patients may feel singled out or rejected, leading to a potential increase in FND symptoms. • Emotional burden "to keep up" the attachment, and demands may become high, particularly on the clinician.

Complex case discussion: the Pressure Cooker method

In this section, we will look more closely at how the PCM can be used to run a complex case discussion. Table 7.6 shows two approaches that can be adopted.

Setting the scene

Good topics to discuss:

- Goals of the complex case discussion: planning interdisciplinary treatment, generate strategies for stuck patients, therapeutic catharsis, FND education. Ask the team what goals they would like to achieve.
- How confident does the team feel working in FND and what is their previous clinical experience working with people with FND?

Table 7.6 Complex case discussions in FND: two approaches

	Unstructured	Structured
Approach to PCM	Bottom-up	Top-down
Style	Slanted towards interactional – with room for education	Slanted towards educational – with room for interaction
FND experience and confidence level	For teams with more experience and confidence	For teams who are less experienced and low in confidence, who benefit from a structured approach
Psychological mindedness	• Psychologically minded teams that have some knowledge of models and principles • Teams that are used to the idea of a reflective space	• Teams who are open to psychology but are more "physical" and have not had much exposure to psychological principles • Teams that are very new and even reluctant towards psychology
"Pressure" level	• Low pressure • More time and "psychological headspace" available to reflect	• High pressure • Structure used as containment during high pressure crisis situations, where there is less "psychological headspace" for the team and strategies are needed more imminently

- How confident does the team feel working with a psychologically driven model and do they have a background or previous experience in mental health?
- Hopes and wishes for the complex case discussion. It is important for the team "to own the space" or it may feel as a forced exercise. Would they like to think more deeply about a person's and family formulation? Offer options if people are quiet.
- Set group rules in the same way as you would do for group therapy with service users, for example maintaining confidentiality about thoughts and feelings, rules around the use of mobile phones, encouraging people to share views but incorporate a "disclaimer" that no one has to share if not comfortable, trying to attend and arrive on time for the group session, respecting each other's opinions even if you disagree.

Case formulation: unstructured approach

In the following section, a new, tried-and-tested "bottom-up" multidisciplinary case reflection method on the basis of the Pressure Cooker Model will be outlined that can be used by teams working with people with FND. This new reflection method consists of the following phases (see Table 7.7).

Table 7.7 Complex case formulations in FND: unstructured approach

Phase	Details
Pre-complex case discussion	• Take some flipchart paper and coloured markers. • The group facilitator should have a "mental model" of the PCM in mind. • You can use different coloured markers, either to highlight the different layers, or to find out what elements were mentioned first and last, as this may have meaning (elements mentioned first may stand out more, whereas elements mentioned last or not at all may be avoided by the team).
Selection	Select a patient that is "stuck" in treatment or elicits strong negative feelings in the team.
Assemble	Assemble as many members of the team and any people interacting with the patient in one reflective group space: • To not miss any information • Cross-validate information between team members • Become aware of inconsistencies and splitting behaviours.
Live build-up of the patient's pressure cooker	Generate observational data, facts and information that stands out by the team members, in a "bottom-up" fashion. • [contents] Tell me what you know about the person and their family? • [process] What have you observed in your sessions with this person, their behaviours, comments? How does this person make you feel? Do you look forward to sessions or the opposite? • [functions] What do you make of that? • What else have you noticed? Are we missing any information? Could we find out from the patient? • As the information from the team starts to stream in, the facilitator writes the information on the empty flipchart paper and starts "live" creating the boxes of the PCM. • Information that cannot be easily integrated in the model can be put in a separate "miscellaneous" box in the corner of the paper, for later integration in the model. • The psychological model is progressively built up in a "live" fashion.
Generate hypotheses	Generation of multiple hypotheses and functions of the behaviours displayed by the patient. • Ask the team about their opinion and views on the functions of the FND • Internal regulation of emotions (keep in mind the FND maintenance cycle, layer 3) • External regulation of emotions (keep in mind the environmental and interpersonal factors, layer 5).
Enrich and deepen the formulation	The model may be further sophisticated as more data is generated by the team. Assimilate this new information into the model.

(Continued)

Table 7.7 (Continued)

Phase	Details
Transition to team pressure cooker	Reflect on the thoughts, feelings and behaviours that the patient generates in the team members • How does it feel working with this person? Their family? What thoughts and feelings come up? • What safety behaviours has the team noticed in themselves and in colleagues? • How has working with this person impacted on their own functioning in the team and in day-to-day life (review the FND SELF CARE – team version).
Live build-up of the team's pressure cooker	Complete a second model for the team reflecting on the formulation. • Focus on the team's pressure cooker – not the individual team member's pressure cooker, as this information is sensitive and personal (although encourage each individual team member to create their own pressure cooker formulation for themselves to review regularly). • What is the team's Overpressure Plug (safety behaviours, Layer 3). • What triggers the safety behaviours? Draw out the "conveyor belt" from trigger to safety behaviour. Draw a straight line with on one extreme the trigger(s) and on the other extreme the team safety behaviours. What steps are in between, what thoughts and feelings drive the safety behaviours in the team? • Generate hypotheses and functions of the behaviours displayed by the team (Layer 5).
Hybrid formulation	• Link the patient and team formulations up with a focus on increasing awareness and uncovering any maladaptive interpersonal cycles, reciprocal reinforcement and systematic re-traumatisation. Is there evidence for any of these systemic processes and person-system co-dysregulation? Does it maintain the FND in the patient?
Strategy generation	• Generation of practical strategies based on the entire formulation and plan a way forward in the treatment for everyone involved.
Strategy implementation and monitoring	• The complex case formulation is an ongoing, dynamic process. Monitor the implementation of strategies by reconvening regularly.

Case formulation: structured approach

Another complex case formulation approach using the PCM is to go "layer by layer" and make it a more structured approach.

Layer 1: Ignition

"Let's talk about the Ignition. What made this person vulnerable? Think about some of their early experiences".

Layer 2: the FND coping triad

"The FND coping triad" consists of three elements, do you remember which three again? Yes, that's right, it's the Sticky left-over food, Cover and the Valve. What element would you like to start with? Is there evidence of a typical FND-style of emotional coping present for the person? (refer to the three most common repeated early childhood strategies: keep self to self, abnormal activities and dissociation).

Layer 3: the Pressure Cooker Chain Reaction (FND maintenance cycle)

What does the chain reaction look like for this person? What is the mechanism of internal regulation? Let's start with the FND symptoms … the Fuel, what triggers have they reported during your session/what do their family note?/have you noticed on the ward? What can we tell about the person's Flames? Do you think this person exhibits dissociative tendencies? In what way? (e.g. language, the way the person talks about emotion or doesn't talk about emotions, any cognitive phenomena such as reported memory or concentration problems? (e.g. brain fog), do they display any behaviours that may suggest dissociation?). Is the person emotionally dysregulated? How does that present? If we pull Layer 2 and Layer 3 together, what do we notice? Does the person fit the PCM formulation?

Layer 4: Facilitating physical factors

Is there anything that we can say about the medico-contextual and facilitating physical factors in FND? (Display the long list of factors from the FND SELF CARE acronym). How is FND impacting on their day-to-day living, their walking, mobilising, accessing the community? Are there any risks? Is the equipment a psychological safety behaviour?

Layer 5: the Kitchen

With respect to environmental and interpersonal factors, what may be the mechanism of the person's strategy for external regulation? What do we know about the family and social situation? What may be the functions of the FND, for both the person and people close to them? Does the family contribute to any reciprocal reinforcement? In what way? How do they manage the dissociative episodes? What might be driving this? Go through layers 1–4. It is possible that not much is known about the family as services tend to be oversubscribed with long waiting lists, or the patient actively prevents the team from liaising with the family. However, it may be worth formulating at least Layer 5, and if there happens to be more information available about the family, then this can be populated in the rest of the formulation.

Bridge to Layer 5 of the team's pressure cooker formulation. Do we contribute to any reciprocal reinforcement or systemic re-traumatisation processes?

For example, when the person has an episode in the waiting room, how is this managed? How do you feel about this person, do you think these emotions filter through in verbal and non-verbal communications? Do you notice any of your own psychological safety behaviours (e.g. starting the session late?). Are there any FND mirrors present, both vertical and horizontal?

It is probably best not to go into personal layers such as individual team members' own coping triangles (layer 2) and their own upbringing (layer 1), in the context of team boundaries and the potential sensitive and personal nature of this information. However, you can encourage individual team members to think about these layers privately during the case formulation and see how this may contribute to their own responses to the person with FND. What is their own process of internal regulation? How do they cope with difficult thoughts and feelings? Give out PCM forms to individual members so they can take it with them and complete for themselves without sharing, as a reflection exercise.

Another solution is to think about the team's collective pressure cooker for these layers and elements. For example, layers 1, 2, 3 and 4 all lend themselves well for that. Layer 4 can be viewed as a self-care element for the team, which is very important when working in this field. It can act as a team building exercise to come up with ways to support each other. Brainstorm how the team can use self-care strategies.

Layer 3 can be enlightening for the team to learn that other members experience the same triggers, thoughts and feelings about the person and their own skills. The team can supportively challenge beliefs together. "How can we help [team member] challenge that belief?" Furthermore, safety behaviours may not previously have been obvious to the team, as some can be very subtle (e.g. delaying the moment you are starting your session), but the complex case discussion can help the team become more aware of their safety behaviours, their functions and their potential impact on maintaining FND (e.g. person with FND missing out on time and opportunities to practise coping skills, or feeling rejected, as other patients are observed to get the full time). You can praise the team for opening their covers by attending the complex case discussion. Challenge any thoughts around tight covers.

Team formulation stage

Both types of approaches eventually lead to a team formulation stage.

- If we look at the processes and elements, and we want to make things better for the person/we want to help the person recover from FND, where do you think should we try to intervene first? Have we tried that yet? Any problems? (resistance to psychology, dropping equipment, problems implementing routine). How can we support the person with this? Brainstorm strategies.

- What areas of the formulation have already been effective for this person. What did we do that helped recovery? Lists team successes.
- What areas are posing challenges? What strategies can we as a team apply? Careful that one discipline is not being singled out as the "culprit".
  - Emphasise that everyone in the team has a responsibility to work on that specific element.
  - Encourage the team to rally extra support for that discipline, for example by doing joint work, taking work out of their hands so they can focus on discipline-specific work.
  - Integrate all disciplines into the model, that is very important, so it becomes a "joined-up" formulation and the team can own the recovery process.

Common issues and solutions

See Table 7.8.

Table 7.8 Complex case formulations in FND: problems and solutions

Problem	Solutions
Low attendance	• Explore the underlying reasons: time–slot, location, staffing issues.
	• Move the group to a location that is highly accessible so that as many people can attend (e.g. ward instead off-ward).
	• Make the group regular. This way everyone has a chance to attend when possible.
Attendance by only junior staff or specific staff	Emphasise that the invitation is for everyone.
	Increase responsibility in individual team members by highlighting that everyone's attention in necessary as:
	• Important information may be missed
	• We don't want to repeat procedures and tests
	• To air feelings
	• FND is a product of the Person x Environment. Recovery is based on reviewing and addressing intra-individual and inter-individual processes.
People walking in and out	Allow this, particularly in busy services. People make an effort to come to the group and are clearly finding meaning.
Quiet people	Ask kindly and gently for their feedback, praise the person for their contribution, and don't push. Staff who do not share or express their views may need more trust in the group and may still highly benefit from the discussions.
People not reflecting on emotions	Model the expression of difficult thoughts and emotions in front of the team, start with yourself and telling them about your own "countertransference"
	Take into account that members from non-psychology disciplines have not had much exposure in the same way as psychologists and other mental health workers.

(Continued)

Table 7.8 (Continued)

Problem	Solutions
Difficulties applying the strategies following formulation	• Write down a summary on the agreed strategies and share with the team • Check in with the team how the application is going, without "monitoring" or "catching people out" and problem-solve any issues with the implementation, for example resistance from the patient or staff (e.g. withholding reassurance) • Role plays to practise skills, for example setting boundaries. Where you play the "staff member version 2.0" and the person plays the patient.
Team not open to formulation of a person	Explore how the space can be used otherwise. The fact that the team is present can be an important marker that they would like to be there. If unable to come up with topics of discussion, offer topics: • Questions about management of FND • Ideas they have and want to bring in • Worries and concerns about patients or staff dynamics • Complex patient that they prefer not to formulate "officially" but to air their own feelings about.
The space becomes a space for unconstructive venting	Although it is important to "vent", it is equally important that this process takes place in a constructive manner. There is also a risk that the space is taken over by venting. Allow venting but also actively note over-venting to the team and use this therapeutically to formulate a patient, by drawing up the team's pressure cooker. Starting a formulation can act as a prompt to draw the team's attention.
Splitting	Regular "FND walk-in clinics" are the antidote towards splitting behaviours. Encourage people to: • Bring ideas, questions and concerns that they have about the patient, family, other staff or the treatment. • Re-iterate the goals of the walk-in: • Meant to be a safe space to talk strategy about FND • It's not meant to monitor, assess or judge individual members. • Praise: "We are all doing a fantastic job at managing the episodes".
People using jargon that others don't understand	Make clear that in terms of knowledge on the person, the team starts at an equal plane and that it is important to use a shared language for everyone to understand.
Strong countertransference	Cultivate compassion for the child that the person with FND was, including their adverse experiences, thoughts, feelings and "survival" coping strategies that they must have felt at that time, and that they may be responding in "child mode" during interactions rather than adult mode.

Complex case discussion: example

The team's Fuel and Flames (i.e. thoughts and emotions that are triggered in individual team members by working with the person with FND) are converted into their own Overpressure Plug ("team psychological safety behaviours"), in the same way as a person with FND's emotions is converted into FND. This psychological conveyor belt starts with a trigger and ends with a safety behaviour as the "product"; however, there are many psychological steps that lie in between these points. The following section will discuss what may happen simultaneously on this conveyor belt for a person with FND and a team responsible for the treatment of the person.

Assessment

Background

Jaden was admitted to the ward for a period of rehabilitation in the context of functional paraplegia, tremors and dissociative episodes, with the latter symptom being his most prominent and bothersome.

Hypothesis #1: Panic attacks

Jaden's initial psychological assessment suggested a possible hypothesis of panic attacks that could explain the occurrence of his dissociative episodes (Figure 7.5).

Initially, the panic model (Clark, 1986) appeared to be consistent with many of the symptoms that Jaden reported. For example, he mentioned high levels of fear in the moment that were consistent with his catastrophic misinterpretations. It was also possible to incorporate his dissociative seizure

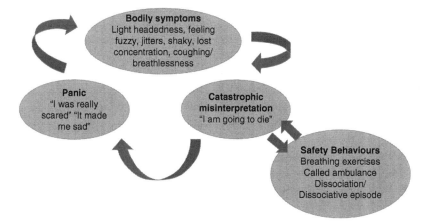

Figure 7.5 Jaden's panic disorder formulation based on Clark (1986).

symptoms into the panic formulation as a safety behaviour. As time went on and several of Jaden's other dissociative episodes were explored with him to plan his panic intervention, thought–belief inconsistencies started to emerge. In addition to fear, he also described feeling sad, which did not entirely match the belief in the panic cycle. Jaden associated his catastrophic misinterpretations mostly with feelings of sadness rather than anxiety, and it seemed that the panic formulation was no longer fitting Jaden's psychological and FND symptoms. Could Jaden experience depression instead?

Hypothesis #2: Depression

Therefore, the first hypothesis of panic attacks was temporarily paused in favour of a new, alternative hypothesis of depression, according to the Six Cycles Maintenance Model (Moorey, 2010). Jaden's vicious flower formulation looked as follows (Figure 7.6).

Although to some extent, Jaden's symptoms fit with a depression formulation, the model did not fully capture all the intricacies of his clinical presentation. For example, the nature of the relationship between Jaden's FND symptoms and depression was initially unclear. It was understandable that Jaden's FND caused him to feel low in mood as it came with significant disabilities, losses

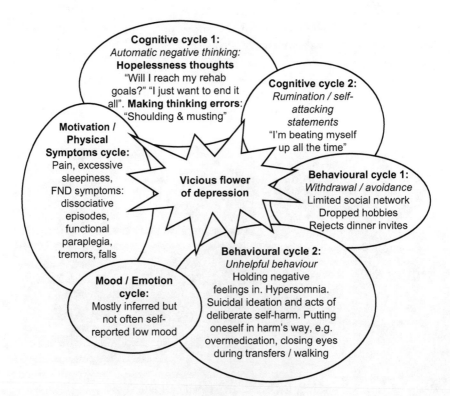

Figure 7.6 Jaden's vicious flower formulation of depression.

and restrictions to his day-to-day activities. However, the FND-depression relationship was harder to see in the other direction: How did the depression contribute or maintain the FND? What mechanism could account for this? Jaden mostly reported "surface level" negative automatic thoughts. If anything, it was unclear whether Jaden experienced depression at all. All the behavioural, cognitive and physical "hallmarks" appeared to be present but were not always consistently accompanied by self-reported feelings of depression and tearfulness, or beliefs around rejection and losses. This discrepancy could also suggest that Jaden was highly dissociated from his emotions.

Furthermore, one defining characteristic of Jaden's symptoms was their instability: the symptoms rapidly alternated on a weekly basis. In the first weeks of his admission, the dissociative episodes would be his most prominent symptom requiring seizure guidelines for his environment. The week after, the episodes stopped, but Jaden's rate of unwitnessed falls exponentially increased, prompting a falls risk assessment with staff becoming more careful in sessions. Over time, the falls became less frequent, but Jaden expressed feeling bothered by the intolerable levels of pain he was experiencing resulting in frequent interactions with the medical and psychological teams to help him manage the symptoms. Towards the end of his admission, Jaden expressed suicidal ideation with a well-formed plan and access to the means, necessitating a thorough risk assessment to help keep Jaden safe. The depression model struggled to account for the rapid changeability and a hypothesis about the underlying functions of these features. In addition, all of Jaden's symptoms shared a considerable risk of self-injury, sufficiently serious to require a range of different management plans and interventions, for example in response to sustaining bruises and wounds during dissociative episodes and falls that needed medical review and care.

Staff interactions

In the first few weeks of his admission, Jaden was settling in well on the ward and developed positive therapeutic relationships with most of the staff. However, as he progressed further into his admission, these positive staff attitudes towards Jaden started to change. Staff was making fun of Jaden's unusual way of managing daily tasks. In addition, during walking practice sessions, Jaden's manner of mobilising was risky and difficult to remediate, no matter what techniques were offered. The team was becoming increasingly frustrated with the lack of his progress. Although staff were not fully aware, the team was barely able to control their non-verbal language towards Jaden including negative facial expressions towards him; a cold and distant approach devoid of any compassion; and eye rolling at each other and deep sighing as he was practising his unusual form of walking in between the double bars. Jaden's dissociative episodes increased in frequency, and he subsequently expressed intent towards deliberate self-harm. The team branded Jaden as an "attention seeker" and manipulating the situation. Although several treatment goals were agreed with Jaden, some goals were "just" met, whilst others were too difficult to reach and stepped down to simpler goals. In the team's eyes, Jaden was doing just enough to stay in the rehabilitation process and not be discharged home. The team felt burnt out and highly frustrated with Jaden, which resulted in a lot of joint sessions "to carry the psychological burden", and staff avoiding Jaden, either by pulling out or terminating his sessions earlier. After several weeks, the team felt that Jaden had made minimal progress and that his small gains were plateauing. As a result, the team recommended early discharge.

Jaden's individual PCM formulation

As more information was coming to light that was increasingly harder to incorporate in the previous two standard CBT formulations of panic and depression, a PCM formulation was applied to Jaden's difficulties to determine whether this could more fully account for the entirety of his clinical picture including the rapidly alternating symptoms and plateauing of rehab (Table 7.9).

Table 7.9 Jaden's Pressure Cooker Model formulation

Kitchen

- Hypothesised *external regulation function* of the FND and other behaviours: FND was not the most prominent issue but part of a wider spectrum of "therapy-interfering behaviours" subsumed under the Overpressure Plug and hypothesised to function as a way to elicit care, soothing and comfort from the environment (the common denominator across all of Jaden's behaviours). Rather than considering each symptom individually, a more parsimonious hypothesis was able to explain the clinical manifestations all at once.
- Jaden's behaviours also tested the boundaries: would the team still care and be present for him, unconditionally, despite these behaviours?

Cover	Overpressure Plug	Valve
Jaden occasionally expressed difficult thoughts and emotions (e.g. anxiety, low mood), but mostly reported "surface level" negative automatic thoughts and emotions in response to what seemed to be "lower-level" stressors (e.g. being late for a session). As the therapeutic relationship became more established, Jaden reported feeling rejected, left out and to his own devices by staff – without reference to any clear emotions and without the ability and willingness to explore this further in sessions.	"Therapy-interfering behaviours" (as viewed by Jaden's treating team): - Dissociative episodes - Sudden tremors during sessions - Falls - Constant reports of pain - Deliberate self-harm/ suicidal ideation. - Putting oneself in harm's way (e.g. "carelessness" during walking) - Hypothesised *internal regulation function*: all behaviours shared features of active and passive self-harm, possible self-punishment or as an emotional release function.	- Jaden exhibited a blocked Valve: his activity levels were completely reduced and he mostly spent time indoors. Jaden did not engage in any enjoyable activities and had dropped many hobbies. His social network was limited to one friend and his immediate family who were also heavily involved in his care.

Warning light

- Jaden was highly preoccupied with his physical symptoms, which showed a tendency to switch in quality on a regular, almost weekly, basis.
- It was difficult to shift his attentional focus away from his physical towards psychological symptoms.

Flames

- He reported these negative emotions in response to lower-level stress triggers.
- Reported feeling rejected by staff.
- Expressed worries about the team thinking he was "putting symptoms on for attention", which fed back into his formulation: if people think he is putting this on, he risks being rejected and becoming a "social outcast" (his worst fear).

Heat

- Although Jaden occasionally expressed feeling distressed, he often struggled to label his emotions and appeared dissociated. He did not express emotions overtly.

Sticky left-over food

- Core beliefs were mostly unclear. Jaden did not share much about his inner world of thoughts and feelings, or his childhood.
- Jaden did report keeping himself to himself as a child.

Pot

- Jaden's risks of hurting himself, either passively or actively, increased substantially in response to the team's rejecting behaviours towards him, particularly for deliberate self-harm and falls.

Ignition

- Did not report any adverse childhood or traumatic events.
- Suspicion of emotional neglect or rejection by a key parental caregiver. Jaden did not disclose a lot about his early upbringing other than that he did not have a good relationship with his father. Details remained vague.
- Range of other rejection experiences, which may have been the "critical incidents" that set off the FND: break-up and fraught relationship with his ex-partner.

Fuel

- Interpersonal triggers: FND worse when around people or in group settings; perception of staff not caring about him (e.g. ignoring, just passing by him or not talking) or caring more about other patients.
- Interpersonal triggers seemed to relate to an amplification of FND symptoms.
- Due to his heightened rejection sensitivity in the context of his past experiences, Jaden likely perceived the team's therapist-interfering behaviours (e.g. being short with him) as major forms of rejection – to some extent rooted in reality.

Safety features

Jaden attended all his sessions and was very organised. He made friends with other peers on the ward and was able to form positive therapeutic relationships with a subset of staff.

Hybrid PCM team formulation

In a way, both Jaden and the team systemically "re-traumatised" each other: Jaden was re-traumatised by repeated rejection, first by a parental caregiver and now by professional caregivers. The team was re-traumatised by the repeated exposure and confrontation of their own psychological vulnerabilities around managing FND. Interestingly, both Jaden and the team experienced the same beliefs and emotions: rejection. This case highlighted the

Table 7.10 Pressure Cooker Model formulation of Jaden's treating team

Kitchen

- The social functions of the team's unhelpful "therapist-interfering" behaviours towards Jaden appeared to serve to (1) reject and create a psychological and physical distance from his "therapy-interfering" behaviours, (2) communicate the adverse nature of Jaden's behaviours directly to him, in a non-verbal way, in the presence of a tight team cover, and (3) retaliation towards Jaden for creating more emotional burden, taking up resources and time. Despite the team's care and compassion, several members grew tired and felt drained by Jaden's behaviours.

Cover	Overpressure Plug	Valve
• Unconstructive venting in the team room on a daily basis. Emotions vented in inappropriate and unproductive ways. • None of the team members discussed the challenging behaviours displayed by Jaden or by themselves. The impact of the behaviours was not discussed with Jaden: the team's cover remained tight.	• Therapist-interfering behaviours: eye rolling, sighing, display of angry facial expressions in sessions, avoiding sessions, doing a lot of joint sessions to share the emotional burden, not planning in as many sessions as for other patients, heavily encouraging discharge. • Splitting behaviours present (1) within the MDT between individual members working with Jaden; (2) between MDT vs nursing team; and (3) between MDT vs patients on the ward.	• Frequent "spill-over" of sessions with Jaden at the expense of other patients' sessions. • Boom Valve: team stayed on longer at work to manage Jaden's behaviours, which adversely impacted on their work-life balance.

Warning light	Sticky left-over food	Pot
• High focus on Jaden's symptoms manifesting as the team speaking a lot about his symptoms during multidisciplinary meetings, overspilling into other patients' slots. Jaden was often on the team's mind: three reflective sessions were organised with a fourth session planned.	Team's negative core beliefs re: working with FND + individual members' early coping strategies • "We are not good enough managing Jaden's behaviours and his recovery from FND". • Team culture: "keeping self to self" in relation to difficult thoughts and feelings about patients.	• Sickness absence rates went up, team started to feel burnt out. • Risk of retaliation towards Jaden increased. • Individual team members were not taking good care of themselves: poor sleep, drinking more alcohol during the week to deal with stress, little time to have a nutritious lunch at work.

Ignition

Jaden's team was relatively new to FND and rotational, spending six to nine months on the unit without any prior FND experience to fall back on. Team members tended to be from physical disciplines with little mental health supervision or knowledge and generally felt de-skilled working with FND patients. *Critical incident:* Jaden's arrival on the ward.

Flames

• Anger, frustration, anxiety about witnessing lack of progress in rehab. Rejection by Jaden towards any strategy conjured up by the team to engage/support Jaden in rehab. Team feeling rejected by Jaden.

• Lack of self-confidence and feeling loss of control about ability to manage Jaden's FND.

• Feeling guilty towards other patients for not spending as much time and effort on their treatment, compared to Jaden's.

Heat

• High Heat: The team's level of discomfort and emotion dysregulation around working with Jaden was strong.

Fuel

Jaden's therapy-interfering behaviours represented the Fuel for the team's therapist-interfering behaviours (subsumed under the Overpressure Plug). Therefore, in the same vein as Jaden, the team's behaviours were driven by interpersonal triggers.

Safety features

Jaden's treating team showed a keen willingness to engage in group reflections, resulting in four reflective sessions in total, the highest number in the team's history. This showed the emotional burden that the team was feeling in response to treating Jaden's difficulties. Although the reflective sessions were characterised by a lot of emotional expression and had a restorative function, the team felt at a loss in terms of generating strategies to manage Jaden's behaviours and implement in day-to-day clinical practice.

power of reciprocal reinforcement in maintaining FND symptoms and provided recommendations for intervention, both for the patient and for the team (Table 7.10 and Figure 7.7).

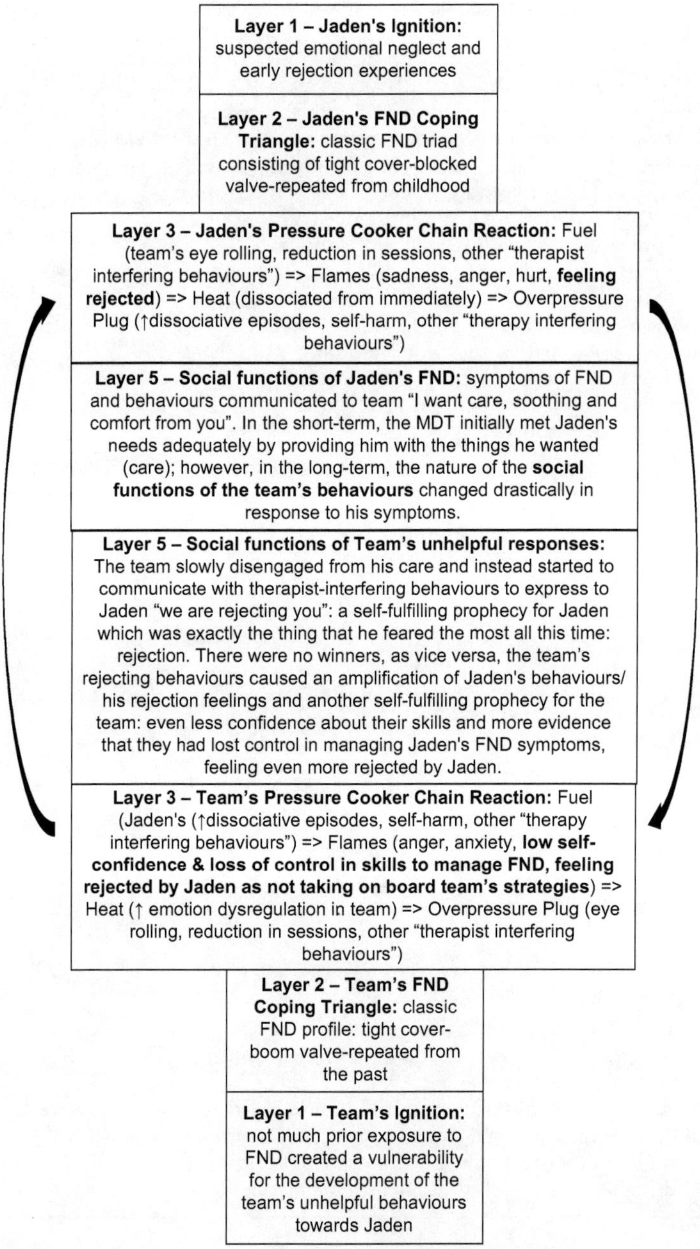

Layer 1 – Jaden's Ignition: suspected emotional neglect and early rejection experiences

Layer 2 – Jaden's FND Coping Triangle: classic FND triad consisting of tight cover-blocked valve-repeated from childhood

Layer 3 – Jaden's Pressure Cooker Chain Reaction: Fuel (team's eye rolling, reduction in sessions, other "therapist interfering behaviours") => Flames (sadness, anger, hurt, **feeling rejected**) => Heat (dissociated from immediately) => Overpressure Plug (↑dissociative episodes, self-harm, other "therapy interfering behaviours")

Layer 5 – Social functions of Jaden's FND: symptoms of FND and behaviours communicated to team "I want care, soothing and comfort from you". In the short-term, the MDT initially met Jaden's needs adequately by providing him with the things he wanted (care); however, in the long-term, the nature of the **social functions of the team's behaviours** changed drastically in response to his symptoms.

Layer 5 – Social functions of Team's unhelpful responses: The team slowly disengaged from his care and instead started to communicate with therapist-interfering behaviours to express to Jaden "we are rejecting you": a self-fulfilling prophecy for Jaden which was exactly the thing that he feared the most all this time: rejection. There were no winners, as vice versa, the team's rejecting behaviours caused an amplification of Jaden's behaviours/ his rejection feelings and another self-fulfilling prophecy for the team: even less confidence about their skills and more evidence that they had lost control in managing Jaden's FND symptoms, feeling even more rejected by Jaden.

Layer 3 – Team's Pressure Cooker Chain Reaction: Fuel (Jaden's (↑dissociative episodes, self-harm, other "therapy interfering behaviours") => Flames (anger, anxiety, **low self-confidence & loss of control in skills to manage FND, feeling rejected by Jaden as not taking on board team's strategies**) => Heat (↑ emotion dysregulation in team) => Overpressure Plug (eye rolling, reduction in sessions, other "therapist interfering behaviours")

Layer 2 – Team's FND Coping Triangle: classic FND profile: tight cover-boom valve-repeated from the past

Layer 1 – Team's Ignition: not much prior exposure to FND created a vulnerability for the development of the team's unhelpful behaviours towards Jaden

Figure 7.7 Hybrid patient-team formulation "Robot".

Table 7.11 shows Jaden's results on a range of outcome measures. At the end of his admission, Jaden self-reported high levels of depression and anxiety. Although the team felt that Jaden was 'putting this on' in order to stay at the rehabilitation facility, given the earlier reflections on the contributions of the team's behaviours to Jaden's symptoms, it is equally likely that Jaden's "iatrogenic" rejection experiences resulted in a deep depression and that he felt not ready for discharge due to an anxiety-provoking "real world". Jaden's challenging behaviours overshadowed this alternative interpretation of his scores.

Although the admission did not result in any significant gains for Jaden and he was discharged with a package of care, his time in the inpatient environment was not deemed as a failed discharge as it enabled the team to gather converging evidence for his presentation, create a formulation by "joining the dots" and linking the different behaviours as serving one function, and signpost him to better suited services (secondary care services). It was not until Jaden was introduced into an interpersonal environment that the narrative around his symptoms became more apparent. Had Jaden not been admitted, no one in the community might have been able to pull all the information together and formulate Jaden's difficulties. This information was

Table 7.11 Jaden's scores on psychology and neurorehabilitation measures

Questionnaire	Measures	Admission	Discharge
PHQ-9	Depressive symptoms	N/A	26 (severe depression)
GAD-7	Anxiety symptoms	N/A	21 (severe anxiety)
HADS-A	Anxiety	N/A	18 (severe anxiety)
HADS-D	Depression	N/A	16 (severe depression)
UK FIM+FAM*	Captures the level of disability and dependency		
• Motor		81	94
• Cognitive		79	81
• Total		160/210	175/210
Modified Barthel Index*	Functional independence in activities of daily living and mobility	13/20	18/20
Neurological Impairment Scale**	Measures a variety of physical, cognitive, affect, communication and behavioural impairments	24/50	17/50
Rehabilitation Complexity Score***	Care needs	13/22	14/22

*Higher scores suggest more independence; **higher scores suggest more severe impairment; ***higher scores mean more care needs.

Table 7.12 Systemic strategies based on the PCM

PCM element	Healthcare professionals	Family and friends
Ignition/Fuel	• A powerful tool to help cultivate and develop compassion and empathy in the team or family towards the person with FND is to explain the link between early rejection experiences (e.g. emotional neglect, abuse), the lack of opportunity to learn helpful coping mechanisms early in life (e.g. emotional expression, building psychologically safe relationships), the necessity of learning survival strategies (e.g. keep self to self), their relationship to current symptoms and care-seeking responses in people with FND, and the notion of feeling cared for as a basic human need that is met in unhelpful ways.	
Flames	• Highlight that patient, family and team all experience the same psychological phenomena – with or without FND. • Normalise common beliefs and emotions in families of FND patients, to help open up a dialogue (e.g. feeling powerless in managing seizures). The person's family is often neglected and not always heard. • Label staff/family feelings in reflective meetings – especially in teams and families that have historically not had much exposure to "emotion labelling". • Explore the family's feelings (and responses) when seeing a loved one experiencing an FND episode or exacerbation, to unearth reciprocal reinforcement patterns.	
Heat	• Provide psycho-education on dissociation, as well as on mirroring mechanisms. • Sometimes a seed needs to be planted and it may take a while for the person to progress. Gains may not be evident immediately. The time between starting treatment and witnessing results may be long, protracted and intolerable, and often requires both the team and family to "sit with the distress" – exactly in the same way that a person with FND will have to "sit with the distress" and stop it from progressing to a seizure. Explore with both systems what distress tolerance strategies can be applied.	
Pot	• FND SELF CARE strategies – similar to those provided to people with FND.	
Sticky left-over food	• Team positive qualities log exercise to build positive team core beliefs: strengths of the team treating FND. • Highlight achievements in the team, for example joint session that went well, positive feedback from a family member praising the team's efforts. • Highlight past treatment successes to show the evidence that the team possesses positive treatment qualities that have clearly worked well in the past, for example recovered patient.	• Family positive qualities log: what are the strengths of the family that can be utilised to develop healthier ways of relating? • Psycho-education on early coping strategies that repeat into adulthood. • Highlight positive experiences in the family unit or relationship.
Cover/sealing ring	• **Opening the Cover:** Encourage "emotion talk" and regular verbal emotional expression in staff and family. Plan in regular team reflective practice and family meetings to achieve the goal of practising emotional expression in a psychological safe space, as well as to manage thoughts and feelings that may drive unhelpful behaviours to patients with FND. • Environmental structuring may be helpful: encourage staff and family to encourage emotion talk with the person with FND.	

PCM element	Healthcare professionals	Family and friends
Valve	• **Watch out for the three Valve profiles** in staff members and whether these mirror or complement patient Valves. • Ensure appropriate work-life balance in teams; for example, staff leaves work in time and attends enjoyable and social activities in their personal life. • **Create social belonging and team cohesion.** Organise team activities that do not focus on FND or the job roles, for example an exercise programme, socials, team building away days.	• Explore family activities that increase cohesion and a sense of belonging. • Respite for main carer of person with FND to allow the 'carer' to pursue individual interests, hobbies, enjoyable activities, other meaningful relationships and meet own personal needs. • Explore the three different Valve profiles in the family unit and whether complementary patterns exist.
Warning light	• Raise insight and help team members making each other aware of heightened focused attention on the patient (including triple reinforcement, "systemic hypervigilance"). • Encourage staff and family with applying re-focusing strategies to support the patient to shift attention away from symptoms.	
Overpressure Plug	• Raise insight into unhelpful behaviours towards people with FND including avoidance, unempathetic responses, overinvolvement and how this may result in **reciprocal reinforcement** and **systemic re-traumatisation**. • Increase team confidence in calling out colleagues if unhelpful behaviours are amplified (now you know that this only perpetuates FND and is therefore a sensible course of action).	• Raise insight into the family's unhelpful responses to the person with FND, for example reassurance, taking away chores and reducing the person's independence, and their impact on maintaining FND.
The Kitchen	**Team support** • Ongoing staff training opportunities (particularly for rotational and bank staff) to increase insight into own contribution to FND and maintaining the rejection experiences and symptoms of people with FND. • Focus the FND education on early intervention, for example clinical psychology, allied health and medical students. • Systemic modelling of these behaviours for other healthcare workers to start managing systemic re-traumatisation.	**FND family education sessions** • Family involvement part and parcel of the treatment programme, from the start. • Organise these meetings regularly rather than a one-off session. • Use these sessions to model healthy relationships with appropriate boundaries.

subsequently handed over to Jaden's community team and GP. Jaden's lack of progress in neurorehabilitation also raised many questions about the damaging impact of patient–team interactions on his persistent FND symptoms.

Systemic strategies

In addition to applying the PCM formulation on your own specific situation, Table 7.12 shows a few more general systemic strategies that may support healthcare professionals and family members in managing their own thoughts, feelings and behaviours to help manage FND symptoms in the person that they have a therapeutic or personal relationship with.

Cultivating compassion: a team exercise

Lack of compassion or compassion fatigue for people with FND is very common, both in FND-specialist and in generic services that occasionally or regularly encounter people with FND (e.g. accidents and emergencies departments). We learned in Chapter 3 that the risk of systemic re-traumatisation is a real risk and crucially maintains FND. One strategy to help counter systemic re-traumatisation is the cultivation of compassion. The following exercise may be useful, particularly for teams that may have some exposure to FND patients but have insufficiently been briefed or learned about the mechanisms of FND (Table 7.13).

Table 7.13 Compassion exercise for teams working with FND

Imagine you receive the following referral:	What are your first thoughts, feelings, clinical and personal impressions? Be honest!
You receive a referral: • 26 year old woman • Drop attacks: 10x a week, each lasting 20 minutes, shaking , on the floor, crying, with accidental self-injury, recovery time: 2-3 days • Host of medical investigations/ seen by two neurologists, pain specialists • Recent visit to Epilepsy Centre for video telemetry for differential diagnosis epilepsy vs non-epileptic seizures. • Whilst in centre, experienced multiple drop attacks. • No accompanying abnormal EEG patterns. Diagnosis: Dissociative seizures • GP / Accidents & Emergency visits: regular • Called ambulance several times this year, on average monthly frequency • Not working, not driving due to seizures • On benefits	People will often not say anything. Be aware that this in itself may be a response and could suggest strong negative beliefs and emotions about the case example that are too negative to express to other people and may cause anxiety, shame or embarrassment about how one is perceived by other colleagues. Example thoughts: • "She sounds complex", "So many health services are involved", "Heart sink" • "Ridiculous that she's taking up services where in fact people with heart attacks and strokes lose out"

- "Oh dear, here we go again, looks like a standard referral, I feel exhausted already"
- "Benefits, wonder whether there are any secondary gains, she's putting the symptoms on to obtain money"

You have now had some time to get to know the patient a little bit better. You have completed your assessment and your new findings are in red.

You receive a referral:

- 26 year old woman
- Drop attacks: 10x a week, each lasting 20 minutes, shaking, on the floor, crying, with accidental self-injury, recovery time: 2-3 days
- Longstanding sexual, physical, emotional abuse and neglect by mother and stepfather with alcohol addiction, emotional and physical needs not met, put herself into care by the age of 13.
- Host of medical investigations/ seen by two neurologists, pain specialists
- Recent visit to Epilepsy Centre for video telemetry for differential diagnosis epilepsy vs non-epileptic seizures. Whilst in centre, experienced multiple drop attacks.
- Slight voice change of the doctor who assessed her re -triggered early abuse experiences: feelings of not being listened to and emotional needs not met.
- No accompanying abnormal EEG patterns. Diagnosis: Dissociative seizures
- GP / Accidents & Emergency visits: regular
- No support network, lives alone, social isolation and mostly spends time indoors
- Called ambulance several times this year, on average monthly frequency
- Not working, not driving due to seizures
- On benefits
- She greatly enjoyed her previous job as a shop assistant and would love to go back but seizures stand in the way

What are your thoughts, feelings, clinical and personal impressions now? If you compare these with the thought contents and feelings you experienced earlier before knowing the newly acquired clinical information: is there a difference and if so, what do you think are the underlying reasons for "the shift" in your thinking about this case? If nothing has changed in your thinking, what may be the underlying reasons and what could help you become more compassionate towards this patient group – bearing in mind that systemic re-traumatisation is a real risk for maintaining FND?

Positively rebuilding FND Theory of Mind

Earlier in Chapter 7, we discussed the concept of healthcare professionals' thoughts and emotions about *themselves in relation to the person with FND*. Lack of confidence and self-efficacy is common in healthcare professionals treating FND and can be powerful forces behind unhelpful behaviours directed towards people with FND. Unhelpful team thinking processes can be actively challenged (Table 7.14).

Management of team splitting in FND

"Joined-up" working

Encourage a joined-up working approach. Use the PCM assessment template to collect information from multiple disciplines. Create a shared, cohesive, multidisciplinary narrative using the PCM formulation to map out and guide the intervention. As a team, stay in regular contact via handovers or any correspondence. Monitor any comments made by patients and families and

Table 7.14 Rebuilding FND Theory of Mind: examples of rational beliefs

Common irrational beliefs	Replace with rational beliefs
I am not able to utilise my full/usual set of skills (e.g. standard CBT models, physiotherapy techniques).	I have been using adapted versions of standard techniques and have diversified my practice with more creative approaches. This shows that I am a versatile clinician.
I worry that the person is not making the gains that I normally see in people with more organic presentations such as stroke/brain injury/or psychological presentations (e.g. depression/panic disorder)…"I must be doing something wrong", "The patient is at fault and being difficult".	FND often has a fluctuating course, which tends to be markedly different from that observed in organic conditions. Given this, it's important for me not to have the same expectations around progress in people with FND compared to people with organic conditions.
	The fluctuating pattern of peaks and troughs often gets ascribed to either the patient or the therapist. The therapist feels like they have failed and responsible when the patient has a set-back. But it's a two-way street.
Reduced self-efficacy, I feel de-skilled, I doubt myself, I am not confident, I question my own abilities about managing FND. I don't know what I'm doing. My confidence levels are low in managing the patient's FND.	I have built up some experience working with FND patients and have had some success helping people to recover. This is the evidence against my low self-confidence beliefs.
	Normalise common beliefs and emotions found in healthcare professionals in relation to people with FND and feelings about their own abilities to manage FND.
I worry that the person relapses, experiences a set-back or shows fluctuations in symptoms during my treatment *[and that this will say something about me, that I am an incapable clinician]*.	Treatment of FND is always multidisciplinary and a two-way street: recovery is the responsibility of both the person with FND and the team. Therefore, even if the person relapses, I cannot ascribe the reasons entirely to myself.
The person has not achieved their goals/ the person still has FND/the person had a set-back/the person's FND symptoms are not abating…I have not achieved anything either. "I must get the person better or else I have not achieved anything in treatment".	Factors outside the person (family) may account for the stalling of progress. For example, due to existing service structures, there is not always time in services to address family factors.

Common irrational beliefs	Replace with rational beliefs
My actions are making/going to make the person worse (e.g. withdrawing support to promote independence).	My actions may indeed make the person worse initially, and this may make me feel sad and guilty towards the person. However, this is only often temporary and will benefit them in the long run, helping them to live their lives to the full. I will be helping them on their road to recovery.
The person is doing well with my other colleagues but not in my sessions, what's going on?	The thoughts and feelings I am experiencing are very normal and nothing to be fearful or ashamed of. Just because my other colleagues do well with the patient doesn't mean I'm doing something wrong. It may well be that I'm pushing the right buttons with the patient who may be resisting my treatment.
I feel distressed seeing the person in distress.	I am only human and there is nothing wrong about experiencing emotions in response to someone else's distress. This shows that I am compassionate and caring.

record verbatim. Encourage all team members to be present for multidisciplinary team or goal planning meetings, not just a selective part of the team, as this can create further splitting.

"Joint" working: create and demonstrate unity

Be mindful of the risks involved in joint working, particularly by reviewing your underlying intentions: are you certain joint working is not a psychological safety behaviour? Would this help or hurt the patient? In splitting situations, undertaking joint sessions between the "accepted and valued" and "split-off and devalued" team members may be very powerful to communicate unity. Openly and consistently back the split-off team member as a core member of the team, and encourage this in other team members to create a unified front, particularly in sessions where the split-off member is not present. Another useful strategy is to learn about or have working knowledge about each other's disciplines and communicate this "transdisciplinary" knowledge to the person with FND. This will demonstrate more unity. Examples of useful phrases include the following: "We work as one team", "We discuss your treatment within the team", "Details from one session trickle down to other disciplines eventually, this is essential to support you in the best way possible", "All disciplines are core to your treatment including [split off discipline]".

Manage your emotions

Ensure that you address the splitting with the patient in a compassionate and gentle way. This is to make the person aware that you are aware, as well as to demonstrate that splitting behaviours are talked about within the team and will eventually trickle down to the split-off person. Compassion is also important to ensure the person does not feel rejected. Provide a safe space for team members to reflect and express emotions about the splitting behaviour, which has the potential to cause psychological injuries, particularly in team members who are not necessarily mental health–trained.

Sharing team reflection

The question arises whether a team formulation about the person with FND should be shared with the person themselves. It is indeed recommended that the formulation is shared in the name of transparency and honesty – two values that the person with FND may not have been exposed to as part of adverse childhood experiences. Sharing the formulation needs to be done sensitively and when the person is psychologically ready. Sensitively means using kind and compassionate language and keeping in mind systemic re-traumatisation. The team shares this formulation, and each team member can explore this with the person. Although the psychologist will often lead and "deliver" the formulation, it does and should not be the sole responsibility of the psychologist as it can cause team splitting and make therapy more difficult for the psychologist. The team should take responsibility and ownership of the formulation. In the spirit of the PCM, the person with FND should be provided with an opportunity to complete their formulation on their environment including family and healthcare professionals. The focus should not be on the person entirely.

8 Using the Pressure Cooker Model alongside CBT models

In previous chapters, we could see the flexibility of the PCM. This model was used as a standalone model that could be applied on patients, family and staff, as well as in a multidisciplinary context representing the different professions involved in the treatment of FND.

In recent years, CBT models or models based on CBT principles have become the mainstay of treatment in FND, both in clinical practice and as part of research trials. Although CBT has proven to be effective for people with FND, particularly investigated in dissociative seizures (e.g. Goldstein et al., 2010; LaFrance et al., 2014; Cope et al., 2017), we have also seen the drawbacks of using CBT, which were outlined in Chapter 1. In this current chapter, we will explore three different relationships between the PCM and CBT models: adjunct, integrated and preparatory. What will become clear from this review is that standard CBT models may prove to be too simplistic to capture the complexity of FND and that the PCM is crucial to understanding and treating FND, warranting a place in clinical practice.

CBT as a standalone model (CBT – PCM)

If during the initial assessment, classic CBT cognitions are encountered that have a good fit to a condition-specific CBT model, it is worth investigating further whether the CBT model can be applied instead of the PCM. As you gather more data and you continue to test your initial hypothesis about this CBT model, you become more convinced that this CBT model is still the right fit for treating the person's psychological difficulties. Sometimes, it is evident that a person with FND needs a CBT model, and it is clinically the correct decision to select and treat the person's difficulties using that CBT model. The following case study will illustrate the use of CBT in a person with FND without resorting to the PCM.

Case study 1: Motor-type FND in a person with obsessive-compulsive disorder

Josh presented with functional tremors and arm weakness that started approximately three years ago after an altercation at a gas station with another

DOI: 10.4324/9781003308980-8

motorist. This resulted in a fight; Josh sustained several punches to the head but did not lose consciousness or his memory. Both individuals were taken into hospital for further treatment. All brain scans came back normal, and Josh was diagnosed with FND.

Although Josh initially exhibited PTSD symptoms following the altercation, these had dissipated at the time of his assessment. During the assessment, Josh struggled to define his current psychological difficulties that he needed help with and described vague "concentration problems" as his most bothersome symptoms. Josh worked in a retail shop and would try to concentrate on a task and then went into a "state of trance", as if he was "frozen in time". He described this state as not being able to go back and unable to go forward, as if he was "encapsulated" and "locked in my body". He did not identify any thoughts, and if asked to move on from this state, this would cause high levels of anxiety. The concentration difficulties had a negative impact on his functioning at work and in his relationship. His sickness absence record had changed dramatically, and the problems at work strained his marriage. Josh' presentation was consistent with obsessive-compulsive disorder.

Figure 8.1 shows the obsessive-compulsive disorder (OCD) formulation (Salkovskis, 1985). In the retail shop, Josh would often experience self-doubt and worries about coming across as incompetent during the completion of work tasks, resulting in anxiety. To reduce his anxiety and avoid his worst fear from happening (coming across negatively), Josh engaged in compulsions (e.g. devote extensive levels of concentration and perfectionism to the tasks) and safety behaviours (e.g. dithering at home and arriving late at work even though this was a self-fulfilling prophecy and made him come across as inadequate to his colleagues). The more concentration Josh applied, the more tremor and arm weakness emerged. These FND symptoms appeared to be a direct consequence of Josh' compulsions of deep thinking and concentrating. The compulsions, safety behaviours and attentional bias on his symptoms maintained the FND and did not allow him to test out his worst fear of looking incompetent. Josh himself felt his fears were irrational.

The OCD maintenance cycle was subsequently "contextualised" and embedded within a longitudinal framework of depression (Beck Judith, 1995). Josh' worst fear of coming across as incompetent stemmed from negative school experiences due to his learning difficulties. His teachers were disrespectful and regarded him as a "failure". Importantly, Josh maintained that it was not the altercation that started his difficulties but rather the disrespectful and condescending manner in which he was treated afterwards by the police officers and the doctors at the hospital that resembled his teacher' responses in childhood and that re-triggered his deeply held core belief ("I'm a fool/inadequate").

Josh engaged and progressed well in his treatment and applied all strategies (see Figure 8.1). The OCD model was clearly capable of accommodating the FND symptoms without difficulty. Although Josh shared some "systemic" issues in his relationship, these did not seem to directly impact on the FND and certainly did not explain most of "the variance" in Josh'

Table 8.1 Josh' scores on psychological questionnaires

Questionnaire	Post-therapy	Interpretation (discharge)
CORE-OM	24 (out of 136)	Just within the "low-level" range
HADS-anxiety	3 (out of 21)	Normal
HADS-depression	4 (out of 21)	Normal
WSAS	12 (out of 40)	Just within the "significant functional impairment" range, nearly subclinical
ATSQ	7 (out of 35)	Low level of self-focused attention
FFMQ – Short Form	• Non-reactivity (7, $z = 3.3$) • Observation (18, $z = 1$) • Aware actions (25, $z = 2.9$) • Description (23, $z = 1.3$) • Non-judgemental (25, $z = 1.7$)	All scores were found to be within normal limits, except for non-reactivity
DERS-SF	Mean: 2.06	$z = .10$ (within normal limits)

CORE-OM, Clinical Outcomes in Routine Evaluation – Outcome Measure; HADS, Hospital Anxiety and Depression Scale; WSAS, Work and Social Adjustment Scale; ATSQ, Attention-to-Symptoms Questionnaire; FFMQ-SF, Five-Facet Mindfulness Questionnaire – Short Form, based on Bohlmeijer et al. (2011) norms; DERS-SF, Difficulties in Emotion Regulation Scale – Short Form.

FND. At the end of therapy, Josh expressed "extreme satisfaction" with the treatment, went back to work in a full-time capacity, picked up enjoyable activities and viewed himself as fully symptom-free, in terms of both the psychological distress and the FND ("100% improvement"). He did not see any reason to further explore any interpersonal mechanisms of the FND, and it was mutually agreed to end the therapy. Table 8.1 shows Josh' results on a range of measures that assessed various FND-related features. NB. Due to embarrassment about his learning difficulties at the start of therapy, Josh had not completed any questionnaires. At the end of therapy, Josh felt more confident engaging with and completing the questionnaires, with the support of his psychologist (Figure 8.2).

PCM as an adjunct model to CBT (CBT+)

As in case study 1, another subset of people with FND will present with clear cognitions and emotions that are highly consistent with an evidence-based CBT model. As the therapy progresses, other interpersonal triggers for the FND may emerge that may benefit from formulating with the PCM. However, the impact of these triggers on the FND or day-to-day life is relatively minimal compared to the primary problem that the person is being treated for with CBT. The treatment of FND in the next case study followed these lines.

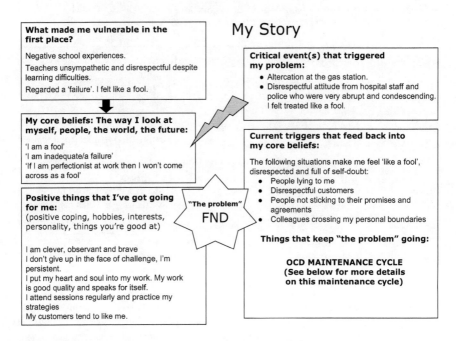

Figure 8.1 Longitudinal formulation of obsessive-compulsive disorder in FND.

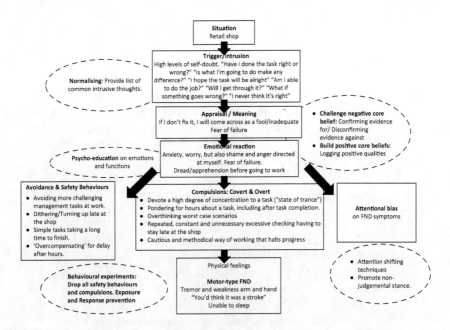

Figure 8.2 Obsessive–compulsive disorder maintenance cycle in FND.

Case study 2: functional dystonia and tremor in a person with social anxiety

Ethan is a 54-year-old man who developed FND approximately 15 years ago following the loss of an important "substitute" parental figure in his life and feeling pain in his back. He stayed indoors for long periods, sometimes for six weeks at a time, and developed severe agoraphobia and social anxiety. Ethan dropped all his hobbies, and his only outing involves shopping with his family. Despite the long course of FND, Ethan was "treatment-naïve"; no one had picked up on the social anxiety before, and as a result, Ethan had never accessed appropriate support to address the social anxiety. Ethan's difficulties were formulated using a slightly FND-adapted CBT model for social anxiety (Clark & Wells, 1995; see Figure 8.3).

Therapy consisted of socialisation to the social anxiety model with Ethan completing several formulations on different feared social situations, creating a social situations hierarchy, and conducting a series of behavioural experiments where he dropped his safety behaviours that tested out his social fears (Table 8.2).

Following therapy for social anxiety and a significant reduction of the motor-type FND, therapy revealed additional interpersonal triggers associated with worsening of the motor features. This was formulated using the PCM. It was concluded with Ethan that these interpersonal triggers, although

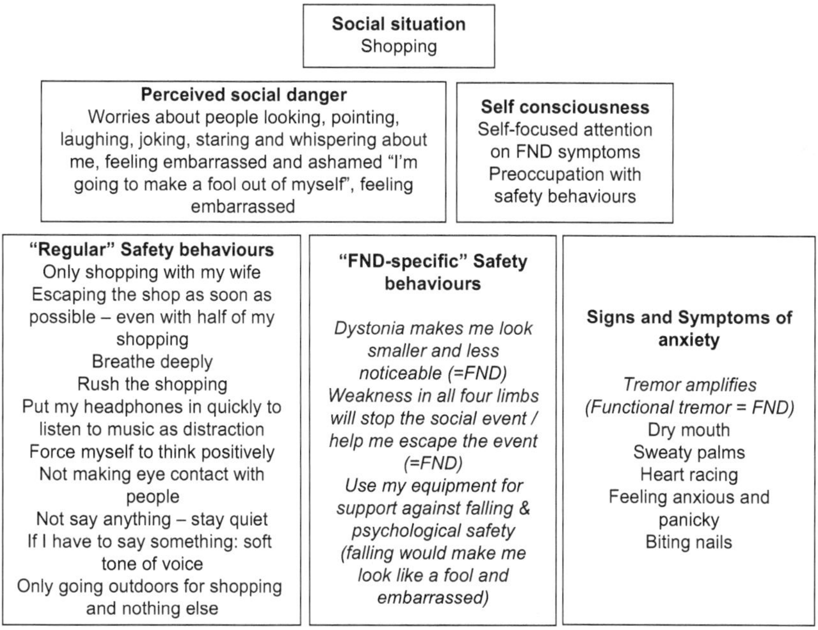

Figure 8.3 Adapted social anxiety disorder formulation in FND (based on Clark & Wells, 1995).

Table 8.2 Ethan's scores on psychological questionnaires

Measure	Start of therapy	End of therapy
PHQ-9	8 (moderate)	2 (mild)
GAD-7	16 (severe)	1 (mild)
HADS-anxiety	15 (top end of moderate range, nearly reaching severe levels)	1 (normal range)
HADS-depression	8 (mild range)	0 (normal range)
Symptom focus (ATSQ)	32/35	10/35
DERS-SF (mean)	2.56 (z = .92), above average	1.44 (z = .92), below average
SPIN (Social Phobia Inventory)	59 (very severe)	2 (none)

present, had only a minor impact on the FND, not in the same drastic way as the social anxiety that was driving the FND (i.e. the "variance" in FND was mostly explained by the social anxiety in this case). Ethan expressed feeling content with both formulations. However, as the social anxiety had been the biggest stumbling block towards living a full life, further treatment based on the PCM was not indicated or commenced and Ethan was discharged (Table 8.3).

In the end, both patients were helped by standard CBT models. The question arises: Why tinker with existing, well-researched evidence-based models that are able to explain the FND and make patients happy? In this situation, selecting a CBT model was the correct choice. The FND symptoms could be accounted for by both CBT models. Although the PCM was helpful in gaining a fuller understanding of the FND, it was almost superfluous when addressing the social anxiety, the core problem contributing to the FND.

Integrated PCM × CBT models: the future?

Imagine that you are working with a patient on a clear-cut CBT problem. You have started making some modest gains in therapy. Trust has started to build in the therapeutic relationship. Gradually, other more important maintaining socio-environmental factors surfaced that seem to be driving the FND symptoms more strongly than the initial psychological difficulty you formulated. Your CBT model loosely fits the data and requires you to change tack towards a treatment approach beyond what a standard CBT model could offer. In such situations, re-formulation with the PCM or an integrated PCM × CBT model may be more appropriate because it adds FND-specific maintaining factors and psychosocial processes that are not incorporated into standard CBT models, for example reduced verbal emotional expression (Cover), abnormal activity levels (Valve) and the social functions of FND (Kitchen). The PCM offers an additional layer with FND-specific features that capture the complexity of FND more fully. In the next section, we will

Table 8.3 Ethan's PCM formulation

Kitchen

Prior to FND, Ethan worked as a mechanic in a hospital and had some exposure to illness models.

Cover
- Tight – Ethan exhibited low levels of assertiveness and did not express his thoughts and feelings about the arguments to people close to him.

Overpressure Plug

Functional dystonia, tremor and limb weakness

Valve
- Bust-after-boom profile: Ethan used to be very active but was now mostly staying indoors.

Warning light
- High symptom focus (= difficult to distinguish from self-focused attention in social anxiety).

Sticky left-over food

"I'm worthless"
Low self-esteem & dashed confidence

Pot
- Use my equipment for support against falling and for psychological safety.

Flames and Heat
- I feel sad and angry about family members treating each other this way and the lack of communication.
- Arguments and people leaving the home re-trigger memories about the traumatic separation and abandonment.
- I feel not cared for and left to my own devices, especially in the context of social anxiety and being dependent on other people to access the community to manage social fears.
- Strong levels of "heat" of the emotions that I feel when arguments happen.

Ignition
- Adverse abusive childhood experiences and a traumatic separation/loss that caused feelings of abandonment. Ethan was not believed and cared for by key people.
- Critical incident: Grief around loss of an important "substitute parent figure", as well as back pain immediately preceded the onset of FND.

Fuel
- Family arguments and strife resulting in people leaving the home and not communicating amongst each other (= perception of loss or losing other important key figures).
- People not believing the FND.

Safety features

"Psychological-mindedness": Ethan demonstrated good insight into the link between mood, anxiety and the FND, for example the tremor worsening when feeling anxious or depressed. Good engagement and actively challenged himself with gradually more difficult behavioural experiments

---

explore the notion of an integrated PCM × CBT model and appropriate
times to use them.

Case study 3: Dissociative episodes and functional motor weakness in a person with social anxiety

Abigail experienced high-frequent, brief, paroxysmal dissociative episodes
that were characterised by vacant staring and "switching off" her mind
impacting on her attention and memory skills. She also presented with more
static functional weakness symptoms that fluctuated in severity. Some days,
Abigail would experience functional left-sided hemiplegic weakness that
rendered her unable to do any activities. On other days, she would regain the
use of all limbs. Abigail mobilised using a powerchair.

During the psychological assessment, it became evident that the FND
symptoms were connected to fears around social situations and negative
judgements from other people. Although Abigail had always been shy and
her social fears pre-dated the onset of FND, she experienced a lot of worries
about how she may come across and was perceived by other people. She was
particularly worried about talking, forgetting words; sounding incomprehensible; losing the train of thought; and eating, writing and walking in public.

To prevent her worst fear ("looking incapable/foolish") from happening,
she engaged in a range of safety behaviours including vacant staring at the
floor ("switching off"), not speaking much and saying the bare minimum,
avoiding social activities and, when unavoidable, shortening or leaving activities prematurely for a quick escape. Although she felt anticipatory anxiety
when entering a social situation, she was found to be jovial, made jokes and
attended therapy groups. Despite the façade of social confidence, Abigail
endured these social situations with great distress and this coincided with the
re-emergence of dissociative episodes.

Although Abigail's safety behaviours reduced her social anxiety in the
short term, they maintained her anxiety long term by preventing her from
testing out that her worst fear of being judged would not happen. The safety
behaviours attracted unwanted attention (e.g. switching off made her look
stern, the powerchair was noticeable, drew attention and made people look at
her). Her increased self-focused attention on safety behaviours further maintained anxiety.

The psychologist decided to select and apply the CBT model for social
anxiety (Clark & Wells, 1995). The FND symptoms (i.e. dissociation: vacant
staring, "switching off", functional weakness) appeared to fit well into the
social anxiety model and were subsumed under the safety behaviours (see
Figure 8.4).

Abigail was treated using this model. Her treatment consisted of graded
exposure using a series of behavioural experiments that aimed to break the
link between her beliefs and safety behaviours to reduce the anxiety. In addition, she practised reality grounding and attention shifting techniques to help

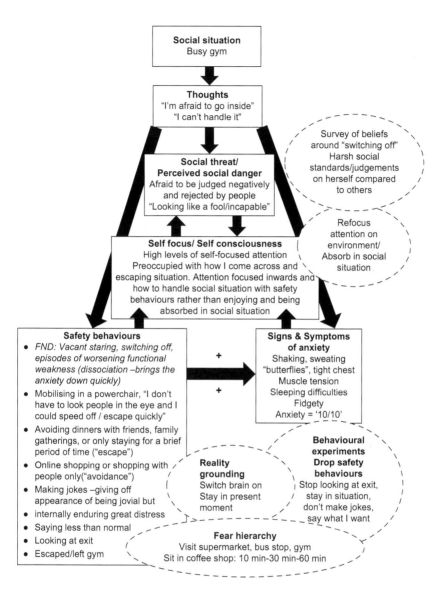

Figure 8.4 Abigail's social anxiety model applied to FND.

with emerging from the dissociative state and shift attentional focus to her environment as opposed to herself. Over time, the anxiety and vacant staring episodes reduced significantly and Abigail started attending more social activities. Although the staring episodes improved, the functional weakness symptoms showed minimal change and Abigail plateaued in her treatment. Reviewing the social anxiety model, the psychologist was wondering whether

Abigail had been dropping all her safety behaviours or whether subtle safety behaviours may have crept in. Abigail's self-report suggested good insight into the social anxiety and the need to drop safety behaviours.

Abigail had mostly been bothered by her cognitive symptoms, particularly attention and memory. She was adamant that she did not mind the motor weakness and preferred to work exclusively on the dissociative episodes. After further exploration and the development of a trusted and psychologically safe therapeutic relationship, it turned out that the functional weakness served another function: this symptom helped to stop the family arguments in the house and make Abigail feel noticed, validated and cared for by the people in her environment. Abigail's partner and children often ended up in heated discussions but as soon as she felt unwell with weakness, the family was supportive and kind to her. Abigail felt overwhelmed and anxious about the deteriorated relationships; she feared her family falling apart and going their separate ways. Although the social anxiety model was helpful for "quick wins" in terms of alleviating some FND symptoms related to anxiety and increasing Abigail's confidence in social situations, the model could not account for this additional function of the FND.

What could the psychologist have done differently in this situation?

Option #1: PCM as an adjunct model

Firstly, the psychologist made the right call to address the social anxiety. The social anxiety was a disabling symptom for Abigail and had a clear link with a subset of her FND symptoms. To address the remainder of her symptoms, the psychologist could have used the PCM as an adjunct model to the CBT model for social anxiety. This would mean one model to treat the social anxiety and the dissociation (i.e. vacant staring episodes and functional weakness that had the function to reduce anxiety; see Figure 8.4) and another model to treat the more social-environmental functions of the functional weakness (see Figure 8.5).

Although progressive hypothesising is common in FND, one could argue that the problem with using both the CBT model and the PCM is the lack of parsimony in accounting for the full range of FND symptoms and the potential to confuse the person with FND. In the spirit of parsimony, adopting one clinical theory that neatly explains the full presentation of FND appears more desirable. Is it possible to merge existing evidence-based CBT models with the PCM to form an integrated model without changing or compromising the core underlying psychological processes?

Option #2: PCM as an integrated model

The next section will describe an example of a merge between the CBT model for panic disorder and the PCM to form a hybrid model that more fully explains the FND presentation of the patient. Please note that the basic psychological processes of panic disorder are left intact in this "upgraded" model. The aim of the hybrid model is not to fundamentally change the

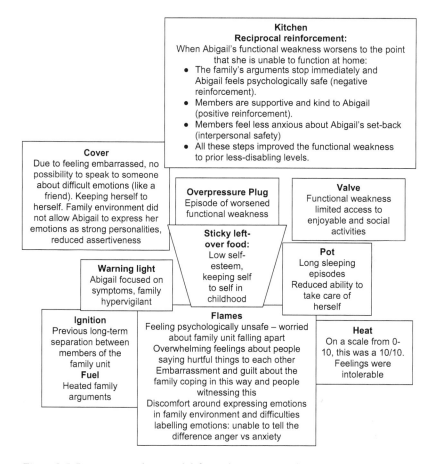

Figure 8.5 Pressure Cooker Model formulation as an adjunct model.

well-researched and evidence-based core mechanisms of the panic cycle. On the contrary, the integration preserves all these processes but presents the same processes in an alternative way, with the addition of FND-specific features that do not fundamentally impinge on the panic cycle processes.

Case study 4: Dissociative motor episodes in a person with panic disorder

Juliette was a 33-year-old female who had a three-year history of experiencing dissociative episodes.

Her first episode started with sudden symptoms of slurred speech, weakness and numbness in the face and limbs whilst at home. This progressed to a mild tremor and an inability to move her leg and speak. Given these symptoms,

Juliette believed that she was having a stroke. An ambulance was called, and Juliette was immediately admitted on a stroke ward in her local hospital. Medical investigations did not show any evidence of an acute stroke, and Juliette was subsequently discharged and followed up in an outpatient neurology clinic. Video telemetry investigations confirmed the diagnosis of dissociative episodes. Her speech and mobility slowly recovered after six weeks.

Following her initial recovery, Juliette experienced regular dissociative episodes lasting for about 20 minutes. A typical episode would "come out of the blue" and emerge in various locations (e.g. at home, at work and in crowded places). Juliette's difficulties were formulated using the CBT model for panic disorder (Clark, 1986). A panic attack would start with a multitude of bodily symptoms, which were misinterpreted in a catastrophic fashion ("I'm going to have a stroke" later replaced with "I'm going to have another episode") causing high levels of anxiety, with its physiological effects further feeding back into the panic cycle. To cope and prevent her worst fear from happening (having a stroke or an episode), Juliette engaged in two sets of safety behaviours. The first set coincided with those found in a "classic" panic cycle and would continue the panic loop, whilst the second set would immediately terminate the panic loop with a dissociative episode. Via negative reinforcement, the dissociative episodes quickly brought down the panic feelings and subsequently became firmly established as a coping habit. Figure 8.6 describes the panic cycle formulation and the treatment regimen that was commenced.

As the therapy progressed, Juliette revealed new information that appeared to have a bearing on the formulation. Juliette disclosed difficult interpersonal dynamics and arguments with her son, which often provoked physical symptoms that she subsequently misinterpreted as signs of an impending dissociative episode. This became a self-fulfilling prophecy and led to an actual dissociative episode with her son and a friendly neighbour engaging in interpersonal safety behaviours (see Figure 8.7). As a result, (1) the panic feelings stopped immediately and (2) the son stopped the argument and did the opposite: caring for Juliette. Figure 8.7 displays this extra dimension of FND-maintaining socio-environmental factors and the treatment strategies emanating from this revised formulation (e.g. family-focused work with the PCM) whilst preserving the original principles of the panic cycle. Juliette decided that that she did not want to pursue a more systemic approach to the FND and preferred to keep her family out of the therapy process. Regardless of this interpersonal trigger, she did well and was subsequently discharged with minimal symptoms. Approximately 1.5 years later, Juliette sought contact with the service and shared that the dissociative episodes had re-appeared. Juliette could not be seen, but the question arose whether the application of the more systemic, integrated PCM × CBT panic model could have made more impact on controlling Juliette's symptoms. It should be noted that although the Flames section describes panic feelings as part of a classic panic cycle, one could argue that Juliette felt "attachment-panic" around the relationship with her son.

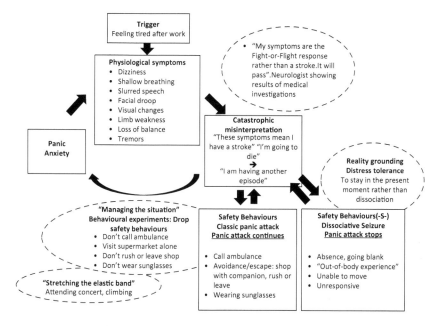

Figure 8.6 Panic disorder formulation with treatment strategies.

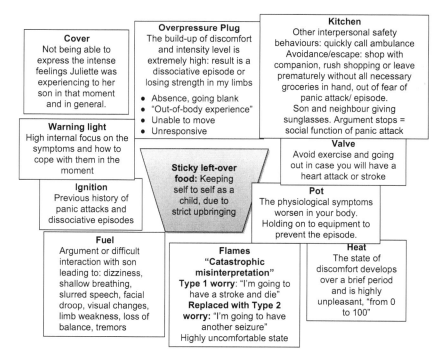

Figure 8.7 Integrated PCM × CBT panic model.

Treatment strategies for panic attacks in FND

In the following section, FND-specific features in panic attacks will be discussed, stage by stage in the panic cycle, as well as useful strategies to support your treatment with the panic model (Clark, 1986) in a person with FND.

PHYSICAL SYMPTOMS

A drawn-out panic cycle often starts with "physical symptoms" at the top of the cycle. List every physical symptom that the person reports but be aware that these may have different functions in FND. For example, FND symptoms such as tremors and pins and needles are often an expression of the underlying anxiety and can easily be subsumed in the "physical" section. However, watch out for FND symptoms such as dissociative seizures, motor paralysis or "switching off": these often are better subsumed under the safety behaviours section in the model. This specific subset of FND symptoms tends to bring down the panic quickly, providing negative reinforcement. The first set of FND symptoms (tremors, pins and needles) do not tend to have that same function in panic attacks. Non-FND symptoms such as heart palpitations, feeling sick or nauseous, hyperventilation or breathlessness, and feeling sweaty are all symptoms that can also be categorised under "physical symptoms".

PANIC COGNITIONS

Classic panic cognitions can be encountered in a person with FND, for example "I am going to have a stroke", "I'm going to have a heart attack" and "I'm going to die". In the early days, panic attacks are often based on these classic beliefs; however, at a later stage, you may find this original belief replaced with "I'm going to have a seizure" or "I'm going to collapse" at the earliest sign of a physical symptom. It is not uncommon for a person to be unable to remember or recount the belief "I've drawn a blank" "It's foggy". It is often helpful to enquire whether this has a positive or negative valence (nearly always the latter).

EMOTION

You may not obtain anxiety or panic as a response from a person with FND. People may not be able to label their internal state and may indicate that they are confused, overwhelmed or angry (mixing the emotion of anxiety up with anger). Ask the person whether it feels negative or positive. Emotion education will be helpful here, including learning about the different motor signatures, and reasons why it is easy to confuse emotions, as well as the different "levels" of anxiety (e.g. scared, fearful, frightened, feeling terror).

SAFETY BEHAVIOURS = FND

Dropping safety behaviours are often the core of treating panic attacks in FND. FND will often be the main safety behaviour that brings down the anxiety or unpleasant internal state quickly and effectively, for example a dissociative seizure or paralysis, rather than tingles (sensory FND symptoms) or tremors. People will occasionally mention fatigue. This can also be viewed as a safety behaviour. Often people with FND who feel suddenly very fatigued do not report feeling anxious or some other unpleasant state; these states appear to be mutually exclusive. FND symptoms often "close the loop" or terminate the panic cycle on the spot – different than in classic panic attacks. This is the internal regulation function of FND. Other more classic safety behaviours can still be found including patients using distraction techniques, calling an ambulance or escaping a situation to manage the panic.

SOCIAL CONTEXT

The social context is not normally part of the classic panic disorder model but will be highly relevant to FND: What happens after the FND symptom emerges? How is the FND externally regulated and reinforced by the environment? Commonly, people with FND will regulate the panic state ("calm down") internally with FND and externally by the environment (e.g. reassurance). This provides double reinforcement of the FND: through the FND the patient's panic will reduce internally providing relief, and externally, the reassurance will further reinforce the FND as a coping habit. Watch out for reciprocal reinforcement and mirroring of the panic attack in the environment: systemic panic may ensue after witnessing the FND/panic attack. You can draw out a regular panic cycle with an added text box that is specifically attached to the FND symptom and safety behaviours section.

COMPARISON

A good technique is to make a comparison between physical symptoms that emerge in the context of FND vs similar physical symptoms in the context of a positive event, for example a sport that elicits the same physical phenomena. The two sets of physical symptoms do not necessarily have to be completely identical but roughly overlap (make sure that the most bothersome FND symptom that takes down the panic state is listed under the safety behaviours). Highlight the similarity in physical symptoms and the difference in thoughts and emotions or internal states between the two situations (FND/panic vs no FND/sports).

BREAKING THE LINKS

The treatment is similar to classic panic attacks without FND and uses psycho-education on the panic cycle to socialise the patient to the model and the fight-or-flight response to address the catastrophic misinterpretation of the physical symptoms, as well as behavioural experiments and encouragement to drop safety behaviours (= FND). However, for people with panic attacks and FND you may provide additional emotion education to help the person label and connect with their emotions; provide reality grounding techniques to halt or slow down the dissociation and drop the safety behaviour that is FND; and ask the environment to stand back rather than intervene and reassure.

Table 8.4 Adjunct vs integrated models in FND

Adjunct model (CBT+)	*Integrated model (PCM × CBT)*
The person has a clearly defined psychological problem that is associated with a specific type of anxiety (e.g. social anxiety).	Initially, the person seemed to experience a clear psychological problem; however, after several sessions, the FND served another function that was not associated with anxiety. The original model has problems explaining the second function of FND.
There are no additional (social) functions of the FND or social functions that drive most of the clinical picture.	
The CBT model is able to incorporate the FND symptom without violating the CBT model's principles (e.g. vacant staring episode as a form of dissociation that is classed as a safety behaviour that helps reduce anxiety and keeps the reinforcement loop going).	The original CBT model is unable to incorporate and easily explain the full range of FND in a parsimonious way. The original CBT model is unable to incorporate the FND symptoms because it terminates the loop (e.g. a non-epileptic episode).
The person is psychologically minded and has sufficient emotional language to work with both a CBT model and the PCM.	The person may be less psychologically inclined and finds it difficult to label emotions, posing a problem for the application of standard CBT models. In addition, two models would cause confusion.
The person has successfully completed CBT treatment for a well-defined anxiety problem but could benefit from an additional "top-up" treatment to fully understand the mechanisms of FND. Even if a CBT model was successfully used, but the mechanism of FND was still unclear, the person may be left with questions: How do my psychological difficulties cause FND? They may worry that they will relapse if they don't understand the mechanism.	
Socio-environmental functions of the FND are less able to explain the variance in the FND presentation than the anxiety disorder that is mostly driving the FND symptoms.	Socio-environmental functions of the FND are prominently present and not paying attention to them in treatment would not do justice to appropriate psychological therapy for the person.

Adjunct vs integrated models

Table 8.4 describes a variety of clinical situations that may guide the choice of one over the other model. These are intended as guidelines to support a clinician with making a choice and should not be regarded as fixed truths.

PCM as a preparatory model to CBT (PCM => CBT)

Occasionally, people with FND experience such extreme levels of dissociation, often present since early childhood, that any type of psychological therapy with CBT would likely halt the process quickly with both the patient and therapist feeling frustrated. An intermediate step before the main treatment is needed for the patient to learn about basic emotion processes, emotion language and "getting in touch with emotions". Sometimes, this may constitute the intervention itself and the FND resolves. At other times, the patient has been made "CBT ready": hidden thoughts and emotions are uncovered that may benefit from further treatment with a classic CBT model. The next two case studies will describe situations where the PCM was used as a "prerequisite" to prepare the patient for further CBT work.

Case study 5: Dissociative episodes in a person with generalised anxiety disorder

Ralph was an 18-year-old male with a five-year-long history of dissociative episodes that emerged following a pedestrian vs car accident. Typical "blackout" episodes lasted for 30 seconds and were characterised by collapses on the floor with temporary unresponsiveness, self-perceived loss of consciousness, and post-episode disorientation and amnesia. Although a diagnosis of post-traumatic stress disorder (PTSD) was initially considered in the context of the accident, Ralph did not report any flashbacks or hypervigilance. Neither did Ralph describe classic panic cognitions. Ralph was unaware of the triggers and drivers of the dissociative episodes. His symptoms greatly impacted on his activities in daily life; he lagged on schoolwork and gave up driving due to road safety issues that dissociative episodes would pose. He avoided busy restaurants and social gatherings and dropped all his hobbies and sports activities, losing touch with his friends. Due to the episodes, Ralph also experienced a high rate of accidental self-injury.

Phase 1: Preparatory therapy with the Pressure Cooker Model

Because Ralph struggled to identify triggers, emotions and thought contents, it was agreed to start the therapy with the PCM to uncover some of these features (see Table 8.5). A preliminary hypothesis of PTSD was still entertained in the background: it was still possible that Ralph was so dissociated from his thoughts and emotions that these needed to be uncovered and outlined first before any trauma-focused treatment could commence.

Table 8.5 Ralph's Pressure Cooker Model formulation

Kitchen

- Hypervigilant parents and siblings suggesting anxiety and worries in Ralph's environment around his dissociative episodes. Supportive partner.
- Social isolation, Ralph lost touch with his friends, despite his friends actively reaching out to him. Ralph explained that he "couldn't be bothered" speaking to them.

Cover	**Overpressure Plug**	**Valve**
• Locked rather than tight: no emotional expression to partner or family. Kept all emotions to himself and appeared very embarrassed exploring anxiety with his parents, partner or psychologist.	• Dissociative episodes with a "loss" of consciousness and unresponsiveness: feeling "nothing".	• Bust-after-boom: previously extremely active and "pushing on" but following the development of the dissociative episodes unable to engage with any activities apart from school but mostly spending time indoors.

Warning light	**Sticky left-over food**	**Pot**
• Ralph mostly used physical language to describe his symptoms and state of being.	Family was not used to expressing emotions	• Significant risk of accidental self-injury requiring medical intervention due to falls in the context of dissociative episodes. • Sleep for long periods after dissociative episodes.

Flames	**Ignition**
• Overwhelmed state with unidentified but highly unpleasant emotions. • Later identified as a progressive build-up of worries and anxiety.	• No traumatic or adverse childhood experiences reported by the patient. Family coping strategies were mainly avoidant and "shoving things under the carpet". • Critical incident: pedestrian vs car accident.

Heat	**Fuel**
• High levels of "heat": the unpleasant internal state would come up fast and strongly, but quickly reduced by dissociation.	• One second before the dissociative episode, Ralph identified a shadow and flashes. • Fuel was initially unclear but later identified as worries that popped up in Ralph's mind.

Safety features

Attended the sessions regularly and engaged with the homework tasks, Ralph was willing to practise techniques in between therapy sessions. Supportive family and partner.

LAYER 1: IGNITION

Ralph's accident was the critical incident that had made him vulnerable towards developing the dissociative episodes. Although he did not report any early trauma or childhood adverse events, nor any problematic parent-child interactions or challenging interpersonal dynamics during his upbringing, he did note a dissociated and "intellectual" style of coping with emotions that was shared within the entire family unit over several generations.

LAYER 2: THE FND COPING TRIANGLE

From an early age, Ralph was used to keep himself to himself and just pushed on – which also constituted his family's main coping habits. These childhood coping strategies repeated into adulthood: Ralph presented with a total lack of verbal emotional expression (locked rather than tight Cover) and a bust-after-boom activity pattern (blocked Valve).

LAYER 3: THE FND MAINTENANCE CYCLE

As the therapeutic relationship grew stronger and Ralph worked through emotion education, he learned to dissect his "feelings of overwhelm" by identifying and labelling the anxiety and worries that made up this internal state. The PCM intervention enabled Ralph to develop emotion language and communicate more clearly and precisely the contents of his thoughts and feelings. It became evident that Ralph worried excessively about a variety of topics including schoolwork and exams; passing out and people's reactions; worry about his family's worrying about Ralph; accidents; death; and terrorism with increased hypervigilance for signs during outdoor trips. Ralph identified his own "Pressure Cooker Chain Reaction": Worries (Fuel, internal psychological trigger) led to a build-up of more worries and anxiety (Flames) but were dissociated from (low Heat) resulting in dissociative episodes (Overpressure Plug).

Ralph's FND coping triangle cultivated the dissociative episodes: Ralph had no recourse to usual helpful channels for stress release. His lack of verbal emotional expression was "total" (locked Cover) as was his lack of enjoyable, relaxation and social activities (blocked Valve). This left no other channel available than to express his anxiety via his body (dissociative episodes).

LAYER 4

When inspecting Ralph's FND SELF CARE acronym, there were two prominent issues that contributed to the maintenance of the FND. Ralph had a tendency towards sleeping long hours, particularly after a dissociative episode. This impacted on his worries in two ways: (1) Ralph's normal sleeping pattern was disrupted leading to even more worries at night about not being able to sleep further feeding the dissociative episodes and (2) although sleep was a direct result of Ralph's exhaustion following an episode, sleep simultaneously had a highly reinforcing effect: sleep cancelled out Ralph's worries and anxiety in the short term. However, in the long term, Ralph's worries and anxiety returned, with "Type 2 worries" added to his "Type 1 worries", further maintaining the dissociative episodes.

There was also a significant risk of accidental self-injury, occasionally severe, requiring medical support. The episodes felt outside Ralph's and his family's control generating more worries.

LAYER 5

Reciprocal reinforcement was prominently present: whenever Ralph experienced a dissociative episode, his worried family would reassure and support him immediately. This served the function to reduce Ralph's episode whilst simultaneously reducing the family's own worries and anxiety at witnessing the episode. Due to his withdrawal from social life, Ralph was isolated and prevented from social opportunities to test out the validity of his worries.

Phase 2: main therapy with the CBT model for generalised anxiety disorder

The PCM enabled Ralph to identify his worries and anxiety. Due to its good fit and ability to manage the intricacies of Ralph's worry processes, the Metacognitive Model for Generalised Anxiety Disorder (Wells, 1995) was selected in the next phase of treatment. Ralph's dissociative episodes were strongly linked to worries. Figure 8.8 shows how a school exam triggered Type 1 worries ("I can't do it"), which accumulated and were amplified via worry processes (e.g. rumination, catastrophising). The worries led to a state of overwhelming anxiety that was accompanied by physiological effects which Ralph struggled to effectively control. With little warning, this highly unpleasant state culminated in a dissociative episode, which instantly and temporarily removed the overwhelming panic, worries and physiological symptoms of anxiety via negative reinforcement (Skinner, 1963). However, after emerging from this dissociative state, Ralph's original Type 1 worries gradually returned. Moreover, the episodes led to a new set of Type 2 worries about future dissociative episodes. The Type 2 worries combined with Type 1 worries and were further subjected to the worry processes, repeating the cycle and strengthening the dissociative episodes as the main coping habit for worries. Figure 8.8 shows the same GAD model but this time re-applied with the techniques that Ralph learned during therapy.

Outcomes

At the beginning of therapy, Ralph experienced approximately 10–15 dissociative episodes a week. On psychological and mood questionnaires, Ralph did not indicate any significant psychological difficulties or adverse impact of the seizures on his day-to-day functioning. His anxiety levels as measured by the HADS fell just within the normal range; the HADS was not able to detect Ralph's worries and anxiety. These scores were expected and consistent with Ralph's high levels of dissociation. Following therapy, Ralph became seizure-free and his scores on post-therapy questionnaires were all found to be in the normal range. This does not mean that psychological therapy had not impacted on Ralph's psychological difficulties. On the contrary, his scores confirmed the qualitative observations that were made at the start of his therapy: Ralph was so dissociated from his emotions and lacked emotion language; he was unable to recognise or describe his emotions. It is therefore not surprising that he rated his mood as normal. Therefore, the underlying reasons for Ralph's normal scores obtained at the beginning vs the end of therapy likely differed. His normal range scores at the beginning were due to dissociation from anxiety, whereas his normal scores at the end suggested "truly" reduced anxiety. Although it was still possible that Ralph demonstrated ongoing dissociation at the end of therapy, the positive behavioural change observed in his dissociative seizure frequency suggested otherwise. Another reason that may have played a role and impacted on his scores was Ralph's embarrassment and reluctance to disclose anxiety. Qualitatively, Ralph was able to avert dissociative episodes during stressful times. He successfully passed his exams and moved on to college. He lived independently and enjoyed a good social network (Table 8.6).

Case study 6: severe functional dystonia and dissociation in a person with suspected social anxiety

The next case study describes a 27-year-old female with the motor-type features of FND.

Claudia was unable to stand or walk without support and used a wheelchair to mobilise. She lived in an adapted home and received support with personal care and daily tasks from her partner. The contrast between her premorbid high level of functioning and current functioning in daily life was significant. Claudia herself explained that she was not bothered by her symptoms and believed these were associated with medication side effects.

During the initial assessment, Claudia mentioned that she did not experience any psychological difficulties and did not quite understand the role of psychology within the multidisciplinary team as part of her care. She was unable to describe any coping strategies "I never have stress" and "I just do". Although she did not report any psychological distress, behavioural observations of safety behaviours (e.g. not making eye contact, sparse conversation and social avoidance) and the physical symptoms of anxiety by the team converged on possible social anxiety.

Despite her reservations about psychology, which continued throughout therapy, Claudia was willing to attend her psychology sessions (Table 8.7).

Layer 1: Ignition

Claudia's early and later life experiences were marked by high levels of emotional disconnection and strong dissociative tendencies that created

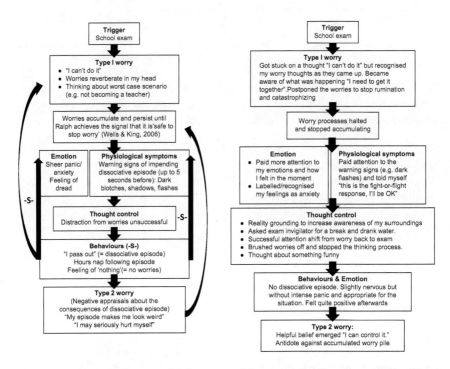

Figure 8.8 Metacognitive Model for Generalised Anxiety Disorder in FND (based on Wells, 1995).

Table 8.6 Ralph's results on psychological questionnaires

Questionnaire	Pre-therapy	Post-therapy
CORE-OM	30 (low level)	9 (healthy range)
HADS-anxiety	7 (normal)	0 (normal)
HADS-depression	0 (normal)	1 (normal)
WSAS-Work and Social Adjustment Scale	4 (subclinical)	0 (subclinical)
ATSQ	24/35	9/35
Therapy experience satisfaction	Extremely satisfied	
Therapy helpfulness in managing the FND	Extremely helpful	
% improvement in FND because of therapy	100%	
Recommend to friend	Extremely likely	

a vulnerability for developing FND. Although no clear-cut critical incident was identified, Claudia's stress-coping resources had started to gradually unravel following years of high pressure in her job, parental and personal relationships that had become an unsustainable way of living.

Layer 2: The FND coping triangle

The FND coping triangle was present and characterised by the three classic FND coping habits (Table 8.8).

Table 8.7 Claudia's Pressure Cooker Model formulation

Kitchen

- Estranged relationship with partner but still living in the same house.
- Significant social isolation with no social network apart from her partner.
- Social function of FND: potentially maintained Claudia's proximity to her partner, even if only for practical and physical care reasons.

Cover

- Locked: Claudia kept herself to herself, minimised psychology and emotions, and made jokes about emotions.
- Reduced assertiveness at work and in her relationship.

Overpressure Plug

- Dystonia, jerky movements and tremors = physical symptoms of anxiety.
- Pain especially headaches and migraines.
- Functional sensory symptoms: reduced sensation and numbness in the arm, leg and face, mirroring reduced emotional sensation or dissociation.

Valve

- Bust-after-boom pattern:
- Prior to developing FND, Claudia did not relax and "kept pushing on", "putting pressure on myself", a self-proclaimed "work-a-holic".
- Outside work: used to be very active and constantly "on the move".
- Stopped working since the FND. Mostly stayed indoors and did not access the community.

Warning light

- Extreme levels of high physical symptom focus that did not leave many "degrees of freedom" for discussion of psychological explanations for FND.

Sticky left-over food

Unclear but suspicion of "I'm worthless"

Mostly kept herself to herself in childhood.

Pot

- Stark dissociation between experience of anxiety vs clear observable physical symptoms of anxiety including tremor, clammy hands, feeling sweaty and nauseous.
- Highly entrenched: equipment and home adaptations.

Flames and Heat

- Strong denial and did not identify with any negative emotions, Claudia mentioned only experiencing positive and neutral moods. Resistance to any psychological interpretation of the FND.

Ignition

- Family of origin adopted very logical and "intellectual" approach to coping with negative emotions. Family relationships were detached and transactional. Life-long complex and strained relationship with father, with high parental expectations: "just pushed on", "kept myself to myself" and did not connect with emotions since early childhood.
- For years, worked in a challenging, high-pressured managerial role and made long hours.

Table 8.7 (Continued)

• Possible social anxiety but highly dissociated from the emotion. • Very logical approach to emotions.	Critical incidents: • Whilst driving to work, Claudia suddenly experienced tremors, jerky movements and muscle spasms in her limbs and trunk lasting for two days. Medically investigated but perceived a lack of care from healthcare services, Claudia felt abandoned. • Previous history of paroxysmal dissociative episodes that ceased and were "replaced" by more motor-type FND symptoms. **Fuel** • 1. Initially unclear but suspicion fell on social situations due to safety behaviours and physical symptoms, particularly in social situations and with people present. • 2. Possible situations that involved some form of rejection and being treated as "less worthy" or "cared for" by other people – although this was never confirmed, for example colleagues overloading patient with work.

Safety features

Engagement was initially problematic, particularly in the beginning stages of therapy.

Despite her reluctance, Claudia regularly attended her sessions and made an effort ("pushed on"). With time, Claudia was able to build a trusted therapeutic relationship and was able to feel as psychologically safe as she could feel when exploring emotions, a topic she did not always feel comfortable with.

Layer 3: The FND maintenance cycle

INTERNAL FUNCTION OF FND

A social situation (Fuel) triggered Claudia's anxiety (Flames). Due to a longstanding background of dissociation that started in early childhood (Sticky left-over food), a dissociative process immediately turned down the heat of the anxiety (low Heat). Claudia was unable to verbalise and emotionally connect with her anxiety nor the underlying dissociative process (tight Cover; first channel out-of-order) and presented with a restricted range of enjoyable and social activities (blocked Valve; second channel out-of-order). This combination cultivated the emergence of FND symptoms: despite her inability to experience the social anxiety, the dissociated "internal turmoil" was expressed via physical symptoms (Overpressure Plug; third channel).

It was hypothesised that the:

• Functional motor symptoms (i.e. dystonia, increased muscle spasms, jerky movement and tremors) reflected the physiological features of the underlying social anxiety.

Table 8.8 Claudia's FND coping triangle

PCM element	Early childhood	Adulthood
Tight "locked" Cover	Kept myself to myself	• Denial of ever having experienced emotional distress.
Boom Valve	Pushed on	• Pushed on in and outside work environment (Boom Valve). • Later transformed to bust-after-boom Valve as stress-coping strategies unravelled: Claudia stopped many meaningful and enjoyable activities.
Overpressure Plug	Cut off my emotions ("intellectualised")	• Dissociation dominated the clinical picture throughout Claudia's life, setting the stage for developing FND. • Reduced "emotional sensation" paralleled reduced physical sensation.

- Functional sensory symptoms (i.e. numbness and reduced physical sensation) mirrored her reduced sensation and disconnection from emotions, particularly anxiety.

Layer 4: Facilitating physical factors of FND

The FND was "omnipresent" in Claudia's day-to-day life. Over the years, she had accumulated various equipment and lived in a fully adapted home environment with a care package, in addition to receiving care from her partner. To the outside world, Claudia presented as very disabled with high care needs. It was hypothesised that the widespread entrenchment of FND in her life and the equipment that Claudia had amassed over the years served as psychological safety behaviours that almost acted as a deterrent for people to question her physical health status and enquire about her psychological well-being. Claudia's physical appearance and adaptations therefore maintained her psychological difficulties and FND.

Layer 5: Social functions of FND

EXTERNAL FUNCTION OF FND

The central theme in Claudia's life was characterised by a perceived lack of emotional care, reduced psychological safety and a sense of feeling abandoned in her distant relationship with her father, job role, current estranged relationship and healthcare services. The FND symptoms provided Claudia with some sense of psychological safety through proximity to people who were at least physically caring for her, for example her estranged partner and treating team.

Psychological formulation = treatment

Claudia's "socialisation" to the PCM and the practice of building a trusted and psychological safe relationship was ultimately the (preparatory) intervention that potentially paved the way for future therapy. Claudia did not entirely share the same thoughts on the formulation; however, perhaps this was another part of the practice: Claudia's psychologist did not reject her for disagreeing, rolled with the resistance and continued caring for her, providing "object constancy". This strengthened the therapeutic relationship and opened the door ajar towards Claudia sharing and labelling an emotion that was connected to thoughts arising from the rehabilitation process. The treatment further focused on psycho-education of emotions and their physiological effects (e.g. fight-or-flight response), as well as dissociation. Joint psychology and physiotherapy sessions helped to reduce the physiological effects of anxiety using breathing techniques that were directly applied in stepping and walking practice.

Outcomes

Some slight improvements were noticeable in FND, more so in the functional sensory than for the motor symptoms. Despite these modest improvements, Claudia's symptoms persisted and she continued to be significantly disabled in her day-to-day life. In PCM language, although Claudia's Cover had "unlocked", it remained tight. She did not express emotions with other people outside the therapy sessions. Her Valve continued to be blocked; her social world was restricted to only a few enjoyable activities. Given these two blocked channels, Claudia remained vulnerable to a heightened risk of FND symptoms.

Claudia's score profile showed some interesting findings (see Table 8.9). At the start of therapy, Claudia denied any psychological difficulties suggesting high levels of dissociation. However, clinically significant scores on the Five Facet Mindfulness Questionnaire - Short Form (FFMQ-SF; Bohlmeijer et al., 2011) and Difficulties in Emotion Regulation Scale - Short Form (DERS-SF; Kaufman et al., 2015) suggested that Claudia self-reported difficulties with her ability to put thoughts and feelings into words, as well as adopting a non-judgemental stance towards her thoughts and feelings. She further reported a tendency towards denial of distress and feeling unclear about the emotions she was experiencing. At discharge, all these scores had reverted to the non-clinical range.

Neuropsychological assessment

As part of the standard clinical work-up, Claudia underwent a comprehensive neuropsychological assessment. Her cognitive profile was generally unremarkable with average scores on tests for most cognitive domains, except for reduced scores on tests measuring mental flexibility and switching between sets. The question arose whether Claudia's reduced mental flexibility may have contributed to her reluctance towards accepting a viewpoint on the FND that was different than her own.

PCM as a preparatory model: final thoughts

The PCM can serve as a useful preparatory model that acts as a bridge or stepping stone towards other psychological treatment models. For example, a person with dissociation and alexithymia who may be at the more severe end of the spectrum, unable to recognise their own distress or recognise emotions, may benefit from practice with the PCM before moving on to models that treat the core of their underlying psychological difficulties. Based on observed safety behaviours in social situations, there may be a suspicion raised that a highly dissociated person experiences social anxiety that they do not connect with and that could highly benefit from treatment using the CBT model for social anxiety, if only they had some extra preparatory training to recognise and connect with their emotions first. Another subset of patients with FND may experience acute PTSD in response to a recent traumatic event or may have held in an unspeakable dilemma for a long time that is ready to be expressed within the therapy space. Both types of patient may benefit from "stabilisation" and consolidation of psychological coping strategies within the context of FND using the PCM before moving on to the phase where the trauma is relived or the unspeakable dilemma released in the therapy space. Other circumstances for use of a preparatory PCM include the situation where both the person with FND and the clinician feel stuck in therapy working with a CBT model without a view towards further movement. In addition, a person with FND may have grown up in a family structure that failed to encourage or invalidated emotional expression. As a result, a person with FND may experience emotions as "foreign currency". They may not be used to speaking or opening up about emotions, which necessitates preparatory work including emotion education and practice with emotional expression which the PCM can easily relate to the emergence of FND symptoms.

If it is very clear that an emotion (e.g. social anxiety) is not recognised as such by the patient, for example, the patient is very disconnected from the anxiety; mixes anxiety up with anger; or only identifies their internal state as highly unpleasant, it may also be possible to use an integrated PCM and refrain from naming the uncomfortable feeling, at least for the time being. However,

Table 8.9 Claudia's scores on psychological questionnaires

Questionnaire	Pre-therapy	Post-therapy
CORE-34	18 (healthy range)	9 (healthy range)
HADS–anxiety	6 (normal)	2 (normal)
HADS–depression	1 (normal)	1 (normal)
WSAS	10 (moderate impact of FND on day-to-day functioning)	3 (subclinical impact)
ATSQ	29/35	17/35
FFMQ – short form	Clinically significant scores on subscales Describe and Non-judging	All scores were within normal limits
DERS – short form	Clinically significant scores on subscales Non-acceptance and Clarity	All scores were within normal limits

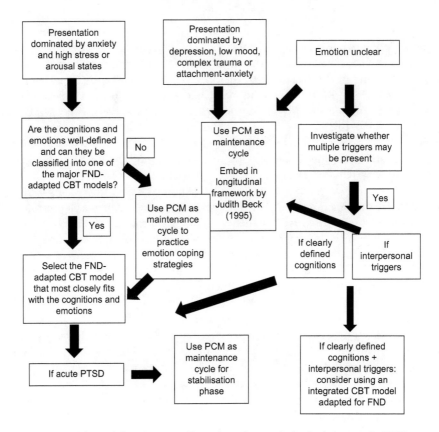

Figure 8.9 Clinical decision tree flow chart for psychological therapy in FND.

this would likely not work in a patient with significant flat affect or an individual who does not recognise any fluctuations or a negative valence in emotions.

Flow chart decision tree

The decision tree in Figure 8.9 could be used as a "rule of thumb": as a first question, ask yourself what type of emotion you have encountered or dominates the clinical picture. Although anxiety and depression often co-exist, emotions will form the basis of your decision what model to select.

Conclusions

The PCM can be used as a standalone model in FND and alongside other CBT models (i.e. adjunct, integrated or preparatory) providing a richer formulation that is capable of fully capturing the FND. Most importantly, incorporating the PCM in daily clinical practice provides an opportunity to treat the patient and family's contribution in parallel with the same model (PCM), giving more credence to the idea that FND is a product of emotion dysregulation between the patient and the environment, and not just the problem of the "patient".

References

Chapter 1

Ahern, L., Stone, J., & Sharpe, M. C. (2009). Attitudes of neuroscience nurses toward patients with conversion symptoms. *Psychosomatics, 50*(4), 336–339.

American Psychiatric Association. (2013). *Diagnostic and statistical manual of mental disorders* (5th ed.). Washington, DC, London: American Psychiatric Association Publishing. https://doi.org/10.1176/appi.books.9780890425596

Aybek, S., Nicholson, T. R., Draganski, B., Daly, E., Murphy, D. G., David, A. S., & Kanaan, R. A. (2014). Grey matter changes in motor conversion disorder. *Journal of Neurology, Neurosurgery & Psychiatry, 85*(2), 236–238.

Bakvis, P., Spinhoven, P., Giltay, E. J., Kuyk, J., Edelbroek, P. M., Zitman, F. G., & Roelofs, K. (2010). Basal hypercortisolism and trauma in patients with psychogenic nonepileptic seizures. *Epilepsia, 51*(5), 752–759.

Barnett, C., Davis, R., Mitchell, C., & Tyson, S. (2022). The vicious cycle of functional neurological disorders: a synthesis of healthcare professionals' views on working with patients with functional neurological disorder. *Disability and Rehabilitation, 44*(10), 1802–1811.

Baslet, G., Dworetzky, B., Perez, D. L., & Oser, M. (2015). Treatment of psychogenic nonepileptic seizures: updated review and findings from a mindfulness-based intervention case series. *Clinical EEG and Neuroscience, 46*(1), 54–64.

Baxter, S., Mayor, R., Baird, W., Brown, R., Cock, H., Howlett, S., ... & Reuber, M. (2012). Understanding patient perceptions following a psychoeducational intervention for psychogenic non-epileptic seizures. *Epilepsy & Behavior, 23*(4), 487–493.

Beck, A. T. (1976). *Cognitive therapy and the emotional disorders.* International Universities Press. New York

Beck, J. S. (1995). *Cognitive Therapy: Basics and Beyond.* New York: The Guilford Press.

Benbadis, S. R., & Hauser, W. A. (2000). An estimate of the prevalence of psychogenic non-epileptic seizures. *Seizure, 9*(4), 280–281.

Bennett, K., Diamond, C., Hoeritzauer, I., Gardiner, P., McWhirter, L., Carson, A., & Stone, J. (2021). A practical review of functional neurological disorder (FND) for the general physician. *Clinical Medicine, 21*(1), 28.

Binzer, M., Andersen, P. M., & Kullgren, G. (1997). Clinical characteristics of patients with motor disability due to conversion disorder: a prospective control group study. *Journal of Neurology, Neurosurgery & Psychiatry, 63*(1), 83–88.

Bowman, E. S., & Markand, O. N. (1999). The contribution of life events to pseudo-seizure occurrence in adults. *Bulletin of the Menninger Clinic, 63*(1), 70.

Brabban, A., & Turkington, D. (2002) The Search for Meaning: detecting congruence between life events, underlying schema and psychotic symptoms. In A. P. Morrison (Ed.) *A casebook of cognitive therapy for psychosis* (Chapter 5, pp. 59–75). New York: Brunner Routledge.

Brown, R. J. (2006). Medically unexplained symptoms: a new model. *Psychiatry, 5*(2), 43–47.

Brown, R. J., Bouska, J. F., Frow, A., Kirkby, A., Baker, G. A., Kemp, S., ... & Reuber, M. (2013). Emotional dysregulation, alexithymia, and attachment in psychogenic nonepileptic seizures. *Epilepsy & Behavior, 29*(1), 178–183.

Brown, R. J., & Reuber, M. (2016). Towards an integrative theory of psychogenic non-epileptic seizures (PNES). *Clinical Psychology Review, 47*, 55–70.

Bullock, K. D., Mirza, N., Forte, C., & Trockel, M. (2015). Group dialectical-behavior therapy skills training for conversion disorder with seizures. *The Journal of Neuropsychiatry and Clinical Neurosciences, 27*(3), 240–243.

Carson, A. J., Ringbauer, B., Stone, J., McKenzie, L., Warlow, C., & Sharpe, M. (2000). Do medically unexplained symptoms matter? A prospective cohort study of 300 new referrals to neurology outpatient clinics. *Journal of Neurology, Neurosurgery & Psychiatry, 68*(2), 207–210.

Carton, S., Thompson, P. J., & Duncan, J. S. (2003). Non-epileptic seizures: patients' understanding and reaction to the diagnosis and impact on outcome. *Seizure, 12*(5), 287–294.

Clark, D. M. (1986). A cognitive approach to panic. *Behaviour Research and Therapy, 24*(4), 461–470.

Clark, D. M., & Wells, A. (1995). A cognitive model of social phobia. In R. G. Heimberg, M. R. Liebowitz, D. A. Hope, & F. R. Schneier (Eds.), *Social phobia: diagnosis, assessment, and treatment* (pp. 69–93). New York: The Guilford Press.

Charcot, J. M. (1889). On sciatica, neurasthenia and hysteria. *Journal of the American Medical Association, 12*(7), 228–230.

Cope, S. R., Smith, J. G., King, T., & Agrawal, N. (2017). Evaluation of a pilot innovative cognitive-behavioral therapy-based psychoeducation group treatment for functional non-epileptic attacks. *Epilepsy & Behavior, 70*, 238–244.

Demartini, B., Petrochilos, P., Ricciardi, L., Price, G., Edwards, M. J., & Joyce, E. (2014). The role of alexithymia in the development of functional motor symptoms (conversion disorder). *Journal of Neurology, Neurosurgery & Psychiatry, 85*(10), 1132–1137.

De Schipper, L. J., Vermeulen, M., Eeckhout, A. M., & Foncke, E. M. (2014). Diagnosis and management of functional neurological symptoms: the Dutch experience. *Clinical Neurology and Neurosurgery, 122*, 106–112.

Edwards, M. J., Adams, R. A., Brown, H., Parees, I., & Friston, K. J. (2012). A Bayesian account of 'hysteria'. *Brain, 135*(11), 3495–3512.

Ehlers, A., & Clark, D. M. (2000). A cognitive model of posttraumatic stress disorder. *Behaviour Research and Therapy, 38*(4), 319–345.

Espay, A. J., Goldenhar, L. M., Voon, V., Schrag, A., Burton, N., & Lang, A. E. (2009). Opinions and clinical practices related to diagnosing and managing patients with psychogenic movement disorders: an international survey of movement disorder society members. *Movement Disorders: Official Journal of the Movement Disorder Society, 24*(9), 1366–1374.

Fobian, A. D., & Elliott, L. (2019). A review of functional neurological symptom disorder etiology and the integrated etiological summary model. *Journal of Psychiatry and Neuroscience*, *44*(1), 8–18.

French, R. (2001). *Getting Along and Keeping Cool: a group program for aggression control.* Perth: Rioby Publishing.

Freud, S., & Breuer, J. (1895). *Studies on hysteria. se, 2.* London: Hogarth, 255–305.

Gardiner, P., MacGregor, L., Carson, A., & Stone, J. (2018). Occupational therapy for functional neurological disorders: a scoping review and agenda for research. *CNS Spectrums*, *23*(3), 205–212.

Goldstein, L. H., Chalder, T., Chigwedere, C., Khondoker, M. R., Moriarty, J., Toone, B. K., & Mellers, J. D. C. (2010). Cognitive-behavioral therapy for psychogenic nonepileptic seizures: a pilot RCT. *Neurology*, *74*(24), 1986–1994.

Goldstein, L. H., Deale, A. C., O'Malley, S. J. M., Toone, B. K., & Mellers, J. D. (2004). An evaluation of cognitive behavioral therapy as a treatment for dissociative seizures: a pilot study. *Cognitive and Behavioral Neurology*, *17*(1), 41–49.

Goldstein, L. H., & Mellers, J. D. C. (2006). Ictal symptoms of anxiety, avoidance behaviour, and dissociation in patients with dissociative seizures. *Journal of Neurology, Neurosurgery & Psychiatry*, *77*(5), 616–621.

Green, A., Payne, S., & Barnitt, R. (2004). Illness representations among people with non-epileptic seizures attending a neuropsychiatry clinic: a qualitative study based on the self-regulation model. *Seizure*, *13*(5), 331–339.

Griffith, J. L., Polles, A., & Griffith, M. E. (1998). Pseudoseizures, families, and unspeakable dilemmas. *Psychosomatics*, *39*(2), 144–153.

Hirsch, C. R., Beale, S., Grey, N., & Liness, S. (2019). Approaching cognitive behavior therapy for generalized anxiety disorder from a cognitive process perspective. *Frontiers in Psychiatry*, *10*, 796.

Janet, P. (1920). The major symptoms of hysteria: fifteen lectures given in the Medical School of Harvard University, Second edition with new matter. *American Journal of Psychiatry*, 78(3), 487–488.

Kanaan, R. A., Armstrong, D., & Wessely, S. C. (2011). Neurologists' understanding and management of conversion disorder. *Journal of Neurology, Neurosurgery & Psychiatry*, *82*(9), 961–966.

Keynejad, R. C., Frodl, T., Kanaan, R., Pariante, C., Reuber, M., & Nicholson, T. R. (2019). Stress and functional neurological disorders: mechanistic insights. *Journal of Neurology, Neurosurgery & Psychiatry*, *90*(7), 813–821.

Klinke, M. E., Hjartardóttir, T. E., Hauksdóttir, A., Jónsdóttir, H., Hjaltason, H., & Andrésdóttir, G. T. (2021). Moving from stigmatization toward competent interdisciplinary care of patients with functional neurological disorders: focus group interviews. *Disability and Rehabilitation*, *43*(9), 1237–1246.

Krawetz, P., Fleisher, W., Pillay, N., Staley, D., Arnett, J., & Maher, J. (2001). Family functioning in subjects with pseudoseizures and epilepsy. *The Journal of Nervous and Mental Disease*, *189*(1), 38–43.

Kuyk, J., Siffels, M. C., Bakvis, P., & Swinkels, W. A. (2008). Psychological treatment of patients with psychogenic non-epileptic seizures: an outcome study. *Seizure*, *17*(7), 595–603.

LaFrance, W. C., Baird, G. L., Barry, J. J., Blum, A. S., Webb, A. F., Keitner, G. I., ... & Szaflarski, J. P. (2014). Multicenter pilot treatment trial for psychogenic nonepileptic seizures: a randomized clinical trial. *JAMA Psychiatry*, *71*(9), 997–1005.

LaFrance Jr, W. C., & Friedman, J. H. (2009). Cognitive behavioral therapy for psychogenic movement disorder. *Movement Disorders, 24*(12), 1856–1857.

Lehn, A., Bullock-Saxton, J., Newcombe, P., Carson, A., & Stone, J. (2019). Survey of the perceptions of health practitioners regarding Functional Neurological Disorders in Australia. *Journal of Clinical Neuroscience, 67*, 114–123.

Lempert, T., & Schmidt, D. (1990). Natural history and outcome of psychogenic seizures: a clinical study in 50 patients. *Journal of Neurology, 237*(1), 35–38.

McCormack, R., Moriarty, J., Mellers, J. D., Shotbolt, P., Pastena, R., Landes, N., ... & David, A. S. (2014). Specialist inpatient treatment for severe motor conversion disorder: a retrospective comparative study. *Journal of Neurology, Neurosurgery & Psychiatry, 85*(8), 895–900.

McMillan, K. K., Pugh, M. J., Hamid, H., Salinsky, M., Pugh, J., Noël, P. H., ... & LaFrance Jr, W. C. (2014). Providers' perspectives on treating psychogenic nonepileptic seizures: frustration and hope. *Epilepsy & Behavior, 37*, 276–281.

Monzoni, C. M., Duncan, R., Grünewald, R., & Reuber, M. (2011). How do neurologists discuss functional symptoms with their patients: a conversation analytic study. *Journal of Psychosomatic Research, 71*(6), 377–383.

Nielsen, G., Stone, J., Matthews, A., Brown, M., Sparkes, C., Farmer, R., ... & Edwards, M. (2015). Physiotherapy for functional motor disorders: a consensus recommendation. *Journal of Neurology, Neurosurgery & Psychiatry, 86*(10), 1113–1119.

O'Connell, N., Nicholson, T. R., Wessely, S., & David, A. S. (2020). Characteristics of patients with motor functional neurological disorder in a large UK mental health service: a case–control study. *Psychological Medicine, 50*(3), 446–455.

O'Sullivan, S. S., Sweeney, B. J., & McNamara, B. (2006). The opinion of the general practitioner toward clinical management of patients with psychogenic nonepileptic seizures. *Epilepsy & Behavior, 8*(1), 256–260.

Petrochilos, P., Elmalem, M. S., Patel, D., Louissaint, H., Hayward, K., Ranu, J., & Selai, C. (2020). Outcomes of a 5-week individualised MDT outpatient (day-patient) treatment programme for functional neurological symptom disorder (FNSD). *Journal of Neurology, 267*(9), 2655–2666.

Reuber, M. (2009). The etiology of psychogenic non-epileptic seizures: toward a biopsychosocial model. *Neurologic Clinics, 27*(4), 909–924.

Reuber, M., Roberts, N. A., Levita, L., Gray, C., & Myers, L. (2021). Shame in patients with psychogenic nonepileptic seizure: a narrative review. *Seizure*.

Salkovskis, P. M. (1985). Obsessional-compulsive problems: a cognitive-behavioural analysis. *Behaviour Research and Therapy, 23*(5), 571–583.

Salkovskis, P. M., & Warwick, H. M. (1986). Morbid preoccupations, health anxiety and reassurance: a cognitive-behavioural approach to hypochondriasis. *Behaviour Research and Therapy, 24*(5), 597–602.

Salkovskis, P. M., Warwick, H. M., & Deale, A. C. (2003). Cognitive-behavioral treatment for severe and persistent health anxiety (hypochondriasis). *Brief Treatment & Crisis Intervention, 3*(3), 353–367.

Schreiber, F. B., & Seitzinger, J. (1985). The stress pressure cooker: a comprehensive model of stress management. *The Police Chief, 52*, 40.

Sharpe, M., Walker, J., Williams, C., Stone, J., Cavanagh, J., Murray, G., ... & Carson, A. (2011). Guided self-help for functional (psychogenic) symptoms: a randomized controlled efficacy trial. *Neurology, 77*(6), 564–572.

Shneker, B. F., & Elliott, J. O. (2008). Primary care and emergency physician attitudes and beliefs related to patients with psychogenic nonepileptic spells. *Epilepsy & Behavior, 13*(1), 243–247.

Skinner, B. F. (1963). Operant behavior. *American Psychologist, 18*(8), 503.

Stone, J. (2009). Functional symptoms in neurology: the bare essentials. *Practical Neurology, 9*(3), 179–189.

Stone, J., Carson, A., Duncan, R., Roberts, R., Warlow, C., Hibberd, C., ... & Sharpe, M. (2010a). Who is referred to neurology clinics?—the diagnoses made in 3781 new patients. *Clinical Neurology and Neurosurgery, 112*(9), 747–751.

Stone, J., Warlow, C., & Sharpe, M. (2010b). The symptom of functional weakness: a controlled study of 107 patients. *Brain, 133*(5), 1537–1551.

Thompson, R., Isaac, C. L., Rowse, G., Tooth, C. L., & Reuber, M. (2009). What is it like to receive a diagnosis of nonepileptic seizures? *Epilepsy & Behavior, 14*(3), 508–515.

Uliaszek, A. A., Prensky, E., & Baslet, G. (2012). Emotion regulation profiles in psychogenic non-epileptic seizures. *Epilepsy & Behavior, 23*(3), 364–369.

United Kingdom Parliament White Paper. (February, 2021). Integration and innovation: working together to improve health and social care for all. Department of Health and Social Care.

Urbanek, M., Harvey, M., McGowan, J., & Agrawal, N. (2014). Regulation of emotions in psychogenic nonepileptic seizures. *Epilepsy & Behavior, 37*, 110–115.

Van der Hart, O., & Horst, R. (1989). The dissociation theory of Pierre Janet. *Journal of Traumatic Stress, 2*(4), 397–412.

Veale, D. (2007). Cognitive–behavioural therapy for obsessive–compulsive disorder. *Advances in Psychiatric Treatment, 13*(6), 438–446.

Voon, V., Brezing, C., Gallea, C., Ameli, R., Roelofs, K., LaFrance Jr, W. C., & Hallett, M. (2010). Emotional stimuli and motor conversion disorder. *Brain, 133*(5), 1526–1536.

Voon, V., Cavanna, A. E., Coburn, K., Sampson, S., Reeve, A., LaFrance Jr, W. C., & American Neuropsychiatric Association Committee for Research. (2016). Functional neuroanatomy and neurophysiology of functional neurological disorders (conversion disorder). *The Journal of Neuropsychiatry and Clinical Neurosciences, 28*(3), 168–190.

Vuilleumier, P., Chicherio, C., Assal, F., Schwartz, S., Slosman, D., & Landis, T. (2001). Functional neuroanatomical correlates of hysterical sensorimotor loss. *Brain, 124*(6), 1077–1090.

Wells, A. (1995). Meta-cognition and worry: a cognitive model of generalized anxiety disorder. *Behavioural and Cognitive Psychotherapy, 23*(3), 301–320.

Wood, B. L., McDaniel, S., Burchfiel, K., & Erba, G. (1998). Factors distinguishing families of patients with psychogenic seizures from families of patients with epilepsy. *Epilepsia, 39*(4), 432–437.

Chapter 2

Alsaadi, T. M., & Marquez, A. V. (2005). Psychogenic nonepileptic seizures. *American Family Physician, 72*(5), 849–856.

Ammerman, A., Smith, T. W., & Calancie, L. (2014). Practice-based evidence in public health: improving reach, relevance, and results. *Annual Review of Public Health, 35*, 47–63.

Beck, J. S. (1995). *Cognitive Therapy: Basics and Beyond*. New York: The Guilford Press.

Bennett, K., Diamond, C., Hoeritzauer, I., Gardiner, P., McWhirter, L., Carson, A., & Stone, J. (2021). A practical review of functional neurological disorder (FND) for the general physician. *Clinical Medicine, 21*(1), 28.

Blascovich, J., & Tomaka, J. (1993). Measures of self-esteem. In J. P. Robinson, P. R. Shaver, & L. S. Wrightsman (Eds.), *Measures of personality and social psychological attitudes* (3rd ed., pp. 115–160). Ann Arbor, MI: Institute for Social Research.

Bowman, E. S., & Markand, O. N. (1999). The contribution of life events to pseudoseizure occurrence in adults. *Bulletin of the Menninger Clinic, 63*(1), 70.

Brown, R. J. (2006). Medically unexplained symptoms: a new model. *Psychiatry, 5*(2), 43–47.

Brown, R. J., Bouska, J. F., Frow, A., Kirkby, A., Baker, G. A., Kemp, S., … & Reuber, M. (2013). Emotional dysregulation, alexithymia, and attachment in psychogenic nonepileptic seizures. *Epilepsy & Behavior, 29*(1), 178–183.

Clark, D. M. (1986). A cognitive approach to panic. *Behaviour Research and Therapy, 24*(4), 461–470.

Clark, D. M., & Wells, A. (1995). A cognitive model of social phobia. In R. G. Heimberg, M. R. Liebowitz, D. A. Hope, & F. R. Schneier (Eds.), *Social phobia: diagnosis, assessment, and treatment* (pp. 69–93). New York: The Guilford Press.

Cully, J. A., Armento, M. E., Mott, J., Nadorff, M. R., Naik, A. D., Stanley, M. A., … & Kauth, M. R. (2012). Brief cognitive behavioral therapy in primary care: a hybrid type 2 patient-randomized effectiveness-implementation design. *Implementation Science, 7*(1), 1–12.

Curran, G. M., Bauer, M., Mittman, B., Pyne, J. M., & Stetler, C. (2012). Effectiveness-implementation hybrid designs: combining elements of clinical effectiveness and implementation research to enhance public health impact. *Medical Care, 50*(3), 217.

Edwards, M. J., Adams, R. A., Brown, H., Parees, I., & Friston, K. J. (2012). A Bayesian account of 'hysteria'. *Brain, 135*(11), 3495–3512.

Gray-Little, B., Williams, V. S., & Hancock, T. D. (1997). An item response theory analysis of the Rosenberg Self-Esteem Scale. *Personality and Social Psychology Bulletin, 23*(5), 443–451.

Hansell, S., Sherman, G., & Mechanic, D. (1991). Body awareness and medical care utilization among older adults in an HMO. *Journal of Gerontology, 46*(3), S151–S159.

Kaufman, E. A., Xia, M., Fosco, G., Yaptangco, M., Skidmore, C. R., & Crowell, S. E. (2016). The Difficulties in Emotion Regulation Scale Short Form (DERS-SF): validation and replication in adolescent and adult samples. *Journal of Psychopathology and Behavioral Assessment, 38*(3), 443–455.

Kroenke, K., Spitzer, R. L., & Williams, J. B. (2001). The PHQ-9: validity of a brief depression severity measure. *Journal of General Internal Medicine, 16*(9), 606–613.

Nie, N. H., Hull, C. H., Jenkins, J. G., Steinbrenner, K., & Bent, D. (1975). Statistical package for the social sciences. San Francisco, CA: McGraw Hill.

Nielsen, G., Buszewicz, M., Stevenson, F., Hunter, R., Holt, K., Dudziec, M., … & Edwards, M. J. (2017). Randomised feasibility study of physiotherapy for patients with functional motor symptoms. *Journal of Neurology, Neurosurgery & Psychiatry, 88*(6), 484–490.

Nielsen, G., Stone, J., Matthews, A., Brown, M., Sparkes, C., Farmer, R., … & Edwards, M. (2015). Physiotherapy for functional motor disorders: a consensus recommendation. *Journal of Neurology, Neurosurgery & Psychiatry, 86*(10), 1113–1119.

Nyein, K., McMichael, L., & Turner-Stokes, L. (1999). Can a Barthel score be derived from the FIM? *Clinical Rehabilitation, 13*(1), 56–63.

Petrochilos, P., Elmalem, M. S., Patel, D., Louissaint, H., Hayward, K., Ranu, J., & Selai, C. (2020). Outcomes of a 5-week individualised MDT outpatient (day-patient) treatment programme for functional neurological symptom disorder (FNSD). *Journal of Neurology, 267*(9), 2655–2666.

Pick, S., Anderson, D. G., Asadi-Pooya, A. A., Aybek, S., Baslet, G., Bloem, B. R., … & Nicholson, T. R. (2020). Outcome measurement in functional neurological disorder: a systematic review and recommendations. *Journal of Neurology, Neurosurgery & Psychiatry, 91*(6), 638–649.

Rosenberg, M. (1965). Society and the adolescent self-image. Princeton, NJ: Princeton University Press.

Rosenberg, M. (1986). Self-esteem research. In *School desegregation research* (pp. 175–203).Boston, MA: Springer.

Schmidt, N. B., Lerew, D. R., & Trakowski, J. H. (1997). Body vigilance in panic disorder: evaluating attention to bodily perturbations. *Journal of Consulting and Clinical Psychology, 65*(2), 214.

Speed, J. (1996). Behavioral management of conversion disorder: retrospective study. *Archives of Physical Medicine and Rehabilitation, 77*(2), 147–154.

Spitzer, R. L., Kroenke, K., Williams, J. B., & Löwe, B. (2006). A brief measure for assessing generalized anxiety disorder: the GAD-7. *Archives of Internal Medicine, 166*(10), 1092–1097.

Swisher, A. K. (2010). Practice-based evidence. *Cardiopulmonary Physical Therapy Journal, 21*(2), 4.

Turner-Stokes, L., Nyein, K., Turner-Stokes, T., & Gatehouse, C. (1999). The UK FIM+ FAM: development and evaluation. *Clinical Rehabilitation, 13*(4), 277–287.

Turner-Stokes, L., Scott, H., Williams, H., & Siegert, R. (2012). The Rehabilitation Complexity Scale–extended version: detection of patients with highly complex needs. *Disability and Rehabilitation, 34*(9), 715–720.

Turner-Stokes, L., Thu, A., Williams, H., Casey, R., Rose, H., & Siegert, R. J. (2014). The Neurological Impairment Scale: reliability and validity as a predictor of functional outcome in neurorehabilitation. *Disability and Rehabilitation, 36*(1), 23–31.

Van Poppelen, D., Saifee, T. A., Schwingenschuh, P., Katschnig, P., Bhatia, K. P., Tijssen, M. A., & Edwards, M. J. (2011). Attention to self in psychogenic tremor. *Movement Disorders, 26*(14), 2575–2576.

Uliaszek, A. A., Prensky, E., & Baslet, G. (2012). Emotion regulation profiles in psychogenic non-epileptic seizures. *Epilepsy & Behavior, 23*(3), 364–369.

Wade, D. T., & Collin, C. (1988). The Barthel ADL Index: a standard measure of physical disability? *International Disability Studies, 10*(2), 64–67.

Wells, A. (1995). Meta-cognition and worry: a cognitive model of generalized anxiety disorder. *Behavioural and Cognitive Psychotherapy, 23*(3), 301–320.

Williams, I. A., Levita, L., & Reuber, M. (2018). Emotion dysregulation in patients with psychogenic nonepileptic seizures: a systematic review based on the extended process model. *Epilepsy & Behavior, 86*, 37–48.

Chapter 3

Aamir, S., Jahangir, S. F., & Farooq, S. (2009). Family functioning among depressive and dissociative (conversion) patients. *Journal of the College of Physicians and Surgeons Pakistan, 19*(5), 300–303.

Adams, C., Anderson, J., Madva, E. N., LaFrance Jr, W. C., & Perez, D. L. (2018). You've made the diagnosis of functional neurological disorder: now what? *Practical Neurology, 18*(4), 323–330.

Ahern, L., Stone, J., & Sharpe, M. C. (2009). Attitudes of neuroscience nurses toward patients with conversion symptoms. *Psychosomatics, 50*(4), 336–339.

Alexander, B. K., Coambs, R. B., & Hadaway, P. F. (1978). The effect of housing and gender on morphine self-administration in rats. *Psychopharmacology, 58*(2), 175–179.

Alper, K. (1994). Nonepileptic seizures. *Neurologic Clinics, 12*(1), 153–73.

Alsaadi, T. M., & Marquez, A. V. (2005). Psychogenic nonepileptic seizures. *American Family Physician, 72*(5), 849–856.

Asadi-Pooya, A. A., Brigo, F., Kozlowska, K., Perez, D. L., Pretorius, C., Sawchuk, T., ... & Valente, K. D. (2021). Social aspects of life in patients with functional seizures: closing the gap in the biopsychosocial formulation. *Epilepsy & Behavior, 117*, 107903.

Bakvis, P., Roelofs, K., Kuyk, J., Edelbroek, P. M., Swinkels, W. A., & Spinhoven, P. (2009a). Trauma, stress, and preconscious threat processing in patients with psychogenic nonepileptic seizures. *Epilepsia, 50*(5), 1001–1011.

Bakvis, P., Spinhoven, P., Giltay, E. J., Kuyk, J., Edelbroek, P. M., Zitman, F. G., & Roelofs, K. (2010). Basal hypercortisolism and trauma in patients with psychogenic nonepileptic seizures. *Epilepsia, 51*(5), 752–759.

Bakvis, P., Spinhoven, P., & Roelofs, K. (2009b). Basal cortisol is positively correlated to threat vigilance in patients with psychogenic nonepileptic seizures. *Epilepsy & Behavior, 16*(3), 558–560.

Bandura, A., Ross, D., & Ross, S. A. (1961). Transmission of aggression through imitation of aggressive models. *The Journal of Abnormal and Social Psychology, 63*(3), 575.

Bandura, A., & Walters, R. H. (1977). *Social learning theory* (Vol. 1). Englewood Cliffs, NJ: Prentice Hall.

Barnett, C., Armes, J., & Smith, C. (2019). Speech, language and swallowing impairments in functional neurological disorder: a scoping review. *International Journal of Language & Communication Disorders, 54*(3), 309–320.

Barnett, C., Davis, R., Mitchell, C., & Tyson, S. (2022). The vicious cycle of functional neurological disorders: a synthesis of healthcare professionals' views on working with patients with functional neurological disorder. *Disability and Rehabilitation, 44*(10), 1802–1811.

Baroni, G., Piccinini, V., Martins, W. A., de Paola, L., Paglioli, E., Margis, R., & Palmini, A. (2016). Variables associated with co-existing epileptic and psychogenic nonepileptic seizures: a systematic review. *Seizure, 37*, 35–40.

Bautista, R. E. D., Gonzales-Salazar, W., & Ochoa, J. G. (2008). Expanding the theory of symptom modeling in patents with psychogenic nonepileptic seizures. *Epilepsy & Behavior, 13*(2), 407–409.

Benabdeljlil, M. (2022). Somatization and Functional Disorders in Migrants and Refugees. In *Neurology in Migrants and Refugees* (pp. 309–322). Springer, Cham.

Benjamin, S., & Eminson, D. M. (1992). Abnormal illness behaviour: childhood experiences and long-term consequences. *International Review of Psychiatry, 4*(1), 55–69.

Bennett, K., Diamond, C., Hoeritzauer, I., Gardiner, P., McWhirter, L., Carson, A., & Stone, J. (2021). A practical review of functional neurological disorder (FND) for the general physician. *Clinical Medicine, 21*(1), 28.

Betts, T. (1990). Pseudoseizures: seizures that are not epilepsy. *Lancet (British edition), 336*(8708), 163–164.

Betts, T. I. M., & Boden, S. (1992). Diagnosis, management and prognosis of a group of 128 patients with non-epileptic attack disorder. Part I. *Seizure, 1*(1), 19–26.

Bhatia, M. S., & Sapra, S. (2005). Pseudoseizures in children: a profile of 50 cases. *Clinical Pediatrics*, *44*(7), 617–621.

Binzer, M., Andersen, P. M., & Kullgren, G. (1997). Clinical characteristics of patients with motor disability due to conversion disorder: a prospective control group study. *Journal of Neurology, Neurosurgery & Psychiatry*, *63*(1), 83–88.

Binzer, M., & Kullgren, G. (1998). Motor conversion disorder. A prospective 2- to 5-year follow-up study. *Psychosomatics*, *39*(6), 519–527.

Bowman, E. S., & Markand, O. N. (1999). The contribution of life events to pseudo-seizure occurrence in adults. *Bulletin of the Menninger Clinic*, *63*(1), 70.

Bronfenbrenner, U. (1979a). Contexts of child rearing: problems and prospects. *American Psychologist*, *34*(10), 844–850.

Bronfenbrenner, U. (1979b). *The ecology of human development: experiments by nature and design*. Cambridge, MA: Harvard University Press.

Brown, R. J. (2006). Medically unexplained symptoms: a new model. *Psychiatry*, *5*(2), 43–47.

Brown, R. J., Bouska, J. F., Frow, A., Kirkby, A., Baker, G. A., Kemp, S., ... & Reuber, M. (2013). Emotional dysregulation, alexithymia, and attachment in psychogenic nonepileptic seizures. *Epilepsy & Behavior*, *29*(1), 178–183.

Brown, R. J., & Reuber, M. (2016). Towards an integrative theory of psychogenic non-epileptic seizures (PNES). *Clinical Psychology Review*, *47*, 55–70.

Carson, A. J., Brown, R., David, A. S., Duncan, R., Edwards, M. J., Goldstein, L. H., ... & Voon, V. (2012). Functional (conversion) neurological symptoms: research since the millennium. *Journal of Neurology, Neurosurgery & Psychiatry*, *83*(8), 842–850.

Carson, A., Hallett, M., & Stone, J. (2016). Assessment of patients with functional neurologic disorders. *Handbook of Clinical Neurology*, *139*, 169–188.

Carton, S., Thompson, P. J., & Duncan, J. S. (2003). Non-epileptic seizures: patients' understanding and reaction to the diagnosis and impact on outcome. *Seizure*, *12*(5), 287–294.

Clark, D. M., & Wells, A. (1995). A cognitive model of social phobia. In R. G. Heimberg, M. R. Liebowitz, D. A. Hope, & F. R. Schneier (Eds.), *Social phobia: diagnosis, assessment, and treatment* (pp. 69–93). New York: The Guilford Press.

Crimlisk, H. L., Bhatia, K., Cope, H., David, A., Marsden, C. D., & Ron, M. A. (1998). Slater revisited: 6 year follow up study of patients with medically unexplained motor symptoms. *BMJ*, *316*(7131), 582–586.

D'Alessio, L., Giagante, B., Oddo, S., Silva, W., Solís, P., Consalvo, D., & Kochen, S. (2006). Psychiatric disorders in patients with psychogenic non-epileptic seizures, with and without comorbid epilepsy. *Seizure*, *15*(5), 333–339.

Deka, K., Chaudhury, P. K., Bora, K., & Kalita, P. (2007). A study of clinical correlates and socio-demographic profile in conversion disorder. *Indian Journal of Psychiatry*, *49*(3), 205.

Demartini, B., Petrochilos, P., Ricciardi, L., Price, G., Edwards, M. J., & Joyce, E. (2014). The role of alexithymia in the development of functional motor symptoms (conversion disorder). *Journal of Neurology, Neurosurgery & Psychiatry*, *85*(10), 1132–1137.

De Schipper, L. J., Vermeulen, M., Eeckhout, A. M., & Foncke, E. M. (2014). Diagnosis and management of functional neurological symptoms: the Dutch experience. *Clinical Neurology and Neurosurgery*, *122*, 106–112.

Dosanjh, M., Alty, J., Martin, C., Latchford, G., & Graham, C. D. (2021). What is it like to live with a functional movement disorder? An interpretative phenomenological analysis of illness experiences from symptom onset to post-diagnosis. *British Journal of Health Psychology, 26*(2), 325–342.

Edwards, M. J., Adams, R. A., Brown, H., Parees, I., & Friston, K. J. (2012a). A Bayesian account of 'hysteria'. *Brain, 135*(11), 3495–3512.

Edwards, M. J., Stone, J., & Nielsen, G. (2012b). Physiotherapists and patients with functional (psychogenic) motor symptoms: a survey of attitudes and interest. *Journal of Neurology, Neurosurgery & Psychiatry, 83*(6), 655–658.

Ekman, P. (1992). An argument for basic emotions. *Cognition & Emotion, 6*(3–4), 169–200.

Espay, A. J., Goldenhar, L. M., Voon, V., Schrag, A., Burton, N., & Lang, A. E. (2009). Opinions and clinical practices related to diagnosing and managing patients with psychogenic movement disorders: an international survey of movement disorder society members. *Movement Disorders: Official Journal of the Movement Disorder Society, 24*(9), 1366–1374.

Fobian, A. D., & Elliott, L. (2019). A review of functional neurological symptom disorder etiology and the integrated etiological summary model. *Journal of Psychiatry and Neuroscience, 44*(1), 8–18.

Gage, S. H., & Sumnall, H. R. (2019). Rat Park: how a rat paradise changed the narrative of addiction. *Addiction, 114*(5), 917–922.

Gardiner, P., MacGregor, L., Carson, A., & Stone, J. (2018). Occupational therapy for functional neurological disorders: a scoping review and agenda for research. *CNS Spectrums, 23*(3), 205–212.

Gardner, D. L., & Goldberg, R. L. (1983). Psychogenic seizures and loss. *The International Journal of Psychiatry in Medicine, 12*(2), 121–128.

Gilmour, G. S., Nielsen, G., Teodoro, T., Yogarajah, M., Coebergh, J. A., Dilley, M. D., ... & Edwards, M. J. (2020). Management of functional neurological disorder. *Journal of Neurology, 267*(7), 2164–2172.

Goldstein, L. H., & Mellers, J. D. C. (2006). Ictal symptoms of anxiety, avoidance behaviour, and dissociation in patients with dissociative seizures. *Journal of Neurology, Neurosurgery & Psychiatry, 77*(5), 616–621.

Goldstein, L. H., Robinson, E. J., Mellers, J. D., Stone, J., Carson, A., Chalder, T., ... & CODES Study Group. (2021). Psychological and demographic characteristics of 368 patients with dissociative seizures: data from the CODES cohort. *Psychological Medicine, 51*(14), 2433–2445.

Gooch, J. L., Wolcott, R., & Speed, J. (1997). Behavioral management of conversion disorder in children. *Archives of Physical Medicine and Rehabilitation, 78*(3), 264–268.

Green, A., Payne, S., & Barnitt, R. (2004). Illness representations among people with non-epileptic seizures attending a neuropsychiatry clinic: a qualitative study based on the self-regulation model. *Seizure, 13*(5), 331–339.

Griffith, J. L., Polles, A., & Griffith, M. E. (1998). Pseudoseizures, families, and unspeakable dilemmas. *Psychosomatics, 39*(2), 144–153.

Gul, A., & Ahmad, H. (2014). Cognitive deficits and emotion regulation strategies in patients with psychogenic nonepileptic seizures: a task-switching study. *Epilepsy & Behavior, 32*, 108–113.

Hadaway, P. F., Alexander, B. K., Coambs, R. B., & Beyerstein, B. (1979). The effect of housing and gender on preference for morphine-sucrose solutions in rats. *Psychopharmacology, 66*(1), 87–91.

Harden, C. L., & Ferrando, S. J. (2001). Delivering the diagnosis of psychogenic pseudoseizures: should the neurologist or the psychiatrist be responsible? *Epilepsy & Behavior, 6*(2), 519–523.

Hoeritzauer, I., Stone, J., Fowler, C., Elneil-Coker, S., Carson, A., & Panicker, J. (2016). Fowler's syndrome of urinary retention: a retrospective study of co-morbidity. *Neurourology and Urodynamics, 35*(5), 601–603.

Jungilligens, J., Wellmer, J., Schlegel, U., Kessler, H., Axmacher, N., & Popkirov, S. (2020). Impaired emotional and behavioural awareness and control in patients with dissociative seizures. *Psychological Medicine, 50*(16), 2731–2739.

Kanaan, R., Armstrong, D., Barnes, P., & Wessely, S. (2009). In the psychiatrist's chair: how neurologists understand conversion disorder. *Brain, 132*(10), 2889–2896.

Kanaan, R. A., Armstrong, D., & Wessely, S. C. (2011). Neurologists' understanding and management of conversion disorder. *Journal of Neurology, Neurosurgery & Psychiatry, 82*(9), 961–966.

Keynejad, R. C., Fenby, E., Pick, S., Moss-Morris, R., Hirsch, C., Chalder, T., … & Nicholson, T. R. (2020). Attentional processing and interpretative bias in functional neurological disorder. *Psychosomatic Medicine, 82*(6), 586–592.

Keynejad, R. C., Frodl, T., Kanaan, R., Pariante, C., Reuber, M., & Nicholson, T. R. (2019). Stress and functional neurological disorders: mechanistic insights. *Journal of Neurology, Neurosurgery & Psychiatry, 90*(7), 813–821.

Kim, Y. N., Gray, N., Jones, A., Scher, S., & Kozlowska, K. (2022). The role of physiotherapy in the management of functional neurological disorder in children and adolescents. In *Seminars in pediatric neurology, 41*(100947).

Klinke, M. E., Hjartardóttir, T. E., Hauksdóttir, A., Jónsdóttir, H., Hjaltason, H., & Andrésdóttir, G. T. (2021). Moving from stigmatization toward competent interdisciplinary care of patients with functional neurological disorders: focus group interviews. *Disability and Rehabilitation, 43*(9), 1237–1246.

Krawetz, P., Fleisher, W., Pillay, N., Staley, D., Arnett, J., & Maher, J. (2001). Family functioning in subjects with pseudoseizures and epilepsy. *The Journal of Nervous and Mental Disease, 189*(1), 38–43.

Ladha, H., Gupta, S., & Pati, S. (2017). Trends in hospital inpatient costs of psychogenic nonepileptic seizures. *Neurology 88*, (P3. 230).

LaFrance Jr, W. C., & Devinsky, O. (2002). Treatment of nonepileptic seizures. *Epilepsy & Behavior, 3*(5), 19–23.

Lancman, M. E., Brotherton, T. A., Asconapé, J. J., & Penry, J. K. (1993). Psychogenic seizures in adults: a longitudinal analysis. *Seizure, 2*(4), 281–286.

Lancman, M. E., Asconapé, J. J., Graves, S., & Gibson, P. A. (1994). Psychogenic seizures in children: long-term analysis of 43 cases. *Journal of Child Neurology, 9*(4), 404–407.

Lehn, A., Bullock-Saxton, J., Newcombe, P., Carson, A., & Stone, J. (2019). Survey of the perceptions of health practitioners regarding Functional Neurological Disorders in Australia. *Journal of Clinical Neuroscience, 67*, 114–123.

Lempert, T., & Schmidt, D. (1990). Natural history and outcome of psychogenic seizures: a clinical study in 50 patients. *Journal of Neurology, 237*(1), 35–38.

Leslie, S. A. (1988). Diagnosis and treatment of hysterical conversion reactions. *Archives of Disease in Childhood, 63*(5), 506–511.

Ludwig, L., Pasman, J. A., Nicholson, T., Aybek, S., David, A. S., Tuck, S., … & Stone, J. (2018). Stressful life events and maltreatment in conversion (functional neurological) disorder: systematic review and meta-analysis of case-control studies. *The Lancet Psychiatry, 5*(4), 307–320.

Macchi, Z. A., Kletenik, I., Olvera, C., & Holden, S. K. (2021). Psychiatric comorbidities in functional movement disorders: a retrospective cohort study. *Movement Disorders Clinical Practice, 8*(5), 725–732.

MacDuffie, K. E., Grubbs, L., Best, T., LaRoche, S., Mildon, B., Myers, L., ... & Rommelfanger, K. S. (2021). Stigma and functional neurological disorder: a research agenda targeting the clinical encounter. *CNS Spectrums, 26*(6), 587–592.

Malhi, P., & Singhi, P. (2002). Clinical characteristics and outcome of children and adolescents with conversion disorder. *Indian Pediatrics, 39*(8), 747–751.

Maloney, M. J. (1980). Diagnosing hysterical conversion reactions in children. *The Journal of Pediatrics, 97*(6), 1016–1020.

Marotta, A., Fiorio, M., Riello, M., Demartini, B., Tecilla, G., Dallocchio, C., & Tinazzi, M. (2020). Attentional avoidance of emotions in functional movement disorders. *Journal of Psychosomatic Research, 133*, 110100.

Maslow, A. H. (1943). A theory of human motivation. *Psychological Review, 50*(4), 370–396.

Mayor, R., Howlett, S., Grünewald, R., & Reuber, M. (2010). Long-term outcome of brief augmented psychodynamic interpersonal therapy for psychogenic nonepileptic seizures: seizure control and health care utilization. *Epilepsia, 51*(7), 1169–1176.

McCormack, R., Moriarty, J., Mellers, J. D., Shotbolt, P., Pastena, R., Landes, N., ... & David, A. S. (2014). Specialist inpatient treatment for severe motor conversion disorder: a retrospective comparative study. *Journal of Neurology, Neurosurgery & Psychiatry, 85*(8), 895–900.

McDade, G., & Brown, S. W. (1992). Non-epileptic seizures: management and predictive factors of outcome. *Seizure, 1*(1), 7–10.

McKenzie, P. S., Oto, M., Graham, C. D., & Duncan, R. (2011). Do patients whose psychogenic non-epileptic seizures resolve, 'replace' them with other medically unexplained symptoms? Medically unexplained symptoms arising after a diagnosis of psychogenic non-epileptic seizures. *Journal of Neurology, Neurosurgery & Psychiatry, 82*(9), 967–969.

McMillan, K. K., Pugh, M. J., Hamid, H., Salinsky, M., Pugh, J., Noël, P. H., ... & LaFrance Jr, W. C. (2014). Providers' perspectives on treating psychogenic nonepileptic seizures: frustration and hope. *Epilepsy & Behavior, 37*, 276–281.

Merkler, A. E., Parikh, N. S., Chaudhry, S., Chait, A., Allen, N. C., Navi, B. B., & Kamel, H. (2016). Hospital revisit rate after a diagnosis of conversion disorder. *Journal of Neurology, Neurosurgery & Psychiatry, 87*(4), 363–366.

Moene, F. C., Spinhoven, P., Hoogduin, K. A., & Dyck, R. V. (2003). A randomized controlled clinical trial of a hypnosis-based treatment for patients with conversion disorder, motor type. *International Journal of Clinical and Experimental Hypnosis, 51*(1), 29–50.

Monzoni, C. M., Duncan, R., Grünewald, R., & Reuber, M. (2011). How do neurologists discuss functional symptoms with their patients: a conversation analytic study. *Journal of Psychosomatic Research, 71*(6), 377–383. Moore, P. M., Baker, G. A., McDade, G., Chadwick, D., & Brown, S. (1994). Epilepsy, pseudoseizures and perceived family characteristics: a controlled study. *Epilepsy Research, 18*(1), 75–83.

Moore, P. M., & Baker, G. A. (1997). Non-epileptic attack disorder: a psychological perspective. *Seizure, 6*(6), 429–434.

Moorey, S. (2010). The six cycles maintenance model: growing a "vicious flower" for depression. *Behavioural and Cognitive Psychotherapy, 38*(2), 173–184.

Nicholson, C., Edwards, M. J., Carson, A. J., Gardiner, P., Golder, D., Hayward, K., ... & Stone, J. (2020). Occupational therapy consensus recommendations for functional neurological disorder. *Journal of Neurology, Neurosurgery & Psychiatry, 91*(10), 1037–1045.

Nielsen, G., Buszewicz, M., Edwards, M. J., & Stevenson, F. (2020). A qualitative study of the experiences and perceptions of patients with functional motor disorder. *Disability and Rehabilitation, 42*(14), 2043–2048.

Nielsen, G., Buszewicz, M., Stevenson, F., Hunter, R., Holt, K., Dudziec, M., ... & Edwards, M. J. (2017). Randomised feasibility study of physiotherapy for patients with functional motor symptoms. *Journal of Neurology, Neurosurgery & Psychiatry, 88*(6), 484–490.

Nielsen, G., Stone, J., Matthews, A., Brown, M., Sparkes, C., Farmer, R., ... & Edwards, M. (2015). Physiotherapy for functional motor disorders: a consensus recommendation. *Journal of Neurology, Neurosurgery & Psychiatry, 86*(10), 1113–1119.

Nunez-Wallace, K. R., Murphey, D. K., Proto, D., Collins, R. L., Franks, R., Chachere II, D. M., & Chen, D. K. (2015). Health resource utilization among US veterans with psychogenic nonepileptic seizures: a comparison before and after video-EEG monitoring. *Epilepsy Research, 114*, 114–121.

O'Connell, N., Nicholson, T. R., Wessely, S., & David, A. S. (2020). Characteristics of patients with motor functional neurological disorder in a large UK mental health service: a case–control study. *Psychological Medicine, 50*(3), 446–455.

O'Keeffe, S., Chowdhury, I., Sinanaj, A., Ewang, I., Blain, C., Teodoro, T., ... & Yogarajah, M. (2021). A service evaluation of the experiences of patients with functional neurological disorders within the NHS. *Frontiers in Neurology, 12*, 656466. doi: 10.3389/fneur.2021.656466

O'Sullivan, S. S., Sweeney, B. J., & McNamara, B. (2006). The opinion of the general practitioner toward clinical management of patients with psychogenic nonepileptic seizures. *Epilepsy & Behavior, 8*(1), 256–260.

Panicker, J. N., Selai, C., Herve, F., Rademakers, K., Dmochowski, R., Tarcan, T., ... & Vrijens, D. (2020). Psychological comorbidities and functional neurological disorders in women with idiopathic urinary retention: International Consultation on Incontinence Research Society (ICI-RS) 2019. *Neurourology and Urodynamics, 39*, S60–S69.

Pareés, I., Kassavetis, P., Saifee, T. A., Sadnicka, A., Bhatia, K. P., Fotopoulou, A., & Edwards, M. J. (2012). 'Jumping to conclusions' bias in functional movement disorders. *Journal of Neurology, Neurosurgery & Psychiatry, 83*(4), 460–463.

Perez, D. L., Matin, N., Barsky, A., Costumero-Ramos, V., Makaretz, S. J., Young, S. S., ... & Dickerson, B. C. (2017). Cingulo-insular structural alterations associated with psychogenic symptoms, childhood abuse and PTSD in functional neurological disorders. *Journal of Neurology, Neurosurgery & Psychiatry, 88*(6), 491–497.

Perez, D. L., Nicholson, T. R., Asadi-Pooya, A. A., Bègue, I., Butler, M., Carson, A. J., ... & Aybek, S. (2021). Neuroimaging in functional neurological disorder: state of the field and research agenda. *NeuroImage: Clinical, 30*, 102623.

Petrochilos, P., Elmalem, M. S., Patel, D., Louissaint, H., Hayward, K., Ranu, J., & Selai, C. (2020). Outcomes of a 5-week individualised MDT outpatient (day-patient) treatment programme for functional neurological symptom disorder (FNSD). *Journal of Neurology, 267*(9), 2655–2666.

Pick, S., Mellers, J. D., & Goldstein, L. H. (2016). Explicit facial emotion processing in patients with dissociative seizures. *Psychosomatic Medicine, 78*(7), 874–885.

Pick, S., Mellers, J. D., & Goldstein, L. H. (2018). Implicit attentional bias for facial emotion in dissociative seizures: additional evidence. *Epilepsy & Behavior, 80*, 296–302.

Pick, S., Goldstein, L. H., Perez, D. L., & Nicholson, T. R. (2019). Emotional processing in functional neurological disorder: a review, biopsychosocial model and research agenda. *Journal of Neurology, Neurosurgery & Psychiatry, 90*(6), 704–711.

Ramani, V., & Gumnit, R. J. (1982). Management of hysterical seizures in epileptic patients. *Archives of Neurology, 39*(2), 78–81.

Rawlings, G. H., & Reuber, M. (2018). Health care practitioners' perceptions of psychogenic nonepileptic seizures: a systematic review of qualitative and quantitative studies. *Epilepsia, 59*(6), 1109–1123.

Razvi, S., Mulhern, S., & Duncan, R. (2012). Newly diagnosed psychogenic nonepileptic seizures: health care demand prior to and following diagnosis at a first seizure clinic. *Epilepsy & Behavior, 23*(1), 7–9.

Reuber, M., Roberts, N. A., Levita, L., Gray, C., & Myers, L. (2022). Shame in patients with psychogenic nonepileptic seizure: A narrative review. Seizure, 94, 165–175.

Reuber, M., Roberts, N. A., Levita, L., Gray, C., & Myers, L. (2021). Shame in patients with psychogenic nonepileptic seizure: a narrative review. *Seizure.*

Robson, C., & Lian, O. S. (2017). "Blaming, shaming, humiliation": stigmatising medical interactions among people with non-epileptic seizures. *Wellcome Open Research*, 2:55. doi: 2 10.12688/wellcomeopenres.12133.1

Rommelfanger, K. S., Factor, S. A., LaRoche, S., Rosen, P., Young, R., & Rapaport, M. H. (2017). Disentangling stigma from functional neurological disorders: conference report and roadmap for the future. *Frontiers in Neurology, 8*, 106.

Rosenberg, M. (1965). Society and the adolescent self-image. Princeton, NJ: Princeton University Press.

Sahaya, K., Dholakia, S. A., Lardizabal, D., & Sahota, P. K. (2012). Opinion survey of health care providers towards psychogenic non epileptic seizures. *Clinical Neurology and Neurosurgery, 114*(10), 1304–1307.

Salmon, P., Al-Marzooqi, S. M., Baker, G., & Reilly, J. (2003). Childhood family dysfunction and associated abuse in patients with nonepileptic seizures: towards a causal model. *Psychosomatic Medicine, 65*(4), 695–700.

Shneker, B. F., & Elliott, J. O. (2008). Primary care and emergency physician attitudes and beliefs related to patients with psychogenic nonepileptic spells. *Epilepsy & Behavior, 13*(1), 243–247.

Skinner, B. F. (1963). Operant behavior. *American Psychologist, 18*(8), 503.

Speed, J. (1996). Behavioral management of conversion disorder: retrospective study. *Archives of Physical Medicine and Rehabilitation, 77*(2), 147–154.

Stephen, C. D., Perez, D. L., Chibnik, L. B., & Sharma, N. (2021). Functional dystonia: a case-control study and risk prediction algorithm. *Annals of Clinical and Translational Neurology, 8*(4), 732–748.

Stone, J. (2009). Functional symptoms in neurology: the bare essentials. *Practical Neurology, 9*(3), 179–189.

Stone, J., Binzer, M., & Sharpe, M. (2004a). Illness beliefs and locus of control: a comparison of patients with pseudoseizures and epilepsy. *Journal of Psychosomatic Research, 57*(6), 541–547.

Stone, J., Burton, C., & Carson, A. (2020). Recognising and explaining functional neurological disorder. *BMJ, 371*:m3745. doi: 10.1136/bmj.m3745 pmid: 33087335

Stone, J., & Carson, A. J. (2013). The unbearable lightheadedness of seizing: wilful submission to dissociative (non-epileptic) seizures. *Journal of Neurology, Neurosurgery & Psychiatry, 84*(7), 822–824.

Stone, J., Sharpe, M., & Binzer, M. (2004b). Motor conversion symptoms and pseudoseizures: a comparison of clinical characteristics. *Psychosomatics, 45*(6), 492–499.

Stone, J., Warlow, C., & Sharpe, M. (2010). The symptom of functional weakness: a controlled study of 107 patients. *Brain, 133*(5), 1537–1551.

Thompson, R., Isaac, C. L., Rowse, G., Tooth, C. L., & Reuber, M. (2009). What is it like to receive a diagnosis of nonepileptic seizures? *Epilepsy & Behavior, 14*(3), 508–515.

Thompson, N. C., Osorio, I., & Hunter, E. E. (2005). Nonepileptic seizures: reframing the diagnosis. *Perspectives in Psychiatric Care, 41*(2), 71–78.

Tojek, T. M., Lumley, M., Barkley, G., Mahr, G., & Thomas, A. (2000). Stress and other psychosocial characteristics of patients with psychogenic nonepileptic seizures. *Psychosomatics, 41*(3), 221–226.

Turgay, A. (1990). Treatment outcome for children and adolescents with conversion disorder. *The Canadian Journal of Psychiatry, 35*(7), 585–589.

Uliaszek, A. A., Prensky, E., & Baslet, G. (2012). Emotion regulation profiles in psychogenic non-epileptic seizures. *Epilepsy & Behavior, 23*(3), 364–369.

Urbanek, M., Harvey, M., McGowan, J., & Agrawal, N. (2014). Regulation of emotions in psychogenic nonepileptic seizures. *Epilepsy & Behavior, 37*, 110–115.

Van Poppelen, D., Saifee, T. A., Schwingenschuh, P., Katschnig, P., Bhatia, K. P., Tijssen, M. A., & Edwards, M. J. (2011). Attention to self in psychogenic tremor. *Movement Disorders, 26*(14), 2575–2576.

Vincentiis, S., Valente, K. D., Thomé-Souza, S., Kuczinsky, E., Fiore, L. A., & Negrão, N. (2006). Risk factors for psychogenic nonepileptic seizures in children and adolescents with epilepsy. *Epilepsy & Behavior, 8*(1), 294–298.

Vroegop, S., Dijkgraaf, M. G., & Vermeulen, M. (2013). Impact of symptoms in patients with functional neurological symptoms on activities of daily living and health related quality of life. *Journal of Neurology, Neurosurgery & Psychiatry, 84*(6), 707–708.

Walczak, T. S., Papacostas, S., Williams, D. T., Scheuer, M. L., Lebowitz, N., & Notarfrancesco, A. (1995). Outcome after diagnosis of psychogenic nonepileptic seizures. *Epilepsia, 36*(11), 1131–1137.

Wilkus, R. J., Dodrill, C. B., & Thompson, P. M. (1984). Intensive EEG monitoring and psychological studies of patients with pseudoepileptic seizures. *Epilepsia, 25*(1), 100–107.

Williams, I. A., Levita, L., & Reuber, M. (2018). Emotion dysregulation in patients with psychogenic nonepileptic seizures: a systematic review based on the extended process model. *Epilepsy & Behavior, 86*, 37–48.

Wood, B. L., McDaniel, S., Burchfiel, K., & Erba, G. (1998). Factors distinguishing families of patients with psychogenic seizures from families of patients with epilepsy. *Epilepsia, 39*(4), 432–437.

Wyllie, E., Glazer, J. P., Benbadis, S., Kotagal, P., & Wolgamuth, B. (1999). Psychiatric features of children and adolescents with pseudoseizures. *Archives of Pediatrics & Adolescent Medicine, 153*(3), 244–248.

Chapter 4

Aamir, S., Jahangir, S. F., & Farooq, S. (2009). Family functioning among depressive and dissociative (conversion) patients. *Journal of the College of Physicians and Surgeons Pakistan, 19*(5), 300–303.

Amir, N., Beard, C., & Bower, E. (2005). Interpretation bias and social anxiety. *Cognitive Therapy and Research, 29*(4), 433–443.

Ball, H. A., McWhirter, L., Ballard, C., Bhome, R., Blackburn, D. J., Edwards, M. J., … & Carson, A. J. (2020). Functional cognitive disorder: dementia's blind spot. *Brain, 143*(10), 2895–2903.

Barkham, M., Margison, F., Leach, C., Lucock, M., Mellor-Clark, J., Evans, C., ... & McGrath, G. (2001). Service profiling and outcomes benchmarking using the CORE-OM: toward practice-based evidence in the psychological therapies. *Journal of Consulting and Clinical Psychology*, *69*(2), 184.

Becerra, R., Preece, D. A., & Gross, J. J. (2020). Assessing beliefs about emotions: development and validation of the Emotion Beliefs Questionnaire. *PLoS One*, *15*(4), e0231395.

Beck, A. T., Epstein, N., Brown, G., & Steer, R. A. (1988). An inventory for measuring anxiety: Psychometric properties. *Journal of Consulting and Clinical Psychology*, 56.893–897.

Beck, A. T., & Steer, R. A. (1990). Manual for the Beck Anxiety Inventory San Antonio, TX Psychological Corporation.

Beck, A. T., Ward, C., Mendelson, M., Mock, J., & Erbaugh, J. J. A. G. P. (1961). Beck depression inventory (BDI). *Archives of General Psychiatry*, *4*(6), 561–571.

Beck Judith, S. (1995). *Cognitive Therapy: Basics and Beyond*. New York: The Guilford Press.

Becker, E., Rinck, M., & Margraf, J. (1994). Memory bias in panic disorder. *Journal of Abnormal Psychology*, *103*(2), 396.

Bédard, M., Molloy, D. W., Squire, L., Dubois, S., Lever, J. A., & O'Donnell, M. (2001). The Zarit Burden Interview: a new short version and screening version. *The Gerontologist*, *41*(5), 652–657.

Beecham, J., & Knapp, M. (1992). Client Service Receipt Inventory (CSRI). Database of Instruments for Resource Use Management.

Bennett, K., Diamond, C., Hoeritzauer, I., Gardiner, P., McWhirter, L., Carson, A., & Stone, J. (2021). A practical review of functional neurological disorder (FND) for the general physician. *Clinical Medicine*, *21*(1), 28.

Briere, J., & Runtz, M. (2002). The inventory of altered self-capacities (IASC) a standardized measure of identity, affect regulation, and relationship disturbance. *Assessment*, *9*(3), 230–239.

Broadbent, E., Petrie, K. J., Main, J., & Weinman, J. (2006). The brief illness perception questionnaire. *Journal of Psychosomatic Research*, *60*(6), 631–637.

Brown, G. W. (1989). Life events and measurement. In G. W. Brown & T. O. Harris (Eds.), *Life events and illness* (pp. 3–45). New York: Guilford Press.

Brown, R. J. (2006). Medically unexplained symptoms: a new model. *Psychiatry*, *5*(2), 43–47.

Brown, R. J., Bouska, J. F., Frow, A., Kirkby, A., Baker, G. A., Kemp, S., ... & Reuber, M. (2013). Emotional dysregulation, alexithymia, and attachment in psychogenic nonepileptic seizures. *Epilepsy & Behavior*, *29*(1), 178–183.

Carlson, E. B., & Putnam, F. W. (1993). An update on the Dissociative Experiences Scale. *Dissociation: Progress in the Dissociative Disorders*, *6*(1), 16–27.

Clark, D. M. (1986). A cognitive approach to panic. *Behaviour Research and Therapy*, *24*(4), 461–470.

Clayton, I. C., Richards, J. C., & Edwards, C. J. (1999). Selective attention in obsessive–compulsive disorder. *Journal of Abnormal Psychology*, *108*(1), 171.

Cloitre, M., & Liebowitz, M. R. (1991). Memory bias in panic disorder: An investigation of the cognitive avoidance hypothesis. *Cognitive Therapy and Research*, *15*(5), 371–386.

Edwards, M. J., Adams, R. A., Brown, H., Parees, I., & Friston, K. J. (2012). A Bayesian account of 'hysteria'. *Brain*, *135*(11), 3495–3512.

Ehlers, A., Hackmann, A., & Michael, T. (2004). Intrusive re-experiencing in post-traumatic stress disorder: Phenomenology, theory, and therapy. *Memory, 12*(4), 403–415.

Epstein, N. B., Baldwin, L. M., & Bishop, D. S. (1983). The McMaster family assessment device. *Journal of Marital and Family Therapy, 9*(2), 171–180.

Feinstein, J. S., Adolphs, R., Damasio, A., & Tranel, D. (2011). The human amygdala and the induction and experience of fear. *Current Biology, 21*(1), 34–38.

First, M. B., Spitzer, R. L., Gibbon, M., & Williams, J. B. W. (2008). Structured clinical interview for DSM-IV axis I disorders (SCID-I). In A. J. Rush, M. B. First, & D. Blacker (Eds.), Handbook of psychiatric measures. Washington, DC: American Psychiatric Publishing.

Goldstein, L. H., Robinson, E. J., Mellers, J. D., Stone, J., Carson, A., Chalder, T., ... & CODES Study Group. (2021). Psychological and demographic characteristics of 368 patients with dissociative seizures: data from the CODES cohort. *Psychological Medicine, 51*(14), 2433–2445.

Graham, K. S., & Hodges, J. R. (1997). Differentiating the roles of the hippocampus complex and the neocortex in long-term memory storage: Evidence from the study of semantic dementia and Alzheimer's disease. *Neuropsychology, 11*(1), 77.

Gratz, K. L., & Roemer, L. (2004). Multidimensional assessment of emotion regulation and dysregulation: development, factor structure, and initial validation of the difficulties in emotion regulation scale. *Journal of Psychopathology and Behavioral Assessment, 26*(1), 41–54.

Griffith, J. L., Polles, A., & Griffith, M. E. (1998). Pseudoseizures, families, and unspeakable dilemmas. *Psychosomatics, 39*(2), 144–153.

Gross, J. J., & John, O. P. (1997). Revealing feelings: facets of emotional expressivity in self-reports, peer ratings, and behavior. *Journal of Personality and Social Psychology, 72*(2), 435.

Gross, J. J., & John, O. P. (2003). Individual differences in two emotion regulation processes: implications for affect, relationships, and well-being. *Journal of Personality and Social Psychology, 85*(2), 348.

Halvorsen J. G. (1991) Self-report family assessment instruments: An evaluative review. Family Pract Res J 1:21–55.

Hansell, S., & Mechanic, D. (1991). Body awareness and self-assessed health among older adults. *Journal of Aging and Health, 3*(4), 473–492.

Hansell, S., Sherman, G., & Mechanic, D. (1991). Body awareness and medical care utilization among older adults in an HMO. *Journal of Gerontology, 46*(3), S151–S159.

Hirsch, C. R., & Mathews, A. (2012). A cognitive model of pathological worry. *Behaviour research and therapy, 50*(10), 636–646.

Hirsch, C. R., Beale, S., Grey, N., & Liness, S. (2019). Approaching cognitive behavior therapy for generalized anxiety disorder from a cognitive process perspective. *Frontiers in psychiatry, 10*, 796.

Horowitz, M., Wilner, N., & Alvarez, W. (1979). Impact of Event Scale: a measure of subjective stress. *Psychosomatic Medicine, 41*(3), 209–218.

Jacobson, N. S., & Truax, P. (1991). Clinical significance: a statistical approach to defining meaningful change in psychotherapy research. *Journal of Consulting and Clinical Psychology, 59*(1), 12–19.

Kapur, N., Kemp, S., & Baker, G. (2021). Functional cognitive disorder: Dementia's blind spot. *Brain, 144*(4), e37–e37.

Kaufman, E. A., Xia, M., Fosco, G., Yaptangco, M., Skidmore, C. R., & Crowell, S. E. (2016). The Difficulties in Emotion Regulation Scale Short Form

(DERS-SF): validation and replication in adolescent and adult samples. *Journal of Psychopathology and Behavioral Assessment*, *38*(3), 443–455.

Kopelman, M.D., Wilson, B.A., & Baddeley, A.D. (1990). The Autobiographical Memory Interview. (Manual). Bury St Edmunds: Thames Valley Test Company.

Kroenke, K., Spitzer, R. L., & Williams, J. B. (2001). The PHQ-9: validity of a brief depression severity measure. *Journal of General Internal Medicine*, *16*(9), 606–613.

Kubany, E. S., Leisen, M. B., Kaplan, A. S., Watson, S. B., Haynes, S. N., Owens, J. A., & Burns, K. (2000). Development and preliminary validation of a brief broad-spectrum measure of trauma exposure: the Traumatic Life Events Questionnaire. *Psychological Assessment*, *12*(2), 210.

Law, M., Baptiste, S., McColl, M., Opzoomer, A., Polatajko, H., & Pollock, N. (1990). The Canadian occupational performance measure: an outcome measure for occupational therapy. *Canadian Journal of Occupational Therapy*, *57*(2), 82–87.

LeDoux, J. (1996). Emotional networks and motor control: a fearful view. *Progress in Brain Research*, *107*, 437–446.

LeDoux, J. (2003). The emotional brain, fear, and the amygdala. *Cellular and Molecular Neurobiology*, *23*(4), 727–738.

Lundh, L. G., Wikström, J., Westerlund, J., & Öst, L. G. (1999). Preattentive bias for emotional information in panic disorder with agoraphobia. *Journal of Abnormal Psychology*, *108*(2), 222.

Maidenberg, E., Chen, E., Craske, M., Bohn, P., & Bystritsky, A. (1996). Specificity of attentional bias in panic disorder and social phobia. *Journal of Anxiety Disorders*, *10*(6), 529–541.

McNally, R. J., English, G. E., & Lipke, H. J. (1993). Assessment of intrusive cognition in PTSD: Use of the modified Stroop paradigm. *Journal of Traumatic stress*, *6*(1), 33–41.

Miller, L. C., Murphy, R., & Buss, A. H. (1981). Consciousness of body: private and public. *Journal of Personality and Social Psychology*, *41*(2), 397.

Morey, L. C. (1991). Personality assessment inventory. Odessa: Psychological Assessment Resources.

Muller, J., & Roberts, J. E. (2005). Memory and attention in obsessive–compulsive disorder: a review. *Journal of anxiety disorders*, *19*(1), 1–28.

Nielsen, G., Buszewicz, M., Stevenson, F., Hunter, R., Holt, K., Dudziec, M., ... & Edwards, M. J. (2017). Randomised feasibility study of physiotherapy for patients with functional motor symptoms. *Journal of Neurology, Neurosurgery & Psychiatry*, *88*(6), 484–490.

Olson, D. H., Bell, R., & Portner, J. (1978). Family adaptability and cohesion evaluation scales (FACES). Unpublished manuscript.

Olson, D. H., Larsen, A. S., & McCubbin, H. I. (1982). The Family Strengths Inventory. St Paul, Mn.: Family Social Sciences, University of Manitoba.

Olson, D. H. (1989). Family assessment and intervention: the Circumplex Model of family systems. *Child & Youth Services*, *11*(1), 9–48.

O'Neill, R., Horner, R. H., Albin, R. W., Sprague, J. R., Storey, K., & Newton, J. S. (1997). Functional assessment for problem behaviors: A practical handbook (2nd Ed.). Pacific Grove, CA: Brooks/Cole.

Pareés, I., Kassavetis, P., Saifee, T. A., Sadnicka, A., Bhatia, K. P., Fotopoulou, A., & Edwards, M. J. (2012). 'Jumping to conclusions' bias in functional movement disorders. *Journal of Neurology, Neurosurgery & Psychiatry*, *83*(4), 460–463.

Petrochilos, P., Elmalem, M. S., Patel, D., Louissaint, H., Hayward, K., Ranu, J., & Selai, C. (2020). Outcomes of a 5-week individualised MDT outpatient (day-patient) treatment programme for functional neurological symptom disorder (FNSD). *Journal of Neurology, 267*(9), 2655–2666.

Pishyar, R., Harris, L. M., & Menzies, R. G. (2004). Attentional bias for words and faces in social anxiety. *Anxiety, Stress & Coping, 17*(1), 23–36.

Porges, S. (1993). Body perception questionnaire. *Laboratory of Developmental Assessment, University of Maryland, 10*, s15327752jpa5304_1.

Rimes, K. A., & Chalder, T. (2010). The Beliefs about Emotions Scale: validity, reliability and sensitivity to change. *Journal of Psychosomatic Research, 68*(3), 285–292.

Salkovskis, P. M., Warwick, H. M., & Deale, A. C. (2003). Cognitive-behavioral treatment for severe and persistent health anxiety (hypochondriasis). *Brief Treatment & Crisis Intervention, 3*(3), 353–367.

Schmidt, N. B., Lerew, D. R., & Trakowski, J. H. (1997). Body vigilance in panic disorder: evaluating attention to bodily perturbations. *Journal of Consulting and Clinical Psychology, 65*(2), 214.

Shields, S. A., Mallory, M. E., & Simon, A. (1989). The body awareness questionnaire: reliability and validity. *Journal of Personality Assessment, 53*(4), 802–815.

Snowden, J. S., Griffiths, H. L., & Neary, D. (1996). Semantic-episodic memory interactions in semantic dementia: Implications for retrograde memory function. *Cognitive Neuropsychology, 13*(8), 1101–1139.

Spitzer, R. L., Kroenke, K., Williams, J. B., & Löwe, B. (2006). A brief measure for assessing generalized anxiety disorder: the GAD-7. *Archives of Internal Medicine, 166*(10), 1092–1097.

Stone, J. (2009). Functional symptoms in neurology: the bare essentials. *Practical Neurology, 9*(3), 179–189.

Stone, J., Warlow, C., & Sharpe, M. (2010). The symptom of functional weakness: a controlled study of 107 patients. *Brain, 133*(5), 1537–1551.

Teodoro, T., Edwards, M. J., & Isaacs, J. D. (2018). A unifying theory for cognitive abnormalities in functional neurological disorders, fibromyalgia and chronic fatigue syndrome: systematic review. *Journal of Neurology, Neurosurgery & Psychiatry, 89*(12), 1308–1319.

Thompson, P. J., Baxendale, S. A., Duncan, J. S., & Sander, J. W. A. S. (2000). Effects of topiramate on cognitive function. *Journal of Neurology, Neurosurgery & Psychiatry, 69*(5), 636–641.

Uliaszek, A. A., Prensky, E., & Baslet, G. (2012). Emotion regulation profiles in psychogenic non-epileptic seizures. *Epilepsy & Behavior, 23*(3), 364–369.

Watkins, P. C., Vache, K., Verney, S. P., Muller, S., & Mathews, A. (1996). Unconscious mood-congruent memory bias in depression. *Journal of abnormal psychology, 105*(1), 34.

Weiss, D. S., & Marmar, C. R. (1997). The impact of event scale—revised. In J. P. Wilson & T. M. Keane (Eds.), *Assessing psychological trauma and PTSD* (pp. 399–411). New York: The Guilford Press, 399–411.

Chapter 5

Ahern, L., Stone, J., & Sharpe, M. C. (2009). Attitudes of neuroscience nurses toward patients with conversion symptoms. *Psychosomatics, 50*(4), 336–339.

Ahles, T. A., Saykin, A. J., Furstenberg, C. T., Cole, B., Mott, L. A., Skalla, K., ... & Silberfarb, P. M. (2002). Neuropsychologic impact of standard-dose systemic chemotherapy in long-term survivors of breast cancer and lymphoma. *Journal of Clinical Oncology, 20*(2), 485–493.

Ahles, T. A., Root, J. C., & Ryan, E. L. (2012). Cancer-and cancer treatment–associated cognitive change: an update on the state of the science. *Journal of Clinical Oncology, 30*(30), 3675.

Almis, B. H., Cumurcu, B. E., Unal, S., Ozcan, A. C., & Aytas, O. (2013). The neuropsychological and neurophysiological profile of women with pseudoseizure. *Comprehensive psychiatry, 54*(6), 649–657.

Alsaadi, T. M., & Marquez, A. V. (2005). Psychogenic nonepileptic seizures. *American Family Physician, 72*(5), 849–856.

Angeli, E., Nguyen, T. T., Janin, A., & Bousquet, G. (2019). How to make anti-cancer drugs cross the blood–brain barrier to treat brain metastases. *International journal of molecular sciences, 21*(1), 22.

Bakvis, P., Roelofs, K., Kuyk, J., Edelbroek, P. M., Swinkels, W. A., & Spinhoven, P. (2009a). Trauma, stress, and preconscious threat processing in patients with psychogenic nonepileptic seizures. *Epilepsia, 50*(5), 1001–1011.

Bakvis, P., Spinhoven, P., & Roelofs, K. (2009b). Basal cortisol is positively correlated to threat vigilance in patients with psychogenic nonepileptic seizures. *Epilepsy & Behavior, 16*(3), 558–560.

Ball, H. A., McWhirter, L., Ballard, C., Bhome, R., Blackburn, D. J., Edwards, M. J., ... & Carson, A. J. (2020). Functional cognitive disorder: dementia's blind spot. *Brain, 143*(10), 2895–2903.

Beck, J. S. (1995). *Cognitive Therapy: Basics and Beyond.* New York: The Guilford Press.

Betts, T. I. M., & Boden, S. (1992). Diagnosis, management and prognosis of a group of 128 patients with non-epileptic attack disorder. Part I. *Seizure, 1*(1), 19–26.

Bhome, R., Huntley, J. D., Price, G., & Howard, R. J. (2019). Clinical presentation and neuropsychological profiles of functional cognitive disorder patients with and without co-morbid depression. *Cognitive Neuropsychiatry, 24*(2), 152–164.

Bigler, E. D. (2008). Neuropsychology and clinical neuroscience of persistent post-concussive syndrome. *Journal of the International Neuropsychological Society, 14*(1), 1-22.

Bowman, E. S., & Markand, O. N. (1999). The contribution of life events to pseudo-seizure occurrence in adults. *Bulletin of the Menninger Clinic, 63*(1), 70.

Boykoff, N., Moieni, M., & Subramanian, S. K. (2009). Confronting chemobrain: an in-depth look at survivors' reports of impact on work, social networks, and health care response. *Journal of cancer survivorship, 3*(4), 223–232.

Brown, L. B., Nicholson, T. R., Aybek, S., Kanaan, R. A., & David, A. S. (2014). Neuropsychological function and memory suppression in conversion disorder. *Journal of Neuropsychology, 8*(2), 171–185.

Castellon, S. A., Ganz, P. A., Bower, J. E., Petersen, L., Abraham, L., & Greendale, G. A. (2004). Neurocognitive performance in breast cancer survivors exposed to adjuvant chemotherapy and tamoxifen. *Journal of clinical and experimental neuropsychology, 26*(7), 955-969.

Clark, D. M., & Wells, A. (1995). A cognitive model of social phobia. In R. G. Heimberg, M. R. Liebowitz, D. A. Hope, & F. R. Schneier (Eds.), *Social phobia: diagnosis, assessment, and treatment* (pp. 69–93). New York: The Guilford Press.

Collie, A., Makdissi, M., Maruff, P., Bennell, K., & McCrory, P. (2006). Cognition in the days following concussion: comparison of symptomatic versus asymptomatic athletes. *Journal of Neurology, Neurosurgery & Psychiatry, 77*(2), 241–245.

Collins, B., Mackenzie, J., Stewart, A., Bielajew, C., & Verma, S. (2009). Cognitive effects of chemotherapy in post-menopausal breast cancer patients 1 year after treatment. *Psycho-Oncology: Journal of the Psychological, Social and Behavioral Dimensions of Cancer, 18*(2), 134–143.

Donovan, K. A., Small, B. J., Andrykowski, M. A., Schmitt, F. A., Munster, P., & Jacobsen, P. B. (2005). Cognitive functioning after adjuvant chemotherapy and/or radiotherapy for early-stage breast carcinoma. *Cancer: Interdisciplinary International Journal of the American Cancer Society, 104*(11), 2499–2507.

Edwards, M. J., Adams, R. A., Brown, H., Parees, I., & Friston, K. J. (2012). A Bayesian account of 'hysteria'. *Brain, 135*(11), 3495–3512.

Edwards, M. J., Stone, J., & Nielsen, G. (2012). Physiotherapists and patients with functional (psychogenic) motor symptoms: a survey of attitudes and interest. *Journal of Neurology, Neurosurgery & Psychiatry, 83*(6), 655–658.

Fardell, J. E., Vardy, J., Johnston, I. N., & Winocur, G. (2011). Chemotherapy and cognitive impairment: treatment options. *Clinical Pharmacology & Therapeutics, 90*(3), 366–376.

Fayette, D., Gahérová, Ľ., Mócikivá, H., Marková, J., Kozák, T., & Horáček, J. (2017). Chemotherapy-related cognitive impairment in patients with hodgkin lymphoma-pathophysiology and risk factors. *Klinicka Onkologie: Casopis Ceske a Slovenske Onkologicke Spolecnosti, 30*(2), 93–99.

Fobian, A. D., & Elliott, L. (2019). A review of functional neurological symptom disorder etiology and the integrated etiological summary model. *Journal of Psychiatry and Neuroscience, 44*(1), 8–18.

Griffith, J. L., Polles, A., & Griffith, M. E. (1998). Pseudoseizures, families, and unspeakable dilemmas. *Psychosomatics, 39*(2), 144–153.

Hammar, Å., & Årdal, G. (2009). Cognitive functioning in major depression-a summary. *Frontiers in Human Neuroscience, 3*, 26.

Hamouda, K., Senf-Beckenbach, P. A., Gerhardt, C., Irorutola, F., Rose, M., & Hinkelmann, K. (2021). Executive Functions and Attention in Patients With Psychogenic Nonepileptic Seizures Compared With Healthy Controls: A Cross-Sectional Study. *Psychosomatic Medicine, 83*(8), 880–886.

Heintz, C. E., van Tricht, M. J., van der Salm, S. M., Van Rootselaar, A. F., Cath, D., Schmand, B., & Tijssen, M. A. (2013). Neuropsychological profile of psychogenic jerky movement disorders: importance of evaluating non-credible cognitive performance and psychopathology. *Journal of Neurology, Neurosurgery & Psychiatry, 84*(8), 862–867.

Hermelink, K. (2015). Chemotherapy and cognitive function in breast cancer patients: the so-called chemo brain. *Journal of the National Cancer Institute Monographs, 2015*(51), 67–69.

Hermelink, K., Bühner, M., Sckopke, P., Neufeld, F., Kaste, J., Voigt, V., ... & Harbeck, N. (2017). Chemotherapy and post-traumatic stress in the causation of cognitive dysfunction in breast cancer patients. *JNCI: Journal of the National Cancer Institute, 109*(10), djx057.

Hurria, A., Somlo, G., & Ahles, T. (2007). Renaming "chemobrain". *Cancer Investigation, 25*(6), 373–377.

Huys, A. C. M., Bhatia, K. P., Edwards, M. J., & Haggard, P. (2020). The flip side of distractibility—Executive dysfunction in functional movement disorders. *Frontiers in Neurology, 11*, 969.

Iverson, G. L., Gaetz, M., Lovell, M. R., & Collins, M. W. (2004). Cumulative effects of concussion in amateur athletes. *Brain injury, 18*(5), 433–443.

Iverson, G. L., Gaetz, M., Lovell, M. R., & Collins, M. W. (2004). Relation between subjective fogginess and neuropsychological testing following concussion. *Journal of the International Neuropsychological Society, 10*(6), 904–906.

Iverson, G. L., Echemendia, R. J., LaMarre, A. K., Brooks, B. L., & Gaetz, M. B. (2012). Possible lingering effects of multiple past concussions. *Rehabilitation research and practice, 2012*.

Jacobson, N. S., & Truax, P. (1991). Clinical significance: a statistical approach to defining meaningful change in psychotherapy research. *Journal of Consulting and Clinical Psychology, 59*(1), 12–19.

Jim, H. S., Phillips, K. M., Chait, S., Faul, L. A., Popa, M. A., Lee, Y. H., ... & Small, B. J. (2012). Meta-analysis of cognitive functioning in breast cancer survivors previously treated with standard-dose chemotherapy. *Journal of Clinical Oncology, 30*(29), 3578.

Kopelman, M.D., Wilson, B.A., & Baddeley, A.D. (1990). *The Autobiographical Memory Interview.* (Manual). Bury St Edmunds: Thames Valley Test Company.

Leon-Sarmiento, F. E., Bayona-Prieto, J., Leon-Ariza, J. S., Leon-Ariza, D. S., Jacob, A. E., LaFaver, K., & Doty, R. L. (2019). Smell status in functional movement disorders: New clues for diagnosis and underlying mechanisms. *Clinical Neurology and Neurosurgery, 177*, 68–72.

Levy, R., & Dubois, B. (2006). Apathy and the functional anatomy of the prefrontal cortex–basal ganglia circuits. *Cerebral Cortex, 16*(7), 916–928.

Magyari, F., Virga, I., Simon, Z., Miltényi, Z., Illés, A., Kósa, K., ... & Illés, Á. (2022). Assessment of cognitive function in long-term Hodgkin lymphoma survivors, results based on data from a major treatment center in Hungary. *Supportive Care in Cancer, 30*(6), 5249–5258.

Marotta, A., Fiorio, M., Riello, M., Demartini, B., Tecilla, G., Dallocchio, C., & Tinazzi, M. (2020). Attentional avoidance of emotions in functional movement disorders. *Journal of Psychosomatic Research, 133*, 110100.

Matsuda, T., Takayama, T., Tashiro, M., Nakamura, Y., Ohashi, Y., & Shimozuma, K. (2005). Mild cognitive impairment after adjuvant chemotherapy in breast cancer patients-evaluation of appropriate research design and methodology to measure symptoms. *Breast cancer, 12*(4), 279–287.

McDonald, B. C., Conroy, S. K., Smith, D. J., West, J. D., & Saykin, A. J. (2013). Frontal gray matter reduction after breast cancer chemotherapy and association with executive symptoms: a replication and extension study. *Brain, behavior, and immunity, 30*, S117–S125.

McWhirter, L., Ritchie, C., Stone, J., & Carson, A. (2020). Functional cognitive disorders: a systematic review. *The Lancet Psychiatry, 7*(2), 191–207.

Metternich, B., Schmidtke, K., & Hüll, M. (2009). How are memory complaints in functional memory disorder related to measures of affect, metamemory and cognition?. *Journal of psychosomatic research, 66*(5), 435–444.

Mohn, C., & Rund, B. R. (2016). Neurocognitive profile in major depressive disorders: relationship to symptom level and subjective memory complaints. *BMC Psychiatry, 16*(1), 1–6.

Moorey, S. (2010). The six cycles maintenance model: growing a "vicious flower" for depression. *Behavioural and Cognitive Psychotherapy, 38*(2), 173–184.

Moretti, R., & Signori, R. (2016). Neural correlates for apathy: frontal-prefrontal and parietal cortical-subcortical circuits. *Frontiers in Aging Neuroscience, 8,* 289.

O'Brien, F. M., Fortune, G. M., Dicker, P., O'Hanlon, E., Cassidy, E., Delanty, N., … & Murphy, K. C. (2015). Psychiatric and neuropsychological profiles of people with psychogenic nonepileptic seizures. *Epilepsy & Behavior, 43,* 39–45.

Pick, S., Mellers, J. D., & Goldstein, L. H. (2016). Explicit facial emotion processing in patients with dissociative seizures. *Psychosomatic medicine, 78*(7), 874–885.

Pick, S., Mellers, J. D., & Goldstein, L. H. (2018). Implicit attentional bias for facial emotion in dissociative seizures: additional evidence. *Epilepsy & Behavior, 80,* 296–302.

Rabins, P. V., & Nestadt, G. (1985). Reversible dementia and depression. *The British Journal of Psychiatry, 146*(2), 212–213.

Rock, P. L., Roiser, J. P., Riedel, W. J., & Blackwell, A. (2014). Cognitive impairment in depression: a systematic review and meta-analysis. *Psychological Medicine, 44*(10), 2029–2040.

Saykin, A. J., Ahles, T. A., & McDonald, B. C. (2003). Mechanisms of chemotherapy-induced cognitive disorders: neuropsychological, pathophysiological, and neuroimaging perspectives. *Semin Clin Neuropsychiatry, 8:* 201–216.

Schagen, S. B., van Dam, F. S., Muller, M. J., Boogerd, W., Lindeboom, J., & Bruning, P. F. (1999). Cognitive deficits after postoperative adjuvant chemotherapy for breast carcinoma. *Cancer: Interdisciplinary International Journal of the American Cancer Society, 85*(3), 640–650.

Schmidtke, K., Pohlmann, S., & Metternich, B. (2008). The syndrome of functional memory disorder: definition, etiology, and natural course. *The American Journal of Geriatric Psychiatry, 16*(12), 981–988.

Shilling, V., Jenkins, V., Morris, R., Deutsch, G., & Bloomfield, D. (2005). The effects of adjuvant chemotherapy on cognition in women with breast cancer—preliminary results of an observational longitudinal study. *The Breast, 14*(2), 142–150.

Silverman, D. H., Dy, C. J., Castellon, S. A., Lai, J., Pio, B. S., Abraham, L., … & Ganz, P. A. (2007). Altered frontocortical, cerebellar, and basal ganglia activity in adjuvant-treated breast cancer survivors 5–10 years after chemotherapy. *Breast Cancer Research and Treatment, 103*(3), 303–311.

Sterr, A., Herron, K. A., Hayward, C., & Montaldi, D. (2006). Are mild head injuries as mild as we think? Neurobehavioral concomitants of chronic post-concussion syndrome. *BMC neurology, 6*(1), 1–10.

Stewart, A., Bielajew, C., Collins, B., Parkinson, M., & Tomiak, E. (2006). A meta-analysis of the neuropsychological effects of adjuvant chemotherapy treatment in women treated for breast cancer. *The Clinical Neuropsychologist, 20*(1), 76–89.

Tannock, I. F., Ahles, T. A., Ganz, P. A., & Van Dam, F. S. (2004). Cognitive impairment associated with chemotherapy for cancer: report of a workshop. *Journal of Clinical Oncology, 22*(11), 2233–2239.

Teodoro, T., Edwards, M. J., & Isaacs, J. D. (2018). A unifying theory for cognitive abnormalities in functional neurological disorders, fibromyalgia and chronic fatigue syndrome: systematic review. *Journal of Neurology, Neurosurgery & Psychiatry, 89*(12), 1308–1319.

Trachtenberg, E., Mashiach, T., Ben Hayun, R., Tadmor, T., Fisher, T., Aharon-Peretz, J., & Dann, E. J. (2018). Cognitive impairment in hodgkin lymphoma survivors. *British journal of haematology, 182*(5), 670–678.

Turner-Stokes, L., Nyein, K., Turner-Stokes, T., & Gatehouse, C. (1999). The UK FIM+ FAM: development and evaluation. *Clinical Rehabilitation, 13*(4), 277–287.

Turner-Stokes, L., Thu, A., Williams, H., Casey, R., Rose, H., & Siegert, R. J. (2014). The Neurological Impairment Scale: reliability and validity as a predictor of functional outcome in neurorehabilitation. *Disability and Rehabilitation, 36*(1), 23–31.

Van Dam, F. S., Boogerd, W., Schagen, S. B., Muller, M. J., Droogleever Fortuyn, M. E., Wall, E. V., & Rodenhuis, S. (1998). Impairment of cognitive function in women receiving adjuvant treatment for high-risk breast cancer: high-dose versus standard-dose chemotherapy. *JNCI: Journal of the National Cancer Institute, 90*(3), 210–218.

Vander Werff, K. R., & Rieger, B. (2019). Impaired auditory processing and neural representation of speech in noise among symptomatic post-concussion adults. *Brain injury, 33*(10), 1320–1331.

Van Wouwe, N. C., Mohanty, D., Lingaiah, A., Wylie, S. A., & LaFaver, K. (2020). Impaired action control in patients with functional movement disorders. *The Journal of Neuropsychiatry and Clinical Neurosciences, 32*(1), 73–78.

Věchetová, G., Nikolai, T., Slovák, M., Forejtová, Z., Vranka, M., Straková, E., ... & Serranová, T. (2022). Attention impairment in motor functional neurological disorders: a neuropsychological study. *Journal of Neurology, 269*(11), 5981–5990.

Vitali, M., Ripamonti, C. I., Roila, F., Proto, C., Signorelli, D., Imbimbo, M., ... & Russo, G. L. (2017). Cognitive impairment and chemotherapy: a brief overview. *Critical Reviews in Oncology/Hematology, 118*, 7–14.

Voon, V., Ekanayake, V., Wiggs, E., Kranick, S., Ameli, R., Harrison, N. A., & Hallett, M. (2013). Response inhibition in motor conversion disorder. *Movement Disorders, 28*(5), 612–618.

Wakefield, S. J., Blackburn, D. J., Harkness, K., Khan, A., Reuber, M., & Venneri, A. (2018). Distinctive neuropsychological profiles differentiate patients with functional memory disorder from patients with amnestic-mild cognitive impairment. *Acta Neuropsychiatrica, 30*(2), 90–96.

Wefel, J. S., Lenzi, R., Theriault, R. L., Davis, R. N., & Meyers, C. A. (2004). The cognitive sequelae of standard-dose adjuvant chemotherapy in women with breast carcinoma: results of a prospective, randomized, longitudinal trial. *Cancer: Interdisciplinary International Journal of the American Cancer Society, 100*(11), 2292–2299.

Wieneke, M. H., & Dienst, E. R. (1995). Neuropsychological assessment of cognitive functioning following chemotherapy for breast cancer. *Psycho-oncology, 4*(1), 61–66.

Zakzanis, K. K., Leach, L., & Kaplan, E. (1998). On the nature and pattern of neurocognitive function in major depressive disorder. *Neuropsychiatry, Neuropsychology, & Behavioral Neurology, 11*(3), 111–119.

Zigmond, A. S., & Snaith, R. P. (1983). The hospital anxiety and depression scale. *Acta Psychiatrica Scandinavica, 67*(6), 361–370.

Chapter 6

American Psychiatric Association. (2013). *Diagnostic and statistical manual of mental disorders* (5th ed.). Washington, DC, London: American Psychiatric Association Publishing. https://doi.org/10.1176/appi.books.9780890425596

Arntz, A., Bernstein, D., Oorschot, M., & Schobre, P. (2009). Theory of mind in borderline and cluster-C personality disorder. *The Journal of Nervous and Mental Disease, 197*(11), 801–807.

Baron-Cohen, S. (2000). Theory of mind and autism: a review. *International Review of Research in Mental Retardation, 23*, 169–184.

Baron-Cohen, S. (2001). Theory of mind in normal development and autism. *Prisme, 34*(1), 74–183.

Baron-Cohen, S., Jolliffe, T., Mortimore, C., & Robertson, M. (1997). Another advanced test of theory of mind: evidence from very high functioning adults with autism or Asperger syndrome. *Journal of Child Psychology and Psychiatry, 38*(7), 813–822.

Barry, J. J., Wittenberg, D., Bullock, K. D., Michaels, J. B., Classen, C. C., & Fisher, R. S. (2008). Group therapy for patients with psychogenic nonepileptic seizures: a pilot study. *Epilepsy & Behavior, 13*(4), 624–629.

Baslet, G., Roiko, A., & Prensky, E. (2010). Heterogeneity in psychogenic nonepileptic seizures: understanding the role of psychiatric and neurological factors. *Epilepsy & Behavior, 17*(2), 236–241.

Beck, J. S. (1995). *Cognitive Therapy: Basics and Beyond.* New York: The Guilford Press.

Benbadis, S. R., Agrawal, V., & Tatum, W. O. (2001). How many patients with psychogenic nonepileptic seizures also have epilepsy? *Neurology, 57*(5), 915–917.

Bennett, K., Diamond, C., Hoeritzauer, I., Gardiner, P., McWhirter, L., Carson, A., & Stone, J. (2021). A practical review of functional neurological disorder (FND) for the general physician. *Clinical Medicine, 21*(1), 28.

Binzer, M., Andersen, P. M., & Kullgren, G. (1997). Clinical characteristics of patients with motor disability due to conversion disorder: a prospective control group study. *Journal of Neurology, Neurosurgery & Psychiatry, 63*(1), 83–88.

Brown, R. J., Bouska, J. F., Frow, A., Kirkby, A., Baker, G. A., Kemp, S., ... & Reuber, M. (2013). Emotional dysregulation, alexithymia, and attachment in psychogenic nonepileptic seizures. *Epilepsy & Behavior, 29*(1), 178–183.

Bullock, K. D., Mirza, N., Forte, C., & Trockel, M. (2015). Group dialectical-behavior therapy skills training for conversion disorder with seizures. *The Journal of Neuropsychiatry and Clinical Neurosciences, 27*(3), 240–243.

Cai, R. Y., Richdale, A. L., Uljarević, M., Dissanayake, C., & Samson, A. C. (2018). Emotion regulation in autism spectrum disorder: where we are and where we need to go. *Autism Research, 11*(7), 962–978.

Canitano, R. (2007). Epilepsy in autism spectrum disorders. *European Child & Adolescent Psychiatry, 16*(1), 61–66.

Cassady, J. D., Kirschke, D. L., Jones, T. F., Craig, A. S., Bermudez, O. B., & Schaffner, W. (2005). Case series: outbreak of conversion disorder among Amish adolescent girls. *Journal of the American Academy of Child & Adolescent Psychiatry, 44*(3), 291–297.

Chen, D. K., Maheshwari, A., Franks, R., Trolley, G. C., Robinson, J. S., & Hrachovy, R. A. (2014). Brief group psychoeducation for psychogenic nonepileptic seizures: a neurologist-initiated program in an epilepsy center. *Epilepsia, 55*(1), 156–166.

Conner, C. M., Golt, J., Shaffer, R., Righi, G., Siegel, M., & Mazefsky, C. A. (2021). Emotion dysregulation is substantially elevated in autism compared to the general population: impact on psychiatric services. *Autism Research, 14*(1), 169–181.

Conwill, M., Oakley, L., Evans, K., & Cavanna, A. E. (2014). CBT-based group therapy intervention for nonepileptic attacks and other functional neurological symptoms: a pilot study. *Epilepsy & Behavior, 34*, 68–72.

Cope, S. R., Smith, J. G., King, T., & Agrawal, N. (2017). Evaluation of a pilot innovative cognitive-behavioral therapy-based psychoeducation group treatment for functional non-epileptic attacks. *Epilepsy & Behavior, 70,* 238–244.

Creeden, K. (2009). How trauma and attachment can impact neurodevelopment: informing our understanding and treatment of sexual behaviour problems. *Journal of Sexual Aggression, 15*(3), 261–273.

Demartini, B., Petrochilos, P., Ricciardi, L., Price, G., Edwards, M. J., & Joyce, E. (2014). The role of alexithymia in the development of functional motor symptoms (conversion disorder). *Journal of Neurology, Neurosurgery & Psychiatry, 85*(10), 1132–1137.

Doss, J., Caplan, R., Siddarth, P., Bursch, B., Falcone, T., Forgey, M., ... & Plioplys, S. (2017). Risk factors for learning problems in youth with psychogenic non-epileptic seizures. *Epilepsy & Behavior, 70,* 135–139.

DuBois, D., Ameis, S. H., Lai, M. C., Casanova, M. F., & Desarkar, P. (2016). Interoception in autism spectrum disorder: a review. *International Journal of Developmental Neuroscience, 52,* 104–111.

Duncan, R., & Oto, M. (2008). Psychogenic nonepileptic seizures in patients with learning disability: comparison with patients with no learning disability. *Epilepsy & Behavior, 12*(1), 183–186.

Edwards, M. J., Adams, R. A., Brown, H., Parees, I., & Friston, K. J. (2012). A Bayesian account of 'hysteria'. *Brain, 135*(11), 3495–3512.

Franzen, N., Hagenhoff, M., Baer, N., Schmidt, A., Mier, D., Sammer, G., ... & Lis, S. (2011). Superior 'theory of mind' in borderline personality disorder: an analysis of interaction behavior in a virtual trust game. *Psychiatry Research, 187*(1–2), 224–233.

Frith, U. (1994). Autism and theory of mind in everyday life. *Social Development, 3*(2), 108–124.

Gardiner, P., MacGregor, L., Carson, A., & Stone, J. (2018). Occupational therapy for functional neurological disorders: a scoping review and agenda for research. *CNS Spectrums, 23*(3), 205–212.

Gray, N., Savage, B., Scher, S., & Kozlowska, K. (2020). Psychologically informed physical therapy for children and adolescents with functional neurological symptoms: the wellness approach. *The Journal of Neuropsychiatry and Clinical Neurosciences, 32*(4), 389–395.

Happé, F., & Frith, U. (1995). Theory of mind in autism. In *Learning and cognition in autism* (pp. 177–197). Boston, MA: Springer.

Herringa, R. J. (2017). Trauma, PTSD, and the developing brain. *Current Psychiatry Reports, 19*(10), 1–9.

Jones, A., Esteban-Serna, C., Proctor, B. J., Yogarajah, M., & Agrawal, N. (2021). An evaluation of initial engagement with a virtual group-based psychological treatment for functional seizures. *Epilepsy & Behavior, 125,* 108384.

Joshi, G., Wozniak, J., Fitzgerald, M., Faraone, S., Fried, R., Galdo, M., ... & Biederman, J. (2018). High risk for severe emotional dysregulation in psychiatrically referred youth with autism spectrum disorder: a controlled study. *Journal of Autism and Developmental Disorders, 48*(9), 3101–3115.

Kim, Y. N., Gray, N., Jones, A., Scher, S., & Kozlowska, K. (2021). The role of physiotherapy in the management of functional neurological disorder in children and adolescents. In *Seminars in pediatric neurology* (p. 100947). WB Saunders.

Kinnaird, E., Stewart, C., & Tchanturia, K. (2019). Investigating alexithymia in autism: a systematic review and meta-analysis. *European Psychiatry, 55,* 80–89.

Klinke, M. E., Hjartardóttir, T. E., Hauksdóttir, A., Jónsdóttir, H., Hjaltason, H., & Andrésdóttir, G. T. (2021). Moving from stigmatization toward competent inter-disciplinary care of patients with functional neurological disorders: focus group interviews. *Disability and Rehabilitation*, *43*(9), 1237–1246.

Koreki, A., Garfkinel, S. N., Mula, M., Agrawal, N., Cope, S., Eilon, T., ... & Yogarajah, M. (2020). Trait and state interoceptive abnormalities are associated with dissociation and seizure frequency in patients with functional seizures. *Epilepsia*, *61*(6), 1156–1165.

Kozlowska, K., Sawchuk, T., Waugh, J. L., Helgeland, H., Baker, J., Scher, S., & Fobian, A. D. (2021). Changing the culture of care for children and adolescents with functional neurological disorder. *Epilepsy & Behavior Reports*, *16*, 100486.

Krumholz, A., & Niedermeyer, E. (1983). Psychogenic seizures: a clinical study with follow-up data. *Neurology*, *33*(4), 498.

Kutlubaev, M. A., Xu, Y., Hackett, M. L., & Stone, J. (2018). Dual diagnosis of epi-lepsy and psychogenic nonepileptic seizures: systematic review and meta-analysis of frequency, correlates, and outcomes. *Epilepsy & Behavior*, *89*, 70–78.

LeDoux, J. (1996). Emotional networks and motor control: a fearful view. *Progress in Brain Research*, *107*, 437–446.

LeDoux, J. (2003). The emotional brain, fear, and the amygdala. *Cellular and Molecular Neurobiology*, *23*(4), 727–738.

Lesser, R. P., Lueders, H., & Dinner, D. S. (1983). Evidence for epilepsy is rare in patients with psychogenic seizures. *Neurology*, *33*(4), 502–502.

Levisohn, P. M. (2007). The autism-epilepsy connection. *Epilepsia*, *48*, 33–35.

Libbon, R., Gadbaw, J., Watson, M., Rothberg, B., Sillau, S., Heru, A., & Strom, L. (2019). The feasibility of a multidisciplinary group therapy clinic for the treatment of nonepileptic seizures. *Epilepsy & Behavior*, *98*, 117–123.

Lin, A., & Espay, A. J. (2021). Remote delivery of cognitive behavioral therapy to patients with functional neurological disorders: promise and challenges. *Epilepsy & Behavior Reports*, *16*, 100469.

Mazefsky, C. A., Yu, L., White, S. W., Siegel, M., & Pilkonis, P. A. (2018). The emotion dysregulation inventory: psychometric properties and item response theory calibration in an autism spectrum disorder sample. *Autism Research*, *11*(6), 928–941.

McFarlane, F. A., Allcott-Watson, H., Hadji-Michael, M., McAllister, E., Stark, D., Reilly, C., ... & Heyman, I. (2019). Cognitive-behavioural treatment of func-tional neurological symptoms (conversion disorder) in children and adolescents: a case series. *European Journal of Paediatric Neurology*, *23*(2), 317–328.

McWilliams, A., Reilly, C., Gupta, J., Hadji-Michael, M., Srinivasan, R., & Heyman, I. (2019). Autism spectrum disorder in children and young people with non-epileptic seizures. *Seizure*, *73*, 51–55.

Meierkord, H., Will, B., Fish, D., & Shorvon, S. (1991). The clinical features and prognosis of pseudoseizures diagnosed using video-EEG telemetry. *Neurology*, *41*(10), 1643–1646.

Metin, S. Z., Ozmen, M., Metin, B., Talasman, S., Yeni, S. N., & Ozkara, C. (2013). Treatment with group psychotherapy for chronic psychogenic nonepileptic sei-zures. *Epilepsy & Behavior*, *28*(1), 91–94.

Mikulincer, M., & Shaver, P. R. (2003). The attachment behavioral system in adult-hood: activation, psychodynamics, and interpersonal processes. In Advances in Experimental Social Psychology, vol. 35. Edited by Zanna M. New York: Aca-demic Press; 53–152.

Milosavljevic, B., Carter Leno, V., Simonoff, E., Baird, G., Pickles, A., Jones, C. R., ... & Happé, F. (2016). Alexithymia in adolescents with autism spectrum disorder: its relationship to internalising difficulties, sensory modulation and social cognition. *Journal of Autism and Developmental Disorders*, *46*(4), 1354–1367.

Miyawaki, D., Iwakura, Y., Seto, T., Kusaka, H., Goto, A., Okada, Y., ... & Inoue, K. (2016). Psychogenic nonepileptic seizures as a manifestation of psychological distress associated with undiagnosed autism spectrum disorder. *Neuropsychiatric Disease and Treatment*, *12*, 185.

Moene, F. C., Hoogduin, K. A., & Dyck, R. V. (1998). The inpatient treatment of patients suffering from (motor) conversion symptoms: a description of eight cases. *International Journal of Clinical and Experimental Hypnosis*, *46*(2), 171–190.

Moorey, S. (2010). The six cycles maintenance model: growing a "vicious flower" for depression. *Behavioural and Cognitive Psychotherapy*, *38*(2), 173–184.

Morgante, F., Matinella, A., Andrenelli, E., Ricciardi, L., Allegra, C., Terranova, C., ... & Tinazzi, M. (2018). Pain processing in functional and idiopathic dystonia: an exploratory study. *Movement Disorders*, *33*(8), 1340–1348.

Morgante, F., Tinazzi, M., Squintani, G., Martino, D., Defazio, G., Romito, L., ... & Berardelli, A. (2011). Abnormal tactile temporal discrimination in psychogenic dystonia. *Neurology*, *77*(12), 1191–1197.

Mul, C. L., Stagg, S. D., Herbelin, B., & Aspell, J. E. (2018). The feeling of me feeling for you: interoception, alexithymia and empathy in autism. *Journal of Autism and Developmental Disorders*, *48*(9), 2953–2967.

Myers, L., Matzner, B., Lancman, M., Perrine, K., & Lancman, M. (2013). Prevalence of alexithymia in patients with psychogenic non-epileptic seizures and epileptic seizures and predictors in psychogenic non-epileptic seizures. *Epilepsy & Behavior*, *26*(2), 153–157.

Németh, N., Mátrai, P., Hegyi, P., Czéh, B., Czopf, L., Hussain, A., ... & Simon, M. (2018). Theory of mind disturbances in borderline personality disorder: a meta-analysis. *Psychiatry Research*, *270*, 143–153.

Neuhaus, E., Webb, S. J., & Bernier, R. A. (2019). Linking social motivation with social skill: the role of emotion dysregulation in autism spectrum disorder. *Development and Psychopathology*, *31*(3), 931–943.

Nicholson, T. M., Williams, D. M., Grainger, C., Christensen, J. F., Calvo-Merino, B., & Gaigg, S. B. (2018). Interoceptive impairments do not lie at the heart of autism or alexithymia. *Journal of Abnormal Psychology*, *127*(6), 612.

Nisticò, V., Goeta, D., Iacono, A., Tedesco, R., Giordano, B., Faggioli, R., ... & Demartini, B. (2022). Clinical overlap between functional neurological disorders and autism spectrum disorders: a preliminary study. *Neurological Sciences*, *43(8)*, 5067–5073.

Normann, E., Antonsen, B. T., Kvarstein, E. H., Pedersen, G. F., Vaskinn, A., & Wilberg, T. (2019). Are impairments in theory of mind specific to borderline personality disorder? *Journal of Personality Disorders,* *34(6)*, 827–841.

Paleari, V., Nisticò, V., Nardocci, N., Canevini, M. P., Priori, A., Gambini, O., ... & Demartini, B. (2022). Socio-demographic characteristics and psychopathological assessment in a sample of 13 paediatric patients with functional neurological disorders: a preliminary report. *Clinical Child Psychology and Psychiatry*, *27*(2), 492–503.

Perry, B. D., Griffin, G., Davis, G., Perry, J. A., & Perry, R. D. (2018). The impact of neglect, trauma, and maltreatment on neurodevelopment: implications for juvenile justice practice, programs, and policy. *The Wiley Blackwell Handbook of Forensic Neuroscience, 1,* 813–835.

Pick, S., Rojas-Aguiluz, M., Butler, M., Mulrenan, H., Nicholson, T. R., & Goldstein, L. H. (2020). Dissociation and interoception in functional neurological disorder. *Cognitive Neuropsychiatry, 25*(4), 294–311.

Pillai, J. A., & Haut, S. R. (2012). Patients with epilepsy and psychogenic non-epileptic seizures: an inpatient video-EEG monitoring study. *Seizure, 21*(1), 24–27.

Plioplys, S., Doss, J., Siddarth, P., Bursch, B., Falcone, T., Forgey, M., ... & Caplan, R. (2014). A multisite controlled study of risk factors in pediatric psychogenic nonepileptic seizures. *Epilepsia, 55*(11), 1739–1747.

Poquérusse, J., Pastore, L., Dellantonio, S., & Esposito, G. (2018). Alexithymia and autism spectrum disorder: a complex relationship. *Frontiers in Psychology, 9,* 1196.

Quattrocki, E., & Friston, K. (2014). Autism, oxytocin and interoception. *Neuroscience & Biobehavioral Reviews, 47,* 410–430.

Ranford, J., MacLean, J., Alluri, P. R., Comeau, O., Godena, E., LaFrance Jr, W. C., ... & Perez, D. L. (2020). Sensory processing difficulties in functional neurological disorder: a possible predisposing vulnerability? *Psychosomatics, 61*(4), 343–352.

Raper, J., Currigan, V., Fothergill, S., Stone, J., & Forsyth, R. J. (2019). Long-term outcomes of functional neurological disorder in children. *Archives of Disease in Childhood, 104*(12), 1155–1160.

Ricciardi, L., Demartini, B., Crucianelli, L., Krahé, C., Edwards, M. J., & Fotopoulou, A. (2016). Interoceptive awareness in patients with functional neurological symptoms. *Biological Psychology, 113,* 68–74.

Ricciardi, L., Nisticò, V., Andrenelli, E., Cunha, J. M., Demartini, B., Kirsch, L. P., ... & Edwards, M. J. (2021). Exploring three levels of interoception in people with functional motor disorders. *Parkinsonism & Related Disorders, 86,* 15–18.

Riquelme, I., Hatem, S. M., & Montoya, P. (2016). Abnormal pressure pain, touch sensitivity, proprioception, and manual dexterity in children with autism spectrum disorders. *Neural Plasticity, 2016*: 1-9 e1723401. Crossref. PubMed.

Samson, A. C., Phillips, J. M., Parker, K. J., Shah, S., Gross, J. J., & Hardan, A. Y. (2014). Emotion dysregulation and the core features of autism spectrum disorder. *Journal of Autism and Developmental Disorders, 44*(7), 1766–1772.

Senf-Beckenbach, P., Hoheisel, M., Devine, J., Frank, A., Obermann, L., Rose, M., & Hinkelmann, K. (2022). Evaluation of a new body-focused group therapy versus a guided self-help group program for adults with psychogenic non-epileptic seizures (PNES): a pilot randomized controlled feasibility study. *Journal of Neurology, 269*(1), 427–436.

Sequeira, A. S., & Silva, B. (2019). A comparison among the prevalence of alexithymia in patients with psychogenic nonepileptic seizures, epilepsy, and the healthy population: a systematic review of the literature. *Psychosomatics, 60*(3), 238–245.

Silver, L. B. (1982). Conversion disorder with pseudoseizures in adolescence: a stress reaction to unrecognized and untreated learning disabilities. *Journal of the American Academy of Child Psychiatry, 21*(5), 508–512.

Silveri, M. C., Di Tella, S., Lo Monaco, M. R., Petracca, M., Tondinelli, A., Antonucci, G., ... & Bentivoglio, A. R. (2022). Theory of mind: a clue for the interpretation of functional movement disorders. *Acta Neurologica Scandinavica, 145*(5), 571–578.

Tager-Flusberg, H. (2007). Evaluating the theory-of-mind hypothesis of autism. *Current Directions in Psychological Science, 16*(6), 311–315.

Tuchman, R., & Cuccaro, M. (2011). Epilepsy and autism: neurodevelopmental perspective. *Current neurology and Neuroscience Reports*, *11*(4), 428–434.

Tuchman, R., & Rapin, I. (2002). Epilepsy in autism. *The Lancet Neurology*, *1*(6), 352–358.

Turgay, A. (1990). Treatment outcome for children and adolescents with conversion disorder. *The Canadian Journal of Psychiatry*, *35*(7), 585–589.

Uliaszek, A. A., Prensky, E., & Baslet, G. (2012). Emotion regulation profiles in psychogenic non-epileptic seizures. *Epilepsy & Behavior*, *23*(3), 364–369.

Urbanek, M., Harvey, M., McGowan, J., & Agrawal, N. (2014). Regulation of emotions in psychogenic nonepileptic seizures. *Epilepsy & Behavior*, *37*, 110–115.

Vassilopoulos, A., Mohammad, S., Dure, L., Kozlowska, K., & Fobian, A. D. (2022). Treatment approaches for functional neurological disorders in children. *Current Treatment Options in Neurology*, *24(2)*, 77–97.

Weiss, K. E., Steinman, K. J., Kodish, I., Sim, L., Yurs, S., Steggall, C., & Fobian, A. D. (2021). Functional neurological symptom disorder in children and adolescents within medical settings. *Journal of Clinical Psychology in Medical Settings*, *28*(1), 90–101.

Williams, I. A., Levita, L., & Reuber, M. (2018). Emotion dysregulation in patients with psychogenic nonepileptic seizures: a systematic review based on the extended process model. *Epilepsy & Behavior*, *86*, 37–48.

Williams, I. A., Reuber, M., & Levita, L. (2021). Interoception and stress in patients with Functional Neurological Symptom Disorder. *Cognitive Neuropsychiatry*, *26*(2), 75–94.

Chapter 7

Clark, D. M. (1986). A cognitive approach to panic. *Behaviour Research and Therapy*, *24*(4), 461–470.

Moorey, S. (2010). The six cycles maintenance model: growing a "vicious flower" for depression. *Behavioural and Cognitive Psychotherapy*, *38*(2), 173–184.

Chapter 8

Beck, J. S. (1995). *Cognitive Therapy: Basics and Beyond*. New York: The Guilford Press.

Bohlmeijer, E., Ten Klooster, P. M., Fledderus, M., Veehof, M., & Baer, R. (2011). Psychometric properties of the five facet mindfulness questionnaire in depressed adults and development of a short form. *Assessment*, *18*(3), 308–320.

Clark, D. M. (1986). A cognitive approach to panic. *Behaviour Research and Therapy*, *24*(4), 461–470.

Clark, D. M., & Wells, A. (1995). A cognitive model. *Social phobia: Diagnosis, Assessment, and Treatment*, *69*, 1025.

Cope, S. R., Smith, J. G., King, T., & Agrawal, N. (2017). Evaluation of a pilot innovative cognitive-behavioral therapy-based psychoeducation group treatment for functional non-epileptic attacks. *Epilepsy & Behavior*, *70*, 238–244.

Goldstein, L. H., Chalder, T., Chigwedere, C., Khondoker, M. R., Moriarty, J., Toone, B. K., & Mellers, J. D. C. (2010). Cognitive-behavioral therapy for psychogenic nonepileptic seizures: a pilot RCT. *Neurology*, *74*(24), 1986–1994.

LaFrance, W. C., Baird, G. L., Barry, J. J., Blum, A. S., Webb, A. F., Keitner, G. I., ... & Szaflarski, J. P. (2014). Multicenter pilot treatment trial for psychogenic nonepileptic seizures: a randomized clinical trial. *JAMA Psychiatry*, *71*(9), 997–1005.

Salkovskis, P. M. (1985). A cognitive-behavioral model of obsessive-compulsive-disorder. *Behaviour Research and Therapy*, *23*(5), 571–583.

Skinner, B. F. (1963). Operant behavior. *American Psychologist*, *18*(8), 503.

Wells, A. (1995). Meta-cognition and worry: a cognitive model of generalized anxiety disorder. *Behavioural and Cognitive Psychotherapy*, *23*(3), 301–320.

Index

203–204, 207, 211, 216–217, 245–246, 259, 278, 319, 326; and ASD 451; in case studies: Abigail 542–545; Claudia 555–561; Ethan 539–540; Leah 443; Rob 401, 404, 412–414; and complex trauma 443; and group therapy 470
social belonging 17, 70, 101, 149, 178, 214, 281, 300, 371, 437, 447, 472, 491, 499, 529
social functions 87, 104, 109–110, 144–145, 167, 172–174, 187, 221, 242, 252, 265, 291, 295–298, 302, 305, 309, 314, 321, 338, 341–342, 422, 424, 448, 460, 493, 505, 524, 526, 540, 550, 559; in case studies: Gabriel 391; Rob 404, 406; Thomas 350, 356–357; *see also* Kitchen (PCM element)
social isolation 2, 80, 83, 87, 102, 120, 122, 129, 147, 149, 178–179, 208, 212, 224, 226, 248, 294, 302, 433, 437–438, 440, 443, 447, 453, 468; and ASD 453; in case studies: Alex 364, 368; Chloe 423; Claudia 557; Gabriel 387, 393; Leah 443; Ralph 552; Rob 413; in children/adolescents 423; and complex trauma 443
social learning theory 12, 157
social media 3, 74, 149, 250, 283, 294, 302, 430
social network 50, 70–71, 87, 120, 149, 178, 208, 226, 245, 248, 253–254, 272, 281, 291–292, 294, 300, 302, 304, 440, 482–483, 552; and ASD 453, 457; in case studies: Alex 373–374; Claudia 557; Gabriel 378, 382, 388, 393; Jaden 520, 522; Ralph 555; Rob 398–399, 401
Social Phobia Inventory 540
social services 1, 24, 149, 153, 183, 219, 222
social skills 26, 52, 208, 280–281, 373, 414, 456–457, 460, 467–468
Socratic method 228
somatisation 115, 124, 187, 303
somatisation disorder 187
spasms 62, 188, 476, 488–489, 558
speech and language therapy 1, 20, 25, 31, 91, 96–97, 153, 193, 310; in case studies: Gabriel 387, 394; Thomas 344, 347, 360
speech problems 58, 61, 63, 65, 83, 90, 102, 187–188, 190, 192–193, 198, 224, 296; in case studies: Gabriel 378, 387–388; Thomas 345

Speed, J. 153
stalking 112, 175
Statistical Package for the Social Sciences 35
Stephen (case study) 450, 456–463
Sticky Left-Over Food (PCM element) 50–51, 82, 107, 110, 115–117, 123–125, 139, 152, 177, 247–248, 255–256, 262, 266, 270–277, 289–290, 292, 299, 302, 308, 310, 312–314, 336, 339; and ASD 458; in case studies: Abigail 545; Alex 369–370, 373; Chloe 424–425; Claudia 557; Esther 435; Gabriel 389, 394; Jaden 523–524, 528; Juliette 547; Leah 444–447; Ralph 552; Rob 400–401, 411, 413–414, 416–417; Stephen 458; Thomas 349–350, 352, 355–356, 358–360, 558; in children/adolescents 422, 424–425; in complex cases 494–495, 497, 515, 523–524, 528; and complex trauma 439, 444–447; and group therapy 470, 485; and integrated PCM/CBT model 541, 545, 552, 557–558; and learning difficulties 433
stigma 23, 168, 170–171, 173, 187
Stigma Scale for Chronic Illness 295
Stone, J. 132
stroke 2, 32, 64, 131, 145, 182, 186, 192–193, 195, 197, 201–202, 218, 229, 237, 244, 246, 322, 344, 420, 437, 456, 501, 530, 532, 538, 546–548
structured FND diary 189, 228, 233, 236–237, 259, 480
substance misuse 205, 376
suicidal ideation 347, 425, 443, 520–521
suicide attempts 49, 369–370, 372, 374, 439
swallowing difficulties 62, 82, 97, 188, 223, 362, 388, 476
systemic re-traumatisation 16, 20, 56, 87, 105–106, 166–167, 170–172, 174, 183, 217, 232, 298, 301–302, 319; and ASD 461; in case studies: Alex 368; Jaden 523–525, 529; Leah 448–449; Rob 401, 405–406; Stephen 461; Thomas 358–360; in complex cases 498, 515, 523–525, 529–530; and complex trauma 439, 448–449; and group therapy 473

team splitting 25, 88, 505, 508–509, 531, 534
temporary escape 229–230